NEW-TOWN PLANNING

NEW-TOWN PLANNING:
PRINCIPLES AND PRACTICE

GIDEON GOLANY

A WILEY-INTERSCIENCE PUBLICATION
JOHN WILEY & SONS, New York ● London ● Sydney ● Toronto

Library of Congress Cataloging in Publication Data

Golany, Gideon.
  New town planning.

  "A Wiley-Interscience publication."
  Bibliography: p.
  Includes index.
  1. New towns.   2.   Cities and towns—Planning—
1945-   I.   Title.

HT166.G6   309.2'62   76-15958
ISBN 0-471-31038-7
Printed in the United States of America

10 9 8 7 6 5 4 3 2 1

TO MY MOTHER

with love and admiration

FOREWORD

The creation of new towns has become a worldwide movement, applied in a variety of situations for a variety of purposes. Gideon Golany's broad-based account of the principles and practice of new town planning meets a widely felt need for fuller, comparative information on this subject.

It is worth asking why interest in new towns has so suddenly expanded. The father of modern new towns, Sir Ebenezer Howard, conceived of the new town as offering a desirable alternative to both rural life and (especially) life in an enormous, crowded city such as London. Howard did not rely on the state to build new towns, but believed that after an initial philanthropic thrust they would prove to be sound, practical business propositions. His memorials in England are the garden cities of Letchworth and Welwyn, which he founded. His successor, Sir Frederic Osborn, believed quite rightly (especially in the changing political climate of Britain) that private initiative could never finance and develop the large number of new towns needed to decongest the large British conurbations. The arguments of Osborn and of the Town and Country Planning Association were very influential in persuading governments to launch, and to sustain, the substantial public new towns program that followed World War II in Britain.

Howard's argument that cities became overgrown and excessively congested is now politically accepted and acted on in many countries, although some economists still question it. This belief is related to a widespread view of new towns as a desirable method of organizing the continuous growth of city regions. The greenbelt and the eight new towns beyond it provided a new structure for the growth of the London region after the war, and this was followed in the 1960s by the designation of an outer ring of larger new towns which are currently being built. In a similar general way new towns have become a central feature of regional plans for the future of many big cities such as Paris, Moscow, and Tokyo. But the enthusiastic advocacy and promotion of new towns is not confined to countries in which government planning is strong and in which explicit strategies of urban growth have been adopted. The "new community" movement in the United States owes a good deal to the belated acceptance by many Americans that there must be a better way to cope with population growth than further accretions to the principal metropolitan areas.

Thus it might seem that Ebenezer Howard's message has finally arrived and that all over the world new towns are suddenly springing up as answers or corrections to the unrestrained growth of the largest cities. Of course many new towns owe their existences primarily to other aims, such as the development or colonization of new territory, the creation of new industries, and the rehabilitation of derelict or rundown areas such as declining coalfields. New towns, in other words, are instruments of economic development as well as social improvement, and the two objectives often march together. At the same time it is true that the great bulk of new town activity is located in proximity to large cities and has a functional relationship to broad zones of urban growth.

The following question then inevitably arises: What difference do these new towns make to the lives of urban people? Do they really represent a preferable alternative to "big city" life, as Howard and others have hoped, or are they just a planned kind of subur-

Peter Self is Professor of Public Administration, University of London; Vice-Chairman of Executive, Town and Country Planning Association; and author of *Cities in Flood* (London, 2nd ed. 1961), which deals with the problems of urban growth, *Metropolitan Planning* (London School of Economics, 1972), and other works.

bia? This question is often evaded by pointing to the technical and economic advantages of "planned communities," such as the advanced acquisition of land, savings in public utility and transportation costs, and so forth. Such advantages undoubtedly exist, and in this era of increased public planning and development, they account for a large part of the appeal and utility of the new town concept. In this sense new towns stand simply for "planned developments," and they attract all the hopes and disappointments, praise and obloquy, associated with this concept, in addition to their economic or technical claims. There is the point too that planners, who often seem to make little impression on the face or life of existing cities, have a better chance to show their paces in the design of a new town—especially if built by an agency that (as in Britain) has powers to buy all the land.

Thus new towns have taken wings (or for some people sprouted horns) from their association with the virtues claimed for public planning and development. This association, which is a natural and important one, needs and deserves close examination, and it is certainly linked with some of the benefits that can be claimed for new towns. But it does not of itself answer adequately the question as to how far new towns change, influence, or transform the lives of people, or how far they promote the social ideals for which they were first conceived and promoted.

It is impossible to assess this large question properly in this short review, but three points may be helpful. First, the social problems of big cities that Howard perceived still exist to some extent, but they have changed somewhat. In place of excessive drunkenness there is excessive crime and delinquency; in place of gross overcrowding and high densities there are traffic snarls and pollution; in place of too much economic activity there is—in some parts of new cities—too little. These changes apply primarily to Western cities, whereas the teeming cities of Asia and Latin America the older problems of excessive crowding and congestion of activities, with the associated dangers to health and welfare, are still intensifying. Moreover all big cities have social problems of anomie and the disruption of kinship links, practical problems caused by long journeys to work and suburban sprawl, and political and managerial problems stemming from the sheer scale of cities and the functional demands that they generate. As cities continue to swell, many of these problems appear to grow also.

It would be disingenuous and naive to suggest that new towns offer a sufficient answer to these various problems. Rather, within the context of existing city regions, new towns should be seen as an essential element in the process of restructuring the urban system. Planning ought not to destroy the distinctive advantages of big city life (such as the variety of occupations and of social and cultural facilities), but ought to balance these more successfully against the drawbacks (such as long work journeys and social fragmentation). Such a policy has many applications to the internal structure of a great city—for example, it points toward a polynucleated pattern instead of the dominance of a swollen business district. But new towns, as a way of organizing *further* urban growth, have the special opportunity of achieving a more balanced scale of values in a new setting. This they will do if they can integrate successfully the decentralizing flows of population and employment, create a good range of local social facilities, and develop against a "green backcloth" that both identifies the new community and provides it with recreation, while also seeking by selective devices to avoid the stigma of a one-class or one-income town.

Such a new town cannot be wholly self-sufficient; it shares the job and cultural opportunities of its surrounding city region. However, it can be a great deal *more* self-sufficient, and with luck and care *more* socially balanced, than are almost all suburbs. It can, in effect, say to its inhabitants: go wider if you like, the opportunities are there, but for *most* purposes we can offer you a good life right here. It is a *most-purpose community*. Of course the extent to which actual new towns realize this potential varies widely. Some (a few only) locate themselves too far from their parent city to flourish, while others (many more) are located much too close for the realization of this most-purpose goal. Also, admittedly, too much cannot be expected of physical planning concepts as such; a great deal depends on methods of economic and social development.

In second place, the dominance of the existing big cities persists in the location of most new towns. Howard's original concept envisaged the creation of an entirely new "social city," composed of a circular group of new towns ranged around a modest-size, new "central city." The latter might have 50,000 people, the new towns 30,000 each, the whole complex a quarter million. If this conception is being realized anywhere in the world, it is here in Canberra, where I write. Milton Keynes might have provided another example if it had been differently and better designed. But for the most part the realization of "social cities" has still to be achieved, although surely representing the next stage in new town evolution.

In the third place one must never allow the macro scale of regional planning to hypnotize one into forgetting the importance of detailed town and neighborhood design. It is at this level that much of the improvement in the health, safety, and welfare of ordinary life is to be realized, if the new town planners are to realize it at all. But that is another long story.

Throughout its history the Town and Country Planning Association of Britain, with which I am proud to have a long association, has stressed the social purposes of new town planning. These introductory remarks have been intended also to emphasize the relationship of this theme to what is now a worldwide movement. In appraising the success of new town projects, it is essential to analyze and appraise their development from a variety of perspectives. Gideon Golany's work provides much essential material for the purposes of such an appraisal, and represents a timely and important contribution to that academic growth point—the study of new towns.

PETER SELF

Canberra, Australia
May 1976

PREFACE

Today's cities are in a crisis caused from both within and without. Their societies, governments, and environments are deteriorating, and at the same time people are migrating from economically weak rural areas to these cities. This migration upsets the traditional ratio of urban to rural populations, aggravates urban problems, and causes urban expansion. This, in turn, threatens vital agricultural land. Also, in developed countries, the middle class and established firms are weakening the tax base of central cities by moving to suburbs, especially when low-income migrants replace these people and firms.

This crisis has been an incentive to both developed and developing countries to seek ways of improving both urban settlements and agrarian regions. Any effective method must be comprehensive, meeting diverse needs rather than merely providing housing. Countries that have developed new urban settlements—especially new towns—have been successful in resolving many of their urban problems and have also made efforts to discover new regions for settlements while protecting agricultural land.

One possible solution for the future is to direct part of the world's urban growth to arid or semiarid regions. Economically feasible methods of desalinization and innovative uses of energy sources available in these regions, especially solar energy, would make such an alternative possible. Doubtless, this kind of development would give impetus to the new town movement and create interest in their planning and construction. Implementation of the new town concept is occurring at a time when planning and construction, as a whole, are operating under uncertain circumstances and rapid changes that affect every facet of our lives. I believe that new towns and new towns in-town (or in-cities) should be conceived only within their regional context to avoid complicating existing problems. Thus, any new town project should be part of overall regional and national policy and plans and their implementation.

One aim of this book is to aid in the understanding of the theory and practice of new town development for their present and future application. Although there have been successful attempts to fill many of the gaps in the literature about new towns during the last three decades, many believe there is still a need to clarify, distinguish, analyze, and define the various elements of new urban settlements, especially those of the new town. My recognition of this need and my belief that a comprehensive treatment (one that describes both recent and expected future changes) of the subject is essential, inspired this book. Thus my prime goal is to analyze comprehensively the principles and practice of new towns for the use of planners, developers, students, teachers, and policy makers concerned with new towns everywhere.

As a product of research, consulting, lectures, and other activities related to new towns, this book encompasses my various experiences over the past 15 years. I hope it will meet the current demands of those concerned with new town development, and perhaps serve as a guide to both theoreticians and practitioners. I anticipate that it will appeal to a wide audience—designers, architects, and librarians; property owners and assessors; real estate agents, building contractors, zoning and planning officials; investors and financial specialists; environmentalists, ecologists, econonomists, and sociologists; and home association directors and other municipal officials.

My task is difficult, since one of my goals is to describe new town planning in an international context rather than in a single national one. Being aware of this scope, I attempt from time to time to compare examples and case studies of the extremes: modern versus traditional societies, developed versus developing economies, and flexible as opposed to controlled management. To show the significance of case studies, I also offer a variety of illustrations of actual new towns developed throughout the world.

I have purposely minimized statistics from case studies in the body of the chapters. My policy has been to analyze the unique nature of each component of a concept and point out the process and tools needed for its planning. Important data concerning new towns are included in the appendix, and the reader already familiar with the tools of urban and regional planning should make his own interpretation of these data.

Since the book focuses primarily on principles and practice, it is mainly concerned with the underlying questions of *what* to do and *how* to do it rather than merely dwelling on the philosophy or history of any given issue. Each chapter focuses on analysis of the planning process rather than only on its technical approach. Also, the structure of each chapter does not necessarily follow its chart on planning, because sections of the chart are discussed in other relevant chapters.

I see new towns as laboratories that experiment with innovative systems for improving the quality of urban life. Therefore the reader should view some solutions offered here as not exclusively related to new towns, but rather as generalizable to established cities. I have attempted to introduce alternative solutions to problems so that planners and developers may select the one most suited to the new or established city. Ultimately, however, a planner must use his own judgment in applying a solution to his project.

For the creation of this book I owe thanks and

apologies to my wife Esther, who has shared with me the ups and downs during the many months of writing this book.

I am grateful to many of my students who have helped in preparing the drawings, among them Thomas Berry, John McDevitt, John Elicker, Wayne Rasmussen, and especially Tom Weaver, who drafted most of the charts. Leslie Fairweather has my thanks for her careful typing. Among those who helped in editing the first draft are Sharman Stanic Mullen, Gary Collison, and Jane Bradford, students in the Department of English.

Joyce B. Buck, my editor, has worked closely with me through all stages in the preparation of this manuscript: without her invaluable assistance the manuscript would never have reached the publisher's desk on time. She well deserves my deepest gratitude for her dedication, talent, and careful treatment of details.

Finally, I am most grateful to the hundreds of friends, individuals, and institutions in the United States, Canada, Venezuela, Mexico, Great Britain, France, Ireland, the Netherlands, Sweden, Finland, Denmark, the Union of Soviet Socialist Republics, Poland, Israel, Pakistan, India, Japan, Australia, and other countries who have helped me by sending data and photographs that I have used in the research and writing of this book.

GIDEON GOLANY

University Park, Pennsylvania
February 1976

CONTENTS

CONTENTS

LIST OF TABLES

LIST OF FIGURES

NEW-TOWN PLANNING

ONE
NATIONAL POLICY FOR URBAN GROWTH AND THE NEW TOWNS

INTRODUCTION

National policies for urban growth became a subject of great interest to many nations after World War II because of accelerating urbanization and the need for large-scale reconstruction. Several countries, such as the United Kingdom, Israel, France, and The Netherlands, have succeeded in developing such policies. A developed country needs a policy for urban growth to solve the main problem of the central city, congestion; a developing country, in which population and economic centers are still in rural areas, needs to focus on regional development. A national policy for urban growth should show a clear strategy for directing this growth. As William Alonso wrote: "A national urbanization policy should include developmental objectives for guiding the phenomenon of growth . . . . "[1]

Chaotic urban growth has also hindered our ability to govern and manage cities. "Governance of our cities . . . has become the art of the impossible."[2] In another statement Daniel P. Moynihan described the circumstances of the local government as a continuous fiscal crisis: "Increasingly, state and local governments that try to meet their responsibilities lurch from one fiscal crisis to another. In such circumstances, the capacity for creative local government becomes least in precisely those jurisdictions where it might most be expected."[3]

This chapter presents issues and problems which urban planners and all of society must face, and describes the necessity for and the difficulties of a national policy for urban growth. The chapter also defines policy, and attempts to make clear that a complex coordinating framework must be assembled before the actual machinery of a policy can be set in motion. Finally, it argues that new towns offer one possible solution to our urban problems.

DEFINITION OF POLICY

Policy is a definite framework of general plans or of fundamental principles selected from several alternatives that have been agreed upon in light of existing and anticipated conditions, to guide and influence present and future decisions or courses of action. Any policy has three important features. First, a policy is more than a statement of general goals and objectives; it is interrelated principles and coordinated systems of regulation or management to achieve certain defined ends. Policy establishes principles by which decisions are made. Thus, instead of being a collection of decisions, policy is a process determining the means to reach defined ends.

Second, a policy must provide a framework of definite strategies. Before it can be formed, a number of alternatives must exist. After a problem has been diagnosed, alternative plans are devised and the consequences of each are anticipated. When agreement is reached on which course of action to follow, a policy is established. Although the agencies involved may disagree on some details, they must agree on the policy's general outlines.

The third feature of a policy is the process of establishing it, which should involve analysis of findings, definition of issues, and statement of a course of action. An analysis of findings should alert a nation and its decision makers to their past and present problems and probable future trends. An accurate and comprehensive analysis should project their future efforts as an aid in setting priorities. A definition of issues generally describes critical forces that create national problems. It diagnoses problems, their causes, and their importance, and this diagnosis should also define potential problems. Statement of a course of action should indicate the interrelated sequential paths and the processes to be followed in solving national problems.

Any policy is always the result of compromise between political leaders and other decision makers after goals and objectives have been considered. Goals establish an orientation; objectives give the details of goals; policies provide specific guidelines for achieving goals and objectives. A national policy must be general yet functional, and a balance of emphasis must always exist between the two. Specifically policy must deal with the effects of urbanization, of population growth, of pollution, and of technological innovations on society. Planners must also shape policy on the basis of social values. "A national growth policy should actually commit the nation to these values."[4] Sometimes, however, a policy may become so general in its effort to gain necessary, wide political support that it loses its effectiveness. In such cases agreement may be achieved for political needs rather than for actual results, and this kind of policy may only give citizens an illusion of governmental activity that helps their morale. Finally, government agencies must not use this type of national policy as an instrument to restrict personal freedom, and a power structure must minimize tension among all national levels while sustaining an effective policy.

NEED FOR A NATIONAL POLICY FOR URBAN GROWTH

Since the end of World War II, governments have had to cope with social phenomena that tax their capabilities. Today, they must coordinate their efforts in formulating and carrying out a plan to deal effectively with these phenomena, since only a unifying national policy will enable traditional governments to alleviate their problems. "One lesson of western urbanization that the developing countries may profitably learn is that it is economic to have an overall policy for guiding the course of urbanization process from the very beginning of development."[5]

"Two problems have shaped national strategies for urban and regional development. One is the lag between growing and depressed areas. The other is the effort to deal with the problems of the metropolis and decentralization."[6] All these problems are dynamic and have a direct or indirect effect on social issues: (1) accelerating urbanization, (2) growing populations, (3) changing transportation, (4) changing environments, (5) increasing middle classes, (6) changing attitudes of young people, and (7) increasing government intervention.

Accelerating urbanization is manifested by the drastic change in the ratio of urban to rural populations, by overconcentrated populations in urban centers and their peripheries, and by increased slum areas. All of these indicate the need for housing and for good public utilities and services. In the last three decades these housing needs have become acute, not only in highly developed countries such as the United States but also in the developing countries of Asia and Africa. In the beginning of this century, populations of most countries lived in rural areas. During the 1930s, migration to urban areas began and has continued to the present day. In developed countries this migration is the result of increased technology; in developing countries it is the spillover of large populations from rural communities. This aggressive migration is a worldwide force with great implications for the development of society and of the environment.

The social cost of accelerating urbanization is the dichotomy between high-density urban communities and low-density rural areas.[7] To alter this pattern and to reduce acceleration, the gap in the middle must be filled. New urban settlements may direct migration, and various forms of settlements may be introduced in depopulated rural regions to halt emigration.

The world's population is increasing tremendously due to technological advances in medicine, medical services, and health conditions. The death ratio has decreased and life expectancy has increased for all age groups, especially infants. Population growth in all countries is accelerating rapidly and occurs mainly in areas where food is in such short supply that growth causes critical problems.

Two different opinions about population growth exist today.[8] Some countries, such as Israel, Canada, and Australia, believe that increased growth means increased strength in terms of a country's human resources. (See Figure 1.1) While these countries have accepted policies that encourage population growth, others, such as The Netherlands, in which it is thought that discouraging growth will improve the standards and quality of living, have adopted policies of no growth. In each case the population growth policy fits the particular conditions of a country, although the overall trend today is toward no growth. In many nations, however, implementation of a no growth policy has faced great religious and cultural obstacles. India, for example, has tried to promote a policy of birth control but has not yet succeeded in implementing it.

Technological developments (railroads, cars, and airplanes) in transportation since the mid-1800s have continually influenced urban patterns and are likely to continue to do so. They have allowed cities to sprawl

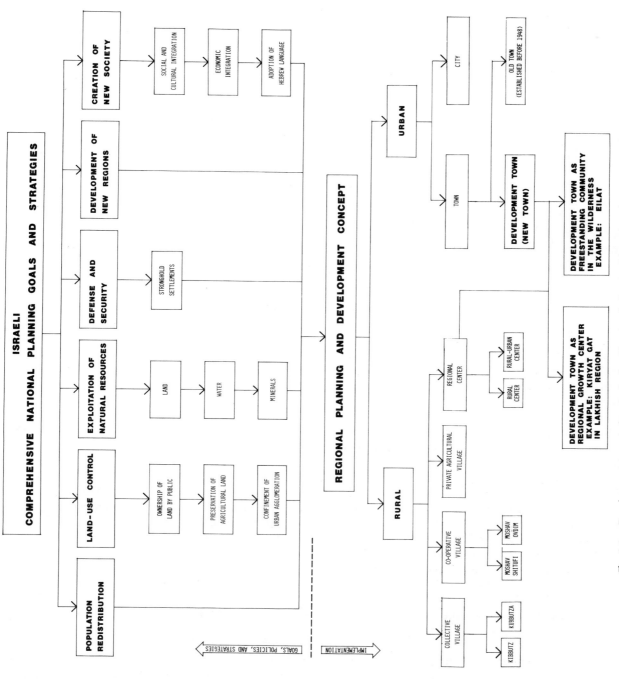

Fig. 1.1. Development towns' place in the Israeli national planning hierarchy. These towns and other settlements are outgrowths of Israel's comprehensive national policy for urban growth and population redistribution.

3

and have linked cities to remote resources. The social implication of these changes is that cities are no longer manageable on a human scale, and man's dependence on transportation is nearly unavoidable. The accelerating growth of transportation, with its concomitant construction, congestion, pollution, and demand for more space, increases population mobility and provides good job opportunities and leisure activities. Transportation growth has diminished travel times between settlements and has increased pressures in congested urban centers.

Changes in the environment, especially those caused by depletion of resources and shortages, have become an important international issues. Urban expansion and speed of exhausting natural resources have disrupted the equilibrium of the physical environment.

The rise of the middle class has influenced national development more than before, not only in highly developed regions such as the United States and western Europe, but also in traditionally nonindustrial, developing areas. Middle-class socioeconomic development has resulted in changes in its standard of living, manifested by increased incomes and education. This rise is similar to that of the Renaissance of western Europe, which produced a new social class that ranked between the extremes of the rich and the poor. Today, this group is rapidly becoming the most influential one in our society.

At present, young people play an important part in determining public opinion. Their dynamism and their effective demands for leisure activities, culture, and amusement show that they should be given more consideration than ever before. Although some think the rebellious attitudes of youth in the nineteenth century were similar to those of young people today, it is doubtful that rejection of traditional systems and institutions was as intense in earlier times.

Contemporary youth will have more to say about planning the future than ever before. Their participation—especially that of young women—in decision making has also increased recently because of the worldwide women's liberation movement which is helping to increase the effective roles of women, not only in labor but in politics and government as well.

Government intervention in the lives of citizens occurs in many ways. Modern democratic societies face a dilemma between balancing the need to maintain personal power and the pressure of technocracy to centralize power for the sake of efficiency. Planning is not merely a course of action to please individuals; it is also a means to ends that benefit society, and as such,

planning that requires coordination and management of growth can support democracy. Contemporary growth in every facet of our lives has become gargantuan and demands management. The more we meet this demand, the more we depend on technocracy; this dependence in turn becomes a part of the dilemma that planning confronts because in its attempt to manage growth, democracy risks self-destruction.

Currently, all the changes discussed above are resulting in rapidly increased development throughout the world, which traditional government systems find extremely difficult to manage. These systems can coordinate their efforts by adopting a national policy and can use all their resources to deal effectively with this development.

Since World War II, eastern European countries and democratic countries of western Europe, such as the United Kingdom and The Netherlands, have recognized the need for a national policy. In the latter two, relatively small, dense populations and limited national resources seem to be the main motives for developing their policies. The United States has recently realized the seriousness of its growth problems, and its citizens are now more willing to accept coordinated solutions. This realization and willingness are the first steps toward formulating a national policy, although each state may have to develop its own policy before the federal government can develop a coordinated national one. (See Figure 1.2.)

COMPONENTS OF A NATIONAL POLICY FOR URBAN GROWTH

A complex of components, differing from one country to another, forms the basis of a national policy, and the emphasis of such components may change with time. However, some components common to most countries are discussed in this section. (See Figure 1.3.)

Coordinated Use of Resources

The traditional concept of self-contained national economy describes its base as consisting of natural resources because their quantity determines a nation's political and economic strength. However, countries poor in natural resources but rich in skilled human ones have shown this concept to be limited. Countries such as Japan have based their economies on manufactured goods produced from imported resources. Recently, many nations have become concerned about the depletion of the world's irreplaceable resources and the negative influence of production on the environment. Thus, one way or another, because of their effect on aggregate urban areas, the use of natural resources must be related to any national policy for urban growth.

In order to use natural resources effectively, especially those which are subject to abuse, governments should at least coordinate their use for the benefit of the majority of the population. This entails effective management of resources by national or regional agencies to avoid abuse that may have a negative effect on a national economy. Such management may support efficient land use to lead to desirable urban growth.

Land. Since land is and will continue to be a major resource, coordinated efforts to manage agricultural land and to preserve forests should be developed. Agricultural land should be designated on the basis of a detailed survey of soil characteristics that should provide data on national land suitability to enable optimal designations of land use according to national needs. From the soil survey a nation may obtain knowledge about the degree of availability of agricultural land and its quality, and may then formulate a national policy for reserving agricultural land. Small, densely populated countries with limited resources, such as the United Kingdom, Israel, and The Netherlands, have an urgent need to develop such a policy. (See Figures 1.4 and 1.5.)

A survey of land suitability may also specify which forests to preserve and may lead to the proper use of forest lands by industries, recreational planners, environmentalists, and ecologists. Misuse of forest land not only disrupts the natural equilibrium but also indirectly affects immediately surrounding agricultural lands and the microclimate of an area. However, the effectiveness of a policy for preserving forests also depends upon the support of other related policies.

Policy for land use establishes any overall future policy for urban growth and determines, to a great extent, the success or failure of that policy. Many elements contribute to the success of land-use policy: (1) patterns of land ownership, (2) land-use control, and (3) land resources. Although many planners have called for national public land banks, it is still policy that makes implementation powerful.[9]

Public land ownership may become a prime force in national development when combined with an existing, clear national policy for urban growth. The effectiveness of planning and implementation of Israeli development towns, collective and communal settlements, and regional development have been successful because of public ownership of 92 percent of the land. On the other hand, the 39 percent of publicly owned land in the United States (federal, state, and local governments) is managed less effectively than that of Israel because the United States lacks a national policy for urban growth.[10] (See Figures 1.6 and 1.7.)

A major concern of any national policy for urban growth is where such growth should occur. Since growth has a direct impact on spatial distribution, a policy must be set for selecting optimal sites for activities, for new settlements, or for expanding existing cities. Consequently, this policy must respond to a related issue: What is the optimal pattern of urban distribution? Both these spatial issues, site selection and pattern of settlements, are direct products of forecasting future changes and demands in three areas —population, resources, and space. When dealing with alternative spatial patterns, one should consider size, functions, and distances between modes, land availability, and the resulting quality of society.

Any strategy for alternative spatial patterns (e.g., settlements or industry) must consider land-use policy. However, there may be many separate national plans directly related to land use, such as transportation, open space and preservations, natural resources, water control and supply, utilities, and agricultural land preservation. Implementation of such plans is not usually coordinated, although a single government may fund them; i.e., there is no national policy for urban growth. The plans may not include long-range national priorities, but may instead be hasty attempts to meet some pressing national needs. Also, if governments have no overall policy, they may not consider the effects of such plans on urbanization and urban sprawl. (See Figures 1.8 and 1.9.)

Water. Water use should be regulated to maintain its quality. Rapid population growth and expansion of industries threaten the water resources of many countries. This is a crucial issue in urban areas, which are rapidly becoming the major consumers of the world's water supply. A policy for water regulation is especially needed in regions with limited water resources.

Financial Resources. Public investments may be a strong and influential tool in directing national development if they are associated with a national policy for growth. In free-market economies, such investments may direct private construction for regional and national development.[10] A policy regulating public financial resources is needed to channel them effectively according to two national priorities: (1) de-

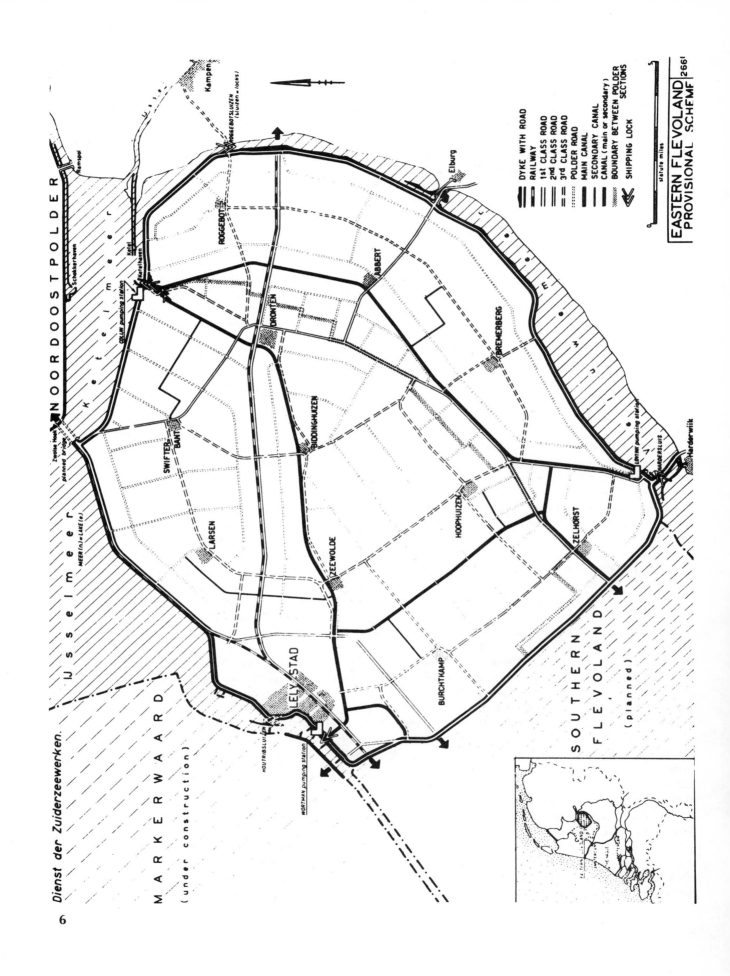

EASTERN FLEVOLAND 266'
PROVISIONAL SCHEME

DYKE WITH ROAD
RAILWAY
1st CLASS ROAD
2nd CLASS ROAD
3rd CLASS ROAD
POLDER ROAD
MAIN CANAL
SECONDARY CANAL
CANAL (main or secondary)
BOUNDARY BETWEEN POLDER
SECTIONS
SHIPPING LOCK

statute miles

Dienst der Zuiderzeewerken.

NOORDOOSTPOLDER

Kampen
Ramspol
Schokkerhaven
Roggebotsluizen (sluizen = locks)
Ketelhaven
COLIJN pumping station
Ketelmeer
Zwolse Hoek
planned bridge

IJsselmeer
MEER (n)= LAKE (e.)

MARKERWAARD
(under construction)

HOUTRIBSLUIZEN
WORTMAN pumping station

LELYSTAD

SWIFTER-BANT
LARSEN
ZEEWOLDE
BIDDINGHUIZEN
ROGGEBOT
DRONTEN
ABBERT
BREMERBERG
HOOPHUIZEN
ZELHORST
BURCHTKAMP

Elburg
LOVINK pumping station
HARDERSLUIS
Harderwijk

SOUTHERN
FLEVOLAND
(planned)

6

Figure 1.2. East Flevoland and the new town of Lelystad. (A) East Flevoland is the third polder reclaimed from the sea by the Dutch. The polder's 135,000 acres were drained in 1957. Dronten is its regional center. (B) Lelystad, begun in 1965, will eventually accommodate a population of 100,000. By 1975 it was 17,000, and by the end of 1976 the population will be over 23,000. The city employs about 70 percent of its population and has a rate of unemployment about 50 percent less than that of The Netherlands in general. The government expects that Lelystad will someday become the capital of a province created from lands regained from the sea. (Courtesy of the Royal Netherlands Embassy and Mr. Bart Hofmeister.)

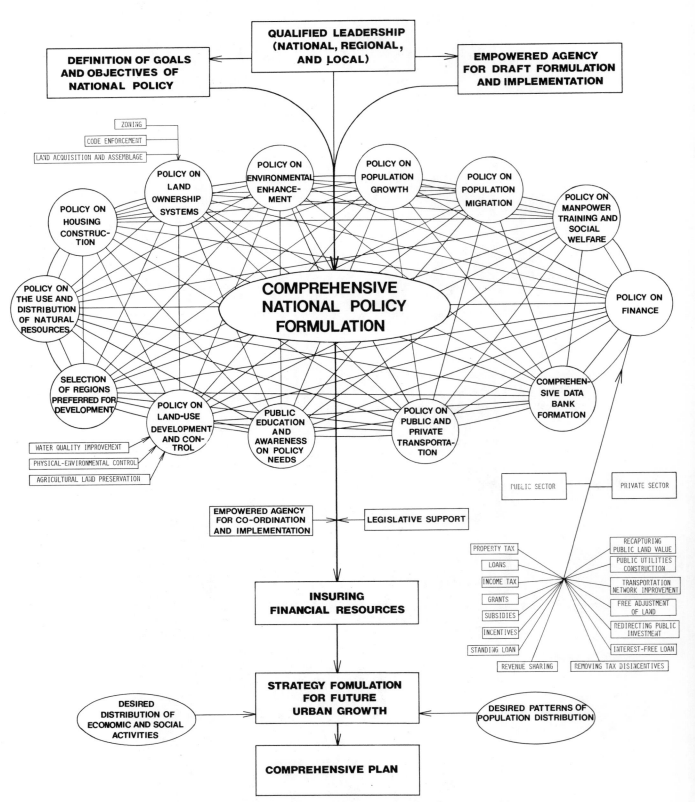

Figure 1.3. A generalized model of a comprehensive national policy and its components.

Figure 1.4. Dutch reclamation of land in Flevoland. (Courtesy of Bijksdienst Voor de Usselmeerpolders Zwolle.)

velopment of regions such as economically depressed and depopulated rural areas or congested urban areas, and (2) projects dealing with problems such as poverty, housing shortages, traffic congestion, and environmental deterioration.

Many nations have used financial incentives successfully to support their national policies for urban growth. This type of policy, combined with a policy for spatial distribution of jobs, can support a desirable spatial distribution of economic growth and thus a desirable settlement pattern. Ultimately, new regional economic centers will yield nationally effective results. National public assistance may have less impact when it covers an entire country than when it is focused on new urban settlements in a few regions. Since private financial resources are insufficient for major development, including new communities, public funds must aid them. The distribution of investments by central, state, or local governments should be coordinated with other policies related to a desired future urban pattern, e.g., rural or urban development, central cities or suburbs, and communication or transportation. This coordination may result in the distribution of investments among top-priority regions.

Population

Policy for population as a component of a national policy for growth should involve such issues as popu-

lation (growth or not growth), a pattern of population distribution, literacy, and training of professional and skilled people and their distribution within a country. Recently, some countries have become concerned about the effects of population growth on natural resources, energy, and food supplies, and about effective ways of maaaging such growth. Other countries have become anxious because of their geopolitical positions or their sparse populations in vast areas rich with resources. Regardless of a country's motivation and desired end for such a policy, it should not be independent of other policies.

Net growth (births minus deaths), immigration, and emigration are the sources of population growth.[12] A strategy for family planning, whether to encourage or to discourage growth, should be carefully considered because of its cultural, religious, and psychological complexity. In addition, any such strategy may take some time to achieve success. A system of taxation and/or incentives can form a second strategy which strengthens implementation of any policy for population growth.

A policy of population redistribution describes how to regulate dispersion of a country's population growth to ease social problems and congestion. To be effective, such a policy should be formed in the context of a national policy that indicates clearly whether to follow a concentrated or a dispersed pattern. (See Figure 1.3.) In formulating a population redistribution policy, such factors as population migration, transportation net-

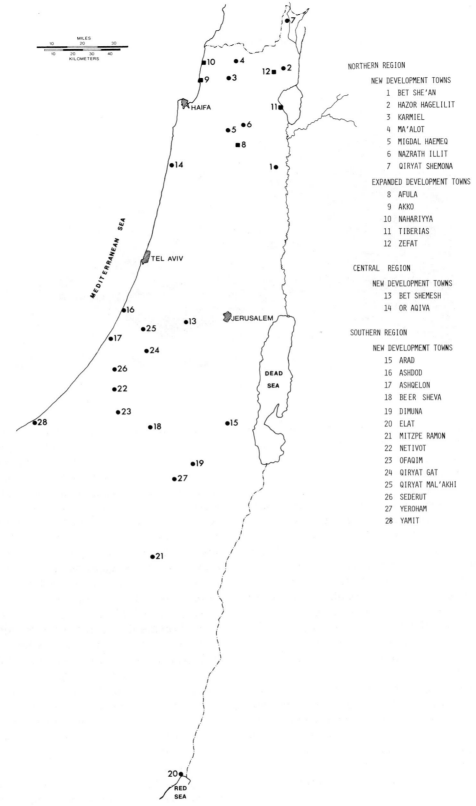

Figure 1.5. Israeli development towns. Israel constructed these towns to redistribute people far from metropolitan areas, to explore natural resources, to act as pioneering, freestanding communities in undeveloped areas, to restore historical sites, and to strengthen the society, economy, and security of the country. These towns are located mainly in the northern (12) and southern (14) parts of the country. Expanded towns have been developed as regional growth centers to stabilize regional urban populations. By 1974, development towns housed 20 percent of Israel's population.

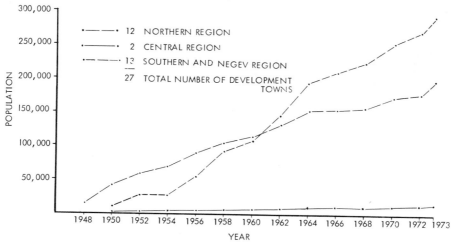

Figure 1.6. Absolute population growth of Israeli development towns by region.

works, job opportunties, and resource allocations must be considered. Economic incentives are also a major means of implementing this type of policy.

The distribution of a population or its settlement pattern in certain areas is related to the size, function, and location of those areas, transportation and communication systems, intensity and quality of social interaction, marketing systems, and quality of environments. Redistribution policy should be considered when it can relieve urban congestion, develop good transportation modes and networks, ease pressure on the physical environment, provide much interaction among people, improve community management, and bring people closer to the natural environment and its resources.

Although it is costly to implement a policy for population redistribution, the social price of no policy for highly urban countries may be higher.[13] The cost benefit of either should be measured by such long-range results as the quality of society.

The literacy and level of skill of a population will directly affect is distribution. Policies for population growth and distribution should be combined with a policy and scheme for training professional and skilled people to meet national needs, and for avoiding excesses and shortages of these personnel in any given geographic area. The two former policies may collapse or be weakened if the latter one is not an integral part of them.

Desired Pattern of Urban Settlements

A national policy for urban growth should generally provide the means to achieve an urban pattern adapted to the socioeconomic and geographic conditions of a region. These settlement patterns can take two directions: the existing urban pattern can be continued and strengthened by directing resources toward its urban areas, or new, diversified patterns can be established away from or close to existing urban areas in the form of new towns, regional growth centers, or satellite towns, and so on. In either case, new urban settlements should relate to the following three basic issues:

(1) Where to locate new urban settlements and how each one relates geographically to the others.

(2) How large a settlement's population should be and the optimum size for its physical development, since settlement size is also related to other settlements in a geographic area.

(3) What the local and regional economic, social, and management functions of a new urban settlement should be.

It may be that developing any urban settlement in light of these issues cannot be effective without the guiding hand of centralized policy and without public awareness. (See Figure 1.10.)

Implementation of Policy

Any national policy for growth dealing with future patterns of urban settlements should treat the issue of urban growth comprehensively. To offer adequate solutions, planners should understand each country and its problems, and citizens should be convinced of the need for a national policy so that they will cooper-

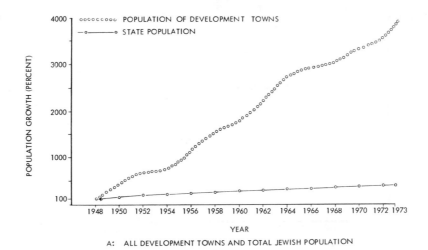

A: ALL DEVELOPMENT TOWNS AND TOTAL JEWISH POPULATION

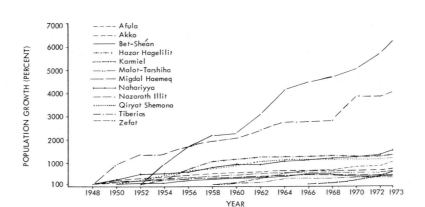

B: NORTHERN DEVELOPMENT TOWNS

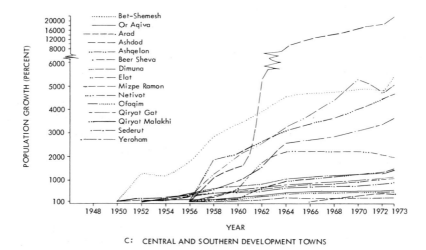

C: CENTRAL AND SOUTHERN DEVELOPMENT TOWNS

Figure 1.7. Relative population growth of Israeli development towns by region. *(A)* Development towns compared to Israel as a whole. *(B)* Northern towns. *(C)* Central and southern towns.

12

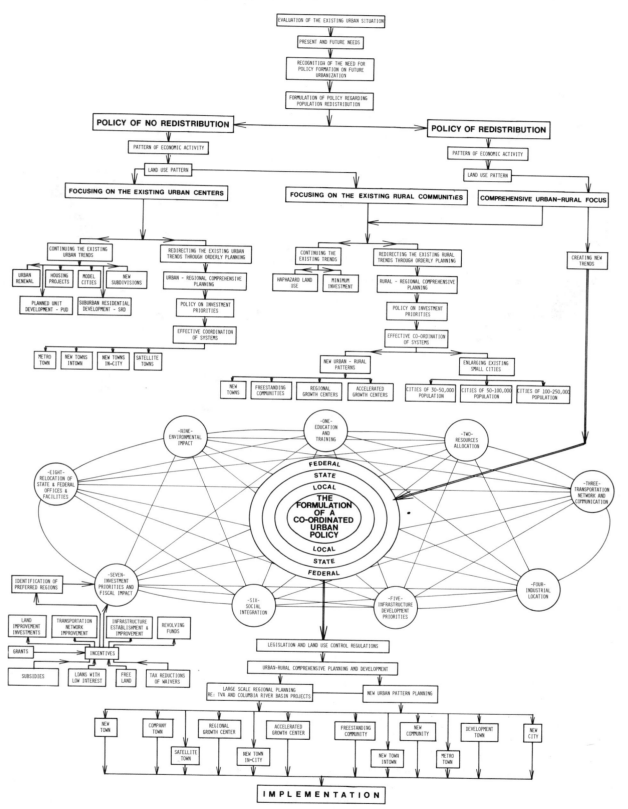

Figure 1.8. The relationship of alternative urban patterns to population redistribution to the United States.

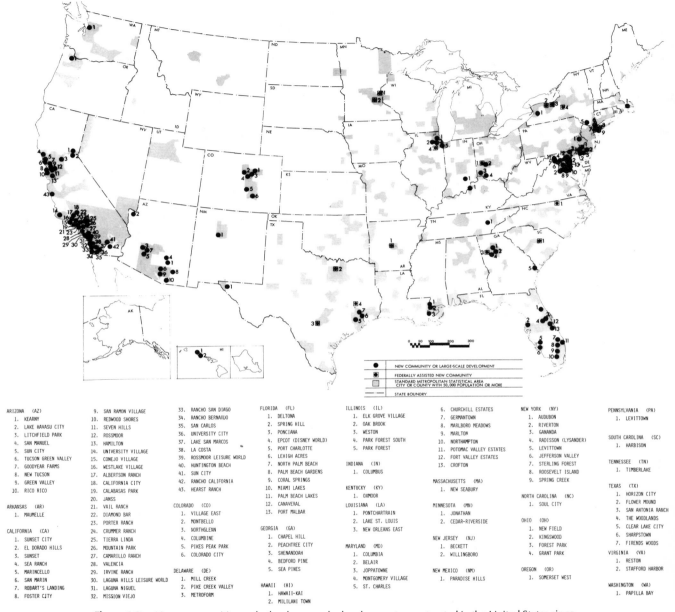

Figure 1.9. New communities and other large-scale developments constructed in the United States since 1948.

ARIZONA (AZ)
1. KEARNY
2. LAKE HAVASU CITY
3. LITCHFIELD PARK
4. SAN MANUEL
5. SUN CITY
6. TUCSON GREEN VALLEY
7. GOODYEAR FARMS
8. NEW TUCSON
9. GREEN VALLEY
10. RICO RICO

ARKANSAS (AR)
1. MAUMELLE

CALIFORNIA (CA)
1. SUNSET CITY
2. EL DORADO HILLS
3. SUNSET
4. SEA RANCH
5. MARINCELLO
6. SAN MARIN
7. ROBART'S LANDING
8. FOSTER CITY

9. SAN RAMON VILLAGE
10. REDWOOD SHORES
11. SEVEN HILLS
12. ROSSMOOR
13. HAMILTON
14. UNIVERSITY VILLAGE
15. CONEJO VILLAGE
16. WESTLAKE VILLAGE
17. ALBERTSON RANCH
18. CALIFORNIA CITY
19. CALABASAS PARK
20. JANSS
21. VAIL RANCH
22. DIAMOND BAR
23. PORTER RANCH
24. CRUMMER RANCH
25. TIERRA LINDA
26. MOUNTAIN PARK
27. CAMARILLO RANCH
28. VALENCIA
29. IRVINE RANCH
30. LAGUNA HILLS LEISURE WORLD
31. LAGUNA NIGUEL
32. MISSION VIEJO

33. RANCHO SAN DIAGO
34. RANCHO BERNAIDO
35. SAN CARLOS
36. UNIVERSITY CITY
37. LAKE SAN MARCOS
38. LA COSTA
39. ROSSMOOR LEISURE WORLD
40. HUNTINGTON BEACH
41. SUN CITY
42. RANCHO CALIFORNIA
43. HEARST RANCH

COLORADO (CO)
1. VILLAGE EAST
2. MONTBELLO
3. NORTHGLENN
4. COLUMBINE
5. PIKES PEAK PARK
6. COLORADO CITY

DELAWARE (DE)
1. MILL CREEK
2. PIKE CREEK VALLEY
3. METROFORM

HAWAII (HI)
1. HAWAII-KAI
2. MILILANI TOWN

FLORIDA (FL)
1. DELTONA
2. SPRING HILL
3. PONCIANA
4. EPCOT (DISNEY WORLD)
5. PORT CHARLOTTE
6. LEHIGH ACRES
7. NORTH PALM BEACH
8. PALM BEACH GARDENS
9. CORAL SPRINGS
10. MIAMI LAKES
11. PALM BEACH LAKES
12. CANAVERAL
13. PORT MALBAR

GEORGIA (GA)
1. CHAPEL HILL
2. PEACHTREE CITY
3. SHENANDOAH
4. BEDFORD PINE
5. SEA PINES

ILLINOIS (IL)
1. ELK GROVE VILLAGE
2. OAK BROOK
3. WESTON
4. PARK FOREST SOUTH
5. PARK FOREST

INDIANA (IN)
1. COLUMBUS

KENTUCKY (KY)
1. OXMOOR

LOUISIANA (LA)
1. PONTCHARTRAIN
2. LAKE ST. LOUIS
3. NEW ORLEANS EAST

MARYLAND (MD)
1. COLUMBIA
2. BELAIR
3. JOPPATOWNE
4. MONTGOMERY VILLAGE
5. ST. CHARLES

6. CHURCHILL ESTATES
7. GERMANTOWN
8. MARLBORO MEADOWS
9. MARLTON
10. NORTHAMPTON
11. POTOMAC VALLEY ESTATES
12. FORT VALLEY ESTATES
13. CROFTON

MASSACHUSETTS (MA)
1. NEW SEABURY

MINNESOTA (MN)
1. JONATHAN
2. CEDAR-RIVERSIDE

NEW JERSEY (NJ)
1. BECKETT
2. WILLINGBORO

NEW MEXICO (NM)
1. PARADISE HILLS

NEW YORK (NY)
1. AUDUBON
2. RIVERTON
3. GANANDA
4. RADISSON (LYSANDER)
5. LEVITTOWN
6. JEFFERSON VALLEY
7. STERLING FOREST
8. ROOSEVELT ISLAND
9. SPRING CREEK

NORTH CAROLINA (NC)
1. SOUL CITY

OHIO (OH)
1. NEW FIELD
2. KINGSWOOD
3. FOREST PARK
4. GRANT PARK

OREGON (OR)
1. SOMERSET WEST

PENNSYLVANIA (PA)
1. LEVITTOWN

SOUTH CAROLINA (SC)
1. HARBISON

TENNESSEE (TN)
1. TIMBERLAKE

TEXAS (TX)
1. HORIZON CITY
2. FLOWER MOUND
3. SAN ANTONIA RANCH
4. THE WOODLANDS
5. CLEAR LAKE CITY
6. SHARPSTOWN
7. FIRENDS WOODS

VIRGINIA (VA)
1. RESTON
2. STAFFORD HARBOR

WASHINGTON (WA)
1. PAPILLA BAY

ate. This policy should also encourage public officials to use it as a way of providing stability in a country.[14] Since policy is not an end in itself, government implementation must be based on five factors: (1) legislation, (2) implementing agents, (3) strategy for implementation, (4) financial resources, and (5) cooperation with all other governmental agencies.

Although legislation can definitely commit a coun-

try to the implementation of a policy, the legislative process is slow; thus it may be difficult to change laws that have been enacted and they may not change as circumstances do. In Israel, public awareness has been substituted for legislation so changes may occur quickly. By contrast, such legislation in the United States has become a political issue.[15] Most countries require legislation not only to implement a policy but

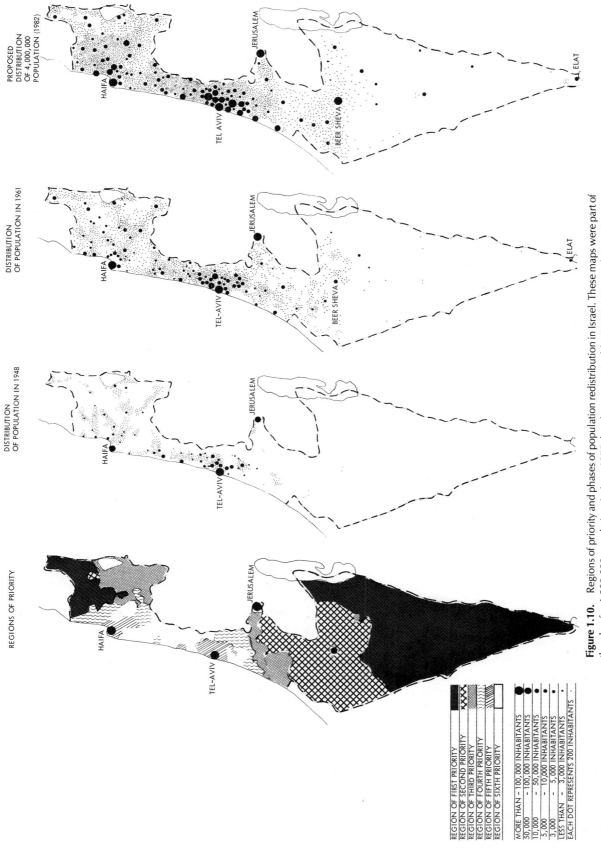

PROPOSED
DISTRIBUTION
OF 4,000,000
POPULATION (1982)

DISTRIBUTION
OF POPULATION IN 1961

DISTRIBUTION
OF POPULATION IN 1948

REGIONS OF PRIORITY

HAIFA

JERUSALEM

TEL AVIV

BEER SHEVA

ELAT

HAIFA

JERUSALEM

TEL-AVIV

BEER SHEVA

ELAT

HAIFA

JERUSALEM

TEL-AVIV

HAIFA

JERUSALEM

TEL-AVIV

REGION OF FIRST PRIORITY
REGION OF SECOND PRIORITY
REGION OF THIRD PRIORITY
REGION OF FOURTH PRIORITY
REGION OF FIFTH PRIORITY
REGION OF SIXTH PRIORITY

MORE THAN – 100,000 INHABITANTS
50,000   – 100,000 INHABITANTS
10,000   – 50,000 INHABITANTS
5,000   – 10,000 INHABITANTS
3,000   – 5,000 INHABITANTS
LESS THAN – 3,000 INHABITANTS
EACH DOT REPRESENTS 200 INHABITANTS

Figure 1.10. Regions of priority and phases of population redistribution in Israel. These maps were part of the plan for 4,000,000 population. In June 1975 the plan was revised for 5,000,000 population. (Source: *The Israel Master Plan and Technical Progress in Israel*.)

15

also to orient public opinion, as has happened in western European countries. The most commonly known feature of this kind of legislation is the concept of eminent domain, which governments use to assemble land.

A public or semipublic implementing agent should have responsibility for executing policy in three ways: planning, development, and maintenance. An implementing agent must also embrace other strategic governmental agencies to gain strength and effectiveness.[16] The implementing body should, however, be least dependent on those agencies to make and execute decisions in following an approved national policy, since a high degree of dependence may hinder implementation and increase its involvement with governmental bureaucracy. It should consist of a small number of highly qualified professionals to work on the optimal alternatives of national urban growth strategy.[17] As a center of experience in comprehensive policy execution, an agent will inform its government of forthcoming trends and will continuously evaluate policy, thus securing continuity of execution relatively free from external political pressure.

Policy may be meaningless if it is not associated with the realization of strategy: "We must seek not just policy, but policy allied to a vigorous strategy for obtaining results from it."[18] Governmental programs always have some direct or indirect impact on existing and future urban growth. In most cases, such programs are actual urban strategy in their implementation whether or not a national policy for urban growth exists. In cases where such policy exists, governmental programs may be measured as they support or detract from the policy.

Strategy is a set of different means to reach the same end (policy). Thus strategy for national urban growth should be flexible enough to cope with national changes while remaining consistent with its policy, and may be interpreted as a framework that may change the emphasis of issues as circumstances change and maintain equilibrium among the components of policy. Since any urban aggregate contains complex problems, strategy must offer alternative solutions, of which new urban settlements may be one. However, it is the responsibility of strategy to set priorities occasionally, although those priorities will be dictated to some extent by the limits of financial resources.

Since implementation of a policy costs vast sums, government must finance it. As the National Committee on Urban Growth Policy stated, "the development of new communities by solely private mechanisms will occur only in those rare circumstances where the dynamics of growth in particular areas will afford a timely and reasonable return on private investment. In most situations, the Committee finds that new kinds of public financing will be required to provide the necessary return on private capital and justify increased involvement of the private sector."[19] Since private investors may or may not join the venture later, public investment will justify public management, coordination, and execution of the policy. Such financial policy becomes a key when a policy exists for investment preferences and their distribution.

The three major financial resources may be used after a project has been initiated. One is resources allocated to various government offices for the implementation of their different programs, such as transportation networks, housing, and employment. A second tool is a taxation policy for private investments, which may encourage or discourage various types of development in different regions by granting tax relief or increases. It may also directly affect land use. The United Kingdom, Israel, and The Netherlands have discovered that taxation is an effective way to encourage or discourage certain kinds of development within their countries. For example, people who move to new towns are given lower income tax rates that those who remain in older towns. A government that wishes to redistribute its population by encouraging movement to new towns might subsidize an industry if it promises to develop in a new town, thus providing job opportunities and encouraging migration. A third resource is a policy for incentives or disincentives for developers, which may support the determination of development distribution. Incentives and disincentives include (1) grants, (2) loans, (3) subsidies, (4) revenue sharing, (5) free land, (6) land improvement, and (7) support for infrastructure or for construction of public utilities.

The public should be aware of the need, the components, and the means of executing a national policy for urban growth. Without this awareness, national attitudes may even work against the policy and render it meaningless. Like planning, any policy is a compromise between political parties and economic forces; therefore it requires public support and understanding to be strong in its implementation.

NEW TOWNS: ONE ALTERNATIVE

A national policy for urban growth should introduce alternative patterns of urban settlements in order to direct urban growth. National policy and a strategy for urban growth will involve diverse variables in their local, regional, and national implementation. The primary variables are

(1) Availability of job opportunities, their distribution, and their aggregated pattern;

(2) flow of public and private investments and their distribution.

(3) density of transportation networks and their modes;

(4) spatial distribution of economic, social, and cultural activities and their intensity.

In considering these variables, a policy naturally deals with both existing settlements and new ones.

Existing Urban Crises

In the past, the creation of urban centers has brought new life and new dimensions to human experience. Today, in contrast, increasing social and environmental deterioration of cities may weaken our civilization. Since the urban crisis is an all-pervasive one involving social, economic, and political factors, it must be resolved by attacking all aspects simultaneously.

Patterns of social behavior in cities are important determinants of the quality of life. Behavior of individuals and groups within a community is a sequence of actions stimulated and influenced by urban forms. In many cities of the United States a high proportion of social disorder exists in urban centers and surrounding areas that decreases toward the fringe of a city.[20] There is also a parallel pattern of socioeconomic disorders such as poverty, slums or low-income housing, unemployment, illiteracy, and lack of services.

Urban centers and their surrounding regions are becoming more and more socially disordered as cities expand. These areas are populated by mixed groups of refugees, aliens, elderly people, migrants, unassimilated groups, unskilled laborers, and segregated ethnic groups. Sometimes new immigrants find themselves caught in the dilemma of conflicting cultures.[21]

Metropolitan areas in most developed countries experience a financial crisis when confronted with the rapid growth of expenditures on the one hand and a decrease in revenue due to the exodus of the population to the suburbs on the other. This crisis leads to a decrease in the level of services or to increased subsidization of the central city by larger governments. It is almost impossible to increase taxes in the central city because business firms and middle- and high-income residents would continue to leave.

Another crisis confronting the central city is the weakening of its educational system. At present, central-city educational facilities fall far behind those found in suburban systems, and consequently central-city children, who need education the most, are receiving the least.

The real problems of today's urban centers are

(1) Their scale and size.

(2) Their inability to govern and manage this scale—large-scale populations result in crowding, congestion and tension, noise, pollution of water and air.

(3) Insecurity and uncertainty.

(4) Migration from central cities to suburbs.

Existing urban crises concentrated in large urban centers have also been amplified by the demand for new housing and additional job opportunities. These demands of growth, when combined with crises in existing cities, raise the question of where to offer solutions; i.e., should growth occur in existing settlements, in new settlements, or in both? The response to this question should grow out of a national policy for urban growth, and any alternative must attack all the demands and crises comprehensively.

Need for New Towns

One of the alternative comprehensive schemes that may alleviate critical conditions of congested urban centers is new towns, which may arise from (1) large-scale expansion of existing urban settlements, and (2) construction of new ones. (See Figure 1.11.)

Planners have viewed new towns as experimental laboratories that can contribute their new experiences to older cities and "afford a chance to break away from conventional developmental thinking and to try new arrangements."[22] Since they are developed literally from the ground up, new towns are pioneers in technological innovation, social management, governmental and economic structures, and urban planning and design. Actually, new-town planners and developers have introduced such innovative techniques of planning and implementation as "new types of building codes, particularly those oriented to performance standards, to test land-use control techniques other than conventional zoning. . . ."[23] Land-use control and building codes in new towns, for example, can be absent or minimal and more flexible than in older urban areas.

New towns may help a country in many ways. As part of a comprehensive policy, they may manage natural resources and use land, water, utilities, and

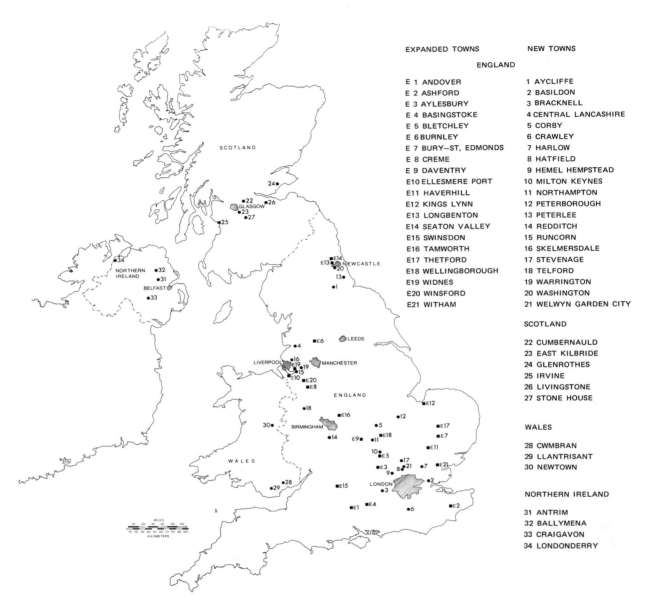

EXPANDED TOWNS	NEW TOWNS
ENGLAND	
E 1 ANDOVER	1 AYCLIFFE
E 2 ASHFORD	2 BASILDON
E 3 AYLESBURY	3 BRACKNELL
E 4 BASINGSTOKE	4 CENTRAL LANCASHIRE
E 5 BLETCHLEY	5 CORBY
E 6 BURNLEY	6 CRAWLEY
E 7 BURY–ST, EDMONDS	7 HARLOW
E 8 CREME	8 HATFIELD
E 9 DAVENTRY	9 HEMEL HEMPSTEAD
E10 ELLESMERE PORT	10 MILTON KEYNES
E11 HAVERHILL	11 NORTHAMPTON
E12 KINGS LYNN	12 PETERBOROUGH
E13 LONGBENTON	13 PETERLEE
E14 SEATON VALLEY	14 REDDITCH
E15 SWINSDON	15 RUNCORN
E16 TAMWORTH	16 SKELMERSDALE
E17 THETFORD	17 STEVENAGE
E18 WELLINGBOROUGH	18 TELFORD
E19 WIDNES	19 WARRINGTON
E20 WINSFORD	20 WASHINGTON
E21 WITHAM	21 WELWYN GARDEN CITY

SCOTLAND

22 CUMBERNAULD
23 EAST KILBRIDE
24 GLENROTHES
25 IRVINE
26 LIVINGSTONE
27 STONE HOUSE

WALES

28 CWMBRAN
29 LLANTRISANT
30 NEWTOWN

NORTHERN IRELAND

31 ANTRIM
32 BALLYMENA
33 CRAIGAVON
34 LONDONDERRY

NEW TOWNS OF THE UNITED KINGDOM

Figure 1.11. New towns of the United Kingdom. The British have located many of these new towns around the major metropolitan areas to solve urban congestion, while locating others in economically depressed areas to improve socioeconomic conditions. Expanded towns were also used to implement solutions to urban problems.

financial resources efficiently. Decentralization and redistribution of human activity may be easily achieved by their establishment, which includes developing industries, commerce, and services to support, to a certain extent, the rational distribution of population. New towns can provide housing and develop superior living areas. They may also serve as focal points for regional development and create new economic structures for new societies. Moreover, the goals of each new town come directly from the type of agency involved in its development: public, semipublic, private, or combinations of these. (See Figure 1.12.)

New towns "hold promise of a market large enough

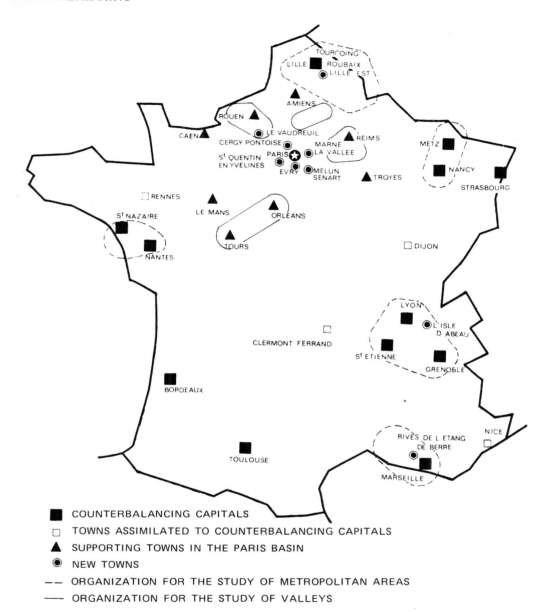

Figure 1.12. French new towns. Currently, France has plans to construct nine new towns. The five around Paris are to decongest it and offer people homes and employment. The other four are to balance the populations of Paris and the provinces. French planners conceive the nine new towns together as an overall solution to French urban problems. However, the French have learned from the experience of the English, and conceive these towns as experiments in city building. (Source: *The Role of French New Towns in Regional Development and Regional Life.*)

to permit technological innovations which, in turn, encourages investment by industry."[24] They may demonstrate what can be achieved by creating a new physical and social environment and may also provide a wide range of employment and a diversity of population.

Alonso, who has criticized the new-communities program in the United States, still admits their importance:" there may be some sense in the limited use of new towns for the testing and development of tech-

nological, physical, and institutional innovations which might be applicable to the expansion and rebuilding of existing cities."[25] The more new towns around the world become a common pattern for our future urban communities, the more they provide a model for improving the physical, socioeconomic, and governmental development of older cities.

If a national policy for urban growth includes an innovative approach for future development to support improving physical and social environments of established cities, then new towns would be an excellent laboratory for such experiments. Areas for innovation may include housing industry, housing management, technology of telecommunication, education, management of social services, economic reform, medical and health services, taxation, governance and citizen participation, delivery of public utilities, disposal of sewage and garbage, transportation systems, and methods of planning and design.

Although we have attempted to view new towns not only in their national context but also as a promising alternative for growth, we should not expect them to introduce social reform or to respond to all national urban problems. However, new towns may be very successful when associated with other programs on a large regional scale, such as that of the Tennessee Valley Authority or of the new towns around London.

In this decade, there has been controversy in the United States about the validity of new communities. One aspect concerns their cost benefit; a second involves mayors of large cities who are afraid that new communities may divert human and financial resources from their cities. Another concern is finances, since optimal marketability of housing is directly related to proximity to metropolitan areas, and it is not feasible to develop private freestanding communities. A fourth concern is that the optimal program of new communities may absorb no more than 20 percent of U.S. population growth.[26]

Those who support new communities have pointed out that the effect of British new towns has outdistanced their financial return. Some also argue that new towns in-town may attract minority groups of a central city and give them a good social and physical environment. These people would not have to leave an existing city. If there is a housing shortage, any project to remedy it should combine with social, educational, and economic reform in a new environment such as a new town.

New towns should not be assessed according to their social, economic, and physical environmental quantity; they should rather be judged by their qualitative impact on their region and their ability to ease national problems. In developing regions the effect of new towns may be significant on economic growth and on population migration stability. Lawrence Susskind has noted: "What is important is not that a new community simply provide jobs but rather that it help to balance a region's economy by making it less subject to cyclical fluctuation, that it promise training and employment opportunities for those presently unemployed, and that it utilizes the construction of the com-

munity itself to promote job training and economic development."[27]

A new town movement may not survive and become effective in a country unless it is preceded by a national policy for urban growth. This combination will make a public commitment to direct its resources at least toward initiating new towns as an alternative way of alleviating national urban problems.

NOTES

1. William Alonso and Elliott Medrich, "Spontaneous Growth Centers in Twentieth Century American Urbanization," Institute of Urban and Regional Development Working Paper no. 113 (Berkeley, January 1970), p. 2.

2. Daniel P. Moynihan, "Toward a National Urban Policy," in *Toward a National Urban Policy*, Daniel P. Moynihan, ed. (New York: Basic Books, 1970), p. 3.

3. Moynihan, p. 15.

4. "First Report of the National Policy Task Force," 2nd ed., *Newsletter of the American Institute of Architects*, January 1972, p.

5. P. B. Desai and Ashish Bose, "Economic Considerations in the Planning and Development of New Towns," in *Planning of Metropolitan Areas and New Towns* (New York: United Nations, 1967), p. 217.

6. Lloyd Rodwin, "British and French Urban Growth Strategies," in *Toward a National Urban Policy*, Daniel Moynihan, ed. (New York: Basic Books, 1970), p. 273.

7. In 1950 the world's population consisted of 698,038 urban (about 28 percent) and 1,786,680 rural (about 72 percent). By 1975 the population was 1,592,289,000 urban (about 40 percent) and 2,436,259,000 rural (about 60 percent), i.e., an 11 percent increase in the urban population. However, in the United States recently the balance has shifted in favor of urban-to-rural migration. (Statistical Office of the United Nations, Dept. of Economic and Social Affairs, *Statistical Yearbook: 1972.* [New York: United Nations, 1973], pp. 80–81, and Roy Reed, "Rural Regions Now Outpacing Urban Regions," *The New York Times* May 18, 1975, pp. 1, 40.

8. "First Report of the National Policy Task Force," p. 10.

9. U.S. Advisory Commission on Intergovernmental Relations, *Urban and Rural America* (Washington, D.C.: U.S. Government Printing Office, 1968), p. 117.

10. U.S. Department of Commerce, Bureau of the Census, *Statistical Abstracts of the United States 1969* (Washington, D.C.: U.S. Government Printing Office, 1969), pp. 190–91.

11. All types of construction in the United States account for 10 percent (or $100 billion) of the gross national product. The public sector accounts for one-third, and the private sector's two-thirds is split almost equally between residential and nonresidential activities. See Robert Gladstone, "Economic and Social Programming: An Overview," (Paper presented at the American Institute of Architects New Communities Conference, Washington, D.C., November 3–6, 1971), p. 4.

12.   The Netherlands has a definite policy for encouraging emigration. In contrast, Israel has a policy for immigration which grew out of vital needs of the country.

13.   James L. Sundquist, "Where Shall They Live?" *The Public Interest,* **18** (Winter 1970), p. 92.

14.   Lloyd Rodwin, *Nations and Cities: A Comparison of Strategies for Urban Growth* (Boston: Houghton Mifflin, 1970), p. 8.

15.   The New York State Urban Development Corporation and the state legislature became involved in a major political issue when they tried to use eminent domain. See Edward J. Logue, *Goals Guidelines Concerns of the New York State Urban Development Corporation* (New York: New York State Urban Development Corporation, 1971) and State of New York, *New York State Urban Development Corporation Act,* as amended through June 1971 (New York: New York State Urban Development Corporation, 1971). (The UDC was disbanded recently.)

16.   Lloyd Rodwin, *The British New Towns Policy: Problems and Implications* (Cambridge: Harvard University Press, 1956), p. 58.

17.   Rodwin, *Nations and Cities,* p. 8.

18.   Moynihan, p. 8.

19.   Donald Canty, ed., *The New City* (New York: Frederick A. Praeger, 1969), p. 171.

20.   Ian McHarg, *Design with Nature* (Garden City, N.Y.: Doubleday and Company, 1971), pp. 187–95.

21.   Robert E. L. Faris and H. Warren Dunham, *Mental Disorders in Urban Areas* (Chicago: University of Chicago Press, 1967), pp. 8–9.

22.   U.S. Advisory Commission on Intergovernmental Relations, p. 155.

23.   U.S. Advisory Commission on Intergovernmental Relations, p. 101.

24.   U.S. Advisory Commission on Intergovernmental Relations, p. 155.

25.   William Alonso, "The Mirage of New Towns," *The Public Interest,* **19** (Spring 1970), p. 5.

26.   Canty, p. 172.

27.   Lawrence Susskind and Gary Hack, "New Communities in a National Urban Growth Strategy," *Technology Review* (February 1972), p. 39.

TWO

THE TERMINOLOGY OF NEW URBAN SETTLEMENTS: DEFINITIONS AND DISTINCTIONS

There have been large discrepancies in terms describing new urban settlements, especially new towns. In recent decades the terms *new town, new community, new town in-town, regional growth center, satellite town,* and others have been used interchangeably. On the one hand, lack of clarification in the meaning of each of these terms has led to much confusion. On the other hand, some planners, designers, developers, and others have used the words to suit their own purposes. Because the term *new town* connotes innovation, private developers have exploited it for commercial purposes. Consequently, these developers have frequently applied the label to settlements that are really subdivisions or regular large-scale housing developments. Thus the specific term for a unique community has become a general term encompassing many new developments planned and implemented in the past few decades.

The United States and other countries of similar urban growth have and will continue to develop more than one type of settlement that can be grouped under the general term *new urban settlement.* The United States in particular has developed a varied and complex set of terms for new settlements because of its pioneering attitude, its constant attempt to be original, and its diversity of issues and potential resources. This constant creation of terms and the confusion of existing ones has created both an academic and a practical need to list, categorize, and clarify all vocabulary dealing with new urban settlements. Such an analysis of specific characteristics of each type of settlement will aid the clear identification of settlements in the future.

The terms introduced within recent decades con-

tain four significant elements: economic base and self-containment, land-use pattern, provision of services, and commuting behavior, the last three factors being integrally dependent on the first. The history of urban experience has shown that a community's economic base strongly influences its character: a community with a diversified economic base has a wide range of socioeconomic groups and provides a variety of job opportunities. The degree of these two factors sets the degree of a community's self-containment. To a great extent the economic base also determines a community's range of social activities, transportation intensity, and power structure. Diversified land use largely supports the development of an assortment of socioeconomic activities. A bedroom community, for example, is limited to a few types of land use and, therefore, does not provide a variety of activities. The number of social services provided through public or private initiative is one motive not only for creating the social identity of a settlement, but also for insuring the future continuity of that community. Since the absence of social services leads directly to intense commuting behavior, the degree of social balance within a settlement is shaped primarily by the amount of services provided. Commuting behavior depends greatly on the variety of an economic base, the diversity of land use, and the number of services provided. Thus, an intense commuting pattern from a community to centers beyond its periphery indicates few economic opportunities, little diversity in land use, and few public facilities and social services within the settlement.

Since an economic base is a dominant factor dictat-

BASIC CATEGORIES

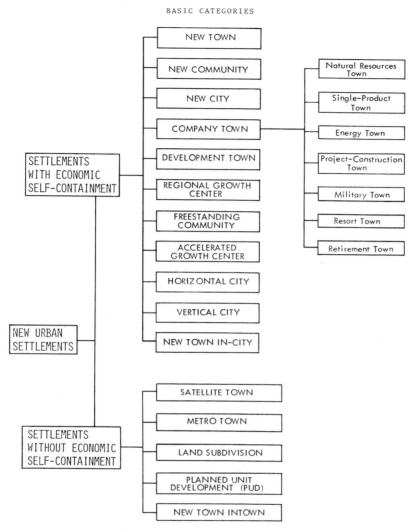

Figure 2.1. New urban settlements.

ing the nature, setting, function, and relation of a settlement to its region, the degree of economic self-containment should define classes of settlements. On this basis, all new urban settlements fall into two major groups: group A, which includes (1) new town, (2) new community, (3) new city, (4) company town, (5) development town, (6) regional growth center, (7) freestanding community, (8) accelerated growth center, (9) horizontal city, (10) vertical city, and (11) new town in-city*; and group B, which includes (1) satellite town, (2) metro town, (3) land subdivision, (4) planned unit development (PUD), and 5) new town in-town.

The settlements in group A are relatively indepen-

dent economically and have physical self-identity. They are not based primarily on a commuting pattern and, in all their dimensions, are relatively self-contained and self-sustaining. Thus, they have diverse socioeconomic groups and include a wide range of land use. Usually these settlements have been carefully, innovatively, and comprehensively planned and developed, to serve purposes and achieve goals other than merely providing housing. (See Figure 2.1.)

By contrast, the settlements included in group B are not economically independent, and are all physically or economically related to an already established urban center. Since major job opportunities exist outside the settlements the majority of their inhabitants form a night population, and the settlements thus have a lower day density. Mainly used as housing centers, these new settlements depend on a pattern of commut-

*The new town in-city is the author's original application of the new-town concept to major sections of a central city. We explain it in detail in Chapter 10.

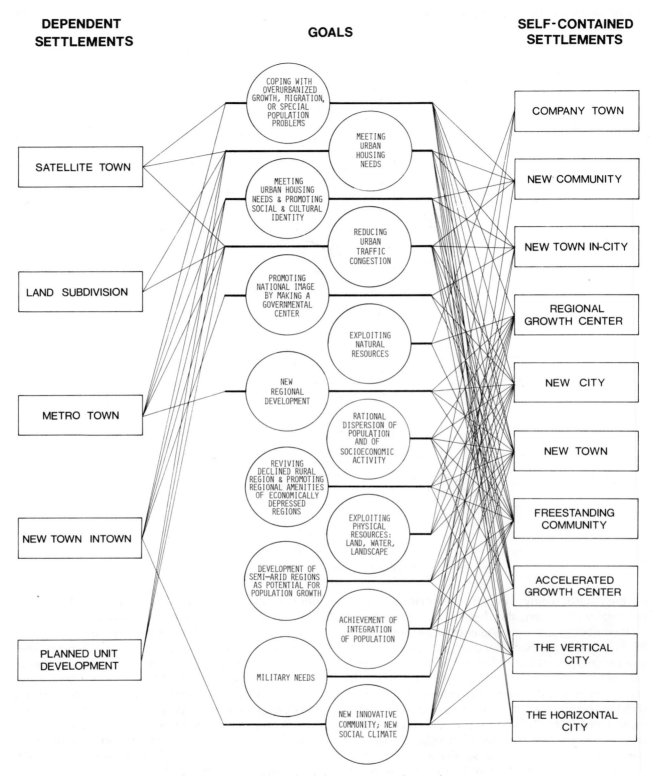

Figure 2.2. Possible goals of alternative new urban settlements.

ing to an established city. Consequently, the social contribution of the population to community life is at best intermittent. Also, since planning of these settlements has traditionally focused more on physical aspects and design than on social considerations and services, citizens rarely participate in local activities, and the community usually lacks community leaders.

These two categories are not exclusive and are mentioned mainly to distinguish settlements for the reader. A public or private developer who wants to build a new urban settlement should first state the goals and objectives he would like to achieve and select the proper settlement accordingly. Figure 2.2 shows 14 possible goals and the settlements that may achieve them. Note that dependent settlements may achieve some of the same goals as independent ones.

NEW TOWN

New-town planning and implementation is one of the oldest concepts in the history of human settlements. The civilizations of ancient Egypt, Greece, Rome, and medieval and Renaissance Europe planned and constructed new towns in order to meet various specific goals and objectives. Their motives involved military, economic, transportation, or religious requirements; the desire to exploit natural resources, build new capital cities, increase regional development, or relieve urban congestion; and the need to improve social, economic, or physical environments. Many philosophers, architects, planners, social scientists, politicians, and others have contributed to the application of the new-town idea, either by their utopian ideas or by participation in the actual implementation of new settlements.

It was only at the turn of this century that new towns were conceived as a comprehensive, unified concept. Ebenezer Howard combined all the positive elements of ancient historical dreams into one integrated philosophy,[1] and since then new-town principles have had an increasing influence on the process of planning and development throughout the world. It is mainly since World War II, however, that an effective, defined new-town movement has actually come into being.

In formulating the concept of a new town,[2] Howard combined elements of the planning process that are still major characteristics of such developments. A new town, built on land strongly controlled under unified public or semipublic ownership, should be distinguished by a combination of town and country life styles and of environments, an uninterrupted greenbelt encircling and intersecting the town, and a well-defined and limited built-up area. One's place of work should be located close to one's residence, and all daily economic needs, social services, and local amenities should be provided for residents. A new town should also be a means of decentralizing industry from congested urban centers. According to Howard, the size of a new town should be fixed and limited, and additional population growth should be absorbed by another new town built on the same principles.[3] All new towns within an area should be connected by rapid transit and "grouped around a Central City. . . ."[4] The distance between any one of them and the heart of the central city should not exceed approximately three and one-quarter miles.[5]

Frederic J. Osborn, a friend and associate of Ebenezer Howard, cited a definition of new town, used interchangeably with the term *garden city* in his preface to Howard's book, *Garden Cities of To-Morrow.* The definition, accepted by the Garden Cities and Town Planning Association in 1919 after consultation with Howard stated: "a Garden City is a Town designed for healthy living and industry; of a size that makes possible a full measure of social life, but not larger; surrounded by a rural belt; the whole of the land being in public ownership or held in trust for the community."[6]

The Association considered the limitation of a town's size to be a major factor in its success, and a greenbelt of rural and agricultural land to be a means of preventing uncontrolled growth. Osborn not only supported these basic ideas[7] but also expanded them when he distinguished between the contemporary new town and its predecessors:

They represent the first modern attempt to apply *scale* to urban development: to define limits of town size and population; to create and retain a measure of relationship between the functional zones within towns and between town and country; to provide some degree of balance of local occupations and residence; and so to arrange and maintain the plan that services and facilities in frequent use are easily accessible to the inhabitants.[8]

Recognizing the need both to reduce urban concentrations which could not in any other way be relieved and to encourage modern industry in sparsely populated and poor agricultural regions, Osborn advanced the concept of new towns as an efficient means of creating pleasant and well-balanced urban settlements.[9]

In the period immediately following World War II, the British government appointed the New Towns Committee to study the promotion of a new-town policy.[10] They focused on three fundamental principles of the new-town philosophy: "decentralization from congested urban areas," and establishment of both "self-contained and balanced communities for work and living."[11]

The recommendations of the New Towns Committee led to the New Towns Act of 1946. Although it did not define new town, the act clearly detailed principles for future new-town planning in England. Such development was to involve the government directly in both the designation of sites and the planning and control of projects. A development corporation would be established to acquire land,[12] act as a housing association,[13] provide public utilities,[14] and manage expenditures.[15] The act also authorized the establishment of a new-town corporation which would be dissolved when its goal had been achieved.[16] Also, according to a 1965 act, a new-town commission would be established to operate the new town, not as an "agent of the Crown" and not as a tax-exempt body.[17] The land acquired for a new town would be transferred from the corporation to the commission, which would be responsible for maintaining the land and its structures.[18]

In the 1950s, worldwide interest in the establishment of new towns became apparent. For example, A. Suquet-Bonnaud formulated a definition of new town that was representative of the type of town desired in Europe during this period. His definition was almost consistent with that of the British:

By "new towns" we meant first of all towns built on a site without any urban concentrations—towns which are large enough to have an independent existence, in other words, self-contained towns with commercial, educational, social and cultural institutions that satisfy all the needs of families and individuals alike; above all, the towns must have a sufficient number of industrial enterprises to create a wide labour market. Such towns are fundamentally different from "satellite towns," . . . they are also different from towns that have been almost entirely destroyed and have been rebuilt on the same site. . . .

We also mean entirely new towns, deliberately created by an act of will on the part of individuals or groups for a given purpose and—most important of all—in accordance with well-established principles and a carefully devised plan, bearing in mind the need for economic and demographic balance.[19]

Doubtless, there have been many attempts to define new town, which have varied from the analysis of the new town as a single unit and its relation to its environs[20] to new-town development on a broader scale. Lewis Mumford, for example, explained that Howard's concept of the garden city was also related to a regional context and to the advantage of grouping such cities in one area. Howard "realized that the advantages of a single city would be multiplied by the creation of 'town-clusters,' groups or constellations of such cities."[21] Thus, a new town could also provide a means of reshaping entire areas through large-scale development.

Most of the recent new settlements that deserve to be called new towns are those in which national governments have had dominant roles in the four major phases of their development which include (1) land assemblage and its financing; (2) establishment of a mechanism for action; (3) construction, planned implementation, and financing; (4) operation of the town, at least in the early stages of development. These governments have also provided incentives for development and for housing, mainly in countries where the public has dominant control of national resources. Examples of such countries are developing countries, where planners and decision makers have respected the new-town philosophy as stated by Ebenezer Howard, or countries such as those of western Europe, where there has been a favorable response of the population to the government's role in national or regional development. (See Figure 2.3.)

To understand precisely what the term new town means, it is necessary to separate, distinguish, and explain each of the five elements commonly associated with its definition: (1) degree of self-containment; (2) extent to which it is a balanced community, (3) diversity of land-use patterns, (4) degree of self-government, and (5) size. The terms self-contained and balanced community are of major significance, since they define the basic differences between new towns and other types of urban developments that have been implemented in the last few decades. We discuss self-containment in detail in Chapter 5. Let us say only that self-containment refers to the degree to which the economy of a new town both produces and consumes all that it needs. Once the idea of self-containment is accepted, then the provisions of employment and housing become the two wheels of new-town machinery essential for the creation of a balanced community.

The British intended that a new town be a "healthy" and "sound" community, including various social, age, and income groups to establish a normal, diverse community which could operate as a "cohesive social unit."[22] A community should provide both places of residence and places of work and, therefore, should not become a dormitory community.[23] In this way, a community may develop a full range of social activities and a way of life related to the various groups. A balanced community should have a positive effect on

Figure 2.3.   Harlow, England. On a designated site of 6320 acres, Harlow features a neighborhood pattern, a town-and-country environment, and separate pedestrian and vehicular systems. Major built-up areas occupy high spots within the site; the valleys are reserved for green open space, communication, and recreation. Harlow's town center includes a municipal building, a shopping and business area, a cultural and entertainment center, wholesale businesses, services, recreation, and transportation terminals. (Courtesy of the Harlow Development Corporation.)

the local tax system and on various local facilities, services, and housing needs. In many new towns, a balanced community has led to the development of local community leaders and self-governance.

Ray Thomas described the most interesting motive behind the concept of a balanced community as "purely social."

Many planners believed, and still believe, that the new towns should aim at an intimate mixture of different social classes. Such a mixture was seen as beneficial to members of the upper and middle classes, who would learn something of the way in which the other half lived. It would be beneficial to members of the working classes who would be provided

with the social leadership which would enable them to lead richer lives.[24]

We discuss the issue of balanced community in more detail in Chapter 4.

The complex relation between the self-containment and balance of a new town is closely connected to land-use patterns. Diverse land use is essential in a new town to accommodate the variety of its elements. We define diverse land use as a mixture of all types of uses required to create a self-contained and balanced community that provides functions characteristic of a city.

This diversity of land use, when considered as a consequence of the self-containment and balance of a new town, distinguishes between new towns and such communities as suburbia which are not self-contained:

In general, "the balanced community" sums up the basic distinction and assumption which is drawn between new towns and other suburban developments—that new towns are composed of a variety of land uses related to the traditional functions of the city, and that this balance between land uses both necessitates and makes possible communities which are socially balanced.[25]

Clearly, diversity in land use creates opportunities for self-containment. In new urban settlements there has always been a high correlation between the degree of diversity and the intensity of commuting from a new town to nearby urban centers.

Thus, self-containment, community balance, and diverse land use all affect the degree of development of the other elements, and the absence of one may even diminish that of the others. Also, the combined existence of these three elements in a new town distinguishes it from other large-scale developments. Moreover, attaining these elements should be a major concern not only in the preliminary stages of development but also in the later stages when a community becomes self-governing.

Self-governance not only makes it possible to provide effective local public services and amenities required by the community but also increases local identity, self-reliance, and community leadership. In practice, self-governance is not achievable in the very early stages of development and requires a span of time, since community leadership must be motivated first: "Effective and responsible self-government will be difficult to achieve [in the new town] until the community has had time to settle down, acquire at least a minimal sense of identity, and develop qualified and experienced local leadership."[26]

Despite governmental independence, however, some new towns may still need to incorporate with adjacent communities to provide joint public utilities and services. In any case, self-governance will add the social identity desirable in a new settlement. A minimum town size is required to justify the provision of local utilities, to support leadership development and, therefore, to achieve self-reliance in governance.

From the planning point of view, a self-contained, self-employed community must be large enough to provide needed services, while permitting the creation of a balanced community, self-familiarity, self-governance, social identity, social interaction, and

urban culture. Thus the optimum size of a community should fall somewhere between the minimum required economically and the maximum desired socially, and this will always be different for each country, since it is related to rates of consumption, commuting behavior, various cultural determinants, levels of services, pedestrian manners, and living standards. Clearly, the determined optimum size of a new town will vary with different circumstances, although self-containment will always be a strong determining factor. We discuss optimum community size further in Chapter 5.

In summary, the new town is defined as a newly built or expanded urban settlement created to combine urban and rural environments. It is a planned community with a distinct confined and compact built-up area surrounded by a reserved greenbelt or agricultural open space and with green and open spaces planned as an integral part of the town. A new town is frequently built on publicly or semipublicly owned land to retain land-use control in its entire urban area. It is relatively independent and has a sound economic base, self-containment, self-sustainment, and self-government. A successful new town provides daily required social, cultural, educational, commercial, and public or private services to satisfy the community and to minimize commuting behavior. A new town has diverse land use that includes industrial, commercial, and service activities. It provides employment opportunities for a wide labor market and a variety of housing for its residents. Any new town should be large enough to support a well-balanced community with a variety of social, economic, age, and other groups to stimulate a town's self-familiarity and identity. Functioning either as a local urban center or as a regional one, a new town is certainly "the antithesis of a suburb."[27]

NEW COMMUNITY

The term *new community* was coined a few decades ago in the United States as a result of this country's unique socioeconomic and political conditions. It describes a new type of settlement similar, but not identical, to a new town. The American Institute of Planners (AIP) envisions the new community as a settlement

built on the expanding edges of existing metropolitan areas and on both new and expanded communities in non-metropolitan areas. To be independent, these new communities should have a sound economic base, a broad range of employment opportunities, a variety of housing types, prices and rents, an internal transportation system as well as convenient access to other communities and metropolitan areas, community facilities, services and amenities and an effective local government. Such settlements could range from small towns of 25,000 population to very large cities with a population of a million or more.[28]

In another definition, the Advisory Commission on Intergovernmental Relations describes new communities as

large-scale developments constructed under single or unified management, following a fairly precise, inclusive plan and including different types of housing, commercial and cultural facilities, and amenities sufficient to serve the residents of the community. They may provide land for industry or are accessible to industry, offer other types of employment opportunities, and may eventually achieve a considerable measure of self-sufficiency. With few exceptions, new communities under development today are within commuting distance of existing employment centers.[29]

However, if one carefully considers either of these definitions, it becomes clear that there are very few, if any, new settlements in the United States today that include all these elements. Actually both definitions are reflections of the wishful thinking of planners and developers rather than accurate descriptions of existing new communities.

New-community definitions generally represent a wide range of opinions and thoughts on a relatively new initiative which has not yet become a state or national movement.[30] Moreover the lack of a definite philosophy behind the American new-communities movement, coupled with the lack of a state or national policy for urban growth, makes it difficult for American professionals and politicians to develop a single acceptable definition of a new community.

Robert Weaver accurately described American new communities as differing greatly from those in the United Kingdom because of contrasting national socioeconomic and political environments. For example, his response to those favoring a reproduction of the European experience in the United States was, "Without going into details at this point, let it be noted that we cannot successfully recreate in this nation approaches and programs which have evolved out of a somewhat different European environment. Recognition of this fact led me a year ago to speak of 'new communities' rather than 'new towns' in America."[31]

Weaver's approach was based primarily on the basic differences in goals and objectives that exist between the United States and Europe. He recognized, for example, that the United States could not adopt the goals of European new-town development: "Whatever the primary role of new communities may be in this nation, it is certainly not to accomplish the stated objectives of the British new towns."[32] This recognition led him to a realistic definition of *new community* as it had been developed in his time for its specific role in America:

A new community is distinguished from even a large subdivision partly by size and location. It should, normally, be planned for a population of 25,000 or more, and some are now being planned for populations of 100,000 or more. It need not be established on wholly undeveloped land, and may even be built around the nucleus of a small existing community, but it requires large tracts of land and, unlike the usual subdivision, will as a practical matter usually be found some distance beyond the nearest built-up area. More basically however, the new community differs from the usual subdivision by reason of the fact that it is planned so as to provide, within its limits, more of the amenities and services required for daily living.[33]

Later Weaver said:

New communities facilitate well-planned, large-scale development. . . . Their greatest economic impact results from their augmenting the supply of residential land in large increments. . . . In them more efficient and effective institutions for education recreation, communications, and transportation could be established.[34]

Although Weaver's definition is somewhat vague, it does specify several elements of a new community: its proximity to an urban center, its size, and its provision of minimum services to its residents. These elements clearly distinguish a new community from suburbia, and they also heighten the contrast between a new community and a new town. The fundamental characteristic of a new community is its major function as a *satellite new community*—the provision of housing. Consequently, such communities have attracted mainly middle-class people.[35]

In the early 1960s,[36] when interest in new communities was growing, a short and different definition was included in the Drafts of Bills Relating to Housing, in January 1964: "The term 'new community' means a locality so established and planned as to provide, on a balanced and internally cohesive basis, the housing, facilities, services, and amenities suitable and appropriate for urban living. . . ."[37]

The National Housing Act in its Title X amendment of 1966 indicated that a development could be considered a new community if it met certain statutory criteria:

in view of its size and scope, [it makes] a substantial contribution to the sound and economic growth of the area within which it is located in the form of—

(1) substantial economies, made possible through large-scale development, in the provision of improved residential sites;

(2) adequate housing to be provided for those who would be employed in the community or the surrounding area;

(3) maximum accessibility from the new residential sites to industrial or other employment centers and commercial, recreational, and cultural facilities in or near the community; and

(4) maximum accessibility to any major central city in the area.[38]

Although this definition is more comprehensive than the ones previously cited, it still considers the provision of housing as a major function of a new community and does not suggest that self-sufficiency is a condition of new communities.

Title IV of the Housing and Urban Development Act of 1968 tried to encourage the type of new community that would

(1) contribute to the general betterment of living conditions . . . by a consistent design for the provision of homes, commercial and industrial facilities, public and community facilities, and open space;

(2) make substantial contributions to the sound and economic growth of the areas in which they are located . . . ;

(4) provide opportunities for innovation in housing and community development technology and in land use planning;

(5) enlarge housing and employment opportunities by increasing the range of housing choice and providing new investment opportunities for industry and commerce . . . .[39]

This definition, which is again broader than that given in the Title X amendment of 1966, considered new communities more comprehensively in terms going beyond housing provisions. Furthermore, it was the first realization that a new community could provide opportunities for innovation. These were the beginnings of the development of self-contained communities, in which major concern would be given to the socioeconomic and transportation patterns rather than housing markets and demands.

The Urban Growth and New Community Act of 1970 added the following elements to the definition of *new community*.

[The new community is a] newly built community or a major addition to an existing community . . . [which should] . . .

(1) . . . provide an alternative to disorderly urban growth, helping preserve or enhance desirable aspects of the natural and urban environment or so improving general and economic conditions in established communities as to help reserve migration from existing cities or rural areas;

(2) . . . be economically feasible in terms of economic base or potential for economic growth; . . .

(4) . . . [be] consistent with comprehensive planning . . .

(6) . . . be characterized by well balanced and diversified land-use patterns . . .

(7) make substantial provision for housing within the means of persons of low and moderate income . . .

(b) . . . be undertaken by a private new community developer or State land development agency. . . .[40]

The Draft Regulations of Title VII clarified the definition of this Act in terms of the size and site of new communities:

(a) [The new community] includes most, if not all, of the basic activities and facilities normally associated with city or town . . .

(b) It must combine these diverse activities in a well-planned and harmonious whole, so as to be economically sound and create an environment that is an attractive place to live, work, and play;

(c) It must contribute to the social and economic welfare of the entire area which it will importantly affect;

(d) It must provide for the creation of a substantial number of jobs, both through development of the project and through the location of business enterprises within the project . . .

(f) It must be designed to increase the available choices for living and working for the fullest possible range of people and families of different compositions and incomes . . . and must be open to all, regardless of race, creed, color, or national origin.[41]

In comparing this definition to others previously cited, it is clear that some notable changes had occurred in the approach to new communities. The first definitions that focused on the new community as a housing center evolved into a description that called for "the basic activities and facilities normally associated with a city" and for the community "to be economically sound" and a "place to live, work and play." This legislated interpretation became a criterion for new-community development and seems to come closest to the definition of *new town*.

There are, however, fundamental elements that distinguish new communities from new towns as developed in England, including land assemblage and land-use control systems, land purchase and development finance, and degree of self-containment and of self-governance.

Private developers have used systems of land assemblage and of land-use control in the majority of American new communities without any public or legislative support. The assemblage process has become most crucial; it is financially speculative and the riskiest of all phases of development. Moreover, since few single developers have been capable of administrating and financing a project of such scale, relatively few new communities have been developed to meet the needs of the United States. In England, by contrast, not only has public land acquisition and eminent domain supported the development of new towns, but land has also continued to be publicly or semipublicly owned as a part of national policy to retain land-use control. Also, European governments have strongly influenced the planning and development of new towns, while in the United States it has been an entirely private responsibility. (We discuss financial differences in Chapter 5.) Only recently has the American government supported some new communities through grants or guarantees to ensure the financial safety of private development.[42]

Although self-containment in the majority of American new communities has not been a major issue, some developments have been planned to meet its basic requirements. In most new communities the immediate function was to meet housing market requirements and provide basic social services. As explained previously, while English new towns have an advanced degree of self-containment in both planning and implementation, the majority of new communities do not have sound economic bases or independent identities. Consequently, they lack the diverse land use characteristic of the typical new town. Several new communities have provided job opportunities, but those jobs were not necessarily filled by local residents. In most of them, daily activities depend on commuting to large, adjacent urban centers.[43]

Thus, a major difference between new communities and new towns is their degree of self-containment, which directly influences the intensity of the commuting pattern, independence, and self-identity. In the United States it seems that the strong ties of neighboring urban centers to new communities cause their self-containment to be less than that of European new towns located within similar distance of urban centers:

"The critical difference between a new town and a new community is in the degree of 'self-sufficiency' of each, which means the percentage of the population expected to live and work within the area."[44] European new towns are also usually large-scale organic expansions of older cities.

Self-governance of new communities also differs from that of new towns. Since new communities have been located close to large urban centers or within the orbit of metropolitan regions, the majority of them are, or are subject to, metropolitan jurisdiction: they have not been given the right to incorporate and establish independent local governments.[45]

The adherence of European new towns to already established national development policies has been absent in American new communities. A comparison of Weaver's definition with that of the AIP shows a difference not only between new communities established up until the mid-1960s and the desired new community as Weaver saw it, but also in the disagreements among American politicians and professional planners about the types of new communities most suitable for the United States. Since European new towns have proved successful, their achievements should serve as goals for American new communities, although these goals will have to be achieved by different means because of situations unique to the United States.

In summary, new communities should be defined primarily as American professionals have described them, and are subject to future change as these urban settlements are further developed. Currently, the new community can be defined as a new, planned large-scale development, built as an expansion of an existing urban center or in a newly developed area on privately owned land. Private developers usually initiate and implement these communities and occasionally receive some governmental support. (See Figure 2.4.)

New communities, which are built to provide a range and high standard of housing on a free-market basis, are planned to be self-contained, self-sustaining, and well-balanced, with a degree of economic opportunity. Those already developed are usually located within commuting distance of adjacent urban centers and are often incorporated with them. They are accessible to a job market, although they are planned to provide employment for their residents.

New communities are planned to have basic local social and cultural services and public utilities, shopping centers, educational facilities, and other daily amenities to enable future independence. They are

Figure 2.4. Lake Anne Village Center, Reston, Virginia. Reston is one of the best examples of a new community. Located 18 miles from Washington, D.C., Reston was planned as a self-contained community providing a wide range of choices in housing, recreation, entertainment, and other facilities to a heterogeneous population. Reston is organized into seven villages, each of which provides community facilities for 10,000 to 12,000 people. Forty-two percent of Reston's gross acreage is dedicated to public use, and by 1974 its population of 23,500 could use any of its 10 public swimming pools, 25 public tennis courts, 19 recreational fields, 25 miles of public walks, and 372 acres of open space. (Courtesy of Gulf Reston, Inc.)

planned for diverse land use, including land set aside for natural green areas and open space. The new community is also viewed as a potential opportunity for innovation in all aspects of urban living.

NEW CITY

New city is a term which planners and developers have recently used to describe an unconventionally large new town.[46] In the United States, the National Committee on Urban Growth Policy promoted the new-city concept to make recommendations for future urban policies as "new measures to further assist exist-ing cities to redesign and rebuild. . . ."[47] Another of their objectives was to find ways of meeting anticipated urban growth through the establishment of large-scale urban centers.[48] (See Figure 2.5.) Planners used the idea of the new city in the planning of Milton Keynes, England, a large-scale settlement with a population of one-quarter million.[49]

A new city may be planned either as a newly developed community or as an expansion of an existing one. Both planning and development can combine private and public sectors, well-coordinated by state, county, and local government agencies which should be authorized to use public funds and to assemble large quantities of land.

Some professionals see the implementation of the new-city concept as an integral part of a national policy for population redistribution and as a means of improving the quality of life now offered by the modern city:

Although the possible goals which have been advanced for new cities are too numerous to mention individually, the major ones seem to be these:

1. Population redistribution to reduce or reverse population flows to large cities;

2. Enhancement of the quality of life for city dwellers; and

3. Enhancement of national or regional employment and income growth.[50]

Not every new city can be constructed anew. Since a new city is a large-scale development which requires a huge area to meet the minimum physical and environmental requirements of planning and design, it may be impossible to find an area that has no existing urban or rural centers. Furthermore, such a site may include existing developments that need to be considered and sometimes included in the plan because of their historical value or the possibility that they may enhance the new development. The planning of Milton Keynes, for example, considered some of the existing villages and towns as integral parts of that new city. In addition to their historical value, which gives the impression of continuity in the settlement process, these centers also add social and cultural meaning to the new city.

The new-city concept includes most of the elements of the new-town concept defined earlier. However, there are several distinct differences between these two settlement types: the new city is primarily distinguished by its scale and magnitude and by its role in the economy, society, and transportation within a region. The population of a new city should be above one-quarter million, and its site should always be some distance from existing large urban agglomerations. Since its role is to provide not only for its own needs but also for the needs of the surrounding region, it should function as a regional growth center with an additional population scattered throughout small communities. A new city should supply social and cultural services, a variety of job opportunities, medical services, and transportation systems. One of the principal goals of a new city should be to enforce and support the economic and population growth of its region and, above all, it should successfully divert migration from other areas and attract this migration to its region. Thus, it can become a large, new urban

center which acts as an effective instrument of urban and regional growth policy as a national goal.

Although the large-scale new city on a regional and national level may be an effective urban focus, the scale and magnitude of a new city can generate a number of new satellite towns in its surroundings. All of these could be confederated or coordinated by one regional government to provide required regional infrastructure.

A combination of public, semipublic, and private enterprise may develop a new city.[51] This joint agency should be the instrument of a national or regional growth policy with legislative power to assemble the required land and pay the necessary compensation.

By virtue of its diversified economic base, a new city can be strongly self-sustaining and self-contained. Yet, to divert people from moving to a metropolis, a new city needs unique appeal. It should make a significant contribution to the increasing demand for housing, employment, and education, especially for low- and moderate-income populations. It may include diverse social classes, races, and age groups and may offer a wide variety of job opportunities. If it has a sound economic base, a new city will have a variety of land uses and a diversity of public facilities and social services needed for a settlement with a population of 250,000 or more.

Good examples of new cities established in this century are capital cities constructed to meet national requirements, such as the creation of a national image or the establishment of a governmental administrative center.[52] Contemporary examples of new cities serving as capitals are Canberra, Australia;[53] Brasilia, Brazil;[54] Islamabad, Pakistan;[55] and Chandigarh, Punjab, India.[56] New cities constructed as capital cities are also called *created capitals*. In each case, governmental policy and funds have supported their construction.[57] (See Figures 2.6 and 2.7.)

In summary, the new city is defined as a large-scale urban community with a population of 250,000 or more, constructed far from a major urban agglomeration on a new or expanded site. A new city is planned comprehensively to stimulate growth in its region and to support desirable balanced national or regional growth, and is initiated and implemented by public, semipublic, or private enterprise.

A new city with a sound economic base should be a self-contained and self-sustaining city which provides a variety of job opportunities for its residents and for the residents of some of its surrounding settlements. It should be self-governed to provide good public utilities and required daily services. As a balanced

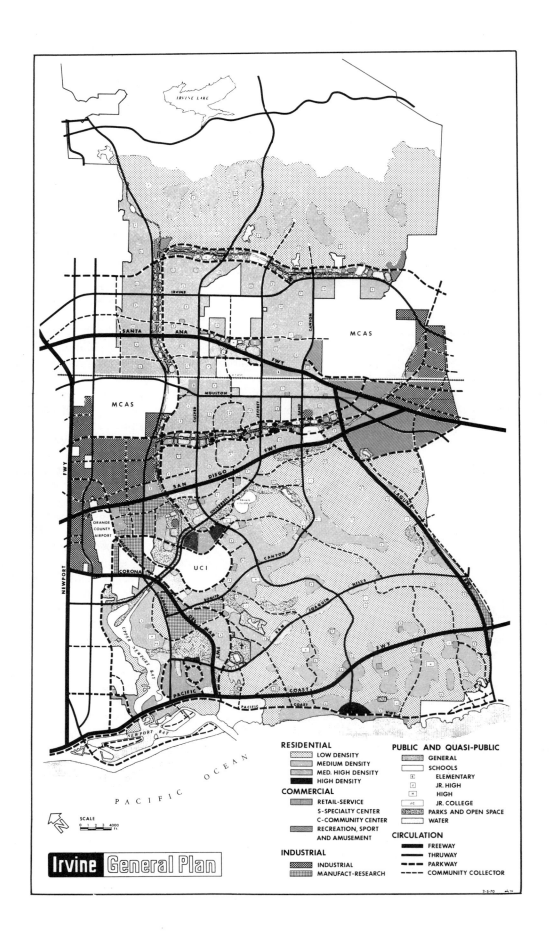

RESIDENTIAL
- LOW DENSITY
- MEDIUM DENSITY
- MED. HIGH DENSITY
- HIGH DENSITY

COMMERCIAL
- RETAIL-SERVICE
- S-SPECIALTY CENTER
- C-COMMUNITY CENTER
- RECREATION, SPORT AND AMUSEMENT

INDUSTRIAL
- INDUSTRIAL
- MANUFACT-RESEARCH

PUBLIC AND QUASI-PUBLIC
- GENERAL
- SCHOOLS
  - E ELEMENTARY
  - J JR. HIGH
  - H HIGH
  - JC JR. COLLEGE
- PARKS AND OPEN SPACE
- WATER

CIRCULATION
- FREEWAY
- THRUWAY
- PARKWAY
- COMMUNITY COLLECTOR

Irvine General Plan

SCALE
0 1 2 3 4000 ft

2-5-70

Figure 2.6. Canberra, Australia: the national capital. Although Canberra originated before 1910, its present structure is relatively new. Five new towns—Tuggeranong, Woden-Weston Creek, Belconnen, Gungahlin, and Inner Canberra—accommodate 27 neighborhoods with a total population of 120,000. The overall configuration of Canberra has been integrated with the topography. The new towns are physically independent, but their commercial and employment centers eventually will all connect with each other and Inner Canberra by a transportation system. This forms the linear spine of the overall pattern. The space between the new towns will be reserved as green open space and also for institutional and commercial activities. (Courtesy of the National Capital Development Corporation.)

community with diverse age, social, and economic groups, it should provide all necessary services and should supply a large range of housing for all income classes.

A new city should also have a diversified land-use pattern which includes residential, industrial, com-mercial, recreational and other uses, and a public mass transportation system to serve the city and its region. Finally, a new city uses a high standard of planning and urban design systems with advanced technological methods and preserves and enhances local and regional natural environments.

Figure 2.5. Irvine, California: a new city planned for a population of 400,000 on an 83,000-acre site. Located close to the Pacific Ocean in Orange County, 40 miles south of Los Angeles, Irvine will occupy 17 percent of the county's total area. Most of the land is owned by a single developer who donated 1000 acres to the University of California. The plan of Irvine features villages ranging in size from 600 to 2000 acres, enhancement of the natural environment, and preservation of agricultural land. Also, Irvine is to accommo-date the major growth in the county, reaching its target population by the year 2000. (Courtesy of The Irvine Company.)

Figure 2.7. Islamabad, Pakistan. In 1960 the Pakistani government selected this site because of its good climate, altitude (1650–2000 feet above sea level), natural beauty, and potential building materials. The government acquired 351 square miles of land through compensation and designated 45,000 acres for the built-up area. The Capital Development Authority empowered to build Islamabad began construction in October 1960. Two years later the first of the city's projected population of 4,000,000 began settling. The development includes typical land uses and a parliament, governmental offices, and the president's home. (Courtesy of the Information Division, Embassy of Pakistan.)

COMPANY TOWN

Although company towns have been developed frequently throughout history, they have become widespread in the last few centuries. Since the Industrial Revolution, this development has been due primarily to the exploitation of natural resources. During this century, however, a variety of company towns have been developed that have not always been related to the exploitation of mineral resources. Thus the general term *company town* encompasses a variety of settlement types, including "any community which has been built wholly to support the operations of a single company. . . ."[58] Although a prominent element in this kind of settlement is the role of the company developer, its most dominant feature is the uniqueness of the company's activities and economy.

Most types of company towns, especially those related to the exploitation of natural resources or dam construction, are usually located in remote areas having little contact with the outside world. To a great extent their location influences the variety of social activities they provide and their demographic structures. A remote site must depend entirely on the developing company to provide amenities.

In some developed countries, the combination of a wealth of natural resources and a pioneering spirit of exploration and technological enterprise has resulted in an urgent need for the creation of company towns. Although natural resources have been a prime motive for the establishment of these towns, a definition of the term encompasses all types of settlements dominated by a single economic force. Thus the nature of all kinds of company towns is the singularity of their economic activity, which justifies their construction and supports their continuity. Accordingly, company towns may be further classified on the basis of this major activity.

Natural Resources Town

Traditionally called a company town, this type of settlement has always been developed primarily to exploit local natural resources[59] and to house the company's labor force.[60] Therefore the town is built close to the industry and its factories. (See Figure 2.8.)

Arthur B. Gallion and Simon Eisner accounted for the flourishing of these natural resources towns during the nineteenth century Industrial Revolution in the United States:

A large supply of labor was needed to obtain the raw products for manufacture, and "company towns" sprung up at mining and lumber camps in various parts of the country. They occupy an infamous place in the annals of American town development. Living in deplorable shacks and shan-

Figure 2.8. Grande Cache, Alberta, Canada: a new town built to exploit natural resources in the Canadian Rockies. Grande Cache is one of 11 new towns implemented under Alberta's New Towns Act of 1956. The province's new towns (except St. Albert) are designed either for oil exploration or extraction of other minerals. Grande Cache, designed for a population of 6000, depends upon McIntyre Porcupine's mine plant, but the Rockies offer the town the chance to diversify its economic base by offering year-round recreational facilities. (Courtesy of Alberta's Government Services Public Affairs Bureau.)

ties, the workers' families were subject to the will of a single employer for their livelihood. Shelter, food, and clothing were supplied through and at terms prescribed by the mining company.[61]

Any plan for such towns was related mainly to the exploitation of resources. In most cases the development of factories led to negative conditions in their physical environment, making them less than an ideal setting for family and social life. Located close to natural resources, these towns usually contained mines and quarries that produced a high rate of water pollution and caused deterioration of the flora and fauna in their surrounding environments. Thus the consequences of short-term interest has often been a lack of concern for the aftermath of a particular private enterprise. A long-range plan would have generated an immediate concern with production and also an awareness of the environmental consequences of that production. In many countries, public involvement in the development of a natural resources town has prevented environmental deterioration.

Ethnic and racial heterogeneity is usually found in this type of company town,[62] and a strong local patriotism is also characteristic of its residents.[63] Since a natural resources town generally employs an unskilled majority and a skilled minority of well-paid workers, one may assume that they develop a savings habit. A high rate of transience and an atmosphere of impermanence exist for the town's predominantly young, single, male population, which rarely participates in social activities. These towns are often very small settlements located in the wilderness where schools are scarce and inadequate. History indicates that these settlements last only as long as their supply of natural resources.

Among the many services required in company towns, adequate medical treatment is most important, especially in mining towns located in remote areas. Services are also in greater demand than in regular towns because of unsanitary conditions and poor management. However, despite the unsanitary conditions, these towns do enjoy the proximity of a vast natural environment, and

many of these isolated communities, especially in the lumber areas, were ideally located with respect to natural facilities. Hunting, fishing, hiking, and winter sports were all readily available and often within walking distance of town. Isolation, therefore, was not always the disadvantage one might suspect.[64]

The building of a natural resources town is usually very costly.[65] The company, as the dominant agency in a natural resources town, not only plays a major part in economics, land ownership, employment, and housing, but also dominates the establishment and control of local governmental regulations and power structure. The company may often act as an arbitrator, "settling quarrels between tenants." Also, "the company assumed the full responsibility of government, being required to furnish all services ordinarily provided by elected city officials. The company alone was the town legislative and executive body."[66] Since political issues have always been of minor interest to a company town's population, there is often an absence of local democratic government. Moreover, "the owners of company towns were sometimes very effective in their control of local political affairs."[67]

Single-Product Town

This type of company town has been developed either according to a controlled, coordinated, and planned economy, as in Russia, or according to a free-market economy, as in the Western world. Although it is not necessarily related to local resources, it is often developed as the result of a national or regional policy of population or industrial redistribution. Generally, single-product towns in the Western world are planned as satellites to major urban areas for market proximity; however, in a controlled economy, they are planned as freestanding towns in the wilderness. These towns operate either one or several kinds of manufacturing focused on or related to one type of product, such as textiles, leather goods, cars, ships, steel, aerospace equipment, or food products. University towns may also be considered as single-product towns. (See Figure 2.9.)

A single-product town is usually populated by a majority of young families and a minority of elderly people. This combination in a small population creates relatively intense social activity supported by local labor organizations. The population is also a combination of skilled and unskilled workers and, in most cases, is stable with a low degree of transience. A wealthy industry supports but, at the same time, either dominates local government or functions as government. Generally, the average income in a single-product town is relatively high compared to the national average, and consequently the purchasing power is also greater than average. Since these towns are often based on export-oriented manufacturing, they require efficient transportation systems.

The economic future of a single-product town is unstable since it depends entirely on one product;

Figure 2.9. Tsukuba Academic City, Japan. Tsukuba is an academic city under construction in Japan to accommodate 43 educational institutions. The site is located 37.2 miles (60 km) northeast of Tokyo on the southern foot of Mount Tsukuba. The projected population of 100,000 persons may eventually reach 200,000. The city is crisscrossed by a pedestrian network. Planned to be free of noise and air pollution, Tsukuba preserves its natural environment and historical heritage. The educational and research institutions will occupy 6671 acres or 60 percent of the total area. The central part of the city will house 60 percent of the total population in medium- and high-rise apartment buildings. It is expected to have a large variety of cultural and social facilities. The city will have centralized air-conditioning and heating systems. The whole city is to be connected to a cable for an information service network; no overhead wires are allowed. Area adjacent to the city is designated as farm and woodland. (Courtesy of the Information Section, Embassy of Japan.)

therefore the town runs the potential risk of sudden economic collapse because of a lack of economic alternatives. Thus, although a single-product town may be doomed to failure unless it diversifies its economic base, in doing so it would no longer be considered a single-product town.

Energy Town

This is a type of settlement developed solely to provide energy resources for local, regional, or national use. Energy towns supply natural gas, petroleum (both crude and refined products), and electricity either from hydroelectric or atomic energy.[68] Those developed during the nineteenth century, when technology was limited, have always had a low-income, unskilled population; in contrast, most of the twentieth-century energy towns were developed as electric and atomic energy centers and, therefore, have a majority of skilled people with relatively high incomes. These towns also usually have a majority of young people with a low degree of transience, which encourages interaction and promotes social activity and recreation. Unless an energy town expands its employment base, however, it will last only for the time it takes to exhaust its supply of resources.

One of the goals of an atomic energy town is to provide shelter for its population and for manufacturing.[69] These towns regularly require enormous amounts of water for their cooling systems, but their location is largely determined by geopolitical strategies rather than by the availability of local natural resources.[70] Since these projects are immense, and their importance extends far beyond their local geographic sites, they are usually publicly created with consideration for security needs.

Project Construction Town

Project construction settlements have been established to develop one specific, usually public, project as part of an overall national policy. Such projects may be related to the construction of dams for water control such as those in The Netherlands since the eleventh century; of structures such as the Egyptian pyramids around 2000 B.C. in the city of Kahun;[71] or of religious shrines, such as those in Greece, the Middle East, and India.[72]

The immense scale of one construction project can motivate the establishment of one of a variety of planned or unplanned new settlements that were not de-

signed as part of an initial project. The Columbia River Reclamation Program, a large-scale regional planning and development project in the Columbia River Valley in the northwestern United States, has been "conceived as a power source, a flood control device, for recreational development, and moreover for irrigation. . . ."[73] The urgent demand for workers to develop such a town often results in disorderly construction.[74]

A project construction town often requires much time for its development. A new settlement springs up close to the project to house building materials and equipment, labor forces and their families, a market focus and, later on, the supervisors of the project's operation. In the early stages of development, most of the population consists of a young, unskilled, relatively low-income labor force.

Once developed, a project construction town may endure only a short time, and although such a town rarely disappears, it can diminish greatly.[75] Contemporary dam construction towns that have changed their economic base have usually become tourist towns, offering water-related recreational activities such as fishing and waterskiing. Such towns have seasonal recreation and combine a variety of population groups including families with young children. Economic conditions in these towns are satisfactory.

Military Town

Such towns, developed to house soldiers and as defense outposts, are usually located strategically in topographical positions overlooking their surroundings or controlling a major passage or port of entry. Military towns are often initiated as temporary campsites and later become permanent constructions. They are frequently pioneering settlements in their respective regions and are always carefully planned and highly organized. Also, because of their efficiency and geographic location, they tend to become regional marketing, administrative, or political centers. In the early stages, their populations are predominantly male.[76] Because of the advantages of their regional location and planning and the changes often made in their economic base, military towns tend to last for long periods.[77] Recently, many of the oldest military towns have become prosperous tourist attractions.

Resort Town

Although this type of settlement has recently evolved mainly to supply a large variety of opportunities in leisure, sports, entertainment, and amusement as one type of economic activity, it is not always based on local climatic resources. Some recreation towns operate throughout the year, but most function only seasonally. They usually attract middle- and high-income people, especially when their recreational focus is on such local resources as snow or the seashore. Most of these towns have many hotels, motels, restaurants, and souvenir shops that support their main activity.

In contemporary times there has been an increasing demand for recreational centers in remote areas, especially in developed countries as part of the national culture.[78] The development of a recreation town requires large initial investments and careful organization by one or several major investors associated for this purpose. These towns are planned, well-organized communities which usually have good transportation systems, accessibility, and parking facilities. They require high standards of communication, especially a maximum separation of pedestrian and vehicular movement. The elimination of noise pollution and the creation of attractive landscapes are essential for making those towns secure and attractive places for both young children and adults. Local populations tend to be diverse, and in most cases, these settlements are governed by the major company controlling the recreational activity.

In France[79] and in the United States, a movement toward the creation of resort towns in remote areas has developed.[80] This phenomenon, however, has often

Figure 2.10. Yanchep Sun City, Australia. Yanchep Sun City is a multimillion dollar residential, country club-style project 35 miles north of Perth, Western Australia, developed by Mr. Alan Bond. Sun City covers 8094 hectares (20,000 acres) of pleasant rolling timbered land and has an Indian Ocean frontage of 10 miles. The area has 60,000 home sites. Its facilities include a golf course, marina, sporting grounds, hotel and motel, equestrian center, 27-chalet holiday village, 90-bay caravan park, and general shops and beach kiosks. When the project reaches a greater stage of development, an aerial view will show that it was designed to resemble a huge ocean cruising yacht. (Courtesy of the Australian Information Service.)

resulted in disorderly development, especially because of avid demands for recreation.[81] Resort towns, widely publicized in the hope of creating a positive image, usually provide good personal services. Examples of these are ski towns, beach and other water-sport towns, towns with special climates required by people with health problems, and entertainment and amusement towns for different age groups. (See Figure 2.10.)

Retirement Town

This new type of settlement exists as a well-organized society with a large middle-class population. Its well-planned environment provides a tranquil setting in a moderate climate, the separation of pedestrian and vehicular networks, large green areas, and sometimes waterfront views. Homogeneity in age level and stability are two characteristics of the retirement town, and many of them provide a good standard of living, special health care and other services, and carefully designed dwellings oriented toward the needs of elderly people.

A retirement town should always be planned to meet the social and mental needs of the elderly who feel a strong desire to be creative throughout their lives. A homogeneous group may prevent such an opportunity. On the other hand, a heterogeneous population will provide the elderly with the opportunity to rejuvenate themselves by interacting with other age groups. Therefore a retirement town should be designed to accommodate the elderly both socially and economically during a sensitive period of life.[82]

In summary, company towns have been successful in stimulating the development of various types of settlements, each focusing on a single product or on the creation of a single environment. The basic motive of their developers is economic. Because of the singularity of their economic base, they can burst forth and flourish, but are always subject to sudden decay which can devastate an environment. Company towns that have been successful in diversifying their economic bases have lost their original identity while gaining the capacity to survive economically.

As a consequence of their original economic bases, company towns lack imaginative, diverse land use. The socially unbalanced populations of these towns usually have homogeneous age groups. Generally since the architectural design of the housing varies little, the character of the landscape often lacks visual appeal. There is always the risk that any kind of development, such as transportation, will focus primarily on the economic needs of a company rather than on the social needs of its community. In many company towns the continuous need for environmental care and improvements has not been the primary consideration. This situation may have been caused by company management acting as a local government, by little social awareness within the town, or by the high rate of worker transience.

DEVELOPMENT TOWN

Israeli planners first conceived of the development town in the early 1950s as new or expanded and rehabilitated towns, developed mainly as melting pots to house new immigrants of diverse origins.[83] Under coordinated policies of population redistribution, exploration of natural resources, and large-scale regional construction, development towns were socially, economically, and physically planned with the economic base, social services, public facilities, and other utilities needed to serve their residents. Development towns were usually planned to be self-contained and self-sustaining communities, with diverse land use and a variety of standardized and governmentally subsidized houses and apartments for low- and middle-income families.[84] Most development towns were designed to function as regional economic service centers related mainly to immediate agricultural domains, and to serve these regions through a transportation network.[85] (See Figure 2.11.)

The central government usually initiates a development town on publicly leased, nontransferable land in semiarid underdeveloped regions,[86] and later opens it to private enterprise that may be supported or subsidized by public funds. Development towns are implemented according to a defined and coordinated policy for urban growth that coincides with investment and incentive policies.[87] The towns are given priority for governmental aid, which supports the development until it matures. When a development town provides full employment possibilities and has its own relatively balanced tax system, governmental priorities diminish, although some governmental aid may continue.

In summary, the development town is a new settlement constructed on undeveloped land or an expansion of an existing urban or rural community. It is established far from any existing urban center in order to meet a national policy for population redistribution and dispersal of socioeconomic activities. The development town functions as a regional center for diverse socioeconomic and administrative activities.

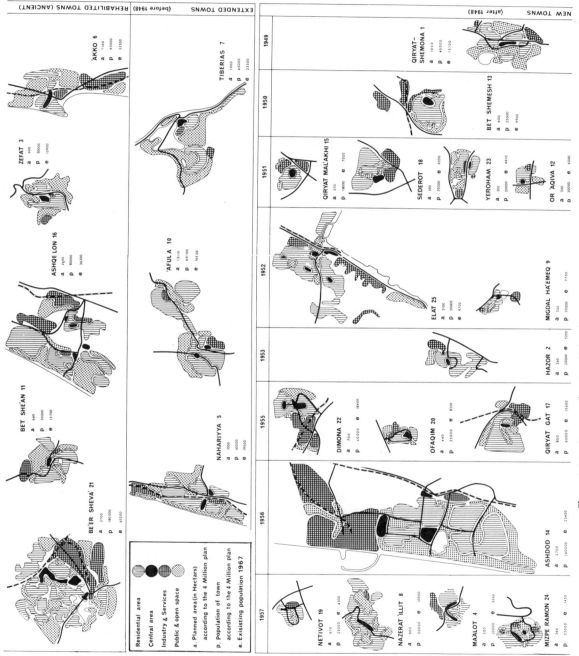

Figure 2.11. Layouts of 25 Israeli development towns. (Source: *Israel Builds.*)

43

In spite of its small size, it may be a self-contained community with an independent economic base and diverse land use. Planned on public land, the development town houses primarily middle- and low-income populations and usually provides subsidized housing, industrial job opportunities, and services. As a balanced community, it also includes a wide variety of age groups.

REGIONAL GROWTH CENTER

Since World War II migration of rural populations to urban centers has caused much anxiety among politicians, planners, sociologists, economists, and citizens. The economic, social, and political consequences of this migratory pattern have formed a two-edged sword, leaving rural areas sparsely populated while overpopulating cities. Moreover, rural communities developed in traditional socioeconomic settings have been losing vitality steadily because of the emigration of their most vigorous age group, young adults. Consequently these communities have not only been in the unenviable position of being unable to provide jobs, but they have also failed to provide basic services for their residents, such as educational facilities staffed by qualified teachers, adequate transportation systems, and varied social activities. As a result, the population distribution has changed to a predominance of elderly low-income people and children with few young adults. The concept of the regional growth center is an attempt to confront and perhaps solve these problems.

India,[88] The Netherlands,[89] Israel,[90] and the United Kingdom[91] have adopted and effectively implemented regional growth centers. Generally, national or regional governmetts have initiated and supported regional growth centers, although there have been ample opportunities for private enterprise to contribute to and evolve specific projects within these centers. It is doubtful, however, that these centers could have ever been implemented without public support.[92]

The first step in the development of a regional growth center is the selection of one geographically centralized rural settlement within an economically depressed region. The objective of such regional policy is to revitalize an existing settlement and to expand it within its region as a self-contained and self-sustaining unit. Also, the center is meant to maximize the cost-effectiveness of infrastructure.[93] Planned for a broad economic base, a regional growth center offers employment not only to its own population but also to those residing in the surrounding areas. Thus a regional growth center differs from a new town, which provides jobs mainly for its own residents. Also, unlike a new town, intense commuting supports a regional growth center. (See Figure 2.12.)

Another basic principle of regional growth centers is the introduction of industry, especially the pairing of industrial and agricultural endeavors, into an economically depressed area. The idea behind these combinations is that most of the industries involved do not require elaborate technical skills. They employ many adults and adolescents and thereby increase individual personal incomes; they also provide job opportunities throughout the year. In this new economy, agriculture with its improved quality and quantity retains its importance, especially in countries with food shortages. Furthermore, a regional growth center becomes a model for its developing region, stimulates local pride, and encourages the development of community leadership.

Since it is planned to attract industry, a regional growth center must provide many industrial location incentives. Areas developed through a regional growth center are successful not only in stabilizing their own populations but also in attracting new immigrants. Governments usually offer industrial location incentives as part of an overall regional or national policy, since the necessity for developing these regions is an integral part of that policy. These incentives are introduced by a variety of means, each of which is related to a unique set of circumstances.

Still another concept in the development of the regional growth center is the planning of an efficient transportation network in a hierarchical pattern, designed to lead to and from the center and to link it with other communities along the way. A regional growth center must provide the minimum services necessary for all its communities. Educational institutions and other services are planned comprehensively and situated in the center to serve its entire region. Development of new industry makes a reasonable improvement of services necessary, which increases the center's employment and attractiveness. A regional growth center is also developed to explore and use the natural resources of its region and, in most cases, provides a significant opportunity for a team of planners to become thoroughly familiar with all the aspects and phases of genuine comprehensive planning.

Since a regional growth center is planned to have basic diverse land-use patterns and also to attract a variety of age and socioeconomic groups, it will also have to provide housing of diverse standards. These centers tend to be structured around a regional government which, in turn, provides public utilities.

Figure 2.12. Cumbernauld, Scotland, looking west toward the extension area. Built to relieve the congestion of Glasgow, Cumbernauld is situated on an original site of 4150 acres and an extension of 3800 acres. The unique town center houses many firms, recreational facilities, a medical center, and a technical college, all under cover. A principle of Cumbernauld's layout is the segregation of pedestrians and vehicles, which was realized through separate networks for each. Footpaths are rare along main roads, and pedestrians can walk from home to the pedestrian precinct of the town center without meeting a vehicle. (Courtesy of the Cumbernauld Development Corporation.)

Furthermore, the small size of each community within the region encourages area-wide governmental structures. Since the nucleus of the population usually was born and bred in a rural atmosphere, their attitudes toward the environment should result in special efforts to prevent any negative environmental consequences.

In summary, a regional growth center is a concentration of new facilities and amenities built on a relatively large scale as an expansion of an existing settlement to revive an economically depressed and sparsely populated region of rural or small urban communities. The center should provide job oppor-

tunities for the surrounding population. A regional growth center is planned as an essential part of a region which, together with its associated rural communities, should form a self-contained and self-sustaining unit.

ACCELERATED GROWTH CENTER

In the 1960s, many of the reasons that motivated the development of the regional growth center led to a similar concept, the accelerated growth center.[94]

Since many members of the National Committee on Urban Growth Policy who were rurally oriented had long believed that something should be done for small towns in the United States, they recommended that states be authorized to create agencies at the state, county, or local levels empowered to use federal financial support for the efficient implementation of a defined state urban growth policy.

According to the Committee, an accelerated growth center would stimulate economic growth and radiate this growth beyond its periphery. Thus, it would provide an alternative to the dynamic sprawling urban center and, theoretically at least, would ease the constant growth pressure of these centers. The accelerated growth center would also have all facilities necessary for self-containment. As such, the region would eventually have a heterogeneous population, offer a variety of job opportunities, and have diverse land use. Furthermore, public initiative combined with private enterprise would construct such centers.[95] This idea, however, has not been implemented. Since the Committee's recommendations only one state corporation in the United States has obtained the power to implement state policy, the Urban Development Corporation (UDC) in New York State.[96] Recently, adverse economic conditions have caused UDC to collapse.

One can interpret the Committee's concern for the implementation of accelerated growth centers as an outcome of its realization of two major issues: the intensive unplanned growth occurring at the edges of cities and the need for an acceptable alternative to absorb this growth. Accelerated growth centers as an alternative to urban sprawl were intended to be interesting and attractive to a mobile and urban-oriented society, to have an orderly integral setting within its planned region, and to be situated at the maximum distance from the large cities at which optional housing markets and accessibility would still be feasible.[97] The location of an accelerated growth center on the outskirts of a metropolitan orbit can be a compromise between the unplanned suburb and the unfeasible freestanding community.

In summary, the accelerated growth center is defined as a settlement initiated by a publicly empowered corporation and developed either on a new site or as an expansion of an already existing urban center. Created to stimulate growth in its region, an accelerated growth center is located on the outskirts of an existing metropolitan center or in a rural region and has a diversified economic base and sufficient employment opportunities for its residents, enabling the center to support itself and its region.

FREESTANDING COMMUNITY

The term *freestanding community* has recently been used in the United States to indicate a new settlement in a rural area far from a metropolis. "Free standing and self-sufficient new communities [are built] away from existing urban centers where there is a clear showing of economic feasibility, primarily built to accommodate population growth."[98] The term has almost the same meaning as that of the original new town: a freestanding community is located far from metropolitan centers as a relatively small, pioneering, self-sustaining unit with its own social identity. This settlement is expected to ease growth pressure in metropolitan areas and to support population redistribution.

The main differences between a freestanding community and a new town are size and degree of economic independence: a freestanding community is smaller and less independent economically. Also, a freestanding community is usually initiated and developed by a private developer on his own land.

The United States Department of Housing and Urban Development (HUD) has envisioned the widespread development of freestanding communities: "Free-standing new communities . . . are economically feasible and will assist in equalizing population growth."[99] Although American public opinion is not yet prepared for an "equalization of population," it is possible that in the distant future population redistribution will be desirable, especially if urban decay continues at its present rate.

In summary, the freestanding community is defined as a settlement with minimum economic self-containment, located in a rural region. This community provides services for both itself and its surrounding region, yet is small enough to be more readily implemented than many other types of urban settlements. Private developers build them on their own land with minimum diversity of land use needed to accommodate a variety of social and economic activities. The freestanding community is a place to work and a place to live.

HORIZONTAL CITY

The horizontal city, an urban concept of the long-range future development of traditional metropolitan aggregates, was first introduced as *Ecumenopolis* by C. A. Doxiadis and his research team.[100] This city is to be a continuous system of constructions, creating a "universal settlement."[101]

One of the major assumptions of Ecumenopolis is that future urban population growth is inevitable; the second major assumption is the size of the modern city is unavoidable. Hence cities quickly expand from town to city, to metropolis, and finally to megalopolis.[102] According to Gottmann's study,[103] most urban centers will eventually be interconnected and will form one continuous urban region with no distinction between separate urban portions.[104] Thus the world will consist of a single city —Ecumenopolis—the "city of mankind."[105]

The Doxiadis research team has determined three major forces which shape present cities into future cities: (1) the attraction of existing urban centers, (2) the attraction of transportation networks, and (3) the attraction of a scenic landscape.[106] Therefore, a major concern in the development of Ecumenopolis is the quality of life it will offer. It is possible that the decay now characteristic of the large city will increase with the even larger dimensions of Ecumenopolis.[107]

A primary concern in attempts to avoid this decay is the size of the community. It may be possible to recapture the old dream of small communities which predominated in various historic periods. According to Doxiadis, communities should be no larger than 7000 × 7000 feet and should house a maximum of 50,000 people.[108] Further, he proposes that small town units be constructed within these huge cities.[109]

A second concern in the creation of the horizontal city to improve the quality of life is the creation of harmony between nature and residents. In the past cities have created this harmony by being of a size that allows short walks from residences to the city center, so that residents could often meet and socialize there. Since this element must be considered in terms of present-day technology, nature should be "converted into a gigantic network with tentacles penetrating deeply into all parts of the universal city so as to reach every residential area—a system of woodlands transformed into parks, intersected by avenues and gardens, within easy reach of our homes."[110] At the same time, transportation networks might be installed underground in order to free the surface of the city for the provision of other amenities and services.[111]

The transportation pattern should also coincide with a regional hierarchical system which is "the circulatory and nervous systems of Ecumenopolis."[112] "This hierarchical pattern provides a basis for the planning and development of both the physical units of which Ecumenopolis will be composed and the

social and administrative units which it will be advantageous to imagine as corresponding to the same hierarchical scheme."[113] There is an urgent need to look ahead and envision the city of the future as a place where billions of people will be happy and safe. A "city of inhuman dimensions" should be built "on the measure of man."[114]

In summary, Ecumenopolis is defined as a future, universal urban settlement proposed to establish an orderly growth within continuous megalopolitan development, and to accommodate the major portion of the world's future population. Ecumenopolis will consist of aggregated, hierarchical town units small enough to create a community identity. Transportation will consist of underground network systems, making all ground surfaces available for other land use.

VERTICAL CITY

The vertical city is a somewhat abstract, radical urban concept developed by Paolo Soleri. Arcology is a giant single structure that could replace the conventional horizontal city by housing approximately 1 million people per cubic mile;[115] it is "the implosion of the flat megalopolis of today into an urban solid of superdense and human vitality."[116]

According to Soleri arcology is meant to be a self-contained and self-sustaining community. Although he did not specify population size, it seems that the expansion of the vertical city would be limited. It is intended to provide one's place of work near one's residence, possibilities for leisure, education, medical care, social institutions, cultural amenities, and age-group integration. Industry will be located in the underground sections of the city. Despite some possible detrimental effects on the quality of society and on the technology of utilities and infrastructure, one may assume that the quality of society and on the technology of utilities and infrastructure, one may assume that the quality of urban life would be improved by eliminating automobiles and replacing them with a vertical public transportation system and the re-establishment of a human scale for distances. According to Soleri, arcology could offer an ideal physical environment. Its compactness could be one way of preserving land as an alternative to traditional urban sprawl. The climate would resemble the regional climate, and pollution would be nonexistent.[117]

An example[118] of an arcology now under development is *Arconsanti,* intended mainly to test the principles of the arcology concept. Arconsanti is located 70 miles from Phoenix, Arizona.[119]

In summary, the vertical city is defined as a super-dense, large-scale settlement which will lead to the total elimination of automobiles and to the preservation of land for open space. The vertical city will be self-contained and self-sustaining, and should, therefore, have all conventional land uses. It should also be a balanced community, including all population groups and providing diverse job opportunities.

SATELLITE TOWN

Satellite town (one of the group B towns, i.e., those not economically independent) is a term applied to a settlement close to a large urban center. This type of town is strongly influenced by the larger city's economy,[120] i.e., economically it is an integral part of a large urban body although it is physically separate from it.[121]

C. B. Purdom described the satellite town of the early twentieth century as

Figure 2.13. Tapiola, Finland: a satellite of Helsinki. Tapiola is located 6 miles from the center of Helsinki, Finland. This new town was established as a private nonprofit enterprise. It's Housing Foundation, Asuntosäätiö, established in 1951, is responsible for the planning, financing, and construction of all buildings and public utilities. The town was planned to be self-contained, and today the majority of its residents work within it. The center was planned for business, administration, cultural, and social requirements of the 16,000 people in the city and the 80,000 people in its region. Another goal of the town was to house a mixed-income population. Accordingly, 80 percent of the housing was allocated for state-subsidized units. The buildings are a mixture of high and low structures integrated with the surrounding evergreen natural environment. Tapiola's planning was the product of an interdisciplinary team which included, among others, architects, sociologists, engineers, landscape architects, and child and youth welfare experts. (Courtesy of the Embassy of Finland.)

an attempt to get new towns built, in place of building suburbs or industrial villages. With that object the term 'garden city' was presented in the form of a town-building project, dependent in some respects upon a city but with a distinct and separate entity as a town, that is to say, not a suburb or part of a parent city.[122]

Therefore, according to Purdom, the terms satellite town and garden city were synonymous in the early part of this century.[123] Osborn, in his preface to Ebenezer Howard's book, also defined the satellite town essentially as a garden city.[124]

To distinguish the character of a satellite town and its features from other settlement types, it is necessary to understand some of its major elements.[125] First, the distance of a satellite town from a major urban center differs from one case to another according to availability of land, accessibility, rate of growth and expansion, transportation network, and degree of dependence. However, the distance should be close enough to justify both a rapid commuting distance and the open space needed to separate the town settlements, and should be far enough to give a physical identity to the satellite town. (See Figure 2.13.)

There should be total economic dependence on the neighboring urban center where the majority of satellite-town residents find their jobs. A satellite town also depends on other urban centers for public services, and social and cultural amenities. Yet it should provide, to varying degrees, some amenities within its own boundaries.[126]

Generally an independent local government runs the town and gives it an identity, so that it is not a suburb of the main urban center. The government of a satellite town could, however, be federated with other adjacent satellite towns or with the major urban center and still retain its own governance.

As a consequence of the above-mentioned elements, the satellite town is usually composed of special social classes. Since it is primarily a bedroom community, the settlement has mainly a middle-class population, larger at night than during the day, and young married or middle-aged workers.

In summary, the satellite town is defined as a new, large-scale urban settlement built within commuting distance on a metropolitan orbit to provide for urban population growth. Primarily a bedroom development with limited types of land use and economically dependent on its adjacent urban center, a satellite town may provide a minimum of required services and educational facilities and, in most cases, an independent government. Many satellite towns provide mass transportation to an adjacent urban center.

METRO TOWN

The term *metro town,* coined by the Baltimore Regional Planning Council in the early 1960s,[127] was also used at that time in Australia.[128] Metro towns are new settlements forming

a metropolis made up of a cluster of new towns surrounding and in symbiotic relationship with the central city. . . .

The word was devised by the Baltimore Regional Planning Council because it suggests three important characteristics of these communities: their intermediate size (between cities and towns); their location; and their social and economic interdependence with each other and with the central city.[129]

The Metropolitan Planning Commission of Kansas City, Missouri, used the concept of the metro town in the early 1970s in the *metro/center:*

a series of new towns or cities within the Kansas City Metropolitan Region. It is a bold idea that would reverse the trends that have brought to so many American cities to the brink of economic and ecological bankruptcy. . . . a high activity core area that would offer employment opportunities, retail outlets, services and recreational facilities necessary to serve about 200,000 people.[130]

In the metro-town concept, new-town principles are modified while still meeting the needs of metropolitan growth and easing congestion in the central city. Thus the metro town is "a new growth point unit,"[131] intended to decentralize development and to achieve orderly population distribution in the metropolitan region.[132] A single authority owns the land and unifies, integrates, plans, and develops it effectively. The metro town should be located in an area where generated land value will be used to further the development.

One purpose of the metro town is to decentralize a central city's socioeconomic activities without overriding the prime functions of the central city within its metropolitan complex; i.e., their relation is symbiotic. In so doing, the metro town should help to reduce city traffic in rush hour periods. Although metro towns form regional clusters that complement each other and in which each unit performs certain functions within this unity for a sound economic base, the prime economic and social institutions of the metropolis should remain in the central city.

A metro town is intended to be a distinct physical entity with adjacent greenbelts. It should have diverse land use and job opportunities in industry and commerce. Although it is not a completely self-contained and self-sustaining community, it should have city and commercial centers, social, cultural, and health facilities, a variety of housing types, and reasonably diverse socioeconomic and age groups.[133] Frequent mass transportation is an essential tool that interrelates all metro towns and their central cities. As in Baltimore and Kansas City, the suggested metro-town unit should have a population of approximately 100,000 to 200,000, similar to many English new towns built in the 1960s.

In summary, the metro town is defined as an integrated regional pattern of satellite communities clustered to form a metropolitan center. Metro towns are built to decentralize some of the central city functions and are usually symbiotically related to it. Metro towns depend on a definite mass commuting network which connects all regional clustered centers. They have a distinct physical form, diverse land use, diverse socioeconomic and age groups, and a variety of job opportunities.

LAND SUBDIVISION

Land subdivision forms an urban pattern by fractionating a large tract of land (usually located in the fringe area of a city) into smaller units, mainly to meet an immediate need for large-scale residential construction. Although it has been considered preparatory work for future urban planning, often subdivision has actually replaced any planning.

In the process of subdividing, a site is mapped out and divided into blocks and individual lots, and streets are outlined for accessibility to the divided lots.[134] This process has introduced many innovative layouts different from those based on the conventional grid design. Subdivision also indicates land ownership precisely by mapping for construction, taxation, and public rights. This method has the added advantage of bringing together individual owners of land to meet the planning and development standards of a city and to make the plan an integral part of urban development.

The public sector usually regulates this process as a means of absorbing the growth of established cities.[135] This development should always be implemented as part of a city's comprehensive plan for urban growth.[136]

Since it is on the periphery of an established urban center, a subdivided development becomes part of an established urban government. Also, since it is not planned, built, or developed to be a self-contained unit, a subdivision relies heavily on its neighboring

city for job opportunities, sociocultural services, and major shopping facilities. However, land subdivision may provide green areas and parks.

Although in most localities the statutory requirements for the approval of a land subdivision plan usually depend on whether it is an integral part of the city's overall plan, often the former is approved and implemented without the latter. In practice, however, approval of a land subdivision plan without a comprehensive city plan would eventually conflict with overall plans for city development, and may even be detrimental to the subdivision itself. In many countries, however, land subdivision has been a major factor in supporting urban growth.[137]

In summary, land subdivision is defined as the fractionating of urban land for the purpose of large-scale development. Frequently occurring at the fringe of a city's jurisdiction, a subdivision is planned to function as a bedroom community to meet a city's growing housing needs. Although it may provide shopping and other facilities, such a development does not provide job opportunities and residents usually commute to other urban sections. Land subdivision is carried out according to the standard regulations of a city.

PLANNED UNIT DEVELOPMENT (PUD)

Planned unit development (PUD) is usually implemented in the marginal areas of an expanding city to absorb its growth. Although its major land use is residential, a PUD may include other land uses such as industrial, commercial, and public open space. PUD is a development program related to a city's overall comprehensive plan.[138]

There is more emphasis on innovative design and planning in PUDs than in land subdivision. As a large-scale development of urban land under single or unified ownership, a PUD is a comprehensive development for providing residential units without the need to subdivide the total tract of land into lots with measured yard sizes. Legislation enables the "inclusion of provisions in the zoning ordinance which authorize the developer to submit his plans for special approval. . . ."[139] Since such approval usually coincides with that which would have been granted if the land were subdivided, the overall gross density is kept consistent with city regulations.

Generally, in contrast to standard land subdivision, a PUD has a variety of housing units, such as row and detached houses, single-family apartments, and high-rise buildings. Clusters can also be grouped as neighborhood units within a PUD area, enabling allocation of space for public needs. In this setting, a PUD also develops a large portion of its land for commercial centers, social services, and industry. Thus, unlike a land subdivision, a PUD functions not just as a residential development and provides another focus or attraction for the city.[140] A PUD eases some transportation and commuting patterns to a city because it provides some of the daily social and economic services required by its residents. Since it is designed to develop the same social identity that a neighborhood unit offers, a PUD has the potential to create a community framework, perhaps even to provide educational and recreational facilities.

PUDs fall within a city's jurisdiction. For the city as a whole, this type of development enables innovative planning and land use, flexibility, an attractive environment, open space, and neighborhood clusters.[141] In the United States many private developers have welcomed the PUD as a means of meeting the pressure of expanding cities, and we anticipate that it will be widely implemented in the coming decade.

In summary, planned unit development is defined as a large tract of land within a city's jurisdiction that is owned and developed under a single or unified ownership as one unit with various dwelling types. Following defined land regulations, PUD is developed under the city's planning and zoning regulations. It introduces some mixture of land use to bring a variety of social groups together, provides for the development of open space to be maintained by the residents of the PUD and is large enough to be built up in stages.[142]

NEW TOWN IN-TOWN

The *new town in-town* is a concept based on the application of some new-town principles within a large city.[143] The main motive for the new town in-town was the urgent need for an effective solution to the problems of dominant large cities. The purpose of a new town in-town is

to revitalize existing urban centers, to stabilize surrounding neighborhoods and to provide a full range of housing within easy access of center city residents. In-town projects have the advantage of being able to tap existing city infrastructure and may represent the best opportunity to provide housing in large amounts for center city residents who wish to remain near their existing jobs. They have the disadvantage of high land prices and fractured land ownership.[144]

A new town in-town tries to revitalize sections of a large city through the development of a wide range of bedroom dwellings and commercial and cultural opportunities. This rehabilitation is intended to provide a better physical environment than that in the major city and to create a new economic focus. Although this concept has not yet been fully developed among those who have written about it, Harvey Perloff seems to have expressed the idea most thoroughly.[145]

A new town in-town is to be implemented in installments to attack urgent problems within a center city through gradual rehabilitation, so that families and businesses will not be dislocated in the implementation stages. The site chosen within a city should have distinctive physical features, such as interesting shopping facilities, and small businesses and artisans operating within the site.[146]

Perloff's idea of a new town in-town emphasizes the functional and monumental elements of the city in an attempt to use their social or cultural aspects for city revival. Thus he sees physical identity as a means of achieving a social unity on which urban social life may focus. This unity would be accomplished in the community by sharing the most modern facilities and services,[147] which would also serve as a means of integration.[148] A lighted center is the focal point of Perloff's concept. It is an important element in the creation of urbanity because it provides an atmosphere for nighttime activity and thus promotes social interaction.[149] (See Figure 2.14.)

A program of neighborhood improvement is also important. Community organizations and neighborhood improvement programs would be established to maintain the community's environment.[150] Perloff has also suggested that the new town in-town provide a mixture of housing.[151] Furthermore, the project should combine both public and private enterprise and be built by a development corporation.

In summary, the purpose of the new town in-town is to revitalize physically and socially blighted sections of a large city through large-scale, staged development that follows a comprehensive plan. However, at best, the new town in-town can cope with only some of the problems of a large city.[152] The new town in-town provides a variety of housing types, neighborhood structures, social and cultural amenities, and educational facilities. It should be established as an integral part of the city with a transportation system linking it to the city center and to its various parts. The new town in-town has a limited variety of land use; also, it may provide limited employment and local services required daily. (See Figure 2.15.)

Figure 2.14. Roosevelt Island, New York. Roosevelt Island is a new town in-town, located on the East River near Manhattan, New York City. The Roosevelt Island Development Corporation was established as a subsidiary of the New York State Urban Development Corporation. The goal of the corporation is to plan and construct the town under the provisions of the Urban Development Corporation law. The town is planned to include a local minibus, keeping all private transportation from circulating. A parking area to accommodate 2400 cars will be provided at the entrance to the island, and the garage will be open 24 hours a day, with a moderate rate for nonresident parking. Residents will park in a designated area. This new town in-town will include two hospitals. (Courtesy of the Roosevelt Island Development Corporation.)

CHARACTERISTIC	NEW TOWN	NEW COMMUNITY	NEW CITY	COMPANY TOWN	DEVELOPMENT TOWN	REGIONAL GROWTH CENTER	FREESTANDING COMMUNITY	ACCELERATED GROWTH CENTER	HORIZONTAL CITY	VERTICAL CITY	SATELLITE TOWN	METRO TOWN	LAND SUBDIVISION	PLANNED UNIT DEVELOPMENT	NEW TOWN INTOWN	NEW TOWN IN-CITY
1. PUBLIC OR UNIFIED LAND OWNERSHIP (SEMIPUBLIC)	●	—	◐	—	●	◐	—	—	—	◐	—	◐	—	—	◐	●
2. CONFINED GREEN BELT	●	●	●	●	●	●	●	●	◐	●	—	●	—	◐	—	●
3. COMBINE TOWN AND COUNTRY	●	●	●	●	●	●	●	◐	◐	●	◐	◐	—	◐	—	●
4. INTERSECTING GREEN OPEN SPACE	●	◐	●	●	●	●	●	●	◐	—	—	—	—	◐	◐	—	●
5. DEFINED AND COMPACT AREA	●	—	●	●	●	●	◐	◐	●	●	—	●	—	●	—	●
6. LIMITED POPULATION SIZE	●	—	—	—	●	◐	—	—	●	●	—	◐	—	◐	—	●
7. BALANCED COMMUNITY	●	◐	●	—	●	●	●	●	●	●	—	●	—	◐	◐	●
8. NEIGHBORHOOD UNITS	●	●	●	—	●	●	●	◐	◐	●	◐	◐	◐	◐	●	●
9. SOUND ECONOMIC BASE	●	◐	●	●	●	●	●	●	●	●	—	◐	—	—	—	●
10. PROXIMATE PLACES OF WORK AND RESIDENCES	●	—	●	●	●	●	●	◐	—	●	●	◐	—	—	—	●
11. LOCAL PROVISION OF INFRASTRUCTURE	●	◐	●	◐	●	●	●	●	◐	◐	◐	●	—	◐	◐	●
12. SUPPORT INDUSTRIAL DECENTRALIZATION	●	◐	●	◐	●	●	●	◐	◐	●	—	●	—	◐	◐	●
13. PUBLIC AS MAIN ENTERPRISER	●	—	—	—	●	●	—	—	—	◐	—	—	—	—	◐	●
14. STRONG PLANNING CONTROL	●	◐	●	—	●	●	◐	◐	—	●	◐	●	●	●	●	●

KEY — NOT APPLICABLE
◐ APPLICABLE IN PART
● APPLICABLE

Figure 2.15. Summary of characteristics of new urban settlements.

NOTES

New Town

1. The ideas of Ebenezer Howard were first published in *To-Morrow: A Peaceful Path to Real Reform* (1898) and later in *Garden Cities of To-Morrow* (1902). *Garden Cities of To-Morrow* was subsequently republished by M.I.T. Press, Cambridge, Massachusetts in 1965.

2. For a more complete description and analysis of Ebenezer Howard's Garden City concept, see Lloyd Rodwin, *The British New Towns Policy: Problems and Implications* (Cambridge: Harvard University Press, 1956). Part II of the book is particularly interesting in its discussion of Newtopia versus Megalopolis. Also see Lewis Mumford's introductory essay to Ebenezer Howard's *Garden Cities of To-Morrow*, "The Garden City Idea and Modern Planning," pp. 29–40.

3. Ebenezer Howard proposed a town with a population of 32,000 and an area of 1000 acres. He also suggested an additional 5000 acres for agriculture as an integral part of the new-town plan. His proposed gross density was 32 people per acre, or an average of 8.3 families per acre (3.7 persons per family). Howard's city plan was greatly influenced by Renaissance design, in which all boulevards led to the central part of the town—a major garden encircled by a central park. The town was intersected by six radial boulevards, forming six equal units, and walking distances did not exceed 600 yards. Howard also suggested a residential lot size of 20 feet × 130 feet. His proposed town was intersected by green boulevards and an avenue which encircled a 115-acre park. Factories and commercial establishments were located on the outskirts of the town. Thus the central part of the town was reserved for clean and attractive functions, and all land uses that could detract from the physical appearance of the town were left for the marginal parts while being conveniently accessible (Howard, chapter 1).

4. Howard, p. 142.

5. Although 3¼ miles was originally one of Howard's basic principles, experience in the early development of new towns in England showed that the distance which was finally accepted was considerably greater. Two garden cities initiated by Howard in an attempt to implement his concept were Letchworth (1904), 35 miles north of London, and Welwyn Garden City (1920), 22 miles north of London (Frederic J. Osborn and Arnold Whittick, *The New Towns: The Answer to Megalopolis* [New York: McGraw-Hill Book Co., 1963], Chapters 4 and 19).

6. Frederic J. Osborn, Preface to *Garden Cities of To-Morrow* (1965), p. 26. See also Osborn and Whittick, p. 11.

7. Osborn and Whittick, p. 11.

8.   Osborn and Whittick, p. 8.

9.   Osborn and Whittick, p. 7.

10.   The Minister of Town and Country Planning appointed the New Towns Committee in October 1945. Chaired by the Right Honorable Lord Reith, it submitted its final report in July 1946. For an explanation of the Committee's goals and findings, see Great Britain, Ministry of Town and Country Planning and Department of Health for Scotland, *New Towns Committee Final Report* (London: Her Majesty's Stationery Office, 1946) and Frank Schaffer, *The New Town Story* (London: MacGibbon & Kee, 1970), pp. 17–18.

11.   Schaffer, p. 17.

12.   The British *New Towns Act, 1946* states that

"The development corporation established for the purposes of a new town may, with the consent of the Minister, acquire by agreement, or may be authorized by means of a compulsory purchase order made by the corporation and submitted to and confirmed by the Minister to acquire compulsorily,—
a) any land within the area designated under this Act as the site of the new town;
b) any land adjacent to that area which they require for purposes connected with the development of the new town;
c) any land, whether adjacent to that area or not, which they require for the provision of services for the purposes of the new town. . . ."
(Great Britain, *New Towns Act, 1946* [London: Her Majesty's Stationery Office, 1946], Section 4[1], p. 4.)

13.   Great Britain, *New Towns Act, 1946,* Section 8(1), p. 8.

14.   Great Britain, *New Towns Act, 1946,* Section 9(2), p. 9.

15.   Great Britain, *New Towns Act, 1946,* Section 11, p. 12.

16.   Great Britain, *New Towns Act, 1946,* Section 15(1), pp. 15–16.

17.   Great Britain, *New Towns Act 1965,* reprint (London: Her Majesty's Stationery Office, 1967), Section 35(3), p. 58.

18.   Great Britain, *New Towns Act 1965,* Section 36(1) and (2), p. 59.

19.   A. Suquet-Bonnaud, "Introduction" (au numéro spécial sur les villes nouvelles), *Urbanisme* **22,** nos. 25–26 (1953), pp. 3–4. Quoted and translated in Jean Viet, *New Towns: A Selected Annotated Bibliogrpphy,* no. 12 (Paris: UNESCO, 1960), p. 16.

20.   A sampling of other formulated definitions of the new town includes the following:

"The New Town is a concept of urban development which is different from any previously known form of community building. It assumes complete control as to planning and use of industrial, residential and community building. It assumes complete control as to planning and use of industrial, residential and community development and growth by private, profit-oriented parties. It is planned to be a self-sustaining, economically viable entity—the antithesis of the typical suburban subdivision which acts as a leech on surrounding industry and a burden on local protective, service, and educational facilities."

(Richard M. Hurd, "City Problems Require Building of New Towns," *Urban Land,* **25,** no. 3 [March 1966], pp. 2, 16.)

"[The new town is] a reasonable autonomous, multi-purpose community providing as full a range of economic activities and population as possible, reflecting the pattern of the larger region of which it is a part. Although the ultimate size of new cities might vary widely

according to the scale and pace of its supporting markets, it should be sufficiently large so that its target population and employment levels take ten or more years to reach."

(Robert M. Gladstone, "Does Building a City Make Economic Sense?" *Appraisal Journal,* **34,** no. 3 [1966], p. 410.)

"New towns should provide for living choices—that is, for a variety of housing types in apartment buildings, row houses, and detached dwellings."

("What New Towns Ought to Be," an editorial in *New Towns: A New Dimension of Urbanism* [Washington, D.C.: International City Managers' Association, 1966], p. 53.)

21.   Howard, p. 36.

22.   Schaffer, p. 1.

23.   Ray Thomas has clearly distinguished between a dormitory community and a balanced community with a sound economic base: "It is generally possible to get housing in one of the London new towns only if there is a job there to go to. By this simple policy the new towns effectively avoided any possible danger of becoming dormitory areas." (Ray Thomas, *London's New Towns* [London: Political and Economic Planning (PEP), 1969], p. 385.)

24.   Thomas, p. 384.

25.   James A. Clapp, *New Towns and Urban Policy* (New York: Dunellen Publishing Co., 1971), pp. 55–56.

26.   Stanley Scott, "Urban Growth Challenges New Towns," in *New Towns: A New Dimension of Urbanism* (Washington, D.C.: International City Managers' Association, 1966), p. 45.

27.   Mumford, in Howard, p. 35.

New Community

28.   Muriel I. Allen, ed., *New Communities: Challenge for Today,* Background paper no. 2 (Washington, D.C.: American Institute of Planners, October 1968), p. 6.

29.   U.S. Advisory Commission on Intergovernmental Relations, *Urban and Rural America* (Washington, D.C.: U.S. Government Printing Office, 1968), p. 64.

30.   Gideon Golany, "New Communities in the United States: Assessment and Potential," in *The Contemporary New Communities Movement in the United States,* Gideon Golany and Daniel Walden, eds. (Urbana, Ill.: University of Illinois Press, 1974), pp. 1–22.

31.   Robert C. Weaver, *Dilemmas of Urban America* (Cambridge: Harvard University Press, 1966), p. 13.

32.   Weaver, p. 19.

33.   Robert Weaver's testimony. See U.S. Senate, *Housing Legislation of 1964: Hearings Before a Subcommittee of the Committee on Banking and Currency* 88th Congress, 2nd session, 1964, p. 368.

34.   Weaver, *Dilemmas of Urban America,* pp. 25–26.

35.   Jerome P. Pickard, "Is Dispersal the Answer to Urban Overgrowth?" *Urban Land,* **29,** no. 1 (January 1970), p. 12.

36.   The sixties reflected the growing interest of the public in encouraging new-community development. Legislation supported a policy for this development more actively than ever before. Although many legislative measures were introduced, not all were enacted. Legislation enacted during this decade includes

Title IV—Land Development and New Communities: Experimental Mortgage Insurance Program for New Communities, "Demonstration Cities and Metropolitan Development Act of 1966," Public Law 89–754, 3 November 1966.

Title IV—Guarantees for Financing New Community Land Development, "Housing and Urban Development Act of 1968," Public Law 90–448, 1 August 1968.

Title VII—Urban Growth and New Community Development, "Housing and Urban Development Act of 1970," Public Law 91–609, 31 December 1970.

37. U.S. House of Representatives, *Drafts of Bills Relating to Housing* (Message from the President), 88th Congress, 2nd session, Title II—Mortgage Insurance Programs, Section 201, Amendment to the National Housing Act (Title X), Definitions (6), p. 22.

38. U.S. "Demonstration Cities and Metropolitan Development Act of 1966," Public Law 89–754, Section 1004(b), in *United States Statutes at Large,* **80,** Part I, p. 1271.

39. U.S. "Housing and Urban Development Act of 1968," Public Law 90–448, Title IV, Section 402, in *United States Statutes at Large,* **82,** p. 38.

40. U.S. "Housing and Urban Development Act of 1970," Public Law 91–609, Sections 711 (a) and 712, in *United States Statutes at Large,* **84,** pp. 26–27.

41. U.S. "Draft Regulations: Urban Growth and New Community Development Act of 1970," Subpart B, Section 32–6, in *Federal Register,* 36 F.R. 14205–14, 13 July 1971.

42. See Title VII, "Housing and Urban Development Act of 1970."

43. Columbia a new community located between Washington, D.C., and Baltimore, Maryland, is a leading new community. Combining a high standard of services with innovative design, Columbia is one of the very few new communities that have tried to build a sound economic base. The interesting phenomena of Columbia is that the majority of its residents commute daily to work outside, while a majority of the local jobs are occupied by outsiders who commute daily from the Baltimore metropolitan region.

44. Edward P. Eichler and Marshall Kaplan, *The Community Builders* (Berkeley and Los Angeles: University of California Press, 1970), p. 24.

45. An analysis of 63 large-scale developments or new communities developed or under construction between 1947 and 1968, conducted by HUD in January 1969, revealed that 78 percent of the projects were within Standard Metropolitan Statistical Areas (SMSAs): 49 projects were in 25 SMSAs. Also, all of the 63 projects were located in 18 states, and over one-third were located in California, Arizona, and Florida. Only 7 projects had their own local governments; 11 were within existing municipal boundaries or were annexed to a city; and a few of those remaining were expected to be incorporated, since surrounding jurisdictions were performing the necessary public functions for these communities. (Pickard, pp. 11–12).

New City

46. The concept of the new city was introduced by Le Corbusier in 1922 as "La Ville Contemporaine." It was to house a population of 3 million with a density of 1200 persons per acre. Le Corbusier dis-played a model of his idea in a Paris exposition on "La Ville Contemporaine." He introduced the concept of a city with 60-story megaskyscraper towers, which could accommodate 5 percent of the ground area. They would be concentrated in the city center and surrounded by wide open spaces. Apartments were 8-story buildings surrounding skyscraper towers, with a density of 120 persons per acre; apartments toward the outskirts were *cite jardins* of single houses. In 1925, Le Corbusier introduced *The City of Tomorrow,* a new version of his concept to the Plan Voisin for the center of Paris. (Le Corbusier, *The City of Tomorrow* [London: The Architectural Press, 1929]).

47. In 1968, a group of senators, representatives, mayors, and governors formed the National Committee on Urban Growth Policy to study the European experience in new-town planning and development in the past decades, and to analyze and evaluate the existing urban crisis in the United States. The Committee recommended the alleviation of current urban congestion by the construction of new cities to absorb future urban population trends (Donald Canty, ed., *The New City* [New York: Frederick A. Praeger, Publishers, 1969], p. 172).

48. The National Committee on Urban Growth Policy proposed the construction of 100 new or expanded cities, each with a population of 100,000, and 10 others with a population of 1 million. Together they would absorb 20 million people, or 20 percent of the total population growth anticipated by the turn of the century (Canty, p. 172). In 1972, the Commission on Population Growth and the American Future estimated that future growth, with a two-child average per family, would add 66 million (based on the total population in 1970) to the population of the United States by the turn of the century (Commission on Population Growth and the American Future, *Population and the American Future* [New York: The New American Library, 1972], p. 20).

49. Milton Keynes was one of the first new cities planned and developed in England, and it is part of Great Britain's new-town program which has developed more than 30 new towns since the New Towns Act of 1946. Milton Keynes, located 50 miles northwest of London, is midway between London and Birmingham. Its designated area of 22,000 acres includes the new city and several existing towns and villages. Its total projected population is 250,000, and in addition to its present population it will provide homes and jobs for 70,000 people by 1981 and for 150,000 by the early 1990s. See Llewelyn-Davies, Weeks, Forestier-Walker and Bor, *The Plan for Milton Keynes,* vols. I and II (Milton Keynes, England: Milton Keynes Development Corporation, 1970).

50. Harvey A. Garn, *New Cities, New Communities and Growth Centers,* an Urban Institute Paper, VI 113–30 (Washington, D.C.: The Urban Institute, March 1970), p. 3.

51. The National Committee on Urban Growth Policy recommended that "the creation of agencies at state, county, or local level with power to use the federal financing tools" be authorized (Canty, p. 173).

52. Jorge E. Hardoy, "The Planning of New Capital Cities," in *Planning of Metropolitan Areas and New Towns* (New York: United Nations, 1967), pp. 232–49.

53. Canberra was created in 1900 when the six Australian states decided to confederate. It was constructed as a capital to serve as the seat of the new government of the Commonwealth of Australia and to function as a symbol of unity and national pride. Although construction began in 1913, it really got underway in 1946 and progressed especially after 1958 (Hardoy, pp. 233–49, and The National Capital Development Commission, *Tomorrow's Canberra* [Canberra: Australian National University Press, 1970]).

54.   The construction of Brasilia was initiated on September 18, 1946, when Brazil's Chamber of Deputies decided to move the nation's capital from Rio De Janeiro on the Atlantic shore to a site 575 miles northwest (925 km) on a virgin site in the wilderness located in the central highlands. The new federal district extended over an area of 1930 square miles. The site was suggested in June 1948, and Congress authorized the project in 1953. On March 16, 1957, the plan was selected and construction began in September of the same year (Willy Staubli, *Brasilia* [Stuttgart: Verlagsanstalt Alexander Koch GmbH, n.d.]).

55.   Islamabad was developed by the Pakistani government when it decided to move the capital from Karachi, on the shore of the Indian Ocean, to the extreme northern part of the country 725 miles (1167 km) away from the old site. The planning started in 1959 (Doxiadis Associates, "Islamabad: The Scale of the City and its Central Area," *Ekistics*, **14,** no. 83 [October 1962], pp. 148–60, and Jorge E. Hardoy, "Two New Capital Cities: Brasilia and Islamabad," *Ekistics*, **18,** no. 108 [November 1964], pp. 320–25).

56.   Chandigarh was created as the new capital of the Punjab province in India. Prepared in 1950 for an ultimate population of 500,000 people, the plan was revised in 1951. Construction began in 1952 (Otto Koenigsberger, "New Towns in India," *Town Planning Review,* **23,** no. 2 [July 1952], pp. 116–19, and E. Maxwell Fry, "Chandigarh: The Capital of the Punjab," *RIBA Journal,* **62,** no. 3 [January 1955], pp. 87–99).

57.   Glenn Stephenson calls new cities that are established as capitals "created capitals." He defines this type of new city as "a capital city which owes its origin and development to government policy and financial support . . . the use of the term 'created capital' is restricted to those capitals that have evolved in a place with no previous urbanization as a result of conscious government policy." (Glenn V. Stephenson, "Two Newly-Created Capitals: Islamabad and Brasilia," *Town Planning Review,* **41,** no. 4 [October 1970], p. 330).

Company Town

58.   James B. Allen, *The Company Town in the American West* (Norman, Oklahoma: University of Oklahoma Press, 1966), p. 4.

59.   The three countries in which natural resources are most commonly found are Australia, Canada, and the United States. The first has developed a significant number of mining towns, especially in the northern parts of the continent. During this century, Canada has developed many company towns for the exploitation of natural resources such as aluminum. During the westward expansion of the United States, the development of the railroad and the discovery of gold and silver initiated land speculation. The development of several company towns of this type was a pioneering effort in remote areas.

One example of a new town constructed in Canada for aluminum mining is Kitimat, British Columbia (Clarence S. Stein, *Kitimat Townsite Report* [Kitimat, B.C.: Corporation of the District of Kitimat, December 1960]). Similar towns have also been constructed in Greece, for example, Aspra Spitia (Th. Dascalopoulos, "New Aluminum Settlement: Aspra Spitia, Greece," *Ekistics,* **16,** no. 94 [September 1963], pp. 170–83).

60.   Many other elements usually included in the definition of the natural resources town and other types of company towns are omitted here because we deal with them in the summary at the end of the section.

61.   Arthur B. Gallion and Simon Eisner, *The Urban Pattern: City Planning and Design* (Princeton, N.J.: D. Van Nostrand Co., 1963), p. 67.

62.   Allen, pp. 101–02.

63.   Allen, p. 105.

64.   Allen, p. 95.

65.   Allen, p. 115.

66.   Allen, p. 108.

67.   Allen, p. 121.

68.   Most recent are the atomic energy towns developed mainly in the United States, such as Oak Ridge, Tennessee, and Los Alamos, Arizona. John O. Merrill described Oak Ridge as an ideal opportunity for the American planner. See John O. Merrill, "Planning a Town for Atom Workers," *Engineering News-Record,* **143** (July 1949), p. 48. Also, this community type tends to grow very quickly. See Ernest A. Wende, "Building a City from Scratch," *Engineering News-Record,* **135** (December 1945), p. 149.

69.   O. Kline Fulmer and Fred N. Severud, "Walled City for the Atomic Age," *Engineering News-Record,* **142** (January 1949), p. 18.

70.   For more information on new towns built for defense needs, see William L.C. Wheaton, Albert Mayer, and G. Holmes Perkins, "New Towns for American Defense," *Journal of the American Institute of Architects,* **15,** no. 1 (January 1951), pp. 4–11. Also see Carroll A. Towne, "Atomic Energy Commission Community Developments: A Planning Policy Built Upon Enlightening Experience," *Landscape Architecture,* **43** (April 1953), pp. 119–23.

71.   It is my thesis that Egypt has always had to depend on a single resource—the Nile. Survival in the desert has been possible only by carefully planned control of the river. Throughout Egypt's history its strong centralized power structure has effectively regulated water. Consequently, a slavery system was established to control seasonal flooding (July-August). Continuing enslavement was necessary to maintain the efficiency of this system, and thus the building of pyramids was designated as the alternate occupation for slaves in other seasons. The need to house slave populations led to the development of many slave new towns. These facts are clearly detailed in the Bible, as in the case of the subjection of the Israeli tribes in the building of some of these new settlements.

72.   Religious towns have been developed in an effort to realize utopian ideals of community living. These towns were intended to provide peace and the perfections of life for members of certain religious sects. Most religious shrine towns, such as Bethlehem and Mecca, have developed from older towns and villages. The holiness of the sites, the construction of new monumental shrines, and an increase in the number of yearly pilgrimages led to the development of services and facilities. In addition to the seasonal influx, pilgrims came to settle in permanent homes in the shrine cities.

73.   M. R. Wolfe, "Urbanisation and a New Town in the Columbia Basin," *Town Planning Review,* **28,** no. 6 (July 1957), p. 112.

74.   Wolfe, p. 120.

75.   Wolfe, p. 116.

76.   See Horst de La Crois, *Military Considerations in City Planning: Fortifications* (New York: George Braziller, 1972).

77.   The Romans established many military towns in North Africa and Western and Northern Europe. Cairo, Egypt, was developed from a campsite established during the Moslem invasions in the seventh century A.D. Several similar military towns were developed

during the Middle Ages and the Renaissance in Europe. Today, countries such as the United States, Russia, and Israel, faced with problems of security and defense, are developing such new settlements, and are motivated, at least in their early stages, by military needs which influence their design and function.

78.   Earl D. Hollinshead, *Land: Recreation and Leisure* (Washington, D.C.: Urban Land Institute, 1970), p. 5.

79.   Hazel Thurston, ''France Finds a New Holiday Coast,'' *Geographical Magazine,* **41** (February 1969), p. 342.

80.   Wendell H. Martin, ''Remote Land Development or Exploitation?'' *Urban Land,* **30** (February 1971), p. 3.

81.   Dan Waldorf, ''Recreation Facilities in a New Town,'' *Official Architecture and Planning,* **29** (November 1966), p. 1695.

82.   Traditional societies (e.g., oriental societies) have been noted for their homogeneous communities. By uniting various age groups within the family, a normal social climate benefits both the elderly and other age groups. The elderly are able to interact with other family members, and consequently an awareness of the strong continuity of generations leads to alleviation of mental depression and feelings of alienation or isolation.

Development Town

83.   Alexander Berler, *New Towns in Israel* (Jerusalem: Israel Universities Press, 1970), p. 58.

84.   Jacob Dash, et al., *National Planning for the Redistribution of Population and the Establishment of New Towns in Israel,* International Federation for Housing and Planning, 27th World Congress for Housing and Planning (Jerusalem: Planning Department, Ministry of the Interior, 1964), p. 23.

85.   Settlement Study Center, *Regional Cooperation in Israel* (Rehovot: National and University Institute of Agriculture, n.d.), pp. 10–15.

86.   Erika Spiegel, *Neue Städte/New Towns in Israel* (Stuttgart: Karl Krämer Verlag, 1966), pp. 15–19.

87.   Benjamin Akzin and Yehezkel Dror, *Israel: High-Pressure Planning,* National Planning Series (Syracuse, N.Y.: Syracuse University Press, 1966), pp. 60–66.

Regional Growth Center

88.   For further information, see Economic Commission for Asia and The Far East, *A Case Study of the Damodar Valley Corporation and its Projects,* Flood Control Series no. 16 (Bangkok: United Nations, 1960).

89.   R. Blijstra, *Town-Planning in The Netherlands Since 1900* (Amsterdam: P.N. Van Kampen & Zoon N.V.,n.d.). See also *Second Report on Physical Planning in The Netherlands,* condensed editions, Parts I and II (The Hague: Government Printing Office of The Netherlands, 1966).

90.   For further information, see Settlement Study Center, *Regional Cooperation in Israel.* See also Ovadia Shapiro, *Inhabited Rural Centers in Israel* (Jerusalem: Settlement Study Center, National and University Institute of Agriculture, 1968).

91.   In the United States, the term *regional growth center* became popular during the Johnson Administration (1963–1968), and the

concept was later advanced by the U.S. Department of Agriculture with the goal of creating a more genuine ''urban-rural balance.'' This term was also adopted by the Appalachian Regional Planning Commission to express their desire to create urban centers within regions which lacked a focus.

92.   Harvey A. Garn, p. 2.

93.   Harry W. Richardson, ''Optimality in City Size: Systems of Cities and Urban Policy,'' *Ekistics,* **34,** no. 205 (December 1972), p. 398.

Accelerated Growth Center

94.   Canty, p. 174.

95.   Canty, p. 174.

96.   New York State, *New York State Urban Development Corporation Act, as Amended through June 1971* (New York: New York State Urban Development Corporation, 1971); Edward J. Logue, *Goals Guidelines Concerns of the New York State Urban Development Corporation* (New York: The New York State Urban Development Corporation, 1970); The New York State Urban Development Corporation and the New York State Office of Planning Coordination, *New Communities for New York,* Report, December 1970.

97.   Canty, p. 174.

Freestanding Community

98.   U.S. Department of Housing and Urban Development, *Draft Regulations,* Section 32.7 (a) (4).

99.   U.S. Department of Housing and Urban Development, Office of New Communities Development, *Outline of New Communities Assistance Programs* (Washington, D.C.: U.S. Department of Housing and Urban Development, January 1971), p. 1.

Horizontal City

100.   Constantinos A. Doxiadis, ''Ecumenopolis,'' *Ekistics,* **13,** no. 75 (January 1962), pp. 3–18. Also see ''The City of the Future,'' *Ekistics,* **20** (July 1965), pp. 4–52.
      In addition to an urban Ecumenopolis, the Athens Center of Ekistics has developed the concept of a Marine Ecumenopolis. It is ''that part of Ecumenopolis located anywhere offshore, possessing mobility and independent facilities.'' (J.R. Stewart, ''Marine Ecumenopolis,'' *Ekistics,* **29,** no. 175 [June 1970], p. 401.)

101.   Constantinos A. Doxiadis, ''Ecumenopolis: Tomorrow's City,'' *Britannica Book of the Year* (Chicago: University of Chicago Press, 1968), p. 38; also Stewart, pp. 400–401.

102.   Doxiadis defines megalopolis as a

''greater urbanized area developed by the gradual merging of many metropolises and cities into one urban system. Its population is calculated in the tens of millions. It is distinct from the metropolis, either because its population exceeds ten million people, in which case it also covers a vast surface area, or because it has incorporated more than one metropolis. Term used since ancient Greece when a city called Megalopolis was created in Arcadia . . . (Doxiadis, ''Ecumenopolis: Tomorrow's City,'' p. 38).''

103.   Jean Gottmann, *Megalopolis: The Urbanized Northeastern Seaboard of the United States* (Cambridge: M.I.T. Press, 1961).

104.   Doxiadis, "Ecumenopolis: Tomorrow's City," p. 26.

105.   Doxiadis, "Ecumenopolis: Tomorrow's City," p. 27.

106.   Doxiadis, "Ecumenopolis: Tomorrow's City," p. 27.

107.   Doxiadis, "Ecumenopolis: Tomorrow's City," p. 28.

108.   Doxiadis, "Ecumenopolis: Tomorrow's City," p. 29.

109.   Doxiadis, "Ecumenopolis: Tomorrow's City," p. 30.

110.   Constantinos A. Doxiadis, "The City (II): Ecumenopolis, World-City of Tomorrow," *The Impact of Science on Society,* **19,** no. 2 (1969), pp. 191–92.

111.   Doxiadis, "Ecumenopolis: Tomorrow's City," pp. 30–32.

112.   Doxiadis, "Ecumenopolis: Tomorrow's City," p. 32.

113.   Doxiadis, "The City of the Future," p. 39.

114.   Constantinos A. Doxiadis, "The Coming Era of Ecumenopolis," *Saturday Review,* March 18, 1967, p. 13.

Vertical City

115.   Paolo Soleri is a world-renowned architect. Early in the 1950s, before introducing the concept of arcology, he introduced another new urban concept—the Mesa City. Mesa City was to be developed on international land "under a world government authority." Its proposed population was nearly 2 million, and structures were to function as "multipurpose social facilities." It was to be "a linear city developing along a man-made waterway," of about 10 km wide and about 35 km long," connected by a "network of roads, railroads, and bridges."

The city was to be developed on a plateau (mesa) in a semiarid area, surrounded by agriculture and open space. The agricultural regions would provide the city residents with food and other required commodities. The regional ecology would be closely controlled by a complex of works, including controlled watersheds, canals, and reservoirs. The city backbone would be comprised of a center for advanced study, a man-made park, and a theological complex. Part of the city would consist of villages, each with a population of approximately 3000, that would be linked by highways above or below ground level, and a pedestrian and bicycle system; no private cars would be permitted. Industry and workshops would be developed in the city center along with living quarters (Paolo Soleri, *The Sketchbooks of Paolo Soleri* [Cambridge: M.I.T. Press, 1971], p. 1).

116.   Paolo Soleri, *Arcology: The City in the Image of Man* (Cambridge: M.I.T. Press, 1969), p. 31.

117.   Soleri, *Arcology,* p. 31.

118.   As one of his proposed designs, Soleri introduced Novanoah I, a city of 400,000 population, with a density of 148 hectares or 60 acres, 1000 meters in height, and 2750 hectares or 6800 acres of covered surface. For Novanoah II, he suggested a population of 2,400,000 with a density of 852 hectares or 345 acres, covering a surface of 2790 hectares or 6900 acres, and a height of 400 to 1600 meters. See Soleri, *Arcology,* pp. 36–39.

119.   For more details on the Arconsanti project, see Soleri, *Arcology,* p. 119. The concept of the vertical city still needs serious study. Specifically, further investigation is necessary of the operational levels of utilities required, such as water supply, sewage and garbage disposal, heating and cooling systems, fire services, medical ser-

vices, food and product supplies; leisure, cultural and other recreational services; daily traffic movement; absorption of natural electricity in high buildings; microclimate of the buildings, sunshine absorption, and the effect of winds. Mainly, arcology must be tested in terms of its possible effects on society.

Satellite Towns

120.   A distinction made by some writers is that satellite towns differ from new towns because they depend on other centers (Clapp, p. 54).

121.   Bernard Weissbourd, "Satellite Communities," *Urban Land,* **31,** no. 9 (October 1972).

122.   C. B. Purdom, *The Building of Satellite Towns: A Contribution to the Study of Town Development and Regional Planning* (London: J. M. Dent and Sons, 1925), p. 22. Purdom claimed that the term originated in Graham R. Taylor, *Satellite Cities: A Study of Industrial Suburbs* (New York: D. Appleton and Company, 1915).

123.   Purdom, p. 23.

124.   Osborn, Preface to *Garden Cities of To-Morrow,* p. 27.

125.   Purdom, p. 24.

126.   W. Fisher Cassie, "The Satellite Town: A Study of the Problems Involved in Recentralised Development," *Journal of the Town Planning Institute,* **29,** no. 2 (January-February 1943), pp. 53–62.

Metro Town

127.   Baltimore Regional Planning Council, *Metrotowns for the Baltimore Region: A Pattern Emerges* (Baltimore: Maryland State Planning Department, June 1962). Also see Marshall Kaplan, *Implementation of the Baltimore Regional Plan Alternatives* (San Francisco: Institute for Planning and Development, 1965).

128.   R. W. Archer, "New Towns for Australia: A Progress Report on the Metrotown Australia Project" (Paper presented to the 39th Congress of Australian and New Zealand Association for the Advancement of Science, Melbourne, Australia, January 6, 1967).

129.   R. W. Archer, "From New Towns to Metrotowns and Regional Cities, Part I," *American Journal of Economics and Sociology,* **28,** no. 3 (July 1969), p. 258.

130.   Metropolitan Planning Commission, *Metro/Center* (Kansas City, Missouri: Metropolitan Planning Commission, October 1971), p. 1.

131.   Archer, "From New Towns to Metrotowns and Regional Cities," p. 257.

132.   Archer, "From New Towns to Metrotowns and Regional Cities," p. 257.

133.   R. W. Archer, "From New Towns to Metrotowns and Regional Cities, Part II," *American Journal of Economics and Sociology,* **28,** no. 4 (October 1969), pp. 385–98.

Land Subdivision

134.   Philip P. Green, Jr., "Land Subdivision," in *Principles and Practice of Urban Planning,* William I. Goodman and Eric C. Freund,

eds. (Washington, D.C.: International City Manager's Association, 1968), p. 443.

135. Green, p. 443.

136. Richard M. Yearwood, "Subdivision Law: Timing and Location Control," *Journal of Urban Law,* **44,** no. 585 (1967), p. 608.

137. Yearwood, p. 597.

Planned Unit Development (PUD)

138. Robert W. Burchell, *Planned Unit Development: New Communities American Style* (New Brunswick, N.J.: Center for Urban Policy Research, Rutgers University, 1973), p. 37.

139. Green, p. 480.

140. Burchell, p. 37.

141. Urban Land Institute, *New Approaches to Residential Land Development: A Study of Concepts and Innovations* (Washington, D.C.: Urban Land Institute, 1961), p. 9.

142. Burchell, pp. 34–43.

New Town In-Town

143. Harvey S. Perloff first introduced this concept in 1955 in an urban renewal project developed in Hyde Park near Chicago. See Harvey S. Perloff, *Urban Renewal in a Chicago Neighborhood: An Appraisal of the Hyde Park Kenwood Renewal Program* (Chicago: Hyde Park Herald, August 1955). Later, in 1965, Perloff elucidated this idea in "New Towns in Town," *Journal of the American Institute of Planners,* **32,** no. 3 (May 1966), pp. 155–61. Also see Albert Mayer, "New Towns and Fresh In-City Communities," *Architectural Record,* **136,** no. 2 (August 1964), pp. 129–38, and *The Urgent Future: People, Housing, City, Region* (New York: McGraw-Hill Book Co., 1967), pp. 76–93. Title VII, "Urban Growth and New Community Development Act, 1970" Part D, Section 740, states that the new town in-town could "provide our cities, which urgently need to augment their inventories of housing (particularly housing for low and moderate income families) and to find s tes for essential public facilities and additional sources of employment, but have virtually no vacant land upon which to build, with a program which will make possible the more rational use of urban land and space that is currently occupied by industrial or commercial uses which though not physically blighted are functionally obsolete or uneconomic, or of land and space that is not usable in its present state because of natural hazards or inadequate development, so that in appropriate cases major rebuilding projects (including new communities intown) may be undertaken without major residential clearance activities and with minimal displacement."

Furthermore, the "Draft Regulations" for the act made reference to "major new-town-in-town development within or adjacent to existing cities, including developments which would help renew center cities or have beneficial effect on the city's tax base. . . ." (Section 32.7 [3]—Specific Eligibility Criteria, Subpart B: New Community Criteria and Standards.)

144. Richard C. Van Dusen, lecture at the New Towns and Planned Communities Conference held by the Practicing Law Institute, July 1971. See James A. Lyons et al., eds., *New Towns and Planned Communities* (New York: Practicing Law Institute, 1971), p. 22.

145. Although Albert Mayer also conceived of the new town in-town, he did not clarify the idea. He drew attention to the potential of implementing the idea of the new town within a large city, but did not explain the feasibility of implementation.

146. Perloff, "New Towns Intown," p. 156.

147. Perloff described the services the new town in-town would provide:

"We should be building the most modern schools, hospitals, libraries, cultural centers, and community centers precisely where incomes are low and density is high, in contrast to our present practice. There is nothing like a modern school with an adequate and attractive play area to give a new-town feeling to a community. . . . A New Town Intown program should work to bring community services and facilities up to the highest level manageable, an effort which might well merit a number one priority for urban renewal (Perloff, "New Towns Intown," p. 157)."

148. Perloff, "New Towns Intown," p. 156.

149. Perloff, "New Towns Intown," p. 157.

150. Perloff, "New Towns Intown," p. 158.

151. Perloff, "New Towns Intown," p. 156.

152. Bruce Sagan in his article, "The Harper Court Experience," *Journal of the American Institute of Planners,* **32,** no. 3 (May 1966), pp. 161–62, explains how a new town in-town development is planned for Hyde Park on the south side of Chicago. It will be called Harper Court and will have an area of 73,000 square feet. The development is planned by the Harper Court Foundation—"a not-for-profit development agency, . . . to develop a center for the small businesses of Hyde Park which have traditionally reflected and enriched the special character of the community" (p. 161). It will use various methods for holding down rents, including long-term financing and limited profit in equity investment. Harper Court, consisting of three major buildings and running at a total cost of $600,000, will be "designed to function as a center for the Hyde Park Community" (p. 162). Plans for the future include a freeway buffered by landscape to improve public transit, a main shopping street, and a program for neighborhood and housing improvement.

THREE
SITE SELECTION: PROCESS, CRITERIA, AND METHOD

In the past man adapted to his environment through his instincts, experience, and wisdom. Since he realized that a depletion of environmental resources would jeopardize his survival, he lived in harmony with his surroundings. He selected his residential site close to water, food, and other resources and near a thoroughfare offering physical security. Consequently, man developed a pattern of site selection to meet the requirements of all his major activities.

In the nineteenth century, industrialization and social economic reform intensified population mobility and subsequent selection of sites for new settlements. This led to the development of new transportation networks such as railways, waterways, and highways, which shifted regional and local population distribution and equilibria among and within settlements. The results of this haphazard development of towns and cities have had far-reaching negative effects on our own urban existence. Today, many cities are paying high prices socially, economically, and educationally, and residents are paying mentally for poor site selection and mismanagement. New towns may offer ways to reduce these costs.

THE PROCESS OF PLANNING

Since he has the power both to plan and to implement new settlements, a developer may perform both tasks simultaneously. This discussion concerns only the planning process. Two of its prime phases involve choosing a region and a locality within it to designate a specific site for a new town. For both, data must be gathered and analyzed concerning cost benefit, patterns of land ownership, and land value. Also, a developer must define and occasionally evaluate his goals and objectives.

Major planning steps and their phases are as follows: (1) definition of goals and objectives of the proposed new town; (2) general regional study, which includes data gathering and analysis; (3) preliminary cost-benefit analysis and recommendations; (4) establishment of the new-town development corporation; (5) choice of a site-selection method and of alternative sites; (6) selection of the preferred site; (7) preparation of base maps; (8) securing financial resources for the project; (9) land assemblage; (10) interdisciplinary planning study; (11) preparation of a comprehensive strategic plan; (12) cost-benefit analysis of the plan; (13) preparation of a detailed developmental plan by priorities and phases; (14) plan implementation. A systematic description of parts of this sequence of actions, which may vary somewhat in practice, follows, and Figure 3.1 gives a schema illustrating this sequence. We defer our detailed discussion of the criteria for selecting a site and one method used till later in this chapter and discuss the remaining parts of the sequence in later chapters. (See Figure 3.2 for the overall process of site selection.)

Defining the Goals and Objectives of the Developer

Before beginning his work, a planner-developer should set tentative goals and objectives (which vary among developers) based on the variety of problems his new town should solve. Such problems may be the

60

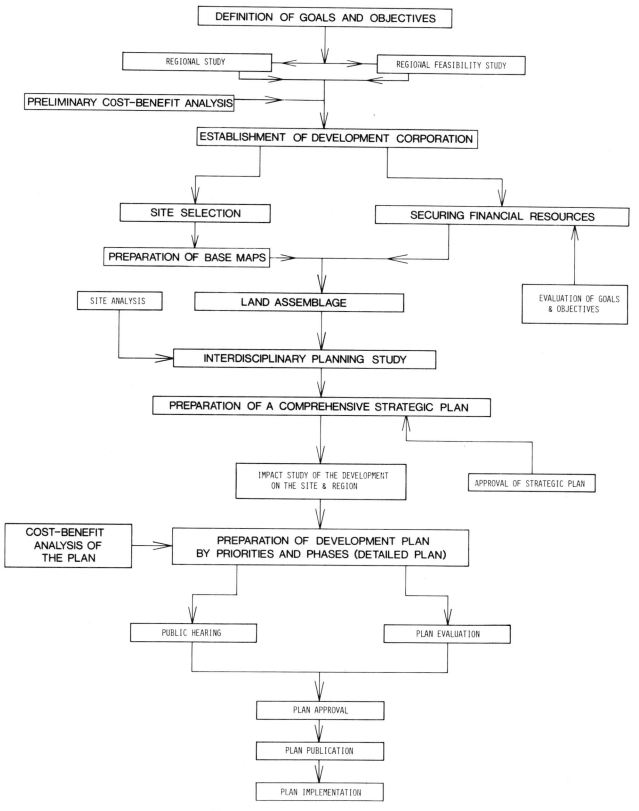

Figure 3.1. Schema of new-town planning.

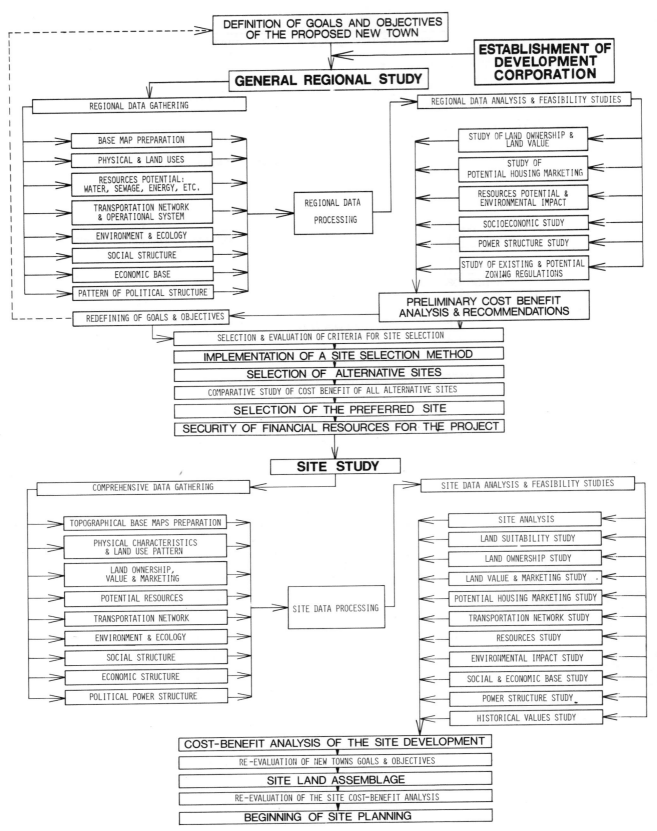

Figure 3.2. Generalized actions and phases of selecting a site.

complicated result of various forces, and a comprehensive solution may best fit the development of a special type of new town. (For the type of new settlement best suited to a particular goal, refer to Figure 2.2.)

When a developer has set goals and objectives he must constantly evaluate and redefine them as surveys gather information. Even after a development has been planned its goals can be revised, if necessary, since parts of a goal may change although its fundamental idea has not.

Regional Feasibility Study

In the earliest planning stage a feasibility study determines the economic, social, physical, and environmental possibilities of a new-town project. (See Figure 3.1.) In estimating feasibility, a developer must consider potential problems relating to population, physical surroundings, or perhaps even to climate, as each affects his project and its goals.

The first regional feasibility study should be followed by a more detailed study of the selected site, since the private developer must find out at an early stage if the project is feasible before he makes an investment. The public developer, on the other hand, may see a new town as part of a national or regional policy for urban growth, which alters the measurement of feasibility.

A feasibility study of a site close to a metropolitan area may involve more aspects and be more expensive and longer than one conducted on a rural site. This study must define regional boundaries within the potential area for a new-town site, although the specific site has not yet been selected.

Defining regional political power structures identifies agents that operate or interrelate communities. Reception of a developer's ideas in a region depends to a great extent upon existing customs. A developer must also contend with the formal and informal power structures of the region and his site. The formal British power structure is a unified national government with undisputed power to execute laws. In the United States, however, central authorities such as federal or state governments have limited authority which allows local governments much independence. An informal power structure composed of unelected community leaders is predominant in Asia, Africa, the Middle East, South America, and in traditional societies based on a tribe, clan, kinship, blood relations, property, or economic system. Coordination with such community leaders may be essential to in-

sure an effective new-town establishment in the region.

Since industry may become the base for local employment, the examination of a site for industry should be comprehensive and detailed including

(1)   Physical conditions—topography, drainage, land suitability, access, availability of sewerage, water supply, and climate.

(2)   Availability of labor, unions, and attitudes of laborers toward organized industry.

(3)   A taxation system within the area.

(4)   Availability of a condition that would attract laborers to live in the area.

(5)   A transportation network—its frequency, condition, and access to the site itself.

Since the site will compete economically with others, its positive elements should at least equal those of other sites within equal distances of markets or consumers.

A site far from urban centers or populated areas may require public incentives or subsidies for industry, since it must compete with other industries located nearer urban centers. Highways, railroads, and airports could be constructed within the area of an industrial complex. A developer could establish facilities required by industry, such as sewage disposal, water supply, high-voltage electric lines, or gas pipelines if industry would locate in the new site. (For further discussion of incentives see Chapter 5.)

Formation of New-Town Development Corporation

A development corporation should be the primary agency responsible for initiation and construction of a new town, including the following:

(1)   Assemblage of the major portion of land, if not all of it.

(2)   Planning for the land.

(3)   Implementation of the plan and development of the site.

(4)   Major social services and public utilities required by the new town until a local government is established.

(5)   Management of all financial resources.

In the United Kingdom, the New Towns Act of 1946 required the formation of a development corporation for every new town financed by the Ministry of Town and Country Planning or by the Secretary of State for Scotland.[1]

The objects of a development corporation established for the purposes of a new town shall be to secure the laying out and development of the new town in accordance with proposals approved in that behalf under the following provisions of this Act, and for that purpose every such corporation shall have power to acquire, hold, manage and dispose of land and other property, to carry out building and other operations, to provide water, electricity, gas, sewerage and other services, to carry on any business or undertaking in or for the purposes of the new town, and generally to do anything necessary or expedient for the purposes of the new town or for purposes incidental thereto. . . .[2]

Every site requires its own corporation to meet the needs of the nation, the region, or the site itself. Development corporations can be of three types: public, private, or a joint venture of the two. The corporation evaluates the goals and objectives of a developer, defines the ultimate objectives of its projects, and determines whether a new settlement is to be a self-contained community or a satellite. It is also the responsibility of a development corporation to manage all the financial aspects of its project, determine strategy, assemble land, and coordinate all parties involved. Four bodies may constitute a development corporation. (See Figure 3.3.)

Interdisciplinary Planning Team. The ideal team should be composed of such professionals as planners, urban designers, architects, sociologists, economists, geographers, geologists, anthropologists, ecologists, housing experts, health planners, political scientists, transportation experts, and computer programmers. This team should constantly evaluate and revise the economic and social aspects of the developmental plan.

Citizens' Advisory Commission. At first, this group may be composed of people of the region and other volunteers who are interested in the new-town project and willing to bring their experience to the development corporation. Later, when the community is settled, local citizens may become members of the commission. To be most effective, a citizens' advisory commission should include people experienced in daily urban life, such as educators, journalists, doctors, psychologists, philosophers, homemakers, religious leaders, age-group representatives, policemen,

and drivers. Although it may sometimes hinder a developer's work, this group can contribute many valuable ideas and establish the harmony necessary for the beginning of a new-town development. It may encourage new local community leaders, construct a local governing body, promote regional cooperation, and improve a new town's image. The commission meeting should be open to everyone who wishes to express an opinion.

Some new towns are constructed on the site of an existing village or of an old urban center since they seek some of the same advantages as earlier settlers, such as good drainage, landscape, climate, accessibility, or other physical features. In these cases, local citizens may make up part of the citizens' advisory commission. The commission should either be appointed by the corporation or operate on a voluntaary basis. The appointment of members should take place after the land has been assembled, unless the public is responsible for land assemblage. Ideally, the commission should provide feedback to the planning team. Since many planners are theoreticians, citizens, who are usually realistic, may react differently.

Board of Directors. The board is a combination of the land owners, investors, regional public representatives, and the representatives of the planning team. The majority of the members will be investors and land owners. As the most powerful body within the corporation, it must approve any decision concerning the new-town project. The board will disband when a new town establishes its own government and the plan has been fully implemented.

Agency for Construction and Maintenance. This body, appointed by the board of directors, has the equipment needed for the construction of new towns according to the board's decision. The agency may remain in existence even after the establishment of the new-town government, to continue the implementation of the plan and to operate those properties still owned by the development corporation.

Potential Financial Resources

Three vital steps in new-town planning and development are (1) insuring financial resources for the whole project; (2) selecting the proper site; (3) assembling land. Both public and private funds are potential financial resources. Theoretically public development advances the interests of the people, while private expansion centers on the personal economics of a

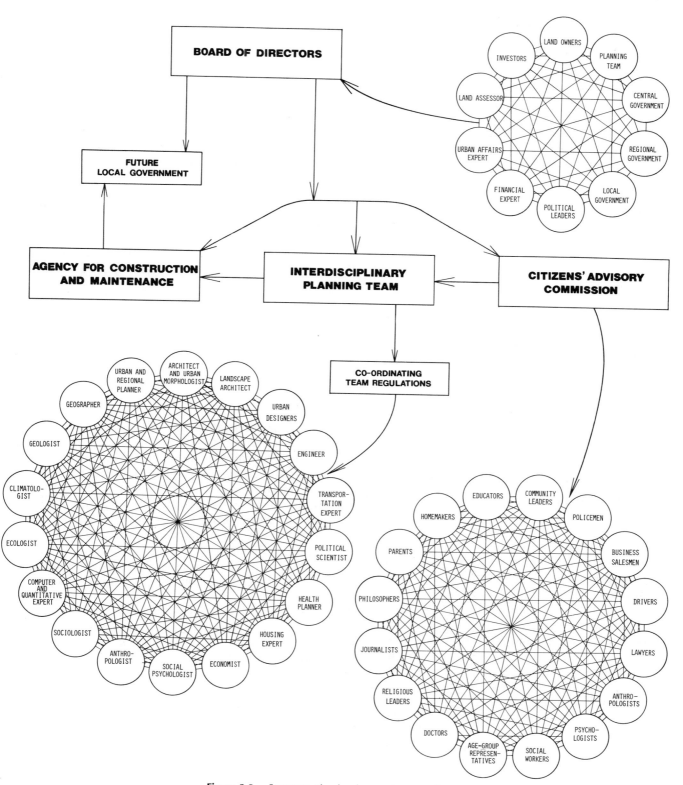

Figure 3.3. Structure of a development corporation.

developer, unless he is ideologically motivated. Ideally both the private and public sectors of a community assume a joint interest in the development of new towns, since forcing private developers to carry the entire financial burden may hinder development.

The public should insure at least a portion of the funds for those parts of a project needed by a community as a whole, such as schools, medical centers, public buildings, green areas and open spaces, sewerage, and roads. The public should also offer subsidies for low-income housing if there is governmental policy to integrate such socioeconomic groups in new towns. In addition, small land owners may invest in a new-town corporation as shareholders.

In a free-market economy such as that of the United States and Canada, where private investment plays a major role in stimulating the economy, the public sector should invest in three areas in the development of a new town. First, the public sector should fund the selection of a new-town site. When the site has been selected, the public must support the private developer of that site. If it is either a national or regional government policy to select a site, public investment and developmental policies should be geared accordingly. These policies have been implemented effectively in the United Kingdom, The Netherlands, and Israel. Land assemblage should have public support since the private developer does not have the power to overcome assemblage problems. The government should therefore have legislative power to support him and to eliminate land speculation which could ruin any project.

After the government has acquired land, it may either be cared for by the government alone, by public and private agencies in a mutual agreement, or returned to a private party. Instead of buying land, a government could simply fix the price of land and allow people to share in a *land bank*. Each party would own a section of the land proportional to the amount he contributed. Any profit from joint ventures would be shared, and profits that go to the public could then be reinvested in the new town. If land assemblage were handled by the public sector, the developer would be free to find innovative techniques to reduce the price of houses or to improve planning or development.

A third area in which government should be involved is subsidizing the construction of public facilities and services for a new town. The establishment of sewage systems, water supply reserves, telecommunications, and schools are projects usually undertaken by a municipality. If a private developer is spared the burden of developing these public facilities,

he can devote his time and efforts to housing and community development.

Land Assemblage

Before selecting a site, a developer should make a detailed inventory of the pattern of land ownership on the prospective site, including (1) maps and lists of the divisions and subdivisions of the land according to size and quadrangular reference; (2) the owner of each land parcel and his address; (3) the current price of a parcel and its market value; (4) the zoning and actual use of the land. (See Figure 3.4.) According to the Land Compensation Act (1961) of Great Britain, a corporation would acquire land by negotiating with owners and compensating them at the market value or a negotiated price.[3] A developer must acquire land discreetly, lest he inadvertently cause speculation to increase land value. He must know all owners and their agents and have alternatives prepared if they refuse his offers. In privately developed towns, speculation can be reduced by having dummy real-estate companies which negotiate for land.[4] Some owners could join the new-town corporation and work with the developer. (For more information about land assemblage see Chapter 5.)

Base Map Preparation

A few regional and site maps should be prepared immediately after a site has been selected. Basic physical information is essential to evaluate the region properly and to aid in selection of a site. Lack of detailed base maps may cause repercussions in later stages. Since a long time is required to prepare these maps, preparation should begin very early in site selection. Aerial photographs should be taken for any site analysis that must be done before maps are available.

A regional base map gives detailed information on all potential sites of a region within a 5- to 10-mile radius of these sites. The scale of this mape should be approximately 5 inches = 1 mile, 1:10,000, or two and one-half times the 7.5-minute maps of the United States Geological Survey. Contour intervals should be 10 or 20 feet. A map on this scale will include an area of 10 to 20 square miles and indicate the following elements:

(1)   All drainage and surface water patterns.

(2)   All topographical features and contour interval lines.

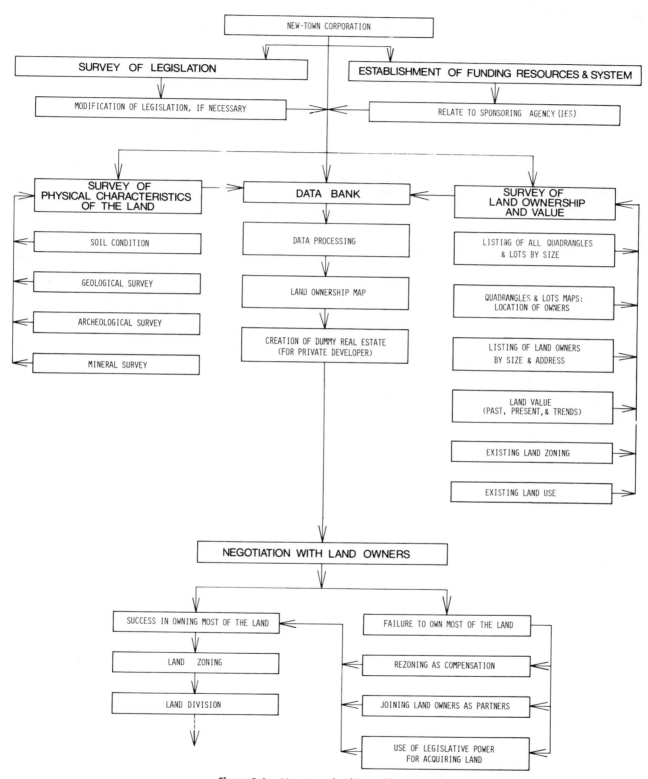

Figure 3.4. New-town land assemblage.

(3)   All transportation networks, communication systems, and infrastructure.

(4)   All political jurisdictions and administrative lines.

(5)   All census tracts or traffic zone lines.

(6)   All existing structures and their functions.

(7)   All wooded areas.

(8)   All names of various sites and settlements.

Information for a regional base map can be obtained from the following sources: (1) governmental survey maps such as those of the United State Geological Survey; (2) current general field surveys; (3) new aerial photographs; (4) Sanborn maps. This map will be used for information on zoning, existing land use, physical characteristics, and other illustrative information about the region.

Preparation of a base map for a site and its vicinity should begin immediately after the final selection of the site because this kind of map will be the most useful one for preparing the strategic or comprehensive plan of the site. The scale of this map should be 10 inches = 1 mile, i.e., approximately 1 inch = 500 feet, or 1:5000. Contour intervals should be 5 feet. The total area shown on a map of this scale will be 25 square miles. The map should include

(1)   All elements included on the regional base map.

(2)   All topographical features and contour intervals of 5 feet.

(3)   All quadrangular lines and their numbers as indicated for land ownership or tax assessment; in some cases this information is prepared in separate maps of the same scale for comparative uses.

(4)   All the unique physical features in the area such as quarries, caves, tunnels, high points, cliffs, shorelines, depressions, and mines.

Information for the site base map may be obtained for the following sources: (1) the same sources as those indicated for the regional base map; (2) special detailed field surveys conducted by the developer; (3) assessor maps; (4) other maps available in the area from the county, township, regional planning commission, and so on.

Detailed site maps are usually prepared after a field survey conducted by engineers for detailed land-use planning and construction. The scale of these maps may be 1 inch = 50 to 200 feet or 1:1000 to 1:2500. Contour intervals may be 1 to 5 feet, and the total area

would be 6 to 9 square miles. The maps should include all the elements of previous maps as well as subdivision lots and their numbers. Although governmental survey maps would provide the most helpful basic information for these detailed base maps, a special survey should be made to insure detailed accuracy of any field survey.

CRITERIA FOR SITE SELECTION

Once developers and planners of a new town understand the process of planning it, they should evaluate the necessary factors in selecting a site. Since this selection will have far-reaching effects on the success or failure of a given new town, all pertinent criteria must be clearly identified. Any criterion must be weighed against all others and be distinguished as either long-lasting or ephemeral. Moreover, great foresight must be used to make a choice that will adapt to all future changes if the new town is to survive.

Except in the case of a specific region the diverse criteria for site selection can apply to nearly any category, and the emphasis given to certain criteria determines their priority. Selection of criteria can also become a political issue despite the existence of a positive attitude toward a town, as has happened in the United Kingdom. Its new-town legislation is purposely vague, on the grounds that inclusion of specific criteria would "limit the discretion of the government in deciding what factors should be considered in the selection of a new town site."[5] In light of this situation, the Ministry of Housing and Local Government has prepared a comprehensive set of criteria for site selection. Generally, however, planners and developers of new towns have accepted the following criteria for selecting new-town sites: (1) physical, (2) social and economic, (3) potential local resource, (4) environmental and ecological, and (5) political.

Physical Criteria

Although emphasis on the component elements may differ from one place to another, one should view physical criteria as they relate to land use. Some sites have special potential related to topography, landscape, and water resources. The developer should learn the policy of a region toward agricultural land, since some countries prefer that construction take place in hilly areas to save the alluvial plains for agriculture. Physical criteria are especially important in areas of floods, erosion, limited available land, and defense problems. Proper accommodation for future growth rather than only for existing needs should also determine site selection.

Physical criteria, as concrete factors, have long-lasting effects. Although they may appear static, physical characteristics are undergoing constant though slow changes. External forces such as temperature, wind, precipitation or other climatic conditions, erosion, and landslides cause this continuous change. Internal forces such as earth movement, volcanoes, and earthquakes may also contribute to changes. Thus planners should consider all diverse existing or potential forces that may bring about any type of change. For planners and developers physical factors are most influential on construction and its cost. Soil characteristics, for example, may largely determine the type of sewerage, degree of erosion, intensity and density of construction, and maintenance of streets.

The topographical condition of a new-town site can dictate the land-use pattern, town shape, intensity of development, and cityscape. Topography consists of elements such as absolute and relative latitude, landform, overall relief of the physical environment, and slope gradient. Low areas may have disadvantages such as poor drainage, potential flooding, and little ventilation; some low land is built up of alluvial soil most suitable for agriculture. Also, large industry usually requires a plain or flat area to allow easy horizontal movement.

One possible land-use pattern integrated with topography reserves the tops of hills for public buildings or for public use, while using strips in between the top and bottom areas for residential buildings. Hillside developments require skillful design and special treatment. Location of houses and buildings in terms of views, curves of the street, and landscapes should all be related to the slope and physical characteristics of the land. It may be possible to design a unique, bounded neighborhood that supports social identity in an area with poor accessibility or steep slopes on three sides.

Steep slopes can erode seriously, especially when free of flora, depending on the combination of soil structure and climate. In semiarid regions, rare but torrential rains intensify erosion. Development of slopes above a 10 percent gradient requires careful design and construction of terraces and landscaping, since conditions of slopes will usually determine the price of the buildings in part. In the United States the lower the slope, the higher the price of land and, consequently, of the building. If the slope is steep, large investments are needed to adjust it to construction needs, thus raising the building cost. However,

slopes may offer the advantage of good views of the surrounding landscape, which some cultures consider as added value for a dwelling. Such dwellings may also gain good ventilation. Since the advantages of slopes may add to the marketability of dwellings, a cost-benefit analysis should be made to compare different areas on slopes.

Topography can place limits on accessibility. Airports, for example, need large, consecutive flat tracts of land for runways. Drainage is also related to topography.[6] Rolling areas are often well-drained and support sewage systems more readily than flat areas which require pumping. Even rolling land may have soil that does not drain well, resulting in the creation of marshes and swamps. On the other hand, transporting water to dwellings at high elevations is expensive. A plain may be adjusted to create a variety of landscapes and townscapes by technical means, but this requires a large investment. The irregular shape of a site may result in wasted space; e.g., marginal areas are frequently unusable because of their unique shapes. However, creative designing can often take advantage of such sites.

Since soil condition relates to all types of construction at a new-town site and to the development of an optimal land-use pattern, a soil structure survey is required. In countries with a shortage of agricultural land or dense rural regions, reservation of good agricultural soil has become a basic national policy.[7] However, if the purpose of some new towns is to provide transportation, financial, economic, and social urban centers for their regions, selection of the new-town site within land reserved for agriculture is inevitable.

A survey of land capability would enable a planner-developer to prepare a basic land-suitability map. Land appearing unsuitable for building or road construction may be reserved as open spaces, woodlands, and green areas, or may be excluded from the site. Areas that seem suitable for both agricultural and urban development require a decision as to which is preferred. Areas with poor natural drainage require extra investment and can perhaps be designated for land use other than built-up areas for exclusion.

The frequency and scale of activity of volcanoes, earthquakes, and landslides should be carefully measured and seriously considered. Cities like San Francisco and Caracas in Venezuela have been paying high prices for their location near serious faults. The construction of a new city close to or over faults can result in serious damage to buildings if the fault moves. A site along a coast may be damaged by tidal waves caused by earthquakes quite far from the site, even

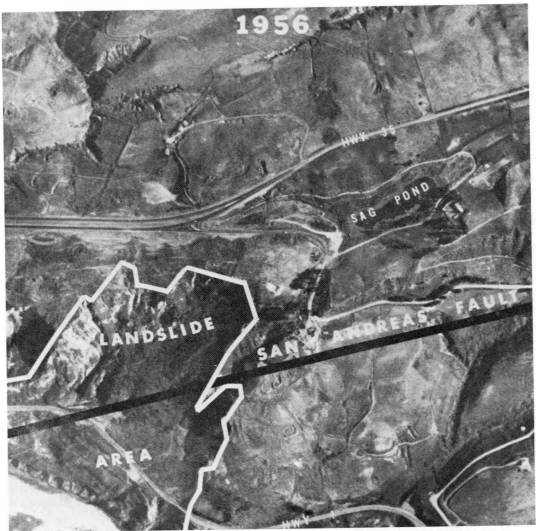

Figure 3.5A.   A hazardous area along the San Andreas fault in California as surveyed in 1956. (Source: U.S. Geological Survey.)

though the site region itself does not have faults.[8] A seismic map and related information about the site and its region should be prepared.[9] (See Figures 3.5A and B.)

Aerial and satellite photographs can be a prime data source, and geologists who have been involved in urban planning can provide advice on site selection and preventative measures. Volcanoes must also be considered, since a city located relatively far from a volcano could still suffer from pollution by tuff (volcanic ash) carried to the city by prevailing winds.[10] Volcanic tuff could cover a city in the same way that Pompeii, Italy, was covered by the ash of Vesuvius.

Information about the emergence and submergence of land is important, especially when developing a seaport. Parts of earth move continuously as a result of constant pressure from global blocks. As time passes, an established seaport can become an inland city, left behind as either emerged or submerged land. In The Netherlands, for example, large parts of the country are submerging.

Although landslides may be considered part of a geological cycle, they can be serious threats to cities in semiarid areas where soil dryness, little or no vegetation, and sudden torrential rains are characteristic. If soil resistance to erosion is minimal, landslides can bring disaster to a neighborhood; with proper precautions, however, landslides can be prevented.[11] In

Figure 3.5B. The fault area as developed by 1966. (Source: U.S. Geological Survey.)

humid regions heavy rains can also lower soil resistance and cause mudslides. In either case, special vegetation can hold soil in place and reduce erosion.

Eolian soil transportation occurs mainly in areas of dry soil free from vegetation;[12] it causes air pollution, building destruction, and inconvenience. Silt, clay, or sand particles eroded by winds can build different types of landforms such as a loess soil type or sand dunes.[13] A body of water or a wide strip of vegetation on the side of a new town facing the prevailing winds can ease eolian soil transportation.

New-town planners should examine all characteristics of the macro- and microclimates of a site and relate their sequences to optimal land use. Such considera-

tions may take place in relation to (1) temperature (which may differ on different altitudes of a site), (2) exposure (in some areas it is desirable and in others not), (3) prevailing wind velocity (daily as related to drainage, water supplies, human activities, and maintenance), and (4) seasonal and daily changes.

In humid climates most rolling land is heavily wooded. Many private developers clear forest land before building instead of removing only those trees representing definite obstacles, even though the cost of mapping and preserving trees is low as compared with the cost of replanting them. The cost of the convenience of such clearing is that it takes many years before the land returns to a state comparable to that which existed before it was developed. Further, a developer loses money because houses surrounded by mature trees have higher market values and better marketability than treeless dwellings.

A planner must consider the value of water to human life, as a major criterion with various uses. The ratio of ground water to runoff depends on the combination of the amount and duration of precipitation, the intensity of evaporation and transpiration, slope conditions, soil character, and geological structure. The amount of run-off water will generally be greater on a rolling area than on a plain and could be reserved in watershed catchment areas and used for landscaping, recreation, or drinking water. On a plain, bodies of water may be a strong, effective element in landscaping that increases its attractiveness. Both proposals may increase ground water and protect it from pollution. Prolonging the shoreline by creating inlets in an urban area is one way of townscaping with water.

Other uses of water may include boating, fishing, water-skiing, transportation, or those planned to affect a local climate. Competing communities consuming local and regional water resources should also be considered to avoid reaching their threshold. Since a site with a large water surface or ground water resources runs the risk of pollution from industries, strict control must be maintained over industrial pollutants. (See Figure 3.6.)

A planner-developer should check all hazards within a site. Fire hazards can exist in woodlands which should be isolated from a future built-up area. Oil and gas storage areas are highly flammable and subject to explosions, so one should carefully note their proximity to a site and the direction of prevailing winds. Airports frequently create problems because of noise and vibrations from low flying planes. A new town's land use must be adjusted to the location of an airport in terms of distance, circulation, and noise

Figure 3.6.   A view of eastern Tapiola, Finland. Tapiola has made abundant use of its bodies of water and its evergreen forest. (Courtesy of the Asuntosäätiö Housing Foundation.)

factors. Perhaps the area between an airport and a residential community can be designated for open space, reservoirs, forests, industrial parks, or playgrounds. Helioports within a town require careful planning because helicopters are very noisy.

Areas subject to flooding are another type of hazard. Size of the water catchment basin should be calculated according to the frequency and amount of precipitation and soil structure to determine the amount of runoff in relation to the capacity of streams. When a river bisects a new-town site, possible flooding can create a problem unless a water control system is developed upstream. Since such an area can be devoted to recreation it may still be located far from the immediate residential area. If an area has heavy rains, the ground may not be able to absorb all the water, which increases flooding. It also can occur in an area with a high slope gradient if the soil does not absorb large enough quantities of water. Areas subject to flooding need not be precluded, however, if they can be developed as recreational open spaces. Other potential hazards that may differ from region to region include high power lines, abandoned quarries and mines, avalanche areas, cliffs, caves, swamps, and karst topography.

Physical elements which intersect a site may be used effectively; e.g., a stream or a river running through a site may become a community's focal point. Damming a river can result in an attractive waterfall and lake within a city. If residential areas are developed on both sides of the water, two separate and often different socioeconomic neighborhoods may result. But if one side of the river were devoted to a residential area while the other became an industrial one, the latter would be vacant at night, which might eventually lead to a negative social atmosphere. Other man-made dividing lines can cause similar problems. A highway or a railroad that bisects a city may create noise and nuisance and may also hinder pedestrian traffic and divide the town into two different socioeconomic sections.

Availability of land tracts large enough to accommodate a designated number of people has always been a serious problem. A tract of land must be large enough to provide all types of land use. Small tracts may encourage a single type of land use, dense population, and increased commuting to adjacent urban centers. The distance of a proposed site from an urban center will affect the size of land parcels and create difficulty in assembling a large enough tract for a new town; i.e., the closer a site is to a city, the smaller the fractions and the more difficult the assemblage. In the United States, a private developer's financial ability to purchase sizeable land parcels will continue to take priority over decisions made by federal or regional authorities as to the best location for a new town.[14]

Access provides the possibility of movement by vehicles or persons, or of transfer of water, sewage, gas, telephone, and other public utilities. Three levels of access exist: underground, used mainly for public utilities and infrastructure; aboveground, used for motor vehicles, waterways, and railroads; and air, used for airplanes and helicopters. Most of the factors that determine the success of these three elements relate to topography, to soil or land condition (the ability of the land to carry land transportation) and to the geological condition (the ability of the ground to support underground construction considering faults, caverns, landslides, and other flaws). Also, movement aboveground will depend on changes in weather conditions. Although new towns are expected to be self-sustaining and self-contained, a portion of the population will always commute to and from the new town. Therefore, to a large extent level of access to a site will dictate housing demand. A new town developed in a wilderness will find itself isolated if it lacks accessibility, especially with regard to the need for labor and goods in the early years of construction. Frequent and efficient public transportation during those years adds a new dimension to the success of such new towns.

Access relates to a variety of other transportation and communication aspects, no matter how developed the site is. Since labor will be hired not only from the site but also from outside, at least for construction needs, regular public transportation to and from work will be required. Otherwise such transportation would become the responsibility of a developer.

If a low-cost development is under consideration, a site within walking distance to places of employment is ideal. But if the site lacks public transit and is over a mile in walking distance from employment or from shopping, then it is poorly located for a development of low-priced housing construction.[15]

An effectively marketable site should have a free flow of traffic and circulation within it, and between it and its surrounding area. Major highways should bypass the site instead of crossing it, but their proximity is critical for the development of a new town. Entrances and exits connecting a new town to a major highway are also necessary.[16]

Social and Economic Criteria

Knowledge of regional social services is necessary to explore the social and economic roles of a new town.

Recreational facilities available within the region should be regarded either as active, such as man-made facilities that provide for daily or seasonal recreation, or passive, mainly natural features. Bodies of water within a region may be used for fishing, boating, or landscaping. Regional facilities for tennis, football, basketball, hiking, water sports, or hunting can be provided. Anticipating the walking distance between the site and recreational areas is also important. Availability of these facilities increases the total value of a development, encourages new migration there, and increases its marketability.

Although the distance between a residential area and a school may not play a major role in locating today's schools, charting the boundaries of existing educational systems is necessary. School district lines usually cross local municipal boundaries, requiring coordination of educational facilities between a new town and its surrounding area. Their cooperation is required to handle this discrepancy so that mutual advantage results. Most new-town residents are young couples with children and high expectations of a school system. Their selection of residences is often influenced by the proximity of a good school system. A developer should understand the complexity of problems related to existing laws which may require new-town residents to send their children to established schools, since being attached to such a school may be undesirable to residents.

The proposed size of a new town will, of course, affect the choice of its site. Although we discuss optimal size in Chapter 5, it is worth mentioning here that a developer must determine how to accommodate a certain population within a given space.

The English New Towns Committee considered the distance between a site to be selected and an urban agglomeration:

Consideration of this problem has usually been limited to an attempt to prescribe a minimum distance, and we suggest that new towns in the Greater London area should be at least twenty-five miles from the center; from other great towns a distance of ten to fifteen miles might be enough. The optimum distance is more difficult to determine. To locate new towns far away from existing great cities, in regions with a relatively sparse population but with good communications and other facilities available, might be very advantageous both in providing a new center of cultural life and a more substantial economic foundation for local government services in the area selected.[17]

Geographic centrality of a site within its region is very important if the new town is to be a regional center. "A regional plan can specify the strategies for regional development, and thus for the location of the new town in view of these strategies."[18] Centrality is essential for shopping, educational facilities, and job opportunities to increase the effectiveness of the new town's marketing catchment area. Centrality can also give a new town its identity and affect its social, economic, cultural, and political strength in the region. However, centrality may overload taxpayers. Health services for an entire region, for example, require hospitals, clinics, and many professionals.

Delineating the boundaries and potential growth of a marketing region is another criterion to be evaluated seriously. Marketability in a region depends on its import-export balance and the purchasing power of its population. Both characteristics help to determine the selection of a site within that region. In a privately developed new town, housing marketing is a major factor in the determination of a site that is greatly influenced by proximity to a large urban agglomeration, where potential markets are found. A marketing catchment region can be divided into three areas:

(1)   Within a 20-mile radius of a new town. These people may move into the new town to improve their housing and enjoy a better school system, better services, and a better society without changing their jobs.

(2)   Within a 100-mile radius of a new town. The people within this area may learn about a new town through the mass media and migrate as a result.

(3)   Within a nation where a town may succeed in gaining a national image; e.g., Columbia, Maryland; Harlow, England; and Arad and Beer Sheva, Israel.

Defining the marketability area will clarify the resource potential of a new town and permit effective evaluation and planning.

Moreover, for a new town designated to rely heavily on industrial development, the quality, variety, and maintenance of sophisticated transportation networks are basic determinants. Linkage of the networks between an industrial park and a national network is essential to the flow of goods. Additional costs of terminals also become an important criterion.

Land value is also related to the value of houses, and both will vary from one place to another. Even if building material prices remain constant throughout an area, labor or land price may differ. Land prices in an area should be studied to predict future trends. The initiative to build a new town will automatically encourage land speculation, which will influence the selection of a site. Some important factors which dictate land value are

(1)   Marketing. Great demand for land increases marketing and land value.

(2)   Land condition, its structure, suitability, and availability for a designated project.

(3)   Access and proximity of the land to highways, transportation networks, and urban centers. Generally the nearer the land is to transportation, the higher its value. However, residential land closer than a certain limit to a highway may decrease in value.

As part of the process of locating new towns within the urban region, new town planners will have to decide whether new towns should be used to counteract market trends in land development or to reinforce these trends within the more adequate development context which the new town community can provide. . . . If the new town is located away from areas of developmental pressure, land values will tend to rise less rapidly within the new town and fringe development will be easier to control. In areas of existing developmental pressures, just the opposite will be true.[19]

Land improvements such as grading, clearance, reclamation, and erosion prevention often make up a large portion of the project cost. A developer should be aware of the cost of land improvement before he selects his site or purchases any land, and not be trapped into buying cheap land with environmental disadvantages that are costly to remove. "Improved land cost equals four times the raw land cost. Land value is becoming non-existent as far as recovering a return on its value."[20] The cost of land improvement is influenced by the cost of labor and machines and by the span of time required to complete the improvement.

A developer should check the availability of and the problems associated with building materials. An intensive survey conducted before selecting the site to determine exactly where building materials are located might reveal some within the region. If materials such as wood are available within the area, it might be economically feasible to use them for building. The cost of local building materials is important in countries which do not produce prefabricated housing. Lack of local materials and of an efficient transportation system could also make site selection difficult. Moreover, competition with other local industries for laborers might be crucial to a project, and the price of labor and the presence of unions should also be noted.

An overall strategy of regional development must be considered for selection of a site and must be applied to all aspects of development, to prevent wasted time, energy and finances, and to avoid political conflicts. "Part of this evaluation will include an appraisal of the regional economic base, and the role which the town will be expected to play in the further development of that base. A full elaboration of regional development strategies will especially have an effect on the location of the new town in relation to other urban centers."[21]

In developing countries, the economic and social issues of a new town are considered on a national scale:

The planning and development of satellite and new towns in developing countries must be viewed as an integral part of the process of economic growth and social change. The over-all objective should be the evolution on the national scale of a suitable hierarchy of settlements conducive to balanced economic development. The crucial role of planned urbanization is one of minimizing the economic and social costs involved in laying the foundations of emerging modern industrial economies.[22]

Potential Local Resource Criteria

Traditionally, most new towns have been developed in relation to their regional and local resources. However, many contemporary new towns wish to achieve their own economic base regardless of their local resources. Resources may be of three types: underground, on the ground, and in the air.

Underground resources such as oil, gas, coal, and iron have motivated the development of many new settlements. Natural landscapes can be important in site selection. Vegetation may enhance recreation or be used to produce paper or lumber. A zoo or botanical garden may increase appreciation of natural wildlife.

Water for drinking, washing, or cooling has been also considered an essential resource in site selection. Availability of water, soil percolation for sewage disposal, and suitable sites for solid wastes are important criteria. Planning sewage and garbage disposal requires careful study of wind, health, and landscaping in relation to land use. Since an individual septic system may pollute ground water if overused, a sewage network may be preferable though more expensive.

Potential sources of energy may include oil, gas, hydroelectricity, coal, wood, or sun in areas with minimal clouds. The availability of high voltage networks close to but not crossing a site may be an essential element in attracting industry to the site. Yet, although they are needed for industrial purposes, power lines may become a burden to the community by creating noise and interfering with residential life. Voltage lines can also be dangerous, especially during electrical storms. Putting a high voltage line underground is expensive, but safer and more practical than lines aboveground; if possible, it should precede any construction. A study of the area's energy should indicate the distribution lines within the site and its vicinity. A utility company may charge a private developer for the main extensions of electrical or gas lines.

Environment Criteria

A site should allow the development of a variety of landscapes to enrich community life style and values. A monotonous site such as a plain creates a drainage problem and requires special landscaping considerations and extra financial investments. However, there are many innovative design methods to overcome its disadvantages. Dutch planners have created variety by using water and vegetation in their designs. Elevating and lowering land to overcome monotony has been used in the United States, although mainly for drainage reasons. Townscape monotony may also be created in a rolling area as a result of poor design.

   If lowlands or flat areas have waterfronts, a variety of recreational activities and landscapes may be possible. However, a waterfront needs walls, a special drainage system, and protection. An impressive view from a high site may become a potential tourist attraction as well as being pleasing to the residents themselves. A high site is easily identifiable and may act as a focal point, creating a positive image.

   Landscape advantages may be gained from the unique characteristics of the view to and from a site, the vegetation, and the natural or artificial landscape. Increasing the aesthetic qualities of a landscape should increase the value of houses as well as migration to a new site. Although man-made landscaping can combine many elements by bringing water to the area or by planting trees, a natural landscape is more valuable in the selection of a site. Moreover, a unique landscape, whether existing or created, will distinguish a new town from its surrounding communities.

   The development of air inversions is undesirable, especially when associated with industrial pollution and topographical constraints which hinder proper ventilation. Fog and inversion combined with smoke may create a serious health hazard. A developer should also ascertain that there are no swamps or dumps near a site that may create unsanitary conditions and noxious odors.

   Development should take place with a minimum of harm to ecology: "site analysis has two elements—the one oriented to human purpose and the other to the site itself as an ongoing system."[23] Any change occur-

ring in one element affects the others and, in the long run, the whole system.

Every site, however disturbed, has had sometime to experience the mutual adjustment of its elements. The surface flow of water has created a drainage pattern, plant and animal life has formed an ecological system, neighboring structures lean against each other, shops have arranged themselves in relation to the resident population, and climate has weathered all alike. Any site is composed of many factors—above, below, and on the ground surface—but all these factors are interrelated and have achieved some sort of balance, whether it is static or moving toward another equilibrium. . . . Site development can have unexpected—often undesirable—effects that pass along the whole chain of living things. A new road may block drainage, induce erosion, overturn soil horizons, kill plants and animals, dispossess human residents, introduce new species, bring in hunters,

Figure 3.7. A preserved landmark in Milton Keynes, England. Bradwell Windmill was saved from dereliction so that future children may understand the past. (Courtesy of the Milton Keynes Development Corporation.)

litterers, or builders, scar the hillsides, pollute air and water, or import exotic chemicals. The entire living community, man included, must adjust to this new situation.[24]

New towns of this century have emphasized combining urban and rural environments by developing a green zone which surrounds or intersects the new town. The English New Towns Committee Report also considered environmental issues: "Areas of exceptional natural beauty or great historic interest should be avoided if their character would be impaired by the siting of a town. A new town, however, need not of itself destroy the beauty of the normal countryside. It may enhance it, and it will bring more people within reach of enjoyment of it. Special care should be taken to safeguard features of particular beauty near new towns."[25] Geologically unique phenomena or geographic sites, such as caves, caverns, or sight-seeing points can become tourist attractions. Criteria such as historic sites or archeological excavations in the vicinity have great educational and economic value, but precautions must be taken to preserve them. Development of historic sites in combination with a new-town site may symbolize the continuity of generations and preserve national history, as in the case of Israeli new towns which bear the names of biblical sites. (See Figure 3.7.)

Although a nearby quarry may provide materials for construction of buildings and other needs, the developer should consider improving its environment for aesthetic or security reasons. A quarry improved by adding vegetation may be used as a water reservoir, swimming pool, or a fishery.

Climatic criteria of a site should be carefully considered. A site located on the slopes facing south (in the northern hemisphere) will enjoy more sunshine than a location facing another direction; a site facing east will have sunshine during the morning, while a western site will enjoy sunshine during the afternoon. The situation would be different in relation to winds, which are distinct factors in arid or semiarid areas.

Noise and pollution produced by such sources as highways, railroads, and high-voltage industries should be studied in relation to the prevailing winds and topographical constraints. Dust may be a major pollutant in arid or semiarid areas where land and air are dry and the soil is easily carried by the wind. Such areas are frequently subject to dust storms which cause health problems and are nuisances to residential areas and vegetation. A water zone or greenbelt separating the developmental area from the dust sources may control dust and make the climate pleasant by reducing high temperatures at the site.

Political Criteria

A planner-developer should investigate the political power structure within a prospective site and its surrounding area to elicit cooperation for such future projects as zoning. Usually the political structures of sites close to large urban centers differ from those in rural areas. A rural site may not generally have as strong a local government to provide adequate services for the community as a development close to an urban center, although this difference may result from variation in systems of taxation. Sites close to or within urban centers may require the developer to adjust his plans and attitudes to existing policies:

Indeed, in a relatively undeveloped area there is likely to be no existing municipal government which is capable of providing services and regulatory functions for a developing new town, and the choice of this kind of an area for a new town community is likely to be dictated to some extent by a preference for open sites. A related question is whether the new town should be put under the sponsorship of an existing community, if one is available.[26]

Political issues in the region of the prospective site eventually become a major concern for a developer. In traditional societies such as those of developing countries, the local power structure is well defined. Technology, integrated too quickly without retaining or properly treating the traditional values of the society, can be socially destructive. Thus a synthesis of social and technological values may be best.

Most new communities in the United States and new towns in the United Kingdom are intended primarily for a middle-class population. A site selected in a low-income region and designated for a middle-class population may lose some of its housing marketability. Communication with local leadership might lay the groundwork for social interaction between the new town and its region and result in effective overall development.

A METHOD

Site selection is the most crucial and far-reaching process shaping the physical and economic development of a city. Although proper selection would be the best investment for the future citizens of a newly built city, they have no say in the selection of the site, since they arrive after the site has been selected and partially developed. At best, citizens may be able to change the land-use plan or the developmental phases of their city.

A variety of forces, most of which are out of the developer's control, such as land availability, financial resources, marketing, or urgency of development, determine the optimal selection of a site. In most cases a public developer finds himself in a better position to select a feasible site with a greater number of alternatives than a private developer, since the government either already owns large tracts of land or has the legislative power to select and acquire land for the optimal site.

Since the ideal site does not exist, any site selected is usually a compromise between more and less desirable elements, such as existing geographic, economic, or political conditions. Moreover, making the development of a new town an integral part of a policy for future urban growth insures a major financial resource for the project and minimizes the interference of short-lived forces that may cause the selection of a less than optimal site. In contrast, a private developer is in a position dictated by local factors:

The decision on new town location will have to be made by a public agency at a governmental level which is superior to the host of counties, towns, cities, and the special districts that inhabit the American urban landscape. A regional or preferably a state planning and development agency would be the logical choice for this responsibility.[27]

Any method for selecting a new-town site should include the following elements:

(1) Minimum subjective judgments and a well-defined rationale for both the process of selection and the actual choice of a site.

(2) Consideration of a maximum number of criteria.

(3) Systematic, quantitative evaluation of contributing factors.

(4) The ability to evaluate more than one site and to have a precise means of making a comparative evaluation among them. These alternatives allow a developer to change his decision about a preferred site if circumstances change, or to face unexpected circumstances that eliminate the preferred alternative.

The method of rating regional cells (MRRC)[28] divides all the region under investigation into small, equal, square cells and rates each on a set of adopted criteria. The cells which accumulate the highest ratings indicate the best potential sites.

This method compared to others,[29] offers the following unique features:

(1) It comprehensively considers all criteria for site selection.

(2) It allows the possibility of rating all criteria equally, or in proportion to each other, or a combination of both.

(3) It allows the elimination of part of a designated region which for some reason no longer warrants consideration, such as existing urban areas.

(4) The rating of criteria can be flexible enough to follow adopted policies under different circumstances.

(5) Although rating factors reflect the planner-developer's judgment, the method allows a modification of the rating pattern when the criteria values change. Criteria ratings may be rationally justified by early research and study of the power, importance, and influence of each criterion. Another solution for minimizing or eliminating subjectivity is that rating decisions can be made by an interdisciplinary team that studies, considers, evaluates, and rates every criterion to minimize intuition in the decision-making process.

(6) Since it considers alternative sites, this method insures steady implementation in a situation where one alternative may be excluded unexpectedly. The possibility of selecting alternatives brings about a flexibility in planning and development when difficulties arise in implementation.

(7) A planner can use this method for any country or geographic region on any scale for any type of land use, not only for site selection. Because of differences in values between one region and another, criteria adopted for evaluation will vary. Therefore a qualified planner must choose both criteria and their values carefully.

(8) An endless number of criteria can be considered, including physical, social, economic, geographic, and others, as long as they can be rated.

(9) The method is simple to use and to interpret.

(10) Rather than limit the investigation to sections of a region, the MRRC enables precise evaluation of the potential of an entire region, providing the chosen site with a regional perspective. MRRC may also be used to compare the potential of different regions.

The approach of MRRC is to quantify the interrelation of the various criteria. Every site has its own unique features and must be evaluated separately. The infor-

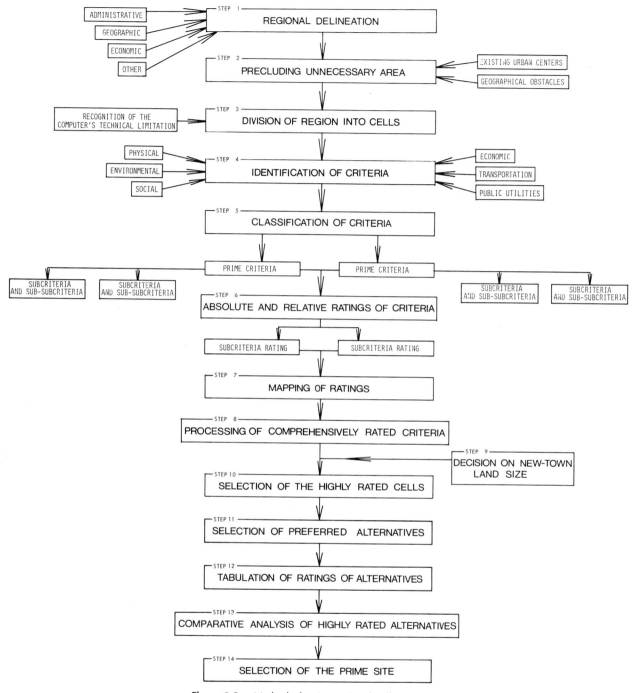

Figure 3.8. Method of rating regional cells (MRRC).

mation, analysis, and methods given here are theoretical, and planners and developers must judge the applicability of MRRC to their particular circumstances.

Time may be the most important factor in selecting the site for a new town, particularly when a special policy must be implemented quickly. Where time is limited, the work of planners and developers on site selection may lead to a compromise rather than full use of MRRC to find the optimal site, since collecting the data which MRRC requires may take too long.

Basic and detailed information is required to make a proper judgment using the MRCC. To explain our method, we will describe an actual study done by this author using the MRRC for a site near the Roanoke Valley in Virginia.[30]

A computer is necessary for maximum accuracy, efficiency, and use of time for modifications and to avoid undue complexity. Computerization offers flexibility in changing ratings, and in elimination or addition of criteria and visual output that is easily interpreted.

Fourteen sequential actions constitute the MRCC which leads to two goals: (1) delineation of alternative sites, and (2) ranking of alternatives by preference, and selection of one as the preferred site. (See Figure 3.8.)

Step One: Regional Delineation

A planner-developer should define and trace precisely on a map the region of his concern. These boundaries may be administrative, political, geographic, or economic. The preferred boundaries are political, since they correspond to statistical or other data prepared by a census bureau, local government, or other agency. While other boundaries may require special surveys or data gathering to acquire the necessary information, the size of a region may affect the degree of detail in the final product. (See Figure 3.9.)

Any subjurisdictional unit that falls within the delineated region should also be indicated, since such information as population changes, density, and marketing may also apply to those units. These data can be used to specify facts and findings that will increase sensitivity ratings.

Step Two: Precluding Unnecessary Areas

After delineating the region it is wise to preclude those areas which would not be considered under any circumstances. Except in the case of a new town in-town, existing urban development can be precluded. A zone of a few miles surrounding an urban center could be precluded, since a new town as a self-contained community and an independent territory stands exclusively within its own greenbelt. Rugged mountains that fall within the delineated region may also be precluded, although some new-town planners would include them as potential areas for innovative types of urban development.

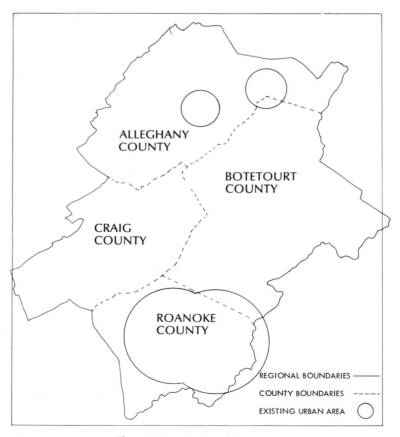

Figure 3.9.   Regional delineation.

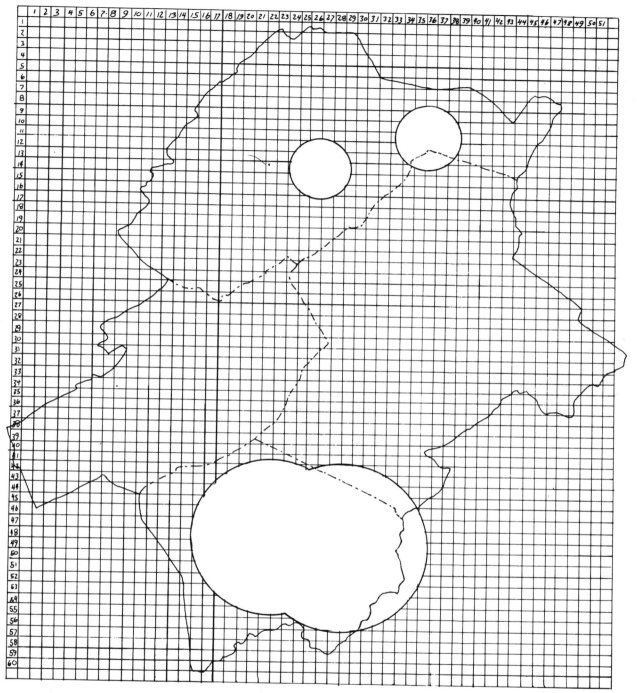

Figure 3.10. Division of region into cells.

Step Three: Division of Region into Cells

This action divides the entire region into small equal squares called cells, which constitute a grid system. To make the size of these cells manageable, each could be designed to correspond to 1, 1/4, 1/16, 1/64, or 1/256 of a square mile (or kilometer). Since each cell will be rated, the size of each will have a direct relation to its detail. Thus the smaller the cell, the more data required and the more accurate the results of the site selection. However, in determining the size of a cell on a map, one should consider the spatial limits of a computer in typing digits and in maintaining the cells as squares.

The boundary lines of a region will rarely be identical with the lines of the cells, and in most cases will divide the border cells into two parts. Therefore we suggest that if the major part of a cell falls within a region it be counted as part of that region. A decision on the included or excluded border cells should be made during this phase, since it will affect consideration of those cells in the following phases when cell-related data are computed.

The third part of this action is the vertical and horizontal numbering of cells for identification using coordinating lines. (See Figure 3.10.) The computer system called Synagraphic Computer Mapping (Symap)[31] or the Computer-Aided Space Allocation Technique (Casat)[32] can chart these coordinates. However, because of the disproportion of vertical and horizontal spacing of computer printers, maps may be distorted.

Step Four: Identification of Criteria

Identification of criteria is one of the most important steps and must be considered carefully and intelligently by the planning team. The list of criteria, their classification, emphasis, preferences, or inclusion can differ from one case to another. Selection, grouping, and priorities of different criteria lead to varying results.

Although physical criteria have been considered important traditionally, it has become increasingly desirable to use social, economic, transportation, and other criteria as equal determinants in selecting a new-town site. Criteria can be divided into two major types: static and dynamic. Most physical criteria would be classified as static. Although some criteria such as climate are dynamic in the long run their cyclic pattern is regular or constant, and thus they may still be considered static. On the other hand, social and economic factors—exports and imports, and migration—are considered to be dynamic, since their cycle can change to an entirely new pattern, although they can be predictable at times. These two major classes may justify giving static criteria higher value or emphasis because of their duration and constancy and the possible influence they exert on dynamic criteria. Yet, a dynamic criterion such as the pattern of land ownership can be considered major in a country such as the United States because of private land assemblage and regarded as minor in other countries such as Israel, where most of the land is publicly owned. The same holds true for water supply in semiarid versus humid regions, highly dense versus depopulated reg-

TABLE 3.1   ONE POSSIBLE CLASSIFICATION OF CRITERIA

Physical	*Social and Economic*
Topography	Demographic structure
Slope	Cultural characteristics
Soil condition	Income level
Land suitability	Job opportunities
Climate patterns	Income tax level
Geological features	Land taxation system
Hazards	Zoning pattern
Water resources	Existing land use
	Land suitability
Environmental	Housing market
Landscape potentialities	Land marketing
Air pollution	Land ownership pattern
Noise pollution	
Water pollution	*Transportation*
Historic sites and tourist	Network pattern
attractions	Proximity to transportation
Flora distribution	network
Fauna distribution	Proximity to urban centers
	Public Facilities
	Proximity to sewage network
	Availability of energy re-
	sources
	Distribution of educational
	facilities

ions, or intensely cultivated land versus sparsely used land.

Criteria may be grouped in countless ways depending on circumstnnces; e.g., as major and minor; as a sequence of interrelated components, such as primary, subprimary, sub-subprimary, and so forth; as physical features, social structures, economic areas, public utilities, governance, transportation, or environmental control.[33] (See Table 3.1.)

Step Five: Classification of Criteria

When criteria have been selected, approved, and grouped according to their importance, comparative rating can begin. To be systematic, one must classify all criteria as primary or subprimary, and so on. In countries such as the United States, a transportation network might be considered a primary criterion because of the dynamic mechanism of the economy and the high mobility of population, whereas in countries such as Israel criteria grouped under physical features would be considered of prime importance because of climatic constraints or defense needs. The comparative rating of the criteria grouped under primary will enable us to divide each according to subcriteria and sub-subcriteria.

Step Six: Absolute and Relative Ratings of Criteria

When criteria have been classified as primary, sub-, and sub-sub, the process of rating may begin. First, one must decide the importance of each primary criterion relative to the others and the maximum possible accumulated rating. Technical limitations of computers dictate using a two-digit number to retain the required size of maps. Thus the total accumulative rating of all primary criteria does not exceed 99. In our case study we assigned a maximum of 24. (See Table 3.2.) To qualify relative importance, one should assign weighted ratings for each primary criterion.

Clearly, some criteria will have a higher rating than others, and weighting is based primarily on determining the relative importance of those criteria in given circumstances. Since changes in weighting may become necessary as circumstances change, different alternatives may be produced.

Ratings should also be assigned to subcriteria whose total does not exceed the rating of their primary criterion. Here again the subcriteria should be rated in relation to each other. Thus some subcriteria will receive a higher rating than others, conditional upon their relative weight. A similar process should be used in rating sub-subcriteria. (See Tables 3.3 to 3.6.)

On the scale of ratings, some subcriteria do not necessarily have characteristics which correspond to each step on the scale. For example, slope characteristics are rated on a scale of 1, 3, 4, and 5 because 2 does not correspond to a condition which exists or the rating is meaningless relative to other subcriteria.

TABLE 3.3 RATING OF PHYSIOGRAPHY

Number of Contour Lines Within One Cell	Change in Elevation Within One Cell (feet)	Rating
0	0	6 (highest)
1	200	5
2	400	4
3	600	3
4	800	2
5	1000 plus	1 (lowest)

TABLE 3.4 RATING OF SLOPE GRADIENT

Degree (%)	Rating
0–8	5
9–15	4
16–24	3
25+	1

TABLE 3.5 RATING OF LAND SUITABILITY

Most suitable for urban development	5
Suitable for most types of land use	4
Most suitable for agriculture	4
Unsuitable for urban development	1

TABLE 3.2 RELATIVE RATING OF PRIMARY CRITERIA

	Rating Highest	Lowest
Physiography	6	1
Slope characteristics	5	1
Optimal land suitability	5	1
Transportation network (comprehensive)	8	1
Potential accumulated rating in a cell	24	

TABLE 3.6 RATING OF TRANSPORTATION SUBCRITERIA

Subcriterion	Proximity to the Network in Miles	Rating Maximum	Minimum
Interstate highway	0–1	4	—
	1–2	—	3
Primary or federal highway	0–1	2	—
	1–2	—	1
State highway	0–1	1	—
Railroad	0–1	1	—
Potential total accumulation on transportation in a cell		8	—

Step Seven: Mapping of Ratings

After the ratings of all considered criteria, subcriteria, and sub-subcriteria for each cell are assigned, they should be processed through an appropriate computer program. Every criterion and subcriterion will have its own map showing the spatial distribution of each rating as well as the similarities or dissimilarities among distribution patterns and the highest and lowest ratings in the cells. By examining the aggregated areas, we can learn which cells are highly rated in each map or which are clearly merged. Extreme rating groups may

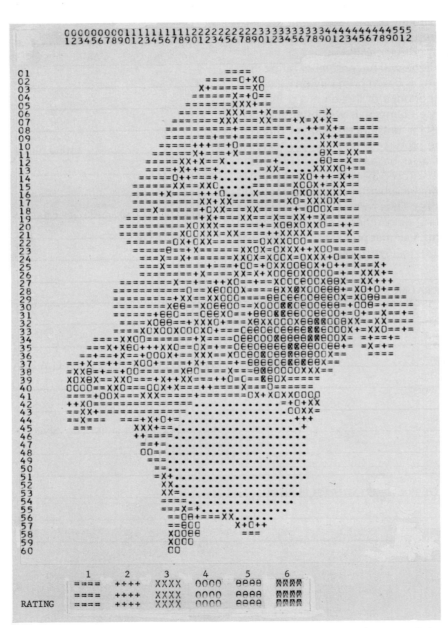

Figure 3.11. Physiographic rating. (*Note:* All the maps for this study were printed using symbols rather than numbers due to technical limitations.)

appear in each map, indicating the strengths or weaknesses of certain areas within a region. (See Figures 3.11 to 3.17.)

The second part in this step is the preparation of a comprehensive map of each primary criterion by combining all the maps of subcriteria. Thus every cell on the comprehensive map will have accumulated ratings of all subcriteria, and the final product will be a comprehensive map for each primary criterion considered. A comparative study of the spatial distribution patterns of primary criteria may be informative. (See Figure 3.18.)

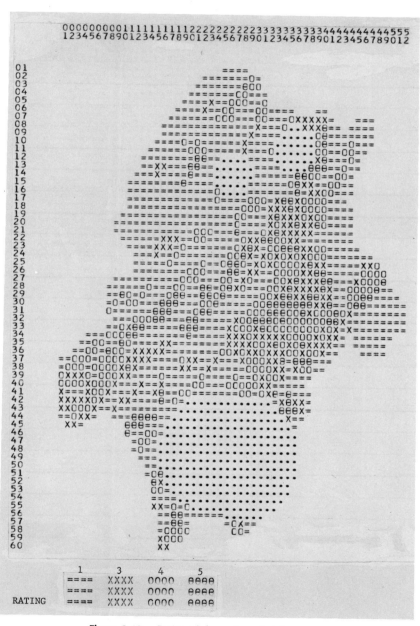

Figure 3.12. Rating of slope characteristics.

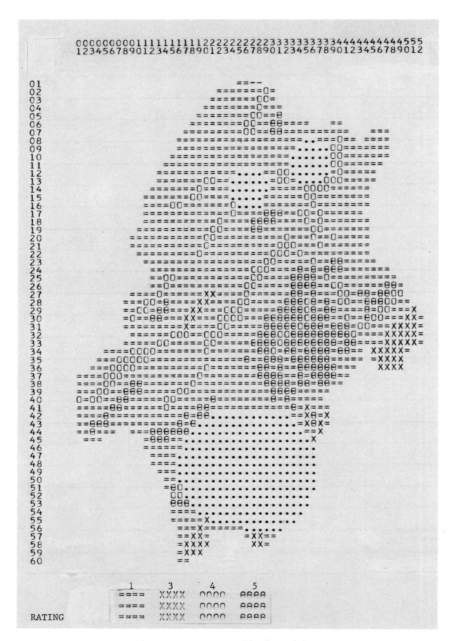

Figure 3.13. Rating of land suitability.

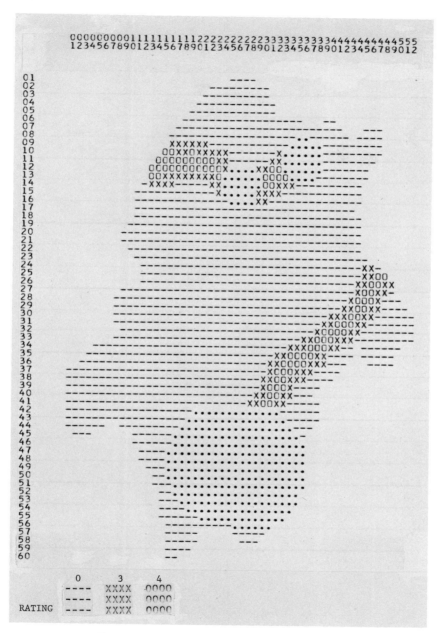

Figure 3.14. Rating of interstate highway network.

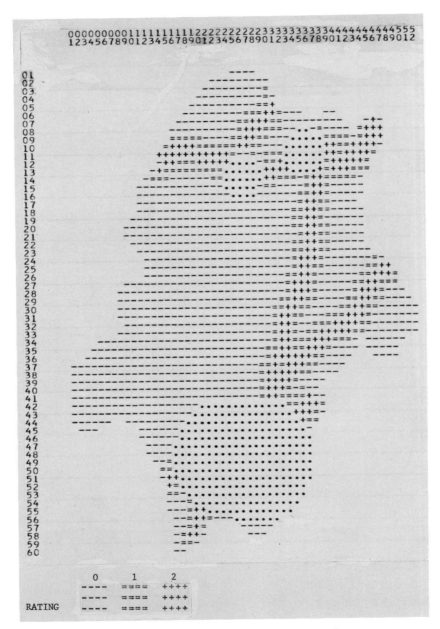

Figure 3.15. Rating of primary highway network.

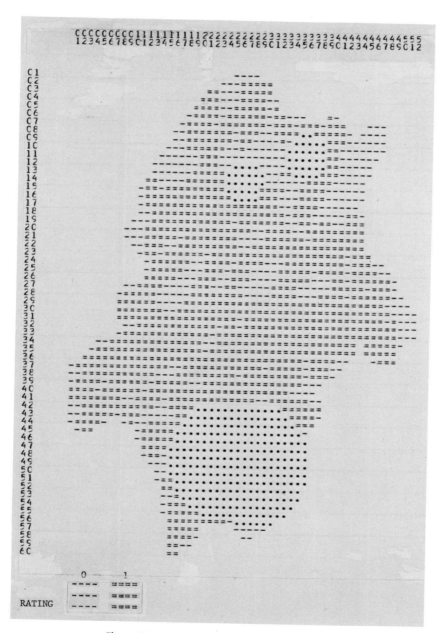

Figure 3.16. Rating of state highway network.

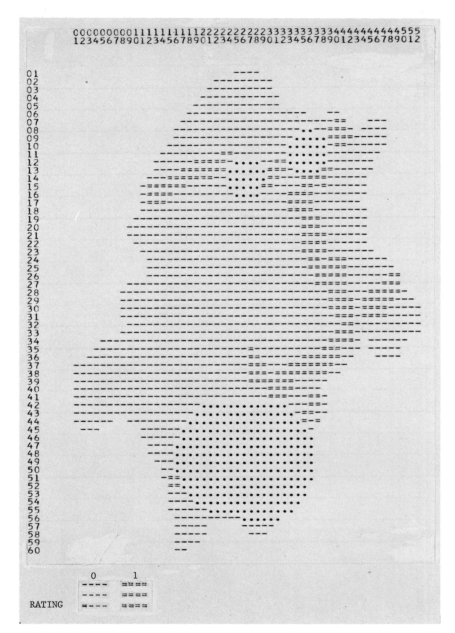

Figure 3.17. Rating of railroad network.

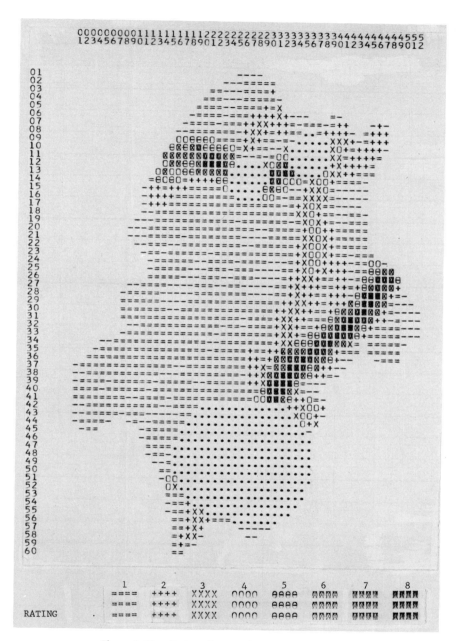

Figure 3.18. Rating of comprehensive transportation.

Step Eight: Processing of Comprehensively Rated Criteria

This step involves computer processing to combine all the comprehensive maps of primary criteria into one final map in which every cell will contain the total of all primary criteria. The final comprehensive map indicates the pattern of rated cells and consecutive aggregation which becomes our major concern. (See Figure 3.19.) This map will show the strengths and weaknesses of the region.

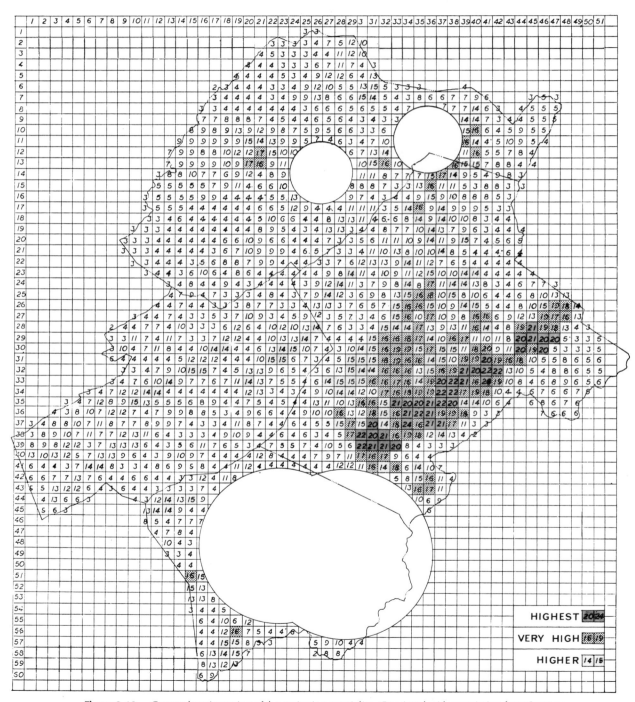

Figure 3.19. Comprehensive rating of the region's potentiality. (Reprinted with permission from *Strategy for New Community Development,* edited by Gideon Golany. Copyright © 1975 by Dowden, Hutchinson & Ross, Inc., Publishers, Stroudsburg, Pa.)

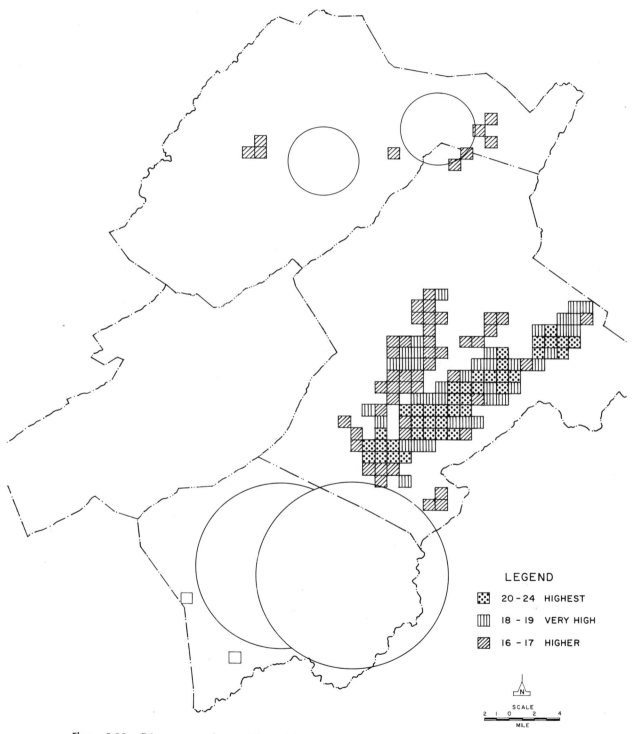

LEGEND

20 - 24 HIGHEST

18 - 19 VERY HIGH

16 - 17 HIGHER

N

SCALE

2 1 0 2 4
MILE

Figure 3.20. Primary area of potential suitability for site selection. (Reprinted with permission from *Strategy for New Community Development,* edited by Gideon Golany. Copyright © 1975 by Dowden, Hutchinson & Ross, Inc., Publishers, Stroudsburg, Pa.)

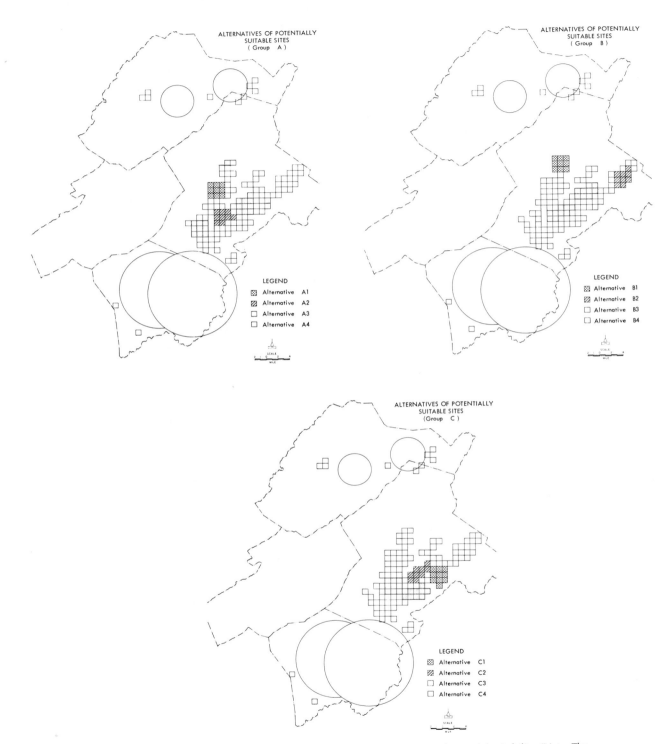

Figure 3.21. Twelve alternative sites delineated within the primary area of potential suitability. *(Note:* The letters and numbers of alternatives do not denote any preference.) (Reprinted with permission from *Strategy for New Community Development,* edited by Gideon Golany. Copyright © 1975 by Dowden, Hutchinson & Ross, Inc., Publishers, Stroudsburg, Pa.)

Step Nine: Decision of New-Town Land Size

To select a site for a new town we must decide the total size of the land required for all possible types of land use. According to the action in step three, all cells are equal, and each one forms one square mile or a square portion of it. To determine required land size, two issues must be considered: (1) the final and optimal population size of the proposed new town, and (2) the gross average density of persons per land unit (acre).

Step Ten: Selection of the Highly Rated Cells

When the decision has been made about the amount of land required, we will know the total number of cells to be selected in the region to form the required amount of land. Our primary concern then should be to select those cells with the following characteristics:

(1)   The cells which have accumulated high or the highest ratings within the region. In our case study, we selected cells which fell between 16 and 24, particularly those which rated 20 to 24, since the maximum total for each cell is 24.

(2)   The selected cells should be in a consecutive cluster, or at least in an overall pattern which supports some new-town urban form such as linear, multinuclear, or radial.

(3)   The total number of selected cells should at least equal the land required to build the new town.

However, since the highest possible rating a cell can have rarely exists, cells with very high accumulated ratings are likely to be scattered geographically and thus not clustered. Thus, our selected cells will be those that are rated closest to the maximum.

Step Eleven: Selection of Preferred Alternatives

According to this approach, we should be able to pinpoint more than one adequate concentration of cells. The various aggregated cells should be considered as alternative sites for a new town. Selected alternative sites may be far from each other, border each other, or even overlap in part. Tracing those aggregated cells with the required number in color will stress their existence and their overall form in comparison to each other. (See Figures 3.20 and 3.21.)

Step Twleve: Tabulation of Ratings of Alternatives

At this stage of the process, we should list those alternatives ranked according to their accumulated ratings.

TABLE 3.7   TABULATION OF ALTERNATIVES IN CITED EXPERIMENT

Alternative Sites in Order of Preference	Accumulated Rating in Nine Required Cells[1]
1	179[2]
2	177
3	176
4	175
5	173
6	172
7	172
8	159
9	158
10	156
11	139
12	134

[1] Every cell has been made equal to 1 square mile. The total amount of land required for a new town of 50,000 people would be 9 square miles, or 9×640 acres = 5760 acres.
[2] In our example the highest rating that could be accumulated in a single cell is 24. Thus, the total rate per site will not exceed $9 \times 24 = 216$.

Since the order will represent our preference, those aggregated cells that accumulate the highest rating will be considered as the primary site. (See Table 3.7.)

Step Thirteen: Comparative Analysis of Highly Rated Alternatives

Although the method introduced here is systematic and quantitative in its approach, there is still a need for a comparative analysis of alternative sites before selecting the final one. When rating regional cells we may be in a position where some criterion could only generally or in part be used quantitatively and spatially. Generalization could also occur because the borderline of clustered cells differed from that of a political jurisdiction or because only general statistical data were available. In this step a re-evaluation and revision of the rating level of all criteria may still be made that could change the results. However, a comparative overview would also spotlight some of the weaknesses in the method's ability to adjust to the region under investigation and support the re-evaluation of the various criteria. Such comparative and comprehensive analyses will also disclose strengths and weaknesses of each alternative.

Step Fourteen: Selection of the Prime Site

The final action is the selection of the prime site for the new town. Both the rating results and the comparative analysis will assist in making the proper decision. Although such a site will be easy to select in this phase, one should keep second and third alternatives in mind in the event that the first choice collapses because of unpredicted complications. However, the optimal choice may not necessarily be the site that accumulates the highest rating for reasons which cannot be measured.

NOTES

1.   Frederic J. Osborn and Arnold Whittick, *The New Towns: The Answer to Megalopolis* (New York: McGraw-Hill Book Co., 1963), p. 88.

"corporations were given ample powers to acquire sites sufficient for complete towns, to undertake all the necessary kinds of development, including the provision of houses, factories and commercial buildings, and were necessary to provide public services, to appoint and employ full-time officers and constructional workers —in fact to have all the powers that an ordinary large-scale developing landowner would possess, plus one or two ancillary powers usually exercised by local authorities. They were not however to replace the local authorities; the site of each town was to be made a separate parish or county district for which the authority would be elected in the ordinary way."

2.   Great Britain, *New Towns Act, 1946* (London: His Majesty's Stationery Office, 1946), Section 2—[2], p. 2.

3.   See James A. Lyons et al., eds., *New Towns and Planned Communities* (New York: Practicing Law Institute, 1971), p. 239.

4.   Edward P. Eichler and Marshal Kaplan, *The Community Builders* (Berkeley and Los Angeles: University of California Press, 1970), p. 61.

5.   Daniel R. Mandelker, "Some Policy Considerations in the Drafting of New Towns Legislation," in *New Towns and Planned Communities,* James A. Lyons et al., eds. (New York: Practicing Law Institute, 1971), p. 271. Mandelker quotes the New Towns Act of 1946: "If the Minister is satisfied, after consultation with any local authorities who appear to him to be concerned, that it is expedient in the national interest that any area of land should be developed as a new town by a corporation established under this Act, he may make an order designating that area as the site of the proposed new town." (Great Britain, Section 1—[1], p. 1.)

6.   Great Britain, Ministry of Town and Country Planning and Department of Health for Scotland, *New Towns Committee Final Report* (London: His Majesty's Stationery Office, July 1946), Section 27—[2], p. 11.

7.   Great Britain, Ministry of Town and Country Planning, Section 27—[5], p. 11.

8.   On the subject of tidal waves, see Robert F. Legget, *Cities and Geology* (New York: McGraw-Hill Book Co., 1973), p. 415.

9.   For more analysis on the interpretation of aerial photography of geological features, see T. Eugene Avery, *Interpretation of Aerial Photographs* (Minneapolis: Burges Publishing Co., 1969), pp. 210–40.

10.   For details see Charles B. Hunt, *Physiography of the United States* (San Francisco and London: W. H. Freeman and Co., 1967), p. 26.

11.   See Legget, pp. 423–36.

12.   Eolian soil transportation occurs when winds carry soil from one place to another. The most commonly known eolian soils are loess and sand dunes. For details see Douglas S. Way, *Terrain Analysis: A Guide to Site Selection Using Aerial Photographic Interpretation* (Stroudsburg, Pa.: Dowden, Hutchinson and Ross, 1973), pp. 261–83.

13.   Way, pp. 262–63. Way defines loess as follows: "Loess materials are composed of unconsolidated or weakly consolidated, silt-sized particles. . . . The mineral content varies according to the source of the parent material. Most loess particles are angular and are typically held together by calcareous cement or binder. Loess is a light-colored material, since it is very porous and well drained vertically." Legget gives another description:

"Loess . . . is very fine grained . . . and usually white or pale yellow in color. It is a transported soil, the particles having been carried into their present position by wind action. Loess is therefore one of the relatively rare eolian soil types. It is often found exposed with almost vertical faces, usually in areas of low rainfall. Microscopic examination shows the soil particles to consist generally of fresh minerals such as quartz, feldspar, calcite, or mica but with other material acting as a binder so that the soil when dry has a relatively hard texture. . . . This binder can give loessal soils considerable dry strength, sufficient to sustain the overburden of 100m or more of dry soil. . . . [A]lthough so satisfactory when dry, they will usually lose much of their strength when water is applied to them. The addition of water generally destroys the binding action of whatever has been holding the individual grains together, and the internal soil structure will, literally, collapse. The previous open texture of the soil mass will be destroyed as the water breaks the bond between adjacent grains and then facilitates their moving together. Even with loess in place, the addition of water to the surface will so destroy the strength of the soil that progressive collapse will take place, possibly leading to considerable settlement of the surface. . . . If such subsidence is not anticipated, its effect can be serious on any structures that may have been built on the dry soil" (Legget, pp. 469–70).

14.   James A. Clapp, *New Towns and Urban Policy* (New York: Dunellen, 1971), p. 164. In the United States, according to Clapp, "the legislation would in effect call for a continuation of site selection and acquisition procedures currently employed by unassisted developers, the primary criterion will continue to be the availability of sizeable parcels which developers can meet rather than any determinations which may be made by the Federal government or regional planning authorities as to the 'best' or desirable locations for new towns."

15.   J. Ross McKeever, ed., *The Community Builders Handbook* (Washington, D.C.: Urban Land Institute, 1968), p. 32.

16.   Great Britain, Ministry of Town and Country Planning, Section 27—[9], p. 12.

17.   Great Britain, Ministry of Town and Country Planning, Section 28, p. 12.

18.   Mandelker, p. 273.

19.   Mandelker, p. 273.

20.   Robert T. Nahas, as quoted in McKeever, p. 300.

21.   Mandelker, p. 273.

22.   P. B. Desai and Ashish Bose, "Economic Considerations in the Planning and Development of New Towns," in *Planning of Metropolitan Areas and New Towns* (New York: United Nations, 1967), p. 219.

23.   Kevin Lynch, *Site Planning,* 2nd ed. (Cambridge: M.I.T. Press, 1971), p. 9. Lynch also notes that "every site, natural or man-made, is to some degree unique, a web of things and activities. That web must be understood: it imposes limitations; it contains new possibilities. Any plan, however radical, maintains some continuity with the preexisting locale. Understanding a locality demands time and effort. The site planner properly suffers a chronic anxiety about this 'spirit of place' " (p. 5).

24.   Lynch, pp. 10–11.

25.   Great Britain, Ministry of Town and Country Planning, Section 27—[6], p. 12.

26.   Mandelker, p. 276.

27.   Mandelker, pp. 271–72.

28.   I first developed the method of rating regional cells (MRRC) for new-town site selection and applied it in 1970–1971 in selecting a site for a new town in the Roanoke Valley of Virginia. That study led to designation of 12 potential sites within a region which consists of four counties and more than 1700 square miles. Because of the availability of materials we are using information on that region in this research, this time by computerizing the rated information. See Gideon Golany, "New Community for Virginia in the Roanoke Valley: Site Selection and Feasibility Study" (State College, Pa.: Gideon Golany Associates, January 1972). Also, Gideon Golany, "Site Selection and Feasibility: A New Town for Roanoke Valley," in *Strategy for New Community Development in the United States,* Gideon Golany, ed. (Stroudsburg, Pa.: Dowden, Hutchinson and Ross, 1975), pp. 129–54.

29.   The most commonly known method is a system of overlaying which may use color or a pattern of distribution for each criterion in separate maps. The combination of overlays should indicate the accumulated distribution of all the patterns. A new combined pattern will emerge from the overlays. For examples of the use of this method, see M. Quoist, *La ville et l'home* (Paris: Les Editions Ouvrieres Economie et Humanisme, 1952); Gideon Golany, *Urban Survey of Existing Residential Quarters in Jerusalem as a Basis for Rehabilitation,* Part D (Haifa: Technion Israel Institute of Technology, 1965); and Ian McHarg, *Design with Nature* (Garden City, N.Y.: Doubleday and Co., 1971).

30.   Golany, "New Town for Virginia" and "Site Selection and Feasibility," pp. 129–54.

31.   L. O. Degelman, *Introductory Manual for Synagraphic Computer Mapping,* version 5, P.S.U. modification 3 (University Park, Pa.: Department of Architectural Engineering and the Graduate Interdisciplinary Program in Regional Planning, The Pennsylvania State University, January 1969).

32.   Richard F. Tomlinson, II, *Computer-Aided Space Allocation Technique,* version 1, modification 0 (University Park, Pa.: Department of Architectural Engineering, The Pennsylvania State University, September 1971).

33.   The criteria used in our experimental case study were mainly physical and included (1) physiographic features, (2) slope characteristics, (3) optimal land suitability, (4) transportation networks and (5) land ownership pattern.

FOUR
SOCIAL PLANNING

INTRODUCTION

Until recently planners of new towns rarely considered social planning or a new town's need for identity as the cornerstone of plans by relating and subordinating all other considerations to those of social livability. Traditionally, the physical aspect of planning has been the most thorough, but recently economics has contributed significantly to planning, and a variety of theories about site selection, industry, distribution of economic activities, and location has been developed. Thus many academic planning programs are now strongly oriented toward economic planning.

Little has been achieved in social planning because of the complexity of contemporary social issues and also because some sociologists have been more concerned with academic studies of society than with finding practical solutions to social problems. Few sociologists have made significant efforts to challenge existing social planning alternatives by analyzing the past and applying their findings to the future. Often solutions offered for social problems have been instantly available and superficial rather than comprehensive and long-range. Unfortunately, since instant solutions are temporary they are undesirable.

Planners of Columbia, Maryland, have related social plans to physical structure; i.e., they first considered such factors as social identity, needs, and social philosophy and then planned Columbia's physical arrangement. In a similar manner, British new towns and those of Western Europe have tried to solve social problems of central cities by reorganizing existing urban populations in new regional patterns such as satellite new towns.[1]

GOALS OF SOCIAL PLANNING

Any social planning, and that of new towns in particular, should carefully answer several major questions before actual plans are begun:

(1)   What are the social goals to be accomplished?

(2)   Are these the only primary goals; and what are other possible goals and their priorities?

(3)   What are the relations and impact of social goals on other goals such as physical, economic, and governmental ones?

(4)   What are alternative means to achieve these goals; i.e., what are the available resources to be used, and under what conditions will planning and implementation take place? What is the cost-benefit ratio?

(5)   For whom will the planning take place, i.e., for what client?

(6)   What planning method will be used?

Social planning should be a goal-oriented system with alternative goals relevant to the changes possible in a dynamic society. Alternative goals are desirable to make citizen participation possible and to allow occasional revision of early goals.

In the first stage of social planning for a new town, social planners should set primary goals and priorities. For obvious reasons, primary goals may differ from one country to another and from one geographic-cultural region to another. Since these goals usually concern the major issues of a country or region, their focuses may vary from integration to assimilation, employment and income improvement, and population redistribution.

One major goal of a social plan is to improve the quality of society. The social planner should identify primary and secondary factors in a prospective community which may support this improvement. His study should show that each community has a unique set of values and, consequently, its own factors which will promote and increase standards of living. Identifying primary and secondary factors will aid the social planner in setting later strategies of implementation and will also aid the developer in budgeting the stages to carry out the plan.

Once the primary goal for a new town is prepared and approved, the social planner should make a detailed plan of implementation that includes stages and time, preferences and priorities, financial resources, alternative goals, and specific people or agencies responsible for fulfilling each aspect of the plan. The planner should also make alternative social plans that are necessary to insure the availability of clear directions a new town may select if it develops interests different from the first alternative presented.

The primary social plan should specify necessary social services including their scope, number and quality for each age group, spatial requirements, skilled and unskilled staff, and occasional research activities to assess community needs and interests. Also, the plan should clearly indicate those existing or planned social services in the surrounding region of a new town and their potential integration with those of the new town.

Several problems of which a planner should be aware are encountered in the early stages of social development. One which is common to all new towns is social imbalance, indicated by a disproportion of sexual and age groups in a new town's population pyramid; the ratios of males to females and of age groups to each other are asymmetric. Usually a large number of children and young people and a very small number of elderly people or no elderly at all live in developing new towns. This asymmetry is also typical of a migrant population, and its instability is similar to that of new towns.

Another element which developing new towns have in common is unbalanced socioeconomic structures. Most new towns in the world, except those in Israel, absorb mainly a middle-income population. One of the arguments against new towns is that they do not solve contemporary problems, especially those of low-income groups. This is true in the United Kingdom, where, for various reasons, only a very small part of new-town populations are from low-income groups. These groups were not well informed about new towns because the mass media did not adequately reach them, and since they were mainly unskilled workers, they were hesitant to move because of existing job security and lack of information about potential jobs in new towns. Research has shown that skilled people are more willing to move and are generally more mobile than unskilled people.[2] Low-income populations are reluctant to take steps that might jeopardize their position or collapse their economic or social lives. (See Figure 4.1.)

COMMUNITY BALANCE

Planners of British new towns have advocated balanced communities as one definite goal of these towns. Heterogeneity is one way of achieving a balanced community in a relatively large-scale settlement if this mixture leads to harmonious relations and interaction and enriches people's lives.[3] Such a community should also provide an opportunity for the existence of a homogeneous group. The communal sharing which homogeneity produces can act as a catalyst to promote local community pride. Moreover, homogeneous groups based on communal factors other than income, such as religious beliefs and ethnic origins, established within a heterogeneous whole community, can play a positive role if these groups are given a planned residential unit of their own.[4] (See Chapter 2.)

Although middle-income families can play a major role in balancing a community, the main challenge in the creation of such a community is to accommodate low-income populations as well as the middle- and high-income groups that often migrate to new towns. Involvement of the public in the scheme and implementation of such a plan has always been essential to insure financial subsidies for the housing needs of low-income people and to attract this socioeconomic segment of society. Moreover, integration or assimilation of this social group can be managed with a higher degree of success than in an old city, since the population of a new town is generally more receptive to change.

Another argument supporting the idea of a balanced community is the need to insure a good standard of equal services for all through local tax income:

Heterogeneity is desirable, because as long as local taxation is the main support of community services, it will help to prevent undesirable inequalities in the level of community services. . . . The increased opportunity for all sectors of the population to make social and cultural choices in a more equalitarian society may also bring about greater heterogeneity in residential areas in the future.[5]

A balanced community is closely integrated with all other features of the new town which make it healthy, alive, and independent.[6] A new town will operate much more efficiently if there is an integral relationship between its degree of self-containment and the extent to which it is a balanced community. Although the main emphasis of a balanced community is on social and demographic aspects, the self-contained community must also have a variety of employment

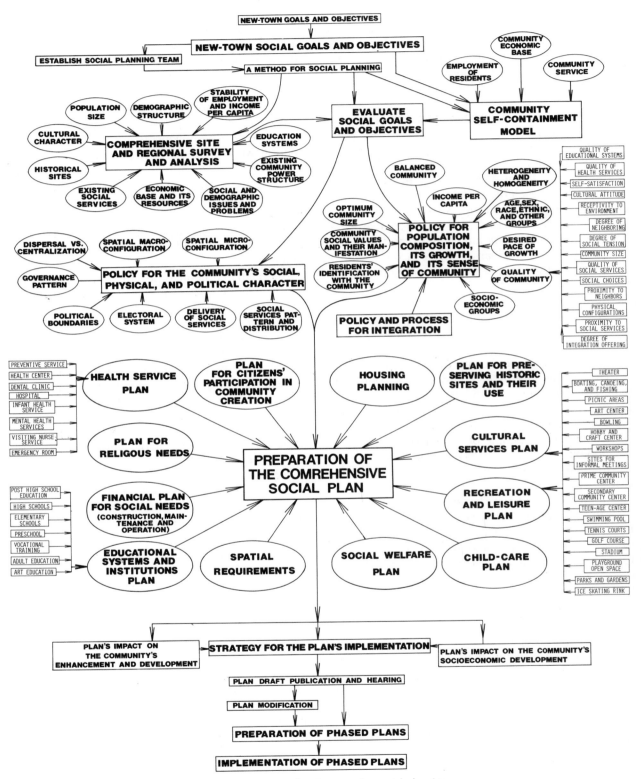

Figure 4.1. Generalized process for social planning.

100

opportunities for its population. Yet, a socially balanced community would not necessarily be a self-employed or self-contained community:

The idea of a balanced community is more complex than that of self-containment, though the origins of the two ideas are partly inter-twined. To some extent a town can be self-contained only if it is 'balanced.' The level of population must more or less match the level of employment or there will be commuting in and out.[7]

POPULATION COMPOSITION

Before we examine each age group, several points should be made about motives for a youthful population to move to new towns:

(1) Jobs are sometimes unavailable in older cities.

(2) Lack of housing in older cities often causes migration to new towns.

(3) Young married people move to new towns because they want to spare their children from the pollution, noise, and tension that exist in big cities, and to provide a better environment.

New towns generally seem to attract predominantly young populations with a large number of children. Age groups also appear to have unequal sex ratios. (See Figures 4.2 and 4.3.)

In the early stages of English new towns and American new communiiies most young married people have many children of kindergarten and early elementary-school age.[8] Although Israel has encouraged a high birth rate in development towns because it is desirable for the country, it was primarily due to the large number of people who came from cultures in which bearing many children was encouraged.

High birth rates cause serious problems in providing services for children that are unique to new towns and should be given top priority by a planner. For example, larger schools than usual with more floor space are needed per 1000 population. In Sweden this problem was solved by building temporary additions to accommodate classes instead of permanent brick or stone buildings. These additions were removed in 10 to 15 years when the community had stabilized and

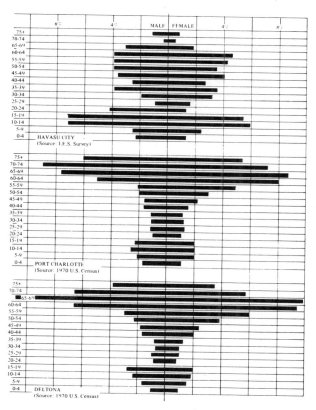
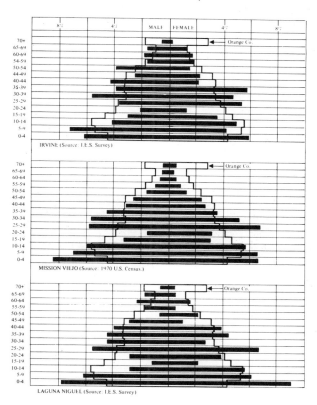

Figure 4.2. Comparison of population pyramids of six privately developed new communities in the United States. Note that Port Charlotte and Deltona are retirement communities. (Source: *Case Studies of Six Planned New Towns in the United States.*)

fewer classrooms were needed. It took British planners many years to realize and to solve this problem. Nearly every new-town plan in England was altered between the time the plan was started and approved because of the change in birth rate just after World War II.

Requirements of this part of the population will have an impact on the land-use pattern. The greater number of children in new towns requires more playground space. High birth rates mean special medical services must be provided for a new-town population, especially for the numerous pregnant women. Also, a medical center or clinic should be located close to residential areas where specialists for women and children are available.

Perhaps the most important group to be considered in new towns are teen-agers because their generation will continue the life of the new town. As parents grow old their children will assume adult roles, continue to fill jobs, provide leadership, and operate the new town.

English new towns have taught us much about teen-agers. It took the English nearly a decade to realize that they had not provided sufficiently for the social life of this group. In early new towns teen-agers had to go to London every evening for social life, and soon they began to find jobs there and move. When

planners realized that the recreational facilities provided in new towns were only for adults, they started changing the emphasis of the facilities. In other new towns such as Columbia, Maryland, the change was so effective that it brought many people from the surrounding area to use the new community's facilities. Residents did not approve of this situation because these incoming people did not pay local taxes to support the facilities. Although social facilities should be planned and constructed specifically for teen-agers, social planners should realize that new towns in their early stages do not have enough teen-agers to support such facilities, therefore teen-agers will find few if any social activities during this phase.

The young-adult and middle-aged groups include those between 18 and 40 years of age. These are major age groups in new towns in terms of size and usually comprise about 50 percent of the total population.[9] More importantly, as the most stable age groups in new towns, they are the nucleus of the society and are responsible for directing social and economic activities.

The last age group is the elderly, 60 years and older. This group includes some people who came to new towns with their relatives and others who chose new towns as places in which to spend their retirement because of attractive environments. Many atypical new towns in California and Florida are retirement communities. (See Figure 4.2.)

Several elements must be considered for the latter age group: (1) Their residences must be close to services to avoid driving because many elderly people are unable to drive. (2) They should not be in an isolated location because this may affect them adversely mentally. (3) They need the support of an urban atmosphere, where they can meet different groups of people and interact with those younger than themselves.

Social planners should also consider the needs of semiinvalid or handicapped people who would like to shop and move around freely. All facilities, including curbs and sidewalks, should be designed to allow partially handicapped people to be mobile. The elderly age group is one of the most desired groups in the community because this population completes the continuum of a normal society: children, teen-agers, the middle-aged, and the elderly. Unfortunately, this continuum is lacking in many existing new towns and is difficult to achieve in the United States because of its highly mobile population. The large size of the country makes it possible for people to move away and thus allows people to break relations with their parents quite easily. In contrast, European countries are much

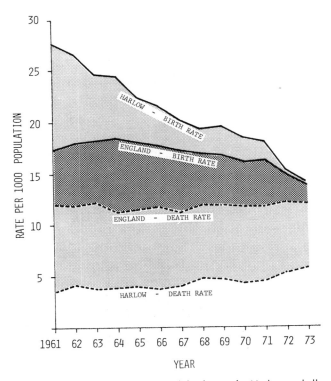

Figure 4.3. Comparative birth and death rates for Harlow and all of England. (Source: *Harlow Expansion 1974.*)

Figure 4.4. Redditch, England: Bungalows for elderly people located on a main footpath near the local shopping center. (Courtesy of the Redditch Development Corporation.)

smaller, and consequently people live closer to their parents. If new communities can provide a place for the elderly to join their married sons and daughters and thereby complete the social structure, the issue of continuity in American new communities may be resolved. (See Figure 4.4.)

The elderly also require particular social and medical services. Some recreational activities do not adequately meet the needs of elderly people, and the elderly require facilities appropriate to their own age group.

Some advantages to having a youthful population in new towns are

(1)   Young people's attitudes.

(2)   Creation of a social climate with minimum conflict.

(3)   The readiness of some young people to volunteer for social services.

(4)   Less distinction among racial, ethnic, and religious groups than in regular cities.[10]

CULTURE IN NEW TOWNS

Webster defines culture as "the act of developing the intellectual and moral faculties especially by education," or the "enlightenment and excellence of taste acquired by intellectual and aesthetic training; behavior typical of a group or class."[11] This definition, however, omits the historical aspect of culture. Culture is a continuous process of transmitting accumulated social and technological achievements from one generation to another to maintain social form and to regulate life. Results of this process change with time. Although they may rebel against their parents, children still learn rules, regulations, and living habits from them and will, in turn, teach their children.

Culture is part of the identity of individual people, of

groups, and of nations. Patrick Geddes was among the first to develop the idea that social planners should consider cultural elements primarily in their plans to further social identity.[12] Understanding culture is necessary to capture the strength, the power, and the nucleus of a society. Traditional societies have established their cultures through many generations building one upon the other. Geddes emphasizes that all elements of such cultures should be understood when planning new settlements.

Planners of new towns should consider several factors related to the history of culture. The first has two parts: traditions which should be revived and developed so that they may become regional or local events, and historical ruins particular to a people's traditions. Natural phenomena used as cultural symbols, such as geographic characteristics, birds, or flowers, are the second factor. A third element is the preservation of historic monuments or settlements. Archeological excavations of biblical sites and burying grounds have been used in Israel to symbolize historic continuity between old and new towns.

Religions often have an identity related to ethnic or racial groups that can strengthen ties between groups in a society, although the religious element was much more important in the past than it is today. The Catholic Church motivated urban development in the Middle Ages, and European medieval cities were all planned with the church as the most important building in the town.

Recreation and leisure are also related to culture, and planners have thoroughly studied them with respect to new towns. By its very nature a new town provides a relaxing environment in which to supply a variety of activities.

The following elements influence leisure in a new-town society:

(1)   Level of per capita income dictates the kind of recreation a person can enjoy or even whether he can afford recreation. The per capita income in India, for example, is very low for the majority of the population, and the standards of living and recreation fall far below any minimum standards for a new town.

(2)   A cultural demand for leisure is not necessarily related to personal income alone. For example, a villager who has just become rich because oil was discovered on his land is not mentally and culturally oriented toward the use of recreational facilities, yet in terms of income he possesses the wealth he needs.

(3)   General attitudes toward leisure and recreation vary from class to class.

(4)   Recreational and leisure facilities must not only be provided but must also be accessible; if these facilities are not readily accessible to the public, they are wasted. Many types of seasonal sports and activities should be introduced to meet the requirements of people of different incomes, ages, and sexes. Recreational facilities designed for year-round use are also economically desirable.

A plan for recreation and leisure is an important aspect of new-town development. Its primary goal should be to provide various daily recreational services for all age groups of the new town's population and, in the long run, for the population of the surrounding area. (See Figure 4.5.)

Recreational facilities should enhance the existing natural resources and beauty of the site and its surrounding area, and should encourage the development of a sense of preserving and maintaining the quality of those natural resources among the site's residents, especially its young members. Services should include open spaces, playgrounds, parks, tennis courts, and swimming pools. Open spaces are a major portion of a land-use plan, ranging from 10 to 40 percent of its total. This range depends on such factors as (1) the proximity of a new town to major urban centers, (2) land value and availability, (3) the amount of land unsuitable for construction, (4) the developer's general policy towards density, and (5) the standards of living of a new town and its nation.

A highly technological society increasingly demands all types of recreational facilities for all age groups. Social changes in an urban society, such as increasing incomes, growth of the middle class, increased communication and transportation to new regions, more vacation days, and early retirement, have resulted in quantitative and qualitative improvements in leisure. Some new towns located in unique natural landscapes will probably attract many outsiders to use the new town's seasonal, physical resources. Since it appears that during the first few decades of new towns a large portion of their populations are less than 30 years of age,[13] social services and their objectives should focus primarily on the requirements of these people.

Standards to be used in determining the recreational needs of a new town can be drawn from national and regional standards and combined with the particular needs of each new town. Final standards and plans will differ from one new town to another, mainly according to location and population composition. In a privately developed new town, highly sophisticated recreational facilities may increase housing marketability.

Figure 4.5. Primary scheme of the city club of Milton Keynes, England. (Courtesy of the Milton Keynes Development Corporation.)

Integrated recreational facilities may save space and maintenance costs for a community. Moreover, when they are properly located in conjunction with residential areas, these facilities may be used effectively by all age groups and may also save time for parents with many children.

SOCIAL INTERACTION AND INTEGRATION

Because of their new social, political, and physical environments, new towns tend to attract people of diverse socioeconomic and cultural backgrounds. Since this diversity may not only add excitement to the community but also may make the population socially unstable, integration is necessary to reduce tension and social conflict in such societies so that they may function successfully, as in uniting a region or country. The United States, Israel, Canada, and Australia, for example, are countries where integration of large numbers of immigrants has been necessary. Social planners need to understand integration and the conditions which facilitate it as one part of the socioeconomic development of a community in order to make proper plans.

Interaction is the mutual or reciprocal action of social groups not necessarily committed to each other. Even if each group retains its own identity, interaction can favor economic and social actions which lay the base for integration. People need a great deal of tolerance and intellectual understanding before they can interact harmoniously; they cannot be forced to do so. (See Figure 4.6.)

Plans for new towns should be carefully prepared to create the best social balance possible. To be socially healthy, at least at the macrolevel, new towns should be heterogeneous in races, cultures, age groups, and personal incomes. The greater the diversity within these factors, the greater will be the kinds of interaction and communication that can occur.

Integration enriches society when it manifests itself by improving the lives of diverse groups in the community. Integration develops when a society socializes informally and when community members share feelings of mutual responsibility and care. Integration also occurs when various groups in the community have diminished or conquered their feelings of inferiority.

As a process, integration has complex implications beyond those of its general meaning. It is a multifaceted phenomenon with at least three components:

Figure 4.6. Experimental flats in Overvecht, Utrecht, The Netherlands. These buildings have common space on every floor, where children can play and adults can meet and socialize. (Courtesy of Gemeente Utrecht.)

(1)   Similar or equal education available to all groups.

(2)   Economic opportunities that do not discriminate among groups.

(3)   Intermarriage between members of socially different groups.

Integration unites various groups into one community and encourages people to accept the values of others. Although integrated groups are still distinguishable, the distinctions may be less apparent than before integration. At this stage, however, it is a reversible process and can be undermined by conflict in the community.

Neither integration nor segregation is a universal, absolute, or eternal remedy. The author believes integration is a desirable means of creating a stable society. However, if the groups of a society want segregation, it should be permitted unless it poses a threat to the community.

Types of Integration

Integration cannot occur unless common values and interests or similar characteristics such as cultural origin, behavioral patterns, personal adaptability, mentality, and (the most decisive factor) income exist as a foundation. Types of integration include (1) social, (2) class or economic, (3) housing, (4) racial, and (5) age group. Racial integration is the most difficult because it involves color as well as cultural background.

Among the catalysts for social integration in new towns are individual expectations, relative youth of their populations, and newness of their environments. In a new town each person, his family, and the community expect more social activity than in established

Figure 4.7. A residential area of Lake Anne Village, Reston, Virginia. This area offers mixed density in housing: apartments, medium- and low-density townhouses, patio homes, and single-family residences. Heron House, the 15-story apartment, symbolizes Reston's dedication to mixed housing. (Courtesy of Gulf Reston, Inc.)

cities. A move to a new town motivates a person to offer and to expect more than he ever did before in order to establish himself. Young married people with children who comprise the majority of new-town populations are more receptive to social interaction or integration than are older people.

In theory, new-town newcomers will immediately

select a residence to avoid stress by settling near people who have values similar to their own, so they will be more demanding in selecting a neighborhood than in choosing a new town as a whole. Also, they may tolerate a heterogeneous new-town community that periodically provides social variation.

In practice, the first wave of newcomers arrives in a

new town that lacks a society or social and economic norms, except for housing and real estate prices and the general image of the new town as the developer has promoted it. Later, the residents will either reinforce the developer's norms or make their own.

Since societies of free-market countries are usually divided into classes, a classless society cannot develop within their new towns. Although equality and integration in new towns may improve the life of a low-income population, a private developer cannot be expected to reduce the gaps between socioeconomic groups. The primary agent which can effect this change is the national government.

The necessity of establishing housing to mix classes and, consequently, to integrate them has often been oversimplified, and planners and social policy makers have only occasionally raised this issue. Other than low-income families may fear risking their real estate

values and may rent rather than buy a house in certain mixed sections of a neighborhood. Local real estate taxes on private housing may differ from those of housing constructed with public funds for low-income people, and this tax system may provoke some legitimate reticence among both low- and middle-income groups attracted to this mixed housing. Each group may analyze the financial and social benefits of this mixture and move to unmixed housing. Those who buy homes in or develop mixed housing should be aware of the difficulties of integration before making efforts to promote it.

Low-income populations are not able to move to new towns without housing subsidies because standards and housing costs in new towns are often higher than those of older cities.[14] Although low-cost mortgages can be obtained, most low-income people still require aid to move to new towns.[15] In Israel, low-

Figure 4.8. Low- and moderate-income housing in Reston, Virginia. Cedar Ridge is the first federal housing project in an American new community. (Courtesy of Gulf Reston, Inc.)

income populations were encouraged to move to new towns by public subsidies for housing provided to the residents themselves; they also knew that they could get a cheaper house in the new town than in their own towns.

Social planning should consider two primary aspects of planning mixed housing for low-income families:

(1)   The ratio of houses for low-income families that society can absorb to the total number of housing units. This ratio should be determined in relation to housing marketing and to the planned image of a community.

(2)   The spatial distribution of those houses within a community.

It should be obvious that the housing type (houses, apartments, attached units, etc.) and unit size will determine, to a large extent, the composition of a new town's society. From the point of view of social planning, housing design should focus on population needs such as those of the handicapped, the elderly, families with a large number of children, and single persons. The impact of each of these groups on a community will probably differ from one culture to another. (See Figures 4.7 and 4.8.)

We can anticipate that diverse ethnic and racial groups who come willingly to new towns will be receptive to some integration in the community. However, even when racial integration is welcomed by the people of a new town, the planners and decision makers would be shortsighted were they to underestimate or ignore the psychological effects of color differences, since such effects could take considerable time to dissipate. During this time, real social and psychological (though not physical) segregation because of color differences can foster the need for self-determination. Racial integration may be achieved, however, if minority groups have equal representation in decision making.[16]

Age-group integration, regarded as easier to accomplish than that of socioeconomic groups, concerns integration among different age groups and within the same age group. Whereas racial differences seem to add tension to age-group integration among teen-age groups, as has happened in Columbia, Maryland, the demographic composition of new-town populations can help accelerate social integration among specific age groups. For example, Columbia has a relatively high ratio of single and divorced people who were attracted to the new community because of its promising opportunities for socializing. This group demands a great degree of socializing which a new town cannot usually provide in its early stages. A small number of elderly persons who move to a new town in its early stages may also want to socialize, but this age group may find itself isolated. The problem becomes more acute when these elderly persons are not capable of driving a car. A solution may be a community group of retired and elderly people, and social institutions for this group readily available to all who need them.

Characteristics of New-Town Newcomers

Newcomers feel mental and social stress caused by moving—feelings of uncertainty and unfamiliarity with the new environment—which may affect every member of the family. This stress continues from the day a family member first considers such a move to the time when the family returns to normal. The duration and emotional effects of this process depend on the existing familial unity which, in turn, depends on culture and maturity, experience, and the ages of family members.

New employment usually associated with moving can create tension, especially for a family head. The effect of this tension is directly related to moving in a given country, the adaptability of each family member, and the family's sense of financial security. Although the lack of initial formality during early stages of life in a new town minimizes class distinctions in socializing, the financial burdens of making a new home contribute to newcomers' tensions. The separation from old friends and the constant desire to make new ones make socializing necessary and may add to family expenses.[17]

Generally a move made willingly by a family to a new physical and social environment generates freshness, excitement, receptivity, and mutual aid within a family. New residents of new towns are constantly trying to establish their status and to play a role in their new society. Accordingly, social events which bring residents into each others' homes motivate them to make new friends. Most people will also associate and integrate primarily with others of equal income regardless of other differences. Thus, integration occurs when individuals or families have established their own status; this is the beginning of a stable community.

Although they prefer a primarily homogeneous society which approximates their existing norms or projected images, newcomers may be willing to accept a

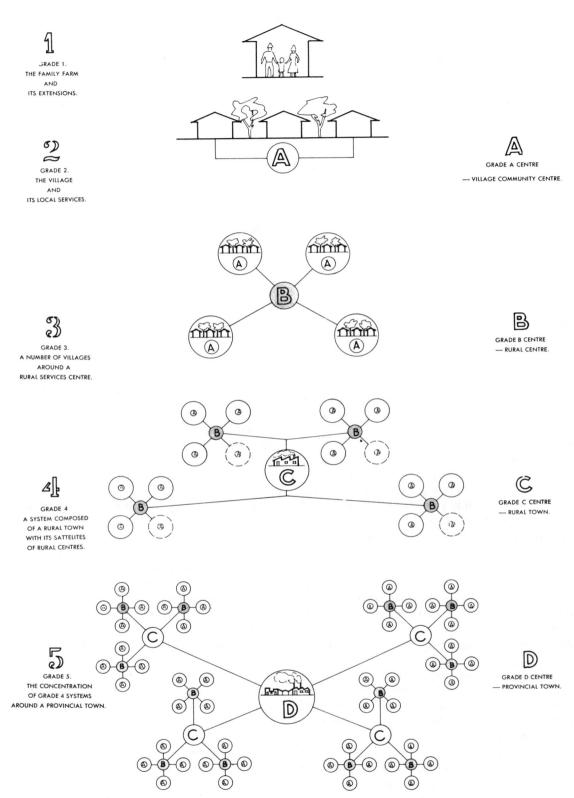

Figure 4.9. The hierarchy of social and other services in Israel. (Source: *Regional Cooperation in Israel.*)

heterogeneous community. Curiosity, social consciousness, and chances for variation can motivate this willingness.

Integration and Delivery of Social Services

A new town should deliver its services, especially social ones, in such a way as to make them accessible and affordable to all residents regardless of income, age, race, or ethnic identity. Health and welfare, child care, recreation and sports, playgrounds, and educational and training institutions can be used to bring residents of various backgrounds together and to foster interaction among them. For the low-income group in particular, obtaining a reasonably priced house is not the only major problem; they also have unconscious stress to adopt a higher standard of living than they used to have along with its daily expenses. Therefore, encouraging integration through social and other services may require taxing these services minimally, if at all, particularly during the early stages of a new town. (See Figure 4.9.)

If social services during the early stages are to be maintained at adequate levels governmental subsidies should finance them, because any new town has an insufficient fiscal base and too small a population to support them. Adequate delivery of services that provide individual and group satisfaction may lessen conflict and increase interaction. People who are forced to seek service outside a new town may be continually dissatisfied with it and have no motive for interaction.

Citizen Participation as a Tool of Integration

In dynamic social conditions, involving people in local social activities helps maintain a nuclear group which continues integration. Citizen participation in new towns depends on three factors: (1) the attitudes and social and educational background of the population, (2) the presence of common issues or problems of concern to the community, and (3) governmental bodies of towns, neighborhoods, or subneighborhoods that are meeting grounds for community action. Here, individuals and groups realize common aspirations, potential community leaders may develop, and housewives may find many ways to use their free time. Government with a high degree of citizen participation may provide a means of integrating a fragmented community. The common interest and shared administrative responsibilities are sound motives for unity and integration.

Local voluntary leadership may emerge in such activities as schools, youth movements, home associations, transportation issues, maintenance of the surrounding environment, and establishment of a community center. A major motive of this emerging local leadership is meeting the needs of children. Parents and children may combine to insure the development of good standards of education and services for themselves. Another important concern is the need of homeowners to protect their rights against the developer. Also, the entire community is interested in its right to make decisions regarding its way of life and the services and public facilities to be provided for it. This interest may sometimes be contrary to the interest of the developer who wishes to insure his economic success and may become a source of conflict between newcomers and the developer.

Physical Forms Related to Integration

Physical configuration can support integration but cannot be its only base.[18] Spatial patterns of neighborhood housing units as well as services, amenities, or facilities required by residents may not only encourage interaction but may also help organize the community. For example, economic or social activities such as shops, transportation, and educational and religious facilities can be meeting places for various age groups.[19] (See Figure 4.10.)

When physical planners determine spatial configurations they necessarily influence social planning; therefore we can say that sparsely distributed residences may hinder spontaneous contact. This will not occur unless people, especially children, congregate at some other center such as one for transportation or communication. For instance, the small number of privately owned cars in early Israeli development towns indirectly supported local social integration.

The effective clustering of houses can ease socializing among unacquainted new neighbors, especially school-age and young groups, during the early parts of their new lives. Proximity alone may not, however, account for many friendships or for integration since affinity of neighbors is directly proportional to the existing degree of homogeneity among them. Limited choices for friendships, as may happen in isolated new towns or company towns, may help the effects of proximity.

Similarity and affinity are crucial to the socialization of children. A large, planned housing block may provide many potential friends for children as well as

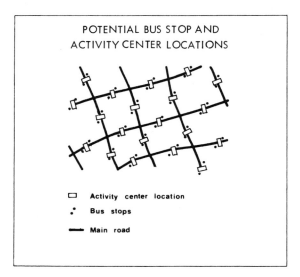

POTENTIAL BUS STOP AND
ACTIVITY CENTER LOCATIONS

☐   Activity center location

⦁   Bus stops

▬   Main road

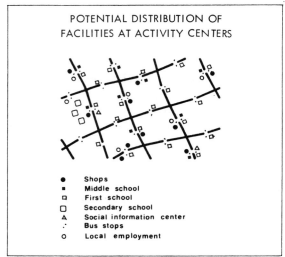

POTENTIAL DISTRIBUTION OF
FACILITIES AT ACTIVITY CENTERS

●   Shops
■   Middle school
▫   First school
□   Secondary school
△   Social information center
⦁   Bus stops
○   Local employment

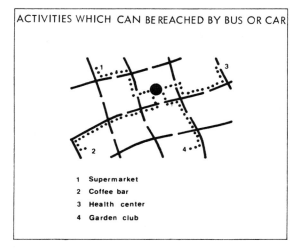

ACTIVITIES WHICH CAN BE REACHED BY BUS OR CAR

1   Supermarket
2   Coffee bar
3   Health center
4   Garden club

ACTIVITIES WITHIN WALKING DISTANCE

●   Shops
■   Middle school
□   First school
⦁   Bus stop
○   Local employment

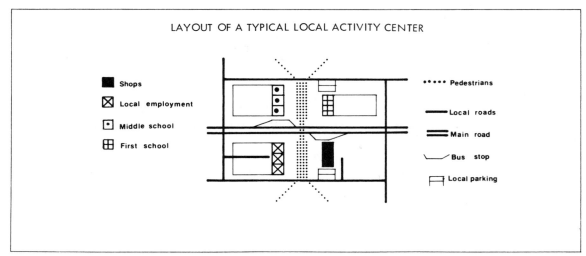

LAYOUT OF A TYPICAL LOCAL ACTIVITY CENTER

■   Shops

⊠   Local employment

▣   Middle school

▦   First school

••••   Pedestrians

──   Local roads

═══   Main road

⌐   Bus stop

⊟   Local parking

Figure 4.10.   Activity centers in Milton Keynes: their proximity to other functions, and a typical layout. (Source: *The Plan for Milton Keynes,* Volume Two.)

112

adults. Affinity has even more importance for the elderly and others who have limited personal mobility and access to transportation than for families. Having neighbors similar to oneself is more important for housewives or mothers with preschool children than for men who are away from home most of the day.

Integration in Neighborhoods

One major goal of a neighborhood is to foster the social identity and social integration of its residents. Neighborhoods are created to make neighboring a stable social system and to develop a sense of community based on existing social understanding, interaction, and integration. Integration is considered easier to attain in neighborhoods than in subneighborhoods and is expected to provide its population with social rather than economic advantages.[20]

Improvement in economic behavior can derive from living among mixed-income groups. Low-income groups may improve their economic image by choosing to change residence from a heterogeneous low-income neighborhood to a higher income area. Family members desiring to be similar to or assimilated with their neighbors try to acquire more education and pay more attention to physical appearances than before, regardless of their income. Nonetheless, this behavior may be mixed with some initial inferiority feelings among low-income family members when they become residents of a new mixed-income group. Thus socioeconomic integration in a new-town neighborhood or its subunit emphasizes social rather than economic integration.

Subneighborhoods help foster personal identity more than larger residential units. If integration is an evolutionary process and a realizable goal in the social lives of people, then a subneighborhood may retain (if it so desires) spatial segregation of its residents to reduce tension. However, segregation should be confined to here.

PLANNING SOCIAL SERVICES IN NEW TOWNS

Services required in areas of health, education, culture, and society must meet the daily, seasonal, and lifetime needs of residents. Adequate new-town social services and facilities require three major ingredients: (1) physical amenities, (2) staffing of services, and (3) teaching the population to use services advantageously.

The younger generation is the most sensitive to and demanding of social services. Moreover, its requirements are unique and need careful attention. Some of its needs include

(1)   Various facilities related to the size of the new town.

(2)   Specific services prepared for that age group, not combined with those of other age groups.

(3)   Services that attract outside participants when a new town is not yet large enough to provide adequately for residents; such services may help to keep the young from traveling to nearby urban centers for evening entertainment.

Low-income families in a new town whose population consists mainly of middle- and upper-income families, where most social services meet the standards of these affluent families, find themselves unable to afford these social services and therefore unable to participate in the social life of the community in a satisfactory way. In some cases housing subsidies for low-income families may be associated with subsidies for social and health services. Public funds from sources outside a new town should aid low-income families at least until the town can collect enough taxes. The sites of social and welfare services are an important factor in determining the intensity of their use. For example, the location of health and day care centers near major economic and social activities may encourage the use of those centers.

Ideally the various services needed by a family should be concentrated in one place. However, it is difficult to achieve this pattern for economic reasons related to neighborhood size. Concentrating services makes it possible to adapt some facilities to more than one activity, such as using the school play field as a playground for children and as a sports field. A multipurpose recreational center used by a wide variety of athletic teams is more economical than a single-purpose center, and may help to develop interest in more than one type of social activity.

Health

There are four major health areas in new towns: mental, physical, and environmental health, and educational and public health services.

It is generally assumed that new towns provide a better social climate than large cities and are therefore conducive to good mental health. Planners have noticed that in older urban centers the closer one goes to the central part of the city, the higher the number of mentally ill people.[21] In recent years, however, more mental health problems have increased in suburban areas.

Mental health services can be developed effectively in a new town when other health services already exist and should operate on two levels: as preventive agencies and as rehabilitative centers. Women other than those who are occupied either by employment or raising many children and teen-agers may require mental health services most: women because of the mental depression which might occur as a result of increased leisure time due to sophisticated technology, and teenagers because of the pressures of growth and adjustment.[22]

Because of the high ratio of young families in a new town, there may be a need for establishing a youth counseling center, a women's center, and a familial counseling center, all of which may function on a voluntary basis to provide necessary services. In its later stages a community may also need a center that provides services for the elderly.

Mental health is largely influenced by the relations one establishes with one's family and neighbors, and by the relaxation one is able to achieve in work, play, and family life. The small size of new towns promotes greater social interaction and allows more intimacy than is possible in larger cities. Many social scientists assume that socializing within small social units can foster harmonious relations among individuals and groups.[23] In small communities people expect little tension from pressure during rush hour or association with hurried patterns of life; they enjoy relaxed social relations and the feeling that children are secure in the neighborhood. Indirectly, new towns may improve relations among family members, since living close to nature and to open space and green areas, and having fresh air and little noise all help reduce tension.

The level of personal participation in local social activities is higher in new towns than in big cities[24] and creates a sense of belonging to the community. Because of the many favorable elements involved, one can assume that the level of mental health in new towns is higher than in large cities.

Some of the following elements promote the physical well-being of people in new towns: adequate public facilities, such as garbage collection, water supply, and sewage treatment; recreational facilities of high quality; transportation networks designed to reduce noise and air pollution and to create clean air. Construction of housing on the macro- and microlevels of a new town, such as window placement to allow more

than adequate ventilation and sunlight, may provide an atmosphere which promotes good physical health.

Health care, i.e., preventive medicine, is a major issue in privately developed new towns and in countries that lack national health insurance. Although many countries of the world have national health insurance, their new towns in predominantly agrarian regions find that they must struggle to develop health-care services because qualified physicians are unwilling to move to isolated regions.

The goals of health-care services are basically the same in all countries: (1) to practice preventive medicine, and (2) to provide a variety of basic and advanced treatment for all age groups. Those services should be accessible and affordable to all local and regional residents regardless of income. Because of their large investment and costly maintenance, health services should treat residents of an entire new-town region to justify their costs and to make full and effective use of their provisions and staff. Services should be comprehensive and operate in new towns located in rural regions where such services are not regularly available.

In planning a system of health care to serve new towns, the social planner should consider four elements: recruitment of highly qualified professional people trained in health service, sophisticated equipment, adequate management, and identification of past and present attitudes among the regional and the national population toward health services. A plan for health-care service should include these elements and should reflect a population's attitudes toward (1) adaptability to changing health services, (2) receptivity to health care and to health service, and (3) health education trends. Health plans which ignore existing trends are difficult to implement unless they are publicized to create necessary awareness. The social planner should also insure that newcomers to new towns are fully informed of existing health-care services available to them.

Health-care or preventive services should be related to the social aspects of new-town life. Establishing a system of health care in new towns will contribute to feelings of satisfaction and pride in their residents. This effect goes beyond the primary goal of a system as a health-care service and may relate the service to concerns of the entire community.

Systems of health care should use the most advanced technological achievements in disseminating knowledge about health care and in bringing services as close as possible to local and regional residents. Telecommunication devices[25] and mobile facilities may provide decentralized services. If possible, at least in their early stages, health services should be related to an established medical school in the area where both qualified professionals and financial resources are present. (See Chapter 6.)

Planning for comprehensive data banks about health conditions in a new town and its surrounding region may result in effective health-care services, and may enable efficient implementation of both health-care and medical-care systems, save effort and money, and predict future demand. These computerized data banks should be updated as the population changes and matures. In regions where health services are scattered, a data bank may be the start of integrating all existing health services.

In countries which lack national comprehensive health insurance, a new-town developer should initiate a local health insurance system. Such a program may be based on prepaid per capita or family insurance and on integration of all agencies providing such services in the region to reduce costs and insure effective operation.

A comprehensive health insurance program should be developed in relation to a person's income to pay for all health and medical needs. In addition to preventive services, the program should include the following: hospitalization, surgery, emergency care, treatment of venereal disease, mental health services, dental services, family planning and counseling, rehabilitation, nursing home care (especially for the elderly), optometric services, and health education for all age groups.

A major issue in new towns is the necessity to move from a system of medical care to a system of health care. Service must shift from diagnosis and treatment alone to preventive measures which help maintain health for all groups in society.[26] New towns provide an opportunity to experiment in this shift for their own benefit and that of established urban centers.

Daily Child-Care Service

The increased number of working mothers throughout the world has resulted in a corresponding need for daily child-care service. Possible contributing factors in this new situation could include migration of families to new towns, since the additional income might be needed to compensate for new family expenses incurred in moving, and consciousness raising by women's liberation movements worldwide. (See Figure 4.11.)

The general goal of a child day care center is to provide organized service by qualified staff to help solve the problem of tending children while parents work. The service should either use volunteers or be inexpensive to be available for all residents. Other goals of a child day care center are (1) to promote the child's mental and physical health, (2) to stimulate communication skills and intellectual ability, (3) to increase confidence in personal ability and self-reliability, (4) to build the child's relations with his family, (5) to free the child's mother for employment, education, or training, and (6) to develop the child's personality, independence, self-expression, and social interaction.

The development of day care institutions in new towns depends on various conditions which may or may not exist in a community. Among these conditions are (1) the number of preschool children (the existence of this age group in a new town would justify the cost of establishing a day care institution); (2) availability of skilled people to run the institution; (3) availability of funds, facilities, and equipment to operate such institutions with high standards; (4) proximity and accessibility of an institution to the residential area which it serves (the location of child day care centers in or near shopping centers, e.g., Reston, Virginia, lets mothers make one trip that includes both facilities); (5) mothers' attitudes toward day care, which are determined by their working conditions, the number of children at home, availability of grandmothers, financial conditions, and sometimes by their cultural backgrounds or psychological constraints.

Day care services for children should vary according to age group and should include nursery, kindergarten, or preschool care. Nursery care is usually provided for children from 2 to 4 years of age for one period of the day; kindergarten care is usually full day care and is offered to children 4 to 5 years old.

Child day care should be decentralized within a new town to meet family needs. Although this approach may conflict with policies of financial saving and of institutional integration, a voluntary, self-organized parental group which would participate in the planning process may help ease this conflict. Doris Wright, a planner of child-care services, outlines four basic systems for child care:

(1) Home care, where child care takes place within the family.

(2) Group home care, where 1 to 5 children are cared for in an "organized home or environment."

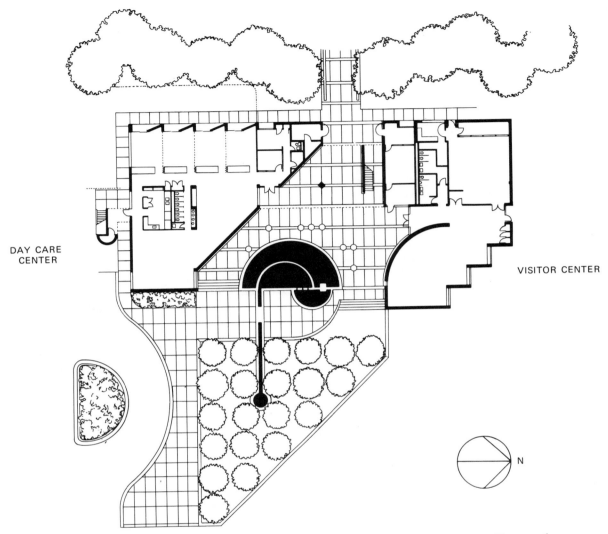

Figure 4.11. Flower Mound, Texas: Plan of the visitors' center, including a day care center. (Courtesy of David A. Crane and Partners.)

(3)   Child-care centers, where up to 25 children are cared for by professional people assisted by paraprofessionals.

(4)   Comprehensive child development centers, where a large number of children (up to 250) are cared for in multiple programs.[27]

Programs of child day care may vary from one new town to another and should be adjusted to individual situations and economic conditions. Wright lists the following as potential programs of child care for new towns:

(1)   Infant and toddler child care.

(2)   Twelve-hour child care.

(3)   Half-day child care.

(4)   Comparative half-day nursery school.

(5)   Hourly child care.

(6)   After-school day care.

(7)   Emergency care.

(8)   Parental involvement and learning (which includes family-life education services and parent-child participation).

(9)   Mobile family outreach services.

(10) Consultant pool.

(11) Cable and television programming.

(12) Food service.[28]

Planning comprehensive programs of child care in new towns may enhance and improve the quality of social and family life; therefore child-care programs are a long-range, justifiable investment for a community. Successful child-care programs may also be one of the most exciting experiences a new town may offer to a well-established urban center. The planner, the developer, and the citizens of a new town should view programs of child care as an integral part of a comprehensive social services program rather than as a separate entity, since the success of child-care programs will contribute immediately and in the future to the enrichment of society.

PLANNING EDUCATION

Educational planning for new towns is a dynamic field because it is related to constantly changing young groups and demands for new educational facilities. Most planners emphasize the importance of this dynamic aspect and, consequently, have difficulty predicting the school population new towns will have. The demand for school facilities changes as the population pyramid of a new town approaches the national one, and it is more difficult to plan floor areas, teachers, equipment, and an operating budget for a new town than for a regular school district.

The primary educational goal of a new town is to provide various training facilities for all age groups of its population (and, in special circumstances, for its regional population). A related goal is to provide educational innovations which may serve as examples for surrounding communities. The latter goal is essential for a new town surrounded by a traditional region, not highly developed technologically, which expects the new town to introduce such innovations. Education in new towns should be accessible to all residents regardless of incomes or ethnic origins.

The Minnesota Experimental City Project, which investigated the role of new towns—the cities of the future—in education, made the following assumptions:

(1) The city is the primary learning laboratory; the entire city is a school.

(2) Every resident of the city is a potential learner.

(3) The learning system is learner-based.

(4) The learning system is dedicated to new fields of knowledge and new ways of improving learning.

(5) The system is a lifelong, continuous process.[29]

Educational facilities may serve a community effectively as meeting grounds for interaction and social integration. Most parents view education as the most valuable service a community can provide for their children and, in many cases, are willing to postpone fulfillment of other desires in order to support their children's education. Preschool, nursery, kindergarten, and elementary school are the components of an educational system that require the most attention in the early stages of a new town. High schools (especially senior high), continuing education, paraprofessional education, and adult training, should be major concerns in the later stages of development when a community has stabilized and has established a wide local tax base that can support it. The development of a normal population at a later stage in the growth of a new town can decrease the need for elementary schools and free some space to be used by senior high schools and centers for adult education. In its early stages the senior high school may be joined to the regional one until the new-town population has grown enough to justify its own facility. Similarly development is possible for such institutions of higher education as community colleges. (See Figure 4.12.)

New towns may have potential use as laboratories for educational experimentation and for reforming school systems simply because such towns accept changes more readily than other communities. The educational system of new towns should provide a wide range of education and training for different age groups: regular instruction should be provided for school-age children, and continuing education should be accessible to the elderly to further their knowledge, to enrich their lives, or to give them a leisure activity.

An educational system should recruit qualified teachers not only to work in a community but also to live there, especially in its early stages. Early establishment of varied social services is necessary to attract qualified educational personnel. Under certain circumstances qualified teachers may be attracted by high salaries, grants, interest-free loans, housing provisions with easy terms, tax releases, or other incentives. Such teachers can be vital to isolated new towns.

New towns developed as satellites to metropolitan centers or in an established region, as for example in the United States, may lie within the boundaries of an existing school system. Such a situation can lead to

Figure 4.12.   A nursery and kindergarten in Lake Anne Village, Reston, Virginia.

conflict between the existing system and the new town and threaten its identity, its independence in deciding matters such as expenditures, quality of the system, and busing, and its functions in educational innovations. Conflicts may hamper relations between the new town and its surrounding region. Therefore, to establish and maintain a coherent position in these circumstances, the new town needs an early, detailed plan.

Location of Educational Facilities

Most planners agree that the location of schools should be determined by the ages of the students and proximity to their homes; i.e., the younger the students, the closer the schools should be to their homes. The elementary school should be located within the neighborhood to serve resident children. In order to justify the school economically and to provide the proper number of teachers, floor areas, equipment, and libraries, planners and architects must determine the minimum size for a school in relation to the size of

a neighborhood. Also, they must know the population density of an area in order to build adequate facilities. For example, the high school may be removed from any particular neighborhood to serve many neighborhoods simultaneously and should be located at their geographic center; it could then serve as a meeting ground for teen-agers. The range of pedestrian students of all ages may be considered in relation to means of fostering communication among residential areas. It is desirable to locate many educational and training institutions close to each other to be efficient and to insure that the selected area will have a day population as large as its night population. (See Figure 4.13.)

The Experimental, Televised University

A new town can be an excellent place for developing an experimental, televised university to serve the town and its region. Residents who are unable to attend a university for various reasons can take televised courses as part of a degree program. A televised university can also serve modern industry by rehabilitating workers. For example, people living in new towns that have been developed to bolster a region's economy often do not know how to operate new machinery; televised university instruction sponsored by industry could train them for new work.

A televised university may also attract professional people to contribute to it and to live in the new town. Thus, the town could become a focus for local education and also a center for meeting the educational needs of a regional population. Further, a televised university should use telecommunication systems to allow communication among students and university faculty, as would be the case in a conventional university, including questions and answers, evaluations, methods of research and surveys, reading guidance, and other instruction.

QUALITY OF SOCIETY

The physical environment of an ideal new town is arranged to foster an ideal social atmosphere whose values differ from one culture to another. Some factors common to all cultures that contribute to each in varying degrees, are

(1)   Self-satisfaction.

(2)   Cultural attitudes.

(3)   Receptivity of people and groups to their social and physical environments.

(4)   Absence of tension in a community.

(5)   Community size and compatibility among residents.

(6)   Human relations and degree of intimacy of friendships.

(7)   Degree of integration offered in a community.

(8)   Variation in social choices offered to different social or age groups.

(9)   Proximity to neighbors.

(10)   Physical forms of micro- and macroneighboring.

(11)   Location and proximity of social services, especially educational facilities and those related to children, such as schools, playgrounds, parks and recreational areas, and swimming pools.

(12)   Quality of social and educational services.

Figure 4.13.   Acre Rigg Secondary School in Peterlee, England. (Courtesy of the Peterlee Development Corporation.)

(13)   Quality and diversity of local institutions.

(14)   Comprehensiveness of health services and their accessibility.

Throughout the planning process, anticipated results should be evaluated against social values to be gained in each alternative presented. In a technological society, social values may be an essential tool in establishing community stability. Again, although social values are dynamic and differ from one condition to another, it is the direct responsibility of the planning team, especially the social planner, to identify the social values of a community, to present alternatives to meet changing conditions, and to weigh them against the planning results of the whole team. Although social values differ from one culture to another, all are related to the following factors:

(1)   Personal and group relations.

(2)   Customs and life style.

(3)   Standards of living and housing patterns.

(4)   Education of family members.

(5)   Behavioral norms and socializing patterns.

(6)   Changes in family and personal expenses.

(7)   Leisure preferences.

(8)   Relations between men and women; specifically, the changing role of women in society, in families, and in associated social positions.

The social values of some age groups, especially those of teen-agers, change from time to time, and these changes may have a direct impact on spatial requirements of such facilities as schools, playgrounds, and community centers. Changes in social values will also directly affect density patterns, size of housing and design units, parking, physical proximity, open space, and even land-use patterns and will result in changes in real estate and land values.

There are five basic indicators of the quality of urban life: quality of physical environment, man's relation to society, quality of housing, impact of network systems, and urban complexity and manageability. The quality of society in well-planned new towns is high in terms of these indicators because of the numerous advantages of new towns and their emphasis on interaction. These advantages include

(1)   Adequate mass transportation in major areas such as shopping centers, places of work, and the social center.

(2)   An effective school system which responds to the needs of a community.

(3)   An attractive natural environment.

(4)   A variety of job opportunities available within the immediate geographic area for men and women who want to learn new skills.

(5)   Satisfactory earnings in new jobs.

(6)   A variety of entertainment for all age groups.

(7)   Safety and security for all residents, and development of pedestrian systems separated from vehicular systems.

(8)   Diversified, integrated land-use patterns.

The quality of society in new towns responds to our major social problems. There are three areas in which new towns may partly or wholly solve these problems:

(1)   Urban areas with rapid growth, mainly those absorbing immigrants, where new, acute physical, socioeconomic, and sociopolitical problems are created, e.g., economic depression and racial tensions in slums.

(2)   Economically and socially depressed and sparsely populated fringe regions, designated or projected for development as part of a national policy either for the use of local natural resources or for solving other acute national problems.

(3)   Rural and traditionally overpopulated regions which are subject to emigration and urgently need to stabilize and create a new regional balance to replace the traditional one.

Two solutions may be available to urbanized countries: new towns in-town or new towns in cities, and new urban centers in arid regions. Agrarian countries, however, may focus on economically depressed and overpopulated rural regions and on developing new cities in arid regions.

A new town in-town may offer a solution to social problems of depressed inner-city areas which does not necessitate relocating people outside the city. Residents (mostly low-income people) would not have to break existing relations with others of their group and would also have the opportunity to integrate with people of other social groups. One thing a new town in-town offers that a regular new town does not is the continuity of social ties that may produce social stability.

Relocating people of minority groups and others willing to live with them may foster integration. If a new town in-town is a self-contained unit rather than a bedroom community, integration of minority groups may occur more easily. Further, we can assume that social tension and conflict in this diverse group would be less than in an isolated new town, since a new town in-town offers established ties as well as new social and economic choices. Thus a new town in-town can offer low-income residents an improved society without any great sense of disorientation or economic stress.

CONCLUSION

New-town communities may respond to the demands for a higher quality of life than is possible in existing urban patterns in some of the following ways: (1) high personal identification with society and greater contribution to public needs, (2) contact with nature, recognition of the need to appreciate natural surroundings, and beneficial use of them, (3) recognition of man's role in his society and in his neighborhood, especially by young age groups, (4) development of good social values in the community, (5) social order and stability along with social and economic security, (6) no or very few social ills and deficiencies, (7) ample employment, (8) a new social and physical environment which offers new opportunities, (9) a high percentage of young people who form a dynamic and energetic society, (10) promotion of promising new local leadership, (11) minimal traffic accidents, (12) relaxation of each person within his sociophysical environment, and less tension and mental pressure, (13) adequate governmental and political structures, and (14) hope for a better environment with freedom from oppression, segregation, and poverty.

Since they provide an opportunity "to start fresh without the handicaps of a preexisting city pattern,"[30] new towns can offer tremendous opportunities in choice for jobs, housing, education, and personal contact to improve the quality of life and to meet man's ever-changing needs.

Social planning, a complicated, multifaceted process, is a primary element in planning a new town that should constantly be revised and evaluated to meet the changes of life. The primary goal of social planning is to improve the quality of society and to increase residents' personal satisfaction with their social and physical environment. Planning teams should realize that people make urban centers, urban centers do not make people. Therefore the role of a qualified social planner is to complete all phases of planning new towns and their implementation and always to be aware of dynamic human needs.

To be efficient, successful, financially resourceful, and convenient, social services should be viewed as comprehensive and integrated projects. As such, they can serve as a meeting ground for a heterogeneous community and can help foster pride and identity among community residents. Social planning as one segment of the overall planning process has the potential to be the focus of the entire process and thus to be an innovative laboratory from which an established urban center can benefit. Although new-town social planning may not solve all the social problems of our urban life, it may alleviate some of them.

Social planning can be an effective instrument if it is continuously associated with constantly revised goals. These goals are extremely important since they are directly related to primary himan needs. Flexibility in social planning and deep understanding of a population's characteristics become the most essential tools of a social planner. To be flexible, a social planner should prepare a set of alternative plans to meet social changes in a population.

A major problem of new towns is on the one hand the need to establish comprehensive social services in the very early stage of their development to increase their marketability, and on the other hand, the small population at this stage that requires those services.

No social plan can be fully successful without the active involvement of its new-town residents. Thus citizen participation in the social planning process may be a cornerstone for the success of a new town.

NOTES

1.   Columbia was planned to have neighborhoods formed by several interrelated housing clusters, and neighborhoods then form villages. For details of the planning concept of Columbia, see Morton Hoppenfeld, "A Sketch of the Planning-Building Process for Columbia, Maryland," *Journal of the American Institute of Planners,* **33,**no. 5 (November 1967), pp. 398–409.

2.   Advisory Commission on Intergovernmental Relations, *Urban and Rural America* (Washington, D.C.: U.S. Government Printing Office, 1968), pp. 14–19.

3.   Herbert J. Gans, "The Balanced Community: Homogeneity or Heterogeneity in Residential Areas?" *Journal of the American Institute of Planners,* **27,** no. 3 (August 1961), p. 177.

4.   Gans, p. 176.

5.   Gans, p. 176.

6.   Great Britain, Ministry of Town and Country Planning and Department of Health for Scotland, *New Towns Committee Final Report* (London: His Majesty's Stationery Office, 1946), Section III—[22], p. 10.

7.   Ray Thomas, *London's New Towns: A Study of Self-Contained Balanced Communities* (London: Political and Economic Planning [PEP], 1969), p. 382.

8.   On the British new towns, see Great Britain, Ministry of Housing and Local Government, Welsh Office, Subcommittee of the Central Housing Advisory Committee, *The Needs of New Communities* (London: Her Majesty's Stationery Office, 1967), p. 8. On the American new communities, see J. A. Prestridge, *Case Studies of Six Planned New Towns in the United States* (Lexington, Ky: Institute for Environmental Studies, University of Kentucky Research Foundation, 1973), p. 16.

9.   A survey of 13 new communities in the United States revealed groups of people under 40 comprise 49.4 percent of the total population, age groups from 40 to 54 include 32.8 percent, and those 55 or older comprise 17.7 percent. See Center for Urban and Regional Studies, *Community Profile: Spring 1973, Columbia, Maryland* (Chapel Hill, N.C.: Center for Urban and Regional Studies, 1974), p. 2.

10.   Christians and Jews worship in the same interfaith building in Columbia. For details on religion in new towns, see Lyle E. Schaller, *Church in New Towns* (Naperville, Ill.: Yokefellow Institute, 1972). Also see Stanley J. Hallett, *Working Papers in Church Planning: Columbia, Maryland* (New York: National Council of Churches of Christ in the U.S.A.), no date.

11.   *Webster's Seventh New Collegiate Dictionary* (Springfield, Mass: G.&C. Merriam Company, Publishers, 1970), p. 202.

12.   Artur Glikson, *Regional Planning and Development* (Leiden: A. W. Sijthoff's Uitgeversmaatschappij N.V., 1955), pp. 70–85.

13.   Prestridge, pp. 12–16.

14.   In their early stages, company towns attract low-income populations, as in Australia and Canada, because an unskilled population provides the labor force and physical power for operations performed there.

15.   J. B. Cullingworth and V. A. Karn, *The Ownership and Management of Housing in the New Towns* (London: Her Majesty's Stationery Office, 1968), pp. 94–104.

16.   For elaboration of this point, see J. Eugene Grigsby, "Views on the Feasibility of Integration," in *New Towns: Why and for Whom?* Harvey S. Perloff and Neil C. Sandberg, eds. (New York: Praeger Publishers, 1973), pp. 189–93.

17.   G. Brooke Taylor, "Social Development," in *New Towns: The British Experience,* Hazel Evans, ed. (New York: John Wiley and Sons, 1972), pp. 124–33. Also see Lucy Thomas and Erich Lindemann, "Newcomers' Problems in a Suburban Community," *Journal of the American Institute of Planners,* **27** (August 1961), pp. 185–93. For newcomers' difficulties see J. H. Kahn, "A Psychiatrist on New Towns," *Town and Country Planning,* **30** (1961), pp. 410–12.

18.   See Barrie B. Greenbie, "Social Territory, Community Health and Urban Planning," *Journal of the American Institute of Planners,* **40,** no. 2 (1974), pp. 74–82.

19.   Qiryat Gat, Israel, for example, has a variety of housing which encourages daily social contacts. See Robert W. Marans, *Social Integration in Housing: A Case Study of Israel* (Ann Arbor, Mich.: Institute for Social Research, the University of Michigan, 1974).

20.   Gans, pp. 176–84. See also Suzanne Keller, *The Urban Neighborhood: A Sociological Perspective* (New York: Random House, 1968), pp. 76–86.

21.   Robert E.L. Faris and H. Warren Dunham, *Mental Disorders in Urban Areas* (Chicago: University of Chicago Press, Phoenix Books, 1967), pp. 1–10, Also see Ian McHarg, *Design with Nature* (Garden City, N.Y.: Doubleday and Co., 1971), pp. 187–95.

22.   Planning Committee of "It's Open for Women," *The Women's Center* (Columbia, Maryland, 1971), p. 2. Also see Donald C. Klein, "Problems and Possibilities for Mental Health Programming in New Communities," in *Planning for the Social Frontier: New Communities in America,* ed. Gideon Golany, manuscript under consideration for publication.

23.   René Dubos, "The Biological Basis of Urban Design," *Ekistics,* **35,** no. 209 (1973), pp. 199–204.

24.   The Columbia Conference Committee, *First Annual Columbia Conference on Community Governance* (Columbia, Md: The Columbia Conference Committee, 1972), pp. 14–15. Also see note 25, Chapter 9.

25.   For a detailed discussion of telecommunication devices and their potential use in health care see Chapter 6.

26.   Minnesota Experimental City, "Health Care," Preliminary Report, part 5.0 of volume V, *Design Strategy Statement* (Minneapolis: Minnesota Experimental City Authority, January 1973), p. 1.

27.   Doris Wright, "Early Childhood Care and Development and Its Implications for New Communities," in *Planning for the Social Frontier: New Communities in America,* Gideon Golany, ed., manuscript under consideration for publication, (p. 15).

28.   Wright, pp. 20–30.

29.   Ronald E. Barnes, "Education," Preliminary Report, part 4.0 of volume V, *Design Strategy Statement* (Minneapolis: Minnesota Experimental City Authority, January 1973), p. 3.

30.   U.S. Advisory Commission on Intergovernmental Relations, p. 107.

FIVE
ECONOMIC PLANNING

INTRODUCTION

Countries have constructed new towns for various reasons:

(1)   To make new capital cities (e.g., Chandigarh, India; Canberra, Australia; Islamabad, Pakistan; Brasilia, Brazil).

(2)   To redistribute population (e.g., Israel and The Netherlands).

(3)   To exploit natural resources (e.g., Canada and Australia).

(4)   To develop either metropolitan or agrarian regions of the country (e.g., England and The Netherlands).

(5)   To ease urban congestion (e.g., France and the United Kingdom).

(6)   To provide housing (e.g., the United States and Sweden).

(7)   To improve the quality of the environment or of transportation (e.g., France and the United Kingdom).

(8)   To revive economically depressed areas (e.g., the United Kingdom and India).

In examining these eight different kinds of new towns, it is obvious that the majority have been developed for complex reasons related to socioeconomic issues. Whatever the purpose for their development, however, establishing a new town is an economic venture which includes such activities as buying and selling land and constructing buildings. Profitability depends upon the intensity of demand for land and for what has been constructed on it. Therefore satellite towns have better housing markets and, consequently, a greater chance of financial success than new towns developed away from existing urban centers. Profitability also depends on the length of time between the pur-

chase of land and the final sale of constructed houses. This period, during which interest costs and land value may vary, is more critical for private developers. Any developer must sometimes wait several years to assess the results of his investments, and most private developers indicate that they would prefer not to invest their money in new towns because their high risks are compounded by the long period of investment.

These risks are well demonstrated by new communities in the United States which private developers have viewed solely as ways to make profit.[1] Such profit-seeking led to the construction of satellite new communities. The British, by contrast, developed new towns in order to achieve national goals. Their strategy was to build new towns that were not satellites or profit-oriented, and only recently have development corporations realized any financial profit.

Economics is a major issue in new towns from their very beginning; only later, when housing has been constructed and people have settled there, do social and political issues arise. The economy of any new town should be based on coordination between the planning and construction of housing and the availability of jobs. In practice, however, local jobs form the base for housing demands and for a new town's degree of self-containment.

Goals

Economic goals rely heavily on the prime and general goals of the new town as the developer conceives them. Although Figure 2.2. illustrates the various types of tentative goals for new urban settlements, in this chapter we discuss various goals that may be common to many of those settlements or to a specific one.

The economic goals and objectives of a new town have far-reaching effects on other goals such as transportation, governance, social characteristics, and land use. Actually, economic goals may determine the

124 ECONOMIC PLANNING

Figure 5.1. The regional town center in Cumbernauld, Scotland. (Courtesy of Cumbernauld Development Corporation.)

foundation of the new town's character and may thus dictate its future development and success. The following are tentative goals which planners may consider in formulating goals for their new towns:

(1) Maximize self-containment and self-sustainment of the community.

(2) Offer various opportunities to increase employees per capita income, to attract low-income people, and to provide an attractive social and physical environment.

(3) Improve the overall infrastructure and tax base of the community and of its surrounding area.

(4) Stimulate economic growth in an economically depressed and depopulated area.

(5) Catalyze agrarian growth in the new town's sur-

rounding settlements and function as a regional growth center which establishes equilibrium between an industrialized new town and its agrarian surroundings. (See Figure 5.1.)

(6) Diversify job opportunities in industry, commerce, and services so that the new town can attract various income groups and skilled workers to form a balanced community;

(7) Optimize land use within the community;

(8) Establish a sound economic base for the new town that will rely on diverse rather than single products to keep the community economically stable;

(9) In a privately developed new town, make a profit to insure the continuity and full development of the project; in a publicly financed new town adhere to national economic goals and to other national

policies. Thus, the fulfillment of economic goals may lead to the attainment of social, environmental, and other goals.

Economic goals and objectives should be integrated with social goals and should not be conceived independently of them.

Economic Planning

From the start, any developer, public or private, should be aware of all phases of economic planning, and their strengths, limits, and sequence. Before beginning construction, he should take the following steps. (For their sequence, see Figure 5.2.)

Site Assessment.   Basic studies of a site to assess existing physical conditions and their strengths and weak-. nesses, and existing social and political systems, utilities, and services, are necessary during early phases and during development. These complex studies require large investments and seem, in some cases, to be endless tasks.

Feasibility Study.   A feasibility study of an entire project and its parts should analyze cost-benefit and potential housing markets. The study should also outline the constraints of a site and its suitability and estimate costs of constructing housing utilities, infrastructure, social services, health and educational facilities, public buildings, and a transportation network. A preliminary study of this type should precede any major planning and should require as little time and money as possible to avoid wasting investors' money in this initial stage. Also, a full feasibility study is essential to save a developer's investment in an entire project.

The costs and benefits of new towns differ among their various types: a self-contained new town differs from a satellite (see Chapter 2), and a privately developed town differs from a publicly developed one.[2] Obviously then, the goals of a new town largely determine its costs and benefits. The time of greatest risk for a private developer is that period between making an investment and receiving a profit. The longer the interval, the greater the interest paid to creditors. Actually, the waiting period for return on investments in new towns is longer than that in regular real-estate developments. In addition, the huge investment of a new-town project excludes small and medium sized private developers. A relatively small number of private developers become potential investors in new towns, and only a few of those may be willing to risk

their money in such ventures. Since the lack of such developers may hinder any new-town movement in a country, public investment is important for new towns, especially if they are part of a national policy.

Securing Finances.   A private developer should secure public funds in the early planning stage in order to minimize his risks. In addition to the obvious ones for construction and front money, funds are needed for taxes on land and unoccupied houses, interest, and other expenses due to the unpredictable duration of construction. Also, a planner-developer should know the amount of tax revenue required to support local services during and after the development of a new town, since tax revenue is directly related to a population and its income and to the type and scale of economic activities located within the community itself. A new town located in a rural area will have too low a regional tax revenue in its early life to support services adequately. Therefore, in order to provide sufficient services, a private developer must receive public funds for them. Also, infrastructure may cost a developer a large portion of his project investment if he is to fund everything alone.

Public agencies and governments usually have more funds than several private developers. Even when governments do not possess the full amount required for a new town, they do have national credit and authority to guarantee such funds and therefore have the potential to make significant investments for new-town development.

Land Assemblage.   Assembling land for a new-town site requires a great deal of the total project funds and will not yield any immediate return. In privately developed new towns, such as those in the United States, this phase will determine the life or death of a project. When a private developer in a free-market economy is not aided by legislation for land acquisition, he must struggle single-handedly with land speculation during assemblage. To succeed, he will need money, time, careful strategy, and administrative talent.

In publicly developed new towns, such as those in the United Kingdom, although land acquisition acts support land assemblage, developers must still compensate private owners at market prices; thus, land purchases still consume a large portion of project funds since much of the land is close to metropolitan areas. The advantage here is that land speculation is minimized, and since most if not all land for development is publicly owned, the system minimizes project risks. Also, in countries such as Israel where the government owns 92 percent of the land, the public can select the optimal site with minimal financial risks. Public financial effort, however, focuses on such other investments for new towns as utilities, infrastructure, social services, education, and planning and implementation.

Planning. Comprehensive and detailed planning of a project must include physical, social, economic, transportation, utilities, and other aspects. Regardless of whether a developer prepares his own plan or hires an outside firm to do so, financial resources for comprehensive planning are required from the earliest stage of land assemblage to the completion of the project. Also, a developer will need a permanent staff when construction has begun for continuous evaluations of plans. Although a developer should know that these expenses will exist for the entire life of his project and should plan accordingly, he needs most of this money in the early years of his project. (See Figure 5.3.)

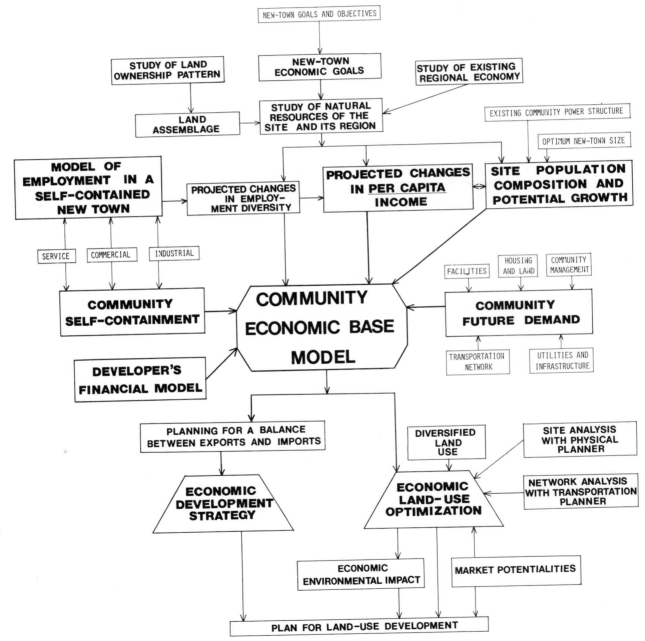

Figure 5.2. Generalized process for economic planning.

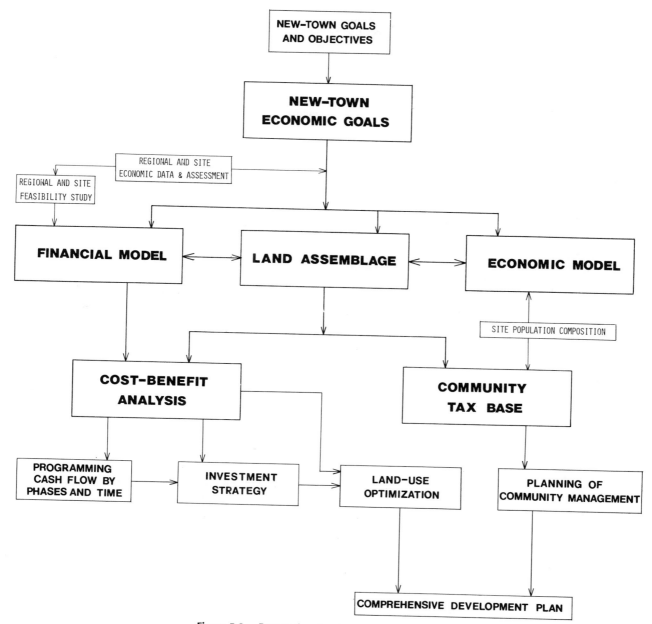

Figure 5.3. Process for planning a new-town economic base.

ECONOMIC BASE OF NEW TOWNS

A developer should define the economic goals and objectives of a new town before he begins to plan its economic base. He should prepare any economic plan in terms of those goals and evaluate achievements against them. (See Figure 2.2 for overall new-town goals.)

A new town with an advanced degree of self-containment has a sound economic base characterized by (1) a sufficient number of jobs provided for its residents, (2) diverse job opportunities, and (3) a mixed economy that includes basic industries. Many new urban settlements do not possess these characteristics in their early years of growth, but the majority acquire them after a reasonably short time. In the

United States, however, most new communities have not acquired all of these characteristics for economic and political reasons. For example, in Reston, Virginia, most of the people still commute to Washington for employment although Reston has some minor industry.

Basic Characteristics

One of the principal ideas of Ebenezer Howard's new-town philosophy was that of a self-contained town, although he did not use this term.[3] A major aspect of self-containment is the provision of a variety of employment opportunities to enable residents to live and to work in a new town.[4] Although it cannot be implemented completely in every new town, there should be a minimum degree of containment that depends on the role of a new town within its region. Some portion of a community may always need services that are unavailable in the new town and therefore would look for them outside it.

Ray Thomas sees self-containment as more desirable than daily commuting when self-containment is directly linked to a goal of providing sufficient employment opportunities.[5] James Clapp defines self-containment as follows: "The use of the terms 'self-sufficient' and 'self-contained' appear to be generally employed to convey the notion that new towns should be developed as relatively self-sustaining communities which should not be totally dependent upon a parent city for employment of its work force."[6]

The English New Towns Committee also considered the issue of self-containment in relation to employment opportunities as one way of achieving it:

Where possible . . . businesses and industries established should include not only factories, shops, and the businesses and services meeting local needs, but head-offices and administrative and research establishments including sections of government departments and other public offices. It is most desirable that proprietors, directors, executives and other leading workers in the local industries and businesses should live in the town and take part in its life. Many professional men and women, writers, artists, and other specialists not tied to a particular location should find a new town a good place in which to live and work. So also should retired people from home and overseas, from every kind of occupation, as well as people of independent means.[7]

However, some commuting is inevitable:

Most of the new towns had been successfully developed as self-contained or complete towns, in that they contained relatively even numbers of jobs and working people. This balance provides only a potential self-sufficiency. The potential can be realised only if the two factors are inter-related: if the people who live in the town are those who work in it; if the jobs in the town are filled by residents. If the two factors are not inter-related there will be cross-movement, with residents travelling out to work elsewhere, while jobs in the town are filled by people drawn from outside. When towns are located within easy travelling distance of each other, some cross-movement is to be expected, for the jobs in one town may not match the occupational skills of the residents. Similarly, its housing may not match the residential needs of the workforce. The new town corporations have tried to inter-relate employment and housing by allocating new town dwellings only to new town workers; and this policy would be expected to keep cross-movement near to the minimum.[8]

Another understanding of self-containment is that it should indicate the degree of a new town's independence in all types of economic services required by a community. Self-contained employment and a little commuting would have great sequential effects on other patterns. Diversified local employment would require a mixture of labor resources—of skilled and unskilled, young and old people, and so on. Consequently, such a condition would generate various daily services required by a population. Clearly then, self-contained employment would have far-reaching effects on other socioeconomic matters which determine the degree of a community's urbanity.

A.A. Ogilvy has considered self-containment comprehensively:

From the start self-containment had a dual meaning. The distinction is worth noting because the two meanings have merged in the past, but in the future may need to be separated. The first meaning refers simply to the facilities that exist in a town. A self-contained area can be defined as one which has a complete range of urban facilities, that is, sufficient employment, shopping, health, education and other facilities adequate for the number of residents. But in general usage this definition has been overlaid by the second meaning, a social purpose. A self-contained town is seen as one in which the townspeople can live full lives, satisfying all their daily needs within the boundaries; the town provides the environment for the life of a complete community; it is 'an experiment in social living.'[9]

Thus self-containment means not only the provision of diversified local job opportunities, but also the provision of an education system; a commercial network; social, cultural, and recreational services for various age groups; and local public utilities, services, and other required amenities for the whole community. It also is synonymous with such terms as self-sufficient, self-sustained, and independent. At the same time, since most settlements cannot maintain complete independence, all are regionally, nationally, or internationally interrelated. Historically, only geographically isolated, autarkic communities were successful in achieving full self-containment.

Since complete self-containment cannot exist, the degree of independence is the important economic characteristic of a new town.[10] The ideal degree, which has become a controversial subject, differs among cultures depending on consumer standards in each society. In practice, self-containment requires not only careful planning but also highly coordinated implementation. This is especially important to meet the goal of providing a place of work close to a place of residence and thus minimizing commuting and maximizing the self-sufficiency of a new town. A specified policy must be adopted to balance the provision of housing with the availability of jobs.[11] The achievement of this balance may require effective and efficient cooperation between newly located employers and housing suppliers, and joint planning and implementation.

Although self-containment may contribute to the overall economic condition of a community, it does not necessarily aid in the upward mobility of low-income population. It may help a few, but most who want to increase their incomes may look for employment elsewhere if their demand for housing is not met.

Sufficient employment in a new town rests on basic economic and social activities. For a new town of 100,000 people in a developed country, employment of approximately 40 percent of the residents provides economic stability.[12] This author classified 96 U.S. cities using 1970 census data and found that mature cities employ about 40 percent of their residents.[13] (See Table 5.1.)

If a new town's economic base is sound, a majority of its residents should live and work there. A person is not permitted to live in an English new town unless he holds a job there; this condition will minimize commuting. In order for people to live and work in a new town, the developer must plan for a variety of land use there. If a new town functions as a regional growth center, people from surrounding regions may seek employment there, and the new town must then provide job opportunities for them.

A new town should have diverse job opportunities in industry, commerce, and services for skilled and unskilled people, different age groups, and both sexes. All three areas of employment should be mutually dependent; i.e., one should complement the others both economically and socially to insure a mixed economy. Such an economy provides stability in employment and production unlike company towns, which are unable to provide such stability. For example, the economy of Kitimat, British Columbia, is based on aluminum production with a few services which focus around this production. Thus, if bankruptcy or economic depression should occur in its industry, Kitimat would face economic stress.

A new town with an industry which produces an exportable product will support a flow of money to the town. When a new town exports material, money flows into the area, but when a new town imports, money is spent outside of the town rather than invested in it. Industries encourage exports, and services or infrastructure, obviously developed to supply the needs of people living in a community, encourage imports.

Each new industry that moves to a new town will strengthen its economy by increasing available jobs and cash flow. A company will move to a new town when it is convinced it will maintain or increase its

TABLE 5.1 PERCENTAGE OF EMPLOYEES IN CLASSIFIED CITIES OF THE UNITED STATES IN 1970

	City Class Size	Population Range	Number of Cities Researched	Number of States Researched	Average Population Size	Average Employees	
						Absolute Numbers	Percentage
1.	50,000	45,000–54,999	12	8	50,300	20,378	40.16
2.	60,000	55,000–64,999	12	11	60,356	23,609	39.11
3.	70,000	65,000–74,999	12	10	70,245	24,535	34.93
4.	80,000	75,000–84,999	12	10	80,085	31,360	37.16
5.	90,000	85,000–94,999	12	8	90,674	36,270	40.00
6.	100,000	95,000–104,999	12	9	100,514	40,928	40.72
7.	110,000	105,000–114,999	12	10	110,276	44,780	40.60
8.	120,000	115,000–125,000	12	9	119,749	45,366	37.88

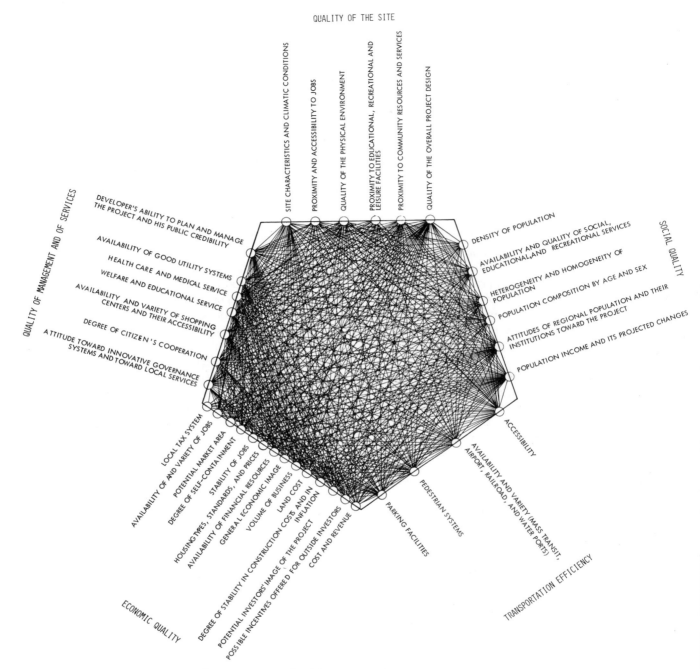

Figure 5.4. Interrelated factors supporting a new-town economy.

profits. Such a move may mean the loss of a large urban market unless transportation of goods is feasible. Other issues a company must consider include availability, cost, and unionization of labor. Companies that require nearby supplementary industries will seek them at alternative sites before reaching a decision about moving to a new town.

The economy of a new town in relation to the four

economic features mentioned above will stabilize when construction is finished and local governance is established. Although an original new-town plan may call for a sound economic base, it may be impossible for one of the following reasons:

(1) Unsynchronized development of housing and jobs. Outsiders who have housing may come into a

new town to find jobs when there are jobs but no housing, or residents who need jobs may commute to find them when there is housing but no jobs.

(2)   Other economic centers within easy commuting distance.

(3)   Prospective employers who do not move to a new town or withdraw from it for some reason.

Factors which support a new town's economy are comprehensive and vary from place to place according to their correlation. Figure 5.4. describes six factors which we discuss elsewhere in detail. The list is not all-inclusive since it does not include goals, policies, strategies, or implementing agents. Developers should examine these factors carefully and weigh their relative importance.

Economic Models

New-town planners should develop an economic model which takes into account all contributing economic variables and their predicted changes during construction. (See Figure 5.3.) A basic model should include the following:

(1)   Phases and subphases of development as related (a) to time periods, and (b) to attaining goals.

(2)   Cash flow and its sources during each developmental phase.

(3)   Alternative courses of action to be considered for each phase of development.

(4)   The possibility of evaluating and occasionally revising the economic goals of the entire project and its segments to measure its achievements and to forecast its success or failure.

When a developer includes these four steps, the model should indicate the feasibility of a project in its first phase and any potential risks during that time, since any decision during this phase may be crucial for the entire project for many years. Any economic model for a new town should consider land and housing values, projected job opportunities, potential income per capita, changes in construction costs, and the reciprocal economic effects of a new town and its region.

Land-use optimization is "the mechanism by which diverse market and financial elements can be integrated into a comprehensive model which is useful in analyzing and planning the development program."[14]

Optimization uses the physical and aesthetic characteristics of land to maximize potential social and economic returns. Since it is a major planning action, physical, social, and economic planners should cooperate in the production of a land-use optimization plan. This team should synthesize information on such factors as land suitability, proximity of uses, their density and intensity, proximity to a transportation network, environmental and aesthetic values, land value, and marketing potential in land and housing. In addition, in privately developed new towns, an economically optimized land-use plan tends to relate to the profit-making goals of the developers.

Optimization of land use and the value of social and economic returns may be estimated by the method of rating regional cells described in Chapter 3. Although it assigns rated values subjectively, it is a rational method for producing optimal economic land use. It is also possible to prepare the optimization plan by a linear programming method.

For solely financial return,

the process of optimization is a systematic allocation of the total site among all potential uses for it. It is leased on the relative profitability available in developing each use to maximize the total value of all profits generated. The generated profits are valued on a time-discounted basis, common to all real estate development practice. The technique used in this optimization is, where appropriate, a linear program.[15]

Another factor of concern to an economic planner is the projection of job opportunities for a new town and its immediate region, detailed enough to include the number of people, types of jobs, level of stability, duration, degree of skills required, and their spatial distribution.

Types of jobs available will determine the income per capita, and this in turn will affect consumption of services and commerce and local tax revenue. Therefore planners of an economic model should relate attracting employers to a new town's goals. For example, if a developer's main goal is to increase individual income he must attract employers who can provide appropriate jobs for meeting this goal. He also may have to develop a concomitant retraining program for unskilled workers to prepare them for these new jobs as one way of encouraging upward social mobility.

The planner of an economic model must consider economic changes in construction costs and inflation. In contemporary internationally oriented economies, the effects of costs and inflation have been increasing worldwide. Since construction costs pay for materials and labor, consideration of these increases may either terminate a project or change its goal.

Economic models should specify the potential reciprocal effects of a new town and its immediate region in light of any existing or proposed regional economic plan. These models should also specify changes in population composition, income, demands for services and, most important, the threshold of local resources such as water, land, and minerals to avoid their abuse.[16] This part of a model is a major consideration in a developing region where advanced technology, sophisticated highways, and infrastructure do not yet exist.

Finally, an economic model should be a framework for analyzing and predicting the economic success or failure of a new town. A comprehensive and systematic model should relate to both the macro- and the microlevel of a new town's economy.

New Towns for Developing Regions

In developing countries, policy makers may need to limit their planning objectives to justify the construction of new towns, whose social and economic effects on rural agrarian areas may be greater than their financial effect.[17] One way to minimize costs in rural regions may be to organize "self-help schemes."[18]

Certainly new towns should be part of a comprehensive regional plan rather than independent units, and this association is even more necessary for an area that is still developing than for a developed one. India, for example, has developed most new towns in relation to a regional plan.[19] (Comprehensive plans in developing countries are usually publicly supported.)

Many developing regions may not have most of the necessary economic tools to establish a strong economic base for new towns. These tools include energy, finances, skill, transportation, and knowledge. Developing regions may not have the energy needed to carry on an industry today, whether that energy comes from oil or wood as fuel or from waterfalls. Some developing regions do have potential energy sources, but very few realize them. One of the richest areas in potential sources is Africa, built on a plateau, with all of its rivers originating in the central region and falling from the plateau to the shore. The hydraulic energy which could be harnessed from these rivers could promote development of new towns in Africa. India also has tremendous potential sources of energy and has developed comprehensive five-year projects for their use. A major project deals with electricity for industry and also for many other purposes.[20]

Since financial resources needed to establish a sound economic base for new towns are unavailable in a developing region, most developing countries depend on outside resources for assistance. Some countries which may be very rich in natural resources such as coal, iron, and oil that could make them financially independent, cannot explore this possibility because of a lack of industry, means of communication, and investment.

A third tool necessary to establish an economic base for regional development and new towns is skilled people. Some developing countries found that even if they acquired the financial resources they needed, they still could not achieve much because they did not have the skilled labor force to go with it.

Developing countries lack a transportation network, without which industry cannot develop. The exportation of products requires sophisticated transportation networks that operate year round and are connected to national networks to insure the flow of goods. Maintenance of these transportation networks should not rely on support from the general population of a new town, but at least in the early stages of development, should rely on a central or regional government.

Most developing regions also lack knowledge of the location and extent of their potential natural resources. Few countries, especially those in the process of developing, have information about their geological structure, water supply, mineral resources, mines, and so forth. These countries also lack knowledge about their human resources, particularly the variety of demographic or social and economic characteristics of their populations. Besides the need for many economic tools, developing regions have a very low rate of technological advancement.

In such regions there are three economic sectors in which new towns could have a major effect: agricultural, industrial, and service. Many developing countries have recently attempted to combine their agricultural and industrial economies and have encouraged new towns to develop industry in agrarian regions[21] (e.g., the production of cotton textiles and fruit juices). Combining these two economic sectors may help to stabilize the population within a region and also attract new residents.

Developing countries accept an agricultural economy most readily because it is the foundation of a growing country's economic structure. The majority of people in these countries reside on farmland, as in India, for example, where more than 80 percent of the people live in rural, agrarian societies. In contrast, 80 percent of the people in the United States live in urban communities. In developing regions, new towns may offer important advantages for an agricultural society, such as improved marketing, delivery service, accessibility to banks, acquaintance with advanced agricultural technology, training facilities, product improvement, regional storage facilities, repair facilities, and accessibility to a large, economic, marketing catchment area.

FINANCIAL PROBLEMS OF DEVELOPERS

Investment by public, semipublic, and private agencies is a critical element in the development of a new town. This is true in housing programs and also in establishing new industry, manufacturing, shops, or any other economic activity. A relatively reasonable per capita income of a new-town population provides an adequate level of purchasing power, especially where a new town provides regional services for its surrounding area.

There is great opportunity for diverse investment in new towns planned to have sound economic bases, especially for companies and corporations which open branches there. Many countries provide tax reductions on investment channeled to their new towns as part of the governmental taxation policy to encourage investment. Moreover, when it establishes a new town as part of a national policy, a government may provide loans, grants, and subsidies to encourage private investment. The greater the investment in new towns, the greater the number of job opportunities and, consequently, the greater the number of new people who settle in them.

When decentralization policies of socioeconomic activity and population redistribution are established, a policy of investment must follow and adjust to them. This applies particularly to the national distribution of housing investments, of mortgages, of highway construction, and of investment in public facilities.

One of the major economic problems facing a private developer is the financial feasibility of a project. Revenue and expenditures in the planning period of a new-town project should produce dividends equal to cost plus profit: the profit should at least be the equivalent of that which he would have obtained from a similar investment in commerce or industry over an equal period of time.

Sometimes a major unexpected or uncontrolled interference such as a flood, earthquake, or fire, may occur and hinder the development of a new town. Building materials may be stolen, or land values may change. Although land value may increase, inflation may decrease the purchasing power of money, causing a developer to lose money in the end. A major difficulty for developers lies in accurately predicting how his investment plan will progress and what unexpected circumstances may arise to hinder it.

Before he can begin the process of land acquisition, a developer must calculate expected population size and density of his new town so that he can acquire the proper amount of land. Table 5.2 presents two statistical models which deal with three possible population sizes: 50,000, 70,000, and 100,000 people, and the table also gives four alternatives for density. Developing a new town for a projected population of 50,000 requires between 3000 and 7000 acres, depending

TABLE 5.2   ALTERNATIVE DENSITY AND LAND SIZE REQUIREMENTS OF A NEW TOWN

Alternative	Total Population	Number of Families[1]	Gross Density per Acre		Total Acres Needed	Equivalent in Square Miles[2]
			Families	Persons		
I	50,000	14,285	5.0	17.5	2,857	4.46
			4.0	14.0	3,571	5.58
			3.0	10.5	4,761	7.44
II	70,000	20,000	2.0	7.0	7,142	11.16
			5.0	17.5	4,000	6.25
			4.0	14.0	5,000	7.81
			3.0	10.5	6,666	10.41
III	100,000	28,571	2.0	7.0	10,000	15.62
			5.0	17.5	5,714	9.08
			4.0	14.0	7,142	11.16
			3.0	10.5	9,524	14.88
			2.0	7.0	14,285	22.32

[1]Based on an average of 3.5 persons per family.
[2]Every 640 acres equals one square mile.

TABLE 5.3   MONEY REQUIRED FOR LAND PURCHASE FOR ALTERNATIVE DENSITIES AND PRICES

Population Size	Required Size in Acres[1]	Money Required for Sites (in thousands of dollars) When the Price of One Acre Is						
		$500	$750	$1,000	$1,250	$1,500	$1,750	$2,000
50,000	2,857	1,428	2,142	2,857	3,571	4,285	4,999	5,714
	3,571	1,785	2,678	3,571	4,463	5,356	6,249	7,142
	4,761	2,380	3,570	4,761	5,951	7,141	8,331	9,522
	7,141	3,570	5,355	7,141	8,926	10,711	12,496	14,282
70,000	4,000	2,000	3,000	4,000	5,000	6,000	7,000	8,000
	5,000	2,500	3,750	5,000	6,250	7,500	8,750	10,000
	6,666	3,333	4,999	6,666	8,332	9,999	11,665	13,332
	10,000	5,000	7,500	10,000	12,500	15,000	17,500	20,000
100,000	5,714	2,857	4,285	5,714	7,142	8,571	9,999	11,428
	7,142	3,571	5,356	7,142	8,927	10,713	12,498	14,284
	9,524	4,762	7,143	9,524	11,905	14,286	16,667	19,048
	14,285	7,142	10,713	14,285	17,856	21,427	24,998	28,570

[1]Required different size of total acres for different gross density alternatives. (See Table 5.2.)

TABLE 5.4   COMPARISON OF COSTS AND REVENUE PER 1000 HOUSING UNITS FOR THREE UNITED STATES CASES

Costs	Prototype (%)	Amherst (%)	Park Forest South (%)
Land acquisition	19	26	21
Land development:			
infrastructure	21	27	13
on-site	42	26	55
Community overhead	5	3	1
Marketing fees and overhead	13	18	10
Total	100	100	100

Source: *Economic and Financial Feasibility Models for New Community Development.*

upon density; developing a new town for a projected population of 70,000 requires between 4000 and 10,000 acres; and a projected population of 100,000 requires from 6000 acres at high density to approximately 14,000 acres at low density.

One problem a private developer faces when beginning a new-town project is land acquisition. Buying land, or at least having an option on land, is his first investment. In 1946 land acquisition in the United States was less than 1 percent of a new-town investment; today it has risen to more than 20 percent, a substantial sum for a developer to raise at the start of his project.[22] If a developer plans for a population of 50,000, he will need from $1.5 million to $3.5 million to buy the necessary land at $500 per acre (See Table 5.3); if he buys land at $2000 per acre, the average purchasing price for most developers, he will need from $6 to $14 million. If the developer plans for 70,000 people, he will need from $2 to $5 million for land at $500 per acre, and from $8 to $20 million for land at $2000 per acre; and for 100,000 he will need from $3 to $7 million for land at $500 per acre and

from $11.5 million to $28.5 million for land at $2000 per acre. Considering the extremes, land acquisition costs could range from $1.5 to $28.5 million for a large, relatively low-density new town.

Land for a privately developed new town could involve 10 to 30 percent of the total project cost and usually must be paid early in the development. Other costs for housing development and other construction can be paid gradually as they occur.[23] The ratio of the land cost to the total cost of the project varies from one project to another; in an area close to an urban center, the ratio is usually high. It will also vary from country to country because of the cost of building materials, labor, and housing market within the area.[24] This ratio has increased due to increased land values: 20 years ago the ratio was 8 to 10 percent; currently it is 15 to 30 percent.[25]

When a private developer obtains land, he must receive approval for his zoning and land-use plan; otherwise it will be impossible for him to develop his new town. Then he must pay property tax on the land from the time of purchase to the time of sale. One solution to this problem is the leasing of undeveloped land to its previous owners for agricultural use, a tactic that will free a developer from paying local taxes on the land and also bring him some income.

Since one of a developer's main goals is to sell a house before or immediately after it is finished, another problem for the private developer is finding

1945—1950

1950—1955

1955—1960

1960—1963

Figure 5.5. Stages of development of Emmeloord, The Netherlands. (Source: *Planning and Creation of an Environment.*)

buyers who are willing to pay good prices for houses in new towns. Discovering a good housing market has caused most private developers to build new towns close to urban areas where the expected demand for housing is high. When a developer starts selling houses, he begins to receive a return on his investment and his risks lessen.

Obviously, infrastructure will be one of the costs of a new town, and includes public utilities, highways, sewer systems, water systems, electric systems, fire service, communication networks, and waste disposal for housing and industry. It is difficult for a new town to attract industry unless sewage services and other infrastructure costs have been paid. Therefore a large portion of infrastructure, such as the water supply network, highways, and sewage system, must be developed at the start of a new-town project.

A major problem of which a developer must be aware when planning a new town is the need for community overhead. This includes maintaining open space, parks, and community centers, which are the kind of investment necessary to increase marketability of a community. It is easy to plan these amenities in great variety if the development project is large in scale. Table 5.4 gives relative costs of major items in three cases.

Since phases of development of a privately developed new town are geared toward the needs of a market, a developer must constantly predict market changes in the immediate region from which the majority of a new town's population will move. Lack of coordination between phases of development and market demand may increase the financial risks of a new town. (See Figures 5.5 and 5.6.)

A private developer must consider three questions concerning his market:

(1)   What is the estimated future growth of a region and where will it take place? The developer must know if the region is subject to rapid or slow growth.

(2)   What portion of a region's market can be captured by a new town? Due to competition, a developer cannot expect to capture the entire market in his region.

(3)   What portion of a market should a developer try to capture?

FINANCIAL PLANNING

Regardless of the type of new-town initiator, public, private, or some combination of the two, planning a

Figure 5.6. Aerial view of Emmeloord, The Netherlands. (Courtesy of the Royal Netherlands Embassy.)

new town's financial base is a cornerstone of its initiation and later of its success. Finances are necessary for investment in development and community operation. For any investor, cohesiveness of his financial policy and its execution determine a new town's success or failure. Public financial resources are better guaranteed and their future development is more predictable than those of private developers. Also, public financial resources are subject to public evaluation and criticism. In any case, financial planning is most essential and includes many elements which require great managerial skill. The following sections discuss the most important of those variables.

Developers' Expenditures and Revenue

Financial feasibility depends on expenditures and revenue which are both determined by time and stage of development.

Basic financial expenditures for development go into the following items:

(1) Early and continuous studies and planning made during the development of a project.

(2) Management of the entire planning and construction, which includes all people employed throughout the project.

(3) Land purchase and assemblage for the entire project.

(4) Site improvement to prepare the land for construction.

(5) Construction of all infrastructure, including road networks, such community facilities as educational and recreational structures, social institutions, and other nonresidential construction.

(6) Construction of residential units, including housing and apartments for rent or sale.

(7) Operational costs of the entire project and of the early stage of community facilities and services.

(8) Payment of principal and interest on loans taken for the development.

(9) Payment of local or regional taxes on any land and property owned.

Recent public concern about and subsequent regulations on environmental quality have led to increased new-town costs. In countries such as the United States where new communities are privately developed, local residents have occasionally succeeded in forcing the developer to change his original development plan and therefore have cost him additional, unexpected expenses.

Revenue from a new-town project comes from various sources and will depend on the degree of demand for it.[26] The following sources may provide a project's income:

(1) Loans, grants, subsidies ,incentives, and bonds.

(2) Land sold to individuals or small developers for the construction of houses, industrial parks, commercial buildings, and recreational facilities. A developer makes a large profit simply by intensifying land use for such purposes as housing, commerce, and industry, and by improving its accessibility, thus increasing the value of the land.[27]

(3) Community services provided or delivered by the developer, including utilities, recreation, and health, social, or other services. (See Figure 5.7.)

(4) Houses sold or rented to community residents and other nonresidential structures. Major variables that influence housing demands are "population size and composition, income levels, the supply and price of housing, consumer tastes and preferences, especially the strength of consumer's desire for housing *vis-à-vis* other goods and services."[28] Although national housing demands have steadily increased

Figure 5.7. Aerial view of the Reston International Center, Reston, Virginia. The center is at the core of Reston's 1300-acre center for business, government, and industry. The conference center is the most extensive in northern Virginia. (Courtesy of Gulf Reston, Inc.)

worldwide, there is no guarantee that an increase will occur at the same rate in each new town. Housing consumption is usually determined by job availability. A second consumption variable related to job availability is the proximity of one's place of work to one's residence. Families with school-age children will always consider the nearness of a school and its quality of education and facilities as another important factor.

(5)   Rented property including land and buildings.

Financial profitability has not been considered as a prime goal or included within the goals of public developers such as those in the United Kingdom and Israel.[29] New towns developed completely or predominantly by the public are usually national tools to achieve social, economic, political, or developmental goals.[30] Privately developed new towns, on the other hand, are viewed primarily as a vehicle for achieving financial profit.[31] Therefore site selection, land-use optimization, degree of economic base, and extent of diversified services have been determined by such a goal. Moreover, the required scale for such develop-

ments has either hindered many developers, brought about a change in their goals, diminished their developments, or caused many of them to go bankrupt or abandon the project. (See Figure 5.8.)

Cash flow is concerned with the dynamics and timing of all expenditures and revenue. A cash-flow model is an effective tool to secure benefit, establish financial awareness and alertness of developers, evaluate a development's plan and timing, establish effective community management and, most importantly, to monitor the financial process to avoid bankruptcy. Therefore a cash-flow model should encompass the planning and development process of an entire project by phases and timing until its completion.

In the early years of projects, a cash-flow pattern usually indicates a negative value. Soundly programmed cash flow is expected gradually to change this pattern from negative to positive toward the end of a project's implementation. "The balance between the scale and timing of negative and positive returns is critical to project feasibility and its acceptability in relation to alternative development projects and investments."[31]

Figure 5.8.   Private enterprise housing in Hemel Hempstead, England. The publicly built English new towns offer some opportunities for private developers. (Courtesy of the Commission for the New Towns.)

A cash-flow model should indicate a developer's expected yearly expenditures and revenue and should also show the scale of investment required during the life of a project and each of its sections. Total profit of a project is part of a cash-flow model, too. Such a model should also offer alternatives to improve financial profit or to avoid lengthy negative results.[32]

Financial Model

A privately developed new town needs huge sums of "front money," commonly known as a long-term "loan plus personal equity."[33] Its availability will set the pace of a development and its marketability. Insufficient sums will retard any early development and will cause a developer to pay taxes and interest before he can obtain any revenue.

A new-town developer, whether public or private, faces a continuous chain of financial challenges and obstacles which he must overcome. (See Figure 5.9.) Therefore he needs to plan a financial model that includes the following considerations:

(1)   Financial resources, especially front money, in each stage of project development.

(2)   The cost-benefit of each part of development.

(3)   Cash flow by phases of development and span of time.

(4)   Alternative courses within the model.

(5)   Identification of potential financial problems that may arise during the life of the construction and preparation of alternative solutions.

(6)   Planning a tax base.

(7)   Planning a community's self-containment and its population composition as they relate to financial concerns.

Some financial planners view linear programming as a good method which may aid a developer of a new town to prepare his financial model. Heroux and Wallace, who developed such a model, state:

Linear programming offers a potentially valuable tool for dealing with the complexities of large-scale developments. The use of linear programming not only serves as a guide to the developer but, more importantly, proposes a framework in which the complexities are recognized and the ability to deal with them constructively is improved.[34]

No financial model of a new town can ignore the nature of two other important issues: a community's economic base and the character and dynamics of its population.[35]

Whether the goal of a new town is profit, socioeconomic quality, or some other end, it is essential for a developer to assume the responsibility of preparing a financial model. After such a model has been conceived, financial planning can be easily managed by a computer program, and the testing of profitability alternatives becomes possible.[36] Such tools may enable developers to prepare a prototype new-town investment model for their use.[37]

Community Tax Base

Bringing industry to a new town will not only provide job opportunities but will also shape its population composition to a certain extent, and will increase the community tax base and revenue. Consequently, local services and amenities will improve. On the other hand, population composition dictated by an industrial type will determine its employee incomes and, therefore, their demand for definite housing types and their local taxes. In sum, the industrial type and its employment have a direct effect on establishing the tax base and revenue of a new town.

Industries will move when the conditions offered in a new town give them a better chance to maximize profits than did previous conditions. Established industries will also seek compensation for loss of market and labor and for moving costs. Therefore industrial contributions to a local tax base will be limited in the early years of a new town's development, while the community will also have a great need for establishing its services. To obtain the necessary funds, a community may have to seek public subsidies.

This problem of attracting industry while building a community's tax base may differ between satellite towns and freestanding communities. Satellite towns offer industrial sites close to labor, markets, existing transportation, and perhaps raw materials. Since such sites can attract industry, these new towns will not have to offer large incentives. In contrast, freestanding communities far from existing large urban centers will have to offer greater incentives than satellite towns to attract similar industries. These conditions detract from the freestanding community's potential tax base and increase its dependence on public subsidies.

Although company towns are built far from urban centers, their companies usually assume responsibility for community services in order to attract labor. These

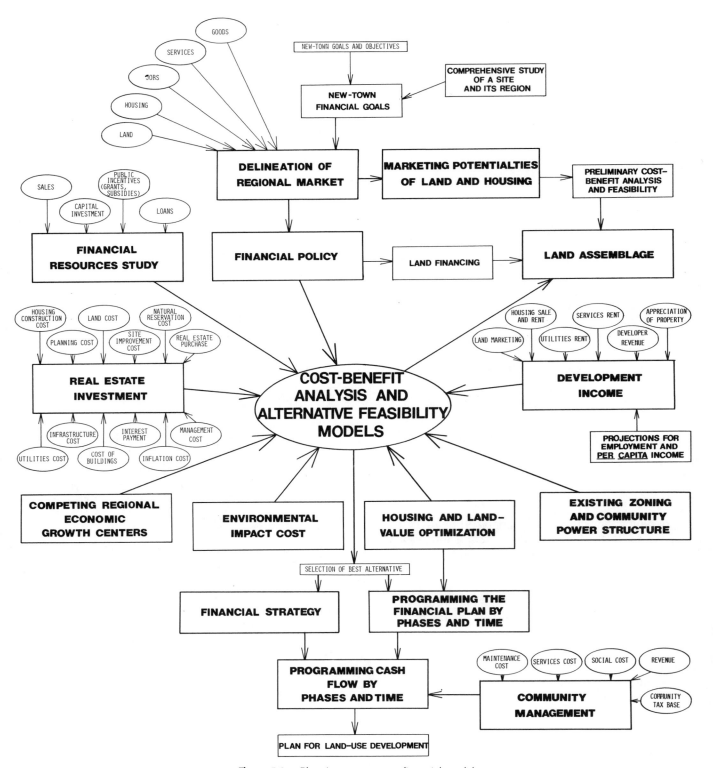

Figure 5.9. Planning a new-town financial model.

companies may also run community government to support their institutions. In such cases a community tax base becomes mainly a matter of company policy and may not even exist. However, if a company town expands its economic base, a local tax base may become necessary.

Some elements mentioned that attract industries may also attract wholesale and retail commercial firms. The latter may consider local and regional markets for their goods more than industry does. Since commercial firms may also be more interested than industry in improvement of local services that benefit them directly, they may expect to pay more local taxes.

Revenue from property and other local taxes is usually low during the early stage of a new town because of its relatively small population, and therefore services will be limited. During this time the combination of expenditures for development and operation of the community, and of a limited tax base, makes the basis of community services weak and may force the community to seek public subsidies.

OPTIMAL NEW-TOWN SIZE

The current growth in urban centers around the world poses many questions for urban planners, developers, and other practitioners. Should urban centers be allowed to grow indefinitely? If so, how could such huge centers be managed? What would be the social implications of such development? Does the urban socioeconomic climate improve or deteriorate with increased size?

The search for the optimal size of a new town is a quest for a compromise between two major viewpoints: maximalist and minimalist. A maximalist claims that the larger a new town is, the greater will be the variety of its facilities and jobs. This variety would generate growth and minimize unemployment, and would keep the younger generation from drifting away from the new town. The result would be a stable economy. Those who advocate large size also claim that services would be cheaper, although they admit that beyond a certain size public utilities might become increasingly costly. The minimalist view, on the other hand, claims that a small new town allows more effective social interaction, strengthens social identity of residents, and provides a better living environment by its proximity to the countryside and to nature.

A major issue which must be considered early in any study of optimal new-town size is the definition of goals and objectives of a new town. A variety of

definitions may be given for the word optimum: "the best or most favorable condition,"[38] "the amount or degree of something that is most favorable to some end; . . . greatest degree attained under implied or specified conditions";[39] "the conditions producing the best results; the combination of conditions that produces the best average result when there is a choice of combinations. The most favorable degree."[40] The questions that must be raised with regard to the word optimum are optimum for what, for whom, and for where? A new town needs an optimal size for many reasons: efficient transportation and movement, fulfillment of economic needs, provision of good services, management of municipal expenses, achievement of social situations and, if necessary, maintenance of defense.

Criteria for Determining Optimal City Size

The criteria used to determine optimal city size form a complex set and must be analyzed before one can determine an optimal size. Optimal new-town size will differ depending on the kinds of criteria used.

The optimum size of cities is quite different from the standpoint of certain criteria from what it is on the basis of others. It is found that even an apparently unitary criterion—e.g., health—may give conflicting indications of the optimum. There is no immediately obvious way on which these various optima may be objectively equilibrated, compromised, weighted, or balanced to yield an unequivocal figure for *the* optimum population for a city. Most theorists proposing a size or size range as the optimum adopt this procedure, or the alternative one of confining attention to a few of the many criteria of optimum city-size that have been proposed in the literature.[41]

Density. The ratio of a city's population to its physical size determines its density. Any change in the city's physical dimensions will, of course, change its density and physical factors such as accessibility. Regarding the optimum size in relation to new-town density, Frederic Osborn suggests:

an optimum or norm for a new town of a population of about 50,000 and a density of about 15 persons a town acre. This cannot be a universal formula, but it is useful as a sort of datum from which the gains and losses of variations upward and downward can be measured.[42]

Function. Size and function of a new town must be examined according to its local and regional relation to other cities in the area. Thus the hierarchical functional pattern of a new town in its geographical region may be determined. Christaller theory indicates three major interrelated elements which build a hierarchy of cities and place an individual city within it: function, size, and distance.[43] A city has a regional function along with its local one, both of which are relative to the functions of other cities and give a settlement its own regional status. There are changeable functions, and emphasis may shift from one to another throughout a city's historical development. Thus a city may change functions, emphasis, and roles as the need occurs. Since size and function are related, one can expect to find a city continuously increasing or decreasing its population. This process of change in function and size is much more frequent and dynamic in free, modern, and competitive economies than in traditional, reserved, closed economies. One can even expect that in a free-market economy the hierarchical sequence of its cities may at some point be broken or disturbed and a new pattern may emerge.

"If one assumes that the hierarchy of inter-related functions of urban centers is a valid concept, then one can arrive at an optimum size for each of the centers on the hierarchy."[44] According to this quotation, the complexity of local and regional functions of a hypothetical city that must be performed to achieve certain of its goals and objectives may be defined, and accordingly, the range or scale of its prospective populations may be indicated. Following the Christaller theory, the higher the number of functions and the greater their diversity, the larger a city's population will be. Exceptions to this pattern are company new towns whose economies are based only on the delivery of one service or industry. Their optimal size is quite predictable because of the clear indication of their economic goals and resources. Since these exceptional new towns are dependent on their natural resources, they usually do not carry any functional position related to their regions. Within such settings, however, they may stimulate a change in the function of other adjacent new towns in a hierarchy.

Also, the geographic location of a new town in relation to a large city would have far-reaching effects on the degree of self-sufficiency, function, and the ultimate town size. Thus the location of a new town far from an urban center tends to support and intensify its self-containment. But such a location could also hamper the development of a high standard of amenities, and could also result in slow population growth. On the other hand, new towns located close to large urban centers could take a longer period of time to achieve independence.

Health. Planners should consider two questions about the relation of city size to residents' health:

(1)   Does a significant correlation exist between city size and health, and if so, what is that correlation?

(2)   Does a significant correlation exist between population dispersion patterns and health, and if so, what is that correlation?

In response to the first question, studies show that the number of physical ills increases to a high proportion as a city's population increases.[45] We may, however, assume that large cities have introduced physical configurations, social constraints, and economic tensions that may have a direct effect on the physical and mental health of their populations. Some factors that may cause tension and disorder include air pollution, noise, congestion, commuting, and lack of contact with nature.

One may also assume that life expectancy is generally higher in small cities than in large ones, and that big cities have a higher ratio of the following ills which cause early death: cancer, nervous breakdown, mental illness, suicide, stomach ulcers, diabetes, tuberculosis, heart disease, pneumonia, intracranial lesions, and nephritis.[46] Although health services in general seem to be better in large cities than in small ones, exposure of large city populations to the causes of illness is far greater than in small cities. Thus, "the populations of these large urban centers are more vulnerable to the long-term, accumulative environmental hazards eventuating in chronic and psychosomatic disorders."[47]

Robert Faris provides an answer to the second question. He found that physical ills and social disorders in established medium size and large cities decrease from the city center toward the periphery, and a correlation exists between city section and number of ailments.[48] From this correlation one may assume that the ratio of physical and social ills from the center to the periphery may be much less in small cities than in large ones. Smaller cities may also have greater social interaction, lower divorce rates, greater unity among families, fewer single and more married people, and proportionately more children than larger cities.

Cost of Services.   The total cost of municipal services for a fiscal year divided by the total number of population gives the average cost of services per capita in a new town. This average differs widely for developed and undeveloped regions, not only because of the differentiation in costs related to the scale and speed of inflation but also because of the different standards of living and services provided in each region. An analysis of local costs of services per capita is the relative comparison of a region with its nation, which shows that the cost of a new town in relation to its size in a particular nation may differ from such costs in another nation. In the United States, "preliminary studies seemed to indicate that municipal operating costs were lowest in communities of from 7000 to 30,000 population. Below and above this population range per-capita municipal expenditures appeared to rise sharply without any very obvious increase in amenity."[49] Also, municipal expenditures of large cities are relatively higher than those of small cities. When considering the efficiency of municipal services in relation to new-town size, planners generally agree that their efficiency "should increase with increasing city-size to a point of diminishing returns, with an optimum size somewhere between the extremes."[50]

Municipal costs per capita are related to costs of individual public services. These latter costs vary widely between technologically developed communities and developing ones since standards of living, quality of services required, and tax bases differ, but "a region can give its inhabitants an adequate range of commercial services when the population of its principal city is somewhere in the neighborhood of 100,000 to 200,000."[51] Since the significance of the costs of public services per capita and the efficiency of these services is related more to city size than any other factor, such services constitute a small part of a city's economy, and are not major economic forces in a self-contained city with a sound economy.[52]

The efficiency of one public service, schools, must usually be considered on the scale of rural village areas of very small size, or of neighborhood size. In the United States, the Advisory Commission on Intergovernmental Relations considered minimum town size for an efficient school system: "a school district needs a minimum of 1000 school-age children to adequately sustain a four-year high school with 300 students. Support for such a school requires a community of more than 3500 people, assuming approximately one pupil per family."[53]

Big cities have a larger proportion of robberies, murders, car accidents, and arrests than small cities. Moreover, the number of police or other security people required in large cities is proportionately higher than in small ones, and this number will continue to grow as big cities increase in size: "it may be generalized that the large city not only experiences a greater relative amount of crime, but also pays proportionately more heavily for it."[54] It seems that this increase in number begins when cities reach a population of 50,000.

In conclusion, every geographic region has its own particular scale and criteria for optimal city size, which are a synthesis of interrelated cultural, social, functional, and economic elements. The elements which contribute to the building of this synthesis and the determination of the optimal range of city size are dynamic. Optimal city size should be determined only after a comprehensive study has been made of those interrelated elements.[55]

The Issue of New-Town Size

Many philosophers and planners, including Plato, Aristotle, Sir Thomas More, Leonardo da Vinci, Ebenezer Howard and his followers, and Lewis Mumford, have considered the issue of optimum city size by setting upper limits for it. Also, atomic scientists considered this issue in light of dispersing urban populations to protect them from nuclear attack.

Various new-town planners and committees have suggested different optimal sizes for new towns based on their own particular justifications. Ebenezer Howard proposed an optimal city size for new towns to be of "a population of 32,000 in the initial garden city and its rural belt, and 58,000 in a later town to be central to an associated group of towns. . . ."[56] Later the New Towns Committee of Great Britain determined an optimal city size for English new towns which closely followed Howard's proposal: "Optimum population suggested for town area is 30,000 to 50,000, but with related district, may be 60,000 to 80,000; in certain cases a smaller population may be sufficient."[57] Related districts are areas within a 10-mile radius of a new town.

The English New Towns Committee considered in its report factors for "optimum normal range" of new-town size which determine the upper level (50,000 persons) and the lower level (30,000) in the built-up area. The "suggested upper limit of the order of 50,000 was based on a balancing of the factors of (a) acceptable internal density, and (b) convenient nearness of homes to workplaces, town centers, schools, and open country."[58] The Committee suggested that under special circumstances the optimal size of some new towns may differ from the normal range. "Special considerations may well justify the creation of a new town with less than 20,000. There are regions in England . . . of low density and remote from any large centre, where a new town could confer great benefits especially on the surrounding agricultural population. . . ."[59]

Optimum size has been increasing constantly since the first English new towns were established after World War II, from 60,000 persons projected for Stevenage (1946) to 250,000 projected for Milton Keynes (1967). Moreover, English planners have tended to increase the projected population size many times throughout the process of their plan prepara-tions. This clearly reveals that the attitudes of new-town planners toward the maximum size of new towns has been changing continually. In the early 1950s, the projected population for most of the new towns was between 30,000 and 50,000, whereas the population projected for plans at the end of the 1960s was be-tween 200,000 and 250,000.

There is no definite agreement among professionals on optimum city size. Some economists, for example, think that the new town with a regional function should have a population somewhere between 100,000 and 200,000.[60] Russian planners, on the other hand,, consider the range of 150,000 to 200,000 as the optimum for a new town.[61] Otis Duncan, who studied the subject thoroughly, considered the attempt to provide an optimum size purely subjective: "Any numerical choice of a figure for the optimum popula-tion is involved in subjective value preferences and impressionistic weighting systems."[62]

In the United States, new-community size varies more than in any other country and depends mainly on the particular developer of a new town.[63] "New towns in the United States also exhibit a wide range of target populations. Rather than being related to any ideal conceptions as to population size, their target popula-tions appear to be more a function of the particular developer's goals, land holdings, market evaluations, or financial capabilities."[64] Albert Mayer, an Ameri-can new-town planner, discusses new-community size in the United States: "Our [American] new towns will not be of any standard size—they can well vary from 50,000 to several hundred thousand, appropriate to the individual location, function, and outlook. But each will be of an approximately pre-determined size modified by 'tolerances.' . . ."[65] As a point of depar-ture, a planner may also describe the acceptable new town in a country by using the average of all cities (excluding the extremely large or small ones) within that country as his prototype. To accomplish this,. the following procedure could be used: (1) Cities of the country should be categorized by degrees of self-containment. (2) The category of self-containment de-sired for the new town should be selected. (3) The size of the selected cities should be determined. (4) Those sizes should be averaged, and this average considered as the optimal size for the proposed new town.

Profile of a City of 100,000

Every city performs certain definite functions for its own population and may also perform some for its

region. Its regional functions are based on complex relations which may be reciprocal both with its im-mediate environs and with other distant regions. Al-though most cities have established their functional relations through a geographiic hierarchy, in highly developed technological societies, the dynamics of transportation systems and the intensity of free economies have interrupted this hierarchy.

Historically the local function of cities has been primarily as economic centers, and it continues to this day. Economic dynamics are a major cause of the growth or decline of cities; i.e., a city's population growth is correlated with its economic growth. Thus additional employment opportunities attract more people to a city, and vice versa. It is therefore feasible for a researcher to trace the various functions of a city of a specific size in a given country when he knows its standard of living, population demands for consumer goods and services, cultural and social standards, per capita income, and other similar determinants. Obvi-ously a city of definite size in a given country has different functions than another city of the same size in another country (e.g., U.S. cities as compared to those of India). Yet we can outline basic functions common to both cities. Also, due to technological differences, two such cities may differ greatly in the number of employees who perform certain functions while pro-ducing the same quantity. Table 5.5 lists some func-tions that a city of 100,000 people usually performs. Since quantity of employees and emphasis of func-tions may vary from one country to another, we did not attempt to quantify the categories.

CONCLUSION

The economic function of a new town should be to stimulate its own economic activities and those of its immediate surroundings. Also, in evaluating the economic impact of a new town, the span of time before any return on the investment is possible be-comes an essential factor. Because of its self-contained economic base, the effect of a new town upon its region is far higher than that of a satellite town de-veloped exclusively as a bedroom community.

An important economic issue in new towns is the spatial distribution of economic activities within a new town and its region. Decentralization or concentration of activities will have an immediate influence on traffic efficiency (and therefore on parking, congestion, acci-dents, trips generated, pollution, safety, and noise); on social behavior (face-to-face contact, age-group in-teraction, commuting, and leisure); on land use (seg-

TABLE 5.5   PROFILE OF A CITY OF 100,000

OCCUPATIONS OF WORKERS

TYPES OF ECONOMIC ACTIVITY

PROFESSIONAL

   ENGINEERS, ARCHITECTS, PLANNERS AND LANDSCAPE PLANNERS

   PHYSICIANS AND SURGEONS

   DENTIST

   OPTOMETRIST

   NURSES

   LAWYERS AND JUDGES

   TEACHERS

   MUSICIANS

   ACTORS AND SINGERS

   PAINTERS

   ARTISANS

   RELIGIOUS CLERGY

   ACCOUNTANTS

   LIBRARIANS

   HEALTH WORKERS

   TECHNICIANS

MANAGERS AND ADMINISTRATORS

SALARIED:

   MANUFACTURING

   RETAIL TRADE

   OTHER INDUSTRIES

SELF-EMPLOYED:

   RETAIL TRADE

   OTHER INDUSTRIES

SALES WORKERS

   MANUFACTURING AND WHOLESALE TRADE

   RETAIL TRADE

   OTHER INDUSTRIES

CLERICAL

   BOOKKEEPERS

   SECRETARIES, STENOGRAPHERS, AND TYPISTS

   OTHER CLERICAL WORKERS

CRAFTSMEN, FOREMAN, AND KINDRED WORKERS

   AUTO MECHANICS

   MECHANICS AND REPAIRMEN

   MACHINISTS

   METAL CRAFTSMEN

   CARPENTERS

   CONSTRUCTION CRAFTSMEN

   OTHER CRAFTSMEN

OPERATIVES

   MANUFACTURING

   TRUCK DRIVERS

   OTHER TRANSPORT EQUIPMENT OPERATIVES

LABORERS

   CONSTRUCTION LABORERS

   FREIGHT, STOCK, AND MATERIAL HANDLERS

   OTHERS

SERVICE WORKERS

   CLEANING SERVICE WORKERS

   FOOD SERVICE WORKERS

   HEALTH SERVICE WORKERS

   PERSONNEL SERVICE WORKERS

   PROTECTIVE SERVICE WORKERS

   PRIVATE HOUSEHOLD WORKERS

SERVICE

   BUS STATION AND NETWORK

   MASS TRANSPORTATION

   RAILROAD

   AIRPORT AND TRAVEL AGENCIES

   TAXI

   TRUCKING SERVICE

   HOTELS AND MOTELS

   BARBER SHOPS

   BEAUTY SHOPS

   AUTO AND OTHER REPAIR SERVICE

   GASOLINE STATIONS

   PLUMBING

   LAUNDRY

   RADIO, TELEVISION, AND TELEPHONE

   OTHER COMMUNICATION

   THEATERS AND CINEMAS

   DANCE HALL, STUDIOS, AND ORCHESTRA

   BOWLING ALLEY AND BILLIARDS

   GOLF COURSE

   SKATING RINK

   COMMUNITY CLUB

   SWIMMING POOLS

   MORTUARIES

   RESTAURANTS

   NEWSPAPERS

FINANCIAL AGENCIES

   BANKS

   TRUST COMPANIES

   INSURANCE AGENCIES

   CREDIT AGENCIES

   REAL ESTATE AGENCIES

PUBLIC INSTITUTIONS

   MUNICIPALITY

   POLICE

   FIRE

   POST OFFICE AND TELEGRAPH

   OTHER GOVERNMENTAL OFFICES

   PUBLIC UTILITIES

COMMUNITY INSTITUTIONS

   SCHOOLS

   HEALTH CLINIC

   HOSPITALS

   CHURCHES

   MUSEUMS AND ART GALLERIES

   WELFARE AND NON-PROFIT ORGANIZATIONS

RETAIL BUSINESS

   CLOTHING STORES

   SHOE STORES

   FOOD STORES

   DEPARTMENT STORES

   GENERAL STORES

   CANDY STORES

   FURNITURE STORES

   APPLIANCE STORES

   BOOK STORE

   PHARMACIES

   LIQUOR STORES

   SALVAGE STORES

   SPORTS STORES

   JEWELRY STORES

   GARDEN SUPPLY STORE

   BUILDING MATERIALS

   FARM EQUIPMENT

   AUTO DEALERS

   PRINTING AND PUBLISHING

WHOLESALE BUSINESS

   CARS

   GROCERIES

   DRUGS

   FARM PRODUCTS

   SCRAP AND WASTE DEALERS

   FURNITURE

   CONSTRUCTION MATERIALS

   LUMBER YARD

MANUFACTURING

   BAKERY

   DAIRY

   FOOD PROCESSING

   BUILDING MATERIALS PLANTS

   BUILDING CONTRACTORS

   LAND DEVELOPERS

   INDUSTRY

   CARPENTRY

regation or integration of uses); and on social, economic, and governmental relations between a new town and its region.

Integrated land use for economic activities does not mean manufacturing and industry alone. Rather, such use is meant to focus on diverse, daily commercial and service needs, especially for offices. In such a pattern there is still an opportunity for industrial sites to be segregated within a new town, a satellite, or regional subcenters such as those in Canberra, Australia.[66] In such cases, a new town may minimize costs in land values, services, utilities, and infrastructure.[67]

There are costs and benefits in constructing any city; some are not measurable in monetary terms: e.g., social well-being, physical and mental health, and self-satisfaction. The high degree of these conditions must be encouraged by quantitative investment.

NOTES

1.   Real Estate Research Corporation, *Economic and Financial Feasibility Models for New Community Development* (Springfield, Va.: National Technical Information Service, 1971), p. 46.

2.   Albert J. Robinson, *Economics and New Towns: A Comparative Study of the United States, the United Kingdom, and Australia* (New York: Praeger Publishers, 1975), p. 3.

3.   Ebenezer Howard, *To-Morrow: A Peaceful Path to Real Reform* (Cambridge: M.I.T. Press, 1965), pp. 41–57.

4.   Ray Thomas, *London's New Towns Planning* (London: Political and Economic Planning [PEP], 1969), p. 382.

5.   Thomas, p. 382.

6.   James A. Clapp, *New Towns and Urban Policy* (New York: Dunellen Publishing Co., 1971), p. 54.

7.   Great Britain, Ministry of Town and Country Planning and Department of Health for Scotland, *New Towns Committee Final Report* (London: His Majesty's Stationery Office, 1946), Section 27, p. 10.

8.   A.A. Ogilvy, "The Self-Contained New Town: Employment and Population," *Town Planning Review*, **39,** no. 1 (April 1968), p. 44.

9.   Ogilvy, p. 38.

10.   Thomas, p. 382.

11.   Ogilvy, p. 40.

12.   This assumes 3.5 members in each family and includes single residents.

13.   Gideon Golany, "New Town Site Selection: Method and Criteria," unpublished study (University Park, Pa.: Department of Architecture, The Pennsylvania State University, 1972).

14.   Michael D. Wilburn and Robert M. Gladstone, *Optimizing Development Profits in Large Scale Real Estate Projects,* Technical Bulletin 67 (Washington, D.C.: Urban Land Institute, 1972), p. 20.

15.   Gregory H. Leisch, "The Economics of New Community Development," in *Strategy for New Community Development in the United States,* Gideon Golany, ed. (Stroudsburg, Pa.: Dowden, Hutchinson and Ross, 1975), p. 206.

16.   J. Kozlowski and J.T. Hughes with R. Brown, *Threshold*

Analysis: A Quantitative Planning Method (London: The Architectural Press, 1972), pp. 60–66.

17.   P.B. Desai and Ashish Bose, "Economic Considerations in the Planning and Development of New Towns," in *Planning of Metropolitan Areas and New Towns* (New York: United Nations, 1967), pp. 218–19.

18.   P.A. Stone, "Financing the Construction of New Towns," in *Planning of Metropolitan Areas and New Towns* (New York: United Nations, 1967), pp. 229–30.

19.   Ved Prakash, *New Towns in India* (Detroit: The Cellar Book Shop, 1969), pp. 1–19.

20.   United Nations Economic Commission for Asia and the Far East, *A Case Study of the Damodar Valley Corporation and Its Projects* (Bangkok: United Nations, 1960).

21.   Otto H. Koenigsberger, "New Towns in India," *Town Planning Review,* **23,** no. 2 (July 1952), pp. 97–105.

22.   William L.C. Wheaton and Robert L. Wagner, "The Economic Feasibility of New Towns," Harvard Studies, *Journal of the American Institute of Architects,* **15,** no. 1 (January 1951), p. 39. This study indicates that the land cost ratio in 1949 was 1.32 percent in Sudbury I (Massachusetts) and 1.53 percent in Sudbury II in 1949. Also see Real Estate Research Corporation, *Economic and Financial Feasibility Models for New Community Development* (Springfield, Va.: National Technical Information Service, 1971), p. 27.

23.   See Edward P. Eichler and Marshal Kaplan, *The Community Builders* (Berkeley and Los Angeles: University of California Press, 1970), pp. 140–59.

24.   For more information, see J. Ross McKeever, *Community Builders Handbook* (Washington, D.C.: Urban Land Institute, 1968), p. 37.

25.   See McKeever, p. 38.

26.   Robinson, p. 15.

27.   Wilburn and Gladstone, p. 16.

28.   Robinson, pp. 15–16.

29.   Frank Schaffer, *The New Town Story* (London: MacGibbon & Kee, 1970), pp. 1–20, 36–49. Also see Jane A. Silverman, "The New Towns of Israel: Unprecedented in Scope and Impact on National Life," *Journal of the American Institute of Architects,* **62** (December 1974), p. 46.

30.   Elizabeth A. Altman and Betsey R. Rosenbaum, "Principles of Planning and Zionist Ideology: The Israeli Development Town," in *Regional Policy: Readings in Theory and Applications,* John Friedmann and William Alonso, eds. (Cambridge: M.I.T. Press, 1975), pp. 692–93.

31.   Ted Dienstfrey, "A Note on the Economics of Community Building," *Journal of the American Institute of Planners,* **33,** no. 2 (March 1967), pp. 120–23. Also see Richard L. Heroux and William A. Wallace, *Financial Analysis and the New Community Development Process* (New York: Praeger Publishers, 1973), pp. 36–37.

32.   Wilburn and Gladstone, p. 24.

33.   Heroux and Wallace, p. 21.

34.   Heroux and Wallace, p. 53.

35.   Donald F. Blumberg et al., "Computer-Based Socio-Economic Evaluation of New Community Proposals" (Jenkintown, Pa.: Decision Sciences Corporation, no date), p. 2.

36.   Dienstfrey, p. 121.

37.   Decision Sciences Corporation, "Basic New Community

Simulation System (NUCOMS)—Preliminary System Description" (Jenkintown, Pa.: Decision Sciences Corporation, no date), pp. 32–48. See also Decision Sciences Corporation, "New Community Fiscal Impact Evaluation System" (Jenkintown, Pa.: Decision Sciences Corporation, no date), pp. 5–26.

38.   William Morris, ed., *The American Heritage Dictionary of the English Language* (Boston: American Heritage Publishing Co. and Houghton Mifflin Co., 1973), p. 922.

39.   *Webster's Seventh New Collegiate Dictionary* (Springfield, Mass.: G. and C. Merriam Co., Publishers, 1966), p. 593.

40.   Frank H. Vizetelly, *The Practical Standard Dictionary of the English Language* (New York: Funk & Wagnalls Co., 1930), p. 797.

41.   Otis Dudley Duncan, "Optimum Size of Cities," in *Cities and Societies: The Revised Reader in Urban Sociology,* Paul K. Hatt and Albert J. Reiss, Jr., eds. (New York: The Free Press, Collier-MacMillan, 1957), p. 772.

42.   Frederic J. Osborn and Arnold Whittick, *New Towns: The Answer to Megalopolis* (New York: McGraw-Hill Book Co., 1963), p. 115.

43.   Artur Glikson, *Regional Planning and Development* (Leiden: A.W. Sijthoff's Uitgeversmaatschappij N. V., 1955), pp. 55–57.

44.   B. Shindman, "An Optimum Size for Cities," in *Readings in Urban Geography,* Harold M. Mayer and Clyde F. Kohn, eds. (Chicago: University of Chicago Press, 1969), p. 258.

45.   Robert E. L. Faris and H. Warren Dunham, *Mental Disorders in Urban Areas* (Chicago: University of Chicago Press, Phoenix Books, 1967), pp. 1–10. Also see Donald Klein, "Problems and Possibilities for Mental Health Programming in New Communities," in *Planning for the Social Frontier: New Communities in the United States,* Gideon Golany, ed., under consideration for publication.

46.   Duncan, p. 763.

47.   Duncan, p. 763.

48.   Faris, pp. 1–10. Also see Ian McHarg, *Design with Nature* (Garden City, N.Y.: Doubleday and Co., 1971), pp. 187–95.

49.   Wheaton and Wagner, p. 36.

50.   Duncan, p. 766.

51.   Colin Clark, "The Economic Functions of a City in Relation to its Size," *Econometrica,* **13,** no. 2 (April 1945), p. 112.

52.   William Alonso, "The Economics of Urban Size," Papers of Regional Science Association, XXVI (1971), pp. 67–83. Also see W. Lean, "Economics of New Town Size and Form," *Ekistics,* **23,** no. 135 (February 1967), pp. 79–82.

53.   U.S., Advisory Commission on Intergovernmental Relations, *Urban and Rural America* (Washington, D.C.: U.S. Government Printing Office, 1968), p. 22.

54.   Duncan, p. 764.

55.   Shindman, p. 260.

56.   Osborn and Whittick, p. 12. Osborn refers to Ebenezer Howard, *Garden Cities of To-Morrow.*

57.   Great Britain, Ministry for Town and Country Planning, Section 294, p. 64.

58.   Osborn, p. 110.

59.   Great Britain, Ministry of Town and Country Planning, Section 21, p. 9.

60.   Clark, p. 112.

61.   N. V. Baranov, "Building New Towns," in *Planning of Metropolitan Areas and New Towns* (New York: United Nations, 1967), p. 209.

62.   Duncan, p. 772.

63.   Jerome P. Pickard, "Is Dispersal the Answer to Urban Overgrowth?" *Urban Land,* **29,** no. 1 (January 1970), pp. 11–12. Pickard introduces a survey made by the United States Department of Housing and Urban Development on 63 large-scale developments built since 1947. The survey indicated that the average projected population of each project is 55,000, with a range between 4000 and 270,000. The populations in all 63 projects would total 1.6 percent of the total U.S. population.

64.   Clapp, p. 58.

65.   Albert Mayer, "Ingredients of an Effective Program for New Towns." *Proceedings of the 1964 Annual Conference* (Washington, D.C.: American Institute of Planners, 1965), p. 188.

66.   The National Capital Development Commission, *Tomorrow's Canberra: Planning for Growth and Change* (Canberra: Australian National University Press, 1970).

67.   Robinson, p. 137.

SIX
SYSTEMS OF TRANSPORTATION AND COMMUNICATION

TRANSPORTATION

In new-town planning, transportation is "not to be treated as an independent variable,"[1] but as a major, integrated part of a plan. Planners should not only approach transportation technically but also socially and economically, since it affects a new town's land use and pattern, future development, and economy. Throughout history interurban transportation has had a great effect, if not the strongest, on the location, growth, and configuration of settlements. Transportation represents the complexity of the mutual influences of urban centers. In spite of its traffic dynamics, transportation routes, once established, remain static unless large investments are made to change their patterns. Local routes, on the other hand, are determined by their original plan and have caused serious problems because they have not been adaptable to technological changes, which helped to shift local gravitational centers to peripheral areas of cities. New towns, however, are expected to overcome this shortsightedness by being adaptable to technology and to provide alternatives for future changes.

Several general characteristics of transportation are common to new towns, new communities, satellite towns, new towns in-town, new cities, company towns, and regional growth centers, but there are unique traffic considerations which result mainly from individual land-use patterns. Cultural habits also affect transportation systems. European traffic systems are based on extensive mass transportation by buses and railways; the American system is based mainly on private cars. Europeans often walk from one place to another, while Americans do not. The Buchanan Report,[2] concerned with finding a solution to traffic problems in cities, identified three main variables which must be measured before a solution can be

found: (1) desired level of usage of vehicles, (2) standard of desired environment, and (3) cost of improving the environment by changing existing physical patterns. The "solution is largely to be found in the unification of the new separated functions of road engineer and planner-architect . . . administrative split-mindedness."[3]

Planning of new towns in most of the world has emphasized the transportation standards and requirements of all socioeconomic classes. In the United States, however, new communities have been established mainly for the middle-class population, which has one or more cars per family and requires a specific level of transportation. Thus, in planning a transportation system for a new community certain assumptions and requirements must be taken into account; for example, the upper middle class will use fewer pedestrian paths, need more garage and parking space, and may have more cars per family than the middle and lower classes. Also, one must assume that mass transportation may be less accepted by new communities than by European new towns, and at present there are few new communities with a plan for a system of mass public transportation. This is due in part to middle-class America's lack of interest in mass public transportation and is one of the major differences between new communities of the United States and new towns of England, Sweden, and Israel.

Traditional planning of transportation in new towns neglected the orientation of thoroughfares toward public buildings and monuments in the city as an element of landscaping. Until now, engineers, who may have a tendency to emphasize the technical aspects of transportation and to neglect its visual or architectural features, have planned transportation systems in new towns. In the early stages of new-town development in Great Britain, traditional transportation systems were unable to cope with traffic needs, such as parking areas, garages, and separation between traffic and pedestrians.[4] In 1958, after the establishment of more than twelve English new towns planners still did not consider traffic congestion seriously and thought it was only a problem faced by big cities. Because of this lack of planning, future traffic congestion problems were inevitable.

The Cumbernauld New Town Traffic Analysis Report[5] in 1959 marked the Ministry of Housing and Local Government's realization of the need for a new traffic system in new towns. In the early studies for Cumbernauld, "a realistic approach to the motor vehicle was incorporated for the first time in a British new town."[6] This approach has had a strong impact on transportation planning for new towns, and English new towns established after 1959 provided for the separation of pedestrian and vehicular traffic and for public transport. Also, subways run under commercial centers or pass alongside them and seldom through them. Such innovation provides examples of solutions that older urban centers may use for some of their transportation problems.

Since most new towns are constructed in undeveloped areas, planners can design optimal transportation systems that may be unconventional yet realistic. Such systems may minimize people's dependence on technology and realize the social implications of these systems. Their corollary may be the choice of little dependence on private cars. When planners choose such systems, they begin by designing pedestrian and then mass-transit systems, which may protect public interest in transportation. However, neither choice should completely eliminate the alternative of using a private car. In short, priorities of planning of such systems should be (1) pedestrian, (2) mass-transit, and (3) private vehicles.

PLANNING TRANSPORTATION SYSTEMS

Transportation networks in new towns are compromises between planners' ideals and complex reality. Transportation has always been dictated by such factors as economics, dynamics, social intensity, physical constraints, financial resources, and political desires. Thus planning transportation in new towns must combine the contribution of team experts before final formulation of a network. Although economists and sociologists may play leading roles in putting together the alternative assumptions for a future development, a final plan should include flexibility, alternatives, and adaptability to future changes. In the long run such

vision may save investments. The most crucial and sensitive section is the center of the new town. Planners may, however, see phases of development of a new town as related to the town center and the transportation network, and may offer an alternative order of constructing sections of the town so that peripheral areas are built before competing the center. This order may keep the center from becoming congested as it is in a typically built town.

Generally, one should consider the following steps in the process of transportation planning for new towns (see Figure 6.1):

1. Define goals and objectives.
2. Study the site and region.
3. Collect data and survey.
   a. physical aspects
      (1) land suitability
      (2) soil hazards and limitations
      (3) availability of quarries and building materials
      (4) projected land-use information and scheme
   b. social and economic aspects
      (1) existing and expected travel behavior of the population
      (2) trends of income
      (3) potential local, regional, and national markets
4. Plan preparation.
   a. pedestrians
   b. highways and streets
   c. town traffic center
   d. local and regional transportation centers
   e. setting in regional network

Goals

It is the responsibility of the transportation designer and the planning team to provide their client with clear goals and objectives for transportation in their new town.[7] The following list gives some of these potential goals:

(1) Provide separate pedestrian and vehicular systems.

(2) Function as a laboratory to demonstrate new systems for the new town and other urban settlements.

(3) Provide (a) convenient access and parking for all community areas, (b) easy modes of interchange among systems and areas, (c) safe movement, (d) little

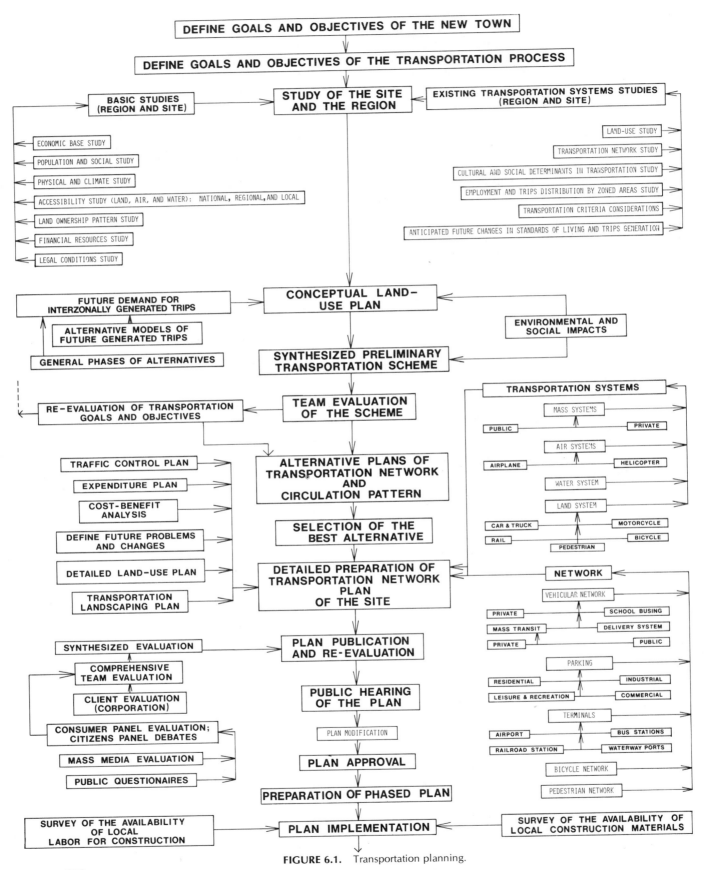

FIGURE 6.1. Transportation planning.

chance for pollution from dust, noise, and vibration, (e) easy commuting and transfer of goods, and (f) flexibility in meeting emergency as well as normal use.

(4) Enhance the landscape by integrating the design of systems and the environment to provide aesthetically pleasing areas for passengers and pedestrians.

(5) Provide a variety of types (land, water, and air) with choices for all age groups and social classes within a new town and its region (frequent public mass transportation and semipublic and private systems must be alternatives if a new town can afford them).

(6) Integrate transportation with land use to meet daily periodic uses and provide an adequate circulation pattern within and among land-use zones.

(7) Provide protection accommodated to a new town's climate.

(8) Develop a hierarchical network consistent with principles of land use within the new town, with regulated speed to minimize the nuisance of transportation and to maintain the network.

(9) Be inexpensive, efficient, safe, durable, easily maintained, usable year round, and easily altered.

(10) Integrate construction, development, maintenance, and operation of infrastructure and utilities.

(11) Function in regional and national networks to provide access to all terminals and to economic markets.

(12) Be consistent with the general goals and objectives of the new town as set by its planners and developers.

As we have explained, the goals of new towns vary, and they will have a direct effect on the planned transportation system. The most important goal affecting a new town's transportation system is self-containment. Relatively independent new towns require a hierarchical network, many parking areas, and efficient circulation and maintenance, while company towns need strong links to their markets, and satellite towns need adequate systems for commuting.

An economic base study of a new town is essential when planning a transportation system. The study should reveal the level of daily trips generated between a new town and its surroundings, and also within itself. Traffic movement from the region to the new town should also be estimated, especially when the new settlement functions as a regional growth center, by providing shopping centers and job opportunities for neighboring areas. In such cases parking space

must also be taken into consideration. However, new-town transportation planners should always view the new town as a part of its entire region; therefore studies should include the site and its region. In this area of transportation planning, as in other areas, it is essential for the transportation planner, the economist, the land-use planner, and other members of the transportation team to coordinate their efforts to insure success.[8]

In considering social factors and economic conditions in urban design, a transportation planner must cooperate with the new town's other planners since correlation between the planning components is vital and builds the comprehensive new-town plan.

Elements of land use, such as density and patterns of zoned areas and their intensity of use, will dictate many features of a new-town transportation plan. Therefore clarification of goals and objectives of land use is desirable before beginning transportation planning. Moreover, such clarification may call for changes in the pattern of land use already set forth, such as industrial land-use location, location of public facilities and buildings, and integration of roads and highways. The effects of zoning and rezoning must also be considered in transportation planning. Rezoning, for example, changes the density of travel and parking patterns but does not affect the capacity of streets and circulation patterns to absorb these changes.

Basic Assumptions for Projecting Traffic in New Towns

If a new town is to be built in an undeveloped area, data for projecting transportation needs may be difficult to gather. However, one may base assumptions on standard traffic data from previous new towns or from existing old towns and neighborhoods. New-town transportation planners may use data available from the area surrounding a proposed new town or may generate data from social groups equivalent to those assumed to be residents of the new town. British planners have made many such assumptions, and planners in other countries are also beginning to use this technique. The following discussion details several of these assumptions.

Increasing ownership and use of private vehicles forces new-town planners to estimate their demands on transportation networks. In England in the early 1960s, for example, the estimate was only 0.2 cars per person.[9] Now the number of cars per person is a little higher. In the United States, the estimate is approaching two cars per family. The corresponding decline in the number of journeys made by public transportation relates to private ownership. European cultures have been strongly oriented toward the use of mass public transportation for many reasons: country scale, mass of low- and middle-income population, and public support. One may not expect the demand for mass transportation to increase rapidly and replace private use, but mass transport may increase its importance in new towns. Modern employment conditions favor shorter and more uniform working hours than ever before. Shortened hours cause two conditions which a planner must consider: rush hours occur at closer intervals, and traffic intensity after the evening rush increases because workers have more leisure time than before.

With the decline of the railroad, most commercial centers are using more commercial vehicles than ever before for industrial purposes. The weight and size of such vehicles dictates their need for space for parking, maneuvering, and movement. They also require well-constructed roads. Planners may assume that bicycles will be in great demand as a means of transportation. They may increase security of movement for pedestrians, especially children, reduce the need for parking space, diminish air pollution and noise, and provide recreation for all age groups of a community. Since it has the advantage of starting its development from nothing, a new town may include a special network for bicycles similar and parallel to that for pedestrians that will underpass or overpass the motor network and lead to every portion of the town. Moreover, one can anticipate that the design, construction, and maintenance of a bicycle network costs much less than a motor vehicle network. Some countries, such as Belgium, The Netherlands, and Luxembourg have used bicycles as the main means of transportation for many years and provide special paths or roads.

Walking has always been a means of travel in any city of a scale to permit it. During this century, changes in vehicular technology and income, and increased city size have lead to less walking. Recently, however, planners have made attempts to make walking a feasible means of travel.[10] Recent research indicates that people like to walk from place to place.

Transportation systems in most English new towns completely separate pedestrians from vehicles. For example, the transportation system of Hook has been designed so that residents can move from one end of the city to the other without crossing any highways or railroads simply by moving above or below them (See Figure 6.2). Long distances between schools and houses are free of interference from roads.

Planners may assume that technological devices will greatly influence the development of transportation, especially in traffic control and new transportation tools. An electronic remote-control system may operate transportation within a new town and its surroundings, and may consist of the five following parts:

(1)   Dial-a-bus systems with arrangements for door-to-door pick-up; dial-busing takes more time to reach a destination than it would by private car.

(2)   Computer measurement of traffic flow in different areas to calculate intensity and adjust flow automatically to insure effective movement.[11] Computer-controlled signaling may also ease congestion and greatly aid in land-use planning since land-use intensity and transportation flow are interrelated. Information gathered by a controlling camera can detect growing problems in transportation and thereby avoid future crises.

(3)   Ultrasonic pickups buried under pavements to help in counting traffic and to feed a central computer, to obtain data to regulate traffic lights.[12]

(4)   Roadway antennas located along the pavement to give advance warnings, advice, weather reports, or instructions to drivers. Signals can be relayed to drivers by radios or "special out-of-band equipment mounted in each car."[13]

(5)   Automatic control for private cars when traveling limited-access, high-speed roads. This system could help drivers avoid collisions and could allow for automatic routing to preset destinations.[14]

The transportation pattern needed by new towns was clarified in a study made for Cumbernauld, Scotland,[15] which estimated the transportation behavior (public and private transportation, walking, and cycling) of the Cumbernauld population at peak hours and then converted this estimate into road capacity. The study assumed that

(1)   70 percent of the families owned cars (a bachelor was considered a family because he is an independent consumer).

(2)   62 percent of the town's cars would be on the road during peak hours. This assumption is an important one, since planners may make the mistake of trying to design road capacity for average traveling hours rather than peak hours.

North

open space

open space

Figure 6.2. Pedestrian network planned for Hook New Town (black areas indicate this network). (Source: *The Planning of a New Town.*)

(3) 45 percent of the population would use their cars to get to work. This assumption still allowed some of the population to use public transportation, walk, ride bicycles, or use any means of transportation other than cars.

The Cumbernauld study provides two lessons later used at Hook and other new towns: (1) motor network systems and pedestrian patterns should be completely separated. For pedestrians the shortest route is the best; for vehicles this is not necessarily so. (2) People habitually avoid underpasses unless they are wide and well-lighted, and tend to cross highways instead. These facts may dictate the use or disuse of a particular transportation system.

Hierarchical Networks

A basic concept assumed as an ideal model for highway transportation is a network of roads connected by

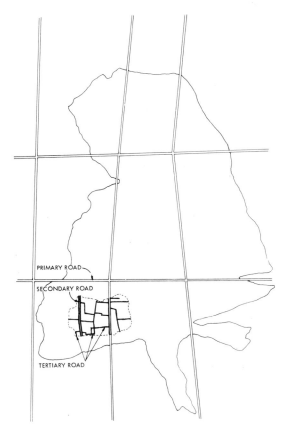

Figure 6.3. The hierarchical system of Mohenjo-Daro (2500–1600 B.C.). Entrances to house opened to B- and C-level streets but not to A-level ones. (Source: *Civilizations of the Indus Valley and Beyond.*)

their size and functions. Toronto, Canada has an excellent example of such a hierarchy. Even ancient cities such as Mohenjo-Daro (2500–1600 B.C.) had effective hierarchies although there were no motor vehicles. (See Figure 6.3.) Most older cities in the United States do not have hierarchical systems; rather, these cities have grid systems of major and secondary highways which have equal use status. One possible classification of roadways follows. (See also Table 6.1.)

National Highways. These are four-lane or more highways designed for medium and long journeys at the highest speeds allowed in a particular region. These highways are used mainly by cars, trucks, and motorcycles and are prohibited to unpowered vehicles and pedestrians. Unfortunately some American cities are crossed by national highways to take advantage of proximity. It is our opinion, however, that the disadvantages and hazards of such an association, such as noise, pollution, congestion, and traffic dangers, far surpass the advantages and should be the determining factors in transportation planning. National highways should never cross a new town, but should bypass it at a reasonable distance to eliminate any adverse effects on the new town. Although new towns should be located away from the influences of national highways, they should still be connected to them.

Regional Highways. These highways mainly link social and economic centers in a region and connect the national highway with the new town. In most cases they pass close to new towns or cross them and are usually medium- or high-speed highways compared to provincial, state, or national ones.

Major Roads. These link neighborhoods, commercial centers, industrial areas, storage areas, communication and transportation centers, cultural and educational centers, residences, and other centers of socioeconomic activity within a new town. These roads should provide easy traffic flow between centers, usually allow from the medium to the highest speeds permitted in the town, and connect with regional highways at free-flow intersections. Major roads may have sidewalks, and pedestrians may cross their connecting highways by means of overpasses or underpasses. These roads have no on-street parking. They also provide a connection between the city and regional roads and are the highest level of internal road in a hierarchy. Usually they have four lanes, but in a small city they may have only two.

TABLE 6.1   FEATURES OF THE TRANSPORTATION NETWORK OF NEW TOWNS AND THEIR LINKAGES

TYPE	PURPOSE	SYSTEM	FEATURES OF CONSTRUCTION	SPEED ALLOWED	NUMBER OF LANES	OTHER CHARACTERISTICS
I. NATIONAL HIGHWAYS (FREEWAY, INTERSTATE HIGHWAY, AUTOBAN, AUTOSTRADA)	* TO LINK URBAN CENTERS, PROVINCES, STATES, OR NATIONAL AND INTERNATIONAL REGIONS * TO TRANSPORT GOODS AND PASSENGERS IN ALL TYPES OF MOTOR VEHICLES FOR LONG- AND MEDIUM-LENGTH JOURNEYS	* BY-PASS URBAN CENTERS * LIMITED ACCESS * NO STOPPING * FREQUENT REST AND SUPPLY AREAS * MINIMUM NUMBER OF CURVES * SHORTEST ROUTE * NO PARKING ALONG THE HIGHWAY * MEDIAN STRIP	* HIGH QUALITY OF CONSTRUCTION FOR HEAVY AND INTENSIVE TRAFFIC * GOOD AND WIDE PAVEMENTS ON BOTH SIDES * WELL MANAGED FOR CLEARING * SECURELY CONSTRUCTED SHOULDERS	* HIGH SPEED	4 OR MORE	* LINE OF BUILDING SET BACK AT LEAST 25 YARDS * FENCE FOR PREVENTING CROSSING OF WILD WILD ANIMALS * IN SOME, TELEPHONES FOR EMERGENCY CALLS * HIGHLY ESSENTIAL FOR INDUSTRIAL REGIONS * PROXIMITY OF NEW TOWNS TO NATIONAL HIGHWAY CAN ACCELERATE TOWN GROWTH AND INSURE ITS SUCCESS
II. REGIONAL HIGHWAYS	* TO LINK VARIOUS URBAN AND RURAL CENTERS WITHIN STATES OR PROVINCES * TO DELIVER MATERIALS WITHIN THE REGION AND LOCALITY AND TO SHIP PRODUCTS OUT ON MEDIUM-LENGTH JOURNEYS	* BY-PASS OR CROSS URBAN CENTERS * CONNECT THE NEW TOWN WITH THE NATIONAL HIGHWAY * INTERSECTIONS EITHER WITH VEHICLES OR REGIONAL HIGHWAY UNIMPEDED OR CONTROLLED BY SIGNALS * NO STOPPING * MEDIAN STRIP	* GOOD QUALITY OF CONSTRUCTION FOR HEAVY TRAFFIC * WIDE PAVEMENT ON BOTH SIDES	* MEDIUM TO HIGH	4	* LINE OF BUILDING SET BACK AT LEAST 25 YARDS * USUALLY HAVE ATTRACTIVE LANDSCAPE * PARKING IS NOT GENERALLY PERMITTED
III. MAJOR ROADS OF A NEW TOWN	* TO LINK THE NEW TOWN WITH THE REGIONAL HIGHWAY * TO PROVIDE UNITY TO THE MAJOR LAND USE OF THE NEW TOWN * TO PROVIDE A FLOW OF TRAFFIC FOR DELIVERY OF MATERIALS TO AND SHIPPING OF PRODUCTS FROM AN INDUSTRIAL PARK	* CONTROLLED INTERSECTIONS * NO PEDESTRIAN ALLOWED TO CROSS OR WALK PARALLEL TO ROAD * NO STOPPING ON MARGINS * MOSTLY CURVED * MEDIAN STRIP	* GOOD QUALITY OF CONSTRUCTION FOR HEAVY AND LIGHT TRAFFIC * WIDE PAVEMENTS ON BOTH SIDES	* MEDIUM	2 TO 4	* LINE OF BUILDING SET BACK 15 TO 20 YARDS * ESTABLISH TERRITORIAL BOUNDARIES FOR MAJOR ZONED LAND-USE UNITS SUCH AS THOSE FOR RESIDENTIAL, INDUSTRIAL, AND COMMERCIAL USES * PARKING IS NOT GENERALLY PERMITTED * USUALLY CAREFULLY PLANNED LANDSCAPE
IV. SECONDARY ROADS OF A NEW TOWN	* TO LINK MAJOR ROADS WITH THE VARIOUS MAJOR SECTIONS OF SINGLE LAND USE * TO FUNCTION AS THE MAJOR SKELETAL ROAD (DISTRIBUTER) WITHIN MAJOR AREAS OF SINGLE LAND USE (E.G., NEIGHBORHOOD, INDUSTRIAL PARK, AND COMMERCIAL AREA)	* LEAD TO THE MAJOR FOCUS OF THE PRIMARY LAND-USE UNIT * INTERSECTIONS CONTROLLED BY STOP SIGNS OR SIGNALS * CAREFULLY LANDSCAPED * NO CROSSING FOR PEDESTRIANS	* GOOD QUALITY OF CONSTRUCTION FOR HEAVY AND LIGHT TRAFFIC * WIDE PAVEMENTS ON BOTH SIDES	* LOW TO MEDIUM	2 TO 4	* LINE OF BUILDING SET RELATIVELY CLOSE (10 TO 15 YARDS) * FORM BOUNDARIES FOR SUBNEIGHBORHOOD UNITS
V. COLLECTOR ROADS OF A NEW TOWN	* TO FUNCTION AS THE MAIN NETWORK OF EACH ZONED UNIT * TO FEED THE SECONDARY ROADS	* INTERSECT WITH SIMILAR AND OTHER ROADS * CAREFULLY LANDSCAPED IN RESIDENTIAL AREAS * INTERSECTIONS CONTROLLED BY STOP SIGNS * ALLOW SIDE PARKING * DESIGNED FOR SPECIFIC PATTERN OF CIRCULATION	* GOOD CONSTRUCTION FOR LIGHT TRAFFIC * HAVE SIDEWALKS SOMETIMES	* LOW	2 OR MORE	* LINE OF BUILDING SET BACK 30 FEET * FORM THE SKELTON OF THE SUBZONED UNITS * DESIGNED TO BE USED MAINLY BY THE LOCAL PEOPLE AND ARE NOT THROUGHWAYS
IV. LOCAL ROADS OF A NEW TOWN	* TO LINK ZONED SUBUNITS AND THEIR SECTIONS * TO LINK BLOCKS AND HOUSING UNITS TOGETHER * TO BE USED AS THE MAIN LOCAL SERVICE NETWORK	* WIDELY INTEGRATED NETWORK INTO ZONED UNITS, ESPECIALLY RESIDENTIAL AREAS * USUALLY CURVED ROADS TO REDUCE SPEED AND TO FORM VARIATIONS IN TOWNSCAPE * PERMIT STOPS OR PARKING ALONG MARGINS * SOMETIMES INTERSECTED CROSSWALKS * PROVIDE SYSTEM OF LOCAL CIRCULATION	* CONSTRUCTED FOR LIGHT AND SLOW TRAFFIC	* VERY LOW	2	* LINE OF BUILDING SET BACK 20 TO 30 FEET * NOT CONDUCIVE TO THROUGH-TRAFFIC * ALSO, SPECIALLY ADJUSTED NETWORK USED BY BICYCLES
VII. CUL-DE-SAC (DEAD END)	* TO ASSURE SECURE MOVEMENT OF RESIDENTS, ESPECIALLY CHILDREN, WITHIN EXISTING TRAFFIC * TO ELIMINATE UNNECESSARY TRAFFIC * TO ALLOW PRIVACY OF MOVEMENT WITH MINIMAL NOISE OF TRAFFIC AND MINIMAL POLLUTION	* CLOSED ROAD AT ONE END WITH SPACE FOR TURNING AROUND * USUALLY SHORT IN LENGTH (NOT TO EXCEED 500') FOR ACCESS OF FIRE AND EMERGENCY VEHICLES * LOWEST LEVEL OF TRAFFIC NETWORK	* DESIGNED FOR LIGHT AND SLOW TRAFFIC	* VERY SLOW (SOMETIMES WITH BUMPS, WHICH IMPEDE SPEED)	2	* LINE OF BUILDING SET BACK 15 FEET
VIII. PEDESTRIAN NETWORK	* TO LINK ALL LAND USE, ESPECIALLY RESIDENTIAL, COMMERCIAL AND SOCIAL * TO INSURE SAFE MOVEMENT FOR ALL AGE GROUPS * TO ENCOURAGE RESIDENTS OF ALL AGES TO KNOW THEIR CITY * TO MAKE A NEW TOWN ON A HUMAN SCALE BY MAKING WALKING A POSSIBLE MEANS OF TRANSPORT	* SEPARATION BETWEEN PEDESTRIAN AND VEHICLES * OVER- OR UNDERPASSES * MAY BE USED BY BICYCLES * LINK A BACKBONE OF HOUSE YARDS * SHORTEST POSSIBLE PATHWAYS	* PAVED * AESTHETICALLY PLEASING WITH SPECIAL SIGHTS * LIGHTED * HAS REST AREAS * LANDSCAPED * ACCESS FOR EMERGENCY VEHICLES	* WALKING	A MINIMUM OF 6.5'	* UNDERPASSES ADEQUATELY LIGHTED BY DAYLIGHT * GRADED (INCLUDING STAIRS, AND ACCOMMODATED TO CHILDREN, PREGNANT WOMEN, ELDERLY AND HANDICAPPED PEOPLE)

Secondary Roads.   These form the internal circulatory system developed within a new town and function as the major skeletal roads (distributor) within areas of single land use. The basic principle of these roads is that motor vehicles circulate around the edges of residential blocks without crossing them, and the basic speeds of this system of roads are from low to medium.

Collector Roads.   These are designed to function as the main network of each zoned unit in a new town and also to feed secondary roads. Collectors link major new-town roads with focuses of activity such as neighborhoods and commercial and industrial centers. Mainly allowing low speeds, collectors provide parking along the sides. In residential areas collector roads are looped to create circulation by entering and leaving the same road within the area. The Cumbernauld study showed that even a new town of 70,000 population needs road junctions for radial roads that cross or interchange with other major local, regional, or national highways. Road junctions may provide easy traffic flow during peak hours and avoid bottlenecks, especially in those new towns which function as regional centers.

Local Roads.   These roads provide for low-level local traffic. They have the lowest speed limits and are the most carefully designed in terms of detail, especially that of any pedestrian system which may cross above

or below them, and also provide for bicycle movement. Although they allow circulation within neighborhoods and commercial areas, they often terminate in a cul-de-sac.

Culs-de-Sac.   These are a pattern of dead-end roads which enable a blocked, built-up area to penetrate the system of roads without crossing or dividing it. They also provide continuous pedestrian circulation within the built-up area without interruption by highways. Culs-de-sac, used extensively in the neighborhoods of ancient cities, were a manifestation of social structure and community philosophy. Today they are used as a means to retain the self-identity of clans or their subunits and to further personal contact, convenience, and propinquity within a population, all of which contribute to community pride. Surprisingly, not many contemporary planners have taken advantage of the cul-de-sac as a planning tool in today's motorized society.

Parking Areas.   These must meet the level of development in a new town, especially in its central part.

Pedestrian Networks.   The last level of this hierarchy is a system of pathways for pedestrians made possible in some new towns by separating pedestrians and vehicles. The network runs from one end of a new town to the other. Usually it is wide enough to allow four people to walk abreast and is designed to be convenient to all age groups and to penetrate all sections of land use, primarily residential, commercial, and social areas.

To summarize, the hierarchical pattern consists of 9 levels: national highways, regional highways, internal roads, major roads, distributor roads, local roads, culs-de-sac, parking areas, and pedestrian networks. In exceptional cases, intermediate roads may function on more than one level. For example, regional highways passing through a new town may serve as major town roads at the same time. However, conflicts may occur, such as differences in speed limits and capacity between the two levels. For long journeys regional highways provide higher speeds than those allowed on major new-town roads. Nevertheless, a major delay may occur where local traffic interferes with regional highways that cross the new town.[16] Therefore, to avoid overloading, it is desirable to have regional highways bypass a new town rather than intersect it. This avoids speed differences and reduces overloading and congestion. (See Figure 6.4.)

Figure 6.4.   Part of the hierarchy of the vehicular network of Stevenage, England. (Courtesy of the Commission for the New Towns.)

TABLE 6.2 TRANSPORTATION CRITERIA

Physical

Total network length compared with population size
Driving view is safe and visible
Wide enough for traffic to meet standards
Signs and directions are clear, do not create doubt
Easy access for police, firemen, and emergency aid
Rest and parking areas
Length of utilities caused by transportation network length

Environmental Impact

Degree of pollution
Degree of noise
Aesthetically pleasing
Impact on water resources and runoff
Impact of ecological systems

Pattern

Accessibility to various land uses
Connection with all transportation centers (e.g., terminals)
Separation between pedestrians and vehicles
Possibility of circulation
Separation of function within a network
Degree of flow
Level of security and safety
Rush-hour traffic flow
Distance from residential area
Degree of integration with economic and social goals
Land-use pattern
Optimal land use
More than one alternative offered in circulation and accessibility
Safe interchanges
Adequate parking

General

Network available in early stage of development
Efficient connection with regional and national networks
Able to modify and expand as technology develops
Introduce a variety of transportation by land, air, and water
Mass transportation accessible to all social groups from all land uses
Maximum choices

Development and Maintenance

Low-cost construction eliminates unnecessary maintenance
Low-cost maintenance
Enable efficient control
Convenient maintenance
Easy access for maintenance (snow removal and repair)
Durable
Usable in most weather conditions

Criteria for Evaluating Transportation Systems

New-town transportation planners and the interdisciplinary team should prepare a set of criteria for evaluating their plan. Such evaluation may be made by a rating method or by any other analytical technique. Value considerations may differ from one new town to another and will also be determined by the availability of financial resources for development. A planner is expected to make his evaluation for the long range of the plan and also for each planned phase of development. A matrix technique may be most helpful. (See Table 6.2 for possible criteria.)

PLANNING PEDESTRIAN SYSTEMS AND THEIR DESIGN

If a planner adopts a model of the separation of pedestrians and vehicles, his first step in planning transportation is to plan and design a pedestrian system for the new town. Any such system should have three provisions:

(1)   Maximum (or total) separation of all vehicles and pedestrians and minimum mixing of powered vehicles and bicycles.

(2)   Safe movement for children and parents from homes to green areas and open spaces, playgrounds, elementary schools, kindergartens and other neighborhood cultural and economic centers.

(3)   Minimum walking to centers of activity, taking into consideration that pedestrians tend to use the shortest possible route.

Complete separation of pedestrians and vehicles is desirable in high-density areas or in the center of a new town where traffic is intense. In less populated areas a small, central pedestrian pathway can lead to each residential unit or pass alongside it. Thus the combination of both settings establishes a continuous pedestrian network radiating from the central part of town to the peripheral parts and beyond.[17] Based on the principle of these patterns, pedestrian pathways can link separate blocks to culs-de-sac and focuses of social activity. In Hook, pedestrian pathways and distributor roads were designed to connect to bridges or underpasses at intervals of 440 yards, where bus stations were also to be conveniently located. "Footpaths must never take the form of pavements running alongside the major roads. It is clearly impossible to prevent some footpaths from adjoining minor service culs-de-sac. This, however, can and should be avoided in detailed planning in most instances, even though service road traffic might not be sufficiently fast or heavy in volume to be very dangerous."[18]

Elements of Design

Barry Benepe describes five elements of planning and designing pedestrian circulation systems: continuity, safety, comfort, convenience, and delight.[19] Continuity provides the shortest way to a destination without detours, direct connections, and established right-of-way for pedestrians. Safety arises mainly from the separation from vehicles. Comfort refers to the ease of walking on smooth, level, dry, wide surfaces with few steps, and protection from weather, pollution, and noise. Convenience means network links to all land uses. Since pathways are intended for observation as well as walking pedestrians may experience delight in discovering attractive elements of a city which riders cannot see from a moving vehicle.

Designs of paths may provide these elements in the following different ways:

(1) By avoiding long, continuous straight lines and using zig-zag lines instead.

(2) By creating variation in the landscape along paths.

(3) By making rest areas available along paths with play space for children.

(4) By creating points of unobstructed view to the open landscape.

(5) By creating "shade stations" along pedestrian paths wherever appropriate for protection.

Moving pavements may assist pedestrians, especially in commercial areas. Pathways may be of different widths to accommodate the peak hours of pedestrian movement: a primary of a minimum width of 23.0 feet, secondary of 11.5 feet, and minor of 6.5 feet in width.[20]

Any design of paths must include access for service vehicles, maintenance, fire, security, and utilities. A planner must consider the legal implications of rights-of-way for such access as well as also the financial implications of building, managing, and maintaining any such system.[21] (See Figure 6.5.)

Paths must be independently lighted to make them safe for use at night, because they do not necessarily follow roads. Lighting may make paths attractive at night and offer views different from those in daylight.

Social Implications

In a new town where people may live within walking distance from the central area, planning pedestrian circulation has social implications. An overall systematically and efficiently designed pattern may offer social advantages that are not possible in vehicular systems. Since people will be walking they may meet casually, and such meetings may support interaction among different social, ethnic, racial, and age groups. Specially designed spaces for such purposes may be scattered along paths (e.g., spaces with benches and small play areas). The safety of pedestrian systems may encourage people to come outside; children may play in areas free of vehicles; elderly people and mothers with small children may walk comfortably away from the noise and air pollution caused by cars. Such a system "has substantial impact on how people feel about themselves and how children feel about their parents,"[22] and also makes it possible for children and parents to spend time together in an open space near home.

Moreover, a wide network of pedestrian systems may enable residents, especially young children, to be familiar with various geographic sections of their urban centers and its environs. This situation will support the development of individual identification with the community, of relaxation, and of physical health. Under this system community members will make full and frequent use of their interaction with nature provided by a new town and its environs.

The focus of a pedestrian network is a town's central area, where socioeconomic and sociocultural activities take place. Much more than any other town, the new-town center may provide a large portion of vehicle-free land for pedestrian movement. (See Figure 6.5).

Land Use

Planners of pedestrian systems should consider the extent to which they influence land use. Residential areas, sociocultural centers, and employment areas of a new town have more potential influence on the reduction of motor vehicle movement than other zoned areas such as shopping centers; social planners should emphasize the former areas in their designs. It is more likely that residents would walk to recreational areas, concert halls, or banks than they would to shopping centers or places of work. Also, people would probably ride bicycles to places of work within close distances more than they would to shopping centers at the same distances. In any case, the presence of a well-designed pedestrian network may encourage residents to walk often. Compact towns would also promote walking among the population if their planners considered pedestrian needs when designing zoned land use.

When effectively designed, pedestrian networks should form an integrated physical configuration with transportation networks and also with all other types of land use. Although it requires investment and energy,

a pedestrian system is safer and less expensive than a motor vehicle system when it is the main alternative for pedestrian movement. Pedestrian networks, when they have been well-designed, (e.g., Reston, Virginia), will increase the walking habits of the population even though walking may not generally be a culturally favored mode of transportation.[23]

VEHICULAR SYSTEMS

Mass Transit

After having planned the pedestrian network, new-town planners should give priority to the planning and

Figure 6.5. Features of pedestrian systems. *A:* Separate pedestrian and vehicular systems in Cumbernauld, Scotland.

Figure 6.5. *B*: Toddlers playing safely away from traffic and within sight of home in Redditch, England.

160

Figure 6.5. C: A pleasant bicycle path and pedestrian overpass in Harlow, England.

Figure 6.5. *D:* Queen Square in Crawley, England, which provides safe shopping.

New Town Pg. Crx. (Ch. 6) C-0609-11

Figure 6.5. *E:* Integrated pedestrian and vehicular systems along the main shopping thoroughfare in the town center of Hemel Hempstead, England.

Figure 6.5. *F:* A pedestrian area in an old city, Utrecht, The Netherlands. (Courtesy of the Commission for the New Towns; Harlow Development Corporation; Cumbernauld Development Corporation; Redditch Development Corporation; and Gemeente Utrecht.)

development of mass transportation. These systems may be public or private. Alternative types of mass transportation are (1) traditional, computer-controlled, or electrically powered systems of buses and minibuses, (2) monorail or dualrail vehicles which move in fixed underground or aboveground paths, and (3) controlled cable cars which move aboveground and cross all other transportation services.

The major advantages of mass transportation are that it minimizes traffic congestion in rush hours, increases safety in the community, reduces the use of private cars and parking areas, and consequently reduces pollution and noise in the community. Mass transit has the potential to support community social life by providing a reliable transportation network, being affordable for low-income groups, and eliminating the need for parents to drive their children to many places. This system may also attract the elderly to the new town, thereby normalizing its age-group structure.

Mass transportation systems are designed to carry large numbers of passengers in an efficient manner, and this is particularly important during rush hours. Although many systems operate mainly during business hours and offer curtailed service in the evening, it is possible for systems to be flexible enough to provide service by appointment at odd times (e.g., Columbia, Maryland). Further, buses can be used for transporting school students during off hours when few passengers use the public transit system. Such use saves school systems the expense of maintaining their own buses and strengthens the transit system.

Mass transportation in many countries is usually a public enterprise or a combination of public and private investment. Like social services, the development of a system in new towns often requires governmental subsidies, especially in the early phases when a community lacks the population to justify the investment and a strong local government to support it. Such subsidies are necessary because systems of mass transportation can influence long-range new-town growth during the early stages.

One may assume that a reasonable percentage of the population in established new towns does not own cars and therefore needs a local bus system. Such a mass transportation system may satisfy the needs of this social group and also avoid problems of congestion. If this service is inadequate in the early stages of new-town development, people may revert to owning cars,[24] and those unable to afford one may not move to such a town. This is a second reason for public subsidies.

The social implications of the availability of mass transportation go beyond whether one can afford a car. If low-income people cannot afford to own and operate a car and move away from a new town, the town's population will become homogeneous. Thus, if social balance is the stated goal of a new town, the transportation system should encourage that goal.

Bus terminals in new towns should be located to connect with regional or national bus systems. For convenience, railroad stations should be located near bus terminals. Generally, (e.g., in Hook) both were to be located in the marginal part of town rather than near the center to avoid splitting the town and causing congestion.

New towns that have been developed as regional growth centers to house regional, industrial, and governmental services need a well-developed traffic center, regional transportation pattern, and a large variety of transportation facilities, such as highways and roads, bus systems, waterways, railroads, and airlines. These needs are especially great for new towns that serve as provincial or national capitals, such as Chandigarh, Brazilia, Islamabad, Qiryat Gat (Lakhish region, Israel), and Canberra.

Rush Hours

Since the greatest volume of traffic within an urban area occurs during rush hours, planners must consider this element when designing transportation in new towns. Roads in a new town and regional roads must be able to absorb the maximum flow in each direction during these times. One may assume that commuters will use all means of available transportation. One may also assume that commuting in a satellite town will be more intense than in a new or company town, since commuting depends on the geographic distribution of the population and the relative availability and diversity of employment in the new town and its surrounding region. To a certain extent regional commuting also dictates the volume of rush-hour traffic within a town, and one must consider this volume and local commuting in the design of town roads. A regional study may be necessary to project potential employment in an area that would lead to workers commuting.

A planner must consider the effects of both mass transportation and privately owned single vehicles on rush hour patterns. Mass-transportation vehicles, whether public or private, are presumably easy to coordinate or control because they are centralized in the hands of a few agencies and follow set routes. With centralized control, these vehicles may be diverted to alternative roads during rush hours if necessary. Pri-

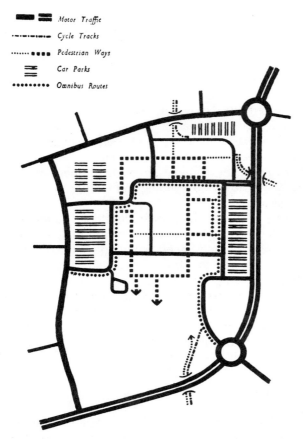

Figure 6.6.   Circulation pattern of the town center of Harlow, England. (Source: *Harlow New Town: Master Plan.*)

vate vehicles do not have definite, constant commuting routes. Since these vehicles usually carry one or two people and their load capacity is much less than that of a mass-transport vehicle, many cars are needed to carry the same number of passengers as a mass-transit vehicle. Therefore in new towns with a high percentage of private car ownership, congestion in rush hours is heavier than in equivalent new towns that have a greater percentage of public vehicles. In new towns, distributing employment areas to peripheral sections can help avoid congestion of streets during rush hours. (See Figure 6.6.)

Parking

After planning pedestrian and vehicular systems, and rush hour, providing adequate parking space is the next challenge for a new-town planner. It is difficult to forecast the amount of parking space required for a new town, especially in its center, which needs many parking facilities in order to function effectively.[25]

In many new communities the calculation of parking needs is based on the "ratio between gross floor area of retail space and gross area of parking space. This may vary between 1:1 to 1:4."[26] The British use a variety of approaches to calculate parking needs. Some new towns based their calculations on such factors as previous neighborhood experience (e.g., Corby), the availability of space (e.g., East Kilbride), shopping frontage (e.g., Harlow and Basildon), different ratios for different commercial functions such as hotel bedrooms, movie seats, shops, and offices (e.g., Hemel Hempstead), census of parked cars (e.g., Welwyn), number of workers and shop and office areas, or the 1:4 ratio of parking space to total population size (e.g., Crawley).[27]

In the early period of new-town development some planners and their clients thought it a luxury to devote a large amount of central land to parking. "The main break-through had already been made at Stevenage"[28] a new town in England, with the establishment of a large-scale regional pedestrian shopping center and parking area. Later, new towns adopted multilevel vehicle parking buildings and shopping centers which made the Stevenage system obsolete. Vallingby, northwest of Stockholm, Sweden, was one of the very early new towns that developed the multilevel town center.

Generally, parking in new towns has not yet become a problem since the availability of parking space meets the requirements of the existing population, but there is no assurance that the situation will remain stable in the future. However, there is always the risk of overproviding for parking within commercial and cultural centers, thus minimizing the use of pedestrian networks connected with those centers.

In the early stages of British new towns, the attitude toward provision of garage space was as poor as that toward parking areas. Later, when the first new towns began demonstrating problems of increasingly crowded and littered streets, planners' attention shifted toward alleviating these problems. The first attempt in this area was the Basildon plan, which provided garages at the end of gardens with entry to apartments from both the garage side and the path side.[29] (See Figure 6.7.)

In the satellite town of Erith in Kent, England, all houses have been raised 12 feet on platforms because of the risk of flood from the Thames River. Spaces under the houses are used as parking areas for each family. The platforms have since been linked by bridges, and some of the subplatform space is also used for gardens. The method of using spaces under buildings for parking areas and gardens has also been

Figure 6.7. Rental housing with integral garages in Milton Keynes, England. (Courtesy of the Milton Keynes Development Corporation.)

employed in development towns in Israel, especially in arid areas to provide shade.

Public transport was poor in many of the early English new towns. The first two—Stevenage and Crawley—provide proof that there was too great a dependence on private cars with no provision for their storage. Also, there was often not more than one garage for every five houses which, in addition to a very inadequate public transportation system, was a cause for discontent that often mounted to bitterness among housewives.[30]

Land Use and Transportation

Careful selection and grouping of land-use categories is important in collecting and analyzing transportation data for a new town. "It seems clear that the number of land-use categories should be held to a minimum."[31] There are five major interrelated land uses which affect transportation: residential, work, shopping, leisure, and education (See Figure 6.8).

Although there is less danger of misuse of land in new towns than in older cities, the possibility of misuse of a transportation network and its facilities is greater than that for any other element. Unlike transportation in older cities, however, new-town transportation has a realistic chance to succeed since it is built on undeveloped land without much interference from surrounding elements.

Employment, Transportation, and Land Use. In planning connections between activity zones in new towns of industrialized societies, a planner should adopt some of the following assumptions:

(1) It is probable that people will choose to live near their place of work. The possibility of their doing so is one of the greatest advantages offered by new towns.

(2) For a distance of less than ½ mile (1 mile equals 1.6 kilometer) between home and work, the majority of employees will most likely prefer to walk.

(3) For a distance between ½ and 1 mile, half of the employees will tend to select different means of transportation, including bicycles and motorcycles, and the other half will prefer to walk to work.

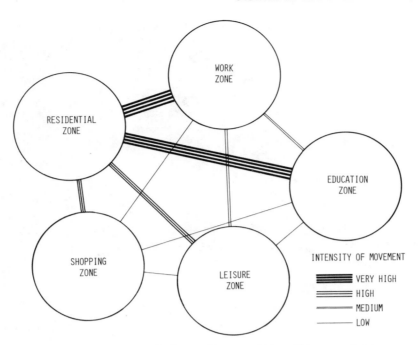

Figure 6.8.   Conceptual scheme of interzonal trips within a new town.

(4)   For a distance of more than 1 mile, a reasonable number of employees will probably prefer to use public transportation if available, or bicycles and motorcycles, rather than a private car.

In a sound, self-contained new town the major source of employment will be industry distributed in different locations throughout the town, followed by commercial establishments located in the geographic center of town. Such an employment pattern can increase the percentage of employees walking to work; moreover, linear industrial areas paralleled by adjacent groups of residential units or located in relation to housing areas may provide more opportunities for walking than concentrated areas. The same result is possible in a central commercial area surrounded by groups of high-density housing. When work is within walking distance, families may own only one car even when the standards of living allow more. The vehicular traffic load in rush hours may be lessened by these various employment patterns which foster walking in new towns.

   The area of a new town will determine to a great extent what means of transportation people will need and use. If distances are short, people will tend to walk. At some limit, however, distances become long enough so that powered transportation seems necessary or even vital. To illustrate the relation between distance and area, let us use a hypothetical,

circular area and vary its radius. Figure 6.9 shows the areas of circles of four given radii and compares three of these areas to the fourth: that of a circle of ¼-mile radius. A circular area with a radius of 1 mile contains approximately 3.14 square miles (2009 acres); an area with a radius of 1.66 miles contains 8.7 square miles (5556 acres), which can accommodate a new town of 100,000 persons. Increases in the area cause the following:

(1)   As Figure 6.9 shows, increasing the city limits by only ¼ mile triples the total area. There is a crucial point at which increasing the peripheral city limits (radius) will result in a drastic shift in the focus of transportation systems from pedestrian to vehicular movement. It seems that a radius of ½ mile is the crucial distance of change. City expansion reduces the proximity of newly developed areas to the city center, and consequently diminishes the tendency of residents to walk to the center and encourages the use of automobiles for commuting.

(2)   In implementing the planning policy of a city, a planner must cautiously integrate land-use diversity, city distance, population size, and density to produce preferred systems of transportation. The alternative to reducing the shift from pedestrian to vehicular movement is to design systems that permit residents to live within walking distances of areas which they use daily.

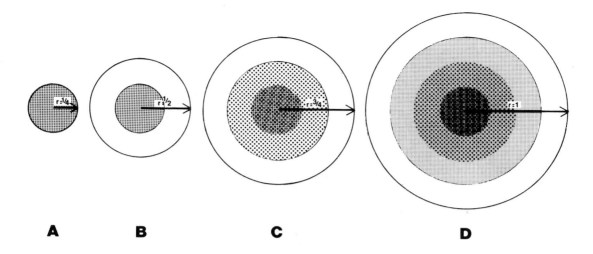

	RADIUS			AREA IN ACRES		
	IN MILES	INCREASE	% INCREASE	TOTAL	INCREASE	% INCREASE
A	0.25	—	—	125.6	—	
B	0.50	0.25	100%	502.4	376.8	300%
C	0.75	0.50	200%	1130.4	1004.8	800%
D	1.00	0.75	300%	2009.6	1884.0	1500%

Figure 6.9. The relation of a city's radius to its area.

Two possible ways of setting such distances are high-density residential areas with major activities at their center—a design creating a compact city such as a vertical city—and spatially decentralized activities, which may require duplication of some services.

Patterns of land use and employment centers affect the pattern of transportation networks and vice versa. Linear, concentrated, dispersed, radial, or polycentric land-use patterns will have parallel transportation patterns. Moreover, each pattern will generate a distinct pattern of trips (mainly during rush hours) correlated to the distribution of employment within a town; i.e., concentrated, sprawled, scattered, or polarized spatial patterns of employment will result in similar trip patterns. Also a consequence of patterns of land use, transportation, and employment, the total length of roads, and the land they occupy determine most of the cost of constructing and maintaining a network. The planners of Milton Keynes tested alternative combina-

tions of patterns in terms of two criteria: accessibility as "total work trip person miles" and cost as investments required to meet peak hours.[33] The study shows that transportation requirements caused by different employment distributions result in different land-use forms. (See Figures 6.10 and 6.11 and Table 6.3.) In this discussion, however, it should be remembered that although transportation is an important factor in selecting a land-use pattern, it is not the critical element.[34]

A secondary consideration of the relation between transportation and land use is how the availability of mass transit affects car ownership and private parking. If residents own cars they must be parked somewhere near homes, if not in one's own garage, and planners should designate such space.

Socioeconomic Considerations. Availability of mass transportation facilities in a new town may determine in part the attitude of the population toward the town.

Three Basic and Extreme Land Use Forms

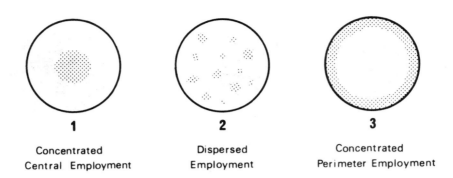

1	**2**	**3**
Concentrated Central Employment	Dispersed Employment	Concentrated Perimeter Employment

Two Additional Land Use Forms

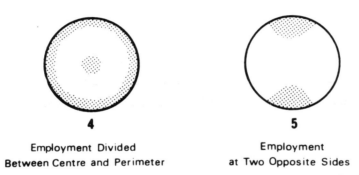

4	**5**
Employment Divided Between Centre and Perimeter	Employment at Two Opposite Sides

Figure 6.10. Five alternative spatial distributions of employment. (Source: *The Plan for Milton Keynes Technical Supplement No. 7 Transportation.*)

One must realize that the behavior of man is influenced to some degree by his living space. Space and variety help satisfy man's needs and affect his composure; transportation can expand that space. In Israel, newcomers who had been advised to migrate to a new town, based their decision partly on the condition of transportation facilities in that town. People realized that a variety of choices and opportunities, and accessibility supplied by that transportation system seemed to extend the geographic dimensions of a town's area. In most cases since those who migrated to new towns came from metropolitan areas, where the number of choices is large, they tended to seek these choices wherever they moved, and new towns seemed to offer such systems.

One must also consider the strong correlation among residential density in a given area, relative location, and distance from socioeconomic and educational focuses, and the need for transportation in a new town. However, residential development would require an intense local transportation network. Industrial land use may not demand equivalent local intensity but may require mainly the condition of sophisticated links with regional and national networks. Planners, however, should be aware of the relation between type of manufacture, land use, and number of workers and their transportation requirements. Thus, there should be differences in transportation requirements between one type of economic activity and another.

Terminals. With the increase of air transportation and the dynamics of social, economic, and administrative activities of the new town, site selection for terminals is required. The following criteria should be considered:

(1)   Accessibility to and from the site as related to the new town and its region, with the least interference with residential areas.

Shaded areas indicate
location of Employment

Residential areas unshaded

Figure 6.11. Preferred alternative land-use plan. (Source: *The Plan for Milton Keynes Technical Supplement No. 7 Transportation.*)

TABLE 6.3 PERSON MILEAGE AND LENGTH OF ROADS OF THE FIVE ALTERNATIVE DISTRIBUTIONS OF EMPLOYMENT

Diagram Number	Person Mileage	Relative Measures of Total Land Requirements for Highest Likely Level of Road Use[1]
1	268,000	340 miles
2	272,000	170 miles
3	319,000	240 miles
4	290,000	220 miles
5	340,000	384 miles

[1]Assumes direct routes and 100% efficient use of good road space in the peak direction.
Source: *The Plan for Milton Keynes Technical Supplement No. 7 Transportation*, volume 1.

(2) Availability of land in consecutive parcels to meet existing demands of the project's future expansion needs.

(3) Zoning of the adjacent land within the site's constraints. Thus, for an airport, such land may not be zoned as residential although it may be open space, agricultural, or forest. Bus or railroad stations should be associated with commercial or industrial zones.

(4) Proximity to residential areas to keep them from nuisances caused by traffic in centers, such as pollution (dust and smoke) noise, or odors.

(5) The overall design of the project should be attractive and pleasing, especially the warehouses of the project. Thus it is essential that construction be integrated with its surroundings.

(6) Physical and environmental characteristics of the site considered in connection with its function, such as soil quality, rock formation, geological limitations, floods, wind, temperature, wildlife, vegetation, and precipitation.

(7) Accessibility and proximity of those transportation centers to each other, such as a bus terminal and a railroad station, and their access to other land uses, such as industrially or commercially zoned areas.

If a new town has a regional economic, social, or administrative role, an airport will increase its importance.[35]

Models for Balancing Generated Trips

When estimating trips, planners should specifically consider the origin and destination of trips (1) within a new town and (2) between a new town and its neighboring communities and region. Local trips generally involve travel among the following zones: residences, places of work, commercial and economic centers, educational centers, and cultural and recreational centers. (See Figure 6.8.) Most trips are made from home to work and vice versa. One may estimate interzonal trips which originate at residences on the basis of the number of dwelling units or the number of resident workers and jobs available. Trips can also be estimated in terms of modes of transportation: walking, mass transit, bicycles, cars, and so forth. Using these estimates, one may then project the number of trips made to or from a neighborhood during a given time (e.g., during rush hour).

One may calculate trips primarily by considering the number of residential units, the average number of employees per residential unit, the standard of living, and the intensity of local and peripheral land use in the generation of a specific number of job opportunities and of social and economic activities.

The distribution of types of interzonal trips generated (walking, bicycling, or driving) will differ among cultures, and a transportation planner must consider such cultural determinants. Generally one can estimate that an average of two trips per day will be made from each residential unit in a new town when the home is located at either the origin or the destination of the trip.[36] Trips made between two points other than from residential units must also be included in this calculation.

The number of trips among a new town, neighboring communities, and its surrounding region are related to the degree of self-containment of the new town on the one hand and the ratio of residents employed within the new town to those employed elsewhere on the other. A new town with a high degree of self-containment and a sound economic base will have many job opportunities, which make commuting outside minimal. It is essential to establish careful coordination in a self-contained community between the types of local job opportunities and the types of housing, to prevent residents from commuting because of a lack of suitable housing that workers can afford or because of a lack of appropriate jobs.

A balanced system of trips may be created by integrating land-use patterns with the transportation system. Even distribution of places of work in conjunction with the number of jobs they generate is one way of establishing traffic equilibrium during peak hours. The goals of a model of balanced generated trips are as follows:

(1)   Achieve a balanced distribution of movement during daily and weekly peak hours.

(2)   Minimize conflict and interaction between pedestrian and vehicular movement.

(3)   Insure the flow of vehicular movement, parking, loading, and unloading.

(4)   Reduce nuisances caused by traffic in residential and recreational areas.

Models can treat all factors affecting transportation and their dynamics comprehensively. In spite of the advantages of such models, there is some reservation among transportation planners about different planning models used in the prediction of generated trips.

The traffic models used to predict trip generation and distribution are subject to statistical errors of the order of ± 20–25 percent. And the assignments to route networks are subject to similar errors.[37]

Despite their sophistication, any of these models must be evaluated constantly to insure their accuracy.

One should also consider the number and frequency of daily or weekly trips made by individuals and families from their residences according to time of movement and desired destinations in the new town, its periphery, and the surrounding region. (See Table 6.4.)

The interference of many factors or forces can disturb the balance of generated trips; one prime factor is the provision of housing conditions which are not contingent upon the types of jobs provided in the same town. The lack of foresight in determining the relation

TABLE 6.4   DAILY AND WEEKLY TRIPS FROM RESIDENCES

Destination	Commuting Time
Work	Morning and evening
Education centers	Morning and afternoon
Shopping	Mainly afternoon
Leisure and recreation	
daily	Evening
weekly	Weekends

of local jobs provided for a low-income or unskilled population to the necessity of providing adequate housing would certainly cause employees to find residences outside the community and commute to their jobs. Also, middle-income residents may look for jobs outside the community when desirable ones are not provided within it. In both cases, daily trips will increase and consequently require changes in the transportation network.

Another factor which may disturb the balance is a change in the intensity of land use (i.e., overuse or underuse). A third factor affecting the balance is an increase in per capita income, which may permit more people to own private cars. This concerns not only traffic movement but parking conditions as well.

A dominant factor affecting a new-town transportation system is the type of community economic base that dictates its land-use patterns and consequently its transportation network. Modifications of the economic base may result in changes in the type, variation, and intensity of land-use patterns, and therefore may effectively control daily transportation.

Trip time is a major parameter in the planning of new-town transportation networks. Minimization of trip time may be accomplished not only by planning effective transportation networks but also by developing public or private mass transportation systems. Trip time may be affected by the distance to be traveled and the efficiency of such systems, and changes in efficiency may also disturb the balance between trips and their time.

COMMUNICATION

The revolution in electronic communications media may be considered a second industrial revolution which will definitely give rise to a social revolution.[38] These new media offer various exciting opportunities that will have a far-reaching effect on our daily lives and on future planning considerations.[39] Many planners anticipate that although future communication will replace trips, there will still be many other factors intensifying transportation. Optimistic planners, however, tend to believe that audiovideo multidirectional systems will lead to decentralized urban centers in new forms. The new two-way audiovideo system, added to existing television, radio, and telephone systems, will provide quicker and more effective ways for worldwide communication.

It appears that communications services can be extended and improved more readily than can transport services since communications facilities have low feasibility and are largely controlled by private firms whereas transport facilities are highly feasible, controversial, and dependent on a public-political decision-making process for implementation. Therefore it is probable that communications will tend to improve faster than transport and a relative shift from real travel to teletravel should result.[40]

Some basic components of an electronic communications system include (1) dial-access information systems, (2) portable videotape recorders and viewers, (3) computer-aided instruction, (4) closed-circuit television, (5) televised teaching programs within universities-without-walls, (6) two-way channel teaching, especially for children who have difficulty commuting to school, (7) videophones, (8) rapid facsimile, (9) audio conferences, and (10) audiovideo conferences.

As it appears now, a two-way electronic communications system will provide new access to (1) remote conferences and actions for daily business needs; (2) local community governance;[41] (3) community affairs and management; (4) safety and security; (5) highly specialized medical treatment and health instruction; (6) scarce educational facilities, such as classrooms; (7) remote data banks, such as library and information files; (8) remote newspapers; (9) entertainment; (10) remote transportation systems. Among all these users, education and business seem to be the best potential consumers of electronic communications.

Electronic Communication and New Towns

Electronic communication for new towns provides "a combination of electronic devices connected into a system by communication links to provide advanced facilities for the residents of new communities."[42] Sophisticated electronic communication should provide video and audio contact in a specific time and place.

New-town planners should consider two main issues of electronic communication:

(1)   What are the existing and foreseen potential electronic communication devices for daily use by individuals and society?

(2)   What will be the future impact of these devices on the social, economic, and political systems and transportation of new towns, and to what extent will this impact require changes in today's urban settlements, land uses, and housing patterns?

In dealing with these issues, new-town planners should outline potential effects on transportation. As it appears now, electronic communication devices may compete with transportation systems or partly replace them with newer and more effective transportation services. The equipment required by electronic communication systems is less than that required by transportation systems and also more flexible for change. Moreover, new towns are more adjustable to the construction of new electronic communication systems than are older towns. Most electronic communication uses cable networks or requires underground construction, together with other utilities such as telephone, electricity, gas, water, and sewage. Installation of these systems is considerably cheaper than transportation systems: "installing a cable into unsettled territory costs about one tenth as much as working beside, under, and around existing streets and sidewalks."[43]

Opportunities of Electronic Communication

Some new-town planners assume that rapid development in electronic communication systems will slow the growth of transportation systems. Improved electronic communication may result in the following changes in urbanization.

Reduced Transportation Systems. The spatial distribution of settlements, especially urban ones, may change to one of new, small, scattered urban settlements. Employment may no longer be connected to a central place, and data banks may be channeled to residences by a new electronic communication system. People could telecommute from their homes, where they would work via closed-circuit television consoles. "The office might cease to exist except as a switchboard and electronic data bank tucked away in any convenient location."[44] Thus advances in the technological development of electronic communication could reduce the use of transportation. Yet, this reduction would occur mainly in business and management as transfer of knowledge and data, as conferences, and as some medical treatment—all of which would not require face-to-face contact—rather than as social interaction. However, videophones and two-way television may help people socialize and may

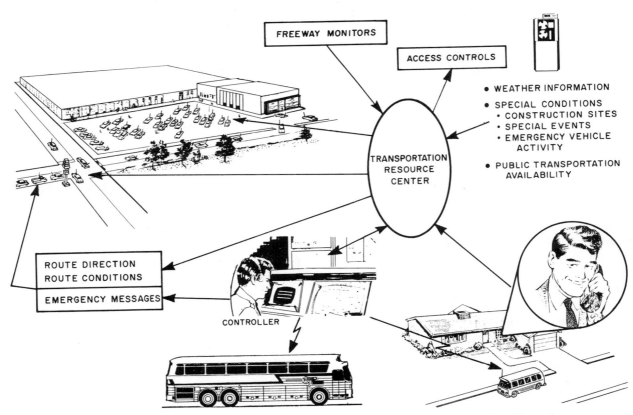

Figure 6.12. Transportation services. (Source: *An Approach to a Total Communications-Electronics System for New Communities.*)

thus partially substitute for transportation. In any case, business and employment trips would still constitute a great number of the total trips made in a community, and their traffic would cause most congestion during rush hours, (See Figure 6.12.)

Conferences of two or more people using electronic communication systems such as videophones or closed-circuit television would save time and money and allow efficient decision making; they would also use less office space. Electronic communications may also reduce or eliminate trips made for information gathering or conferences. If we consider the absence of the telephone in our society, we can imagine the number of trips made each day to fulfill our needs.

Increase in the use of communications, especially electronic ones, may decrease the demand for travel. Although one may argue that electronic communication might generate travel, since a phone conversation could often stimulate the desire for a face-to-face meeting, electronic conferences could also replace such meetings and thus reduce travel. Finally, if electronic communication could substitute for some trips, then new, smaller, less congested urban settlements may be possible in the future, rather than the existing aggregated metropolitan areas.

Decentralization. In the history of human settlements, transportation networks determined the location and aggregation of urban centers. Moreover, improvements in transportation networks have not caused the dispersion of settlements as might be expected, but they have caused overconcentration of urban centers. Improved electronic communication may result in the decentralization of economic and administrative activities, which in turn may affect the development of new land-use patterns by eliminating the need for central offices. Remote branch offices and electronically transferred documents are some of the possibilities that could reduce time-consuming travel and aid effective decision making.

Electronic communication offers the potential for decentralization of office activities which provide most employment in large urban centers. Among many of these centers, office activities depend more on communication than on manufacturing and selling, which rely heavily on transportation facilities. Thus offices might be major potential consumers of new electronic communication devices and act as an effective force in decentralization. Ever since offices have been located in central cities, employers have complained about the lack of parking areas, fear and insecurity of their employees, lack of good workers, noise, pollution, expensive services, high taxation, lim-

ited possibilities for expansion, high rent, and similar conditions.[45] We anticipate that the tendency to move will continue and will be accelerated by the new communications devices.

Improved Social Services. New communications devices, such as one- and two-way video-dial access, may improve social welfare and the political process, health service, governance, safety, and entertainment. Electronic communication is most important as a potential tool for improving education. Since part of the educational process today is the storage of large amounts of precise information in books, microfilms, video- and audiotapes, films, computers, radio, and television, electronic communication may make such information readily available to teachers and students.

The diverse potential uses of electronic communication for education are mostly directed toward the following aspects:

(1) Common education, where different age groups, especially adults, have easy access to resources for education. This would also apply to homebound children who could be "present" in class by two-way closed-circuit television. Moreover, laborers or professionals may be able to join a university-without-walls or televised university without interrupting their work.

(2) Storage and transfer of large quantities of information for education, and the presentation of this information to consumers in a selective manner. The system could provide dial-access arrangements by which students and teachers could call information from central data banks. Recorded videotaped information could be played upon request to many schools at the same time through fixed cables, as Ottawa, Canada, and North Framingham High School in Massachusetts have done in experimental systems.[46]

(3) Release from face-to-face contact between educator and student, and opportunity for a student to select his own learning time; also, provisions for slow children to review information or catch up with the class by means of supplementary materials, and for rapid learners to use supplementary materials.

In a period of pressing need for common and inexpensive education, electronic communication has the potential to meet these needs.

Technology could bring about far more productive use of the teacher's and the student's time. Of particular importance is its capacity to provide instruction that is truely tailored to each individual student; the traditional resources of teacher and textbook are not sufficiently flexible by themselves. Moreover, technology could help educators base instruction more systematically on what is known about learning and communication, not only guiding the basic research, but also providing the strategies for applying research findings. . . . technology's greatest boon could be to make education more democratic. Access to the best teaching and the richest opportunities for learning is inevitably inequitable because of the constraints of economics, geography, or other factors having nothing to do with a student's ability to learn. Through television, film, and other forms of telecommunications, however, the remote rural college and the hard-pressed ghetto school could share the intellectual and esthetic advantages of the best institutions and the richest community resources.[47]

New towns may provide their residents, especially women, with more free time than do established urban centers, and this new free time may be used for adult education. Electronic communication could be an effective tool to meet such demands by means of two-way video and dial-access systems. Educational programs using electronic communication systems could not only be more effective, but could also be less expensive than traditional programs. "A society hurtling into the age of the computer and the satellite can no longer be held back by an educational system which is limping along at the blackboard-and-textbook stage of communication."[48]

One of the major disadvantages in educational programs using electronic communication systems is the lack of personal contact. Retaining the merits of traditional educational programs is desirable, and using both traditional and new programs is ideal. Therefore the value of electronic communication systems should be measured and evaluated by their capacity to increase and improve learning rather than by their technological, innovative achievements.

Health Services. The contributions of electronic communication systems to medical health services could bring about a far-reaching revolution in the distribution and effectiveness of those services in developed as well as developing societies. In an economically or socially depressed rural region, those sophisticated communication tools could improve the infrastructure and the delivery of health services and permit full use of medical resources throughout the new town.

A physician could use electronic communication systems for consultation, counseling, diagnosis, instructions for treatment, checkups, and examination of findings made with such instruments as X rays. Elec-

tronic communication systems could also allow him to hire paraprofessionals related to his service to increase and spread knowledge about health-care needs, and could even help him to contact relatives of patients when necessary.

The new communication system could be especially effective when used in new towns which also function as regional growth centers within areas of widely spread rural communities. Countries with a serious shortage of physicians and health-care staffs, or with an uneven distribution of these professionals between urban and rural settlements, could benefit most from this new system. These countries could save manpower and money and still maintain good health services. Thus, new towns may be an effective tool for introducing electronic communications services to such countries.

Additional opportunities in which electronic communications could be used for health education include two-way video networks for conferences, discussions, giving instructions in emergencies, and instant transmission of information and diagnosis from one place to another. This system could save the lives of people during war as well as in peace time, when time is a critical factor, by relaying diagnoses and treatment to all people involved via two-way video. Some other uses of the system include

(1)   Instant storage and transfer of patients' records.

(2)   Supervision of basic medical care and training for health-care personnel.

(3)   Interviewing patients by computer with automated medical questionnaires in conjunction with their medical records.

(4)   Counseling of patients by psychiatrists over remote distances. This method could even result in patients being more comfortable during these counseling sessions than in face-to-face meetings.[49]

Governance and Management. A new-town government may attempt to offer a democratic way of life in which every resident enjoys and participates equally in community life and has a voice in its development.[50] To do so, local government should increase communication among citizens and the community as a whole, and between governments. Open-channel, two-way video and audio communication could bring new-town governmental meetings to all citizens and allow all of them to participate in decision making. This system may not only increase the sensitivity of citizens to community issues, but it may also accelerate the responsiveness of publicly elected community representatives because they may thus receive criticism continuously.

A two-way video communication system may intensify interaction between citizens and local officials, direct thinking and decision making, create community understanding and, above all, strengthen local identity among citizens. A two-way audiovideo communication system may also enable local new-town officials to explain and provide detailed information on taxation systems, revenues and expenditures, service conditions and instructions, and development and planning issues and phases. This information could be provided in an open communication between citizens and government. Such a system may also deliver high quality, basic daily services to a community efficiently, inexpensively, and conveniently.

Entertainment. Subscribers may entertain themselves through one-way video, dial-access channels from a community resource center, along with information on weather, news, stock conditions, sports results, special events, sales, job opportunities, or shopping services.[51]

New towns offer a chance to incorporate such a community-oriented communications system as an integral part of the total living environment. New communities possess a unique opportunity to establish a 'sense of community' among its previously unacquainted residents. Broadcasts of local government meetings, school and athletic events, schedules of community events, local news programs, religious services, and minority programs perform both an assimilative and entertainment function. With the provision of at least 30 channels, a wide spectrum of community-related programs can be added to the existing offerings of commercial networks to provide the range of programs required to satisfy diverse tastes.[52]

Safety. Electronic communication systems could be used for detection of robbery, burglary, and vandalism, for fire prevention, for detection of gas leaks, for weather alerts, for national emergencies, for reserve calling, and for monitoring traffic intersections. Safety and security alarm systems in homes or on properties connected with a central guard patrol might

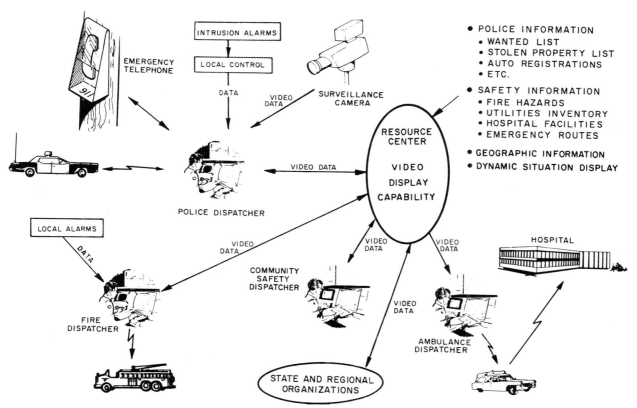

Figure 6.13. Safety and security services. (Source: *An Approach to a Total Communications-Electronics System for New Communities.*)

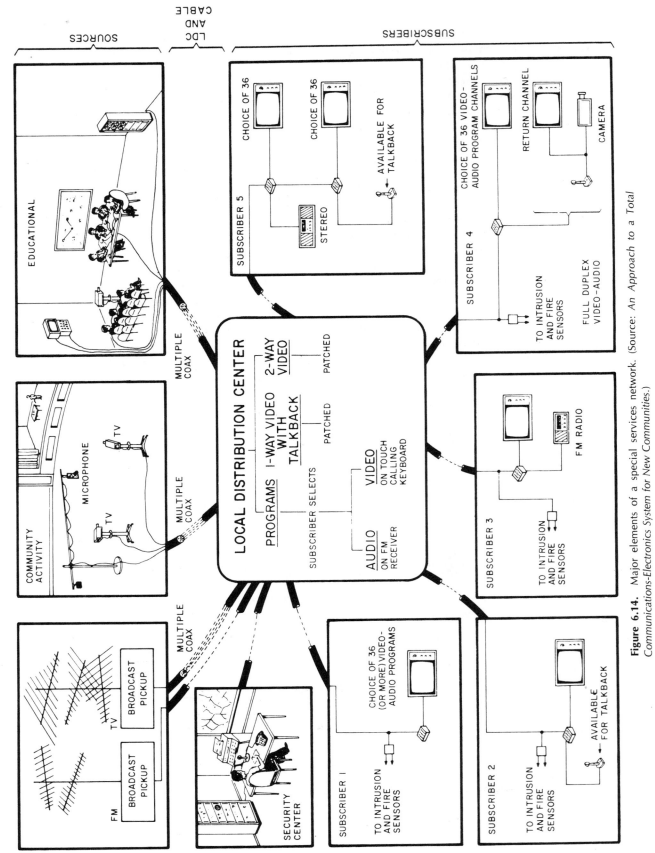

Figure 6.14. Major elements of a special services network. (Source: *An Approach to a Total Communications-Electronics System for New Communities.*)

178

be installed in new towns during their construction; alarms could be connected to cable television to alert authorities. (See Figure 6.13.)

CONCLUSION

Planners should relate transportation goals not only to their technological feasibility and achievement but also to the social goals of a community. Phases of development and achievement should also be equalized among the separate parts of a new town. Failure of new towns to solve some transportation problems is not necessarily the fault of planners, but can sometimes be traced to limitations which restricted them, ways in which plans were implemented, or to financial conditions imposed by governmental policy.

With a controlled and rationally planned land-use pattern a new town provides a good opportunity for the transportation planner. But planners must make local and regional economic base studies in the early stages of development to project land use and make assumptions about transportation.[53] These studies may provide a new-town transportation planner with "realistic information on future land-use patterns."[54] Moreover, because of relatively efficient land-use control in new towns and the expectation of a high degree of resident cooperation, one may assume that changes to improve traffic circulation, such as widening streets, will be welcomed by a new-town population.

In an age of intense mobilization, a person needs to identify with at least a portion of his town. Therefore, neighborhoods where a quiet, open green area separated from traffic movement forms a nucleus of surrounding blocks, and where children can play safely and adults can walk and relax without seeing a car, are necessary. People need to feel loyalty to their immediate residence to achieve the identity their ancestors felt with small towns or villages of the past.

Regardless of our attitude or philosophy toward the effects of modern technology on the future of our society, electronic communication systems will have a strong impact. Such devices could be an effective tool in diminishing barriers among socioeconomic, racial, religious, age and other groups, in establishing good national and international relationships, in bridging geographic distances, and in bringing urban activities to rural areas.[55] Although there may be some doubt about its advantages for future urban settlement or for educational systems, electronic communication offers great advantages for the general advancement of communities. The newly constructed new town and the pioneering, receptive attitude of its young population would support the implementation and success of electronic communication devices more than an established city. (See Figure 6.14.)

Electronic communication may connect a geographically remote area to the activities of a social neighborhood, and could bring more unity to the culturally and linguistically diverse world. Thus proximity would no longer be a basic requirement for neighboring.

With the rapidity of technological change in our environment and the accelerated mechanization accompanying such change, we anticipate that transportation and communication will share a major portion of the innovations that occur. Innovations in transportation relate to energy, types available, and spatial orientation (i.e., vertical and horizontal transportation systems), including

(1) Sidewalks moving at different speeds.

(2) Computer-controlled bus or jitney service.

(3) Air-cushioned tracked vehicles.

(4) Cable-suspended vehicles with central computer control.

(5) Monorail types of network systems.

(6) Electric minibuses driven at a fixed rate.[56]

New towns are ideal laboratories for the development of innovations to meet the challenges of today's motor age with which existing cities can hardly attempt to cope. One innovative transportation program is in Columbia, Maryland:

The recommended transit system would consist of 300 six-passenger vehicles operating automatically on 17 miles of two-way exclusive right-of-way and ten 25-passenger buses operating as a feeder service to the automatic system. A majority of the trip origins and destinations in Columbia would be within a 3-minute walk of one of the 46 stations on the exclusive right-of-way. The system would attract around 17 percent of the trips and is financially feasible.[57]

NOTES

1. Norman A. Abend, "Transportation Inputs in New Town Planning, "Traffic Quarterly, **23,** no. 4 (April 1969), p. 260.

2. Great Britain, Ministry of Transportation, Traffic in Towns: a Study of the Long Term Problems of Traffic in Urban Areas, Buchanan Report (London: Her Majesty's Stationery Office, 1963). Also see the summary report: Great Britain, Ministry of Transportation, Traffic in Towns (Hammondsworth, England: Penguin Books, 1964).

3.   Paul Ritter, *Planning for Man and Motor* (Oxford, England: Pergamon Press, 1964), p. 110.

4.   John Tetlow and Anthony Goss, *Homes, Towns and Traffic* (London: Faber & Faber, 1965), pp. 97–98.

5.   L. Hugh Wilson, *Cumbernauld New Town Traffic Analysis Report* (Cumbernauld, Scotland: Cumbernauld Development Corporation, 1958).

6.   Tetlow and Goss, p. 98.

7.   Robert D. Stevens and George J. Bacalis, "Transportation For a New Town," *Highway Research Record,* no. 367 (1971), pp. 9–16.

8.   Henry K. Evans, "Transportation Planning Criteria for New Towns," *Highway Research Record,* no. 97 (1965), p. 31.

9.   Greater London Council, *The Planning of a New Town: Data and Design Based on a Study for a New Town of 100,000 at Hook, Hampshire* (London: Greater London Council, 1965), p. 78.

10.   Barry Benepe, "Pedestrian in the City," *Traffic Quarterly,* **19,** no. 1 (January 1965), p. 29.

11.   Leo I. Bluestein, "Innovative Communication Systems for New Communities," in *Strategy for New Communities Development in the USA,* Gideon Golany, ed. (Stroudsburg, Pa.: Dowden, Hutchinson and Ross, 1975), p. 234.

12.   L.M. Smith, ed., *An Approach to a Total Communications-Electronics System for New Communities* (Waltham, Mass.: GTE Laboratories, 1971), p. 30.

13.   Smith, p. 30.

14.   Smith, p. 30.

15.   See Wilson.

16.   Greater London Council, p. 81.

17.   Greater London Council, p. 86.

18.   Greater London Council, p. 86. For a different pedestrian system, see Llewelyn-Davies et al., *The Plan for Milton Keynes,* Volume 2 (Milton Keynes, England: Milton Keynes Development Corporation, 1970), pp. 279–300. Also see Peat Marwick Kates and Company, *The Plan for Milton Keynes, Technical Supplement No. 7: Volume 2. Transportation* (Milton Keynes, England: Milton Keynes Development Corporation, no date).

19.   Barry Benepe, pp. 32–34.

20.   James Antoniou, "Planning for Pedestrians," *Traffic Quarterly,* **25,** no. 1 (January 1971), p. 59.

21.   Antoniou, pp. 64–70.

22.   Robert E. Simon, Jr., "The Private Developer and Title VII New Communities," in *Strategy for New Community Development in the United States,* Gideon Golany, ed. (Stroudsburg, Pa.: Dowden, Hutchinson and Ross, 1975), p. 163.

23.   Alan M. Voorhess, "The Transportation System," in *New Towns for America: The Design and Development Process,* James Bailey, ed. (New York: John Wiley and Sons, 1973), p. 77.

24.   Marjorie A. Salley, "Public Transportation and the Needs of New Communities," *Traffic Quarterly,* **26,** no. 1 (January 1972), p. 38.

25.   Ritter, p. 109.

26.   Ritter, p. 109.

27.   Ritter, p. 109.

28.   Tetlow and Goss, p. 100.

29.   Tetlow and Goss, p. 105.

30.   "Transport in New Towns: A Change of Emphasis," *Town and Country Planning,* **35** (1967), pp. 385–86.

31.   Abend, p. 254.

32.   Greater London Council, p. 145.

33.   Peat Marwick Kates and Company, *The Plan for Milton Keynes. Technical Supplement No. 7: Volume 1. Transportation* (Milton Keynes, England: Milton Keynes Development Corporation, 1969), p. 33.

34.   Peat Marwick, vol. 1, p. 34.

35.   Linda Liston, "The Case for the Airport New Town," *Industrial Development* (July/August 1969), pp. 3–9.

36.   Evans, p. 33.

37.   Evans, p. 38.

38.   U.S. Commission on Instructional Technology, *To Improve Learning: A Report to the President and the Congress of the United States* (Washington, D.C.: U.S. Government Printing Office, March 1970), p. 6.

39.   Kas Kalba, "Telecommunications for Future Human Settlements: a Plannnng Framework for Minnesota Experimental City," *Ekistics,* **35,** no. 211 (June 1973), p. 330.

40.   Richard Harkness, *Communication Innovations, Urban Forum and Travel Demand: Some Hypotheses and a Bibliography* (Springfield, Va.: National Technical Information Service, 1972), p. 3.

41.   Bluestein, pp. 235–36.

42.   Smith, p. 42.

43.   Bluestein, p. 230.

44.   Harkness, p. 1.

45.   Leland F. Smith, "Is There a Future?" *Urban Land,* **30,** no. 5 (May 1971), p. 6.

46.   Bluestein, p. 231.

47.   Commission on Instructional Technology, pp. 6–7.

48.   Commission on Instructional Technology, p. 7.

49.   Smith, pp. 14–21.

50.   Bluestein, pp. 235–36.

51.   Smith, pp. 35–37.

52.   Smith, p. 37.

53.   Abend, p. 249.

54.   Abend, p. 250.

55.   Kalba, pp. 329–30.

56.   Robert U. Ayres et al., "Evaluation of New Urban Transportation Systems," *Highway Research Record,* no. 367 (1971), pp. 17–19.

57.   Stevens and Bacalis, p. 9.

SEVEN
THE CONCEPT OF A NEIGHBORHOOD UNIT AND ITS PLANNING

INTRODUCTION

The new-towns planning movement has reacquainted planners with two significant concepts. The first is the provision for a pedestrian pattern totally separated from vehicular networks. The second concept, which most concerns us in this chapter, is that of social and organizational identity in the form of a neighborhood unit. Since its beginning in the ancient cities of the world, the neighborhood unit has been of interest to many different professions concerned with urban life. The continuous degeneration of some elements of today's large cities has once again brought sociologists, planners, decision makers, and others to view the neighborhood unit as one promising solution to degeneration. Social and physical planners in particular have conceived neighborhoods as a combination of the preindustrial pastoral village and a means of fulfilling modern planning necessities. Many developers have misinterpreted the real nature of the neighborhood unit as a residential aggregate designed to provide only housing and some minor services. New-town planners should view the neighborhood as a unit of complex components focused on human needs rather than physical configurations. Many planners and sociologists hope that the neighborhood unit may be the means to retain urban culture and establish a new, positive, urban social climate. This hope stems in part from the fact that residents of planned neighborhoods rate their communities higher than those of less planned areas.[1] Also, the fact that the planning of the post-World War II English new towns was based on and became associated with the neighborhood unit concept is cause for such hope, although recently there have been reservations about the success of the neighborhood in English new towns.[2] (See Figure 7.1.)

In general, planners expect a neighborhood unit to (1) introduce physical order into a chaotic, fragmented urban aggregate; (2) "reintroduce local, face-to-face" contact into "anonymous urban society, thereby helping people to regain some sense of community;" (3) encourage people to form "local loyalties and attachments and thereby offset" personal detachment caused by extensive social and residential mobility; (4) stimulate personal "feelings of identity, security, stability, and rootedness" in a threatening world; and (5) "provide a local training ground for the development. . .of loyalties to city and nation."[3] Similar to an ancient neighborhood, a modern new-town neighborhood may also be based on give-and-take relations, especially among immediate neighbors.

DEFINITION

To understand the concept of what a neighborhood should do, let us begin with a definition of neighborhood: "the area within which residents may all share the common services, social activities and facilities required in the vicinity of the dwelling."[4] However, neighborhoods are not just territories; they function to provide a collective social identity for their residents. Thus a neighborhood is "the people collectively who live in the vicinity . . . the condition of standing in the relation of a neighbor . . . a district considered with reference to a given characteristic,"[5] or it is "local areas that have physical boundaries, social networks, concentrated use of area facilities, and special emo-

Figure 7.1.   Country atmosphere provided in rental housing in Milton Keynes, England. (Courtesy of the Milton Keynes Development Corporation.)

tional and symbolic connotations for their inhabitants. . . ."[6]

One characteristic implicit in these definitions is scale. As such terms as "local" and "in the vicinity" imply, the scale of a neighborhood is that of walking distance rather than driving distance. This scale allows facilities and services needed in daily life to be close enough to link individuals and families within a neighborhood. Most modern planners accept the provision of these distances as a goal for neighborhoods: "it will be on the basis of bringing a larger number of institutions and facilities within walking distance of the home."[7]

The crucial characteristic of a neighborhood, however, is social identity. The overwhelming psychological need to belong, to identify with a group, applies directly to the development of a neighborhood. Many factors contribute to this personal identification. In the past, kinship and family ties provided much of this sense. Proximity, often lacking in large urban centers, is also important. A balance between social homogeneity and social heterogeneity and a continuous age structure in a population are desirable characteristics to foster a personal sense of belonging.

Often what we may call a landmark for identity unifies neighborhood residents. In a neighborhood there may, for example, be a consensus that it is safe, and this belief serves to unite all residents of that neighborhood. There may also be a concrete symbol that unifies a neighborhood. Whether dynamic, such as an image of moral value a community holds in common, or static, such as a monument or a particular service of notable quality, these landmarks create a sense of belonging. This sense results in communal pride, which fosters a sense of identity and community.[8] (See Figure 7.2.)

Actually, it is hard to find within a contemporary urban technological society a neighborhood which embraces all those features and characteristics. Many physical planners tend to view the neighborhood unit merely as a distinct residential entity, since spatial forms are easily implemented and may be immediately perceived.[9] Physical forms support the creation of an image by local people and outsiders, and they leave a distinct impression on both visitors and local residents. Also, physical form may foster local identity and pride. Many sociologists, on the other hand, see the neighborhood unit as a chain of social

Figure 7.2. Restored Tudor cottages on Sun Square, Hemel Hempstead, England. (Courtesy of the Commission for the New Towns.)

systems designed to improve the quality of society within a harmonious and balanced community and to tie residents together physically and socially.

In our previous definition and in the following parts of this chapter we conceive the neighborhood as a unit in which all factors including physical boundaries, society, utilities and services, transportation networks, government, and others contribute to the formation of the whole unit, and in which the absence of one or more factors detracts from its quality.

HISTORICAL DEVELOPMENT

The idea of the neighborhood is not new; the first records we have are of the early Mesopotamian villages where nomadic tribes established either temporary or permanent settlements. These tribes contained the essential characteristics of a neighborhood, and when they settled together the subgroups which had been formed earlier were already arranged in a close physical setting within the total communal arrangement. It is important to note that the nomadic community first organized society, and only later did it

settle in a definite area and arrange itself physically. (See Figures 7.3 and 7.4.)

The development of the neighborhood system within the early village depended on two important characteristics of tribal society: communal sharing and blood relations. Since it was to the economic advantage of the people to share the means of cultivation, mainly equipment and livestock, communal housing was also erected. However, there is a size, depending on the culture and behavior of a people, beyond which the communal system breaks down: the number of people, amount of land, equipment, and livestock become too unwieldy to function communally. Therefore the larger the village community, the greater the possibility of having the total community divided into economic groups. These groups keep the communal setting intact and functioning. Blood relations defined the smallest social unit of a tribe: the biological family of man, wife, and children. This unit was in turn related by blood to other units of a tribe or clan. Of all loyalties, including religious and economic relationships, blood relations have traditionally been the strongest.

Based on tribal or clan relations, neighborhoods

came into existence to strengthen individual relationships with a society and to provide a definite culture. A neighborhood was an expression of communal desire and thus reflected the need of each person to identify himself with a subgroup or subunit of a total community where he built, together with others, his private image of his immediate community and his general identity with his community as a whole. In this way, physical proximity manifested a definite psychological desire. Thus we see in the early village the origin of the neighborhood. ''Before the city came into existence, the village had brought forth the neighbor: he who lives near at hand, within calling distance, sharing the crises of life, watching over the dying, weeping sympathetically for the dead, rejoicing at a marriage feast or a childbirth.''[10]

Early cities also possessed neighborhoods; however, they were modified to meet urban economic needs. The motive for forming a neighborhood changed as cities introduced an economic system new to the history of human settlements: amalgams of people drawn together by common economic interests. Despite the adjustments of the neighborhood to meet the emergence of an urban economic system, there is a basic distinction between the values of a city and a village and the motives for forming each. Villages originated primarily because of common social interests and needs; cities were organized primarily because of individual economic interests and needs.

With the economic motive in settling, a variety of socioeconomic classes and a mixture of sociophysical arrangements were introduced that were alien to the communal village. Thus with the change from village to city, we see a change not only in physical arrangement and social composition but also in social values, and we face the problems so familiar to twentieth-

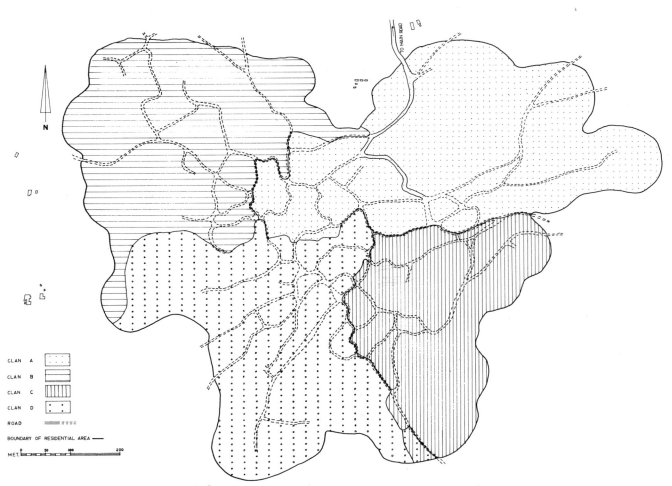

Figure 7.3. Kinship neighborhoods in a traditional Israeli village, 1963. Homogeneous clans settled in four distinct territories to establish an ancient heterogeneous village which still exists today.

Figure 7.4. Territorial and kinship neighborhood segregation in a traditional Israeli village in transition. (Numbers 1 to 11 are the old segregated neighborhoods and 12's are new mixed neighborhoods.)

century urban man: "What we call morality began in the mores, the life-conserving customs, of the village. When these primary bonds dissolve, when the intimate visible community ceases to be a watchful, identifiable, deeply concerned group, then the 'We' becomes a buzzing swarm of 'I's', and secondary ties and allegiances become too feeble to halt the disintegration of the urban community."[11]

The classic planned cities of the Greeks contrast sharply with ancient unplanned cities. These first planned cities, developed about the fifth century B.C., combined social and political identity in the concept of the city-state. It was based on establishing a quota for the population of a city. No one could live in a given city unless he had been born there or was accepted by its council or citizens. This established social identity. The citizens of a city-state elected their own governmental officials; they minted their own coins and made their own calendars; they established their own foreign policy independent of the cities adjacent to them. Socially, the city-state was a new version of the Mesopotamian neighborhood, except that its social structure was planned.

The neighborhood of medieval cities also contri-

buted its social characteristics to the concept of neighborhoods. In this neighborhood different socioeconomic groups lived together: the master, the laborer, and the craftsman. Further, craft guilds, which grouped people according to religious or economic agreements, developed during this period.

Physically, the medieval city combined elements of the ancient Mesopotamian cities and the grid system of the Greeks and the Romans. The streets of these cities were winding and narrow, providing protection from inclement weather and encouraging social interaction among residents. However, such cities were organized into a series of quarters each of which possessed its own character. The physical closeness of individual residential units resulted in unplanned social integration. A city consisted of several self-contained quarters formed on the basis of occupational or religious identity.

During the Renaissance, the idea of all socioeconomic groups living together was discarded. Middle- and upper-class people, wishing to establish their own identity, moved outside the medieval city walls; the low-income populace remained inside. This was the beginning of segregation based on income and

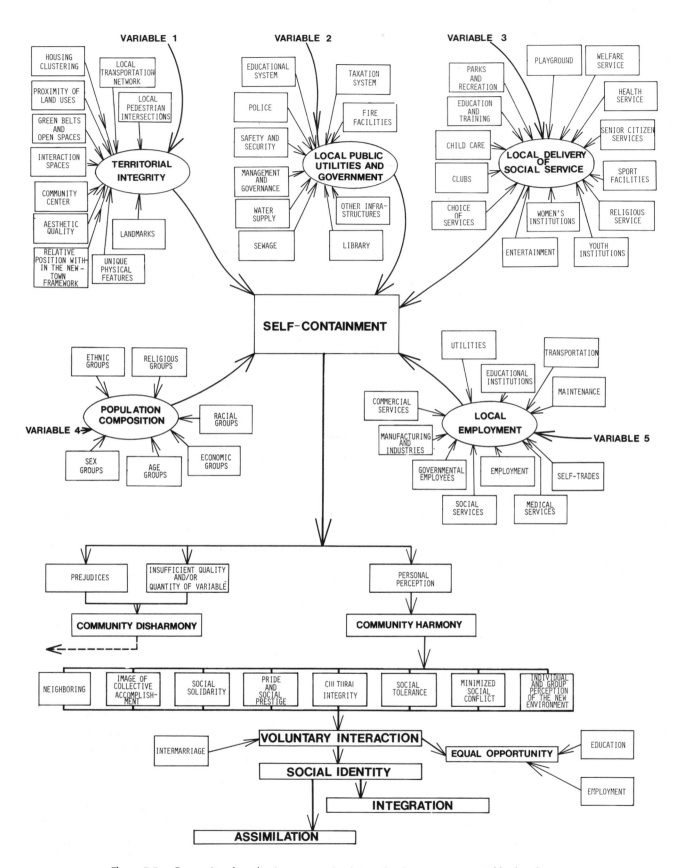

Figure 7.5. Composite of mechanisms supporting integration in a new-town neighborhood.

the foundation for today's middle- and upper-class neighborhoods.

The Industrial Revolution introduced rail and, later, automobile traffic which supported a population shift from rural to urban centers. This movement created slums along vehicular routes into the city and around its boundaries. As streets became more important than neighborhoods, the establishment of these neighborhoods resulted in a population classed by income as the railroad and automobile split the city into sections. Although earlier most people had lived within walking distance of work, the rapid expansion of cities increased the influence of transportation.

The twentieth century has seen a revival of interest in the neighborhood. Even in the early decades of this century, many scholars regarded the social issue as the important one, and "Cooley, Park, Woods and Ward may be fairly regarded as setting the sociological framework within which Perry's delineation of the neighborhood unit took place. . . ."[12] Clarence Perry, the formulator of the neighborhood concept in the United States, defined six fundamental physical planning principles: schools, boundaries, open spaces, institutional buildings, retail districts, and the internal street layout.[13] Perry's main goal in the neighborhood was to produce social interaction, and the physical layout was a means to this end.

The English post-World War II new towns have applied neighborhood planning concepts which have centered around community buildings, schools, shopping centers, open space for interaction, and the use of wide, green open spaces as boundaries. The

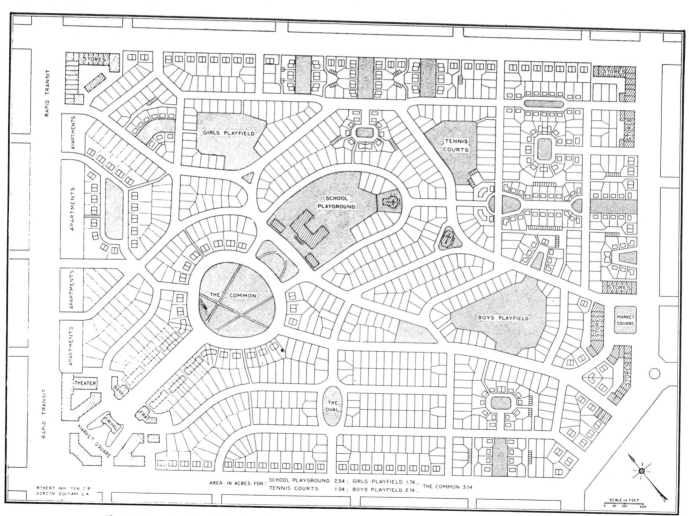

Figure 7.6. Perry's neighborhood unit. (Source: *Neighborhood and Community Planning*, Regional Survey, Volume 7.)

English New Towns Commission considered the neighborhood as an identifiable unit: "New Towns were to be constructed on a 'neighborhood' basis, with services which would make each area relatively self-contained for day to day needs, even more important would be the attainment of local or neighborhood balance."[14] (See Figure 7.5.)

In the early 1950s, however, neighborhoods did not stress their social benefits. As a result of this failure, a debate arose late in the 1960s concerning the validity of the British new-town neighborhoods. In 1954 Lewis Mumford predicted this debate when he commented that the idea had been accepted in principle but not in actual practice.[15] Perry's neighborhood concept and that presented by the Dudley Report[16] in 1944 differed in three major elements: location of shopping centers, location of open spaces, and neighborhood size in relation to school size.[17] (See Figure 7.6.)

Despite some rejection of the neighborhood structure developed in Britain in the fifties and sixties, such as in Milton Keynes and Telford, planners retained three basic ideas of the neighborhood concept. These were (1) size, as related to school catchment area, walking distances, and service considerations; (2) location of facilities to serve overlapping residential catchment areas (e.g., Milton Keynes), to replace the centralized services of the neighborhood, and to form a flexible rather than rigid structure; and (3) a city layout which favors subdivision of large units into smaller ones.[18] The neighborhood unit has undergone many changes in physical form, but the impetus behind it remains the same: to provide a setting where people not only can live comfortably but also can socialize and find an identity within a defined community.

Some contemporary neighborhoods, like those in the United States, are segregated by common income (low, middle, or high), by ethnic identity (Italian, Irish, Puerto Rican, etc.), or by race (black, yellow, or white). Contemporary planned neighborhoods attempt to break down this segregation and to establish diverse social, economic, ethnic, or racial groups in the same area. In keeping with this social goal, the ideal new-town neighborhood houses a cross section of these groups. In practice, we cannot expect that every neighborhood unit will be able to overcome the real-life obstacles which stand in the way of reaching this goal. However, if integration is adopted as a goal, a neighborhood may function as an experimental meeting ground. In this way a new-town neighborhood may contribute to meeting national or regional goals that require the acceptance and support of many deci-

sion makers. Thus such a goal may greatly affect the overall plan of a new town and its neighborhoods.

MODERN PLANNED NEIGHBORHOOD UNITS

From a discussion of the history of the neighborhood concept, we can infer several important characteristics relevant to modern neighborhoods. Since no one characteristic defines a meaningful neighborhood, combinations of these characteristics are essential. The first and most important characteristic is a personal sense of communal unity and identity that allows a person to find his place and define his role in his community. This characteristic is the result of creating a community organized around social activities: the greater the social sense, the greater the sense of unity and identity. Sharing systems and neighboring are two important means of promoting unity and identity; a local, effective, political power structure is another. Identification with and responsibility toward a community are encouraged when residents govern themselves. Conversely, a sense of identity and responsibility may lead to a desire for self-government. The more residents determine a course of action for issues of their own immediate concern, the more responsible and effective they feel. A fourth factor in promoting unity and identity is the provision of services which enables a neighborhood to be relatively self-contained and thus reinforces a feeling of social identity. With the inclusion of services, a neighborhood ceases to function only as an aggregate of housing—a dormitory; it now meets the routine daily needs of its residents. These services should include public utilities, cultural amenities (for all ages and both sexes, and for all cultural, religious, and ethnic groups), educational and training facilities, and recreational opportunities. Residents may attain a great sense of community if these services are provided by the local government. The new town would then provide only those services that neighborhoods could not provide.

To produce these desirable characteristics, a neighborhood must be effectively and efficiently designed and include the walking-distance scale it needs. Thus any nonresidential buildings designed to be used by a community should be located to be accessible by foot to all residents of the community. As was mentioned in Chapter 6, this walking communication pattern should be separated from the vehicular network. The design should separate the neighborhood from nuisances such as noise pollution and undesirable climatic effects. Since the visual impression of a neighborhood is

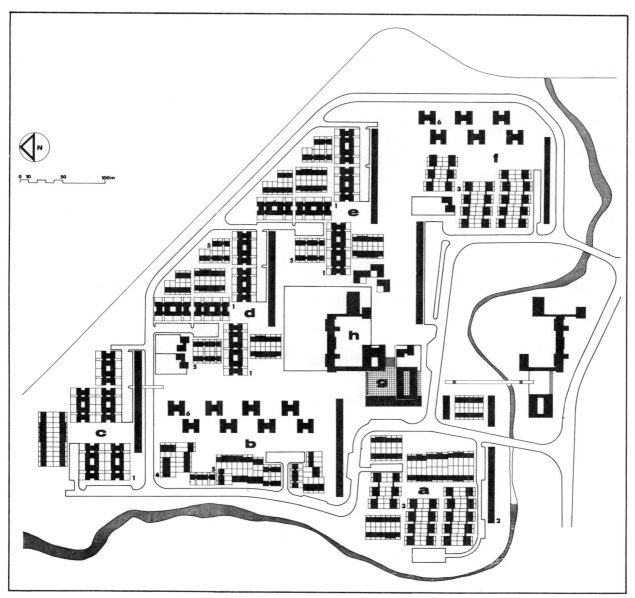

Figure 7.7. Layout of an experimental neighborhood in Qiryat Gat, Israel. Each of the six subneighborhoods houses between 175 and 200 families and surrounds a central open space. These open spaces are connected through a pedestrian network. (Source: *Israel Builds.*)

also an important part of its design, it needs a concrete focal point—a visual landmark to encourage personal identity and local pride. Perhaps, too, because of the small scale of a neighborhood, the visual impression of the natural environment is very great, and a designer should integrate it into the plan of residential areas. (See Figure 7.7.)

Social Integrity

Regardless of the population of a neighborhood, its main goal should be to establish social identity and unity. Other than using and/or recognizing the practical advantages of living in a planned neighborhood, there should be a basic feeling of personal or family

Figure 7.8. Residential neighborhoods in Shannon, Ireland. (Courtesy of Shannon Free Airport Development.)

satisfaction among its residents. "Even if people have only casual relations with neighbors, even if they do not have a clear sense of the boundaries of an area, nor make concentrated or exclusive use of local facilities and services, they may have a special feeling for a given place, a special sort of pride in living there, a sense of attachment transcending physical inconvenience or social undesirability."[19] The quality of its society and of services offered, rather than merely its physical configuration, contribute most to a neighborhood's reputation.

The "urban neighborhood should be regarded both as a unit of a larger whole and as a distinct entity in itself. . . . There are certain other facilities, functions or aspects which are strictly local and peculiar to a well-arranged residential community."[20] The characteristics of society and population, rather than planned physical forms, give a residential agglomeration the self-identity of a neighborhood. (See Figure 7.8.)

Unplanned neighborhoods illustrate the validity of this theory. "Even in the undifferentiated rectangular plan of Manhattan, a plan contrived as if for the purpose of preventing neighborhoods from coming into

existence, distinctive entities, like Yorkville, Chelsea, and Greenwich Village, nevertheless have developed, though they lack any architectural character, except that conditioned by the successive dates of their building."[21] An ideal neighborhood possesses this intangible identity and unity, and its residents have a sense of belonging, of being a part of an identifiable community.

Sharing Systems

Sharing systems within a neighborhood help most in establishing its unity. Unlike the ancient neighborhood based on common origins, a modern neighborhood should be founded on the basis of sharing. Further, the degree to which a neighborhood shares may be the strongest single factor that defines a contemporary urban section as a neighborhood. The first level of sharing is that of common residences. In many cultures, residential sharing associated with proximity and social affinity (see Chapter 4), whether vertical or horizontal, increases this degree of sharing and thus strengthens residents' identification with their neighborhood. Second, the sharing of services contributes to a high degree of distinct neighborhood identity. Services may be daily, occasional, or seasonal, such as schools and other educational centers, playgrounds, parks, sports, and health centers, clinics, shopping and community centers, or other essential facilities. The diversity of services, their accessibility and proximity to neighbors, and their quality and quantity are strong forces in establishing and retaining the identity of a neighborhood. A third sharing element is the degree to which local residents are concerned with happenings in the community and are willing to defend the collective interests of their area, whether it be services, environment, or social quality. The degree to which citizens participate in community life and its accomplishments and share the responsibility of operating neighborhood machinery contributes in decision making and, thus, in forming a neighborhood with a strong identity. The fourth area of common sharing is in self-operated neighborhood services. Residential services offered primarily by outsiders rather than by local residents limit an area's identity and diminish residents' attachment to their area.

Since sharing brings people together, it is the basic element of a neighborhood on which new-town planners should focus. Their consideration of the degree of sharing is essential to avoid relying on superficial physical forms as the only means of creating identity in a neighborhood. Many developers and some planners fail to understand this issue in determining the meaning of neighborhood identity. A combination of the four elements mentioned here seems to be a basic requirement for neighborhood planning and development. The degree to which sharing in all forms is accomplished will determine to what extent the residents of a neighborhood have a sense of belonging.

In addition, a major motive for establishing neighborhood units is the decentralization of services and the reduction of transportation needs in a new town. However, low-income families, more than middle- or high-income groups, tend to prefer services close to their homes; this also applies to the elderly, children, housewives, and immobilized people.[22] It is efficient for a large city as well as a new town to distribute (hierarchically or otherwise) the delivery of services among residential areas to coincide with sharing in neighborhoods. To strengthen its unity, neighborhood services may be offered only or mainly to local residents. If a neighborhood tax-base system and government are to be adopted (interrelated and complemented to the entire new-town tax base), then local

services such as education or leisure may charge outsiders a higher fee than local residents.

It is the human network which should be emphasized in the modern neighborhood to make it a neighboring system. "The sociological conception of neighborhood emphasizes the notion of shared activities, experiences, and values, common loyalties and perspectives, and human networks that give to an area a sense of continuity and persistence over time."[23] In the existing wilderness of a large urban agglomeration, neighborhoods may be blessed new societies. In this sense, reintroducing and re-experimenting with this concept is desirable for both new and established cities. When a sharing system is established within a new-town neighborhood, it may foster a sense of continuity in the community which will tie the people to their future expectations of the area. When it is used by all residents, sharing should deepen and strengthen communal ties. In this sense, at least, a neighborhood may create the pastoral society of rural communities and reroot it within an urban environment.

Neighboring

We anticipate that established neighboring relations may develop over a long period from exchanging, borrowing, assisting, gossiping and exchanging information into intimate friendships. Thus neighboring may be a limited relation which is a reliable source of socializing for children and housewives, and a relation which precedes friendship.[24] On the other hand, the self-reliance of a neighborhood may weaken the mutual need of neighbors for borrowing and exchanging although it may not change socializing patterns. Neighboring has its own norms and regulations dictated by various cultural, physical, or even climatic conditions. In some countries (e.g., the United States) residents may establish contact with new neighbors by presenting a homemade cake; in others (e.g., Israel) they may offer bread and salt to express peace. In the early stages of moving to new towns, new neighbors raising young children have mixed feelings of curiosity, uncertainty, and some anxiety, especially concerning their children's socialization. "The role of the neighbor fits into a network of social roles and its explicitness depends on the nature of the social organization, including the density of settlements, the distance between dwelling units, the economic well-being of the inhabitants, the degree of co-operation demanded or permitted among residents, and the general trust placed by individuals in nonrelatives."[25]

Neighbors in a new town may replace absent relatives and may thus intensify neighboring. Thus we can assume that neighboring in a new-town neighborhood or its subunit may become more effective than it is in a large city that has lost much of its neighborhood character; exceptions to this assumption are the ethnic, racial, or religious groups who migrated (nearly collectively) to large cities. Centrality of services and institutions and, to some extent, mass media and mass transportation associated with modern society are factors that have weakened neighboring and the neighborhood unit. Since newcomers to a new town may wish to intensify their neighboring to replace the loss of old neighbors and social environment and also because they see neighboring as a means of interacting with local society, they are generally not selective in their early neighboring. It is also more likely that neighboring may grow into friendships among new-town newcomers if the neighbors are of a homogeneous group. Further, proximity in residential units may produce much socializing among children, housewives, and elderly, relatively nonmobile people, and among people who do not own cars, cannot afford them, or are not physically able to take public transportation.

The neighborhood, however, was never meant to be the exclusive provider of friendship and friends. In new towns, such opportunities are provided by the various new-town institutions outside neighborhoods. They are not social enclaves and are not meant to be the only opportunity for social intercourse for a population.

Governance

Recently there has been an increasing interest among residents of large cities to establish and retain an organization that can exercise local control over matters of common interest to their community.[26] In the United States the extensive annexation of small towns by large cities, and their resulting political control, has worked against communal identity and self-government and has diminished the political identity of neighborhoods.

One advantage of establishing neighborhood governments within a new town is reducing the risk that a centralized power will develop an absolute government, as has happened in established cities. This balancing of political power between neighborhood governments and a central government may encourage citizen participation, promote local leadership, and improve relations and contacts between voters

and elected officials. Local government for a neighborhood does not mean separation from a central new-town government. Laws and regulations of both bodies should be complementary rather than contradictory. Neighborhood power is chartered by a central government, which is formed jointly with all neighborhood representatives. A central government may be a federated power, and the neighborhood government should be the communal responsibility of all citizens. (See Chapter 9.)

Self-Containment

New towns and their neighborhoods require self-containment for sound social composition. Ideally, in both, one's work is near one's residence. Some planners view neighborhood self-containment as a concept that has been extended to the new town. In the neighborhood, as in the new town, however, "self-containment is not an end in itself,"[27] and planners view the neighborhood as an entity that provides job opportunities for its residents together with daily shopping and social facilities. The difference between the self-containment levels of the neighborhood is a matter of degree and also exists between the new town and the established large city.

A primary neighborhood goal is to provide maximum possible daily services within a short distance from its residents. This does not mean, however, that a unit should be self-contained and self-sufficient in all services, since even a new town may not be able to reach such independence alone. The decentralization of new-town services among its neighborhoods may not only ease family life within a neighborhood but should also decrease the number of trips taken to the new-town center and thus indirectly solve some traffic problems. "Neighborhood unit organization seems the only practical answer to the giantism and inefficiency of the over-centralized metropolis."[28] If the neighborhood unit within a new town provides most daily facilities for all age groups, its effect on the younger generation and on family life as a whole may be beneficial.

If self-sufficiency in providing services for a new town is desirable and the neighborhood concept is accepted, some services will be duplicated between the neighborhoods and the town center while others may be distributed in hierarchies (of size and function) between the two. In any case, neighborhood development should not diminish the social, economic, and administrative roles of the new-town center. A neighborhood shopping center will not, however, provide for all local needs since this would require a larger number of consumers to justify its position economically than is compatible with the neighborhood concept. Thus a new-town center should provide a larger variety of services than a neighborhood. The balancing of the relation between the new-town center and neighborhoods is one of the prime issues facing new-town planners the resolution of which will require the efforts of the entire planning team. The distribution pattern of educational and health-care services may be a key to this problem.

Although self-containment is suggested here for the neighborhood unit to provide daily, local, immediate services and facilities, it is not the purpose of a neighborhood to be an impractical, totally independent island within its urban surroundings. Instead, the planner should design a neighborhood as an integral coherent segment of the overall new town linked to the new-town tax system, public utilities, services, and especially to its government. Despite its described comprehensive self-containment and self-identity, a total new-town community will be able to use and enjoy those services and amenities provided by any neighborhood unit. A relatively self-contained balanced neighborhood that offers employment opportunities and delivers daily social services is an essential contributor to the formulation of a sound economic base for its new town. It is also clear that friend and family cross-neighborhood relations will form and establish interneighborhood socializing.

PLANNING PROCESS

In planning a neighborhood, as in designing an entire new town, there are complex factors for planners to consider. Since the scale of a neighborhood compared with that of new towns is large, planning details are important. Here again the comprehensive work of an interdisciplinary team is essential, but the major roles will be those of a social planner, an urban designer, and an architect. This team must consider the following major issues: social composition, site selection, criteria for planning design, and determination of optimal size of the neighborhood unit.

Optimal Size of a Neighborhood

Implicit in the preceding discussion of the neighborhood concept is that to maintain proximity, a sense of identity, and necessary services, there must be a limit

to the physical size and population density of a neighborhood so that the unit will not lose its social interaction and unity while providing effective services. "As with the city itself, the main thing to recognize in neighborhood units is that there is an upper limit of growth and extension; and that, to define the unit and keep it in form, there must be both a civic nucleus to draw people together and an outer boundary to give them the sense of belonging together."[29] This issue of size has become a cornerstone of planning which has a direct effect on density, land-use patterns, degrees of services and utilities, self-sufficiency, and governmental patterns. The neighborhood unit should be large enough to support necessary daily local services, especially schools, yet small enough to produce local neighboring and community identity.

As we noted earlier, the scale which provides the easiest means of interaction is walking distance. This means that the average, middle-aged resident should be able to walk comfortably between the boundaries of a neighborhood. Another way of examining the issue is to ask: What is the optimal distance between a residence located at the periphery of the neighborhood and its geographic center where services are located? There is a variety of opinion on the subject, but ½ to ¾ mile is generally considered the most desirable distance. This would set the diameter of a neighborhood at about 1 mile and its optimal physical size at less than 1 square mile or 640 acres. Beyond that size, we must assume that residents either have to develop a habit of walking or rely on a vehicle for social communication and services. Table 7.1 depicts a model of the quantitative sequences when alternative maximum walking distances are considered.

However, since optimal physical size also depends on the population density one must consider preferences for both density and distance in setting maximum limits. As the Table shows, the optimal distance of 1 mile provides a reasonable population size in the low-density portion of the model, while the optimal distance of ¾ mile provides almost the same total population in the high-density portion. Thus, for nearly the same population (5000 to 6000) the preference would be for a short distance with high density or a relatively long distance with low density.

Since it is a basic, essential community service planners should use the school as a fundamental requirement and point of departure for basic size calculations. "The school building may offer the focal point around which many common interests of families may be organized with minimum need for special physical facilities."[30] We will focus our discussion on the elementary school because many planners believe

TABLE 7.1 QUANTITATIVE ALTERNATIVE NEIGHBORHOOD SIZES RELATED TO DIMENSIONS OF A DESIGNATED AREA AND PROXIMITY

Alternative	Total Population	Total Number of Families*	Alternative Gross Density Per Acre — Families	Alternative Gross Density Per Acre — Persons	Total Area Needed — In Acres	Total Area Needed — In Sq. Miles**	Total Number of Employees — Avg. of 1.0 Persons	Avg. of 1.5 Persons	Avg. of 2.0 Persons	Radius of Area Required in Miles
I	2,500	675.6	3	11.1	225.2	.352	675	1013.4	1351.2	.112
			4	14.8	168.9	.264				.084
			5	18.5	135.1	.211				.067
			6	22.2	112.6	.176				.056
			7	25.9	96.5	.151				.048
			8	29.6	84.5	.132				.042
			9	33.3	75.0	.117				.037
			10	37.0	67.6	.106				.034
			11	40.7	61.4	.096				.031
			12	44.4	56.8	.089				.028
II	3,000	810.81	3	11.1	270.3	.422	810	1,216	1621.5	.134
			4	14.8	202.7	.317				.101
			5	18.5	162.2	.253				.081
			6	22.2	135.1	.211				.067
			7	25.9	115.8	.181				.058
			8	29.6	101.4	.158				.050
			9	33.3	90.1	.141				.045
			10	37.0	81.1	.127				.040
			11	40.7	73.7	.115				.037
			12	44.4	67.6	.106				.034
III	3,500	945.9	3	11.1	315.3	.493	946	1,419	1,892	.157
			4	14.8	236.5	.370				.118
			5	18.5	189.2	.296				.094
			6	22.2	157.7	.246				.078
			7	25.9	135.1	.211				.067
			8	29.6	118.2	.185				.059
			9	33.3	105.1	.164				.052
			10	37.0	94.6	.148				.047
			11	40.7	86.0	.134				.043
			12	44.4	78.8	.123				.039
IV	4,000	1081.08	3	11.1	360.4	.563	1,081	1621.6	2,162	.179
			4	14.8	270.3	.422				.134
			5	18.5	216.2	.338				.108
			6	22.2	180.2	.282				.090
			7	25.9	154.4	.241				.077
			8	29.6	135.1	.211				.067
			9	33.3	120.1	.188				.060
			10	37.0	108.1	.169				.054
			11	40.7	98.3	.154				.049
			12	44.4	90.1	.141				.045

Alternative	Total Population	Total Number of Families*	Alternative Gross Density Per Acre — Families	Alternative Gross Density Per Acre — Persons	Total Area Needed — In Acres	Total Area Needed — In Sq. Miles**	Total Number of Employees — Avg. of 1.0 Persons	Avg. of 1.5 Persons	Avg. of 2.0 Persons	Radius of Area Required in Miles
IX	6,500	1756.7	3	11.1	585.6	.914	1,756	2,635	3,513	.291
			4	14.8	439.2	.685				.218
			5	18.5	351.4	.548				.174
			6	22.2	292.8	.457				.145
			7	25.9	251.0	.392				.125
			8	29.6	219.6	.343				.109
			9	33.3	195.2	.305				.097
			10	37.0	175.7	.274				.087
			11	40.7	159.7	.249				.079
			12	44.4	146.4	.228				.073
X	7,000	1891.8	3	11.1	630.6	.984	1,891	2,837	3,783	.313
			4	14.8	472.9	.738				.235
			5	18.5	378.4	.590				.188
			6	22.2	315.3	.492				.156
			7	25.9	270.3	.422				.134
			8	29.6	236.5	.369				.117
			9	33.3	210.2	.328				.104
			10	37.0	189.2	.295				.094
			11	40.7	172.0	.268				.085
			12	44.4	157.7	.246				.078
XI	7,500	2027.0	3	11.1	675.7	1.056	2,027	3,040	4,054	.34
			4	14.8	506.8	.792				.25
			5	18.5	405.4	.633				.20
			6	22.2	337.8	.528				.17
			7	25.9	289.6	.452				.14
			8	29.6	253.4	.396				.13
			9	33.3	225.2	.352				.11
			10	37.0	202.7	.317				.10
			11	40.7	184.3	.288				.09
			12	44.4	168.9	.264				.08
XII	8,000	2162.2	3	11.1	720.7	1.126	2,162	3,243	4,324	.36
			4	14.8	540.5	.845				.27
			5	18.5	432.4	.676				.22
			6	22.2	360.4	.563				.18
			7	25.9	308.9	.483				.15
			8	29.6	270.3	.422				.13
			9	33.3	240.2	.375				.12
			10	37.0	216.2	.338				.11
			11	40.7	196.6	.307				.10
			12	44.4	180.0	.281				.09

Left group

Section V — 4,500 — 1216.21

Index	Density	Value	Value	Decimal
3	11.1	405.4	.633	.202
4	14.8	304.1	.475	.151
5	18.5	243.2	.380	.121
6	22.2	202.7	.317	.101
7	25.9	173.7	.271	.086
8	29.6	152.0	.238	.076
9	33.3	135.1	.211	.067
10	37.0	121.6	.190	.061
11	40.7	110.6	.173	.055
12	44.4	101.4	.158	.050

1,216 — 1,824 — 2,432

Section VI — 5,000 — 1351.4

Index	Density	Value	Value	Decimal
3	11.1	450.5	.704	.224
4	14.8	337.8	.528	.168
5	18.6	270.3	.422	.134
6	22.2	225.2	.352	.112
7	25.9	193.1	.302	.096
8	29.6	168.9	.264	.084
9	33.3	150.2	.235	.075
10	37.0	135.1	.211	.067
11	40.7	122.9	.192	.061
12	44.4	112.6	.176	.057

1,351 — 2,027 — 2,702

Section VII — 5,500 — 1486.5

Index	Density	Value	Value	Decimal
3	11.1	495.5	.774	.246
4	14.8	371.6	.581	.185
5	18.5	297.3	.465	.148
6	22.2	247.7	.387	.123
7	25.9	212.4	.332	.106
8	29.6	185.8	.290	.092
9	33.3	165.2	.258	.082
10	37.0	148.6	.232	.074
11	40.7	135.1	.211	.067
12	44.4	123.8	.193	.061

Section VIII — 6,000 — 1621.6

Index	Density	Value	Value	Decimal
3	11.1	540.5	.843	.268
4	14.8	405.4	.632	.201
5	18.5	324.3	.506	.161
6	22.2	270.3	.422	.134
7	25.9	231.7	.361	.115
8	29.6	202.7	.316	.100
9	33.3	180.2	.281	.089
10	37.0	162.2	.253	.080
11	40.7	147.4	.230	.073
12	44.4	135.1	.210	.067

1,621 — 2,432 — 3,243

Right group

Section XIII — 8,500 — 2297.3

Index	Density	Value	Value	Decimal
3	11.1	765.8	1.190	.378
4	14.8	574.3	.896	.285
5	18.5	459.5	.717	.228
6	22.2	382.9	.597	.190
7	25.9	328.1	.512	.163
8	29.6	287.2	.448	.142
9	33.3	255.3	.398	.126
10	37.0	229.7	.358	.114
11	40.7	208.8	.326	.104
12	44.4	191.4	.298	.095

2,297 — 3,445 — 4,594

Section XIV — 9,000 — 2432.4

Index	Density	Value	Value	Decimal
3	11.1	810.8	1.260	.401
4	14.8	608.1	.949	.302
5	18.5	486.5	.759	.241
6	22.2	405.4	.632	.201
7	25.9	347.5	.542	.172
8	29.6	304.1	.474	.151
9	33.3	270.2	.422	.134
10	37.0	243.2	.379	.121
11	40.7	221.1	.345	.109
12	44.4	202.7	.316	.100

2,432 — 3,648 — 4,865

Section XV — 9,500 — 2567.6

Index	Density	Value	Value	Decimal
3	11.1	855.9	1.340	.426
4	14.8	641.9	1.000	.318
5	18.5	513.5	.801	.255
6	22.2	427.9	.668	.212
7	25.9	366.8	.572	.182
8	29.6	320.9	.501	.159
9	33.3	285.3	.445	.142
10	37.0	256.8	.401	.128
11	40.7	233.4	.364	.116
12	44.4	214.0	.334	.106

2,567 — 3,851 — 5,135

Section XVI — 10,000 — 2702.7

Index	Density	Value	Value	Decimal
3	11.1	900.9	1.401	.446
4	14.8	675.7	1.054	.335
5	18.5	540.5	.843	.268
6	22.2	450.5	.703	.223
7	25.9	386.1	.602	.191
8	29.6	337.8	.526	.167
9	33.3	300.3	.468	.149
10	37.0	270.3	.421	.133
11	40.7	245.7	.383	.121
12	44.4	225.2	.351	.112

2,702 — 4,053 — 5,404

* Assumes 3.7 people per family
** 640 acres = 1 square mile

195

that a high school may easily be a joint effort between two or more neighborhoods. "Educational authorities . . . point out that a school district needs a minimum of 1000 school-age children to adequately sustain a four-year high school with 300 students. Support of such a school requires a community of more than 3500 people, assuming approximately one pupil per family."[31]

Some planners believe that the population of a neighborhood needed to support the basic facility of a school will be around 5000. Others think a neighborhood may function with a maximum population of 10,000.[32] Generally, then, a population of 7000 seems most desirable.

The neighborhood unit should at least be large enough to justify the establishment of a well-developed local elementary school. Since the size of an elementary school will vary among geographic areas and from one time to another, the size of the neighborhood unit will differ according to the place and time in which it is planned. The basic concept here is that young adults with small children constitute a large percentage of the population, consume many services, and require an environment based on the proximity of various land uses within a walking distance of one-half mile.

These two variables, walking distance and school size, may dictate the size of a neighborhood unit. They may then, indirectly, partially determine the variety and quantity of services offered. This variable has a circular function: size in part dictates range of services, and range of services in part dictates size.

The provision of services in a neighborhood is aimed at reducing the need to commute to other parts of a new town for daily needs, thus providing a hierarchy of services within the whole city and, above all, creating social unity within the neighborhood population. The kinds and number of services expected by a population are highly flexible since they depend entirely on the living standards and culture of a country. For example, daily food shopping may have a great deal more to do with culture and tradition than with the availability and size of a refrigerator.

The services required in a neighborhood are those

Figure 7.9.   Galley Hill Community Center Workshop in Milton Keynes, England: an area for arts, hobbies, and even for car repair. (Courtesy of the Milton Keynes Development Corporation.)

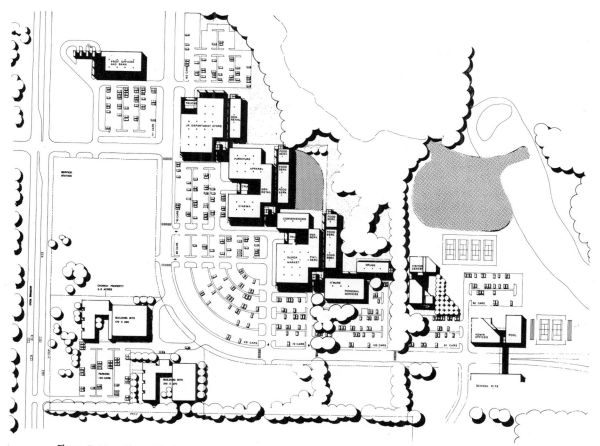

Figure 7.10.   Plan of Timber Creek Village Center, Flower Mound, Texas. (Courtesy of David A. Crane and Partners.)

needed daily or frequently by neighborhood residents. Ideally, some of these services might include an elementary school, a community center, a kindergarten or nursery school, outdoor and indoor recreational facilities for adults and children, parks and gardens, a religious center, a library, and restaurants. Medical aid should be available through a children's clinic, a school inspection service, a diagnostic laboratory, an emergency health center, a food inspection laboratory, a general clinic, dentists, and a home nursing service. A neighborhood may provide local mass transportation and rescue equipment, such as ambulances and fire-fighting equipment, and may also fulfill local shopping needs with food and clothing stores, barber and beauty shops, a stationery store, and a post office. (See Figures 7.9–7.11.)

The planning of local services and shopping areas within a neighborhood should not conflict with or substitute for such activities in a new-town center. The two centers should complement each other but not compete. To encourage social unity among residents,

a neighborhood should provide self-contained services as an integral part of entire town services. Thus the ties with the town are not only physical but also social and administrative. The services of a neighborhood, especially those that are socially oriented, will develop its social identity through the promotion of citizen participation in activities. By its nature and setting a neighborhood should help eliminate social segregation and bring about interaction.

Some have argued that small neighborhood size is required to establish social interaction and a feeling of unity among residents. Others believe that new technology in transportation and communication has diminished the validity of a defined social unit. Thus there seems to be no single universal formula that will determine the optimal size for all types of societies, and this leads to the conclusion that a separate judgment should be made for each case. Regardless of its size, a neighborhood after planning should remain constant to avoid changes in land use, the overuse of services and utilities, and an increase in taxes.

Figure 7.11   Gadebridge neighborhood center in Hemel Hempstead, England. (Courtesy of the Commission for the New Towns.)

Criteria for Site Selection

A site that includes all the optimal aesthetic, convenience, and health requirements rarely exists. Moreover, a neighborhood is designated primarily in conjunction with the site selection for the entire new town. The general site for a new town may already have been selected, and the neighborhood site may have to be chosen within that context. Thus a compromise with the whole town site may be required for designating that land portion that is to become a neighborhood. There may be fewer possibilities offered for neighborhood sites than for the new-town site. Despite this and other handicaps faced by a planner, there are basic criteria that one should use in evaluating a neighborhood in addition to those criteria used to evaluate the entire new-town site. (See Chapter 3.) In his evaluation a planner should decide an adaptability of a site to the general conceptual plan of the neighborhood and its policy.

The water and sewage system and the adaptability of topography to their installation are of major impor-tance. A thorough analysis of any necessary adjust-ments the water and sewer networks will have to make to the topography will provide a clear idea of the capital investment necessary for the changes. An ex-amination of other geological formations is needed not only for the safety and convenience of the residents of a neighborhood, but also for the safety and facilitation of building construction, road construction, and the laying of ground utilities. Also, the suitability of land and its capability for development have a great impact on the economic investment required per land unit and the intensity with which it may be used.

A second criterion in choosing a site is its visual and environmental quality. This involves various ele-ments, one of which is the view and landscape values lost or gained in selecting the site as a whole or in part. A landscape study should examine the topography and vegetation of the site, and both the daytime and nighttime views. Value can be added to a landscape by adjusting the design to the existing landscape to cap-ture its advantages or by adjusting the landscape to a design.

The examination of a site in reference to potential foul odors and air pollution is a second element of visual and environmental quality. This examination should include a determination of prevailing winds and the location of such possible polluting factors as industry, garbage dumps, sewage plants, fertilized agricultural land, motor traffic networks, and polluted streams. Conducted at various times of day, an examination should not only include the distance from sites to potential polluters and the direction of winds, but should also consider normal wind velocity to determine the extent of pollution concentration when it reaches a site.

A related element is the amount of existing or projected noise pollution. The location of its sources, such as airports, highways, railroads, and factories is a primary factor in evaluating the environmental quality of a site. Often, for instance, a distance of 2 or 3 miles from a highway is still not enough to diminish the sounds of trucks and buses at a site to a suitable level, especially at night.

A fourth point to be assessed in the evaluation of a site's landscape and environmental qualities is the possibility of health hazards. Potential hazards may arise from swampy areas within or near the site that could breed disease-carrying insects; from insects carried from adjacent farms; from polluted water sources such as ponds, streams, or lakes; from abandoned caves usually populated by special insects and bats; or from refuse dumps and junk yards. Obviously a determination of the existence of these hazards is of major importance to residents.

Figure 7.12. Aerial view of a neighborhood center in Hemel Hempstead, England. (Courtesy of the Commission for the New Towns.)

A fifth element is the potential for harmony between the development of the site and the natural environment. To enhance the sociophysical aspects of a neighborhood, a mutually advantageous arrangement between the development and the flora and fauna of the area must be achieved. Thus the visual and environmental aspects of the site should be analyzed and accommodated into the development of the site. (See Figure 7.12.)

Accessibility is a third criterion in the site selection process. Easy access to transportation and communication networks should be available to and from the site and within the site. There should also be adequate space for the circulation of vehicular and pedestrian patterns to and from the site and within it. Convenient access to public utilities such as water, sewer, and communication cables is essential.

The last criterion is climate—an important factor that is seldom seriously considered. Temperature, its seasonal extremes and daily changes, generally affects humidity and comfort. Temperature and wind can sometimes be controlled at the macrolevel if there is careful site planning. Orientation is yet another climatic consideration. In the northern hemisphere orientation to southern slopes will provide more exposure to sunshine than eastern or western orientation, while northern exposure will have little or no sunshine at all. The orientation of an entire neighborhood and also its individual buildings should be considered. The combination of prevailing winds and precipitation is important with reference to the orientation of a whole neighborhood site, individual buildings, and the placement of windows and doors in those buildings.

Planning Design Criteria

Planners should consider the basis of an overall policy for design in the very early planning stages and later establish an actual comprehensive design. This policy may be formulated by asking some basic questions: What type of residents will the neighborhood have? Does the population structure require segregation or integration? For what age groups will either segregation or integration be required? The answers to these questions will determine whether the design will result in segregated villages or an aggregate neighborhood. What is the cultural behavior of the population? Do they often have social celebrations that require special spacing, or are they individually oriented people? Is the prospective neighborhood likely to be self-governing or strongly dependent on the central government of the new town? Using a policy formulated

from the answers to these questions as a basis, planners should develop design criteria.

These criteria should include access to different parts of the neighborhood and distances between them. The facts to be considered here are movement and age groups: some residents will walk and others will use bicycles or cars, but not all of them will use the same means. Various age groups in differing numbers will need different land uses at various hours of the day, and this should be provided for within a neighborhood's physical framework. Consideration of these two facts should lead to land-use arrangement that provides maximum accessibility from one part of a neighborhood to another and a minimum need for powered transportation. (See Figure 7.13.)

Planners of neighborhoods should know the threefold function of neighbors: "as helpers in times of need and as sources of sociability and information."[33] Various cultures stress these elements differently, and planners who are aware of the prevalent one within the society for which they are planning will be able to determine the relevant physical form. They should also know that each of these three values is stressed differently by various income groups. "Middle class individuals place relatively greater stress on sociability; upper class residents, on the preservations of class codes and traditions; and working class residents, on help in crisis."[34] Which of these functions is stressed will determine not only a clustering of housing and different land-use densities, but may also dictate the need for various local social services, such as community centers, coffee rooms, clubs, and sports facilities. Thus a neighborhood composed of people from various income groups would require a wider range of services than a community of one social class. A neighborhood that comprised a low-income group may feel the need for internal local services more than one with a middle- and high-income population. The latter two groups may feel that the new-town center is as important as any local center.

In view of the size and location of services, transportation, and land-use functions, the neighborhood unit described here should be part of a hierarchical pattern within a whole new town. It should not be planned as a segregated unit by function and land use. The effect of service and land-use patterns on the development of the social pattern in a city is immense. However, the cost benefit of a hierarchical system should not be the only consideration, if the quality of society is a prime concern. The various hierarchies of functions and land-use patterns vary and may occasionally bring families to these different sites. The hierarchical pat-

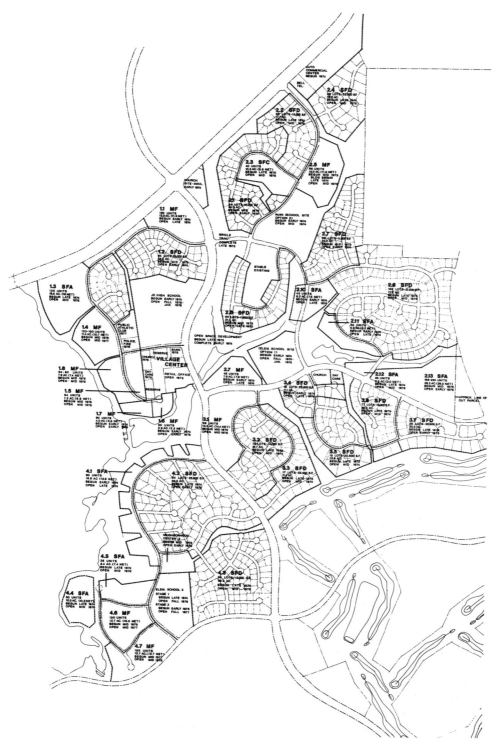

Figure 7.13. The land-use plan and phasing of Glenloch Village, Peachtree City, Georgia. (Courtesy of David A. Crane and Partners.)

tern should begin with a small street and move through a subneighborhood grouping and a new-town center to a regional center. Some overlapping of services among different sites is inevitable in any such pattern.

Regardless of how hierarchies are distributed, a design plan should assure that no changes in zoning laws or land use of the area adjacent to a neighborhood can occur that would affect its quality. Since the area adjacent to a neighborhood is usually designated as an open space (park, playground, wooded area), there may be continuous political pressure to change this land use. Even though changes in land use may keep the adjacent area an open space, such development may affect the quality of a neighborhood: e.g., the development of a highway, airport, or garbage disposal plant.

The establishment of neighborhood boundaries mentioned earlier is a desirable criterion. Definite physical boundaries support the formation of local identity and a sense of neighborhood unity. These include natural geographic boundaries, such as rivers, slopes or mountains, forests or green areas, open spaces, or man-made limits, such as planted tree zones, agricultural strips, railroads, major highways, avenues, or streets. A neighborhood may also have a distinctive social appearance: a hierarchy of the population by density, ethnic affiliation, race, or religion. Neighborhood boundaries may function as a barrier between two parts of a new town, such as a major highway, or as a unifying element and a meeting ground between separated parts, such as a body of water or a green area. Although jurisdictional or geographic neighborhood boundaries have an explicit psychologic and symbolic effect on both outsiders and local residents, the availability and quality of local services and the local social mechanism make an urban section a neighborhood unit. However, physical boundaries may have special meaning when they coincide with other boundaries such as social or service-related limits.

A neighborhood unit should also have primary and secondary internal landmarks to reinforce personal identification with the area and to serve as visual cues within an area's geographic complexity. These landmarks may be special trees, open-space squares, fountains, monuments, buildings, or any other form that might contribute a sense of distinctive identity.

It may be socially desirable to design those landmarks functionally, to be used for meetings by various groups, e.g., children, the elderly, or housewives. In keeping with this principle, the various residential and business sections of a neighborhood should be architecturally designed to establish a visual distinction among them. This distinction should be reinforced by the remainder of the planning pattern which should eliminate nonlocal traffic, provide paths and open areas, and provide a sense of self-sufficiency.

If socializing is considered to be the most important function of a neighborhood, then the physical planner must include elements conducive to socializing in his criteria. Socializing may be encouraged by the physical proximity of residential units, by an increase in population density, by closeness to common functional spaces, or by accessibility increased by intense local commuting patterns (pedestrian or vehicular). Physical planners must adapt these factors to each case. At the microlevel, physical planners may consider various elements within the building units themselves, such as communal spaces for laundry and other services, and communal recreational space, stairways, back doors, and backyards. However, planners should carefully consider the unique cultural or behavioral determinants of privacy and communal acceptance among each age and social group within a neighborhood since such consideration may help avoid conflict between socializing and personal privacy. This is one of the major issues facing planners who consider neighborhood socializing to be one way of improving the quality of society.

Physical planners should keep in mind that in a highly developed technological society physical proximity is not the sole factor in determining socializing among neighbors of a new-town neighborhood. Although physical closeness may establish face-to-face interaction, it would require the existence of other elements, such as personal desires, similarly, or common interests to make socializing effective.

Although it is essential to the creation of a neighboring climate, proximity should be only a supporting element. Neighbors do not necessarily become friends. Tensions may be created among persons with clashing personalities who live close to each other. The physical configuration of housing in a neighborhood should offer residents more than one opportunity for interaction as an outlet for tension caused by the design form. This is also true for childrens' playgrounds or playing space. Recent experience reveals that young families are the first to move into a new neighborhood. The presence of families tends to make a neighborhood stable and, assuming that at least some of the families remain in that neighborhood a long time, provides continuity within it. However, it is also advantageous to design "pockets" of rental housing and apartments devoted mainly to the young within a neighborhood. Such housing helps continuous, social rejuvenation of a neighborhood.

Proximity should not under any circumstances undermine personal privacy. The neighboring bond is group-oriented, and its progress or regression will be affected to some extent by the physical clustering of neighbors. Friendship, being selective and individually oriented, is another reason for the need of variation and choice in a design.

Kinship, clanship, or any other blood relation are formed mostly on a nonselective basis and will not disappear even when they are neglected. Friendship, in contrast, is a product of an active response and interest of people and is likely to vanish if ignored by one of them. A neighborhood may stimulate interaction and consequently friendship when the physical plan is designed mainly for such social results. Unlike an established city neighborhood, proximity in a new-town neighborhood may add to friendship if so desired by its people, but it will not provide the option of selecting neighbors since all the residences of a new neighborhood will be occupied at approximately the same time.

Social space for immediate neighbors varies among cultures and also depends on the climate of an area; thus design requirements will vary. The design may have to consider such elements as patios, front doors, backyards, gardens, or indoor areas. If the neighborhood is to include many children, special design consideration should be given to their needs. Often parents choose a neighborhood because of the degree of safety and convenience it affords their children.[35] Special social space in the immediate neighborhood is essential to encourage social bonds among children. The design must then provide safe areas such as those provided by dead-end streets and minimal traffic. Thus physical closeness can be effective when the design elements are related not only by proximity but also by function: door to door, backyard to backyard, and so forth.

To insure the social effect of a neighborhood, planners should view the unit as a complex of many subunits and sub-subunits that allows real neighboring contact. Designers should structure the basic social unit (10 to 40 families) physically and socially to create social interaction and neighboring relations among all residents regardless of age. The neighborhood and its subunits should multiply physically and socially from this small unit. The size of the base unit may vary from one culture to another, but will probably be between 10 and 40 families. Some space should be provided for communal use, the size of which may vary according to available space and living standard. Such common social space may be playgrounds, gardens, tearooms, swimming pools, tennis courts, or similar areas that draw people together. A variety of physical clustering designs could be introduced to support socializing. The 10 to 40 families social unit provides a range within which individuals and families may retain intimate social contact and be socially satisfied.

CONCLUSION

A neighborhood unit is a sociophysical aggregate that forms its own characteristic unity and differs from other urban surroundings. Thus a neighborhood is distinguished by physical integrity bounded by identifiable landmarks or geographic features; by social, socioeconomic, ethnic, religious, or cultural characteristics; by a common sharing of social or other services, facilities, or amenities (those services necessary for a self-contained neighborhood), by a developed neighboring pattern and community identity; and by criteria that provide a neighborhood with its unique landscape, cityscape, and architectural identity.

The establishment of the modern neighborhood as a social unit is not a re-creation of the ancient village neighboring system. It is rather the recognition that modern urban man of overurbanized society requires a social unit to belong to and needs to regain his social balance by face-to-face interaction in a neighboring system. Neighborhood planners who stress the social benefit of the unit expect the neighborhood to offer informal relations among neighbors and active consumer-participants in its social services. Social isolation of people and the mental consequences stressed in large urban centers may be reduced or diminished in a neighborhood. It is noteworthy that a highly mobile society tends to weaken kinship relations, and in a rapidly urbanized society such as that of the United States personal isolation may easily become an imposed social pattern and lead to depression and mental illness. Thus a neighborhood unit may be an alternative to isolation while residing in an urban environment. The neighborhood is a successful planning experiment where social and physical factors may be combined.

A neighborhood unit should not be regarded solely as a physical entity; it should be a unit synthesized from the society, education, economy, transportation, government, and physical form of a new town. The focus of this synthesis is the recognition of socializing and intimate relationships between residents as the means to improve the quality of society.

A neighborhood unit and a new town as a whole should interact socially, economically, and physically. The combined shapes of neighborhood units should determine the form of a whole town. A new town should be viewed as a dynamic entity.[36] To face this process of change on the one hand, and to retain the neighborhood unit's distinction and identity on the other, a new-town designer-planner should envision the desired future interrelation and integration between the two elements—the town and the neighborhood. The same may be said of the relations between the integrity and identity of the town center and those of the neighborhood unit. An overall new-town plan should clearly specify the relation among integrative processes for the town center, the neighborhood unit, and the new town as a whole. Although this issue is considered one of the most challenging for a new-town designer-planner, it is essential to resist the rigidity normally associated with a planned neighborhood unit. Built-in, flexible alternatives are necessary if an overall plan is to remain viable.

At the same time, the plan should relate a new town to its region. Only on those various but interrelated planning scales (subneighborhood, neighborhood, town center, new town, and region) can social goals be implemented and effective. Those who have introduced the social themes of the neighborhood never meant it as a segregated social entity isolated from its regional context. It is concern about a town network as a whole that leads to the development of a neighborhood concept.

It seems that cultures, such as those of the Mediterranean, where personal relations are open, warm, friendly, and intimate, are more prone to support an ideal socializing pattern in a neighborhood than highly industrialized or extremely urbanized cultures where personal relations tend toward isolation and individualism. In all groups, children of all ages and women are the most receptive to the social form and sharing pattern of a neighborhood unit. Therefore such units, which have a high proportion of young married families with many children, have the potential to be successful.

Some elements of the neighborhood themes introduced here coincide with a "neighborhood of collective responsibility."[37] This calls for the collective responsibility of a neighborhood to provide such mutual public services as fire, police, schools, and recreation, encourages the development of local leadership, and seeks a tax base system that may support a sense of community and local identity. However, the increase in population mobility may lead to heterogeneity instead of homogeneity, destroy the sense of collective responsibility gained over a period of time in a neighborhood, and weaken its social solidarity. In spite of this mobility, self-management should be recognized as a strong tool in promoting the use of local resources. The benefit of social vitality of the unit has a far-reaching effect on neighborhood unity and on the new-town political structure.

The sociophysical planning of a neighborhood is a process that affects every sector of life, and constantly changing social values also necessitate other changes. Recently an increased understanding of this process has accelerated the involvement of the social scientist in the planning process.

NOTES

1. Robert B. Zehner, "Neighborhood and Community Satisfaction in New Towns and Less Planned Suburbs," *Journal of the American Institute of Planners,* **37,** no. 6 (November 1971), p. 384.

2. Anthony Goss, "Neighborhood Units in British New Towns," *Town Planning Review,* **32,** no. 1 (April 1961), pp. 81–82.

3. Suzanne Keller, *The Urban Neighborhood: A Sociological Perspective* (New York: Random House, 1968), p. 126.

4. American Public Health Association Committee on the Hygiene of Housing, *Planning the Neighborhood,* 2nd ed. (Chicago: Public Administration Service, 1960), p. 1.

5. Frank H. Vizetelly, ed., *The Practical Standard Dictionary* (New York: Funk & Wagnalls Co., 1930), p. 766.

6. Keller, pp. 156–57.

7. Lewis Mumford, "The Neighborhood and the Neighborhood Unit," *Town Planning Review,* **24,** no. 4 (January 1954), p. 264.

8. Keller, pp. 30–31 and 108.

9. Arthur B. Gallion and Simon Eisner, *The Urban Pattern: City Planning and Design* (Toronto: D. Van Nostrand Co., 1963), pp. 250–64.

10. Lewis Mumford, *The City in History: Its Origins, Its Transformations, and Its Prospects* (New York: Harcourt, Brace and World, 1961), pp. 14–15.

11. Mumford, *The City in History,* p. 15.

12. Gilbert Herbert, "The Neighborhood Unit Principle and Organic Theory," *Sociological Review,* **11,** no. 2, new series (July 1963), p. 171. Also see Charles Horton Cooley, *Social Organization: A Study of the Larger Mind* (New York: Charles Scribner's Sons, 1909); Robert E. Park, "The City: Suggestions for the Investigation of Human Behavior in the Urban Environment," in *The City* (Chicago: University of Chicago Press, 1925), pp. 1–46; Robert A. Woods, "The Neighborhood in Social Reconstruction," *Publications of the American Sociological Society,* **VII,** Meeting held in Boston, Mass., December 28–31, 1912; and J.H. Ward, *The Social Center* (New York: D. Appleton and Co., 1913).

13. Clarence Perry, "The Neighborhood Unit," in *Neighborhood and Community Planning* (New York: Committee on the Regional Plan of New York and Its Environs, 1929), pp. 34–35. Also see American Public Health Association, pp. 102–03.

14. B.J. Heraud, "Social Classes and the New Towns," *Urban Studies,* **5,** no. 1 (1968), p. 37.

15.   Mumford, "The Neighborhood and the Neighborhood Unit," p. 256; and Anthony Goss, "Neighborhood Units in British New Towns," *Town Planning Review,* **32,** no. 1 (April 1961), p. 66.

16.   Great Britain, Central Housing Advisory Committee, *Design of Dwellings,* Report of the Design of Dwellings Subcommittee of the Central Housing Advisory Committee appointed by the Minister of Health and the Minister of Town and Country Planning on site planning and layout in relation to housing (London: His Majesty's Stationery Office, 1944).

17.   Goss, pp. 66–67.

18.   Andrews Blowers, "Planning Residential Areas," in *Planning and the City* (Walten Hall, Milton Keynes: The Open University Press, 1973), pp. 122–26.

19.   Keller, p. 108.

20.   Perry, p. 34.

21.   Mumford, "The Neighborhood and the Neighborhood Unit," p. 257.

22.   Keller, p. 105.

23.   Keller, p. 91.

24.   Keller, p. 44.

25.   Keller, p. 26.

26.   Milton Kotler, *Neighborhood Government: The Local Foundations of Political Life* (Indianapolis: The Bobbs-Merrill Co., 1969), p. X.

27.   Ray Thomas, *London's New Towns: A Study of Self-Contained and Balanced Communities* (London: Political and Economic Planning [PEP], 1969), p. 382.

28.   Mumford, "The Neighborhood and the Neighborhood Unit," p. 266.

29.   Mumford, "The Neighborhood and the Neighborhood Unit," p. 263.

30.   American Public Health Association, p. 1.

31.   U.S. Advisory Commission on Intergovernmental Relations, *Urban and Rural America* (Washington, D.C.: U.S. Government Printing Office, 1968), p. 22.

32.   Herbert, pp. 174–75.

33.   Keller, p. 152.

34.   Keller, p. 153.

35.   Gerald D. Suttles, *The Social Construction of Communities* (Chicago: University of Chicago Press, 1973), p. 38.

36.   Herbert, p. 165.

37.   Keller, p. 141.

EIGHT
LAND-USE PLANNING

INTRODUCTION

Traditional planners of new towns considered land use their dominant element. Though it is still the most important, planners now realize the value of other factors as well. Effective land-use planning requires consideration of all components of the environment that exist before the new town's creation and the environment to be created by the new town. A plan will not be effective, however, if planners treat each of these components disjunctively; i.e., a comprehensive land-use plan should interrelate all elements that form a community. Also, because land is a concrete form, any land-use plan must be flexible enough to change established uses either to correct mistakes or to accommodate changing needs.

Land requirements surely differ from one new town to another, depending on densities of use, population, living standards, scales of service, and other cultural and geographic factors. Because such differences exist, we will limit our discussion to the unique nature of land use in new towns and to the elements considered in planning. A planner may determine standards such as densities and land allocation for a given new town after comparing statistics from case studies such as we provide in Appendix A.

Goals and Objectives

The process of preparing the goals and objectives of land use combines the effort of all planning team members with developers, decision makers, and concerned politicians, who are later joined by the town council and citizens when these goals are to be revised or the plan is to be re-evaluated. Along with the chief planner-designer of the new town there are specific team members who primarily formulate the goals: sociologist, economist, transportation expert, and physical planner-designer. The goals and objectives of

land use are a synthesis of all other formulated goals. Thus when land-use goals are to be re-evaluated, their reciprocal impact on all other goals should be cross-checked. Also, as with other goals, those of land use should be flexible to meet changes required by modern life.

Land-use goals, like many others, should include working goals that specify the realization of a general goal in any given phase. In this way planners and implementors, whatever their status, may properly interpret the practical implications of the land-use goals. Thus working goals may minimize misunderstanding and maximize communication among all concerned.

The following are some tentative goals that new-town planners may use to formulate goals for their land-use plan:

(1) Focus on all unique physical, geographic, historic, and cultural characteristics of the site and its region.

(2) Enhance the surrounding natural environment and protect the physical and ecological equilibrium of the site and its region.

(3) Achieve an optimum use of the land to minimize destruction of its balance.

(4) Recognize the thresholds of the site's resources and avoid crossing them during the new town's life.

(5) Support the creation of a good society by a socially oriented design for land use (see Chapter 4).

(6) Formulate an overall design in all levels that encourages the use of a pedestrian system within an accessible, attractive environment.

(7) Maximize traffic segregation from residential areas, establish safe access and movement, and minimize trips generated between land uses by decentralizing services.

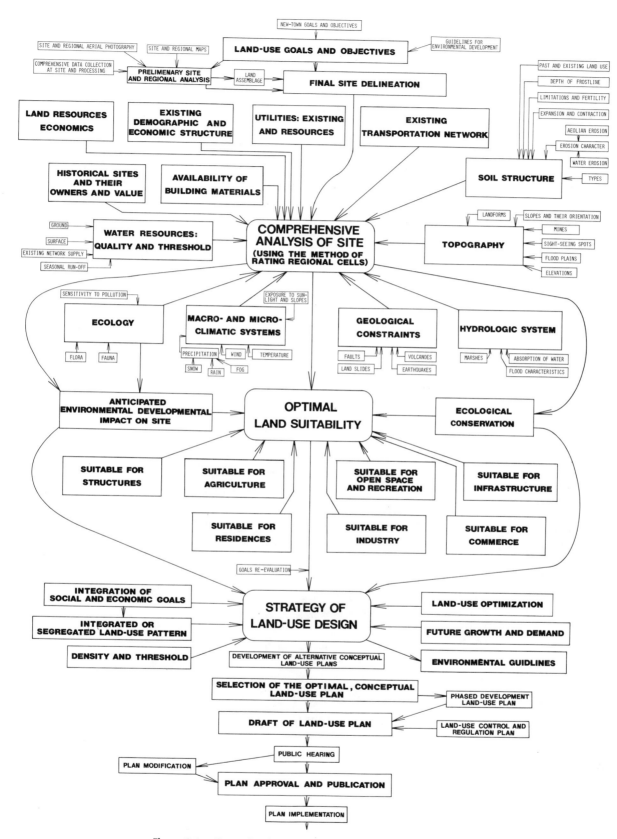

Figure 8.1. Generalized process of planning land use in new towns.

207

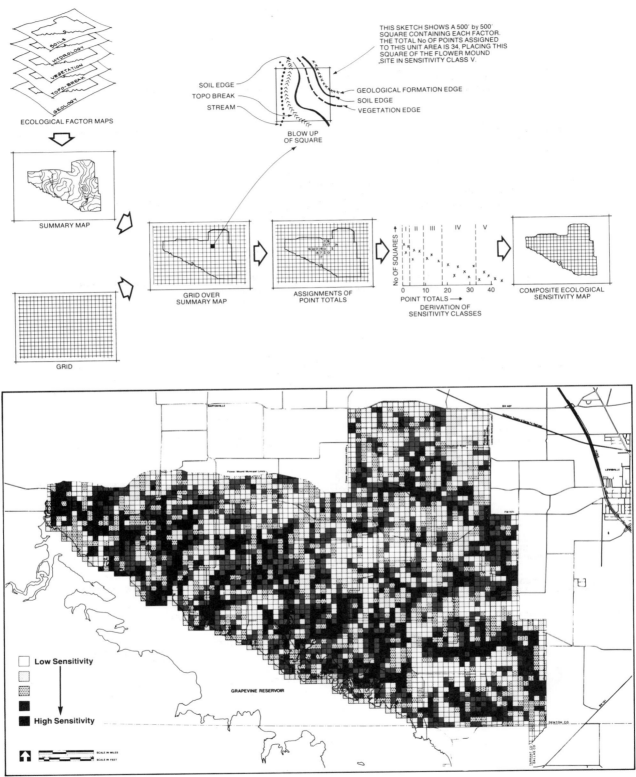

THIS SKETCH SHOWS A 500' by 500' SQUARE CONTAINING EACH FACTOR. THE TOTAL No OF POINTS ASSIGNED TO THIS UNIT AREA IS 34, PLACING THIS SQUARE OF THE FLOWER MOUND SITE IN SENSITIVITY CLASS V.

SOIL EDGE
TOPO BREAK
STREAM

GEOLOGICAL FORMATION EDGE
SOIL EDGE
VEGETATION EDGE

BLOW UP OF SQUARE

ECOLOGICAL FACTOR MAPS

SUMMARY MAP

GRID

GRID OVER SUMMARY MAP

ASSIGNMENTS OF POINT TOTALS

DERIVATION OF SENSITIVITY CLASSES

COMPOSITE ECOLOGICAL SENSITIVITY MAP

No OF SQUARES

POINT TOTALS

Low Sensitivity

High Sensitivity

GRAPEVINE RESERVOIR

SCALE IN MILES
SCALE IN FEET

Figure 8.2. Ecological sensitivity of Flower Mound, Texas. The method of overlayed maps was used to obtain the final sensitivity map. (Source: *Flower Mound New Town.*)

(8)   Introduce a flexible pattern that includes undesignated portions of land which may accommodate future changes, especially in relation to the town center.

(9)   Offer a variety of housing designs and densities that will effect the community's social balance (see Chapter 4).

(10)   Minimize municipal costs for construction, management, and maintenance of utilities and infrastructure through an efficient land-use pattern.

(11)   Formulate a system of land-use control and its enforcement that are accepted and enhanced by the residents.

Finally, the planning team should offer its clients alternative goals (or parts thereof) so that they may select the most suitable or consider other alternatives when original goals are to be re-evaluated throughout the process. All goals should be made public to alert citizens to future development of their community.

The Process of Planning

The sequence of comprehensive land-use planning proceeds from deciding what land to develop to when and how to develop it. In Chapter 3 we discussed how to choose a site; now we must concern ourselves with the sequential actions that lead to a land-use plan and its implementation. Having chosen a site, a developer should then decide what types of land use his new town will have, what their sequence of development will be, and what methods he will use to reach his ultimate goal. Figure 8.1 shows a generalized process of planning land use for new towns.

Although planning land use is a complex process, there are several major steps we should point out: stating land-use goals and objectives, comprehensively analyzing a site, surveying optimal land suitability, developing land-use design strategy, and preparing a final land-use plan.

Land-use planning should encompass both physical characteristics and constraints and socioeconomic possibilities. Land potential should include soil composition, land suitability and land value. Soil composition maps, which delineate all soil types of a designated site by physical and organic characteristics, should clarify the strength and the limitation of any soil. The planner should interpret this information to determine the potential use of each soil. (See Figure 8.2.)

Planners should document all necessary information about the site. Land suitability maps designate land according to its physical capability, regardless of any planner's conceptual interest. This designation of suitability should include at least the following types of uses: building construction (including residential, commercial, and industrial), transportation construction, recreation, and agriculture. Although it depends on a soil composition map, a final land suitability map

TABLE 8.1   CLIMATIC ASPECTS FOR DESIGN OF RESIDENCES

Temperature	Wind	Precipitation

Variation
  a.   day
  b.   night
  c.   seasonal
  d.   daily average
  e.   seasonal extremes
	Variation
	  a. daily
	  b. prevalence
	  c. temperature
		Type
		  a. rain
		  b. snow
		  c. dew
		  d. hail
		  e. humidity

Orientation and exposure
  a.   buildings
  b.   windows and openings
  c.   pedestrian pathways
	Proximity
	  a. industrial
	  b. pollution
	  c. garbage
	  d. sewage
		Quantity
		  a. daily
		  b. seasonal
		  c. frequency
		  d. duration

Solar energy
  a.   heating
  b.   energy for running machines
	Orientation
	  a. streets
	  b. neighborhoods
	  c. entire city
		Design
		  a. roofs
		  b. storage
		  c. runoff
		  d. landscaping

Figure 8.3. Town center of Leaf Rapids, Manitoba. The center contains everything normally found on a main street, but here it is integrated under one roof in a climate-controlled environment. (Courtesy of the Leaf Rapids Corporation.)

will be entirely different from such a map. Designations may be flexible since some sections of a site may suit more than one purpose. Such flexibility should enable a planner to formulate land suitability alternatives, thereby providing a flexible, final, land-use plan.

A land value map should index the value of various sections of a site for three categories: (1) market value, calculated from past, present, and future values, (2) subjective value of topographical characteristics, and (3) values of proximity.

By integrating soil composition, land suitability, and land value, a planner may produce a land potentiality map that is later combined with socioeconomic variables to produce final alternative land uses. A planner may integrate these three characteristics by using the MRRC as explained in Chapter 3; this

method will give a comprehensive map of their combined ratings. The technique of overlayed maps may produce similar results.

Many planners have ignored climate because they thought of buildings as fortresses against nature. However, if they want to have efficient living spaces, planners must use methods not only to eliminate climatic disadvantages but also to enhance its advantages. Table 8.1 lists aspects of temperature, wind, and precipitation which planners and designers might consider.[1] (See Figure 8.3.)

In addition to a physical land-use plan, a new town needs a socioeconomic plan to summarize its social and economic characteristics. This should include desired housing density as a cultural determinant, types of occupations (manufacturing, commercial, and services), and space and proximity as a product of cultural behavior. As an example, it is worth noting that the adjustment of Japanese society to spatial requirements and proximity to various uses is totally different from that of American society. A thoughtful and comprehensive analysis of social, cultural, and economic determinants of a designated community may help to produce a comprehensive map of socioeconomic values to be combined with a land potentiality map.

If the land-use plan follows the site analysis informa-

tion, then the plan will be limited to a product of the site's limitations and advantages, and its final product of development will be in harmony with the site and its natural environment. Under these conditions, the plan will reflect the site's limits and will regulate development so as not to cross the threshold of its resources such as water, natural beauty, soil stability, or climate.

A conceptual land-use plan is a preliminary expression of general ideas of land use that precedes the actual land-use plan. Often there are several alterna-

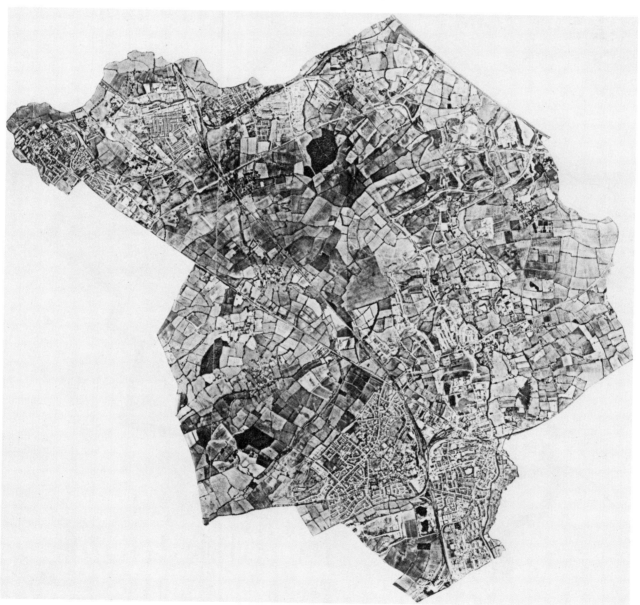

Figure 8.4. The site of Milton Keynes, England, which encompasses existing development. Rural centers will be preserved as the nuclei of expansion. Most of the site taken by Milton Keynes was agricultural land which will be lost to urban expansion. (Source: *New City.*)

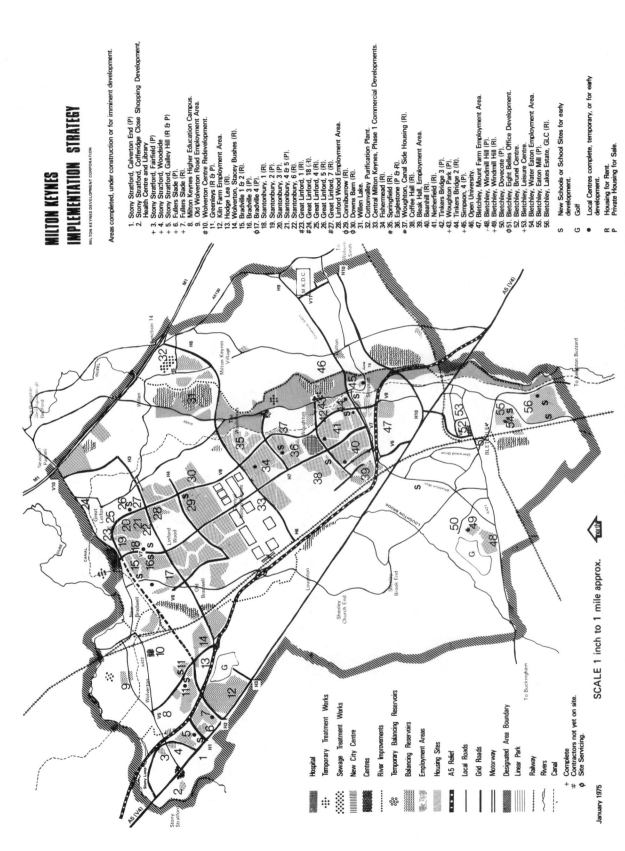

MILTON KEYNES
IMPLEMENTATION STRATEGY

MILTON KEYNES DEVELOPMENT CORPORATION

Areas completed, under construction or for imminent development.

1. Stony Stratford, Calverton End (P)
2. Stony Stratford, Cofferidge Close Shopping Development, Health Centre and Library
+ 3. Stony Stratford, Fairfield (P)
+ 4. Stony Stratford, Woodside
+ 5. Stony Stratford, Galley Hill (R & P)
+ 6. Fullers Slade (P)
+ 7. Fullers Slade (R)
8. Milton Keynes Higher Education Campus.
9. Old Wolverton Road Employment Area.
10. Wolverton Centre Redevelopment Area.
11. Greenleys (R & P).
12. Kiln Farm Employment Area.
13. Hodge Lea (R).
14. Wolverton, Stacey Bushes (R).
15. Bradville 1 & 2 (R).
16. Bradville 3 (P).
Φ17. Bradville 4 (P).
18. Stantonbury, 1 (R).
19. Stantonbury, 2 (P).
20. Stantonbury, 3 (P).
21. Stantonbury, 4 & 5 (P).
22. Stantonbury, 6 (R).
#23. Great Linford, 1 (R).
#24. Great Linford, 18 (:3).
25. Great Linford, 4 (R).
26. Great Linford, 5 (R).
#27. Great Linford, 7 (R).
28. Linford Wood Employment Area.
Φ29. Conniburrow (R).
Φ 30. Downs Barn (R).
31. Willen Lake.
32. Cottonvalley Purification Plant.
33. Central Milton Keynes, Phase 1 Commercial Developments.
34. Fishermead (R).
35. Springfield (R).
36. Eaglestone (P & R).
37. Woughton, Canal Side Housing (R).
38. Coffee Hall (R).
39. Bleak Hall, Employment Area.
40. Beanhill (R).
41. Netherfield (R).
42. Tinkers Bridge 3 (P).
+43. Woughton Park (P).
44. Tinkers Bridge 2 (R).
45. Simpson, 4 (P).
46. Open University.
47. Bletchley, Mount Farm Employment Area.
·48. Bletchley, Windmill Hill (P).
·49. Bletchley, Windmill Hill (R).
50. Bletchley, Dovecote (P).
Φ51. Bletchley, Eight Belles Office Development.
52. Bletchley, Brunel Centre.
+53. Bletchley, Leisure Centre.
54. Bletchley, Water Eaton Employment Area.
55. Bletchley, Eaton Mill (P).
56. Bletchley, Lakes Estate, GLC (R).

S   New Schools or School Sites for early development.

G   Golf

•   Local Centres complete, temporary, or for early development.

R   Housing for Rent.
P   Private Housing for Sale.

Hospital
Temporary Treatment Works
Sewage Treatment Works
New City Centre
Centres
River Improvements
Temporary Balancing Reservoirs
Balancing Reservoirs
Employment Areas
Housing Sites
A5 Relief
Local Roads
Grid Roads
Motorway
Designated Area Boundary
Linear Park
Railway
Rivers
Canal

+ Complete
# Contractors not yet on site.
Φ Site Servicing.

January 1975

SCALE 1 inch to 1 mile approx.

Figure 8.5. Implementation strategy of Milton Keynes, England. (Courtesy of the Milton Keynes Development Corporation.)

Figure 8.6. Strategic plan of Milton Keynes, England. (Courtesy of the Milton Keynes Development Corporation.)

213

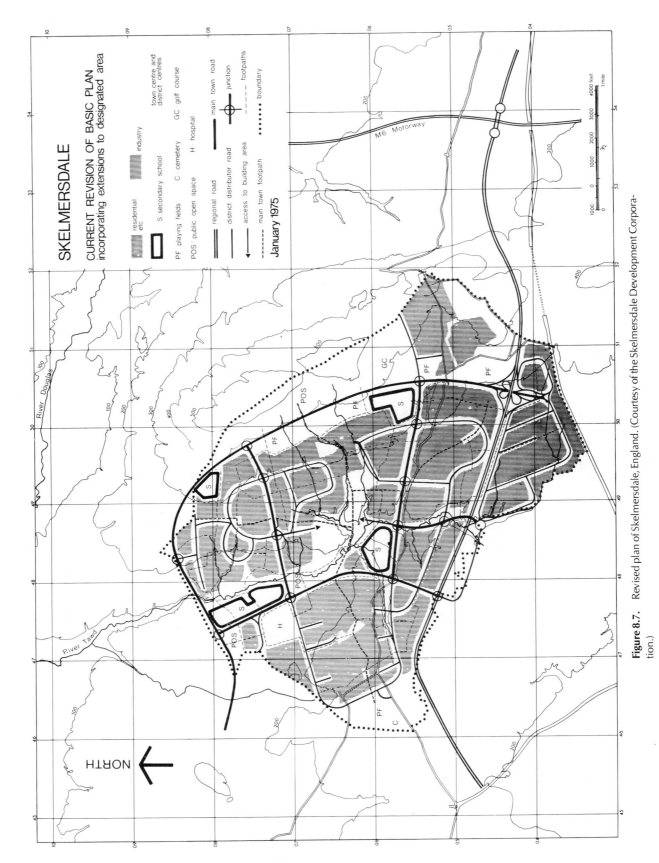

SKELMERSDALE

CURRENT REVISION OF BASIC PLAN
incorporating extensions to designated area

residential
etc

industry

S secondary school

town centre and
district centres

PF playing fields   C cemetery   GC golf course

POS public open space   H hospital

regional road

district distributor road

access to building area

main town footpath

main town road

junction

footpaths

boundary

January 1975

M6 Motorway

NORTH

River Douglas

River Tawd

Figure 8.7. Revised plan of Skelmersdale, England. (Courtesy of the Skelmersdale Development Corporation.)

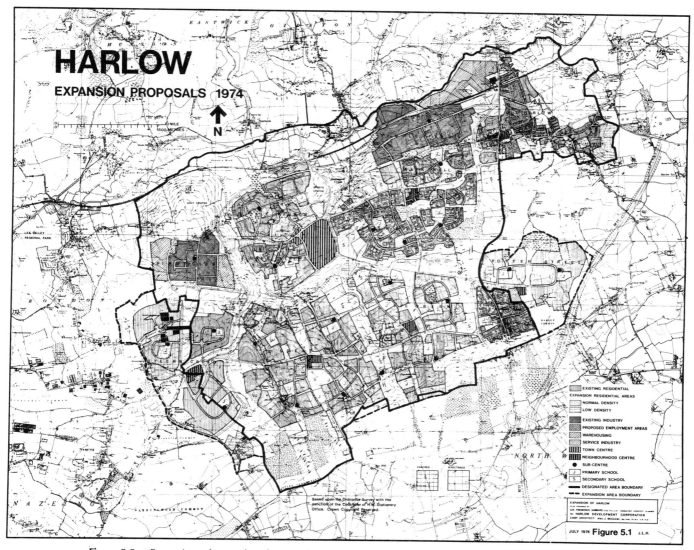

Figure 8.8. Expansion scheme of Harlow, England. Harlow, a new town, has grown to the point that its original site has been expanded. (Source: *Harlow Expansion 1974: Technical Papers.*)

tive conceptual plans that are constantly revised till one is chosen as final. Usually the conceptual plan has been a drawing that included major land uses; occasionally it has been a verbal outline. Its function has been to generate understanding and agreement among the parties involved, especially among team members. A conceptual plan also publicizes the project for nonprofessionals.

Any comprehensive land-use plan should be a series of plans for development phases that may terminate either by completing definite time periods or by definite targets for development. Each plan should state the goals and objectives of a phase, the development to occur, cash flow, and the duration of the phase. A plan should also state explicitly the subsequent actions to be undertaken to reach its target. Also,

planners may wish to prepare alternate plans for each phase. Although the first few phases should be very detailed, subsequent ones need not be since they will be implemented much later and by then conditions may have changed. (See Figures 8.4, 8.5, 8.6.)

Any plan is dynamic and should be revised occasionally. In addition as planners gain experience during early phases, they may be able to improve plans for later aspects. (See Figures 8.7 and 8.8.)

A Comprehensive Survey and Analysis

Any physical analysis is insufficient for land-use planning if it does not include a complementary concept: the cultural landscape. ''The new geographical survey and its product, the maps, give the planner new dimensions for his thinking and practice. The survey no longer describes only the nature of a place and its physical geographical properties; it views it also as a source of livelihood and work; . . . it is capable of giving us a comprehensive view of cultural phenomena by charting the *cultural landscape* created within our environment, by natural and human interaction."[2]

While these remarks relate primarily to regional planning, the importance of this concept for land-use planning in new towns is clear. First, a new town cannot be an isolated phenomenon, even if it were to attain the ideal of full self-sustainment. A new town interacts with the rest of society, especially within its geographic region. To insure that the regional society does not change the carefully planned equilibrium within a new town (by building factories around its perimeter, for example), a new town must be part of a regional plan for improvement and development.

Second, a new town must be designed to preserve the culture of the society in which it is built. The people of the region, their institutions, and their customs are a cultural product, just as the flora and fauna of one region are natural products. Patrick Geddes, one of the first to emphasize the interdependence of society and land, argued that there are three major categories—he called them "notations of life"—involved in man's habitation of the natural world: place, folk, and work.[3] To study any one of these alone, Geddes argued, is not to study it at all, since each of the categories is real only in relation to the other two. Each category is defined by the others so that each has no separate identity.

Although the three notations of life are essentially equal, place is fundamental since it has historical meaning beyond folk and work. A study of place concerns hydrology, geology, climatology, botany, and a survey of place would produce maps describing topography, drainage, and other physical characteris-

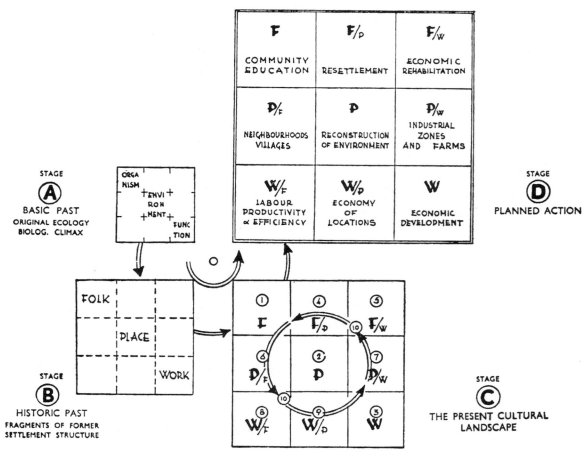

Figure 8.9.   The main subjects of a cultural landscape survey using the Geddes notation. (Source: *Regional Planning and Development.*)

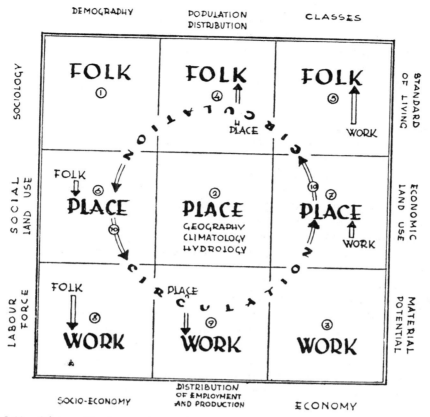

DEMOGRAPHY   POPULATION DISTRIBUTION   CLASSES

SOCIOLOGY

STANDARD OF LIVING

ECONOMIC LAND USE

SOCIAL LAND USE

LABOUR FORCE

MATERIAL POTENTIAL

SOCIO-ECONOMY   DISTRIBUTION OF EMPLOYMENT AND PRODUCTION   ECONOMY

Figure 8.10. Schema of the stages and main subjects of a survey and planning of a region using the Geddes notation. (Source: *Regional Planning and Development.*)

tics. However, unlike traditional surveys of physical features, the maps produced would only contribute to the design of a comprehensive plan; they would not control the plan absolutely. The study of folk adds population features. A survey of folk would produce maps of the sociologic and demographic features of an area. Finally research of work, or the economic features and potential of an area, rounds out the initial phase of a comprehensive survey.

Surveys of areas of influence among the three primary elements follow the initial survey in Glikson's adaptation of Geddes. Figure 8.9 is a schematic representation of these survey areas. The survey of place yields two separate surveys of place/folk and place/work. The first of these, place/folk, would consist of maps of the influence of society upon location: maps of buildings and cultural activities, residential locations, and densities, and so on. Maps of place/work, in contrast, would indicate land use for income production: agricultural land, industrial areas, mines, and so forth. Such maps include channels for movement of goods and services and various economic spheres of influence.

The initial study of folk yields to studies of folk/place, the relation of land forms and spatial characteristics to the life of society, and to folk/work, the relation between population and economic resources. Folk/place would produce maps of population density over the region and would define rural, suburban, and urban environments. Qualitative maps would indicate health, living conditions, types of occupations, and other information directly related to location. Folk/work, on the other hand, would be concerned with economic structure and its effect upon the population. The study of folk/work would produce maps of economic classes, employment and unemployment, living conditions, and similar information.

Finally, an analysis of work/folk, the economic potential of the work force, and work/place, the economic possibilities for a defined space, complete the study of work. Work/folk would yield an analysis of special skills of the population, and so on. Work/place would be an analysis of occupational opportunities within the area and of maps that show the distribution of various categories of industries and services.

In addition to these nine aspects of a survey, a tenth

must be added to complete the study of cultural landscape: circulation. While the other nine aspects may provide a relatively complex picture of the significant interrelation within a region or area, they do not account for the life of the region until circulation, or the interaction of elements, is charted. Circulation studies would consist of a set of maps defining the flow of messages, goods and services, people, and so on. These maps would allow a planner to understand the energy of a region, and thus would permit him to calculate future energy and plan for effective use of regional energy distribution, exchange, and growth.

A planner may understand a region thoroughly by adding the dimension of time (see Figure 8.10). By combining it with an understanding of the present cultural landscape, a planner will be able to approach the point where planning is integrated with regional potential. This historical survey would consist of four parts. First, study of the basic past would determine the biologic capabilities of the area by attempting to reconstrict the climax development of the area before the intervention of human society. Maps of the basic past would define biologic functions, ecological equilibrium, and climax landscape. Thus the study of the basic past would permit planners to envision the physical and biologic potential untainted by encrustations of civilization, and this knowledge would enable the planner to use the physical and biologic capabilities of the area most effectively.

The second and third phases of the historical survey chart the cultural landscape of the area from the beginning of time to the present. These studies result in maps of how the society within and beyond its borders has used and currently uses the area. The survey of the historic past, although incomplete because no reconstruction of history can include all aspects and details, will show what has been done, thereby indicating what has been possible and impossible. It will reveal how well an area has been developed according to its potential, and what areas contain unrealized potential, either in manpower, natural resources, or cultural development.

When all information about a cultural landscape has been gathered and classified, a planner will have assembled a complex model of an area that can allow regional and local planning to proceed. This kind of comprehensive information gathering will, of course, require sophisticated interpretation, but the thoroughness of this comprehensive planning proposed by Geddes and elaborated upon by Glikson can lead to innovative development that coordinates all of the life functions of a community and its environment. This approach should permit planners to avoid past mistakes arising from incomplete or superficial knowledge of the complex relations and interactions that create the character of a community and of a region.

PRINCIPLES

New-town planners should prepare a strategy of land-use design. We suggest five issues for consideration which affect all other variables of a land-use plan: segregated or integrated uses, their proximity, densities, systems of land-use control, and environmental enhancement.

Segregation or Integration

There seem to be two popular models of patterns for urban land use. One represents a city as a society in which each is under constant change and renovation. Individuals and groups should have access to daily services on a human scale within a city's mechanism and integrated land-use pattern. Accordingly, mixed land use is essential to operate a city effectively. This model is a unit of social cells. Social scientists, religious leaders, educators, and others who favor social value as a prime concern in community and individual life may use it. Another model represents a city as a unit of economic cells whose major function is the transfer and trading of goods and products both within the city and to its region. To do this, a city must operate its entire transportation network efficiently and establish an interrelated system of segregated land uses. People who favor growth because it generates economic activity, such as politicians, decision makers, and financiers, may prefer this model. (See Figure 8.11.)

Can a city realize both models? If an equilibrium between the two is established and retained, a community may enjoy the advantages of both. However, disturbances may arise from economic pressures, such as congested transportation and parking to the detriment of pedestrian systems, concentrated utilities and infrastructure to the detriment of parks, green areas, and open space, and overintensified industrial aggregates to the detriment of housing and public buildings. Since it is the result of conscious planning, a new town may provide an exciting laboratory for testing these two models of cities.

For example, the following types of land use require total or partial segregation from residential areas to avoid strong negative impact: (1) heavy and some light industries, (2) wholesale businesses and warehouses,

Figure 8.11. A segregated industrial park in Columbia, Maryland. (Courtesy of the Howard Research and Development Corporation.)

(3) major highways or terminals, (4) some utilities, and (5) major recreational and sport centers. Some of these uses, especially those that have large open spaces and do not create a nuisance, may serve as buffers between neighborhoods. Land uses that may be integrated with residential areas include

(1)   All educational land use.

(2)   Health services of nearly all types. Hospitals would require a buffer zone to residential areas.

(3)   Social and cultural institutions such as community centers and clubs, theaters, and religious centers.

(4)   Stores, including all types of retail shops. Those in a new-town center may be mixed with special residential areas, or small centers may be built in neighborhoods or subneighborhoods.

(5)   Offices, including public, semipublic, or private ones, that may create a "dead" zone at night and become crime centers if they are not mixed with residential areas.

Such mixed land uses may foster more social activity than segregated uses. (See Figure 8.12.)

Proximity

A policy regarding the proximity of land uses should be included in the earliest development of a conceptual plan. The most important distance is that between the extreme border of a neighborhood and the nearest activity center (neighborhood or town center). This distance may be a tool to encourage use of a pedes-

Figure 8.12.   Integrated land use in Columbia, Maryland. Note the hierarchy of the vehicular network, the clustered housing pattern, the neighborhood (upper right), the shopping mall, and the lake. (Courtesy of the Howard Research and Development Corporation.)

trian network and socializing within a compact city. Most planners have accepted 0.62 miles (1 km) as a reasonable distance for encouraging most people to walk.[4] This radius describes an area of 1.2 square miles (or 3.14 square km). Planners who intend to foster good social relations try to accommodate a variety of land uses in this area— residential, commercial, services, educational, recreational, and open space. Decisions about proximity have a direct influence on densities. Proximity is also influenced by using green areas, open spaces, and agricultural land to divide one major land use from others. If proximity is considered to be related to social variables and to transportation, then the city may be planned as sociophysical cells. For this reason, planners have concluded that neighborhoods are desirable. For detailed discussions of this point see Chapters 4 and 7.

Density and Spatial Requirements

When proximity is regarded as an essential principle of land-use planning and its effect on society is recognized, a planner should consider the integral factor of density. There is no universal standard for density, but it is usually affected by the following variables:

(1)   Cultural, social, and psychological adaptability of people to new living conditions, including new neighbors and other people.

(2)   Per capita income and standard of living in a country.

(3)   Suitability of land for buildings and utilities without exceeding the threshold of its resources.

(4) Cost of construction and maintenance, and taxation as related to site size.

(5) Availability of land and its market value, which may dictate the intensity of land use and consequently its density.

Various factors determine land value. The most obvious elements affecting value are landscapes, their aesthetic richness, and the quality of their air and water. Other factors are the result of existing or planned development. Accessibility to infrastructure, utilities, and transportation affect construction costs for most types of land use and, hence, its value. Accessibility in turn relates to the proximity of land to other economic or social centers and their values. Policies of taxation may also determine land value by affecting the cost of both development and maintenance. All these factors combined affect the density of any land use because they determined much of its cost.

Gross density is the number of people per gross land unit required for a new town—measured either in "acres per thousand population" or "persons per acre."[5] Some planners refer to this as gross gross density. Such density refers to all types of land use. Differences in densities between new towns result from differences in living standards, land consumption, total available land, its value, and changes in community size and per capita income.

Table 8.2 shows 14 alternative population sizes and 11 possible gross densities within new towns. The alternatives indicate land requirements, employment, and proximity as measured by radii of required areas.

In general, gross density of new towns in early stages of development is less than that of established cities in the same country. However, spatial requirements may be similar to those in established cities due to the fact that the general standard of living is the same. "Planning for space standards . . . are in fact very similar to those already adopted in the larger existing towns."[6] Appendix A shows various gross densities of single land uses in different new towns around the world.

Some people may believe low densities in new towns to be one step toward improving the environment. Such densities, however, require large investments for the construction of utilities and infrastructure that have caused heavy local taxation.[7] This in turn has discouraged low-income people from moving to such new towns. Thus the lesson to be learned from this may be that to integrate income groups new towns must integrate land uses to ease the community's tax burden.

Gross density may also be defined by the number of users. For example, in industry it is the number of employees per gross land unit, and in commercial use, gross density is the number of employees per unit of floor area. Obviously, gross density of a single land use must correspond to densities of other uses.

The ratio between requirements of different land-use types vary between new towns from one country to another and also among new towns in the same country. Although developers and planners formulate the policy for such variation, it is a result of the unique condition of the project, its site, region, projected population, land price and availability, and the standard of living.

Planners, urban designers, and architects use different ways to calculate net density. It is therefore always necessary to specify the terms used in order to compare data. For example, net residential density may be the total number of units or occupants per land unit, or the residential floor area per person.

In setting alternative standards of density, a new-town planner must support the developer's policy and help him choose the best standard for reaching his goals and objectives. This standard, once set, will be difficult to change because alterations in infrastructure are costly, and not making necessary changes can lead to defects in environmental systems.

Control

Standards of proximity and density may be ineffective if a new town does not follow the principle of land-use control. To have effect, land-use control should be jointly accepted by all citizens, regardless of their status. The education of residents should be a cornerstone for their cooperation. Without controls a developer's planning and development may completely erode. Land-use control varies and may include comprehensive planning, laws and regulations, police power for regulatory purposes and systematic code enforcement, public ownership of essential land, and taxation.

By use of these controls, land use can proceed according to design and meet the following needs:

(1) Land-use control should be directly related to environmental control. Limitations of the natural environment should be recognized prior to planning.

(2) The quality of development within a given area should not exceed the capacity of that area to carry the

TABLE 8.2 ALTERNATIVES OF DENSITY, TOTAL LAND SIZE, EMPLOYMENT NUMBER, AND RADIUS
AS RELATED TO VARIOUS POPULATION SIZES IN NEW TOWNS

Alternative	Total Population	Total Number of Families*	Alternative Gross Density Per Acre — Families*	— Persons*	Total Area Needed — In Acres	— In sq. Miles**	Total Avg. of 1.0 per Family	Number Employees Avg. of 1.5 per Family	of Avg. of 2.0 per Family	Radius of Area Required in Miles
I	35,000	9,459	15	55	636	1.0	9,459	14,189	18,918	.56
			14	52	673	1.1	9,459	14,189	18,918	.58
			13	48	729	1.2	9,459	14,189	18,918	.60
			12	44	795	1.2	9,459	14,189	18,918	.63
			11	41	853	1.3	9,459	14,189	18,918	.65
			10	37	945	1.4	9,459	14,189	18,918	.69
			9	33	1,060	1.6	9,459	14,189	18,918	.73
			8	30	1,166	1.8	9,459	14,189	18,918	.76
			7	26	1,346	2.1	9,459	14,189	18,918	.82
			6	22	1,590	2.5	9,459	14,189	18,918	.89
			5	18	1,944	3.0	9,459	14,189	18,918	.98
II	40,000	10,810	15	55	727	1.1	10,810	16,215	21,620	.60
			14	52	769	1.2	10,810	16,215	21,620	.62
			13	48	833	1.3	10,810	16,215	21,620	.64
			12	44	909	1.4	10,810	16,215	21,620	.67
			11	41	975	1.5	10,810	16,215	21,620	.70
			10	37	1,081	1.6	10,810	16,215	21,620	.73
			9	33	1,212	1.8	10,810	16,215	21,620	.78
			8	30	1,333	2.1	10,810	16,215	21,620	.81
			7	26	1,538	2.4	10,810	16,215	21,620	.87
			6	22	1,818	2.8	10,810	16,215	21,620	.95
			5	18	2,222	3.5	10,810	16,215	21,620	1.05
III	45,000	12,162	15	55	818	1.3	12,162	18,243	24,324	.64
			14	52	865	1.4	12,162	18,243	24,324	.66
			13	48	937	1.6	12,162	18,243	24,324	.68
			12	44	1,022	1.6	12,162	18,243	24,324	.71
			11	41	1,097	1.7	12,162	18,243	24,324	.74
			10	37	1,216	1.9	12,162	18,243	24,324	.79
			9	33	1,363	2.1	12,162	18,243	24,324	.82
			8	30	1,500	2.3	12,162	18,243	24,324	.86
			7	26	1,730	2.7	12,162	18,243	24,324	.93
			6	22	2,045	3.2	12,162	18,243	24,324	1.01
			5	18	2,500	3.9	12,162	18,243	24,324	1.12
VIII	70,000	18,918	15	56	1,273	1.9	18,918	28,377	37,836	.80
			14	52	1,346	2.1	18,918	28,377	37,836	.82
			13	48	1,458	2.3	18,918	28,377	37,836	.85
			12	44	1,590	2.5	18,918	28,377	37,836	.89
			11	41	1,706	2.7	18,918	28,377	37,836	.92
			10	37	1,890	3.0	18,918	28,377	37,836	.97
			9	33	2,120	3.3	18,918	28,377	37,836	1.03
			8	30	2,332	3.6	18,918	28,377	37,836	1.08
			7	26	2,692	4.2	18,918	28,377	37,836	1.16
			6	22	3,180	5.0	18,918	28,377	37,836	1.26
			5	18	3,888	6.1	18,918	28,377	37,836	1.39
IX	75,000	20,269	15	55	1,363	2.1	20,269	30,404	40,538	.82
			14	52	1,442	2.3	20,269	30,404	40,538	.85
			13	48	1,562	2.4	20,269	30,404	40,538	.88
			12	44	1,704	2.7	20,269	30,404	40,538	.92
			11	41	1,828	2.9	20,269	30,404	40,538	.95
			10	37	2,036	3.2	20,269	30,404	40,538	1.01
			9	33	2,272	3.5	20,269	30,404	40,538	1.06
			8	30	2,499	3.9	20,269	30,404	40,538	1.12
			7	26	2,884	4.5	20,269	30,404	40,538	1.20
			6	22	3,408	5.3	20,269	30,404	40,538	1.30
			5	18	4,166	6.5	20,269	30,404	40,538	1.44
X	80,000	21,620	15	55	1,454	2.3	21,620	32,430	43,240	.85
			14	52	1,538	2.4	21,620	32,430	43,240	.88
			13	48	1,666	2.6	21,620	32,430	43,240	.91
			12	44	1,818	2.8	21,620	32,430	43,240	.95
			11	41	1,950	3.0	21,620	32,430	43,240	.98
			10	37	2,162	3.4	21,620	32,430	43,240	1.04
			9	33	2,424	3.8	21,620	32,430	43,240	1.10
			8	30	2,666	4.2	21,620	32,430	43,240	1.15
			7	26	3,076	4.8	21,620	32,430	43,240	1.24
			6	22	3,636	5.7	21,620	32,430	43,240	1.35
			5	18	4,444	6.9	21,620	32,430	43,240	1.49

Section XI — 85,000 — 22,972

15	55	1,545	2.4	22,972	34,458	45,944	.88
14	52	1,635	2.6	22,972	34,458	45,944	.90
13	48	1,771	2.8	22,972	34,458	45,944	.94
12	44	1,932	3.0	22,972	34,458	45,944	.98
11	41	2,073	3.2	22,972	34,458	45,944	1.02
10	37	2,297	3.6	22,972	34,458	45,944	1.13
9	33	2,576	4.0	22,972	34,458	45,944	1.19
8	30	2,833	4.4	22,972	34,458	45,944	1.28
7	26	3,269	5.1	22,972	34,458	45,944	1.39
6	22	3,864	6.0	22,972	34,458	45,944	1.53
5	18	4,722	7.4	22,972	34,458	45,944	

Section XII — 90,000 — 24,324

15	55	1,636	2.6	24,324	36,486	48,648	.90
14	52	1,730	2.7	24,324	36,486	48,648	.93
13	48	1,874	2.9	24,324	36,486	48,648	.97
12	44	2,044	3.2	24,324	36,486	48,648	1.01
11	41	2,172	3.4	24,324	36,486	48,648	1.05
10	37	2,432	3.8	24,324	36,486	48,648	1.10
9	33	2,726	4.3	24,324	36,486	48,648	1.16
8	30	3,000	4.7	24,324	36,486	48,648	1.22
7	26	3,460	5.4	24,324	36,486	48,648	1.31
6	22	4,090	6.4	24,324	36,486	48,648	1.43
5	18	5,000	7.8	24,324	36,486	48,648	1.58

Section XIII — 95,000 — 25,674

15	55	1,727	2.7	25,674	38,511	51,348	.93
14	52	1,827	2.9	25,674	38,511	51,348	.95
13	48	1,979	3.1	25,674	38,511	51,348	.99
12	44	2,159	3.4	25,674	38,511	51,348	1.04
11	41	2,317	3.6	25,674	38,511	51,348	1.07
10	37	2,568	4.0	25,674	38,511	51,348	1.13
9	33	2,879	4.5	25,674	38,511	51,348	1.20
8	30	3,167	4.9	25,674	38,511	51,348	1.26
7	26	2,654	5.7	25,674	38,511	51,348	1.35
6	22	4,318	6.7	25,674	38,511	51,348	1.47
5	18	5,278	8.2	25,674	38,511	51,348	1.62

Section XIV — 100,000 — 27,024

15	55	1,818	2.8	27,024	40,536	54,048	.95
14	52	1,924	3.0	27,024	40,536	54,048	.98
13	48	2,084	3.3	27,024	40,536	54,048	1.02
12	44	2,272	3.6	27,024	40,536	54,048	1.06
11	41	2,440	3.8	27,024	40,536	54,048	1.10
10	37	2,702	4.2	27,024	40,536	54,048	1.16
9	33	3,030	4.7	27,024	40,536	54,048	1.23
8	30	3,334	5.2	27,024	40,536	54,048	1.29
7	26	3,846	6.0	27,024	40,536	54,048	1.38
6	22	4,546	7.1	27,024	40,536	54,048	1.50
5	18	5,556	8.7	27,024	40,536	54,048	1.66

Section IV — 50,000 — 13,512

15	55	909	1.4	13,512	19,728	27,024	.67
14	52	962	1.5	13,512	19,728	27,024	.69
13	48	1,042	1.6	13,512	19,728	27,024	.72
12	44	1,136	1.7	13,512	19,728	27,024	.75
11	41	1,220	1.9	13,512	19,728	27,024	.82
10	37	1,351	2.1	13,512	19,728	27,024	.87
9	33	1,515	2.4	13,512	19,728	27,024	.91
8	30	1,667	2.6	13,512	19,728	27,024	.91
7	26	1,923	3.0	13,512	19,728	27,024	.98
6	22	2,273	3.6	13,512	19,728	27,024	1.06
5	18	2,778	4.3	13,512	19,728	27,024	1.18

Section V — 55,000 — 14,864

15	55	1,000	1.6	14,864	22,296	29,278	.71
14	52	1,058	1.7	14,864	22,296	29,278	.73
13	48	1,146	1.8	14,864	22,296	29,278	.76
12	44	1,250	2.0	14,864	22,296	29,278	.79
11	41	1,341	2.1	14,864	22,296	29,278	.82
10	37	1,486	2.3	14,864	22,296	29,278	.86
9	33	1,667	2.6	14,864	22,296	29,278	.91
8	30	1,833	2.9	14,864	22,296	29,278	.96
7	26	2,115	3.3	14,864	22,296	29,278	1.03
6	22	2,500	3.9	14,864	22,296	29,278	1.12
5	18	3,056	4.8	14,864	22,296	29,278	1.23

Section VI — 60,000 — 16,216

15	55	1,091	1.7	16,216	24,324	32,432	.74
14	52	1,154	1.8	16,216	24,324	32,432	.76
13	48	1,250	2.0	16,216	24,324	32,432	.79
12	44	1,364	2.1	16,216	24,324	32,432	.82
11	41	1,463	2.3	16,216	24,324	32,432	.85
10	37	1,622	2.5	16,216	24,324	32,432	.90
9	33	1,818	2.8	16,216	24,324	32,432	.95
8	30	2,000	3.1	16,216	24,324	32,432	1.00
7	26	2,308	3.6	16,216	24,324	32,432	1.07
6	22	2,727	4.3	16,216	24,324	32,432	1.17
5	18	3,333	5.2	16,216	24,324	32,432	1.29

Section VII — 65,000 — 17,567

15	55	1,182	1.8	17,567	26,351	35,134	.77
14	52	1,250	1.9	17,567	26,351	35,134	.79
13	48	1,354	2.1	17,567	26,351	35,134	.82
12	44	1,477	2.3	17,567	26,351	35,134	.86
11	41	1,585	2.5	17,567	26,351	35,134	.89
10	37	1,757	2.7	17,567	26,351	35,134	.94
9	33	1,970	3.1	17,567	26,351	35,134	.99
8	30	2,167	3.4	17,567	26,351	35,134	1.04
7	26	2,500	3.9	17,567	26,351	35,134	1.12
6	22	2,955	4.6	17,567	26,351	35,134	1.21
5	18	3,611	5.6	17,567	26,351	35,134	1.34

* Assumes 3.7 people per family
** 640 acres = 1 square mile

load and stress of development; thus growth should not pass the threshold of any given area.

(3) Adaptability of a definite land-use pattern in a given physical environment should require local examination of the mutual influence of nature and any planned urban development.

Planners of any projected land-use development should seriously consider any existing land-use control system and its level of effectiveness, because failure to do so will cause ineffective implementation of a new town's plan. Thus it is necessary to understand the nature of the power structure that stands behind the existing land-use regulations, codes, and enforcements.

No zoning can be effective unless a government adopts clearly stated rules and regulations, makes them public, and implements and enforces them. Policies of taxation, investment, and incentives are the most effective tools of land-use control. Any system of controls must be legally defensible, harmonious with planning goals and objectives, and administratively feasible.[8]

Maintaining a Natural Equilibrium

Developing land for human habitation interferes with the land's natural physical balance. Residents of agrarian villages understood the characteristics of nature, and their society knew that its survival depended upon cooperation with natural phenomena. Urban society, on the other hand, has not depended on local natural resources. Improvements in transportation and communication that permitted large numbers of people to form urban communities also reduced social knowledge of cooperating with the local environment. The result of this decreased knowledge is that the rate of urban growth has usually corresponded directly to the rate of natural destruction.

The conflict between nature and urban society cannot be avoided, but planners may help resolve it satisfactorily if they consider the natural environment in all stages of a comprehensive plan. The first step is to understand the processes of the natural world. The physical environment has been built from numerous elements that have been brought into equilibrium. Direct interference with the process of any single element can indirectly influence other related elements and the entire system. Stress on nature will also lead to stress on the society that lives within the bounds of their system. (See Chapter 3.)

Until recently, however, man did not realize the tremendous stress his civilization places upon the existing balance of nature. Although planners of urban expansion have often tried to substitute a man-made equilibrium for the natural one that existed, the failure of urban development has usually been the result of an inability to see the interrelation of all parts. Thus the solution to one problem has itself introduced a new stress.

To say all this is not to say, as extreme ecologists may, "Don't touch." There will be land development as populations grow or migrate, and there must be development to correct the conditions of many urban areas. But planners must recognize what ecologists, biologists, and other specialists in the natural and physical sciences have learned, and they must be able to apply knowledge from these disciplines. If this knowledge is neglected by the planner or developer, he may provide short-term relief while insuring long-term imbalance and decay.

Planning that aims at establishing a favorable equilibrium among natural and human elements must be concerned with the long-range needs of man and of the natural world, and such planning must begin with the knowledge that nature and humanity are closely intertwined. From this point of view, recent concerns with the negative results of poor land use became very important.[9]

By bringing the countryside into the residential areas as natural and developed open space, a new town can provide residents with an attractive, psychologically pleasing environment in which to live. If open space, agricultural land, wooded land, or playground areas, jointly or separately, are planned to intersect the residential area or to establish boundaries for its territory, they may help create a sense of closeness to nature. The function of natural boundaries for residential areas may also serve the purpose of physical self-identity for a neighborhood that will support personal neighborhood identities. However, any areas reserved as open space to border residential or other structured environments should be planned thoughtfully and carefully to enhance nature. This policy is one of the major issues anticipated by planners, developers, residents, and users of a new town. Among its many advantages, the educational results for young people and the relaxed environment for a community as a whole are the most beneficial.

PRACTICE

After defining the prime principles to be adopted by a new-town planner, we must clarify the practice of land-use planning—the contents of a land-use plan. The new-town plan is a general framework for policy formulation of the optimal designated uses of various sections of the site. Such policy should be the basis for detailed plans of each section. The plan indicates in a clear form the overall network of communication and transportation. In its comprehensive pictorial and written expression the plan is also meant to inhibit the misuse of land. Although a land-use plan may be only a combination of physical variables, its best form should be a synthesis of the social, economic, political, and other goals and of the physical limitations of the site as a planner-developer and others conceive them. Almost no variable in the land-use plan can be isolated and treated individually without considering its reciprocal impact. Therefore the success or failure of a planner-developer will depend to some extent on his ability to realize and predict these mutual impacts. Because of our limited ability as human beings and as planners to predict precisely the resulting forms of the interrelated variables, and because of the dynamic technological and social changes occurring in our time, land-use plans should retain some flexibility to meet those changes. Land-use plans should also be evaluated and modified occasionally after their completion. Unlike other items, land is irreplaceable. Soil may require thousands of years to return to its existing form, and construction errors resulting from inadequate land-use planning may cause immense damage for which money may not compensate.

Conventional land-use plans categorize uses as residential, industrial, commercial, transportation, institutional, agricultural, open space, recreational, conservation and, occasionally, unassigned. Generally land for housing is the largest use: about 50 percent, except in those new towns with high-density residential use. Open space uses 20 percent, and education and industry use 10 percent each; the rest is used for transportation and commerce.[10] In the following sections we will discuss most of these land uses.

Residential Land Use

Residential land use is the main type in size and in function. In a bedroom community, 85 to 95 percent of the land may be used for residential development. The provision for diverse land uses in a new town, however, prevents development of such one-sided communities. In most cases new-town residential land will occupy between 30 and 50 percent of the total land area, though residential use may be as high as 65 percent of the total in regions where land for development is scarce. (See Appendix A.)

To insure that residential land will enhance the living conditions of a new-town population, planners and developers should have the following objectives. Housing in new towns may be a tool for social accomplishment. Designers and planners certainly influence a new town's society when they decide to segregate or to integrate housing, to define housing size and type, and to establish certain forms and horizontal and vertical densities. Design policy for housing should be consistent with a new town's goals and objectives. Formulation of housing goals may lead to the re-evaluation of the new town's goals and objectives. Thus it is necessary for the housing experts to work closely with the new-town social planner before making their final decision and presenting it to the interdisciplinary team.

People who build their own homes is one possible method of meeting housing value increases and encouraging self-reliance and creativity among individuals and groups.[11] A rural or agrarian community may accept self-constructed housing because of its economic advantages. Self-construction may require preparatory work by a developer (especially the public) of a new town that may include the following:

(1) Alternative housing plans available to potential newcomers.

(2) A variety of forms that change the combination, to avoid overall standardization and to encourage variety in buildings.

(3) Use of building materials available in the surrounding area that may integrate buildings harmoniously with their surroundings.

(4) Detailed plans and material provided to each self-help resident who joins the program. Also, a building expert should follow the construction so that residents meet code requirements and basic building regulations.

(5) Loans available with low or no interest for all who would like to join the program.

Implementation of such plans may strengthen residents' ties to their area and thus become a social instrument for community identity and pride.

Housing Layouts.   Regardless of how housing is constructed, its configuration and grouping affects economic and social activities. New towns, as laboratories for urban design, have used a variety of layouts for residential areas that include clustered, curvilinear or rectilinear, polycentric, concentric, radial, and the Radburn pattern. (See Figure 8.13.)

Figure 8.13. The Radburn layout. This superblock residential configuration aligns housing around green areas which are only for pedestrians. (Source: *Neighborhood and Community Planning.*)

The rectilinear or grid layout, known to the Greeks by the fourth century B.C., is the pattern of most cities in the United States. Simple in design and implementation, the pattern is often monotonous because standard forms and sizes are set for lots, buildings, and streets. However, this simplicity makes it easy for strangers to acquaint themselves with an area. The grid system allows good distribution of traffic and supports the formation of neighborhoods when formed in a hierarchy. The layout of rectangular blocks may use more infrastructure than other layouts.

Since this type of layout may distribute all traffic evenly, it may be necessary to place traffic lights at nearly every street corner. Also, nuisances (pollution and noise) exist almost equally on all blocks.

Compared with others, such as the clustered or curvilinear layout, the grid allows integration of commercial, industrial, and other land uses within residential blocks. Thus blocks designated as green areas may eventually be converted to other uses. The system is especially adaptable to flat areas, but may ignore the topography in other areas. (See Figures 8.14 and 8.15.)

Figure 8.14. A linear layout in Grande Cache, Alberta, Canada. (Courtesy of the Alberta Government Photographic Service.)

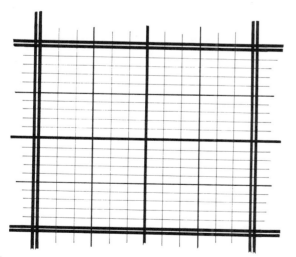

Figure 8.15. Schema of a hierarchical transportation network in a grid system. This system may eliminate major cross-traffic from neighborhoods and may enable access to them, mainly for those who live or have business there. This pattern has been developed in Los Angeles, California, and Toronto, Ontario.

The curvilinear layout combines the linear form of the grid with curved lines to adapt a design to local topography. Although this layout has some variation in townscape, it often remains uniform in sizes of lots, buildings, and street widths. The curvilinear layout has been widely used in new towns and other large-scale developments since the 1950s. It allows more green areas and reduces the total length of streets as compared with the grid layout, but construction of infrastructure may be almost as costly.

Clustered housing is a recent innovation in new towns and other large-scale developments. This layout groups single, detached, or attached housing around dead-end streets to save a central open space for communal use. It allows relatively high densities and variety not available with other forms,[12] and may decrease the cost of each unit compared to that of conventional layouts.[13] The culs-de-sac serve two functions: first, they restrict traffic to residents, their friends, and service vehicles. This allows safe pedestrian movement and quiet areas far from major highways. Second, the layout fosters social interaction among its residents, which may lead to local social identity. Residents may use the common green area for recreation and leisure and should be responsible for its maintenance. Green areas in this layout may be stretched along the backyards of houses to form a special pedestrian pathway between the boundaries of the superblocks and thus improve their environmental quality. This leads to greater marketability and land value.[14]

The clustered layout offers further advantages over the grid and curvilinear layouts. This form allows

mixed land uses not available in the other designs. Costs of constructing and maintaining infrastructure, utilities, and streets are lower than for conventional layouts.[15] The clustering decreases the length of streets and with it the amount of paved surface. Therefore, rainfall as runoff is less and may enrich groundwater. The reserved green areas may foster a country environment and lead to reserved woodlands not available in conventional patterns.[16] For a comparison of a conventional subdivision and a clustered layout on equal parcels see Table 8.3 and Figure 8.16.

Density. A major goal of the residential area is to create an attractive atmosphere where people will be active during the day as well as at night, and this requires diverse land use. Each residential unit within a neighborhood should have convenient access to nearby recreational facilities, shopping areas, medical services, neighborhood centers, schools, and offices such as banks and loan services. By providing local space for recreational and other services the new town prevents overloading of transportation corridors while it makes minor services readily available for its inhabitants.

In a new-town center or in designated sections within a neighborhood, mixed density may be desirable to bring together a mixed population and justify economically the variety of immediate services. Thus apartments, high-rise buildings, and single detached

TABLE 8.3 COMPARISON OF LAND USE IN A CONVENTIONAL SUBDIVISION AND A CLUSTERED LAYOUT OF EQUAL SIZE

	Conventional Subdivision	Cluster Subdivision
Acres in streets	32	24
Linear feet of street	22,500	16,055
Percent of site in street	29	19
Acres in building sites	80	41
Dwelling units	590	604
Acres of usable open space	0	51

Source: *Cluster Development.*

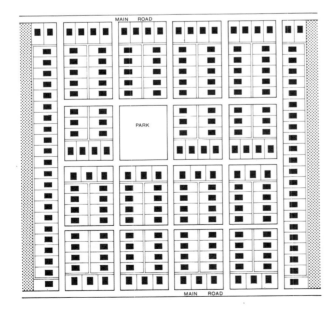

A: GRID

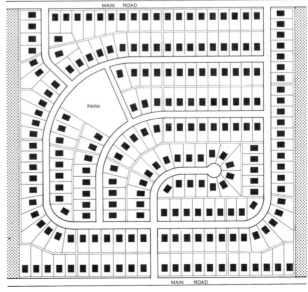

B: CURVILINEAR

Figure 8.16.   Comparison of three alternative designs for a 50-acre site.

units may also meet the housing needs of various groups, such as single people, young married couples, elderly, or low-income people. (See Figure 4.7.)

To insure that the positive features of residential density are maintained, the residential land-use plan must contain provisions for zoning restrictions, laws, and regulations as well as for community education, to develop and maintain a positive community image. If the members of the community have a clear idea of the value and importance of density for the quality of life within their community, they themselves will control density. (See Figure 8.17.)

A recent comparative study between a prototypic, high-density development of 70 percent apartments and 30 percent townhouses and a development of single-family residences, of which 75 percent were layed out in a grid and 25 percent were clustered, revealed that the high-density pattern saves 44 percent of the capital investment cost of the low-density development. "The largest cost savings are for housing construction, although significant savings are also found for roads and utilities (55% lower in high-density 'planned' than low-density 'sprawl') and land consumption."[17] The cost share of a local government in constructing services in a high-density prototype is less than that in low-density sprawl construction.

Planned high density generates less air and water pollution than low density does since they "use less energy per unit." The study found that "overall reduc-

tion in air pollution emissions from home energy consumption and transportation is 45%." Energy used in high-density dwellings is less than that in low-density sprawl, and the saving in consumption may even be 14 percent, resulting from reduced use of gas and electricity and transportation demand. In a well planned, high-density development, saving in energy may reach 44 percent.[18]

Industrial Park

This section describes the basic principles of industrial land use through the study of an industrial park. We discuss this, and later a commercial park, to acquaint readers with development that can be adapted to any scale. (See Figure 8.18.)

An industrial park is a tract of land, zoned and subdivided with special utilities, transportation, services, and management, and planned comprehensively for the sole use of industries.[19] Industries move to an industrial park to improve their working environment, obtain efficiency, provide space for transportation and expansion, and to enjoy good services. In designing an industrial park a new-town planner must consider area requirements, percentage of built-up area, off-street parking and loading facilities, limits of building heights, storage areas and their regulations, setback of buildings from highways and roads, dis-

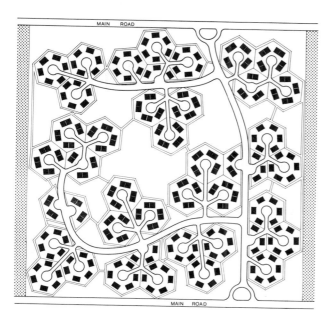

C: CLUSTER

QUANTIFIED SUMMARY OF THE THREE LAYOUTS

	GRID	CURVILINEAR	CLUSTER
	HOUSING LAYOUTS		
DWELLING UNITS	207	216	272
STREET LENGTH*			
MAJOR (34'wide)	9,541	6,932	3,494
MINOR (26'wide)	1,048	325	—
LOCAL (18'wide)	—	—	4,993
TOTAL AREA*	351,642	244,138	239,820
AREAS*			
LOT AREA			
TOTAL	1,681,848	1,792,000	1,091,420
PERCENT	77.4	82.5	50.2
STREET AREA			
TOTAL	351,642	244,138	239,820
PERCENT	16.2	11.2	11.05
PEDESTRIAN PATH			
TOTAL	64,374	64,374	97,620
PERCENT	2.9	3.0	4.05
PARK			
TOTAL	75,150	72,500	744,154
PERCENT	3.5	3.3	34.7
STREET FIXTURES			
STOP SIGNS	12	8	11
TRAFFIC LIGHTS	10	2	2
STREET SIGNS	20	8	4
FIRE HYDRANTS	20	16	15
INTERSECTIONS			
MAJOR-MAJOR	10	6	4
MAJOR-MINOR	10		13
MINOR-MINOR	10	4	13
UTILITY LINES	9,436	6,932	8,487

* Length in feet and area in square feet

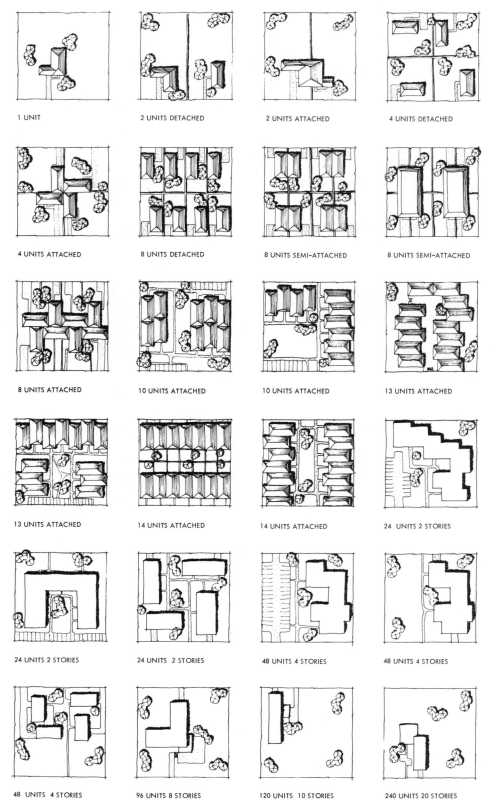

Figure 8.17. Comparative densities of residential units in 1 acre. The potential use of 1 acre may depend on the value of density a community adopts. The implementation of density may vary in a vertical or horizontal form. In either case density will have an immediate impact on the environment by dictating the availability of space for movement within the acre, the landscaping and, most important, the load of utilities and infrastructure systems in its immediate surroundings.

230

Figure 8.18. An industrial center in Columbia, Maryland. (Courtesy of the Howard Research and Development Corporation.)

tances between buildings, fire regulations and code requirements, basic requirements for building appearances, landscaping requirements, minimum building safety requirements, and maintenance regulations. An industrial park may reduce maintenance costs, release a single firm from site development, allow small industry to enjoy a variety of local services usually required by large ones, increase property values over time, offer safety and security, provide social services for employees, and save taxes.[20]

Industrial parks may cover an area of 100 to 200 gross acres and may even reach 500 acres. One firm may require up to 25 acres. Privately developed industrial parks usually attract small firms that require an average of 2 acres.[21] The average number of workers per gross acre of industrial land is 6 for heavy industry, 22 for light industry, and 16 for an industrial park. For a self-contained new town, where 30 to 35 percent of the working labor force is in industry, we may expect

that for every 1000 new-town population, industry will consume a total of 12 acres for all types, or 2 acres for light industry and 10 acres for heavy industry.[22] Lot size will depend on the size of the firm and should expand as a firm grows. Equal lots may be desirable for flexibility in expansion.

The planning and development of an industrial park in a new town may require consideration of various factors. In general, the site selection of an industrial park requires investigation of its relation to the overall new-town land-use plan, all physical and environmental criteria, and the evaluation of the sequential impact of the site's development on the new-town community and on other land uses.

Planners of a new town should develop an industrial park in visual harmony with its environment. Such consideration should refer not only to outlook, shape, and color of the buildings, but also to the maintenance mechanism, such as by-products, open outdoor storage, and disposal. The exposure of industry to highways requires special landscaping and attention to building design to insure an attractive view from the road. A park also needs buffer zones to control any nuisances it may cause.

Access and Transportation.   The parking, loading, and maneuvering of trucks consumes a substantial portion of land in an industrial park. It may also take more area to accommodate employees' cars than their work space or a research laboratory.[23] An area for rights-of-way may use 10 to 15 percent of the gross land, and building coverage may range from 20 to 50 percent of the total land. The ultimate coverage may exceed 60 percent.[24]

Convenient access for vehicles to local, regional, and national transportation networks is a prime factor in attracting industry and supporting its success. Highways in good condition for traffic of heavy loads are especially essential for the import of raw materials and export of heavy industrial goods. A network is also important for employees commuting to the industrial park from the new town and from the surrounding region, especially in rush hours. Also essential for an industrial park is the parking space within the site and convenient movement and circulation for large trucks. An accessible network should not cross or bypass residential areas, and should avoid pollution, noise, and vibration.

Heavy industry may require access to a railroad; therefore the allocation of land for rail, switching, parking, and for a cargo terminal will consume a large portion of land with rights-of-way.[25] Ninety percent of American industrial parks are served by rail.[26] Similar land consumption may be required by other land or air transportation.

The use of track and trains in an industrial park requires avoiding intersections of roads with rails. A planner may overcome this problem by planning a diagonal rail branch interlaced with roads or interconnected rail and roads entering the lot from opposite sides.[27]

An airport is another type of transportation that must be considered for land use, including the site and its proximity to other land uses, its noise and pollution, and the total land required for the facility, its access, and for hangars. Airports that serve an industrial park require high quality and large capacity, large open land with a flat terrain for runways and for buildings, extensive utilities, and rapid land transportation. It is also important to consider that the site may not appeal equally to every industry. Unattractive factors of an airport such as vibration, noise, pollution, electrical

disturbances, or transportation prices may hinder some industries.[28]

Availability of waterways in a new town may be a strong additional factor in the development of an industrial park and require a large land tract for docks and warehouses. Ports require integration with land transportation, especially railroads, for the transfer of goods.

Infrastructure and Utilities.   Planning and development of the infrastructure and services, such as water supply and sewage network, energy, transportation networks, and telecommunication systems, all of which result in land consumption and allocation, are necessary to attract industry. In most cases the construction of utilities should precede the development of industrial projects.

Many planners now agree that placing public and private utilities underground is the best method for preserving aesthetic values aboveground and insuring minimally disruptive repair, expansion, and addition to existing utilities. In addition to the aesthetic values gained from underground installation, it will be less expensive and more effective for the community to coordinate all utilities in a comprehensive plan that will release the municipality from re-excavation. At least six utility systems could be combined into one underground utilidor network: sewage, water, telephone, electricity, gas, cable television and other communications systems.[29]

Most industries consider the availability of water supply and a sewage network at reasonable prices as essential requirements for their needs. The network, water storage areas, and a plant for purification and recycling and systems control require special integrated land use which should be taken in account for construction and maintenance. The site also will attract industry when water is available in large quantities and is durable and cheap enough to satisfy existing and potential needs. Large quantities of water may be required for cooling, heating, or fire protection.

Natural gas, electricity, and telephone networks require land especially when they are constructed underground. An industrial park will also require land for dumping waste and garbage to follow health regulations. Such land must be ample to absorb additional waste from future pressing growth.

Although most industries require flat or graded land for horizontal movement, the selected site must be free from flood hazards and have good drainage. Occasionally expenses for sewage pumping must also be considered.

Environmental Impact. A new-town planner must analyze the environmental impact of the industrial park development and its growth on the site itself, its environs, the total new town, and on the exhaustion of local and regional resources such as water, land, and air. The land must be suitable for heavy construction and vehicular movement, must not be located in an area subject to air inversion or fog, must have soil that is not subject to damaging erosion, must not be suitable for agriculture, and must not be in the most attractive area of the new-town site where residential development is best.

Proper climate is important in land for industries, especially those that contribute to air pollution, noise, or odors. An early survey of data on the macro- and microclimate of the potential site is essential; a site where prevailing winds carry all nuisances away from the new town is best.

In a privately developed new town it is difficult to predict land requirements for industrial parks because of uncertainty about the types of industries they will attract and because of outside competition. Publicly developed new towns usually enjoy a condition in which industries are initiated, subsidized, or supported by the public, who may direct and influence the decision about the location of those industries. Spatial requirements may also differ completely from one industry to another and will depend on factors such as the number of workers, social conditions offered, size of raw materials, and their by-products, machines and equipment required, product size, marketing system, and storage. Thus the land-use plan of the industrial park should be general and flexible. At first it may offer skeletal networks of local roads and utilities; the detailed plan may be developed as industries commit themselves to the park. A planner should study various plans of relevant industries to establish his own code and spatial requirements for his industrial park.[30]

Despite the many advantages of a segregated industrial park, its major disadvantage is being depopulated at night. This situation may support a negative social climate at night when the isolated industrial park is not in operation. Another disadvantage of overconcentration is rush hour traffic, which may be overcome by highly sophisticated alternative points of access.

Industries are usually segregated because of their large size requirements and their type. Some small industries and manufacturing may be integrated with other land uses when they do not have a negative environmental impact. Such integration may ease commuting and contribute to transportation efficiency. (See Chapter 7.)

The strong environmental and ecological concern of new-town developers causes them to support research and light industries that will not have a negative impact on the town's environment.[31] In any case, the types of industries brought to the new town will have an impact on the composition of the population they attract. Although employment will include residents of the immediate surrounding region, we may assume that the majority of employees will come from the new town itself. Therefore when planning industrial use, one must also consider employee housing which will meet their standards.

An industrial park may also require accommodations for restaurants, child care centers for working mothers, and some other social services for employees in their free time. Thus the goals and objectives of an industrial park should coincide with the social and economic goals of the new town.

Commercial Land Use

In spite of its economic importance in a new town, commercial land use is not a large portion of the total. Unlike industrial use, major commercial space is in vertical rather than horizontal forms. Commercial uses include land for buildings to house commercial activities and their employees, warehouses, and parking lots and structures. Most commerce needs flat areas or land that can be graded, and infrastructure and utilities must be available. Solid waste collection may require special consideration. The land must also be suitable for heavy construction since commercial buildings usually have more than one floor. Location of this type of land use should be close to all residential areas and other land uses, and should be accessible to vehicles and pedestrians. Land selected for commercial use should be free from floods, erosion, or landslides.

The scale of the commercial development will depend on the market catchment area and its population size, income, buying habits, and access to transportation networks, on other competing commercial centers in the area, and on supply and demand. Planners may consider potential purchasing power per capita as market capture together with the required expenditure to determine commercial space requirements.[32] Factors such as selection of a convenient and accessible site, quality of commercial facilities in the area, variety of goods offered, and a pleasing environment may also support commercial activities. Commercial land may be integrated with other uses, such as residential, office, or transportation, or it may be segregated in a commercial park. When designed well, such a park may improve the environment by making it pleasing

Figure 8.19. Kodak House and Hempstead House, office buildings in Hemel Hempstead, England. (Courtesy of the Commission for the New Towns.)

and attractive. Landscaping is essential here, especially in parking areas and areas of public gatherings. Commercial parks may also contribute much to the social well-being of a new-town community and boost its regional image. (See Figure 8.19.)

Development of commercial land use requires consideration of climate. Landscaping, shadowing, and covering or protecting areas from stresses from temperature, wind, or precipitation may be necessary to attract outsiders and encourage movement.

Shopping Center. A shopping center is "a group of commercial establishments, planned, developed, owned and managed as a *unit* related in location, size, and types of shops to the trade area that the unit serves; it provides on-site parking in definite relationship to the types and sizes of stores."[34] (See Figure 8.20.)

A shopping center may serve three areas: a neighborhood, a community, and a region. Obviously the last mentioned may serve all three areas and should be large scale in operation and in variety. A regional shopping center may be located within or adjacent to

the new town, and must have good access in either case. Such a center includes all types of furniture, restaurants, food and drug stores, clothing, domestic goods, and even car repair facilities and may range in size from between 300,000 to 1 million square feet. To be economically feasible, a regional shopping center should serve a population of 150,000. In the United States, such centers are generally designed to serve a catchment area with a population of 150 to 400,000.[34]

A new-town community shopping center serves mainly its community and sells a large variety of goods, furniture, and food. A community shopping center must have easy access and an average gross leasable area ranging between 100,000 and 300,000 square feet. Such a center requires 10 to 30 acres of land when it serves a population of 40,000 to 150,000.[35]

A neighborhood shopping center may serve a population of 5000 to 40,000 and offer goods, food, drugstores, dry cleaning laundry, and shoe repair services, and book stores for daily needs. A neighborhood center's size may range from 50,000 to 100,000 square feet, and it would need from 4 to 10 acres of site area.[36]

Food stores are major items in the neighborhood center, and general merchandise is important in both the community and regional centers. In the latter, merchandise may comprise over 50 percent of total sales. (See Table 8.4.)

In planning a shopping center, the new-town planner must consider its economic and physical feasibility, and delineate the marketing area, accessibility, and land availability and value. (See Figure 8.21.) The site must be large enough to accommodate future expansion. Land value is lower before the development is built than when expansion is needed. Since utilities are essential for the development, a planner should check their proximity to the site and consider the cost of extending them. He should also check adjacent uses and their mutual impact.

Selection of tenants for a shopping center should be made when a central managing body is formed, which will make rules and regulations for all the tenants. The floor plan should be prepared for the desired tenants to coincide with the original goals of the shopping center; variation in shops may be an additional factor for its success. Tenants should be selected during the planning process in order to adjust units to their needs.

In a severe climate it is desirable to cover all structures under one roof. Such design attracts families with children, enables them to spend more time, and makes shopping a kind of social venture. Interior decoration and landscaping can make the shopping center attractive and foster local community pride. Building layouts may have different shapes, but they must be convenient for shoppers' movement and circulation within the complex. It is also important to arrange the shops in relation to each other. On a large paved area

Figure 8.20. A shopping center in Elizabeth, Australia. Note the integration of the center and transportation. (Courtesy of the South Australia Housing Trust.)

TABLE 8.4   GOODS AND SERVICES OF A SHOPPING CENTER

Food and Food Service	*General Merchandise*
supermarket	department store
bakery	variety stores
meat	ladies', men's, and children's stores
dairy	shoe store
candy	furs
restaurant	fabrics
cafeteria	luggage
	leather goods

Home Furnishings	*Other Retail*
furniture	hardware
lamps	automotive supply and general repairs
appliances	garden shops
floor coverings and carpets	hobby shops
curtains and drapes	books and stationery
radio, television, and music store	flowers
interior decorator	tobacco store
glassware	drugstore
cutlery	sporting goods
	jewelry
	liquor and wine stores
Services	sewing machines
	cosmetic shops
banks	camera shop
finance companies	toy stores
post office	
insurance office	
beauty shop	
barber shop	
watch repair	
shoe repair	
dry cleaning	
laundry	

Source: This list is based in part on *The Community Builders Handbook,* pp. 318–319.

in a hot or cold climate walks require protection from sun, rain, or snow. (See Figure 8.22.)

For determining the amount of parking space for a shopping center, planners have used various criteria, such as the estimated rush hours of purchasing, gross floor area of the building, gross sales area, or "gross leasable area."[37] Trucks and parking for loading should be separated from those of shoppers. Entrances and exits should be considered, with many alternative routes available to avoid congestion. Setback lines of buildings and of parking should be ample for safety from traffic. Circulation alternatives are essential for traffic movement. Walking distances from parking to the building should be acceptable for the community; moving sidewalks may also be useful. A large, paved parking area would require landscaping. Light in the parking area and within the structure is also necessary.

Business Park.   A business park is a consecutive tract of land zoned and subdivided with special utilities, infrastructure, services and management, and planned comprehensively for the dominant use of such businesses as offices, office-oriented facilities, and complementary services. A business park may be efficient and may improve its environment. It may be used by a single corporation or by many tenants.[38] Although business parks usually serve a metropolitan area, they may still be located in a new adjacent town and accommodate employees within the new town itself.

A business park, like a shopping center and an industrial park, is a comprehensive entity established to achieve uniformity in a large unit development, although one restricted to offices may not have the same attraction as a shopping center or an industrial

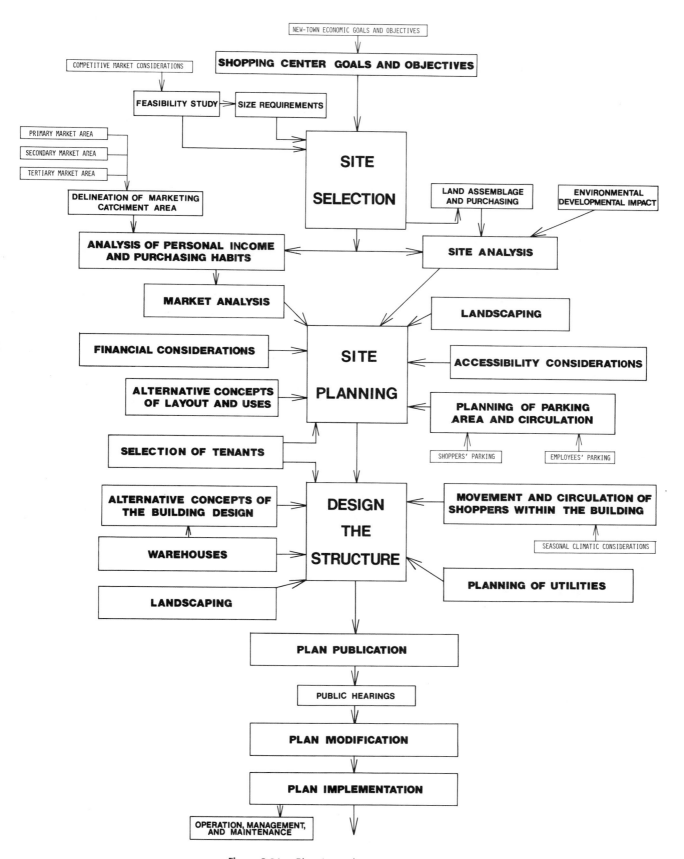

Figure 8.21. Planning a shopping center.

237

park. A planner may provide variation by integrating housing units, shopping, restaurants, hotels, banks, or similar facilities.

Some requirements for a business park are similar to those for a shopping center or industrial park: access, site selection, parking needs, and architectural attractiveness. New telecommunication devices and proximity to an airport and other rapid transit are also essential.

In the United States, the business park is a newly emerging concept of large-scale commercial land development. New cities developed as provincial or national capitals have also developed a type of business park in the form of a public office campus, as in Brasilia, Brazil, and Islamabad, Pakistan. Like the industrial park, the office or business park has a daytime population, and may be almost empty at night. (See Figure 8.23.)

If a business park is not developed in the downtown section of the new town, it is necessary to provide easy access between the two. A business park may provide larger space, relatively low land value, and more potential expansion than a downtown location. It may also offer good management and an attractive environment.

A company town may be a new urban settlement that develops all three types—an industrial park, a business park (as headquarters), and a shopping center—jointly or separately.

Town Center. This portion of land use in the new town should be its unifying center and should be accessible from all parts of town for vehicles and pedestrians. The center should have a convenient circulation pattern for traffic and enough parking area for consumers. Traffic circulation should lead in and out

Figure 8.22. The exhibition area in a shopping center of East Kilbride, Scotland. The hall is in the air-conditioned, centrally heated Plaza shopping development in the town center. (Courtesy of the East Kilbride and Stonehouse Development Corporation.)

Figure 8.23. A commercial center in Irvine, California. (Courtesy of The Irvine Company.)

of the area, but the center should be closed to cross traffic.

A town center should be designed functionally and artistically to be a meeting ground for all sections of the community and its neighborhood units. To become a community focus, the center's land use should be integrated without distracting neighborhood centers. The diverse land use should encompass residential areas including non-car users to increase its nighttime activities, various commercial activities, handicraft and art shops, town and regional private and public offices, an arts and music center, educational facilities, and a communication center. (See Figure 8.24.)

It is also essential that the functions of a town center respond in details of their design to special segments of the community, such as the handicapped, and make the area accessible to them by a variety of techniques such as mobile sidewalks and alternatives to stairways.

Public indoor and outdoor land uses of the town center should relate functionally and integrate themselves to establish continuous use. Playgrounds for young age groups may be close to shopping centers or to public service land use. An open green area should be separated from vehicles, but may be used by social groups for free meetings. The center should provide attractive and special space for public gatherings, which should be protected from the weather. (See Figure 8.25.)

Climatic limitations should be considered in designing the integrated sections of the center. Tropical climates need shading all through the center and along the connecting lines for various types of land use so that pedestrians will continue using the area. This sheltering pattern is necessary to avoid rain and overexposure, and controlled ventilation will also be required. Similar considerations may exist in arid and

Figure 8.24. The town center of Tapiola, Finalnd. (Courtesy of the Museum of Finnish Architecture.)

semiarid places, and opposite requirements may be needed for snowy areas. In semiarid regions where much rain may fall within short periods, surfaces of the centers may decrease water absorption and increase surface water, and consequently flood the center. A similar process may occur in a center located in a tropical region that has intense precipitation. In arid regions, large paved areas (for parking) in centers may increase ground heat radiation and make it unsuitable for use by pedestrians and cars. Here trees must be used to break winds and sandstorms and also to provide increased shaded areas.

The public space in the town center should use natural daylight; at night it should be lit up to encourage use and establish secure feelings.

Artistically the town center should be a noticeable landmark within the entire new town to establish its image and residents' identification, a place that people

are attracted to which responds to their social or economic needs. Geographically the center is best when it is almost equally close and accessible to all other land use.

Open Space, Recreation, and Conservation

Recreational and conserved open space plays a large part (up to 40 percent) in establishing a desirable living environment for new-town residents. Open space can provide the aesthetically pleasing natural environment lacking in most sections of contemporary cities, and careful use of such space in a comprehensive land-use plan can avoid the inequality between private and public open space that often exists in purely residential communities. Careful use of open space could avoid

1 COMMERCIAL CORE
2 RESIDENTIAL
3 LAKESHORE ENTERTAINMENT
4 GOVERNMENT OFFICES
5 SERVICE TRADES
6 PARKLANDS
7 CLUBS & INSTITUTIONS
8 COMMERCIAL
9 GENERAL HOSPITAL

Figure 8.25. Plan of the town center of Belconnen, Australia. (Source: *Seventeenth Annual Report*. 1 July 1973–30 June 1974.)

Figure 8.26. Public baths and open space in East Kilbride, Scotland. (Courtesy of the East Kilbride and Stonehouse Development Corporation.)

undesirable mixing between industrial and residential land uses, and could increase or strengthen territorial identity of neighborhoods and of a new town. By limiting its scale and by innovative land-use design, open space can be made valuable and easily accessible to all residents of a new town. (See Figure 8.26.)

Open space for a new town falls into two categories: developed and undeveloped. Undeveloped open space consists of land that naturally has a high value for recreation or for wildlife preservation and a fairly low value for construction. Developed open space, which usually comprises the larger proportion of open space within a new town, should be carefully designed to enhance the environment. (See Table 8.5 and Figure 8.27.)

Land for open space and green areas have become typical features of new towns as planners have attempted to combine town and country atmospheres. The amount of such use varies greatly from place to place; some new communities have reached 20 percent of their designated areas.[40] Agricultural land may be combined with green areas to assure its existence. Also, open space surrounding public buildings may establish buffers for dividing various land uses. (See Figure 8.28.)

To ensure control of land zoned as open space within a new town and to minimize the risk of changing its use, it should be publicly owned and maintained by a local new-town government.[41] The public may acquire land by aquisition and eminent domain, condemnation, long period lease, gift, voluntary agreement, easement, exchange, or by reservation as public open space.[42]

It is essential that the open space land-use plan be based on long-range trends and goals. Increasing disposable income, especially when coupled with a shortened work week, means there will be a large demand for usable recreational space. Trends in recreational habits also warrant strong consideration.

One of the new urban settlements that may devote a large portion of its area to recreation is the resort or retirement town. Although many of the former use

TABLE 8.5   VARIOUS USES OF OPEN SPACE

Developed	Undeveloped
Green open space between residential units and other intersecting uses	Woodlands
	Hunting areas
Green open space between major land uses	National or state reservations
	Fringe areas of new town
Bodies of water	
canals	Bodies of water
rivers or tributaries	rivers
lakes	lakes
waterfalls	ponds
swimming pools	
(indoor or outdoor)	Cliffs and steep slopes
racing areas	
boating	Flood plains
skiing	
fishing	
Waterfront: sea, river, lake	
Skiing	
Parks	
Golf courses	
Tennis courts	
Playgrounds	
Gridirons	
Basketball courts	
Horse trails and race courses	
Agriculture	

land seasonally, it is possible for such a town to offer year-round activities. Because the town's economy rests on recreation, maintenance is a primary consideration. Many countries that have recognized the economic significance of resort towns now plan and support them. (See Chapter 2.)

Skiing is a growing sport in the United States; in 1970 it was estimated that 3 million Americans enjoyed it. Many skiers love luxury, and the majority of them can afford it; some have purchased ski homes as a second home. The skier is willing to travel long distances to indulge in the sport. (The major ski areas in the United States are in the Rocky Mountains and the New England states).

Skiing requires the development of auxiliary facilities and services such as motels and hotels, re-

staurants, clubs, special transportation to ski areas, specialized shops, and fast lift services. The quality and variety of facilities are most important for skiers. Availability of rental facilities is very important, especially for beginners. Major runs of a ski area are 1 or 2 miles or more and should offer a range of slopes from beginner to expert. The first category seems more important than the latter, since beginners insure the potential increase of users and the demand for skiing. Thus a ski school in the area would provide more appeal. Expert skiers tend to stay longer (a week or more) than beginners (a weekend). A developer must provide adequate access to the project area and maintain roads and airports.

Another sport for which planners may allocate space is snowmobiling, which is increasing in popularity especially in the United States.

Controlled small bodies of water may be a prime sale element for housing in any new town, especially for families with children. Lake and waterfront communities are usually marketable.[44] (See Figure 8.29.)

The residential land-use plan must not only provide open space in terms of parks, playgrounds, picnic areas, and so on, but must also design open space that is accessible and valuable to the residential community. While some open space may merely increase the aesthetic quality of a residential area, most such areas must be designed to be useful to the residents and an asset to the community. Open space must therefore be varied and be planned for a number of uses rather than for a single use. Variety in physical characteristics and uses help insure that a heterogenous population will use the open space. (See Figure 8.30.)

Development and maintenance of open space and recreational land use enhance an environment and society. Attractive open space designed with adequate facilities will help educate children and provide a relaxing environment for adults.

Open space land should be provided in the new town within walking distance of the town and its surrounding area. The location of a new town in a regional setting brings the residents close to the open space because of the town scale.

CONCLUSION

The realization of land-use planning is the product a community receives. Since this development is deter-

Figure 8.27. Castle Eden Dene from Lady Mary's Walk, Peterlee, England. (Courtesy of the Peterlee Development Corporation.)

mined by a variety of factors that shape the final new-town environment, planners should not isolate any one factor but should instead try to manage their interrelated effects. Crucial factors for development include quality of residents, cultural standards and habits, receptivity to land-use control, transportation networks, and available finances.

The land-use pattern as this product is far more

influential on the quality of society than many people realize. Land-use planning is not just a designation of definite uses; it is rather an effective tool in the comprehensive planning of a new town that may support the environment of its whole community. Areas designated for residential use should be integral parts of the entire community. Thus the design of residential land should respond to social, governmental, and economic structures.

Innovations seem to be one of the most promising areas of land-use planning and implementation. Planners should realize that new ideas may be meaningless and ephemeral unless they are associated with social, governmental, and economic reforms. Above all, planners should publicize novel plans to prepare the community for changes innovations may cause. The domed city is one of the most significant comprehensive land-use plans prepared recently.

Theoretically planners may consider a domed new town for an extremely cold area to establish a controlled and regulated microclimate in a newly explored region. Since a domed new town requires concentrated land uses, it establishes a high-density population within intense use of a site. The city may form one

Figure 8.28.   Integrated public buildings and green areas in Elizabeth, Australia. (Courtesy of the South Australia Housing Trust.)

Figure 8.29.   The Water Gardens of Hemel Hempstead, England. (Courtesy of the Commission for the New Towns.)

megastructure. High quantities of energy will be needed to regulate the town's microclimate. Domed cities may have unconventional impact in at least two ways. One pressure is on the social and psychological adaptability of residents, because such density may force too much personal contact, diminish privacy, and thus produce social tension; the other is the quantity of air pollution and noise. Utilities systems and infrastructure operation may also pose serious environmental problems. To some planners or architects a domed new town may seem to be economically and socially efficient because of the proximity of its land uses and the release from using motor vehicles. To ease those problems and others a domed new town may be designed as interconnected, separate domed structures for distributed land uses. (See Figure 8.31.)

Practically, a domed new town may not be feasible in our time because of its cost benefit. The Minnesota

Experimental City Project, which considered the domed city as one of its alternatives, reached the following conclusions:

(1)   Preliminary cost benefits indicate the unfeasibility of doming the entire urban megastructure.

(2)   A domed megastructure accumulates large quantities of snow or huge amounts of rain water at its dome margin, equivalent to 100 percent of the entire occupied city surface.

(3)   Because of its structural integrity, the city is to be built as a complete unit that will require the major portion of its capital investment in the early phase of the city's construction.[45]

The Minnesota Experimental City Project suggested a macrourban form that combines domed sections of the city with a domed/gallery system to accommodate outdoor public activities and with houses developed in a linear, horizontal pattern that may relate to the indoor, public domed galleries and to the outside natural environment.[46] The proposal called for an interior transportation system along the galleries and an outside major linkage.

In summary, we must mention that there are no universal standards, rules, or regulations in land-use planning and its implementation. This is especially true in items such as density and land-use control. In making decisions about land use the planning team should rely on a synthesis of three considerations: (1) the analysis and interpretation of cultural, historic, geographic, social, economic, and other significant characteristics of the site; (2) an evaluation of the experience of applicable new-town case studies; and (3) personal professional judgments.

Figure 8.30. Big Canyon area of Irvine, California. The golf course is integrated with the clustered residential area. Note the clustered apartment buildings (bottom) and the curvilinear layout of the residential area (top). (Courtesy of The Irvine Company.)

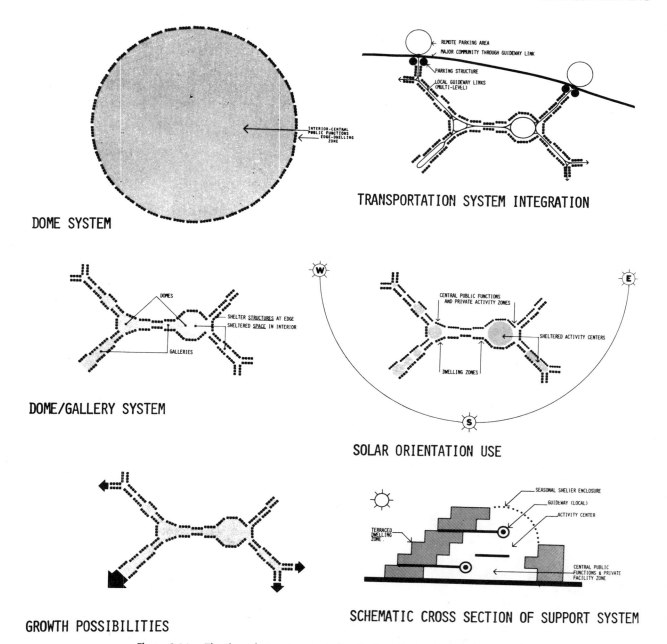

Figure 8.31. The domed city. (Source: *Urban Design: Design Strategy Statement.*)

NOTES

1. Balwant Singh Saini, *Building Environment: An Illustrated Analysis of Problems in Hot Dry Lands* (Sydney: Angus and Robertson, Publishers, 1973).

2. Artur Glikson, *Regional Planning and Development* (Leiden: A. W. Sijthoff's Uitgeversmaatschappij N.V., 1955), p. 76.

3. Glikson, pp. 73–85. See also Sir Patrick Geddes, *Cities in Evolution* (New York: Harper and Row, 1968).

4. Neil Pinney, *Urban Design: Design Strategy Statement,* Pre-liminary Report, vol. V, part 1.0 (Minneapolis: Minnesota Experimental City Authority, 1973), p. 34. Also see Greater London Council, *The Planning of a New Town: Data and Design Based on a Study for a New Town of 100,000 at Hook, Hampshire* (London: Greater London Council, 1965), p. 86.

5. Robin H. Best, *Land for New Towns* (London: Town and Country Planning Association, 1968), p. 8.

6. Best, p. 35.

7. Real Estate Research Corporation, *The Costs of Sprawl* (Washington, D.C.: U.S. Government Printing Office, 1974), pp. 3–24.

8. John L. Hyson, "Land Use Controls: Who Watches the Watchers," *Urban Land,* **33,** no. 3 (March 1974), p. 5.

9. Edmund N. Bacon, "7 Principles for an Urban Land Policy," *Urban Land,* **30,** no. 4 (April 1971), pp. 4–5.

10. Best, p. 18.

11. P. A. Stone, "Financing the Construction of New Towns," in *Planning of Metropolitan Areas and New Towns* (New York: United Nations, 1967), p. 230. U.S. Department of Housing and Urban Development, *Special Report on Techniques of Aided Self-Help Housing: Some Examples of U.S. and Overseas Experience* (Washington, D.C.: U.S. Government Printing Office, 1973), 24 pp.

12. Urban Land Institute, *New Approaches to Residential Land Development: A Study of Concepts and Innovations* (Washington, D.C.: Urban Land Institute, 1970), p. 23. Also see the table in Fig. 8.16.

13. Urban Land Institute, *The Pros and Cons of Cluster Housing* (Washington, D.C.: Urban Land Institute, 1969), p. 13.

14. William H. Whyte, *Cluster Development* (New York: American Conservation Association, 1971), p. 12; and Urban Land Institute, *Innovations vs. Traditions in Community Development* (Washington, D.C.: Urban Land Institute, 1963).

15. Whyte, pp. 16–22.

16. Urban Land Institute, *The Homes Association Handbook,* rev. ed. (Washington, D.C.: Urban Land Institute, 1970), pp. 63–78.

17. Real Estate Research Corporation, "The Costs of Sprawl," *Real Estate Report,* special issue (1974), p. 5.

18. Real Estate Research Corporation, p. 5.

19. Robert E. Boley, *Industrial Districts Restudied* (Washington, D.C.: Urban Land Institute, 1969), p. 10; and J. Ross McKeever, ed., *The Community Builders Handbook* (Washington, D.C.: Urban Land Institute, 1968), p. 449.

20. McKeever, p. 450.

21. Boley, p. 6.

22. Joseph DeChiara and Lee Koppelman, *Planning Design Criteria* (New York: Van Nostrand Reinhold Co., 1969), p. 247.

23. Dorothy A. Muncy, "Planning Guidelines for Industrial Park Development," *Urban Land,* **29,** no. 11 (December 1970), p. 4.

24. Boley, p. 7.

25. Robert E. Boley, *Industrial Districts: Principles in Practice* (Washington, D.C.: Urban Land Institute, 1970), pp. 10–11.

26. Boley, *Industrial Districts Restudied,* p. 6.

27. DeChiara, pp. 250–51.

28. Boley, *Industrial Districts: Principles in Practice,* p. 12.

29. Utilidor is an innovative underground tunnel built to accommodate all city utilities and their networks. The utilidor facilitates the addition of new utilities and repair and maintenance of existing ones. See Walter A. Lyon, "Innovation in Pollution and Environmental Control," in *Innovations for Future Cities,* Gideon Golany, ed. (New York: Praeger Publishers, in press.)

30. Boley, *Industrial Districts: Principles in Practice,* pp. 27–194.

31. Richard L. Heroux and William A. Wallace, *Financial Analysis and the New Community Development Process* (New York: Praeger Publishers, 1973), pp. 72–73.

32. Heroux and Wallace, p. 75.

33. McKeever, p. 264.

34. McKeever, p. 266.

35. J. Ross McKeever, *Shopping Center Zoning* (Washington, D.C.: Urban Land Institute, 1973), p. 10.

36. McKeever, *The Community Builders Handbook,* p. 265.

37. McKeever, *The Community Builders Handbook,* p. 264. Also see Urban Land Institute, *Parking Requirements for Shopping Centers: A Survey* (Washington, D.C.: Urban Land Institute, 1965), pp. 6–9.

38. J. Ross McKeever, *Business Parks, Office Parks, Plazas and Centers: A Study of Development Practices and Procedures* (Washington, D.C.: Urban Land Institute, 1970), p. 8.

39. A new-town center may include the following functions: shopping and commercial uses, grocery stores, offices, residential areas, clubs and community center, theaters, cinemas, a music hall, a library, parking areas, playgrounds, educational centers, transportation, telecommunication, restaurants, a public bath, a swimming pool, and a health center.

40. Jonathan Development Corporation, *Jonathan New Town: Design and Development* (Chaska, Minn.: Jonathan Development Corporation, 1971), p. 44.

41. William H. Whyte, *Securing Open Space for Urban America: Conservation Easements* (Washington, D.C.: Urban Land Institute, 1968), p. 7.

42. Whyte, *Securing Open Spaces,* pp. 7–20.

43. Urban Land Institute, *Land: Recreation & Leisure* (Washington, D.C.: Urban Land Institute, 1970), p. 29.

44. Carl Norcross and Sanford Goodkin, *Open Space Communities in the Market Place,* Technical Bulletin 57 (Washington, D.C.: Urban Land Institute, 1966), pp. 59–62; and William B. Rick, *Planning and Developing Waterfront Property* (Washington, D.C.: Urban Land Institute, 1967).

45. Pinney, p. 26.

46. Pinney, pp. III, 28–30.

NINE
GOVERNMENT AND GOVERNANCE SYSTEMS

INTRODUCTION

Government can be defined as "the continuous exercise of authority over and the performance of functions for a political unit."[1] Government is usually thought of as a political unit: "the organization, machinery, or agency through which a political unit exercises authority and performs functions. . . . " Another aspect of government is "the complex of political institutions, laws and customs through which the function of governing is carried out in a specific political unit."[2] As planners, however, we would like to view it differently. Rather than thinking of government—the body whose responsibility it is to provide and maintain public facilities and social services—we think of governance: the citizens' concept and philosophy of the system and methods of managing their political lives, a system of upholding their rights and interests as individuals and as a community which has self-identity within a defined territory. This principle of governance supported the Greek city-states and should support modern governmental institutions.

The existing state system focuses on government rather than governance, and we can anticipate that the existing system will become more centralized and therefore interfere more with the local level than ever before. New towns, however, should stress the governance concept, which focuses on citizen participation in government and thus on their strong self-identity. If the establishment of new towns could strengthen governance, older urban centers could profit directly from this experience in solving the urban governmental crisis discussed in Chapter 1. Being new, and therefore free from the city's commitments, the new town could function as an experimental laboratory which re-evaluates existing governance systems and reforms them.[3]

Goals and Objectives

Goals of local and regional governance systems differ from one condition to another, but we may expect new-town governance to achieve the following basic goals and objectives:

(1)   Develop maximum citizen participation in decision making and in the developing of a city and region socially, economically, and environmentally.

(2)   Foster a sense of community among residents: "to convert residents into citizens."[4]

(3)   Provide high-standard required utilities, infrastructure, and social, educational, health, and welfare services that the community needs, or manage their delivery.

(4)   Provide equal access of residents to all services, utilities, and infrastructure.

(5)   Plan and implement a tax system to support provision of services, retain effective land-use control, and protect the interest of individual citizens and the public.

(6)   Implement comprehensive management and planning for community development and establish a strategy for coordinated control of the development to protect public needs and private rights.

(7)   Develop and enhance the natural environment and provide a positive social climate for the satisfaction of residents.

(8)   Ensure diverse equal employment opportunities for all citizens.

Since local government receives its power from its residents, the government's major goal is to protect public needs and rights. Thus goals of governance and of a community are two sides of the same coin: i.e., "the task of animating the citizen to his duty to participate in the democratic process of which he is the heart."[5] Any governance, efficient though it may be, cannot be meaningful if it does not gain the support of its citizens and meet their goals and objectives.

Planning Process

In a new town built from scratch, it is necessary to plan the governance system in the early stages to face construction issues and problems.[6] Surprisingly not every new town does. The developer, especially a private one, may not have the time required to organize local government because he is committed to the construction process. Early governance may also be improvised. Some countries which have developed many new towns have not realized this problem and thus detract from the quality of their community building.

The Soviet Union, which has developed nearly 1000 new towns, has failed to respond to the needs for the early planning of governance. In Soviet new cities, which were mostly constructed as company towns to meet industrial development, "city governments were an afterthought: they could do little more than ratify industrial actions. . . ."[7] It seems that the pressing interest in immediate production took precedence over good planning of governments. Consequently, many new industrialized cities do not have adequate public utilities and social services and fall behind many other established cities.[8]

This does not mean that the first government of a new town should be structured in a final form. An early government which is rigid may stall the development and its governmental pattern for a long time.[9] Also, a short term government may respond to pressing needs rather than to long-range requirements, although any of its decisions will have long-range influence.[10]

In planning the development of a local governance system, a new-town planner must consider the following major steps (see Figure 9.1.):

(1)   Define the prime goal of the future government and the working goals of each stage of its development within the context of the new town's goals.

(2)   Study the existing power structures, governments, and community affairs within the site.

(3)   Study all legislation, regulations, and codes existing or planned for the area and the new-town site to reveal constitutional limits, and seek modifications necessary to meet goals and objectives.

(4)   Study existing and forthcoming tax systems within the site and its surroundings to support the preparation of a detailed, phased plan for a tax system.

(5)   Study existing public utility networks and infrastructure.

(6)   Formulate policy focused on three major issues: taxation, land-use control and development, and prospective intergovernmental relations; and formulate a local policy for attracting investment.

When most studies have been finished and a policy has been formulated, the planning team should study all potential innovative forms of local governments. This special study, combined with the knowledge gained about the site and the region, should lead to the selection of the most desirable and suitable form of governance.

This step of the process concerns the phased comprehensive plan and that of public utilities and infrastructure. The governance plan should also include a phased fiscal plan for utilities, and plans for taxation, land-use regulation, and community affairs. Before the plan is implemented, separate bodies should administer the construction process and the responsibilities of local government. Although each responsibility is assigned to a separate group in the early developmental phases, it is essential that the two coordinate their work effectively. Moreover, in the early stages of development, conventional governmental responsibilities are usually assigned to an appointed body because of the absence of a reasonably sized electorate.

Any governance plan should introduce the phases of its development and the impact of each phase on other development. The development of qualified local leadership to be trained for new positions and the creation of constant citizen awareness of community needs, and citizen participation, should be prime sections of the governance plan. The phased plans for public utilities, infrastructures, social services, education, and other conventional local government assignments should be checked against tax revenues and the cash-flow model of the government to insure continuity of their maintenance.

Issues and Problems

The problems and issues of intergovernmental relations are complex. Whether a new town is a public or private development, the community will deal with three levels of government: state, county or regional,

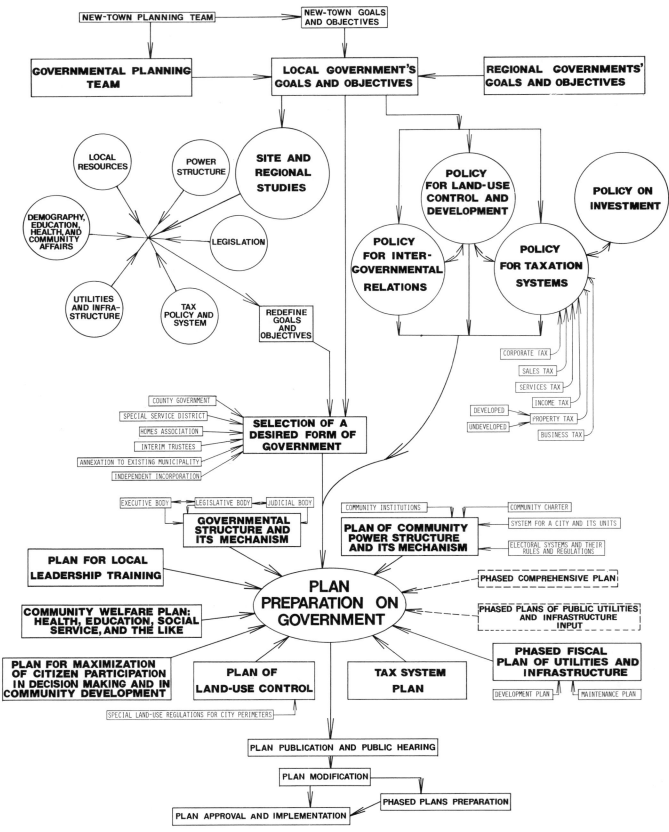

Figure 9.1.   Generalized planning process of new-town governance.

and local power structures. The effectiveness of these relations stems from the existence (or nonexistence) of policy at the state level. In a financially supported new town the central government will dictate many decisions for the new-town government, and the latter may lose some of its local political identity. In such cases "local governments tend to become administrative mechanisms for implementation of national policies, rather than dynamic centers of authority in their own individual right."[11]

The most difficult procedure for a recently created community is to confront any existing local or regional government. The community immediately needs such vital services as water supply, sewage treatment, and garbage collection, and usually establishes a single body to manage them, because in most cases the established government is not prepared to provide these services.

In a development within a weak rural county, governmental plan preparation for both the site and the county may become the responsibility of a public developer, when the county lacks planning. Another problem of such a county government is the lack of adequate subdivision and effective land-use control and developmental regulations combined with a lack of suitable administrative organization. In rural areas, county governments are ill-equipped to meet local needs for public utilities. Yet a private developer is required to develop such facilities in the early stages, and to invest his money before he can sell houses to new residents. In addition, he might be required to pay local tax to the county for land holding or for services he is not receiving.

To stimulate further growth and development, a developer needs to establish a proper body for building and furnishing required services such as schools, sewage treatment, and water supply. For some developers the establishment of a subsidiary or independent company to construct and operate the required public services proved to be a sound investment. Another possibility is to enter into a contract with the nearest government furnishing the public services needed by a new town. Such an arrangement often enhances the quality of the established government's services.

The creation of a subordinate service or taxing area within a county is another possibility for providing public utilities. This requires a new town to be completely under the jurisdiction of a county government, even for purposes of taxation. Such an arrangement may require an early investment by the county. To avoid burdening the established community with more taxes, it may be necessary to create a special

agency to provide the services. This agency may issue bonds and obtain capital for financing projects with its own revenue. Thus the municipality will not bear the burden of financing and the operational budget will affect equally all who benefit from it.

One of the crucial periods in governance of a new town is the transitional period,[12] when citizens start to assume responsibilities, begin to provide new-town services, and implement developmental policy according to their plans. It is best to prolong this period so that citizens will become knowledgeable about the operation of governance. The length of the period will be determined by the type of relationship built up between the developer and community leaders and by the extent of their preparation to assume responsibility. To minimize confrontation, the citizens and the developer might find it necessary to form a joint body for effective coordination and to function as a local governing body. Moreover, a series of phases for the transitional period would insure stability and continuity of governance with minimum interference.

In a publicly developed new town we may assume that the overall institutional structure of the country has (generally) favored the establishment of the new town. Since the project stems from the existence of a national policy we may expect support occasionally from different governmental branches. This may be true for financial, advisory, moral and, most important, legislative support, and at first the new-town development corporation enjoys all these benefits. In any case, the development corporation is empowered for a defined purpose: construction of the new town and maintenance of its real estate. Neither the central government nor the development corporation (for obvious reasons) will seek to govern the community during its existence, and both will seek a governmental plan to be implemented within a certain period. In these circumstances the process for the three forces (central government, development corporation, and community) is definite, and any argument they may have will probably focus on the exact time that the community will be eligible to elect local officials. This eligibility may be granted because of a community's size and maturity. Issues and problems that may occur regularly during this time are the transfer and maintenance of public real estate planned and constructed for public use (e.g., playgrounds, schools, gardens, streets, etc.) to the new government, the continued dependence of the new government on subsidies from the central government and the corporation to enable the operation of the new government's machinery and, finally, the problem of obtaining leaders and staff to assume operation of the new system.

In a privately developed new town the transitional period for a local government will be most difficult for both the community and its developer. On the one hand a conflict of interest may arise, centered on the differences in the goals and objectives of each. On the other hand, a central government that would naturally protect individual and community interests is usually lacking. Associated with this absence is the lack of legislation to support the rise of a new community within an established political entity. Since both lacks stem mainly from the absence of a national policy for urban growth, public financial subsidies will not be channeled to the local community. The following issues and problems may arise from such conditions: the transitional period is prolonged to suit the needs of the private developer; services may be provided on a profit basis that may not necessarily protect the community; continuous tension may exist between the developer and the community that may hinder the development or even cause a change in its ultimate goal; and finally, when local government is established it may not have complete power because it relies on central legislation for support.

In both cases the problem of finding a qualified government staff may be solved by filling such positions with people from the developer's staff who have valuable experience to contribute to their jobs.

It may also be advisable to hold elections more often than usual to discover the potential leaders living within the new-town community. Such an arrangement may encourage citizen participation in the electoral process.

ALTERNATIVE GOVERNANCE FORMS

Among the interrelated crises in our large cities is the governmental one in which government continues to execute power in a traditional way without being fully effective while the communication gap between the government and its citizens increases. Most planners realize that the modern urban center has grown so much in size and complexity that it is almost unmanageable.

Governmental costs are rising so rapidly that both the scale and the quality of services are deteriorating. To preserve their independence many cities resort to high taxation which, in several central cities, is almost crippling. However, despite high taxes collected from a variety of overlapping governmental agencies, urban problems grow more serious.

Governance reform in established cities has become almost impossible to achieve. However, since new towns are generally built from scratch, they may introduce potential reform in governance which may in turn guide the established city. New-town planners should review potential governance forms and select the best alternative for their case. There are several possible forms of governance a new town may adopt: (1) independent incorporation, (2) annexation, (3) interim trustees, (4) homes association, (5) special service district, and (6) county government.

Independent Incorporation

Independent incorporation forms a unified body granted legal power by a higher government to perform standard municipal functions within its defined, restricted area. This is one of the most commonly used forms of new-town government and is effective because it is founded on a well-structured legislative procedure. Incorporation may use the traditional electoral process and a central municipal council, or a reformed, decentralized structure throughout the community. In either case, the democratic process is its legal foundation. This system is more receptive to innovation and reform in its early years than it would be later, and we can expect intense citizen activity throughout the process.

Since such action requires a certain size population for economic justification, and a degree of maturity, a new town cannot incorporate in the early stage of its development; actually incorporation is sometimes impossible because of the lack of county and state law. Thus incorporation brings with it all the complex problems of an independent city.

In countries with comprehensive new-town legislation, such as the United Kingdom, there are built-in procedures for new towns to incorporate when they have reached a certain population size or quality of services. In countries with little experience with new towns, such as the United States, there are no uniform procedures among the states for a mature new town to incorporate.

Annexation to an Existing Municipality

When it falls within the municipal boundaries of an incorporated urban center that is economically dominant, a new town is subject to annexation. Problems for the new town are inherent in the arrangement: the new town must compromise its goals with those of the established community, which provides essential services. The annexation must be planned carefully, since the more hasty the annexation, the greater will be the risk of abandonment of the new town's original plan and of loss of social identity.[13]

Another type of annexation that often causes its own distinct problems is annexation to a county. When a proposed new-town site falls outside the municipal boundaries of an incorporated city but inside the boundaries of a county, the new town is subject to annexation by the county. This process is one of conflict and confrontation because the new town may become almost as effective as the county: the new town will be able to offer social services, educational systems, and other services equal or superior to those that already exist in the county. Although the new town will pay taxes to the county, the county's residents will use many of the new-town facilities. In addition, the growing new town will probably provide employment opportunities for the county's residents. Thus the new town, technically under the jurisdiction of the county, has much to offer its parent; and until the new town is sufficiently mature to break away and incorporate itself independently, this dilemma will be a constant source of confrontation with the county.

Interim Trustees

This is a new solution which has been used mainly in Israel, where the major responsibility for new-town construction is a governmental function. The concept calls for a public agency, appointed by the state, to run the municipal functions from the new town's origin until its maturity. The new town has matured when it has a sufficiently large population to justify self-government, capable local leadership, and a gradually self-sustaining tax system. The taxation policy of the new town is designed to ease the tax burden on new residents, who are mostly low-income people. In the early years of the new town, the central government subsidizes most local services. The central government through one of its appropriate departments, such as the Department of Interior, appoints a committee to manage the municipal functions of the new town. In general, government officers representing appropriate departments, local leadership, and experts in various fields such as urban affairs, municipal issues, financial management, and so on, and voluntarily chosen for their expertise, comprise this committee. It implements government policy directly and may manage the new town very efficiently because it releases the community from traditional, paid municipal machinery.

An election of a local government council is held after several years, when the community has matured.

Until then, however, the agency functions to protect the local community's interests, in conjunction with the central government's policy, by developing and maintaining a minimum standard for public utilities and necessary services. In the absence of local legislation and regulations, the agency has legislative power granted by the central government.

In addition to its functions for the new town, the agency could also be authorized to construct necessary areawide services for the county when this is economically feasible. Thus the new town could function as a catalyst for improving and promoting county services.

Homes Association

Homes associations are defined as "incorporated non-profit organizations operating under recorded land agreements for the maintenance of private and common property."[14] Their powers can range from the management of open space and community facilities to the provision of mass transportation systems and energy distribution.

Members of the homes association are homeowners who pay dues. Although they do not require public funds, the effectiveness of home associations is limited. First, they are limited, special purpose institutions and thus are not designed for general governmental planning and decision making. Second, they are influenced by the developer, usually private, who is often reluctant to relinquish his power. Since he is well-organized, the developer is able to implement his goals more effectively than the residents.

In Columbia, Maryland, the homes association is the Columbia Park and Recreation Association, established to take care of various public services when it became clear that it was not possible to use a "special district."[15] The services of the association are also available to local industries and businesses. The association manages the development and maintenance of services which a local municipality would regularly manage. Those services include parks and open space, golf courses, tennis courts, swimming pools, lakes, and possibly roads, water supply, sewage treatment, child day-care programs, and supervision of the operation of a bus system.

Special Service Districts

Special districts are nonprofit organizations established by law to execute special services required by local citizens. This is a common method and may be used whether or not a local municipality exists. When a municipality exists, special districts may be formed to provide services required by more than one locality and thus disregard municipal boundaries.

Special service districts provide essential services such as water supply, sewage disposal, or garbage collection on an interim basis, but do not have representative decision making and are not practical for long-term functions. Special districts may issue bonds to finance their services.[16]

County Governments

County governments usually exist prior to the initiation of a new town. They can be classified as urban —large, powerful, financially strong—and rural —small, weak, and underfinanced. They usually perform the local functions for unincorporated new towns. Any new town built within a strong county may be annexed by it. In a weak county a new town may incorporate when it becomes the dominant political area because of its population size. Any county, however, may involve an unincorporated new town in continuous conflict with county officials that focuses on taxes, services, and zoning.

In the United States, the issue of local government formation is very complex due either to the absence of state legislation or to the conflict with other powerful groups such as the county.

Due to varying circumstances, including State practices and customs and an evaluation of services available and cost involved, new communities have frequently remained unincorporated within a county. In Virginia and Maryland, where a number of new communities are being developed, incorporations are limited, with urban counties providing the government for a number of unincorporated communities. In California, the decision to incorporate appears to hinge on whether satisfactory service arrangements, including the formation of special districts, can be accomplished under the county government. On the other hand, if the area of the new community lies in several competing incorporated places, detachments and a new incorporation may be the preferred approach.[17]

In a sparsely populated area where county government services are not meeting adequate standards, a new town may enrich the quality of the county's management.

When he is informed about these alternative governance forms, a new-town planner may help his project to avoid repeating the mistakes of established cities. On the other hand, he may make the new town a leading example for established cities.

ALTERNATIVES OF INNOVATION AND REFORM

New-town development is an excellent opportunity to reform governmental structure and governance. In established cities, governance is difficult to reform since it is enforced by existing legislation which takes time,

TABLE 9.1   SUGGESTED MODEL FOR ELECTED GOVERNMENT OF A NEW TOWN OF 75,000 POPULATION

Unit	Population			
	No. of Villages	No. of Neighborhoods	Total Families per Unit	Total Population per Unit[1]
Village	1	—	250	750
Neighborhood	10	1	2,500	7,500
Town	100	10	25,000	75,000

Unit	Electoral System		
	Voters[2]	Elected Representatives on Council	No. of Citizens Electing Constituents for Each Member
Village	500	3	165
Neighborhood	5,000	10	750
Town	50,000	30–50	1,500–2,500

[1]Average of 3.0 persons per family.
[2]Assumes 2 voters per family.

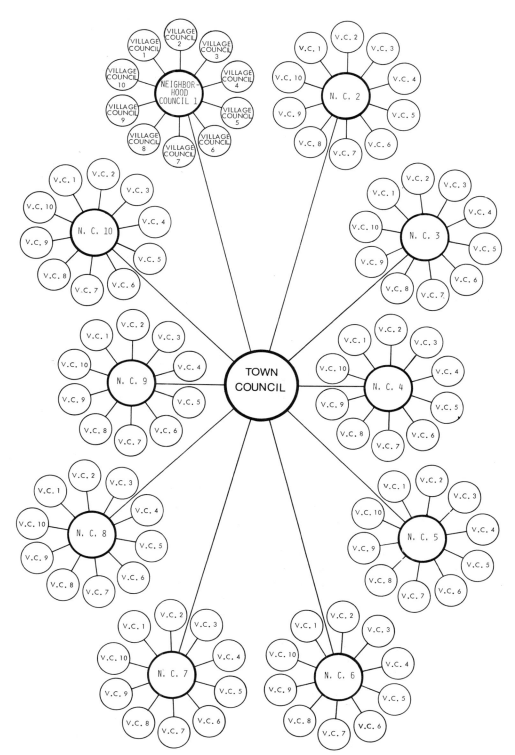

Figure 9.2. Schematic diagram of proposed decentralized governance units: hierarchy of representatives in a new town of 75,000 population.

energy, and political maneuvering to change. Also, political power structures, often composed of personal or group structures, are complex and rigid and impede reform. In such cases, goals must be compromised to bring about reform. Also, since changes take a long time to complete, when they come they may either be too late or require further change.

A new town, at least in its first decade, is a dynamic and receptive center of young people willing to accept change. Successful governance reform in their new town might be more acceptable as an example to an established city than if reform were proposed by only one city leader, without evidence of its feasibility. Finally, the new town is usually not susceptible to most governmental maneuvering and provides an opportunity to start without prior commitments.

Decentralization

Sociologists and public management experts favor decentralized operation as one method of easing crises in large cities. "Much discussion has ensued as to what new instrumentalities can make city government more responsive, efficient, and effective than it is. . . . The two strategies most often mentioned are lateral integration . . . and decentralization, and these are defined as complementary. In fact, a combination of centralized policy-making and decentralized operations is often seen as an appropriate strategy."[18]

David Rogers makes a distinction between decentralization of decision making and of the operational system: "Delivery systems that centralize policy-making while decentralizing operations are more efficient and effective than those that centralize or decentralize both."[19]

Many believe that decentralization is necessary to increase voters' roles in decision making and their sense of community; others argue that decentralization is costly and inefficient.[20] However, since the basic premise of decentralization is social rather than economic, areawide interdependent services may enable small units to provide technological and economic efficiency. Effective government does not necessarily imply efficient service; rather such government exercises good communications between voters and elected officials.[21]

New towns can provide an opportunity for decentralization of functions within a centralized power structure. Recently many governance planners have advocated decentralization, where services and citizens councils are taken to the neighborhood level and to neighborhood halls. This advocacy also favored dividing the central city into small manageable community governments.[22]

Governance reform should seek primarily to promote the average citizen to participate in governance by maximizing his involvement in community decision making. This concept could be implemented through a hierarchical pattern of governance systems by which subcommunity groups are defined, voluntarily or otherwise. Every unit is confined as a social, territorial, and governmental cell with its own rights for identity and local services. This hierarchical pattern calls for the confinement of the new town and its community to small units of villages of 750 people each, and of neighborhood units of 10 villages or 7500 people, each of which will have its own village council and neighborhood council. The community as a whole, then, will establish the third level in the pattern of councils. This new-town community, composed of 10 neighborhoods, will have a total population of 75,000. In this structure a new-town community could be enlarged by adding more neighborhoods without changing the density, size, and land use of each established unit. (See Table 9.1 and Figure 9.2.)

According to this hierarchical pattern every unit will have the right to conduct its services the way it wants, but it may choose to buy services from a larger unit. The village population will be represented in their own elected council, in their neighborhood council, and in the town council. Thus there will be a sharing of power, with a village unit making its own decisions either in the village council or, if necessary, in its citizens assembly. We can anticipate that in this hierarchical pattern citizen participation in community life and decision making in governance will be more intensive and extensive than that in the centralized structure of an established community. This hierarchical system should give much meaning to community life, stimulate its identity and, finally, improve individual responsibility and the closeness of social groups.

The nature of a governmental system is isolation and proliferation of its bureaucracy. A new town, however, may seek to confederate with the government of its immediate region without losing its self-identity while sharing responsibilities. (See Table 9.2.) A planner should learn which governmental services are provided by the new-town region, their quality and scale, and the extent to which such services may be shared with the new town. He also should determine which services could ultimately be provided by the new town to its region. Fire protection, water supply, sewage and garbage disposal, health services, recreation, mass media, telecommunication, transportation, and education are among the services that may become a joint endeavor and may be used as the foundation for other mutual social and economic activities. For the new town such cooperation is especially essential in its early stage of development. (Also see Chapters 4 and 5.)

Public agencies may direct or supervise part of all these services, but they may not necessarily operate them. These services could be contracted to a private body, and should bring about a minimum standard for essential services in the new town. These areawide services should be financed equally by the regional population, and a planner-developer should also plan services available to prospective newcomers as they prepare to move to the new town.[23]

Citizen Participation

"One of the most important functions of local government is to convert residents into citizens by affording them the opportunity to acquire civic experience through participation in governing, through sharing responsibility for public decisions. Local self-government also legitimates authority. Citizen participation in local decision-making inevitably influences the character of services and helps to determine the beneficiaries of government programs."[24]

When a nucleus of citizens has settled, a new town can offer them an excellent opportunity to participate in their governance.[25] Their motives may be

(1) The "newness" of the new town, which may create a positive image for citizens and motivate them to maintain the town's standards to insure the value of their homes.

(2) Citizens' high expectations for the new environment, which may lead them to invest more money and time than they would in a conventional place, and thus develop interest and awareness of their new environment, which are the basic elements needed for the development of a citizen participation movement.

(3) Maintenance of a good educational system.

(4) The opportunity to serve on citizens' advisory boards and affect issues of major importance to the communities, neighborhoods, and villages of a given new town. (See Chapter 3 for details of such boards.)

(5) The expected enduring conflict of interest between the developer and citizens about issues of major concern, which may crystallize a nucleus of citizens concerned about the future of the community, especially on the issue of alternative forms of governance.

(6) The fact that women in the new towns have found themselves with more free time than they had in the established city, which allows them to volunteer to be active in the community.

Citizen participation may be encouraged by developing intensive and effective communication between residents and officials. We can expect the decentralization of power, of the decision-making process, and of action among the neighborhood and villages of the new town to bring citizens closer to officials and to action. The use of new media may strengthen this process, too. Some of these media are opening all government meetings to the public; granting charters to small groups to make petitions, acquire, investigate, ask for re-examination of decisions that have been made by the government or request similar actions; televising government meetings to the whole community in two-way channels, enabling community voting through computerized television on issues of concern rather than leaving it to the government (see Chapter 6); and delegating power to committees of local citizens to make decisions and take action on specific issues. It is also a most beneficial investment to program school curricula to include the theory and practice of local governance of the community.

Citizen participation in decision making should also be fostered in a manageable form beginning in the smallest community cells. In this practical form, citizens in their residential units should be able to be well informed, react, express opinion, influence, vote, and make decisions on local matters of concern. If a developer does not consider and properly channel citizen participation so it is based on harmonious relations and mutual faith and interest, it may become detrimental to the progress of the development. A developer, however, should keep in mind that "citizen control can retard development, but so can a sense of alienation by citizens or interminable bureaucratic review and control."[26]

The concept of citizen participation is a corollary of governmental decentralization. We believe that central policy making leads to central power, which in turn leads to diffuse communication between voters and their representatives and to citizen apathy. Also, central power structures support the growth and influence of economic and social pressure groups in obtaining decisions favoring their interest. Decentralizing power to the neighborhoods and various community sections may diminish the influence of such pressure groups and strengthen voters. If the choice in government is between (1) centralized power for the sake of efficiency, without citizen par-

TABLE 9.2. CENTERS OF AUTHORITY AND INFLUENCE IN COLUMBIA

	STATE			
	DECISION MAKER	STAFF – S	PRESSURE GROUP	DECISION MAKER
EARLY CHILDHOOD ED. (NURSERY & DAY CARE)		DEPT. OF SOCIAL SERVICES STAFF	MD. DAY CARE COMMITTEE	
PUBLIC TRANSPORTATION		DEPT. OF TRANSPORTA-TION	LEAGUE OF WOMEN VOTERS	
RECREATION PROGRAMS				COUNTY COUNCIL COUNTY EXEC. (PARKS & REC. BD.) BD. OF EDUCATION
PARKS & RECREATIONAL FACILITIES				COUNTY COUNCIL COUNTY EXEC. (PARKS & REC. BD.) (PLANNING BD.) (PUBLIC WORKS BD.)
PRIMARY & SECONDARY EDUCATION		DEPT. OF ED. STAFF		COUNTY COUNCIL COUNTY EXEC. BD. OF ED.
PUBLIC SAFETY				COUNTY COUNCIL COUNTY EXEC.
FIRE				COUNTY COUNCIL COUNTY EXEC. (FIRE BD.)
WATER, SEWER			BALTIMORE REGIONAL PLANNING COUNCIL	COUNTY COUNCIL COUNTY EXEC. (PUBLIC WORKS BD.)
GARBAGE				COUNTY COUNCIL COUNTY EXEC. (PUBLIC WORKS BD.)
ELECTRICITY, GAS	(PUBLIC UTILITIES COMMISSION)		LEGAL ADVOCATE FOR CONSUMERS	
ROADS — COUNTY				COUNTY COUNCIL COUNTY EXEC. (PUBLIC WORKS BD.) (PLANNING BD.)
ROADS — STATE		MD. STATE HIGHWAY ADMIN. STAFF		
PLANNING & ZONING			BALT. REGIONAL PLANNING COUNCIL	COUNTY COUNCIL COUNTY EXEC. (PLANNING BD.) (ZONING BD.)
BUILDING — ARCH. REVIEW				
BUILDING — CODES				COUNTY COUNCIL COUNTY EXEC. (PUBLIC WORKS BD.)
HEALTH		DEPT. OF HEALTH & MENTAL HYGIENE STAFF		COUNTY COUNCIL COUNTY EXEC. (MENTAL HEALTH ADVISORY COMM.) HOW. CO. HOSP. STUDY COMM.
SOCIAL SERVICES	(DEPT. OF SOC. SER-VICES & EMPLOY-MENT)	DEPT. OF SOCIAL SERVICES & EMPLOY-MENT STAFF	MD. CONF. OF SOCIAL WELFARE; WELFARE TASK FORCE	COUNTY COUNCIL COUNTY EXEC.
ENVIRONMENTAL PROTECTION		DEPT. OF NATURAL RESOURCES	ZERO POPULATION GROWTH; LEAGUE OF WOMEN VOTERS	COUNTY COUNCIL COUNTY EXEC. (HOW. CO. SOIL CONSERVATION DIST.) (ENVIRONMENTAL BD.)
ARTS				
SOCIAL REFORM			WOMEN'S CENTER; LEAGUE OF WOMEN VOTERS	

DECISION MAKER: LEGAL AUTHORITY • (DELEGATEE) LIMITED AUTHORITY DELEGATED BY DECISION MAKER • STAFF HIRED BY DECISION MAKER T

*STAFF & (DELEGATEE) ALSO ACT AS PRESSURE GROUPS IN ATTEMPTING TO INFLUENCE THE ACTIONS OF THE DECISION MAKER

SOURCE: FIRST ANNUAL COLUMBIA CONFERENCE ON COMMUNITY GOVERNANCE

TABLE 9.2. *Continued*

| COUNTY | | COLUMBIA | | |
STAFF – S	PRESSURE GROUPS	DECISION MAKER	STAFF – S	PRESSURE GROUPS
	HOW. CO. CHILD DEVEL. CORP.	CA EXEC. COMMITTE (OPERATIONS COMM.)	CA STAFF	HRD; EARLY CHLHD. ED. BD; VILLAGE ASSN. BDS. NURSERY CO-OPS; ROSLYN RISE; JOINT BDS.
		CA EXEC. COMMITTEE (OPERATIONS COMM.)	CA STAFF	COLUMBIA TRANSPORT. COMM. JOINT BDS; VILLAGE ASSN. BDS; HRD
DEPT. OF PARKS & RECREATION STAFF	WEST HOWARD REC-REATION ASSOC; LEAGUE OF WOMEN VOTERS	CA EXEC. COMMITTEE (OPERATIONS COMM.)	CA STAFF	HRD; VILLAGE ASSN. BDS; JOINT BDS; VILLAGE REC. COMM; COL. AQUATIC ASSN.
DEPT. OF ED. PLANNING & ZONING PUBLIC WORKS; REC. & PARKS STAFFS	LEAGUE OF WOMEN VOTERS	CA EXEC. COMMITTEE (OPERATIONS COMM.)	CA STAFF	HRD; VILLAGE ASSN. BDS; JOINT BDS; VILLAGE REC. OPEN SPACE & PATHWAY COMMS; FRIENDS OF OPEN SPACE; VILLAGE ARCH.COMM.
DEPT. OF ED. STAFF	HOW. CO. NOMINATING FEDERATION; STATE SENATOR; PTA'S & TEACHER'S UNIONS; LEAGUE OF WOMEN VOTERS			PTA'S; VILLAGE ED. COMM; HRD; COLUMBIA COUNCIL; VILLAGE ASSN. BDS.
POLICE DEPT. STAFF	STUDY ACTION GROUP IN RACISM			VILLAGE ASSN. BDS; HRD; JOINT BDS; COL. COUN.
				HRD
DEPT. OF PUBLIC WORKS STAFF				HRD
DEPT. OF PUBLIC WORKS STAFF	COUNCIL FOR ENVIRONMENTAL QUALITY			
	PLANNING BD.			HRD
DEPT. OF PUBLIC WORKS	CIVIC ASSNS.			
		(HRD)		VILLAGE ASSN. BDS; JOINT BDS; COL. TRANS. COMMITTEE; COLUMBIA COUNCIL; NEIGHBOR-HOOD ASSNS.
	COUNTY COUNCIL; HOW. CO. LEGISLA. DELEGTN; CIVIC ASSNS.			
DEPT. OF PLANNING & ZONING STAFF	CIVIC ASSNS; LEAGUE OF WOMEN VOTERS; HOW. CO. FAIR ZONING COMM. FARM BUREAU	(HRD)		VILLAGE ASSN. BDS; JOINT BOARDS; VILLAGE ARCH. COMM.
		HRD (ARCH. COMM.) (VILLAGE ARCH. COMMS.)	HRD & VOLUNTEER RESIDENT STAFF	VILLAGE ASSN. BDS; JOINT BDS; NEIGH. & TOWNHOUSE ASSN. BDS; BUILDERS
DEPT. OF PUBLIC WORKS STAFF	CIVIC ASSN. HOW. CO. BLDRS. ASSN.			HRD; BUILDERS
DEPT. OF HEALTH	HOW. CO. ASSNS. OF COMMUNITY SERVICES; HOW. CO. MENTAL HEALTH ASSN; HOW. CO. MEDICAL SOC. ZERO POPULATION GROWTH	COLUMBIA HOSP. & MEDICAL PLAN BD. (ADMIN. JOHNS HOPKINS) (FINANCE: CONN. GEN.)		MEMBER ADVISORY COUNCIL OF CHMP; COLUMBIA COUNCIL
DEPT. OF SOCIAL SERVICES STAFF; FRIENDSHIP EXCHANGE	HOW. CO. ASSN. OF COMMUNITY SERVICES; WOMEN'S CENTER; LEAGUE OF WOMEN VOTERS	CA EXEC. COMMITTEE FRNDSP. EXCHANGE BD. AWARENESS, INC. BD; GRASSROOTS INC. BD; COL. COOP. MINISTRY BD. (OPERATIONS COMM.)	CA STAFF FRNDSHIP EX. STAFF AWARENESS STAFF GRASSROOTS STAFF COL COOP. MIN. STAFF	COMMUNITY SERVICES ADVISORY COMM; COLUMBIA COUNCIL; WOMEN'S CENTER
	COUNCIL FOR ENVIRONMENTAL QUALITY; LEAGUE OF WOMEN VOTERS	CA EXEC. COMM. (HRD)	HRD STAFF	VILLAGE NEIGH. & TOWNHOUSE ASSNS; COLUMBIA COUNCIL; MIDDLE PATUXET VALLEY ASSN; VILLAGE ARCH. COMMS.
		CA EXEC. COMMITTEE		AD-HOC COMM. FOR THE PERFORMING ARTS
	WOMEN'S CENTER; STUDY ACTION GROUP IN RACISM			WOMEN'S CENTER

) CARRY OUT ACTIONS • PRESSURE GROUP* GROUP WITH NO LEGAL AUTHORITY WHICH ATTEMPTS TO INFLUENCE ACTIONS OF DECISION MAKER

ticipation in community life, or (2) decentralized power within a hierarchy of functions with high costs and citizen involvement and satisfaction, we believe the second alternative is the better choice for society.

Governance Residential Unit (GRU)

We suggest this concept to enable a group of new-town residents to establish their own system of self-governance, if they so desire, within the total framework of their new-town government. This alternative form may be used when a hierarchical system is not applicable, although some points of the GRU could be used in the hierarchical system. Major basic requirements are essential for the GRU.

The total number of residents in the GRU should be large enough to justify the establishment of a mechanism of self-government, but the number should also be small enough to retain its social identity and territorial proximity. The optimum GRU size is 5000, but not less than 3500, the number that would justify an elementary school.

The GRU should have the basic services required to support self-governance. These should include mainly the social and educational services essential to the subcommunity and to individual families: nursery school, kindergarten, elementary school, a community center for adults and the elderly as well as for children, recreational services, such as playgrounds for different age groups, and swimming pools, and basic clinical services, such as first aid and medical care primarily for women and children.

The GRU should be located within the municipal boundary of the new town and should be close to its structures. The GRU could have an independent physical territory which supports its local self-government. Residents should have common interests, such as an interest in a special form of education or services, or should have a more basic bond, such as a similar age group, race, ethnic origin, or religion. Sharing motivates personal creativity and social interaction.

Only GRU residents will participate in elections for its council. The GRU in turn will send its own representatives to the new-town council.

The primary advantages of the GRU can be summarized in the following points: the GRU can establish effective communication between its governing body and its residents, because of the residents' proximity, the community size, and the residents' familiarity with their elected representatives. Thus there will be a mutual and intensive influence between residents and government. The GRU system may also strengthen the

residents' identity and individual consciousness regarding their government, a quality that is being lost in most large, established cities. Overall, the GRU system can create citizens' interest, intensify their participation in community activities and, finally, lead to a sharing of responsibilities. A GRU may increase the contributions of citizens regularly left out of community activities, such as women and teen-agers. In other words, the GRU can replace government institutions with governance systems.

It should be remembered that decentralization of functions with centralization of policy, and the promotion of GRU through a hierarchical system, cannot be accomplished unless a comprehensive plan is prepared. Therefore physical, social, and economic planning should take place in an integrated comprehensive way; otherwise consideration of the proposed idea would fail to achieve its goal and probably could not operate effectively.

Another consideration is the need for adequate organized training for the community and its leaders in community management and leadership training to achieve an effective result. Without such systematic formal training, comprehensive, productive results are doubtful.

Tax Reform

It has long been believed that established cities have been suffering a financial crisis and that there is a need for comprehensive financial reform. Perhaps the new town as an experimental laboratory for innovative taxation systems could teach established cities. This reform should focus primarily on the following issues:

(1)   Efficiency in the governmental machinery and in tax collection.

(2)   A taxation policy that would encourage the establishment of a balanced community in which different income groups are integrated and taxed at a graduated rate, by income, number of people per family, and floor area in their homes.

A first step in this direction would be to collect all local taxes in one yearly bill. This would increase efficiency by reducing bureaucracy, increase coordination between different agencies, and foster feelings of cooperation among citizens by eliminating endless bills. A second step would be to eliminate duplicate taxes. Reform might equalize the level of services among the individual neighborhood or residential units, regardless of their total tax base. Also, revenue sharing between local governments and the provincial or state government might aid tax reform.

An increase in the local government's tax base could also be stimulated by a sharing, between the developer and the local government, of profits resulting from government improvements of the community's environment. For example, road development and other utilities constructed in an undeveloped area in the community will increase land value, and a percentage of this increase may be returned to the local government.

Another way to ease the local tax burden would be to educate residents about the advantages of voluntarily implementing various services, such as day-care centers, public libraries, and clinics. Voluntary work would also be excellent education for the participants. Finally, new-town citizens could participate in operating the local government's tax base by becoming its stockholders.[27]

CONCLUSION

Governance is the art of making residents into citizens who share responsibilities. To implement such governance, a new town free from established power structures may be "for testing new forms and processes of local self-government" from which established cities could benefit.[28]

Ideal governance should be based on horizontal communication through all cells of a community: house, block, residential cluster, village, neighborhood, town, and region. Also, vertical communication should flow through its agencies, service institutions, local councils, regional council, and mayors and other decision makers. A telecommunication system used by educated, concerned citizens may support such a goal.

The distribution of power greatly influences the effectiveness of local government and delivery of its services. "The size of political bodies, the scale of constituencies and geographic units of participation also affect who participates in what, and to what effect."[29]

Although we conventionally view governance as decision making by elected officials, it is essential to understand that governance is also a long- or short-term process for citizens and all local agencies that affect the lives of individual residents. Awareness of the mechanism of all these components should enable the governance planner to form the coordinating process and have governance approach its ultimate goals. In this level of governance, citizens dedicated to defend public interest may play an effective role in the process.

Decentralization of power structures and management of services by villages and neighborhoods may attract many usually apathetic citizens to participate in community affairs (e.g., low-income groups). This system should not only strengthen the construction of community democracy, a spirit of volunteering, and its social coherence, but should also support the continuity of the new town's construction by the developer.

In developing a democratic system, every segment of the community becomes important. In a time when technology is accelerating its dominance, democracy increases in importance as a tool for the dignified survival of community spirit.

One of the unfortunate conditions of the large city is that the immense scale of its bureaucracy keeps government remote from local citizens. Also staffs of low quality and service fragmented among a large number of agencies have become detrimental to large cities. Volunteers in a new town may shorten this gap between bureaucrats and ordinary citizens.

A conflict between the public or private developer and the early residents that stems from the provision of democratic relations and may hinder implementation is sufficient reason for establishing a governing body very early. The significance of democracy has been its ability to unite all conflicting and interested groups under one umbrella on an equal basis, with tolerance and mutual understanding.

NOTES

1. *Webster's Seventh New Collegiate Dictionary* (Springfield, Mass.: G.& C. Merriam Co., 1966), p. 361.

2. *Webster's*, p. 361.

3. James M. Banovetz, ed., *Managing the Modern City* (Washington, D.C.: International City Management Association, 1971), pp. 18–43.

4. Royce Hanson, "Issues in Democratic Development of New Towns," *Ekistics,* **34,** no. 201 (August 1972), p. 83.

5. James McKeller, "Public Control vs. Public Action," in *New Towns in America: The Design and Development Process,* James Baily, ed. (New York: John Wiley and Sons, 1973), p. 135.

6. Stanley Scott, "Local Government and the Large New Communities," *Public Affairs Report,* **6,** no. 3 (June 1965), p. 2.

7. William Taubman, *Governing Soviet Cities: Bureaucratic Politics and Urban Development in the USSR* (New York: Praeger Publishers, 1973), p. 54.

8. Taubman, pp. 70–71.

9. Stanley Scott, "The Large Scale Communities: Ultimate Self-

Government and Other Problems," *Public Affairs Report,* **6,** no. 5 (October 1965), p. 3.

10.   Scott, "Local Government and the Large New Communities," p. 2.

11.   Research and Policy Committee, *Modernizing Local Government* (New York: Committee for Economic Development, 1966), p. 9.

12.   Royce Hanson, *Managing Services for New Communities* (Washington, D.C.: Washington Center for Metropolitan Studies, 1972), p. 16.

13.   U.S. Advisory Commission on Intergovernmental Relations, *Urban and Rural America* (Washington, D.C.: U.S. Government Printing Office, 1968), p. 93.

14.   David R. Godschalk, "The Future of Citizen Participation in New Communities," in *Planning for the Social Frontier: New Communities in America,* Gideon Golany, ed., under consideration for publication.

15.   Royce Hanson, *New Towns: Laboratories for Democracy* (New York: The Twentieth Century Fund, 1971), pp. 42–47.

16.   Hanson, *New Towns: Laboratories for Democracy,* pp. 51–52.

17.   U.S. Advisory Commission on Intergovernmental Relations, pp. 89–90.

18.   David Rogers, *The Management of Big Cities: Interest Groups and Social Change Strategies* (Beverly Hills, Ca.: Saga Publications, 1971), pp. 17–18.

19.   Rogers, p. 153.

20.   Research and Policy Committee, *Reshaping Government in Metropolitan Areas* (New York: Committee for Economic Development, 1970), p. 17.

21.   George J. Washnis, *Municipal Decentralization and Neighborhood Resources* (New York: Praeger Publishers, 1972), p. 371.

22.   Washnis, p. V.

23.   Hanson, *Managing Services for New Communities,* p. 3.

24.   Hanson, "Issues in Democratic Development of New Towns," p. 83.

25.   In the new community of Columbia, Maryland, only 34 percent of the residents were not active in community affairs; 63 percent were not active prior to moving to Columbia. Moreover, 68 percent of the residents indicated that it was easier for them to be involved in community affairs in Columbia than where they had lived before; 64 percent of those indicated as reasons the new-community spirit and the new opportunity. See *First Annual Columbia Conference on Community Governance* (Columbia, Md.: Columbia Conference Committee, 1972), pp. 14–15.

26.   Hanson, *New Towns: Laboratories for Democracy,* p. 55.

27.   The Minnesota Experimental City suggested that the city be managed as "a corporate model with the citizens as stockholders." (Minnesota Experimental City, Volume III: *Areas for Study and Experimentation* [Minneapolis: University of Minnesota, 1969], p. 52).

28.   Hanson, *New Towns: Laboratories for Democracy,* p. 8.

29.   Hanson, *New Towns: Laboratories for Democracy,* p. 56.

TEN
NEW TOWN IN-CITY:
NEW URBAN VENTURE

INTRODUCTION

A major objective of the new-town movement has been to ease congestion in large urban centers. Control of population growth may be feasible in the future, but it will always be much more difficult to ease the problems of overconcentration in certain areas. There has been, and always will be, a trend toward increasingly large cities.[1] The dynamism of the city continues to attract people of all ages and income levels, yet despite its magnetism, sections of the large city are rapidly becoming deteriorated, unsafe, and unhealthy places for living. The problems that the urban center poses for the future are complex and critical; therefore, as planners, we should direct our major efforts toward improvement of these areas.

The new town in-town (see Chapter 2) can significantly improve some aspects of the city. Yet within any city there are large areas that are almost or completely decayed, and therefore it does not pay in terms of money and effort to rehabilitate or remodel these areas. Instead, a comprehensive approach can prevent wasted time and money.

One viable means of improving both physical and social environments is through the application of the original new-town concept within decayed areas of the central city or its surrounding regions.[2] As such a possibility, we propose the new town in-city. The author has developed this concept over the period of time spanning several of his new-town seminars conducted at different universities. The concept combines many ideas presented in ancient and contemporary theories for both new-town development and central city improvement. Furthermore, the concept is unique and new in its comprehensive approach and its emphasis. Combining the new-town principles, the new town in-city would be characterized by a greenbelt and designated open space; unified land ownership under a public or quasi-public agency; a limited population size; a well-developed neighborhood setting; close proximity of place of work and residence; and provision of public utilities and social services. In addition the new town in-city would be a self-contained and balanced community with a relatively sound economic base, and would support the central city in the decentralization of industry and control of population densities and land uses.

Traditional planning often attacks the specific and most urgent problems within a given region of a metropolis. Yet this kind of planning seldom considers that the interaction of human beings and their behavior is always a result of diverse forces, and that the city is an organic mechanism with all the characteristics of a live body. A solution to one problem does not necessarily solve other complex problems related to it. Thus the new town in-city, when planned comprehensively, is intended not only to solve the pressing problems of an area but also to improve significantly the total environment of that area. When completed, the new town in-city will be largely independent of the metropolis socially, economically, governmentally, and physically, and yet will also be a strong focal point of the entire city, still able to fulfill its comprehensive objectives.

BASIC PLANNING VARIABLES

The first step in planning the new town in-city is the choice of a suitable site within the metropolis. Indicative of such an area is not only the deterioration of its structures, but also the existence of inefficient utilities (e.g., water and sewage systems and garbage collection), poor housing conditions, and abandoned buildings. Minimum public and social services, good quality streets and roads, and green park areas and playgrounds are usually absent. This section of the city is also characterized by a general apathy of individuals and groups toward their social and physical environments, by a destructive attitude of young people toward local utilities, and by the lack of local community leaders. Often the area is further distinguished by a strong homogeneity of age or income groups. In order to achieve the most effective results, the site for the new town in-city should be totally cleared prior to implementation.[3]

The concept of the new town in-city could also be applied to sections of the central city which already have a distinctive social character due to a predominance of certain population groups. Development of the new town in-city plan under such circumstances could be implemented gradually, stage by stage, and local community residents could be relocated when houses are completed and jobs become available.

Greenbelt and Open Space

Among the distinctive traits of the new town in-city are a greenbelt and many open green areas; both are vital to achieve a pleasing environment. Greenbelts divide and distinguish both the new town from its surrounding city and the various different land uses within the town itself. Open areas create numerous possibilities for recreation and leisure. Physically, both greenbelts and open spaces account for the unique appearance of the new town in-city; socially and psychologically their effects are far-reaching.

The greenbelt is a strictly zoned, continuous strip of open land following the circumference of the new town.[4] Its first function is to create a territorial distinction between the new town and the rest of the city. In this respect the greenbelt will effectively eliminate from residential areas the noise and air pollution of major highways that necessarily cross the metropolis. These major highways, aside from their national and regional functions, could act as collectors or distributors between the various units of the central and outer city, but such highways should always be lined up along the center of the greenbelt. On the one hand, this would create a country atmosphere for a driver when he is actually in the heart of an urban center—a country atmosphere which the metropolis, in most cases, has entirely lost because of an ever-increasing need for construction space.

On the other hand, for both outsiders and residents, the distinct physical form of the town would create a feeling of the unique community in a large "alienated" atmosphere. Thus the greenbelt would promote a

sense of belonging to a specific territory.[5] The greenbelt would enable some urban dwellers to achieve the local identity which the large metropolis denies them, and could possibly help to transform the apathy so common among city dwellers into a real concern for their environment.

Greenbelts could be put to uses other than open space and wooded areas to benefit the community. For example, part of the large belt surrounding the entire community could function as a heliport; the greenbelt could also be sited for artificial lakes, parks, and other recreational facilities, experiments in agriculture, and perhaps even an open zoo. If the new town in-city is located in or close to a waterfront, the greenbelt could be replaced by a canal. Careful design of this waterway would not only vary the landscape but could also provide for a variety of water-related recreational activities.

The planner should carefully decide the size of these dividing greenbelts or water belts. Their widths and sizes will inevitably vary, but their scales should be determined on the basis of local factors such as overall density, land market value, variation of land uses, land suitability, and especially pollution elimination.

A scattered pattern of small green areas and open spaces within the community will strengthen the kind of environment the new town in-city seeks to achieve. Parks, playgrounds, flower gardens, and wooded and other open spaces should be provided within the neighborhoods, industrial parks, commercial centers, and other land uses of the new town. Such open spaces should meet the various requirements of all age groups and be within walking distance of the major focus of daily activities. To insure safety and to allow for extensive use, these areas should be well lighted at night[6] and should never be located along or close to roads and streets; they would be most valuable located close to high-density residential areas.

Open spaces and green areas are essential in creating a positive physical environment and in motivating the avid participation of town residents. Obviously, the maintenance system of these areas is as important as their design. In the long run, conscientious and continuous maintenance by both residents and local municipalities will determine the effectiveness of green areas.

The new town in-city concept as a development within the central city is unconventional in its allocation of land for greenbelts and open spaces. Yet such new-town principles are feasible for implementation within the city. Since the entire area is first cleared, both the planner and the developer are free to designate land uses as necessary in the creation of a total environment and to introduce a variety of innovative designs. If space is limited, then increasing or decreasing density in one or more sections will make the creation of these areas possible.

Although crowded conditions are a problem urban redevelopment tries to solve, its single dwellings are not the only means of combating the poor living conditions in high-density areas. Innovatively designed apartment buildings and attached dwellings will improve these conditions just as effectively. In any case, the value of green areas is inestimable. Not only are they a means of improving facilities and providing recreational opportunities, but they are also essential in promoting the community spirit and unity characteristic of the genuine new town. Thus their creation is a first priority in the development of the new town in-city.

Size

The size of the new town in-city is a crucial factor in its future development. Since the pace of community development within the city far exceeds that of any other type of new town outside a metropolitan area, the housing market within this city is obviously more intense than in a rural community. Thus one could easily anticipate that the new town in-city would reach its full development within a relatively short period, and the issue of controlling future growth becomes a major early consideration in its planning.

An examination of development and planning history reveals that crucial problems have occurred when various forces caused changes in the original planned land use and density of a designated area. In large cities an increase in population size and density that exceeded the capacities of facilities led to a decrease in the quality of life and environment. Similarly, uncontrolled growth was disruptive to the unity of the area. Since the new town in-city is intended to provide an environment of superior quality and to be self-sustaining, any unrestrained expansion could defeat its purposes. Economic independence depends heavily on the provision of job opportunities within the town for most of its residents. The quality of life is greatly influenced by a decrease in the commuting pattern and a tightly structured neighborhood pattern; both could not be maintained if a large influx of new residents were permitted.

The new town in-city should be designated for a limited fixed population size, which would justify hierarchical patterns of all services and amenities.

Using the conclusions of economists, one can generally assume that the population of the new town in-city should be approximately 100,000.[7] (For a further discussion of size, see Chapter 5.)

Since it is located within a large urban center, the size of a new town in-city could be related to the degree of economic independence desired by the development corporation. When this size has been determined it should be specified in the community constitution, and there should not be any future fluctuation. Any population spillover should be directed to another new town in-city or to other areas developed within the central city and its environs.

The greenbelt encircling the new town in-city will complement this concept of limited town size. Since land designated as greenbelts will not change its use, nor will its ownership be transferable, future expansion of the town or gradual merging with the surrounding metropolis will be impossible. Other land-use patterns should also be held constant, especially to prevent changes in the originally planned density. Changes in the original land-use pattern should only be permitted if innovative technology, such as an improved transportation or communication system, necessitates adjustments.

Table 10.1 illustrates 14 alternative sizes of new towns in-city, each related to another 11 alternatives of gross densities, total land needed, total number of employees, and radius of land for possible pedestrian movement. The 11 density alternatives for each of the community sizes do not exceed the average gross density existing in the central city.[8]

Limited city size would create community stability; enhance familiarity, social interaction, and local identity; and develop a local urban image for the new-town population.[9]

Transportation and Proximity

Since a steady increase in car use has greatly influenced our socioeconomic and physical environment patterns, an efficient transportation system must be a major concern in planning a new town. One of the most effective means of coping with transportation intensity has been a hierarchical ordering of all transportation means (see Chapter 6). This systematic arrangement is essential in planning the new town in-city.

The principal elements that determine the location of roads and highways are points of origin and destination, function, and overall purpose within the com-

TABLE 10.1 ALTERNATIVE DENSITY AND LAND SIZE REQUIREMENTS FOR A NEW TOWN IN-CITY

ALTERNATIVES	TOTAL POPULATION	TOTAL NUMBER OF FAMILIES *	ALTERNATIVE GROSS DENSITY PER ACRE		TOTAL AREA NEEDED**	
			*FAMILIES	PERSONS	ACRES	SQ. MILES
I	10,000	2,702	23	85.1	117.509	.184
			22	81.4	122.850	.192
			21	77.7	128.700	.201
			20	74.0	135.135	.211
			19	70.3	142.248	.222
			18	66.6	150.150	.235
			17	62.9	158.983	.248
			16	59.2	168.919	.264
			15	55.5	180.180	.282
			14	51.8	193.050	.302
			13	48.1	207.900	.325
			12	44.4	225.225	.352
II	15,000	4,054	23	85.1	176.263	.275
			22	81.4	184.275	.288
			21	77.7	193.050	.302
			20	74.0	202.703	.317
			19	70.3	213.371	.333
			18	66.6	225.225	.352
			17	62.9	238.474	.373
			16	59.2	253.378	.396
			15	55.5	270.270	.422
			14	51.8	289.575	.452
			13	48.1	311.850	.487
			12	44.4	337.838	.528
III	20,000	5,405	23	85.1	235.018	.367
			22	81.4	245.700	.383
			21	77.7	257.400	.402
			20	74.0	270.270	.422
			19	70.3	284.495	.445
			18	66.6	300.300	.469

ALTERNATIVES	TOTAL POPULATION	TOTAL NUMBER OF FAMILIES *	ALTERNATIVE GROSS DENSITY PER ACRE		TOTAL AREA NEEDED**	
			*FAMILIES	PERSONS	ACRES	SQ. MILES
VI	35,000	9,459	23	85.1	411.281	.643
			22	81.4	429.975	.672
			21	77.7	450.450	.704
			20	74.0	472.973	.739
			19	70.3	497.866	.778
			18	66.6	525.526	.822
			17	62.9	556.439	.869
			16	59.2	591.216	.924
			15	55.5	630.631	.985
			14	51.8	675.676	1.056
			13	48.1	727.651	1.137
			12	44.4	788.288	1.232
VII	40,000	10,810	23	85.1	470.035	.734
			22	81.4	491.400	.768
			21	77.7	514.801	.804
			20	74.0	540.541	.845
			19	70.3	568.990	.889
			18	66.6	600.601	.938
			17	62.9	635.930	.994
			16	59.2	675.676	1.056
			15	55.5	720.721	1.126
			14	51.8	772.201	1.207
			13	48.1	831.601	1.299
			12	44.4	900.901	1.408
VIII	45,000	12,162	23	85.1	528.790	.826
			22	81.4	552.826	.864
			21	77.7	579.151	.905
			20	74.0	608.108	.950
			19	70.3	640.114	1.000
			18	66.6	675.676	1.056

Group	Population	Area			
IV	25,000	6,756	17	62.9	317.965	.497

			17	62.9	317.965	.497
IV	25,000	6,756	16	59.2	337.838	.528
			15	55.5	360.360	.563
			14	51.8	386.100	.603
			13	48.1	415.800	.650
			12	44.4	450.450	.704
			23	85.1	293.772	.459
			22	81.4	307.125	.480
			21	77.7	321.750	.503
			20	74.0	337.838	.528
			19	70.3	355.619	.556
			18	66.6	375.375	.587
			17	62.9	397.456	.621
			16	59.2	422.297	.660
			15	55.5	450.450	.704
			14	51.8	482.625	.754
			13	48.1	519.751	.812
			12	44.4	563.063	.880
V	30,000	8,108	23	85.1	352.526	.551
			22	81.4	368.550	.576
			21	77.7	386.100	.603
			20	74.0	405.405	.633
			19	70.3	426.743	.667
			18	66.6	450.450	.704
			17	62.9	476.948	.745
			16	59.2	506.757	.792
			15	55.5	540.540	.845
			14	51.8	579.151	.905
			13	48.1	623.701	.975
			12	44.4	675.675	1.056

Group	Population	Area			
IX	50,000	13,512	17	62.9	715.421	1.118
			16	59.2	760.135	1.188
			15	55.5	810.811	1.267
			14	51.8	868.726	1.357
			13	48.1	935.551	1.462
			12	44.4	1013.514	1.584
			23	85.1	587.544	.918
			22	81.4	614.251	.960
			21	77.7	643.501	1.005
			20	74.0	675.676	1.056
			19	70.3	711.238	1.111
			18	66.6	750.751	1.173
			17	62.9	794.913	1.242
			16	59.2	844.595	1.320
			15	55.5	900.901	1.408
			14	51.8	965.251	1.508
			13	48.1	1039.501	1.624
			12	44.4	1126.126	1.760

* 3.7 members in the family
** every sq. mile = 640 acres
1 acre = 4,840 sq. yard

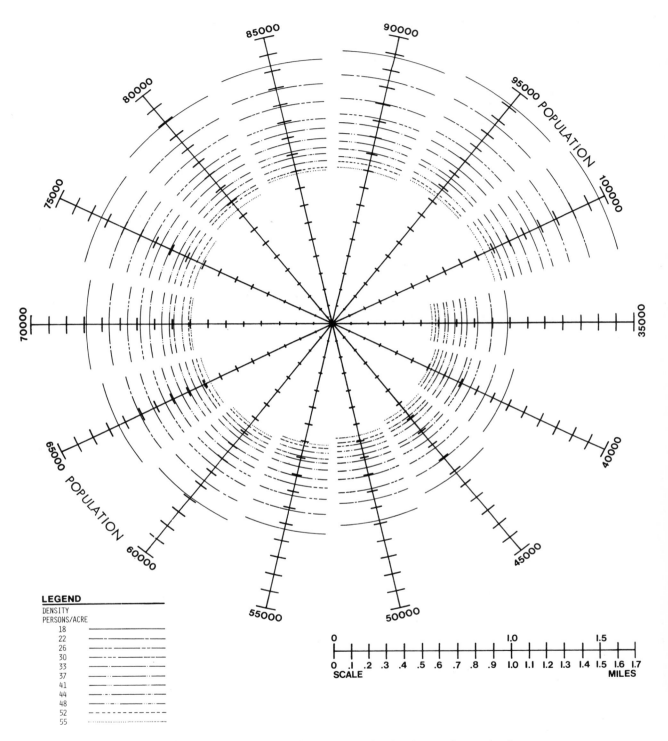

LEGEND

DENSITY
PERSONS/ACRE

18	
22	
26	
30	
33	
37	
41	
44	
48	
52	
55	

Figure 10.1. Alternative gross densities and populations related to the stimulation of walking in a new town in-city.

munity. Since major highways are not of direct benefit, they should not cross the new town but should be redirected and aligned along the center of the greenbelt. Access to them should be through regional access roads, which may also link the new town in-city and similar developments within the metropolis.

A public transit system should be combined with the private transportation network, connecting not only the various sections of the new town in-city, but also the new town and other portions of the central city and its metropolitan area. This suggested public transit, whether under- or aboveground, should operate 24 hours a day and be free for town citizens; there should be a charge for outsiders. Such a public transit network may reduce the use of the car, and may in time be the dominant means of transportation, establish local pride, and further help to establish the identity of the new town in-city. A major element in this transportation system is the pedestrian walkway (see Chapter 6).

Figure 10.1 clearly illustrates the various alternatives of new town in-city size with various densities that could be related to the development of a pedestrian system within the town. Note that the largest population size (100,000) combined with the lowest density (18 persons per acre) provides a maximum radius of 1.7 miles from the center to the periphery of the town. On the other hand, the smallest distance of the same community size is less than a mile when its density is as high as 55 persons per acre. A prime advantage of the new town in-city is the closeness of its different land uses, which may reduce transportation and encourage interaction. Even with a population of 100,000 the maximum distance between the new town center and its periphery, the new town in-city allows walking for young people. This proximity becomes meaningful when one's place of work is in the same town.

Doubtless, the new town in-city must overcome obstacles that do not generally exist in the development of a new town located far from the metropolis. The cleared site would enable comprehensive design of a transportation network while coping with the traffic network beyond the site of the new town in-city. It will not be easy to redirect major highways or other throughways; this will require the cooperation of city government and may necessitate changes in the transportation network of closely related sections of the city. Nevertheless, the new town in-city accomplishments socially, economically, and governmentally, will make the meeting of such requirements in physical planning worthwhile.

SOCIAL STRUCTURE

The major achievement of the new town in-city will be the creation of a healthy, diverse social environment. Since social rather than physical aspects should initially determine physical design, sociologists and professionals in related fields will play significant roles in planning the new town in-city. A team of these professionals will help to foster a positive social climate for the community—unique in contrast to the almost total absence of social interaction in modern, large urban centers.

A prime objective of the new town in-city is the integration of diverse population groups. Heterogeneity will create a variety of socializing choices for residents of the town that will lead to a closely-knit community with a clearly defined unity. Balanced heterogeneity will also make the community as a whole an attractive place for outsiders. A steady influx of outsiders (city residents and visitors) should provide the new town in-city with the kind of activity that accounts for the magnetism of most resort or recreational centers, and thus make it a focal point of the metropolis.

This heterogeneous population should be multifaceted, and should include a variety of cultural, age, ethnic, religious, and racial groups. Although diversity is a prime goal, complete integration is not absolutely essential; thus any single group could organize and voluntarily choose a certain section of the community as its domain. However, although a group could comprise the majority within an area, it should not monopolize it completely. (See Chapter 4 for a general discussion of integration and Chapter 7 for a discussion of integration in neighborhoods.)

The clustering of identical population groups could add to the appeal of the new town in-city. The clearly defined character of some of its sections is responsible for much of the charm of the European city. This accounts for a unique cultural distinction that the new town in-city could also establish in time. On the other hand Israel, for example, has illustrated that the initial separation of various groups is, in the long run, a method of solving segregation problems.[10] Thus in some countries that consider integration a primary objective, this kind of grouping might also prove successful.

Characterized by extensive innovation and high standards of living, new towns generally attract the middle echelon of society. The central city, however, usually houses many low-income groups; therefore the new town in-city must be flexible enough to prevent the displacement of this low-income population. Subsidized housing would offer an excellent opportunity for people with low incomes to enjoy the conveniences and comforts they rarely can afford. However, in the new town in-city subsidized housing should be interspersed with other types to prevent the usual grouping of low-income families and thus insure against the neglect of any single area in the community. Also, mixture of housing types would lead to the psychological well-being of people who usually suffer the alienation and resentment common to poverty-stricken groups.

Social Services

Heterogeneity of population will require diverse social services and facilities. There is probably no better way of promoting social interaction and future integration than through a sharing of services.[11] The sharing of social and cultural services is most effective in creating an environment for social interaction. Therefore both the neighborhood and the town center will be strong focal points and will help to generate a positive image of the community.

The neighborhood center will offer residents daily

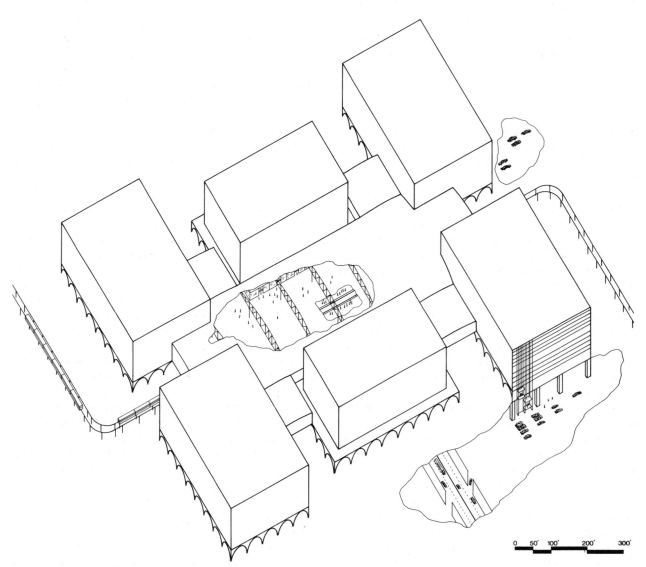

Figure 10.2. A bird's-eye view of a schematic plan of a comprehensive town center for a new town in-city. Serving both the town and its peripheral region, the town center is based on an aboveground mass transportation system (linking various parts of the town and city) and underground parking. The entire ground level is kept free for pedestrian use and green area.

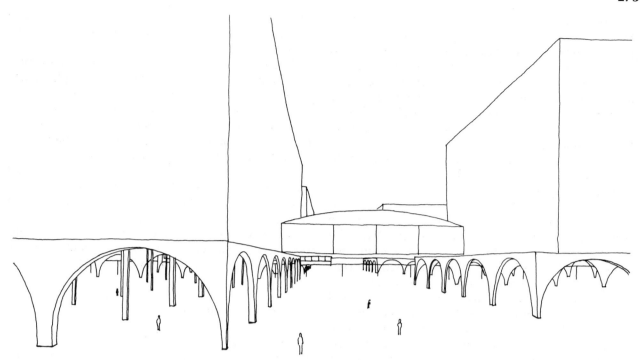

Figure 10.3. A ground-level view of Figure 10.2.

required services and facilities close to their homes. These services will be oriented primarily toward the needs of young children, to insure their safety and to ease the anxieties of parents who must raise their children in an urban environment. The neighborhood center will provide child day-care centers, elementary schools using the most advanced technology in cable and mass-media education, and ample playgrounds and recreational facilities. The center may also provide some services required by older people such as stores, sports facilities, an adult education program, and perhaps a modest art center.

The town center will be a more elaborate complex than the neighborhood center (see Figures 10.2 and 10.3). As a major social and cultural center it will combine an auditorium, theaters, a museum, and restaurants. A multipurpose shopping plaza with child-care facilities will be one of the major attractions of the center. The town center should fill two roles: it will provide all required services and amenities for the community, meeting physical needs and offering a choice of cultural and recreational facilities; it will also attract a number of outsiders. In both cases the town center will be a major focus for social activity and entertainment.

The arrangement of facilities in both the neighborhood and the town defines the hierarchical system of

services designed for the new town:[12] services are arranged for maximum convenience and efficiency.[13] For example, the new town in-city would have to supply the health services required by its populace, and the efficiency of these services will depend largely on their locations within the new town in-city. Obviously, they should be located close to residential areas and be especially accessible for mothers. The site for a local hospital would also require careful selection to guarantee maximum efficiency. The new town in-city will offer a highly sophisticated and innovative system of services and facilities. This will add to the social environment of the town and also to the character of the new town in-city as a model for the surrounding metropolis.

Although the new town in-city will have its own social identity and will provide all the services and facilities required by its population, it may not be socially independent of the surrounding metropolis. New-town residents may go into the city for a greater diversity in cultural amenities or in services than is available in the new town in-city, while city residents will frequently use the facilities offered in the new town. In this sense the new town in-city will be unconventional—a steady influx of outsiders and an occasional outward movement of the population will increase opportunities for social interaction and thus improve the social environment of the new town. Further, because the new town in-city will also function as a center for an area larger than its own, it may in time become a regional center for that area. The surrounding metropolis could construct some enterprises (e.g., a new art center) in the new town in-city either because the new-town environment would be conducive to the success of that establishment or simply because space is lacking in the city.

The new town in-city could break the eternal cycle of extreme poverty and unbalanced social environment generally associated with the large city. Because of its innovative nature, the new town in-city will probably attract a good number of young people whose energy, imagination, and time could well be directed to programs of improvement and constructive work within the community. A well-planned transportation system, a decrease in the commuting pattern, and pedestrian walks will decrease daily tensions and pressures. Many opportunities for leisure and pleasure will add to the relaxed atmosphere of the whole community. Comfort coupled with modern conveniences for all income groups and opportunities to mix and choose freely should prevent the growth of hostilities generally characteristic of the central city. As a result of these features, relations on all levels should improve dramatically. Family ties will be stronger, a healthy interaction between groups will prevail, and community spirit will bind all residents together, providing them with common interests and the common goal of maintaining the community's image.

Neighborhoods

The social identity of the new town in-city will originate in the well-planned neighborhood unit. Unfortunately, rapid growth within the city in recent decades has resulted in the almost complete disappearance of the neighborhood structure. Attempts to re-establish it have concentrated mainly on providing improved and sophisticated housing without much regard to community climate. Traditionally the neighborhood has been a major element in the improvement of housing conditions and also in the cultivation of a strong community atmosphere;[14] the new town in-city aims to create both. Through innovative design and the highest standard of conveniently located services, the practical aspects of living will improve. At the same time the neighborhood will act as an agent in motivating social identity.[15] Local governance and other neighborhood committees, and development of neighborhood leaders, will promote individual participation in

neighborhood activities and thus create the unique character of each community unit within the new town.

As a point of departure, the smallest subneighborhood unit of a 1 acre lot could be physically planned to insure this sense of identity. Sophisticated circulating roads or culs-de-sac would facilitate entry and exit and also insure the safety of the residents. All houses would face a center courtyard—a green area designated solely for the use of that unit—and access to it may be possible only from the homes. Since the courtyard would provide a safe place for children to play and also serve as a meeting place for unit residents, it would become a center of activity and a focus for social interaction. A complex of many clustered units designed to embrace a neighborhood center would be linked by a pedestrian network (Figure 10.4).

ECONOMIC STRUCTURE

The economic base of a community is a major determinant in its overall character. As explained earlier, the social environment of the new town in-city will be greatly influenced by location of employment and residence, land-use patterns, and housing mixture —initially these are all economic concerns. Just as the new town in-city is planned to provide its own infrastructure, it should also sustain its own relatively sound economic base.

Employment opportunity is the essential key to the new town in-city project in terms of its economic and social setting. Without it, this concept will not only lose its significance and uniqueness, but the new town will be a repetition of many other programs that have been introduced in the central city (e.g., the model city or urban renewal). Employment opportunity will be consistent with the population structure allocation, the demographic character, the diversity of the required balanced community, and the demand for a variety of housing types. However, the new town in-city should be planned and implemented to be self-contained; to have a sound economic base for its daily needs and employment opportunities primarily for its residents; and to provide health, education, and social services.

Place of Work and Residence

Careful coordination between location of place of employment and residence can be an effective method of controlling commuting patterns and town size. Such an arrangement will also prevent the new

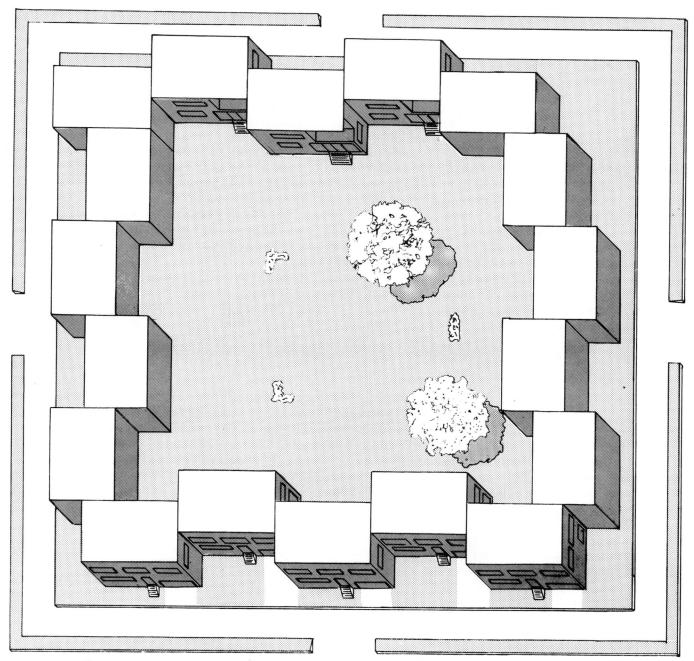

Figure 10.4. General scheme of a proposed subneighborhood unit of attached houses. Each housing unit faces a patio exclusively for the residents as commonly shared space. It is a 1-acre unit comprised of 18 housing units.

town in-city from becoming a bedroom community (see Chapter 5). Although it would be impossible to establish all places of employment close to residences, the new town in-city should be planned and implemented to insure maximum proximity. There are several ways of achieving this goal. First, residences could be limited mainly to those who have jobs in the community,[16] as has been successfully accomplished in many new towns in England.[17] Second, the town's development corporation and the industries and businesses admitted to the community could work together to provide housing for their prospective employees, or even provide housing as part of the fringe benefits of the employment package. To achieve any measure of success, a well-coordinated and comprehensive policy would have to be formulated in the early stages of development.

The allotment of land parcels for housing construction to each firm in proportion to the number of jobs it provides should guarantee an adequate number of housing units for both skilled and unskilled labor forces in the industry. However, a single section should not be developed by one firm; instead, several firms should share an area to guarantee heterogeneous population groups and housing types. This will improve employer-employee relations.

Despite these measures a resident may change jobs after he has settled in the new town. One way of insuring the above-mentioned policy is to build non-rental housing units supplied by a firm and returnable to it at market price if an employee leaves; another alternative is a specially designed taxation system.[18] Residents who work within the new town in-city might be exempted from some property and local income taxes, while residents employed outside would pay higher taxes. Moreover, people who reside outside the new town in-city but work within it should be required to pay local government taxes to the town since they are using some of its services. This would be a good incentive for finding employment within the town rather than in the surrounding city.

We anticipated that many industries and commercial concerns that do not have adequate space to expand within the central city, or have difficulties in recruiting qualified employees because of their location would want to relocate in the new town in-city. Therefore the new development could readily attract industry and could also, indirectly, ease the problems of the surrounding city. On the other hand, a careful selection process would determine which industries or commercial enterprises would most benefit the new town in-city. Industry would be confined to light ones, and strict pollution controls would be followed at all times to preserve the community's environmental quality. Similarly, commercial enterprises would be carefully selected on the basis of the services and facilities they supply. They should fulfill the requirements of the citizens, yet add to the diversity of the new town's character.

Land Assemblage

Perhaps the greatest obstacle in implementing the new town in-city concept is the acquisition of a suitable area within the city. Legislation may be required to enable the assemblage of land and to prevent land speculation. The first initiative should be public, yet the primary financial responsibilities should be the burden the central or state governments rather than the city government, which could not possibly have the resources for such a project. These financial resources would serve, in part, to establish a profit foundation and thus enhance the idea of a joint venture for both large and small private developers. Land cost in a new town in-city may constitute a large portion of the project's developmental cost, which may be much higher than those of any other settlement type. Therefore a highly sophisticated and innovative design and planning device should be introduced to overcome the high-density requirement of a new town in-city project.

When interests have been secured the new town in-city corporation, combining public and private enterprise, should be established. The public would play the major role in this corporation; the principal revolving fund would be granted jointly by the national and state (or provincial) governments. The corporation would function a the planner and developer of the new town in-city and would be responsible for the daily required services in the early stages of construction prior to the establishment of the locally elected government. It would own all land, leasing it to various contractors for development, and would thus guarantee diverse housing and provide the necessary controls in the early phases of development.

LAND-USE PATTERN AND HOUSING

The sites chosen for the new town's industries and commercial enterprises would dictate residential land use to some extent. In an effort to locate homes close to places of employment, residential clusters would be situated near industrial complexes. Similarly, each neighborhood would have easy access to the town center, the focus of commercial activity. The greenbelt, open spaces, and parks would clearly distinguish between the various land uses and thus define the identity of each. Obviously, all land uses should be aimed at meeting the specific needs of the new town rather than the needs of the central city as a whole. The intention to establish a sound and diversified economic base, services, and commercial and other activities will in turn require a corresponding variation in land use; thus such diversity will be a direct consequence of the economic function. On the other hand, a combination of land uses would enrich community

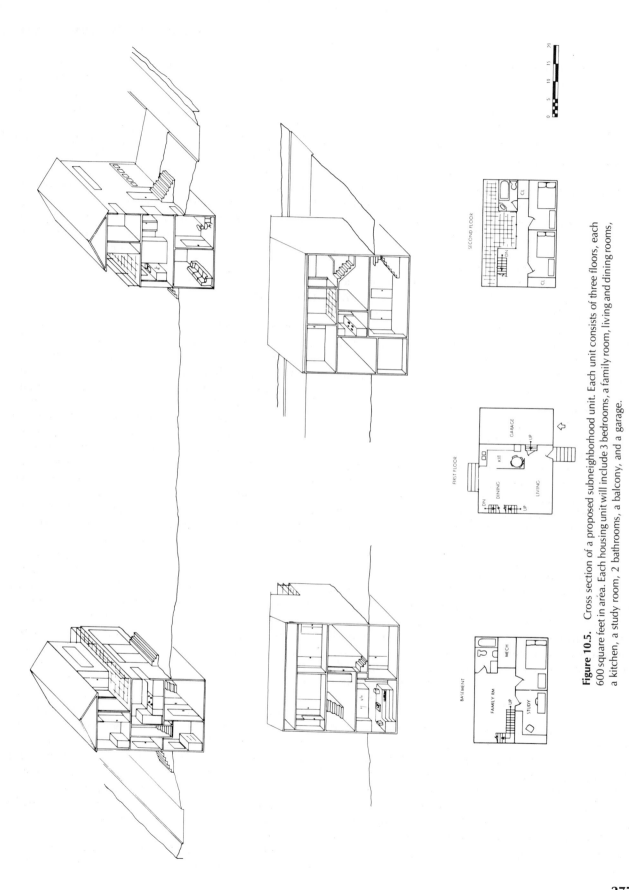

Figure 10.5. Cross section of a proposed subneighborhood unit. Each unit consists of three floors, each 600 square feet in area. Each housing unit will include 3 bedrooms, a family room, living and dining rooms, a kitchen, a study room, 2 bathrooms, a balcony, and a garage.

277

life and ease or diminish traffic congestion during rush hours, since places of work will be decentralized within the new town in-city. Consequently, a pedestrian pattern will be accepted by a reasonable portion of the population. Figure 10.1 and Table 10.1 illustrate the optimum radius of all land required for optimum walking distances in relation to the new-town population size. Since such distances will be much shorter if land uses are diversified, there will be a major correlation between the optimum new town in-city population size, density, total space required, and the development of its diverse land use.

Evidently the diversity of economic base, land use, and social groups in the new town in-city will require a variation in housing units. Housing will vary in type, size, and cost to meet the demands of a heterogeneous population. The leasing of land to various contractors will achieve much of this housing variety, and all design in the new town in-city will use the innovative methods and the most recent technological advances. Thus the new town will be an experimental laboratory in housing construction that will benefit the central city in the long run, while providing the highest standards for community living.

Although subsidized housing will be a major objective, subsidies will have to be granted through a reformed system to protect low-income groups. Skyrocketing housing prices, generally characteristic of a new-town development, often result in the resale of subsidized units at a much higher than original cost. In time, therefore, the subsidies disappear. In the new town in-city subsidized units will be returned to the corporation if the original purchaser desires to move, to be resold to a low-income family. This will guarantee a continuation of the subsidized portions of the community for low-income groups.[19]

Limitation of population size and control of land-use patterns will be facilitated by close regulation of the new town's in-city housing market. Since all land will be leased and not purchased, the corporation will never lose its ability to regulate land use. Also, the housing projects will partially restrain the influx of outsiders who are not employed in the new town. However, the most efficient means of controlling the construction and rental of housing units will be the planned density of the community, established as part of the original community constitution.

Although the new town in-city will provide all types of housing, one of its most interesting features will be the attached unit. For example, housing units in the neighborhood may be attached to encircle an acre of common, green open space for its residents (Figure 10.4).

The most common type will consist of three split levels (Figure 10.5). This housing design is aimed at retaining in the new town in-city the original gross density of that section of the central city without detracting from the quality of neighborhood living. To accomplish this, we suggest that part of the housing unit be constructed underground. Although unconventional, this would be an effective way of achieving adequate living space for average families, especially those with many children. Furthermore, the development of these houses will provide good homes, opportunity for social interaction, security, privacy and, above all, a stimulating environment.

GOVERNANCE

When the new town in-city reaches maturity, a local, authorized, independent citizens' association would be established. This kind of citizen participation may help to create a healthy community spirit and should insure governance proceedings that will directly benefit the entire community. The association would constitute its own laws and regulations, yet could not make changes in the original constitution formulated by the new-town development corporation: policies concerning land ownership, land use, and community size would be unalterable. Eventually the new town in-city citizens' association would be in charge of maintaining the development, but all profits from the project would go to the still-existent development corporation to be invested for community improvements.

The board of directors of the association would comprise representatives of the development corporation and of the citizens. Although corporation controls will always be necessary to retain land use and to insure direct adherence to all other regulations, the citizens—the community representatives—will be the major decision makers of the corporation. These community representatives will be elected from the body of town citizens that forms the association, and will include those who have been accepted as residents of the town and who pay the required monthly or yearly fee used to operate the town and its services. Priorities for establishing job opportunities such as new industries and shops should be given to local residents, and houses or apartments should be sold first to those who have already been accepted as citizens and members of the community. Membership would be open to every person, regardless of age, race, religion, or ethnic origin.

Membership fees will be based on income level, family size, house size, and the number of corporation shares owned by the member. Similarly, the power of each member will be proportional to his initial investment in the community development; thus business may have a greater voice in governance than the individial residential homeowner. The local government will be a close working arrangement between citizens and their elected representatives, industrial and commercial concerns, and corporation officials.

Self-governance should not only be considered in terms of efficiency and local governmental cost expenditure. It is the social flavor of the self-governance system that is most important in the short or long run of community development. Self-governance could contribute to the promotion of citizen responsibility toward the comprehensiveness of his environment.

The establishment of local independent governance is essential to insure a strong local identity and efficiency in social services and infrastructure. Once organized, it could be partially or fully federated with similar new town in-city projects or with the central city. Federation might be required for the coordination of services and utilities and for practical economic reasons. For example, although the new town in-city is planned to provide its own public utilities, social services, and other facilities, cooperation with other government units could improve the diversity of available services. Thus taxation would be by the governments of the new town in-city and the city in proportion to the services offered. Despite federation, however, the new town in-city association should always preserve its own identity.

Obviously this suggested form of governance means the decentralization of municipal government. Since such a change involves city politicians, we can anticipate that relinquishing power may be one of the most difficult obstacles encountered. Nevertheless, in breaking with convention, the governmental system proposed for the new town in-city could bring about significant reform and improvement in the management of the central city.[20] (See Chapter 9 for a discussion of decentralization.)

INNOVATIVE LABORATORY

Comprehensive innovation, typical of most new-town developments, will be the main theme of the new town in-city—in housing design and construction, in transportation and all means of communication, in educational facilities, in governance, and in cultural amenities.

We also hope that the new town in-city will overcome a problem common to most new towns,

difficulty in attracting low-income populations. The high standard of living which innovation produces is a major deterrent; also, low-income groups may feel they will not integrate easily with the middle-income population that usually forms the majority in a new town. An innovative, subsidized housing system, great variety in housing prices, and a well-rounded social environment should help to ease this dilemma.

Finally the new town in-city, as a model, should have an advantage over other new towns: because of its location, it could make significant contributions to the central city and to the surrounding metropolis. When a new practice has proven successful in the new town, it will be readily available for implementation within the central city. Eventually the model of a single new town in-city development could lead to noticeable improvements within various sections of a central city region.

CONCLUSION

Although the new-town concept has been widely implemented, its application in the form of the new town in-city is revolutionary. In view of the many obstacles it must overcome, the new town in-city may not seem a feasible project. The assemblage and clearing of city land will be difficult tasks, as will the continuation of strict controls on land use and size. It will also be difficult to arrange satisfactory cooperation between public and private enterprise; the proposed form of self-governance will doubtless be difficult for some city politicians to accept. The fact that if the new town in-city is to prove successful it must be completely implemented poses still another problem. It would involve drastic change, and therefore the concept may be too radical for immediate acceptance by the general population. Finally, the project will require great financial resources, much energy and, above all, belief in and devotion to the concept.

On the other hand, if the trend toward city living continues, the new town in-city may offer a promising future for rapidly deteriorating urban centers. The modern city can accurately be described as socially bankrupt, with urgent problems that require immediate attention. Housing renewal projects are helping to a certain extent, and the new town in-town with its gradual rehabilitation is another partial solution to the urban crisis. Perhaps in many cases we are wasting valuable time on partial projects that are oriented toward a single, narrow goal. Thus the new town in-city may be the only comprehensive solution for areas of the city which are beyond repair.

The development of the new town in-city may serve to unify the central city and also to stimulate areawide interest and concern among private enterprises in terms of investment and site selection for their economic activities. In this phase, private investors can play a significant role in its development. The new town in-city may also be an essential and effective tool to improve the central city tax system in the long run, rather than a financial and social burden on the central city.[21]

If expenses seem high, one should remember that the returns from such a development may far outweigh initial investments. The new town in-city may create the kind of environment that has been lost in the large city. The fast disappearing "community" would be re-established, thus restoring a positive social environment. Well-planned transportation systems, quality housing, parks and recreational areas, and strict pollution controls would significantly repair the physical environment of the city. Participation in government would restore public interest and individual rights, and the entire project would inspire the pride and concern for our city environment that is practically nonexistent today. Thus the new town in-city would find its supporters—politicians and central city mayors working for genuine improvement; groups who strongly favor the large city as their place of residence (e.g., racial and ethnic minorities); and all concerned citizens and professionals who are deeply involved with the betterment of living conditions in the entire city (e.g., ecologists and sociologists).

The urban center is as it exists today for the most part an agglomeration—a mere collection of disparate elements without any purposeful arrangement or structure. Certainly "urban renewal can and must address itself to reorganization, to structuring the city, to recognizing the vestiges of and helping to create a somewhat cellular structure. . . ."[22] The development of many new towns in-city would accomplish a restructuring of the city into a continuous network of urban communities that would coalesce while retaining their separate identities. Thus each new town in-city would fulfill some function of the whole city as a part of the urban complex. Such functional differentiation and distribution could be on two levels: types of employment opportunities and economic activities, and recreation, leisure, and sociocultural activities. One long-range effect of the development of several new towns in-city could also be to support spatial decentralization of the human activities within the central city, and to moderate density distribution and ease traffic or parking congestion. *Conurbation* is the ultimate achievement of the new town in-city

concept—the transformation of disorganized cities into well-arranged and coordinated urban complexes.[23]

Thus the new town in-city can accomplish much for a designated section of a city, and eventually for the metropolis as a whole. Although innumerable obstacles exist to the implementation of this kind of new town, its potential makes the endeavor worthwhile. It is time to replace the false notion that growth equals progress with real advancement through the improvement of the quality of life. The new town in-city, comprehensively planned and oriented toward many goals, is not merely a new land-use pattern, but rather a social and economic reform mechanism. It will inevitably solve some of the most critical problems confronting us today.

NOTES

1.   Sylvia Fleis Fava, ed., *Urbanism in World Perspective: A Reader* (New York: Thomas Y. Crowell Co., 1971). Also see Jean Gottmann, *Megalopolis: The Urbanized Northeastern Seaboard of the United States* (Cambridge: M.I.T. Press, 1965).

2.   For the purposes of this study, the central city is defined as that part of the metropolis in which there is the highest combined population density, transportation generation, and economic activity within the metropolitan region. For descriptions of central city features, see Peter Marris, "A Report on Urban Renewal in the United States," in *The Urban Condition: People and Policy in the Metropolis*, Leonard J. Duhl, ed., with the assistance of John Powell (New York: Simon and Schuster, 1963), pp. 113–34; Lyle Fitch, "Eight Goals for an Urbanizing America," in *The Conscience of the City*, Martin Meyerson, ed. (New York: George Braziller, 1970), pp. 67–68; Harold Mayer, "The Pull of Land and Space," in *Metropolis on the Move: Geographers Look at Urban Sprawl*, Jean Gottmann and Robert A. Harper, eds., (New York: John Wiley and Sons, 1967), pp. 23–35.

3.   Possible locations suitable for the implementation of the new town in-city in the United States are New York, Philadelphia, Chicago, Washington, D.C., or St. Louis; in Canada, Montreal (Pointe St. Charles); in Great Britain, London; in India, Calcutta; and in Japan, Tokyo.

The metropolitan area of New York City would be a good site for a new town in-city since the city has conditions which meet the needs of such a project: (1) many sections of its central city already have all the signs of social, physical, economic, and political deterioration; (2) at present, New York State is the only one in the country that has claimed the power of eminent domain to implement such a project; (3) th city is still the gateway to the United States and a window on the outside world; its cosmopolitan nature introduces various social problems but could be a significant experiment; (4) New York City already has many blighted built-up areas which are abandoned or deteriorated and could, therefore, be potential areas for the project.

4.   F. J. Osborn, in his preface to Ebenezer Howard's *Garden Cities of To-Morrow*, defines greenbelt, country belt, agriculture belt, and rural belt as synonymous: "They describe a stretch of countryside around and between towns, separating each from the others and

predominantly permanent farmland and parkland, whether or not such land is in the ownership of a town authority." He describes greenbelt as "a narrow strip of parkland more or less encircling part of a built-up metropolitan or large urban area." (Ebenezer Howard, *Garden Cities of To-Morrow* [Cambridge: M.I.T. Press, 1965], p. 27).

5. It is commonly known that sense of territory is a basic instinct of humans and other animals; it establishes and enforces feelings of security and belonging. Strong senses of territory have developed among tribal, clan, or patriarchical communities where social values have also been substantial.

6. Perloff also included in his concept of the new town in-town the necessity to construct a "Lighted Center for activities and social exchange." (Harvey S. Perloff, "New Towns in Town," *Journal of the American Institute of Planners,* **32,** no. 3 (May 1966), p. 158.

7. For details on optimum city size and the relationship of economic base and self-containment, see Otis Dudley Duncan, "Optimum Size of Cities," in *Cities and Society: A Revised Reader in Urban Sociology* (New York: The Free Press, 1957), pp. 759–72; William Alonso, "The Economics of Urban Size," *Regional Science Association,* **26** (1971), pp. 67–83; Manuel Gottlieb, "The Theory of Optimum Population for a Closed Economy," *Journal of Political Economy,* **53,** no. 4 (December 1945), pp. 289–316; W. Lean, "Economics of New Town Size and Form," *Ekistics,* **23,** no. 135 (February 1967), pp. 79–82; David Darwent, "Externality, Agglomeration Economies and City Size," Institute of Urban and Regional Development Working Paper No. 109 (Berkeley, January 1970).

8. Number of persons per acre in selected large cities in the United States in 1960 is shown in the following table:

City	Population	Land Area (sq. mi.)	Population (sq. mi.)
Boston, Mass.	697,197	48	14,586
Cleveland, Ohio	876,050	81	10,789
Detroit, Mich.	1,670,144	140	11,964
New York, N.Y.	7,781,984	315	24,097
Bronx	1,424,815	43	33,135
Brooklyn	2,627,319	76	34,570
Manhattan	1,698,281	22	77,195
Queens	1,809,578	113	16,014
Richmond	221,991	60	3,700
Philadelphia, Pa.	2,002,512	127	15,743
Washington, D.C.	763,956	61	12,442

Source: *Planning Design Criteria.*

Peter Hall indicated that in 1962 the Paris density was 114 persons per acre or 73,960 people per square mile; the inner city of London in 1961 had 43 persons per acre or 27,520 per square mile (*The World Cities* [New York: McGraw-Hill Book Co., 1966], p. 62). According to the 1970 U.S. census (U.S. Department of Commerce, Bureau of the Census, "Number of Inhabitants," *United States Summary,* 1970 Census of Population, pp. 187–88), there were 26,343 persons per square mile of land area inside the central city of New York and 2,001 outside the central city. Thus, density was 41 persons per acre. In Boston, central city density was 22 persons per acre; in Chicago, 23 persons per acre, and in San Francisco, 17 persons per acre.

9. The idea of limited size of the city as related to social and other issues has been frequently discussed throughout history, before Ebenezer Howard's concept of city size. Plato (428/427–348/347 B.C.) discussed city size. In *The Republic* he referred to the need of a size "neither large nor small but, one and sufficing" with sound

economic base of the city that would fulfill the daily needs of its citizens (B. Jowett, trans. [New York: Vantage Books: A Division of Random House, no date], pp. 61–67 and 132–33). In *The Laws* Plato also referred to city size and territory (A.E. Taylor, trans. [London: J.M. Dent and Sons, 1934], p. 119). Plato suggested that the city be limited to 5040 landholders.

Aristotle (384–322 B.C.) also discussed city size in *Politics and Athenian Constitution,* which relates his discussions with Plato. Aristotle thought that size was related to the function of the city and should be limited: "Citizens must know one another's character" (John Warrington, trans. [London: J. M. Dent and Sons, 1959], p. 198). Hippodamus (fifth century B.C.), a Greek architect and city planner, also suggested limiting the city population to a fixed number. According to Aristotle, Hippodamus thought that the city should "consist of 10,000 souls divided into three classes—one of artisans, one of farmers, and a third of professional soldiers for defense" (Aristotle, *Politics and Athenian Constitution,* p. 46).

Sir Thomas More (1478–1535) in *Utopia* referred to an ideal imaginary island of cities with a definite population size. In 1516 he introduced the idea of an island consisting of 54 cities of 6000 families each with the same laws and regulations for constant distances (Sir Thomas More, "Utopia", in *Ideal Empires and Republics* [New York, William H. Wise and Co., 1901], pp. 163 and 173).

10. When faced with a major conflict among diverse cultural groups of immigrants, some Israeli development towns introduced voluntary segregation clustered around an integrated center for social and economic activities of the whole community. Thus segregation has been temporarily accepted as a means for future integration. See Settlement Study Center, *Regional Cooperation in Israel* (Rehovot, Israel: National and University Institute of Agriculture, no date).

11. For details on services for new communities, see Royce Hanson, *Managing Services for New Communities* (Washington, D.C.: Washington Center for Metropolitan Studies, 1972).

12. Morton Hoppenfeld, "A Sketch of the Planning-Building Process for Columbia, Maryland," *Journal of the American Institute of Planners,* **33,** no. 5 (November 1967), pp. 398–409.

13. A team research report of the Ministry of Housing and Local Government of Wales on the issue of services as related to new towns concluded that "the team considers that the pattern of local services for residential areas should ideally fulfill three requirements: The conveniences of the users, the requirements of the agencies who provide the services, and general planning requirements such as economy of space." (Great Britain, Ministry of Housing and Local Government, Welsh Office, Sub-Committee of the Central Housing Advisory Committee, *The Needs of New Communities* [London: Her Majesty's Stationery Office, 1967], pp. 28–29).

A sophisticated innovative health service such as would be essential in the new town in-city should include a variety of health services justified by the population size, beginning with a local hospital and ending with home visit child-care units.

14. See Milton Kotler, *Neighborhood Government: The Local Foundations of Political Life* (Indianapolis: The Bobbs-Merrill Co., 1969). Also see Suzanne Keller, *The Urban Neighborhood: A Sociological Perspective* (New York: Random House, 1968).

15. The traditional neighborhood developed throughout history in the ancient cities of the world has evolved mainly from voluntary segregation of ethnic, religious, or social groups. These cities were successful in easing social tension and establishing stability among residents.

16.   In the English new towns, "after acceptance by the development corporation a firm moving could expect to get housing for all of its employees within the town. The firm could bring its existing employees and they would be given priority on the corporation's waiting list irrespective of their previous housing need or the location of their previous residence" (Ray Thomas: *London's New Towns: A Study of Self-Contained and Balanced Communities* [London: Political and Economic Planning (PEP), 1969], p. 387).

17.   Ray Thomas stated that "the main feature of these procedures [for allocating housing] is that employment came first. It is generally possible to get housing in one of the London new towns only if there is a job there to go to. By this simple policy the new towns effectively avoided any possible danger of becoming dormitory areas" (Thomas, p. 385).

18.   Tax systems coinciding with a "policy of place of work close to place of residence" may be rated according to a formula based on the combinations of place of work and place of residence as related to the size of the new town in-city. Classes in such a formula may include the following: (1) people who live and work in the community, (2) people who live in the community and work outside, (3) people who work in the community but live outside, (4) people who live in the community but do not work, and (4) firms located in the community, measured by building footage, total product value, number of employees, and quantity of service needed, such as water supply and sewage. The formula may also consider yearly membership per capita paid by residents, or number of municipal bonds purchased by all citizens.

19.   As housing and housing coordination in English new towns illustrate

"A major element in the attraction for employers was the housing allocation procedures. The availability of new subsidised rented dwellings was an important incentive for their employees to move with the firm, and a bait to attract new employees. Governmental planning in the new towns was certainly not restrictive in any way on industrial growth. It is probably easier for the industrialist to expand rapidly in the new towns than it is anywhere else. There was

a powerful and experienced development corporation ready and anxious to help" (Thomas, p. 386).

20.   The Research and Policy Committee of the Committee for Economic Development (U.S.A.), in their concluding statement on the issue of centralization versus decentralization of the local government, indicated that today's growing support for decentralization may be paradoxical. In its recommendation, the Committee stated that "to gain the advantages of both centralization and decentralization, we recommend as an ultimate solution a governmental system of two levels. Some functions should be assigned in their entirety to the area-wide government, others to the local level, but most will be assigned in part to each level." (*Reshaping Government in Metropolitan Areas* [New York: Committee for Economic Development, February 1970], p. 19).

21.   One of the goals of housing renewal has also been tax improvement. "The most straightforward aim of urban renewal is the reconstruction of the tax-base" (Peter Marris, p. 117).

22.   Albert Mayer, "New Towns: And Fresh In-City Communities," in the series, "Architecture as Total Community: The Challenge Ahead," *Architectural Record*, **136,** no. 2 (August 1964), p. 138.

23.   Conurbation is an aggregation of a continuous network of urban communities, where each unit has its own distinct physical, political, and economic identity. Conurbation has been effectively developed and preserved through strict national policy in land-use control in the western portion of The Netherlands. The conurbation policy has recently led to the development of the "city region" concept, which is also based on distribution of urban aggregations by function, size, and distance in a hierarchical pattern within the conurbation. For further details, see The Netherlands, *Second Report on Physical Planning in The Netherlands,* Parts I and II (The Hague: Government Printing Office of The Netherlands, 1966); Gideon Golany, *An Analytical Approach to Optimal Future Location and Distribution of Urban Areas of "Conurbation Holland" Into The Netherlands* (The Hague: Institute of Social Studies, 1965).

A

DATA DESCRIBING THE PLANNING AND DEVELOPMENT OF NEW URBAN SETTLEMENTS

TABLE A1   DEVELOPMENTAL COMMUNITIES IN CANADA

Name of Community	Economic Activity	Approximate Date Established	Population 1951	1956	1961	1966
Newfoundland						
Badger	woodcutting	n.a.			1,036	1,192
Buchans	lead, zinc, and copper mining	1926	1,944	2,413	2,463	2,159
Corner Brook	pulp and paper	1915	2,000	23,255	25,185	27,116
Gander	air transportation	1953			5,725	7,183
Goose Bay	military airbase	1941			3,040	2,364
Grand Falls	paper mills	1909	5,064	6,064	6,606	7,451
Stephenville	near air force base	1940		3,762	6,043	5,910
Wabana	iron ore	1894			8,026	7,884
Wabush (Lab.)	iron ore				151	2,669
Nova Scotia						
Brooklyn	pulp and paper	1928	1,282	1,312	1,308	1,245
Dominion	coal mining	n.a.	3,143	2,964	2,999	2,960
Glace Bay	coal mining	1858	25,586	24,416	24,186	23,516
New Waterford	coal mining	1908		10,381	10,592	9,725
Reserve Mines					2,715	2,710
Stirling	lead, zinc, and copper mining	1952	124	200		
Sydney Mines		1952	—	8,731	9,122	9,171
New Brunswick						
Atholville	pulp and rayon	1929			2,145	2,291
Black's Harbour	fish packing	1920	1,533	1,546	1,297	1,701
Fundy Park (townsite)	park administration	1950	10			
Marysville	cotton manufacturing	1862	2,152	2,538	3,233	3,572
Minto					1,319	1,231
Oromocto	military training complex	1952	—	661	12,170	14,112
Quebec						
Arvida	aluminum smelting	1926	11,078	12,919	14,460	15,342
Asbestos				8,969	11,083	10,534
Baie-Comeau	pulp and paper	1937	3,972	4,332	7,056	12,236
Belleterre	gold mining	1942	1,011	899		
Bevcourt	gold mining	1953	13			

283

Name of Community	Economic Activity	Approximate Date Established	Population			
			1951	1956	1961	1966
Bourlamaque	gold mining	1934	2,460	3,018	3,344	4,122
Burnt Creek	iron mining	1951	1,049			
Chandler	pulp manufacturing	1914	2,326	3,338	3,406	3,608
Capais	copper mining	1953		380	2,393	2,459
Chibougamau	lead, zinc, copper, and gold mining	1952	—	1,262	4,765	8,902
Clarke City	pulp and paper	1902	643	834	816	713
Crabtree Mills	pulp and paper	1907	983	1,103	1,313	1,509
Dolbeau	pulp and paper	1927	4,307	5,079	6,052	6,630
Donnacona	pulp and paper	1912	3,663	4,147	4,812	4,815
Duparquet	pulp and paper	1932	1,485	1,144	978	
Forestville	pulp and paper	1944	709	1,117	1,529	1,572
Gagnon	iron ore	1960			1,900	3,999
Gatineau	pulp and paper	1926	5,771	8,426	13,002	17,727
Great Whale River	gold mining	1956			718	849
Halet	gold mining	1939	250			
Isle-Maligne	aluminum smelting and hydro	1924		1,761	2,070	
Kewegama	gold mining	1934	200			
Kilmar	magnesite mining and milling	1916			116	172
La Tuque				11,096	13,023	13,554
Malaretic	gold	1937		6,818	6,998	6,606
Murdochville	copper mining	1953		1,694	2,951	3,028
Noranda	copper and gold mining and milling	1927	9,672	10,323	11,477	11,521
Normetal	copper and zinc mining and milling	1937	1,486	1,892	2,285	2,110
Perron	gold mining	1944	585			
Port Cartier					3,458	3,537
Port Menier	pulp logging	1926	654	438	475	463
Rapide Blanc	hydro	1934			319	286
Riverbend	pulp and paper	1925	278	260		
Rouyn				17,076	18,716	18,581
Schefferville	iron ore mining	1954		1,632	3,178	3,086
Sept-Isles	iron ore transport	1951	1,866	5,592	14,196	18,950
Tee Lake	lumber milling	1941	422	122	206	483
Temiskaming	pulp	1919	2,787	2,694	2,517	2,799
Val d'Or	gold mining	1934		9,876	10,983	12,147
Vimy Ridge Mine	asbestos mining	1918	317	272	230	207
Thetford Mines	asbestos	1876	15,095	19,511	21,618	21,614
Ontario						
Abitibi Canyon	hydro	1932	146			
Ajax	munitions—now light industry	1941	4,710	5,683	7,755	9,412
Atikokan	iron mining	1945	5,855	2,609	6,674	6,240
Batawa	shoe manufacturing	1914	500		754	692
Blind River				3,633	4,093	3,617
Cameron Falls	hydro		242	337	254	235
Caromat	pulpwood logging	1948	341	484	386	462
Central Patricia	gold mining	1936	332	51	70	175
Chenaux Rapids	hydro	1948	127			
Cobalt				2,367	2,209	2,211
Cocheneur	gold mining	1939	429	524	539	755
Coniston	nickle and copper smelting	1934	2,292	2,478	2,692	2,692
Copper Cliff	nickel and copper smelting	1901	3,944	3,801	3,600	3,505
Creighton Mines	nickel and copper mining	1900	2,105	1,792	1,727	1,463
Deep River	atomic power generation	1945	2,043	3,176	5,377	5,573

TABLE A1 (*continued*)

Name of Community	Economic Activity	Approximate Date Established	1951	1956	1961	1966
Delore	cobalt smelting	1918	283			
Des Joachims	hydro	1950	160			
Elliot Lake	uranium mining	1954	—	3,791	13,790	6,640
Espanola	pulp and paper	1919	3,535	4,381	5,353	5,567
Falconbridge	nickel and copper smelting	1928	1,056	1,273	1,138	1,097
Frood Mines	nickel and copper mining	1930	109	124		
Haley Station	magnesium production		83	150	186	180
Hawkesbury	pulp and paper		7,194	7,929	8,661	9,188
Heron Bay South	pulpwood logging	1938	168	192	136	87
Hillsport	pulpwood logging	1952	25	233	179	173
Iroquois Falls	pulp and paper	1951	1,342	1,478	1,681	1,834
Island Falls	hydro		79	105	111	134
Jamestown (WaWa)	iron mining	1946	527	2,749	4,040	4,577
Kapuskasing	pulp and paper	1921	4,687	5,463	6,870	12,617
Keewatin	lumbering, pulp and paper			1,949	2,197	2,089
Kirkland Lake	gold	1911			15,484	14,008
Leitch Mines	gold mining	1936	181		191	
Levack	nickel and copper mining	1938	1,833	2,929	3,178	3,025
Lively	nickel and copper mining	1950		2,840	3,211	3,169
Longlac	pulpwood logging	1938	696	865	1,125	1,315
Madsen	gold mining	1938	650	601	666	566
Manitouwadge	copper mining	1954		877	2,006	2,893
Marathon	pulp and paper	1945	1,358	2,404	2,568	2,532
McKenzie Island	gold mining	1935	556	303	482	327
Nephton	nepheline and syenite mining	1949	84	79	86	83
Nobel	explosives manufacturing	1915	149		693	520
Pickel Crow	gold mining	1934	412	341	281	287
Pine Portage	hydro	1948				
Red Rock	pulp and paper	1944	878	1,275	1,316	1,414
Renabie	gold mining	1947	387			
Schreiber	railway transportation	1890	1,939		2,230	2,188
Smoky Falls	hydro	1928	95	83	45	63
Smooth Rock	pulp manufacturing	1917	1,102	1,104	1,131	1,191
Starratt Olsen	gold mining	1948	145	136	137	129
Steep Rock Lake	iron ore mining	1952	150	80		
Stevens	pulpwood logging	1946	460	233	599	660
Sturgeon Falls	pulp and paper	1901	4,962	5,874	6,288	6,430
Terrace Bay	pulp and paper	1947	1,114	1,567	1,901	1,896
Throne	pulp and paper	1950	267	401	416	488
Virginiatown	gold mining	1937	1,489	1,694	2,009	1,471
Manitoba						
Bissett	gold mining	1937	813	770	857	584
Churchill	railway and ocean transportation	1931	250		1,878	1,689
Flin Flon	copper, lead, and zinc mining and smelting	1929	9,899	10,234	11,104	10,201
Leaf Rapids	copper and zinc mining	1971				
Lynn Lake	copper and nickel mining	1951	225	1,218	2,082	2,174
Pine Falls	pulp and paper	1926	958	1,082	1,244	1,233
Sherridon	copper, zinc, and gold mining	1930	778	88	43	117
Snow Lake	gold mining	1937	552	659	881	1,349
Thomson	nickel mining	1958	—	—	3,418	8,846
Wasagaming	parks administration	1933	39		136	124

TABLE A1 *(continued)*

Name of Community	Economic Activity	Approximate Date Established	1951	1956	1961	1966
Saskatchewan						
Hudson Bay				1,421	1,601	1,957
Lanigan	potash development	1964	410		516	11,000 (proposed)
Reserve	logging and lumbering	1928	270	279	202	187
Uranium City	uranium mining	1952	—	1,794	1,660	1,665
Alberta						
Alexo	coal mining	1920	170			
Banff	parks administration	1888	3,000		3,429	2,896
Bellevue	coal mining	1906	1,884	1,419	1,323	1,174
Blairmore	coal mining	1917	1,933	1,973	1,779	1,779
Bow City	coal mining	1943	130			
Coal Valley	coal mining	1922	250			
Coleman	coal mining	1903	1,961	1,566	1,713	1,507
Cynthia	oil drilling and development	1956		65	139	139
Devon	oil drilling and development	1949	842	1,429	1,418	1,283
Drayton Valley	regional center	1955	—	2,588	3,352	3,352
Foothills	coal mining	1912	210	224		
Grande Prairie	regional center		2,664	6,302	8,352	11,417
Hays	regional center	1953		109	62	32
Hinton	pulp manufacturing	1956	203	948	3,529	4,307
Jasper	parks administration	1914	1,969		2,360	2,500
Lodge pole	oil drilling and development	1955		500		
Luscar	coal mining	1921	557	301		
Merrcoal	coal mining	1912	977	972		
Nordegg	coal mining	1912	1,500		42	133
Redwater	oil drilling and development	1949	1,306	1,065	1,135	1,050
Robb	coal mining				271	272
Waterton Park	parks administration	1911	167		—	200
British Columbia						
Blubber Bay	limestone processing	1908	263	243	167	205
Bralorne	gold mining	1931	643	613	670	531
Britannia Beach	copper mining	1900	1,600	771	775	770
Caycuse	logging	1927		346	369	308
Ceepeecee	fish packing	1926	200			
Copper Mountain	copper mining	1923	1,061	1,039		
Emerald Mine	lead and zinc mining and milling	1947	500			
Field	parks administration	1905	375		—	395
Holberg	logging	1942	440	236	117	200
Honeymoon Bay	lumber milling	1943	602	415	518	539
Ioco	oil storage	1922	333	335		
Kemano	hydro	1953		577	255	325
Kitimat	aluminum smelting	1953		9,676	8,217	9,782
Michel	coal mining	1898	593	524	591	340
Namu	fish processing	1893	257	168	159	225
Nickel Plate	gold mining	1904	250			
Nitinat	logging	1928	250		175	138
Ocean Falls	pulp and paper manufacturing	1909	2,825	2,832	3,056	2,800
Pioneer	gold mining	1928	600	114	226	60
Port Alice	pulp manufacturing	1917	1,038	1,073	952	1,000
Port Edward	fish processing	n.a.	338	786	887	1,006
Port Mellon	pulp manufacturing	1918	250	360	284	341

Name of Community	Economic Activity	Approximate Date Established	Population			
			1951	1956	1961	1966
Powell River	pulp and paper manufacturing	1910	2,700	9,969	10,748	12,500
Prince Rupert	port	1909	8,546	10,498	11,987	14,677
Radium Hot Springs	parks administration	1927	50		306	320
Sparwood	coal mining	1939	125	245	295	381
Tadanac	ore smelting	1922	479	325		
Torbrit Mines	silver mining	1947	150			
Woodfibre	pulp manufacturing	1912	548	776	729	524
Toubou	lumber milling	1919	846	1,328	1,153	1,120
Zincton	gold mining	1941	125			
Northwest Territories						
Aklavik (Inuvik)	regional center	1957	1,118	1,445	1,248	
Con Mine	gold mining	1938	500			
Discovery Mine	gold mining	1950	50		203	159
Frobisher Bay	regional center	1957	353	351	1,426	1,631
Giant Mine	gold mining	1945	376		611	599
Negus Mine	gold mining	1939				
Norman Wells	oil drilling and development	1932	95	183	297	199
Pine Point		1961	—	—	1	459
Port Radium	uranium mining	1944	311	412	526	470
Yellowknife	regional center	1939	2,724	3,100	3,141	3,741
Yukon Territory						
Calumet	lead and zinc mining	1946	134	366	377	198
Elsa	lead and silver mining	1946	141	193	395	529

Source: *New Towns: The Canadian Experience.*

TABLE A2   FACTS AND FIGURES OF NEW TOWNS IN THE UNITED KINGDOM

	Date of designation	Area designated (hectares)[1]	Distance from nearby city (kilometres)[2]	POPULATION At designation	POPULATION (Estimate) 31 December 1973	POPULATION Ultimate
Great Britain:						
Stevenage	November 1946	2,530	50 —London	7,000	74,000	105,000
Crawley	January 1947	2,450	48 —London	10,000	71,000	79,000
Hemel Hempstead	February 1947	2,420	47 —London	21,000	73,000	80,000
Harlow	March 1947	2,560	40 —London	4,500	81,000	90,000
Aycliffe	April 1947	1,000	19 —Durham	60	24,000	45,000
East Kilbride	May 1947	4,140	14·5—Glasgow	2,500	69,000	100,000
Peterlee	March 1948	1,080	16 —Durham	200	25,600	30,000
Hatfield	May 1948	950	32 —London	8,500	25,000	30,000
Welwyn Garden City	May 1948	1,750	35 —London	18,500	40,000	50,000
Glenrothes	June 1948	2,300	50 —Edinburgh	1,100	31,500	70,000
Basildon	January 1949	3,120	48 —London	25,000	83,700	140,000
Bracknell	June 1949	1,900	45 —London	5,000	40,000	55/60,000
Cwmbran	November 1949	1,260	29 —Cardiff	12,000	43,200	55,000
Corby	April 1950	1,770	37 —Leicester	15,700	51,200	83,000
Cumbernauld	December 1955	3,150[4]	24 —Glasgow	3,500	36,300	100,000
Skelmersdale	October 1961	1,670	21 —Liverpool	10,000	37,700	80,000
Livingston	April 1962	2,700	24 —Edinburgh	2,100	20,200	100,000
Telford[3]	December 1968	7,790	48 —Birmingham	70,000	92,500	220,000
Redditch	April 1964	2,910	22·5—Birmingham	32,000	45,000	90,000
Runcorn	April 1964	2,930	22·5—Liverpool	28,500	44,800	100,000
Washington	July 1964	2,120	9·5—Newcastle	20,000	35,000	80,000
Irvine	November 1966	5,040	42 —Glasgow	40,000	47,600	120,000
Milton Keynes	January 1967	8,800	80·5—London	40,000	61,000	250,000
Peterborough	July 1967	6,400	133·5—London	80,500	94,400	185,000
Newtown	December 1967	600	149 —Cardiff	5,500	6,500	13,000
Northampton	February 1968	8,000	106 —London	131,000	138,000	230,000
Warrington	April 1968	7,460	24 —Manchester	124,000	132,000	230,000
Central Lancashire	March 1970	14,250	32 —Liverpool	235,000	240,500	430,000
Stonehouse	August 1973	2,700	12·5—Glasgow	7,900	7,900	70,000
Northern Ireland:						
Craigavon	July 1965	25,900	48 —Belfast	40,000	74,000	180,000
Antrim	July 1965	113,680	28 —Belfast	7,000	41,000	50,000
Ballymena	August 1967		44 —Belfast	21,000	56,000	80,000
Londonderry	February 1969	34,700	116 —Belfast	72,000	82,000	100,000

[1]One hectare = 2·5 acres.
[2]One kilometre = 0·621 mile.
[3]Part of Telford was originally designated as Dawley new town in January 1963.
[4]Includes 1,470 hectares in extension area designated in April 1973.
Source: *The New Towns of Britain*, 1974

TABLE A3   NEW COMMUNITIES AND OTHER LARGE-SCALE DEVELOPMENTS CONSTRUCTED IN THE UNITED STATES SINCE 1948

New Town	County	Population	Acres
Arizona			
1. Kearny	Pinal	4,000	1,300
2. Lake Havasu City	Mohave	60,000	16,500
3. Litchfield Park	Maricopa	75,000	13,000
4. San Manuel	Pinal	6,000	700
5. Sun City	Maricopa	55,000	10,700
6. Tucson Green Valley	Pima	15,000	2,900
7. Goodyear Farms	west of Phoenix	50,000	13,000
8. New Tucson	east of Tucson	100,000	16,500
9. Green Valley	south of Tucson	25,000	11,000
10. Rico Rico	north of Nogales	—	55,000
Arkansas			
1. Maumelle	Pulaski	45,000	2,044
California			
1. Sunset City	Placer	110,000	12,000
2. El Dorado Hills	Eldorado	75,000	9,800
3. Sunset	Sacramento	150,000	—
4. Sea Ranch	north of San Francisco	—	5,000
5. Marincello	Marin	—	2,100
6. San Marin	Marin	20,000	2,200
7. Robert's Landing	San Francisco	—	—
8. Foster City	San Mateo	35,000	2,600
9. San Ramon Village	Alameda	72,000	4,500
10. Redwood Shores	Redwood City	60,000	4,700
11. Seven Hills	Alameda	60,000	6,000
12. Rossmoor	Conta Costa	16,000	2,000
13. Hamilton	south of San Jose	100,000	11,500
14. University Village	Santa Barbara	14,000	4,000
15. Conejo Village	Ventura and Los Angeles	87,000	11,000
16. Westlake Village	Los Angeles	68,000	12,000
17. Albertson Ranch	Ventura and Los Angeles	100,000	11,500
18. California City	Kern	—	101,000
19. Calabasas Park	Ventura and Los Angeles	15,000	3,000
20. Janss	Ventura	80,000	11,000
21. Vail Ranch	Los Angeles	—	87,000
22. Diamond Bar	Los Angeles	80,000	8,000
23. Porter Ranch	Los Angeles	43,000	4,100
24. Crummer Ranch	Los Angeles	50,000	6,300
25. Tierra Linda	Los Angeles	250,000	4,000
26. Mountain Park	Los Angeles	60,000	10,000
27. Camarillo Ranch	Pomona	—	4,600
28. Valencia	Los Angeles	250,000	4,000
29. Irvine Ranch	Orange	270,000	32,000
30. Laguna Hills Leisure World	Orange	30,000	2,500
31. Laguna Niguel	Orange	80,000	7,900
32. Misson Viejo	Orange	80,000	11,300
33. Rancho San Diego	San Diego	—	—
34. Rancho Bernardo	San Diego	26,000	5,400
35. San Carlos	San Diego	35,000	5,000
36. University City	San Diego	—	13,000
37. Lake San Marcos	San Diego	6,000	1,700
38. La Costa	San Diego	—	2,700
39. Rossmoor Leisure World	Orange	30,000	3,600
40. Huntington Beach	Orange	10,000	1,000

New Town	County	Population	Acres
41. Sun City	Riverside	11,000	1,700
42. Rancho California	Riverside	80,000	41,000
43. Hearst Ranch	San Simeon	—	—
Colorado			
1. Village East	Denver	10,000	1,000
2. Montbello	Denver	35,000	3,000
3. Northglenn	Adams	30,000	2,700
4. Columbine	Denver	—	—
5. Pikes Peak Park	Colorado Springs	35,000	4,300
6. Colorado City	south of Pueblo	30,000	5,000
Delaware			
1. Mill Creek	north of Wilmington	13,000	1,300
2. Pike Creek Valley	New Castle	20,000	1,200
3. Metroform	New Castle	—	—
Florida			
1. Deltona	Volusia	75,000	15,000
2. Spring Hill	Hernando	75,000	10,000
3. Ponciana	—	—	—
4. Epcot (Disney World)	near Orlando	20,000	27,000
5. Port Charlotte	Charlotte	53,000	—
6. Lehigh Acres	Lee	51,000	—
7. North Palm Beach	Palm Beach	25,000	9,600
8. Palm Beach Gardens	Palm Beach	70,000	6,100
9. Coral Springs	Broward	60,000	10,400
10. Miami Lakes	Dade	25,000	1,900
11. Palm Beach Lakes	Palm Beach	70,000	7,000
12. Canaveral	west of Cape Kennedy	43,000	2,500
13. Port Malbar	Brevard	—	—
Georgia			
1. Chapel Hill	Atlanta	12,000	1,100
2. Peachtree City	Fayette	15,000	15,000
3. Shenandoah	Coweta	70,000	7,200
4. Bedford Pine	Atlanta	—	78
5. Sea Pines	north of Savannah	—	—
Hawaii			
1. Hawaii Kai	Honolulu	56,000	6,000
2. Mililani Town	Honolulu	56,000	3,000
Illinois			
1. Elk Grove Village	Cook	58,000	5,800
2. Oak Brook	DuPage	25,000	3,600
3. Weston	west of Chicago	50,000	4,700
4. Park Forest South	Will	60,000	1,600
5. Park Forest	Cook and Will	34,000	2,700
Indiana			
1. Columbus	west of Columbus	—	1,500
Kentucky			
1. Oxmoor	west of Louisville	15,000	1,100
Louisiana			
1. Pontchartrain	north of New Orleans	—	—
2. Lake St. Louis	north of New Orleans	20,000	2,600
3. New Orleans East	New Orleans	250,000	32,000

New Town	County	Population	Acres
Maryland			
1. Columbia	Howard	110,000	14,000
2. Belair	Prince George	30,000	3,800
3. Joppatowne	Harford	10,000	1,300
4. Montgomery Village	Montgomery	30,000	2,200
5. St. Charles	Charles	79,145	6,980
6. Churchill Estates	Montgomery	35,000	3,300
7. Germantown	Montgomery	—	—
8. Marlboro Meadows	Prince George	31,000	1,200
9. Marlton	Prince George	48,000	2,300
10. Northhampton	Prince George	35,000	2,800
11. Potomac Valley Estates	Montgomery	21,000	3,000
12. Fort Lincoln (Washington D.C.)	Washington, D.C.	—	—
13. Crofton	Anne Arundel	15,000	1,300
Massachusetts			
1. New Seabury	Barnstable	16,000	3,000
Minnesota			
1. Jonathan	Carver	50,000	2,300
2. Cedar-Riverside	Hennetin	31,250	100
New Jersey			
1. Beckett	Gloucester	60,000	6,100
2. Willingboro	Burlington	50,000	4,500
New Mexico			
1. Paradise Hills	Bernalillo	70,000	8,500
New York			
1. Audubon	—	—	—
2. Riverton	Monroe	25,632	2,125
3. Gananda	Wayne	55,800	4,733
4. Radisson (Lysander)	Onandaga	18,355	2,760
5. Levittown	Nassau	68,000	5,000
6. Jefferson Valley	—	—	—
7. Sterling Forest	Orange	60,000	20,000
8. Roosevelt Island	New York	17,000	121
9. Spring Creek	New York	—	2,000
North Carolina			
1. Soul City	Warren	44,000	5,180
Ohio			
1. New Field	Montgomery	40,000	4,032
2. Kingswood	north of Dayton	—	1,700
3. Forest Park	Hamilton	35,000	4,000
4. Grant Park	Clermont	50,000	7,500
Oregon			
1. Somerset West	north of Portland	40,000	6,600
Pennsylvania			
1. Levittown	Bucks	68,000	5,000
South Carolina			
1. Harbison	Lexington and Richland	23,075	1,730
Tennessee			
1. Timberlake	London and Monroe	—	—

TABLE A3 *(continued)*

New Town	County	Population	Acres
Texas			
1. Horizon City	east of El Paso	—	—
2. Flower Mound	Denton	64,141	6,156
3. San Antonia Ranch	Bexar	87,972	9,318
4. The Woodlands	Montgomery	150,000	16,939
5. Clear Lake City	south of Houston	150,000	15,000
6. Sharpstown	Houston	35,000	4,000
7. Friends Woods	Harris	—	—
Virginia			
1. Reston	Fairfax	75,000	7,400
2. Stafford Harbor	Stafford	35,000	5,000
Washington			
1. Papilla Bay	north of Seattle	40,000	6,600

TABLE A4   PROXIMITY OF SOME NEW COMMUNITIES TO MAJOR URBAN AREAS

New Community	Distance (miles)	Major Urban Center	New Community	Distance (miles)	Major Urban Center
Arizona			**New York**		
Lake Havasu City	153	Las Vegas, Nevada	Ganada	12	Rochester
Litchfield Park	18	Phoenix	Lysander	12	Syracuse
			Riverton	10	Rochester
Arkansas			Roosevelt Island	within	New York City
Maumelle	12	Little Rock			
			North Carolina		
California			Sea Pines	40	Savannah
Foster City	18	San Francisco	Soul City	45	Raleigh-Durham
Irvine Ranch	40	Los Angeles			
Laguna Niguel	50	Los Angeles	**South Carolina**		
San Ramon Village	24	Oakland	Harbison	8	Columbia
Valencia	30	Los Angeles			
Westlake Village	10	Los Angeles	**Tennesse**		
			Timberlake	30	Knoxville
Georgia					
Peachtree City	20	Atlanta	**Texas**		
Shenandoah	35	Atlanta	Flower Mound	20	Dallas
			San Antonio Ranch	20	San Antonio
Illinois			The Woodlands	30	Houston
Elk Grove	20	Chicago			
Park Forest	30	Chicago	**Utah**		
Park Forest South	30	Chicago	Stansbury Park	25	Salt Lake City
Louisiana			**Virginia**		
Lake St. Louis	35	New Orleans	New Franconia	25	Washington, D.C.
Nouville	7	Baton Rouge	Reston	20	Washington, D.C.
Pontchartrain	25	New Orleans			
			Washington		
Maryland			Padilla Bay	75	Seattle
Columbia	25	Washington, D.C.			
St. Charles	25	Washington, D.C.	**Washington, D.C.**		
			Fort Lincoln	within	Washington, D.C.
Minnesota					
Cedar-Riverside	downtown	Minneapolis			
Jonathan	20	Minneapolis			

TABLE A5 NATIONAL CAPITAL DEVELOPMENT CORPORATION POPULATION PROJECTIONS —CANBERRA CITY DISTRICT

Year Ending June	*Previous Projection to 1980			New Projection to 1985		
	Total Projected Population	Annual Growth	Percentage Growth	Total Projected Population	Annual Growth	Percentage Growth
1974	184,000	15,000	8.8	184,000	18,000	10.8
1975	202,000	18,000	9.8	206,000	22,000	12.0
1976	224,000	22,000	10.9	230,000	24,000	11.7
1977	246,000	22,000	9.8	255,000	25,000	10.9
1978	270,000	24,000	9.8	280,000	25,000	9.8
1979	297,000	27,000	10.0	306,000	26,000	9.6
1980	328,000	31,000	10.4	332,000	26,000	8.5
1981	—	—	—	358,000	26,000	7.8
1982	—	—	—	385,000	27,000	7.5
1983	—	—	—	413,000	28,000	7.2
1984	—	—	—	441,000	28,000	6.8
1985	—	—	—	471,000	30,000	6.8

*Based on a continuation of the 10.3 per cent actual Australian Public Service Act employment growth 1960-1970.

The major difference between the two projections is the more rapid population build-up now expected in the next few years. By 1980 the difference in the projections is of little significance.

Source: *National Capital Development Commission Seventeenth Annual Report.*

TABLE A6 POPULATION GROWTH PERCENTAGE IN ISRAELI DEVELOPMENT TOWNS

Development Town	1948	1950	1952	1954	1956	1958	1960	1962	1964	1966	1968	1970	1972	1973
NORTH
Afula	100	247	383	399	475	547	569	599	662	650	654	674	691	758
Akko	100	937	1,394	1,394	1,737	1,942	2,091	2,411	2,731	2,760	2,794	3,874	3,851	4,057
Bet-Shean	—	100	127	160	247	346	349	379	445	431	431	413	393	417
Hazor Hagelilit	—	—	100	283	723	1,083	1,182	1,293	1,293	1,293	1,305	1,293	1,296	1,354
Karmiel	—	—	—	—	—	—	—	—	—	100***	**	**	421	666
Malot-Tarshiha	—	—	—	—	—	100	157	171	325	332	339	360	358	385
Migdal Haemeq	—	—	100	942	1,728	2,200	2,257	3,085	4,142	4,485	4,685	5,028	5,703	6,285
Nahariyya	100	290	522	551	644	813	920	923	1,085	1,161	1,202	1,271	1,381	1,579
Nazarath Illit	—	—	—	—	—	100	177	371	565	634	674	857	855	1,028
Qiryat Shemona	—	100	—	274	629	740	888	1,029	1,111	1,118	1,133	1,118	1,118	1,192
Tiberias	100	219	291	297	313	352	378	401	421	419	424	430	426	455
Zefat	100	237	334	349	405	427	453	496	548	556	565	565	589	621
TOTAL NORTH	100	318	454	519	673	813	894	1,003	1,156	1,186	1,202	1,316	1,369	1,506
CENTER
Bet-Shemesh	—	100	1,276	1,190	1,823	2,857	3,333	3,904	4,547	4,714	4,714	4,857	4,814	5,428
Or Aqiva	—	—	100	141	152	190	254	349	447	497	497	526	527	546
TOTAL CENTER	—	100	1,850	2,005	2,699	3,952	4,795	5,914	7,119	7,571	7,571	7,881	7,845	8,571

SOUTH

Arad	407	432	330	**	100***	—	—	—	—	—	—	—	—	—
Ashdod	22,009	18,422	17,168	14,566	12,328	8,858	5,319	1,552	1,118	421	100	—	—	—
Ashqelon	903	843	786	749	723	686	556	500	431	376	282	245	100	—
Beer Sheva	1,089	1,027	932	867	813	749	621	512	433	307	124	174	100	—
Dimuna	1,502	1,357	1,285	1,160	1,080	965	691	262	200	100	—	—	—	—
Elat	5,090	4,759	5,309	4,400	3,781	3,236	2,545	2,036	1,272	349	163	100	—	—
Mizpe Ramon	**	3,071	3,333	3,222	3,222	3,222	1,777	644	297	100	—	—	—	—
Netivot	4,697	4,429	4,053	3,659	3,409	3,106	2,651	2,159	1,893	100	—	—	—	—
Ofaqim	501	497	490	466	450	439	339	230	199	100	—	—	—	—
Qiryat Gat	1,164	1,060	997	942	881	814	665	526	365	100	—	—	—	—
Qiryat Malakhi	1,475	1,395	1,263	1,177	1,130	1,067	855	745	698	478	290	100	—	—
Sederut	297	283	278	250	245	232	196	130	109	100	—	—	—	—
Yeroham	3,641	3,382	3,121	2,855	2,716	2,601	1,520	953	664	454	217	100	—	—
TOTAL SOUTH	2,183	2,008	1,876	1,684	1,573	1,406	1,095	809	664	433	204	209	100	—
Total in Development Towns	3,880	3,552	3,332	3,013	2,919	2,710	2,202	1,798	1,555	1,158	753	697	421	100
Total State Population	392	375	357	339	327	312	288	266	252	232	213	202	167	100

* The first year's population is the base equal to 100%.

** Data not available

*** 1965

Note: All data are from the Israeli Central Bureau of Statistics and refer only to the Jewish population. The data for 1948 and 1972 are from the official census, and all others are estimates made each 31 December. The data from 1972 are from Population and Households for Localities and Statistical Areas, Population and Housing Census 1972, Series No. 4, 1974.

	(a) Population			
	Original	Proposed[1]	31 Dec. 1974	Males
LONDON RING				
Basildon	25,000	103,600 / 134,000	84,900	22,600
Bracknell	5,149	55–60,000 / 55–60,000	41,300	14,448
Crawley	9,100	—[3] / 85,000	71,000	25,500
Harlow	4,500	undecided	82,250	20,498
Hatfield	8,500	—[3] / 29,000	26,000	18,000
Hemel Hempstead	21,000	65,000 / 80,000	73,000	20,150
Stevenage	6,700	80,000[6] / 100–105,000	74,800	24,500
Welwyn Gdn City	18,500	—[3] / 50,000	40,000	17,000
Total: London Ring	98,449	—	493,250	162,696
OTHERS IN ENGLAND				
Aycliffe	60	undecided / 45,000	25,000	n.k.
Central Lancs.	235,638	420,000[8] / not estimated	242,500	77,000
Corby	15,700	undecided / 83,000	53,750	18,551
Milton Keynes	40,000	200,000 / 250,000	64,000	n.k.
Northampton	131,120	244,000 / 260,000	145,400	44,125
Peterborough	81,000	182,000 / n.a.	98,000	38 200
Peterlee	200	28,000 / 30,000	26,500	2,700
Redditch	32,000	70,000[12] / 90,000	49,730	14,400
Runcorn[13]	28,500[14]	70–75,000 / 100,000	48,213	n.k.
Skelmersdale	10,000	73,000 / 80,000	39,000	11,540
Telford	70,000[14]	225,000 / 250,000	94,200	28,800
Warrington	122,300	201,500 / 225,000	133,000	40,300
Washington	20,000	65,000 / 80,000	39,000	11,097
Total: Others in England	786,518	—	1,058,293	—
WALES				
Cwmbran	12,000	55,000 / 55,000	43,000	10,320
Mid-Wales (Newtown)	5,000	11,500 / 13,000	6,700	2,946
Total: Wales	17,000	—	49,700	13,266
Total: England and Wales	901,967	—	1,601,243	—
SCOTLAND				
Cumbernauld	3,000	70,000 / 100,000	38,500	6,800
East Kilbride	2,400	82,500 / 90,000+	71,500	16,050
Glenrothes	1,100	55,000 / 70,000	32,500	8,161
Irvine[16]	34,600	116,000 / 120,000	50,100	14,322
Livingston	2,000	70,000 / 100,000	22,470	5,187
Stonehouse	7,250	45,000 / 70,000	7,800	1,000
Total: Scotland	50,350	—	222,870	51,520
Total: Great Britain	952,317	—	1,824,113	—

* includes cost of assets constructed for sale.
n.k. – not known.   n.a. – not available.
[1] Two figures are given: the first is the population size when planned migration is to stop; the second is the proposed ultimate population, allowing for natural increase.
[2] Some of these schools have closed since the date of designation.
[3] Planned migration has already stopped.
[4] Excludes 9,000 employed at Gatwick airport adjacent to designated area.
[5] Includes those employed in industrial area adjacent to designated area.
[6] Under review.
[7] Excluding College of Further Education.

Source: *Town and Country Planning*, **43,** no. 2 (1975).

(b) Total employment			(c) Schools (in brackets no. of school places)		(d) Estimated capital expenditure by DCs and NTC	
Females	Total	Date	No. before designation[2]	No. completed from designation to 31 Dec. 1974 (est.)	Housing since designation to 31 Dec. 1974 £m	Total (incl. housing) to 31 Dec. 1974 £m
16,400	39,000	Dec. 1974	7 (2,600)	29 (19,490)	93·700	135·100
8,566	23,014	Oct. 1974	4 (1,260)	20 (8,500)	41·535	63·295
16,600	42,100[4]	June 1973	7 (1,176)	30 (24,184)	35·874	51·120
14,696	35,194	Oct. 1974	5 (815)	37 (27,155)	53·700	92·000*
9,000	27,000[5]	Dec. 1974	4 (1,280)	16 (6,230)	9·698	14·585
16,140	36,290	Dec. 1974	11 (3,520)	44 (18,775)	30·129	49·226
13,000	37,500	Dec. 1974	2 (600)	57 (22,900)[7]	40·059	63·460
11,000	28,000	Dec. 1974	5 (2,100)	23 (9,500)	14·701	26·003
105,402	268,098	—	45 (13,351)	256 (136,734)	319·396	494·789
n.k.	10,500	Dec. 1974	—	18 (7,500)	18·200	28·600
47,000	124,000	Sept. 1974	133 (45,426)	n.a.[9]	17·000	22·500
8,163	26,714[5]	Sept. 1974	7 (3,060)	24 (11,300)	26·746	32·108
n.k.	36,000	n.a.	28 (8,057)	19 (6,630)	26·896[10]	92·817
32,875	77,000	Dec. 1974	60 (20,600)	18 (7,980)	21·500	45·250
18,300	56,500	Dec. 1974	32 (15,600)	22 (4,822)[11]	28·738	56·174
4,200	6,900	Dec. 1974	—	22 (10,436)	21·032	30·280
9,200	23,600	Dec. 1974	18 (6,522)	24 (n.k.)	21·256	41·226
n.k.	19,207	Oct. 1974	10 (3,340)[14]	20 (5,950)	37·886	53·375
6,660	18,200	Dec. 1974	7 (1,218)	20 (10,090)	38·458	63·212
14,200	43,000	Dec. 1974	26 (12,430)[14]	35 (9,650)	29·000	68·000
22,300	62,600	Dec. 1974	66 (19,270)	18 (5,440)	4·300[10]	16·000[10]
6,101	17,198	Dec. 1974	13 (3,923)	18 (6,866)	29·911	48·343
—	521,419	—	400 (139,446)	258 (86,664)+	320·923+	597·885+
7,010	17,330	Dec. 1974	9 (1,975)	27 (10,530)	25·891	37·341
1,634	4,580	Dec. 1974	6 (1,900)	2+2 extns (1,100)	3·565	7·810
8,644	21,910	—	15 (3,875)	29+2 extns (11,630)	29·456	45·151
—	811,427	—	460 (156,672)	543+2 extns (235,028)+	669·775+	1,137·825+
5,300	12,100	Dec. 1974	2 (515)	19 (12,415)	43·612	62·851
15,150	31,200	Sept. 1974	1 (550)	26 (19,890)[15]	56·960	86·300
6,743	14,904	Dec. 1974	1 (200)	12 (8,418)	26·000	42·000
7,478	21,800	Mar. 1975	15 (8,450)	7 (6,000)	10·171	22·703
2,664	7,851	Sept. 1974	2 (285)	10 (6,040)	27·954	47·674
750	1,750	Sept. 1974	3 (1,000)	—	0·067	2·020
38,085	89,605	—	24 (11,000)	74 (52,763)	164·764	263·548
—	901,032	—	484 (167,672)	617+2 extns (287,791)+	834·539+	1,401·373+

8 Year 2001.
9 Figures are only available for development carried out by or on behalf of the development corporation.
10 Excluding land purchase, but in Warrington includes £1m for acquisition of private dwellings for rented accommodation.
11 Including major extensions to existing schools.
12 Subject to implementation of West Midlands Regional Study.
13 Runcorn estimates under 31.12.74 refer to 1.10.74 throughout these tables.
14 Figures revised since 1973.
15 Including 1,890 temporary places.
16 Irvine estimates under 31.12.74 refer to 31.3.75 throughout these tables.

TABLE A8 POPULATION GROWTH OF BRITISH NEW TOWNS, 1951–1971.

New Town Group	*Population 1951*	*1951–61 increase*	*per cent*	*1961–71 increase*	*per cent*	*1951–71 increase*	*per cent*
I	60,743	103,953	171·1	39,335	23·9	143,288	235·9
II	82,726	225,287	272·3	171,069	55·5	396,354	479·1
III	14,478	2,853	19·7	54,532	314·7	57,385	396·4
IV	183,025	23,065	12·6	60,855	29·5	83,920	45·9
V	520,212	29,726	5·7	38,405	7·0	78,131	15·0
All New Towns	861,184	384,884	44·7	364,196	29·2	749,078	87·0
Great Britain	48,854,303	2,429,589	5·0	2,694,646	5·3	5,124,235	10·5

Source: *Town and Country Planning,* **43,** no. 2 (1975).

TABLE A9 POPULATION STRUCTURE 1961 CENSUS: SKELMERSDALE, ENGLAND

	AGE GROUP									
PERCENTAGE OF POPULATION	**0-4**	**5-14**	**15-24**	**25-34**	**35-44**	**45-54**	**55-64**	**65+**	**TOTALS**	**YEARS AFTER FIRST OVERSPILL**
England & Wales	**7.9**	**15.0**	**13.2**	**12.6**	**13.6**	**13.9**	**11.8**	**12.0**	**100.0**	
Bracknell	**13.9**	**19.4**	**10.4**	**19.6**	**16.8**	**9.5**	**5.1**	**5.3**	**100.0**	**10**
Aycliffe	**14.6**	**20.5**	**10.5**	**22.2**	**17.1**	**7.8**	**3.7**	**3.6**	**100.0**	**11**
Peterlee	**17.9**	**21.9**	**11.0**	**23.5**	**13.8**	**5.6**	**3.4**	**2.9**	**100.0**	**11**
Basildon	**13.0**	**19.4**	**11.6**	**18.4**	**14.7**	**9.3**	**6.3**	**7.3**	**100.0**	**10**
Harlow	**14.6**	**22.3**	**10.3**	**20.3**	**17.1**	**8.2**	**3.8**	**3.4**	**100.0**	**11**
Hatfield	**11.0**	**19.2**	**12.0**	**16.3**	**16.7**	**11.9**	**7.0**	**5.9**	**100.0**	**10**
Hemel Hempstead	**10.9**	**20.0**	**10.8**	**16.3**	**17.1**	**11.3**	**6.8**	**6.8**	**100.0**	**11**
Stevenage	**14.0**	**20.6**	**11.0**	**20.4**	**16.9**	**8.8**	**4.5**	**3.8**	**100.0**	**11**
Welwyn New Town	**11.3**	**18.9**	**12.1**	**16.0**	**15.6**	**12.4**	**7.5**	**6.2**	**100.0**	**10**
Corby	**12.8**	**20.7**	**14.4**	**15.9**	**14.8**	**11.8**	**6.4**	**3.2**	**100.0**	**9**
Crawley	**12.4**	**20.8**	**9.9**	**18.9**	**18.0**	**9.7**	**5.2**	**5.1**	**100.0**	**11**
Cwmbran	**12.3**	**18.9**	**11.3**	**18.2**	**16.3**	**10.5**	**6.7**	**5.8**	**100.0**	**9**
Glenrothes	**16.0**	**22.4**	**10.8**	**20.0**	**14.6**	**8.1**	**4.5**	**3.6**	**100.0**	**9**
East Kilbride	**15.0**	**20.7**	**9.3**	**19.6**	**17.0**	**9.0**	**5.1**	**4.3**	**100.0**	**11**
Cumbernauld	**12.5**	**17.9**	**11.8**	**19.6**	**14.1**	**10.8**	**7.7**	**5.6**	**100.0**	**4**
Kirkby	**15.3**	**31.1**	**11.3**	**14.5**	**14.8**	**7.3**	**3.2**	**2.5**	**100.0**	**8**

Source: *Skelmersdale New Town Planning Proposals.*

TABLE A10 AGE STRUCTURE OF BRITISH NEW TOWNS 1971 (percent)

New Town Group	0–9	10–19	20–29	age group 30–39	40–49	50–59	60+
I	17·6	18·2	13·6	12·5	15·6	11·1	11·3
II	21·8	18·2	15·3	13·9	13·6	8·6	8·7
III	27·1	15·0	18·9	15·1	10·2	6·5	7·2
IV	19·8	14·9	15·6	12·7	12·3	10·5	14·2
V	17·4	14·4	13·6	11·8	12·6	11·8	18·7
All New Towns	19·5	16·1	14·7	12·7	13·1	10·3	13·5
Great Britain	16·5	14·4	14·1	11·6	12·4	12·0	18·9

Source: *Town and Country Planning,* **43,** no. 2 (1975).

TABLE A11 HARLOW'S SECOND GENERATION AGE STRUCTURE, 1972

Age Groups	Males			Females			All Persons	
	Single	Married	All	Single	Married	All	Total	% of Total Population
20 - 24	1540	1475	3015	960	2265	3225	6240	7.8
15 - 19	3495	80	3575	3040	300	3340	6915	8.7
10 - 14	4445	-	4445	4100	-	4100	8545	10.7
5 - 9	4565	-	4565	4375	-	4375	8940	11.2
0 - 4	4085	-	4085	3780	-	3780	7865	9.9

Source: *Harlow Expansion 1974.*

TABLE A12 SOCIAL CLASS STRUCTURE

SOCIAL CLASS	GREAT BRITAIN	HARLOW
	1971 %	1972 %
1. PROFESSIONAL	4.4	4.0
2. INTERMEDIATE NON-MANUAL	18.4	14.2
3. SKILLED NON-MANUAL AND MANUAL	48.9	59.8
4. PARTLY SKILLED	18.6	15.9
5. UNSKILLED	7.4	5.1
6. NOT STATED	2.3	1.0
	100.0	100.0

Source: *Harlow Expansion 1974.*

TABLE A13   NEW COMMUNITIES WITH TITLE VII GUARANTEES, APRIL 2, 1974

Name of new community	State	Federal commitment		Proposed population	Employment	Housing		Area	
		Amount	Date			Low-moderate	Other	Acres	Hectares
Jonathan	Minnesota	21·0	2/70	50,000	18,150	3,870	11,530	8,194	3,317
St Charles	Maryland	24·0	6/70	79,000	14,890	4,940	19,780	6,980	2,825
Park Forest South	Illinois	30·0	6/70	110,000	28,000	5,800	31,400	8,163	3,304
Flower Mound	Texas	18·0	12/70	64,000	16,450	3,660	14,660	6,156	2,492
Maumelle	Arkansas	7·5	12/70	45,000	—	1,220	4.070	2,044	827
Cedar Riverside	Minnesota	24·0	6/71	31,000	4,600	5,540	6,960	100	40
Riverton	New York	12·0	12/71	25,000	11,180	3,200	4,180	2,125	860
San Antonio Ranch	Texas	18·0	2/72	88,000	17,990	10,310	9,162	9,218	3,772
The Woodlands	Texas	50·0	4/72	150,000	40,000	12,930	47,375	16,939	6,857
Gananda	New York	22·0	4/72	55,000	12,890	3,730	17,200	4,733	1,916
Soul City	N. Carolina	14·0	6/72	44,000	18,000	4,980	8,340	5,180	2,122
Radisson 2	New York	(1)	6/72	18 000	600	2,500	2,500	2,760	1,117
Harbison	S. Carolina	13·0	10/72	23,000	6,100	1,850	5,550	1,730	700
Roosevelt Island 3	New York	(1)	12/72	17,000	7,500	2,750	2,250	121	49
Shenandoah	Georgia	40·0	2/73	70,000	29,600	6,900	16,100	7,200	2,915
Newfields	Ohio	32·0	10/73	40,000	4,500	2,950	9,900	4,000	1,619
Beckett	New Jersey	35·5	10/73	60,000	14,300	5,000	15,000	6,100	2,469
Totals	—	361·0	—	969,000	244,750	82,130	226,587	91,843	37,201

1. State projects, eligible for federal grants
2. Previously Lysander
3. Previously Welfare Island

Source: Town and Country Planning, **43**, no. 2 (1975).

TABLE A14 PROFILES OF 16 NEW COMMUNITIES IN THE SPRING OF 1973

PERCENT OF RESPONDENTS

CHARACTERISTIC	COLUMBIA	ELK GROVE VILLAGE	FOREST PARK	FOSTER CITY	IRVINE	JONATHAN	LAGUNA NIGUEL	LAKE HAVASU CITY	NORTH PALM BEACH	PARK FOREST	PARK FOREST SOUTH	RESTON	ROSSMOOR LEISURE WORLD	SHARPS-TOWN	VALENCIA	WESTLAKE VILLAGE
RACE																
WHITE	79.9	99.0	91.4	92.8	95.5	96.5	99.5	99.9	99.4	91.2	89.8	95.3	100.0	94.9	97.5	97.2
BLACK	18.7	0.0	8.6	2.6	2.0	2.0	0.0	0.0	0.6	6.3	10.2	4.3	0.0	4.5	1.0	1.9
OTHER	1.4	1.0	0.0	4.5	2.5	1.5	0.5	0.1	0.0	2.4	0.0	0.4	0.0	0.5	1.5	0.9
AGE OF HOUSEHOLD HEAD																
UNDER 40	76.3	53.1	61.6	52.4	53.1	83.9	37.7	30.6	24.6	50.5	73.5	69.1	0.0	60.9	59.7	34.1
40 - 54	16.6	39.5	30.8	38.1	33.6	11.4	32.8	29.0	30.6	30.4	19.5	23.5	0.0	27.5	31.8	43.1
55 OR OLDER	7.1	7.4	7.5	9.6	13.4	4.7	29.4	40.5	44.9	19.1	7.1	7.4	100.0	11.6	8.5	22.7
HOUSEHOLD COMPOSITION																
UNMARRIED ADULT(S), NO CHILDREN	18.8	8.7	5.2	16.4	13.5	14.7	8.7	8.0	14.0	9.5	11.6	18.5	41.7	22.2	9.1	13.3
MARRIED COUPLE, NO CHILDREN	18.3	18.2	18.4	23.6	27.1	18.4	34.3	44.3	42.6	25.6	24.0	17.0	58.3	21.6	25.9	31.3
UNMARRIED ADULT(S) WITH CHILD(REN)	5.3	4.7	3.0	3.3	5.5	14.4	5.3	2.8	4.0	4.9	2.5	5.3	0.0	5.1	2.5	5.3
MARRIED COUPLE WITH CHILD(REN)	57.6	68.3	73.4	56.7	53.9	52.5	51.7	44.8	39.5	60.0	61.9	59.3	0.0	51.0	62.5	50.1
HOUSEHOLDS WITH CHILD(REN) UNDER 6	38.3	29.8	39.9	25.6	24.8	53.7	24.6	15.8	14.2	30.8	40.9	32.6	0.0	30.0	36.1	23.9
HOUSEHOLDS WITH CHILD(REN) 6 - 13	36.0	47.7	49.1	37.4	33.6	29.7	31.2	28.8	26.3	43.0	33.8	38.1	0.0	29.6	37.9	34.3
HOUSEHOLDS WITH CHILD(REN) 14 - 20	9.8	30.9	28.7	16.9	24.7	6.4	23.5	25.5	22.8	21.3	15.1	14.4	0.0	21.3	23.1	28.2
EDUCATION OF HOUSEHOLD HEAD																
HIGH SCHOOL GRADUATE OR LESS	16.9	44.4	39.6	23.8	20.4	38.1	21.3	57.6	35.0	33.4	26.2	15.4	33.7	15.2	21.4	19.1
SOME COLLEGE OR COLLEGE GRADUATE	36.6	44.9	39.2	59.5	45.5	41.9	53.1	33.0	43.5	41.8	53.9	35.0	46.2	55.6	55.2	52.3
GRADUATE OR PROFESSIONAL TRAINING	46.6	10.7	21.2	16.7	34.1	20.0	25.6	9.4	21.5	24.8	19.9	49.5	20.2	29.2	23.5	28.6
EMPLOYMENT STATUS OF HEAD AND SPOUSE																
ONLY HOUSEHOLD HEAD EMPLOYED	55.7	56.6	57.8	60.5	62.1	58.3	52.5	42.2	40.5	55.9	52.3	68.0	10.6	59.2	59.8	66.2
BOTH HEAD AND SPOUSE EMPLOYED	39.2	40.2	38.4	36.2	27.4	34.0	26.2	31.4	32.0	34.8	42.1	26.0	1.0	31.6	34.3	18.7
NEITHER EMPLOYED	4.1	2.7	3.8	3.3	8.5	5.0	20.8	23.1	27.5	6.4	4.5	4.6	87.5	7.1	4.0	12.6
OCCUPATION OF HOUSEHOLD HEAD																
PROFESSIONAL OR MANAGERIAL	76.0	42.2	48.7	57.5	64.5	52.1	60.7	34.7	65.6	53.0	48.2	77.6	71.3	66.0	66.8	63.1
OTHER WHITE COLLAR	12.7	22.9	19.1	24.1	22.1	22.7	15.9	13.1	16.7	22.3	24.9	12.9	17.2	19.3	13.9	24.1
BLUE COLLAR	11.4	34.9	32.1	18.5	13.4	25.3	23.4	52.1	17.6	24.8	26.9	9.6	11.4	14.8	19.4	12.8
FAMILY INCOME IN 1972																
UNDER $10,000	15.9	8.0	12.8	9.1	6.0	40.1	5.9	32.7	15.5	16.1	12.3	14.4	45.7	21.6	5.7	4.7
$10,000 - $14,999	20.9	25.1	34.6	15.8	19.4	25.4	25.0	36.3	20.2	25.8	25.5	13.9	37.2	22.5	15.0	14.6
$15,000 - $24,999	38.7	55.0	45.0	51.4	51.6	28.9	47.9	24.3	42.3	44.5	50.2	40.2	10.6	39.7	62.3	44.9
$25,000 OR MORE	24.4	11.9	7.6	23.8	23.0	5.6	21.2	6.7	21.9	13.5	12.0	31.6	6.4	16.1	17.0	35.8

COMPILED FROM INFORMATION GATHERED BY THE CENTER FOR URBAN AND REGIONAL STUDIES, UNIVERSITY OF NORTH CAROLINA

TABLE A15   SUMMARY OF THE ENVIRONMENTAL AND PERSONAL EFFECTS OF SIX PATTERNS OF DEVELOPMENT[a]

Community Development Pattern (10,000 Units)

	I Planned Mix	II Combination Mix (50 Percent PUD, 50 Percent Sprawl)	III Sprawl Mix	IV Low-Density Planned	V Low-Density Sprawl	VI High-Density Planned
Environmental effects						
Air pollution						
Pollutants from private automobiles (CO, HC, NO$_x$)	70% of emission levels in community III; differences result from variation in auto use among development patterns.	83% of emission levels in community III.	CO: 3,628 pounds per day HC: 437 pounds per day NO$_x$: 427 pounds per day	81% of emission levels in community V.	CO: 4,040 pounds per day HC: 487 pounds per day NO$_x$: 475 pounds per day	50% of emission levels in community V.
Pollutants from residential heating (particulates, SO$_x$, CO, HC, NO$_x$)	100% of emission levels in community III; differences are a function of housing type, not development pattern.	100% of emission levels in community III.	Particulates: 83 pounds per day SO$_x$: 3 pounds per day CO: 2 pounds per day HC: 184 pounds per day NO$_x$: 554 pounds per day	100% of emission levels in community V.	Particulates: 108 pounds per day SO$_x$: 4 pounds per day CO: 2 pounds per day HC: 240 pounds per day NO$_x$: 720 pounds per day	61% of emission levels in community V; differences reflect housing mix and variation in energy use by housing type.
Water pollution and erosion						
Volume of sediment from erosion (average annual)	Slightly greater than III due to land-budget variation in developed acreage.	Virtually 100% of III.	4,431 tons per year.	89% of V; difference results from variation in developed acreage.	7,170 tons per year.	60% of V; difference results from variation in developed acreage.
Pollutants from sewage effluent (BOD, COD, N, P, SS, FCB)	No variation by housing type or development pattern. Sewage volume is a function of population, and its resulting pollutants a function of treatment level. Sewage volume is approximately 4.5 billion liters per year.	Same as I.	Same as I.	Same as I.	Same as I.	Same as I.
Pollutants from storm run-off (BOD, COD, N, P, SS, FCB)	99% of III; small difference results from more paved area (road length) in III.	Same as I.	Total run-off volume is approximately 7.8 billion liters per year.	93% of V; difference results from variation in amount of paved area.	Runoff volume is approximately 9 billion liters per year.	Runoff and its resulting pollutants are the lowest in this community. Volume is approximately 7.1 billion liters per year.
Pollutants from sanitary landfill leachate (BOD, N, P, FCB)	No variation by housing type or development pattern. Solid-waste volume disposed of in landfills is a function of population; amount of pollutants is largely a function of soil characteristics and quality of operation.	Same as I.	Same as I.	Same as I.	Same as I.	Same as I.
Noise	Where open-space buffer strips separate highways from residential areas and where careful planning locates dwellings only along minor streets, noise impact will be significantly less than in sprawl alternatives.	A less efficient traffic pattern is likely here as compared with I; some buffering of noise can be expected, although some homes may be located along busy arterials.	Where buffers and setbacks are absent, high level of noise irritation is likely.	Lower density means more auto use and hence more auto noise than in I. However, noise impacts are spread over a larger area.	Buffers more likely to be lacking than in III. Much higher total auto use than I means greater transportation noise, although spread over a larger area.	High density causes concentrated traffic flows which must be compensated for with buffers and setbacks.
Vegetation and wildlife	Less species disruption where significant tracts of land are preserved as permanent open space. Degree of adverse effect depends on ability of species to adapt to human proximity.	Greater disruption than in I, as few large open areas can be retained.	Similar to II. Leapfrog development pattern leaves only small pockets of undisturbed area.	Low-density development decreases the amount of open land preserved in its natural condition. Careful planning can protect areas of special significance as species habitats, e.g., woodlands, swamps.	Virtually no land will be left totally undisturbed, thus eliminating habitats and causing a disruption in ecological balance.	Least adverse effect through careful planning to conserve special habitats and through high-density development, which preserves large tracts of undisturbed land.

Visual effects	Development controls for retention of visually pleasing natural features and careful building design are likely to occur.	Individual developments may be well designed; however, lack of overall control will result in the haphazard spreading of urban uses in a manner that lowers the visual quality of the community.	Similar to II.	Similar to I.	Similar to II.	Similar to I.
Water and energy consumption						
Water use (gallons per year)	Same as III. Water consumption is largely a function of household size, housing type, and lawn-sprinkling demand.	Same as III.	Approximately 91 million gallons per year.	94% of V; difference reflects varying needs for lawn sprinkling.	Approximately 117 million gallons per year — greater sprinkling and household use than in III.	65% of V; difference reflects variations in residential consumption and sprinkling uses by housing type.
Energy use (billion Btus per year)	86% of III; difference reflects variation in gasoline used for auto travel, and electricity consumption a function of housing type, with apartment units consuming less than single-family homes.	92% of III; difference reflects variation in gasoline used for auto travel.	Approximately 3,416 billion Btus per year.	92% of V; difference reflects variation in gasoline used for auto travel.	Approximately 4,145 billion Btus per year.	57% of V; difference reflects variations in residential power consumption by housing type and decrease in auto use in high-density planned areas.
Personal effects						
Travel time	Auto travel time is estimated at 62% of III. Greater time spent in bicycle travel or walking. Time saved is largely a function of better planning and location of facilities and services.	Auto travel time is estimated at 81% of time consumed in III.	Estimate of almost 3 hours per day spent in auto travel by the average household. Park and travel time need results from "leapfrog" development pattern, which increases travel distances.	Time spent in auto travel is 33% greater than in I owing to lower density but is 20% less than in V owing to better planning of facility and service locations.	Similar to III, with slightly greater travel time due to longer travel distances and greater likelihood of auto use.	Auto travel time is 52% of V, owing to decreased auto use, more walking. Somewhat less than I owing to greater density of development and increased proximity of facilities and services.
Traffic accidents per year, both fatal and nonfatal, intersection and nonintersection	64% of III; difference results from variation in total vehicle miles traveled, lengths of road, street widths.	82% of III.	694 accidents per year.	80% of V; 33% greater than I owing to increased auto use and road length.	743 accidents per year, 7% more than in III owing to greater auto use and road length.	47% of V; difference reflects decreased auto use, shorter road length, wider road widths in high-density areas.
Crime	Same as III; no variation by development pattern. Differences are a function of housing type.	Same as III.	1,460 crimes per year, 5% of which are crimes to persons.	Same as V; no variation by development pattern. Differences are a function of housing type.	1,300 crimes per year, 5% of which are crimes to persons.	20% more crime than in V, due to higher density.
Psychic costs Design, natural features, leisure facilities and services, socioeconomic status, investment	More varied design, safer vehicular circulation pattern; emphasis on preserving open space; wide variety of community activities encouraging group participation. Residents are willing to bear the cost of higher-quality services, many of which are provided by community associations. Likely to have a wide range of housing prices and a heterogeneous population.	Residents of planned unit developments will reap psychic benefits in design, preservation of open space, availability of leisure activities. In other ways, costs and benefits will be similar to III.	Housing shows little design variation; land development reflects a desire to economize on direct costs; public services are not likely to be extensive. Leisure activities oriented around home and family. Likely to be homogeneous with regard to race, income, education.	Same as I.	Same as III.	Same as I.

Source: **Real Estate Research Corporation,** *Environmental and Economic Effects of Alternative Development Patterns, Task II, Detailed Cost Analysis,* August 1973, pp. 16–17.

Abbreviations as follows: CO, carbon monoxide; HC, hydrocarbons; NO_x, nitrogen oxides; SO_x, sulfur oxides; BOD, biological oxygen demand; COD, chemical oxygen demand; N, nitrogen compounds; P, phosphorus compounds; SS, suspended solids; FCB, fecal coliform bacteria.

Reprinted with permission from *Strategy for New Community Development in the United States,* edited by Gideon Golany. Copyright © 1975 by Dowden, Hutchinson & Ross, Inc., Publishers, Stroudsburg, Pa.

TABLE A16   PROJECTIONS OF SCHOOL POPULATION FOR FLOWER MOUND NEW TOWN, 1973–1988

Year	Pre-School	Elementary School	Middle School	High School	Total (E+M+H)
1973	222	383	177	177	737
1974	467	748	378	386	1,512
1975	645	1,143	608	615	2,366
1976	990	1,485	843	874	3,202
1977	1,262	1,750	1,038	1,043	3,831
1978	1,564	2,045	1,237	1,323	4,605
1979	1,905	2,392	1,456	1,626	5,474
1980	2,268	2,768	1,687	1,944	6,399
1981	2,951	3,623	2,134	2,505	8,262
1982	3,595	4,435	2,585	3,021	10,041
1983	4,203	5,197	2,956	3,481	11,634
1984	4,788	5,923	3,454	4,040	13,417
1985	5,357	6,614	3,927	4,621	15,162
1986	5,781	7,100	4,288	5,113	16,501
1987	6,148	7,530	4,609	5,593	17,732
1988	6,490	7,911	4,888	6,040	18,839

Source: *Flower Mound New Town.*

TABLE A17   WAYS IN WHICH PEOPLE HAD BETTERED THEMSELVES BY MOVING TO EAST KILBRIDE: SAMPLE SURVEY

	Head of Household (Husband)		Wife		Other Head of Household		Other Adult		Total	
	No.	Percentage	No.	Percentage	No.	Percentage	No.	Percentage	No.	Percentage
Better House	250	63·1	89	55·6	32	54·2	9		380	60·7
Better Job	23	5·8	7	4·4	1	1·7	1		32	5·1
Better Neighbours	10	2·5	5	3·1	4	6·8	—		19	3·0
Better chance for the children	33	8·3	22	13·7	3	5·1	—		58	9·3
More open space	22	5·6	7	4·4	6	10·2	—		35	5·6
Better living conditions	43	10·9	21	13·1	7	11·9	1		72	11·5
Safer community	5	1·3	2	1·3	2	3·4	—		9	1·4
Other reasons	10	2·5	7	4·4	4	6·8	—		21	3·4
Total	396	100·0	160	100·0	59	100·0	11		626	100·0

Source: *East Kilbride 70.*

304

TABLE A18 STUDENT POPULATION AND EDUCATIONAL INSTITUTIONS, PARK FOREST SOUTH, ILLINOIS

Year	Number of Students			Number of Schools		
	Elementary (K-6)	Jr. H. School (7-8)	High School (9-12)	Elementary (K-6)	Jr. H. School (7-8)	High School (9-12)
1970	651	193	361	—0—	—0—	—0—
71	1,142	338	635	1	—0—	—0—
72	1,830	542	1,017	2	—0—	—0—
73	2,788	826	1,548	3	—0—	—0—
74	3,746	1,110	2,081	5	1	—0—
75	4,704	1,394	2,613	6	1	1
76	5,662	1,678	3,146	8	2	1
77	6,620	1,961	3,678	9	2	1
78	7,578	2,245	4,210	10	2	1
79	8,536	2,529	4,742	11	2	1
80	9,494	2,813	5,274	13	3	1
81	10,452	3,097	5,806	14	3	2
82	11,410	3,381	6,339	15	3	2
83	12,367	3,664	6,871	17	3	2
84	13,325	3,948	7,403	18	4	2
85	14,284	4,232	7,935	19	4	2
86	15,242	4,516	8,468	20	4	3
87	16,199	4,800	9,000	21	5	3
88	17,157	5,084	9,532	22	5	3
89	17,791	5,272	9,884	23	5	3
90	17,902	5,304	9,946	24	5	3

Average students per school:

Elementary (K-6)	746
Junior High School (7-8)	1,061
High School (9-12)	3,315

Source: *Project Agreement Between The United States of America and Park Forest South Development Company.*

TABLE A19   PRIMARY INSTITUTIONAL RESPONSIBILITY (INITIAL ENUMERATION)

SERVICE	PROVIDER	Existing	New
Coordination			
Planning—			
Role Definition	Task Force		x
Social Planning	Town Government	x	
Functional Planning	Providers of Service	x	x
Convenor	Community Foundation		x
Education			
Planning	LISD/Junior College District/Colleges	x	
Pre-School	LISD	x	
	Churches	x	
	Local Groups	x	x
Elementary	LISD	x	
Secondary	LISD	x	
Community College	Junior College District	x	
Continuing Education	Local Colleges	x	
Health			
Planning	Medical Foundation		x
<u>Centralized</u>			
Medical Arts Office	Entrepreneurial	x	x
General Hospital	Entrepreneurial/Local Hospital	x	
Resource Center	Local Medical School/Medical Foundation	x	x
<u>Decentralized</u>			
Group Practice	Entrepreneurial	x	x
Clinic	Medical Schools/Medical Foundation	x	
Private Physician	Entrepreneurial	x	x
<u>Access</u>			
Pre-Paid Insurance	Foundation/Carriers	x	x
Para-Professional	Local Medical Schools	x	
Ambulance	Medical Foundation/Entrepreneurial	x	x
Outreach	Medical Foundation/Community Foundation		
Telecommunications	Local Medical Schools	x	
Religion			
Planning	Interfaith Consortium	x	
Free Standing	Denominations	x	
Multi-Faith	Consortium/Interfaith Groups	x	x
Recreation			
Planning	Town Government/MUD	x	x
Contemplative	MUD		x
Unstructured	MUD/Community Foundation/		
	Homeowners Association		x
Structured	MUD/Community Foundation/		
	Homeowners Association		x
Spectator	MUD/Community Foundation/		
	Homeowners Association/Entrepreneurial		x

TABLE A19   *(continued)*

SERVICE	PROVIDER	Existing	New
Community Arts			
Planning	Community Foundation		x
Network			
Film	Community Foundation/Local College/ Junior College	x	x
Libraries	Town Government/LISD/Local College/ Junior College	x	
Theatre	Entrepreneurial/Junior College/ Local College	x	x
Lecture/Concert	Entrepreneurial/Community Foundation	x	x
Dance/Music	Entrepreneurial/Local College/ Junior College	x	x
Street Scene	Community Foundation		x
Artist-In-Residence	Community Foundation		x
Employment			
Planning	Developer	x	
Industrial Park	Entrepreneurial/Developer	x	x
Retail			
Planning	Developer/Entrepreneurial	x	x
Special Opportunity	Entrepreneurial	x	x
Community	Developer/Entrepreneurial	x	x
Town	Developer/Entrepreneurial	x	x
Regional	Developer/Entrepreneurial	x	x
Safety and Security			
Planning	Town Government	x	
Institutional	Town Government	x	
Development Pattern	Developer	x	
Housing			
Planning	Developer/Entrepreneurial/Non-Profit	x	x
Low/Moderate	Developer/Entrepreneurial/Non-Profit	x	x
Moderate	Developer/Entrepreneurial/Non-Profit	x	
Upper Income	Developer/Entrepreneurial/Non-Profit	x	
Governance			
Planning	Town Government	x	
Symbol	Town Government	x	
Consensus	Town Government/Community Organizations/ Foundation	x	x
Provider of Limited Services	Town Government/Foundation	x	x
Protector of Minority Viewpoints	Town Government/Community Organizations/ Foundation	x	x
Resident			
Planning	Organizations/Foundation	x	
Definition of Objectives/ Programs	Organizations/Foundation	x	x
Accountability	Town Government/Organizations/ Foundation	x	x

Source: *Flower Mound New Town.*

TABLE A20 COST ANALYSIS FOR SIX PATTERNS OF DEVELOPMENT (IN THOUSANDS OF DOLLARS)

Community Development Pattern (10,000 Units)

Cost Category	I Planned Mix		II Combination Mix 50 Percent PUD, 50 Percent Sprawl		III Sprawl Mix		IV Low Density Planned		V Low Density Sprawl		VI High Density Planned	
	Cost	Percent of Total Cost	Cost	Percent of Total Cost	Cost	Percent of Total Cost	Cost	Percent of Total Cost	Cost	Percent of Total Cost	Cost	Percent of Total Cost
Capital Costs: Summary												
Open space/recreation	2,968 (111% of III)	1	2,826 (105% of III)	1	2,684	1	2,968 (111% of V)	1	2,684	1	2,968 (111% of V)	1
Schools	45,382 (100% of III)	13	45,382 (100% of III)	12	45,382	12	45,382 (100% of V)	9	45,382	9	45,382 (100% of V)	16
Public facilities	16,216 (99% of III)	5	16,441 (100% of III)	4	16,453	4	16,259 (98% of V)	3	16,615	3	16,304 (98% of V)	6
Transportation — streets and roads	27,077 (84% of III)	8	29,768 (92% of III)	8	32,353	9	33,770 (89% of V)	7	37,965	7	22,862 (60% of V)	8
Utilities	33,227 (86% of III)	9	36,042 (93% of III)	10	38,684	10	47,444 (77% of V)	10	61,974	12	22,432 (36% of V)	8
Subtotal	124,870 (92% of III)	35	130,459 (96% of III)	35	135,556	36	145,823 (89% of V)	30	164,620	32	109,948 (68% of V)	38
Residential	214,172 (100% of III)	60	214,172 (100% of III)	58	214,172	57	318,291 (99% of V)	65	320,400	62	160,300 (50% of V)	56
Total exclusive of land	339,042 (97% of III)	95	344,631 (99% of III)	94	349,728	94	464,114 (97% of V)	95	485,020	94	270,248 (56% of V)	94
Land (developed area and vacant improved)	18,491 (80% of III)	5	23,531 (102% of III)	6	23,105	6	25,692 (87% of V)	5	29,539	6	16,814 (57% of V)	6
Total capital cost	357,533 (96% of III)	100	368,162 (99% of III)	100	372,833	100	489,806 (95% of V)	100	514,559	100	287,062 (56% of V)	100
Present value (exclusive of land)												
Present value at 5%	270,173		272,183		277,261		367,557		377,325		216,502	
Present value at 10%	221,431		221,191		226,088		299,528		302,391		178,311	
(Comparison of results at 10%)	(98% of III)		(98% of III)				(99% of V)				(59% of V)	
Incidence of cost Government/private (%/%)	16/84		21/79		24/76		12/88		19/81		18/82	
Cost to the household Capital cost service charges/taxes (%/%/%)	47/38/15		43/37/20		41/37/22		81/7/12		75/6/19		26/56/18	

Operating and Maintenance Costs

Open space/recreation	380 (146% of III)	2	320 (123% of III)	2	260	1	380 (146% of V)	2	260	1	380 (146% of V)	2
Schools	9,643 (99% of III)	49	9,652 (99% of III)	49	9,737	49	9,643 (99% of V)	46	9,737	46	9,643 (99% of V)	51
Public services	5,103 (94% of III)	26	5,296 (98% of III)	27	5,405	27	5,165 (95% of V)	25	5,575	26	5,164 (93% of V)	27
Transportation — streets and roads	260 (100% of III)	1	260 (100% of III)	1	261	1	354 (89% of V)	2	396	2	209 (53% of V)	1
Utilities	4,186 (100% of III)	21	4,187 (100% of III)	21	4,188	21	5,269 (100% of V)	25	5,280	25	3,497 (66% of V)	19
Total year 10 operating costs	19,572 (99% of III)	100	19,715 (99% of III)	100	19,851	100	20,811 (98% of V)	100	21,248	100	18,893 (89% of V)	100
Cumulative year 10 operating costs	125,265		117,299		109,489		133,186		116,827		120,919	
Present value												
Present value at 5%	95,526		88,860		82,377		101,567		87,804		92,212	
Present value at 10%	74,913		69,210		63,710		79,651		67,822		72,315	
(Comparison of results at 10%)	(118% of III)		(109% of III)				(118% of V)				(107% of V)	
Incidence of cost — year 10 Government/private (%/%)	54/46		60/40		60/40		51/49		56/44		55/45	
Cost to the Household — year 10 Service charges/taxes (%/%)	50/50		44/56		44/56		52/48		46/54		49/51	

Note: Residential operating and maintenance costs are not estimated.

TABLE A21   NEW COMMUNITIES PROJECT DATA SHEET, APRIL 2, 1974 (MILLIONS OF DOLLARS)

Community Name	State	Commitment Amount	Commitment Date	Guarantee Issues Amount	Guarantee Issues Date	Guarantee Issues Interest	Bond Sale[a]	Housing L/M	Housing Other	Population	Jobs	Acres	County
Jonathan	Minnesota	21.0	2/70	8.0 13.0	10/70 6/72	8.500 7.200	NP	3,874	11,531	49,996	18,152	8,194	Chaska, Carver
St. Charles	Maryland	24.0	6/70	18.5 5.5	12/70 11/73	7.750 7.950	NP	4,946	19,784	79,145	14,890	6,980	Charles
Park Forest South	Illinois	30.0	6/70	30.0	3/71	7.000	NP	5,800	31,400	110,000	28,000	8,163	Will
Flower Mound	Texas	18.0	12/70	14.0	10/71	7.600	NP	3,667	14,659	64,141	16,454	6,156	Denton
Maumelle	Arkansas	7.5	12/70	6.9	12/71 12/73	7.625	PP	1,220	4,073	45,000		2,044	Pulaski
Cedar Riverside	Minnesota	24.0	6/71	24.0	12/71	7.200	NP	5,539	6,961	31,250	4,609	100	Minneapolis, Hennetin
Riverton	New York	12.0	12/71	12.0	5/72	7.125	NP	3,204	4,816	25,632	11,180	2,125	Monroe
San Antonio Ranch	Texas	18.0	2/72					10,314	9,162	87,972	17,990	9,318	Bexar
The Woodlands	Texas	50.0	4/72	50.0	8/72	7.100	CB	12,938	47,375	150,000	40,000	16,939	Montgomery
Gananda	New York	22.0	4/72	22.0	12/72	7.150	CB	3,735	17,200	55,808	12,890	4,733	Wayne
Soul City	North Carolina	14.0	6/72	5.0	3/74	8.100	NP	4,980	8,346	44,000	18,000	5,180	Warren
Radisson (Lysander)	New York	Eligible finding	6/72				CE	2,500	2,500	18,355	600	2,760	Onandaga
Harbison	South Carolina	13.0	10/72					1,850	5,550	23,075	6,100	1,730	Lexington, Richland
Roosevelt Island (Welfare Island)	New York	Eligible finding	12/72				CE	2,750	2,250	17,000	7,500	121	New York
Shenandoah	Georgia	40.0	2/73	25.0	3/74	8.200	CB	6,900	16,100	70,000	29,621	7,200	Coweta
Newfields	Ohio	32.0	10/73	18.0	11/73	7.90	CB	2,353	12,861	40,000	10,556	4,032	Montgomery
Beckett[b]	New Jersey	35.5	10/73					5,000 (est.)	20,000 (est.)	60,000	14,300	6,100	Gloucester

[a] NP, negotiated placement; PP, private placement; CB, competitive bidding; CE, certificate of eligibility, no guarantee involved; and L/M, low- and moderate-income housing.

[b] Offer of commitment not yet accepted.

Reprinted with permission from *Strategy for New Community Development in the United States*, edited by Gideon Golany. Copyright © 1975 by Dowden, Hutchinson & Ross, Inc., Publishers, Stroudsburg, Pa.

TABLE A22 CALCULATED REVENUES AND EXPENDITURES: PARK FOREST SOUTH, ILLINOIS

Type of Expenditure	Amount ($000)
Land Acquisition	$ 19,320
Land Improvements	93,966
Commercial and Administrative Expenses [a]	9,332
Income Taxes	20,359
Bond Interest	33,124
Bond Call Premium Fees	328
HUD Initial Fee of 3 Percent	900
Other HUD Fees	4,310
Total Expenditures	$181,639

[a] Document 15A shows the total figure for "Commercial and Administrative" costs as $14,869,875. This is due to the inclusion of the HUD initial fee of $900,000 and the other HUD fees of $3,310,000.

Source of Revenue	Amount ($000)
Sale of Land	
Residential	$164,871
Commercial	13,296
Industrial	19,401
Land Subtotal	$197,568
Interest from Investment	4,430
Total Revenues	$201,998

Source: Developing a Methodology for the Evaluation of Proposed New Communities.

TABLE A23 REVENUES AND EXPENDITURES 1966–1974: COLUMBIA, MARYLAND

Year	Assessment Revenues	User Fee Revenues	Total Revenues	Operating Expenses	Capital Expenditures	Interest	Total Expenses	Surplus or (Deficit) for Year
1966	$	$	$	$ 10	$ 99	$ 4	$ 113	$ (113)
1967				49	1,628	69	1,746	(1,746)
1968	92	113	205	504	1,869	273	2,646	(2,441)
1969	157	268	425	948	1,183	400	2,531	(2,106)
1970	351	333	684	1,324	1,049	476	2,849	(2,165)
1971	619	546	1,165	1,937	2,721	659	5,317	(4,152)
1972	961	876	1,837	2,411	476	925	3,812	(1,975)
1973	1,400	1,167	2,567	2,915	1,768	2,037	6,720	(4,153)
1974	1,800	1,418	3,218	3,597	4,878	1,270	9,745	(6,527)
Total	$5,380	$4,721	$10,101	$13,695	$15,671	$6,113	$35,479	$(25,378)

[a] Year ending April 30.
Source: "The Briefing Book, 1974."

TABLE A24   PROTOTYPE NEW COMMUNITY

	Percent
Acres Absorbed	
Residential	
Above Market	
Medium Density	8
Low Density	33
Total Above-Market Land	41
Below Market	
Medium Density	3
Low Density	11
Total Below-Market Land	14
Total Residential Land	55
Commercial [1]	4
Industrial [1]	8
Public Acreage	
Public Recreation and Open Space	13
Streets and Services	13
Other (public, Institutional, etc)	7
Total Public Acres	33
Total Acres Absorbed	100

[1] 800 nonmanufacturing jobs at 80 employees per acre; 400 manufacturing jobs at 20 jobs per acre; 200 employed in schools, etc. Total employment of 1,400 persons.

Note: Some figures do not adde due to rounding.
Source: Real Estate Research Corporation.
Source: *Economic and Financial Feasibility Models for New Community Development.*

TABLE A25 PROTOTYPE NEW COMMUNITY: DEVELOPMENT COSTS PER 1000 HOUSING UNITS (IN THOUSANDS OF DOLLARS)

Costs 1/	0	1	2	3	4	5	6	7	8	9	10	Total
Land Acquisition	663											663
Land Development												
Major infrastructure												
Town Roads	113	68	45	45	45	45	45	45				452
Water Distribution	33	19	13	13	13	13	13	13				130
Sanitary Sewer	24	15	10	10	10	10	10	10				98
Storm Drainage	14	9	6	6	6	6	6	6				57
Total Infrastructure	184	110	74	74	74	74	74	74				737
On Site												
Water, sewer and storm drains	21	42	53	53	53	53	42	42	42	21		422
Grading	56	34	62	44	62	36	25	8	8	4		
Interior streets	34	69	86	86	86	86	69	69	69	34		688
Total On Site	111	145	200	183	200	174	136	118	118	59		1,444
Total Infrastructure and On-Site Costs		255	274	256	274	248	210	192	118	59		2,181
Community Overhead												
Public recreation and open space		30	15	15	15	15						90
Other (public, institutional, etc.)		15			15		15					45
Structures			30									30
Total Community Overhead		45	45	15	30	15	15					165
Marketing, Fees and Overhead		23	46	58	58	58	58	46	46	46	23	462
Total Costs	958	323	365	329	361	320	267	253	165	105	23	3,469

Development Year

1/ Costs include all capital costs by developer for land acquisition and land development of all properties (residential, public, commercial, and industrial) within the new community. Costs usually paid by government bodies (e.g., school buildings) are not included here.
Note: Some figures do not add due to rounding.
Source: Real Estate Research Corporation.

Source: *Economic and Financial Feasibility Models for New Community Development.*

313

TABLE A26 PROTOTYPE NEW COMMUNITY: DEVELOPMENT REVENUE PER 1000 HOUSING UNITS
(IN THOUSANDS OF DOLLARS)

	Revenue per Unit or Acre Base Year 1/	Development Year											Total
	Per Unit	0	1	2	3	4	5	6	7	8	9	10	
Revenues													
Residential													
Above Market													
Medium Density	$3,400		48	89	132	126	146	138	112	135	124	74	1,124
Low Density	$5,600		79	221	260	304	287	335	281	259	310	122	2,458
Total Above Market			127	310	392	430	433	473	393	394	434	196	3,582
Below Market													
Medium Density	$2,900		20	21	34	35	37	39	27	43	30	32	318
Low Density	$3,200		15	47	50	52	55	58	60	42	67	23	469
Total Below Market			35	68	84	87	92	97	87	85	97	55	787
Total Residential			162	378	476	517	525	570	480	479	531	251	4,369
	Per Acre												
Commercial	$25,000		100	–	55	–	61	–	63			251	279
Industrial	$15,000		30	47	66	69	73	57	–				342
Total Revenues			292	425	597	586	659	627	543	479	531	251	4,990
Total Cost (from preceding page)		958	323	365	329	361	320	267	253	165	105	23	3,469
Cash Flow Before Financing		-958	-31	60	268	225	339	360	290	314	426	228	1,521
Cumulative Net Cash Flow Before Financing		-958	-989	-929	-661	-436	-97	263	553	867	1,293	1,521	
Discounted Rate of Return													17.7%

1/ Appreciated 5 percent per year in real value.
Note: Some figures do not add   due to rounding.

Source: Economic and Financial Feasibility Models for New Community Development.

TABLE A27   PROTOTYPE NEW-COMMUNITY DEVELOPMENT COSTS AND REVENUES EXPRESSED AS A PERCENT OF TOTAL COST

Costs	0	1	2	3	4	5	6	7	8	9	10	Total
Land Acquisition	19											19
Land Development												
Total infrastructure	5	3	2	2	2	2	2	2	1			21
Total On Site	3	4	6	5	6	5	4	4	3	2		42
Total Community Overhead		1	1		1		1		1			
Marketing, Fees and Overhead		1	1	2	2	2	2	1	1	1	1	13
Total Cost	28	9	11	9	10	9	8	7	5	3	1	100

Some numbers do not add due to rounding.

Revenues	0	1	2	3	4	5	6	7	8	9	10	Total
Residential												
Above Market												
Medium Density		1										32
Low Density		2										71
Total Above Market		4	9	11	12	13	14	11	11	12	6	103
Below Market												
Medium Density												9
Low Density		1										14
Total Below Market		1	2	2	2	3	3	3	2	3	2	23
Total Residential		5	11	14	15	15	16	14	14	15	7	126
Commercial		3	—	2	—	2	—	2				8
Industrial		—	~	2	2	2	2	—				10
Total Revenues		9	12	17	17	19	18	16	14	15	7	144
Total Cost (from Table 6-A)	28	9	11	10	10	9	8	7	5	3	1	100
Cash Flow	-28	1	2	7	6	10	10	8	9	12	7	44
Discounted Rate of Return												17.7%

Note: Some figures do not add   due to rounding.

Source: *Economic and Financial Feasibility Models for New Community Development.*

315

TABLE A28   COMPARISON OF KEY PHYSICAL AND ECONOMIC ELEMENTS PER 1000 HOUSING
UNITS FOR THE PROTOTYPE, AMHERST, AND PARK FOREST SOUTH

	Prototype	Amherst	Park Forest South
Total Acreage	230	281	231
Residential	125	117	142
Commercial	10	12	12
Industrial	20	58	25
Public	75	94	52
Market Housing	750	530	783
Below-Market Housing	250	470[3]	217
Development Period	10	10[1]	20
Net Residential Density (Units per Net Residential Acre)	8	9	7
Gross Population Density[2] (Population per Acre in Total Community)	15	11	15

1/ Limited development beyond ten years to 15 years.
2/ Assumes 3.4 persons per unit in Prototype and Park Forest South, but only 3.1 in
   Amherst because of its strong university orientation. At 3.4, Amherst would have
   a gross population density of 12.
3/ Amherst includes housing for students as well as low- and moderate-income families
Source: *Economic and Financial Feasibility Models for New Community Development.*

316

TABLE A29 COMPARISON OF COSTS AND REVENUES PER 1000 HOUSING UNITS FOR THE PRO-
TOTYPE, AMHERST, AND PARK FOREST SOUTH (IN THOUSANDS OF DOLLARS)

	Prototype		Amherst		Park Forest South	
	Per 1,000 units ($000)	% of Total cost	Per 1,000 units ($000)	% of Total cost	Per 1,000 units ($000)	% of Total cost
Costs						
Land Acquisition	$ 663	19%	$1,812	26%	$1,098	21%
Land Development						
Infrastructure	$ 737	21%	1,855	27%	$ 669	13%
On Site	1,444	42	1,836	26	2,962	55
Total Land Development	$2,181	63%	$3,691	53%	$3,631	68%
Community Overhead	165	5	211	3	58	1
Marketing Fees and Overhead	462	13	1,241	18	533	10
Total Costs	$3,471	100%	$6,955	100%	$5,340	100%
Revenues						
Residential Land	$4,369	126%	$4,942	71%	$6,819	127%
Commercial Land	279	8	471	7	484	9
Industrial Land	342	10	1,326	19	641	12
Utilities	N.A.	-	N.A.	-	780	15
Developer Fees	N.A.	-	130	2	N.A.	-
Total Revenues	$4,990	144%	$6,874	99%	$8,723	163%
Revenues – Costs	1,519	44%	-81	-1%	3,383	63%
Rate of Return Before Financing	17.7%		N.A.		9.9%	

Notes: Some numbers do not add because of rounding.
     Without subsidy, Amherst costs exceed revenues before financing.
     Prototype is for ten years; Amherst is nearly all completed in ten years; Park Forest South is scheduled for 20 years. Because of real land appreciation, the longer time period results in much greater revenues for Park Forest South.

N.A. = Not applicable
Source: *Economic and Financial Feasibility Models for New Community Development.*

TABLE A30   PRESENT VALUE OF MAJOR FINANCIAL ELEMENTS OF THE PROTOTYPE NEW COM-
MUNITY (IN THOUSANDS OF DOLLARS)

| | Total Value | Discounted Present Value | | | Percent of Net Cash |
| | | Discount Rate | | | |
		5%	7.5%	10%	Flow at 7.5%
Land Acquisition Cost	664	664	664	664	110%
Land Development Costs (Infrastructure)	737	646	609	577	101%
Land Development Cost (On Site)	1,444	1,193	1,093	1,008	182%
Residential Revenue	4,369	3,332	2,940	2,610	488%
Commercial Revenue	279	235	218	202	36%
Industrial Revenue	342	285	261	240	43%
Public Land Donation	165	144	135	127	22%
Overhead and Marketing	462	358	318	284	53%
Net Cash Flow	1,521	851	602	396	100%

Source: *Economic and Financial Feasibility Models for New Community Development.*

TABLE A31 FINANCIAL RESULTS OF BRITISH NEW TOWNS FOR THE YEAR ENDING MARCH 31, 1974 (FIRST 28 NEW TOWNS)

	Year's profit and loss (excluding adjustments for depreciation written back)				Net capital advances at 31.3.74 £	Average rate of interest %
	General Revenue* (before tax) £	Ancillaries £	Disposals* (before tax) £	Total £		
Aycliffe	− 175,467	− 4,911	+ 221,157	+ 40,779	22,039,208	7·02
Basildon	− 531,761	− 402,794	+ 1,039,738	+ 105,183	94,403,391	6·59
Bracknell	+ 348,382	− 109,896	+ 630,954	+ 869,440	44,280,651	6·53
Corby	+ 298,335	—	+ 379,689	+ 678,024	26,191,295	6·53
Cwmbran	+ 64,217	− 14,035	+ 377,218	+ 427,400	32,738,820	6·62
Harlow	+ 2,124,785	+ 97,308	+ 1,532,424	+ 3,754,517	61,326,558	5·55
Peterlee	− 508,588	− 14,834	+ 192,853	− 330,569	29,529,422	6·97
Stevenage	+ 1,282,760	—	+ 1,449,959	+ 2,732,719	66,703,379	6·18
8 England and Wales	+ 2,902,663	− 449,162	+ 5,823,992	+ 8,277,493	377,212,724	—
Crawley	+ 1,626,769	—	+ 1,190,713	+ 2,817,482		
Hatfield	− 5,939	—	+ 568,584	+ 562,645		
Hemel Hempstead	+ 2,014,847	—	+ 789,574	+ 2,804,421	102,330,547	5·12
Welwyn Garden City	+ 385,235	—	+ 718,341	+ 1,103,576		
	+ 4,020,912	—	+ 3,267,212	+ 7,288,124	102,330,547	5·12
12 England and Wales	+ 6,923,575	− 449,162	+ 9,091,204	+ 15,565,617	479,543,271	—
Central Lancs.	− 410,295	− 7,694	− 2,109	− 420,098	10,910,997	12·01
Mid-Wales (Newtown)	− 51,657	− 76,969	− 1,500	− 130,126	5,190,855	9·58
Milton Keynes	− 1,332,125	− 1,415,857	+ 831,781	− 1,916,201	67,526,039	10·13
Northampton	− 266,962	—	+ 24,850	− 242,112	28,059,830	11·77
Peterborough	− 1,375,572	− 25,207	+ 306,334	− 1,094,445	36,774,362	10·08
Redditch	− 1,185,437	− 195,980	+ 147,837	− 1,233,580	49,746,350	8·95
Runcorn	− 390,407	− 388,658	+ 123,437	− 655,628	52,444,581	9·11
Skelmersdale	− 749,514	− 7,176	+ 40,886	− 715,804	62,482,248	8·26
Telford	− 1,648,485[1]	− 938,943	− 351,137	− 2,938,565	68,374,358	9·09
Warrington	− 1,422,005	− 108,790	+ 53,394	− 1,477,401	25,338,251	10·12
Washington	− 555,580	− 64,942	+ 445,832	− 174,690	38,543,420	9·18
	− 9,388,039	− 3,230,216	+ 1,619,605	− 10,998,650	445,391,291	—
23 England and Wales	− 2,464,464	− 3,679,378	+ 10,710,809	+ 4,566,967	924,934,562	—
Cumbernauld	− 268,372	—	+ 63,000	− 205,372	61,252,010	7·49
East Kilbride and Stonehouse	+ 732,629	—	+ 953,403	+ 1,686,032	68,768,267	6·37
Glenrothes	− 306,578	− 6,898	+ 90,015	− 223,461	35,421,621	6·72
Irvine	− 489,169	—	+ 29,561	− 459,608	19,796,416	9·74
Livingston	− 618,767	—	+ 123,925	− 494,842	45,365,866	8·13
5 Scotland	− 950,257	− 6,898	+ 1,259,904	+ 302,749	230,604,180	—
28 Total: Great Britain	− 3,414,721	− 3,686,276	+ 11,970,713	+ 4,869,716	1,155,538,742	—

* Several towns have made provisions in their accounts for Corporation Tax, but for comparison purposes these have been ignored.
1 Excludes deficiency on derelict land reclamation of £90,335.

Source: *Town and Country Planning*, 43, no. 2 (1975).

TABLE A32 INDUSTRY IN 29 BRITISH NEW TOWNS TO DECEMBER 1974

	(a) Before designation			(b) Completed from designation to 31 Dec. 1974 (est.)			(c) Under construction at 31 Dec. 1974 (est.)	
	No. of occupiers	No. of employees	Size (sq. ft)[2]	No. of occupiers	No. of employees	Size (sq. ft)[2]	No. of units	Size (sq. ft)[2]
LONDON RING								
Basildon	20	438	144,714	185	20,966	6,133,678	17+8 extns	401,475
Bracknell	7	179	48,250	74	9,589	2,788,495	—	—
Crawley	23	1,529	222,000	93	18,319	4,930,510	—	—
Harlow	6	333	n.k.	302	20,450	6,643,569	5 extns	159,180
Hatfield[3]	8	900	10,000	77	1,568	439,850	—	—
Hemel Hempstead	36	6,200	n.k.	77	14,000	4,187,957	1+4 extns	134,320
Stevenage[4]	5	1,700	371,000	49	16,200	3,540,000	3+2 extns	31,700
Welwyn Garden City	69	10,000	1,994,594	24	4,002	1,483,900	1	41,700
Total: London Ring	174	21,279	—	824	105,094	30,147,959	27+19 extns	768,375
OTHERS IN ENGLAND								
Aycliffe	97	8,994	3,486,297	—	—	—	5+3 extns	219,668
Central Lancs.	380[5]	55,000[5]	17,000,000[5]	n.a.[6]	n.a.[6]	n.a.[6]	22[6]	140,000[6]
Corby	3	n.k.	n.k.	55	5,720	1,607,465	3	48,654
Milton Keynes	86	12,000	n.k.	102	n.k.	1,635,300	7	325,000
Northampton	419	29,200	7,526,000	153	6,220	1,866,000	45	870,000
Peterborough	n.k.	23,000[7]	6,290,000	n.k.	4,800[7]	1,310,000	35[8]	800,000[8]
Peterlee	—	—	—	49	4,100	1,394,044	3	246,000
Redditch	108	12,600	3,413,750	235[9]	5,812	2,479,909	11+10 extns	541,160
Runcorn[10]	30	8,000	n.k.	81	3,775	1,860,970	4+4 extns	1,369,240
Skelmersdale	12	981	328,078	100	10,600	3,737,291	11+3 extns	434,130
Telford	100	15,000[11]	5,300,000	232	20,800	2,204,417	89+2 extns	859,472
Warrington	n.k.	32,800	5,401,440	13[6]	475[6]	379,406[6]	27[6]	610,070[6]
Washington	10	3,614	759,375	186	7,795	2,840,698	30	246,804
Total: Others in England	—	201,189+	—	1,206+	70,097+	21,315,500+	292+22 extns	6,710,198+
WALES								
Cwmbran	20	6,800	1,500,000	110	5,053	1,090,453	5+2 extns	222,723
Mid-Wales (Newtown)	7	900	350,000	27	815	185,000	5	120,000
Total: Wales	27	7,700	1,850,000	137	5,868	1,275,453	10+2 extns	322,723
Total: England and Wales	—	230,168+	—	2,167+	181,059+	52,738,912+	329+43 extns	7,801,296+
SCOTLAND								
Cumbernauld	3[12]	171	151,000[12]	149	7,400	2,804,872	19	155,150
East Kilbride	3[13]	314	173,200[13]	306	19,410	6,018,500	14+2 extns	194,800
Glenrothes	4	1,884	750,000	141[14]	8,979[14]	2,466,236[14]	22+1 extn	216,000
Irvine	58[15]	6,000	2,479,000	81	7,000	2,147,000	12+1 extn	280,487
Livingston	3	70	89,500	74	5,570	2,175,809	11	371,000
Stonehouse	6	790	90,750	—	—	—	—	—
Total: Scotland	77	9,229	3,733,450	751	48,359	15,612,417	78+4 extns	1,217,437
Total: Great Britain	—	239,397+	—	2,918+	229,418+	68,351,329+	407+47 extns+	9,018,733+

n.k. – not known.
n.a. – not available.

1 Industry in this table refers to all industrial enterprises covered by Section 21 of the Local Employment Act 1960.
2 Gross floor area.
3 Figures do not cover substantial industrial area adjacent to designated area.
4 Basis of calculations amended since last year.
5 Amended to exclude warehouses.
6 Figures are only available for development carried out by or on behalf of the corporation concerned.
7 Last year's figures incorrect.
8 Figures are only available for development carried out on corporation land.
9 Includes 16 existing buildings renovated, improved and re-let.
10 Runcorn estimates under 31.12.74 refer to 1.10.74.
11 Figures revised since 1973.
12 Now demolished.
13 Two firms totalling 59,075 sq. ft have closed down.
14 Figures at 30.9.74.
15 Irvine estimates under 31.12.74 refer to 31.3.75.

Source: Town and Country Planning, **43**, no. 2 (1975).

TABLE A33   EMPLOYMENT SUMMARY: FLOWER MOUND, TEXAS

Project Year	Total Population	Total Employment	Retail Employment	Office Employment	Industrial Employment	Educational Employment	Civic, Recreation and other Employment
1972....	—	—	—	—	—	—	—
1973....	1,176	332	29	—	300	—	3
1974....	2,615	670	29	—	600	—	6
1975....	4,176	1,293	348	—	900	35	10
1976....	6,101	2,051	711	—	1,260	70	10
1977....	8,628	2,615	1,030	—	1,500	70	15
1978....	11,568	4,513	1,030	1,493	1,800	170	20
1979....	15,183	5,253	1,640	1,493	2,100	170	30
1980....	19,232	6,464	2,221	1,493	2,400	305	45
1981....	23,513	7,623	2,555	1,568	2,800	640	60
1982....	28,508	8,316	2,584	1,717	3,200	740	75
1983....	34,010	9,317	2,686	1,866	3,600	1,075	90
1984....	39,900	10,086	2,860	2,016	4,000	1,110	100
1985....	45,587	11,400	3,005	2,240	4,900	1,145	110
1986....	51,562	12,788	3,049	2,464	5,900	1,245	130
1987....	57,785	14,702	3,194	2,688	7,100	1,580	140
1988....	64,141	16,454	3,237	2,912	8,540	1,615	150

Source: *Project Agreement Between The United States of America and Flower Mound New Town, Limited.*

TABLE A34   FUTURE EMPLOYMENT SITUATION IN HARLOW, ENGLAND

	1974	ADDITIONAL WORKERS	1989	% AVERAGE GROWTH RATE P. A.
MANUFACTURING	16,200	5,800	22,000	2.4%
SERVICE SECTOR	15,600	9,400	25,000	4%
OTHERS	2,000	-	2,000	-
TOTAL	33,800	15,200	49,000	3%

Source: *Harlow Expansion 1974.*

TABLE A35 SERVICE WORK FORCE IN HARLOW, ENGLAND: ADDITIONAL WORKERS TO 1989

	1974 WORKERS	ADDITIONAL WORKERS	TOTAL 1989
COMMERCIAL EMPLOYMENT : SHOPS	3,600	2,800	6,400
COMMERCIAL EMPLOYMENT : OFFICES	2,700	2,100	4,800
LOCAL AUTHORITIES	3,200	1,950	5,150
PUBLIC UTILITIES AND SERVICES	3,000	1,950	4,950
WAREHOUSING AND SERVICE INDUSTRY	3,100	600	3,700
	15,600	9,400	25,000
BUILDING TRADES, AND EMPLOYMENT IN PREMISES NOT UNDER AEGIS OF CORPORATION	2,000	-	2,000
	17,600	9,400	27,000

Source: *Harlow Expansion 1974.*

TABLE A36 GROWTH OF SERVICE EMPLOYMENT IN HARLOW, ENGLAND: 1965–1973

YEAR	NUMBERS EMPLOYED			% OF TOTAL EMPLOYMENT
	MALE	FEMALE	TOTAL	
1965	4900	4700	9600	37%
1966	5400	5200	10600	38%
1967	6300	5800	12100	41%
1968	6400	6100	12500	41%
1969	7100	6600	13700	44%
1970	7500	7000	14500	43%
1971	8000	7300	15300	44%
1972	7900	7400	15300	46%
1973	7700	7900	15600	46%

Source: *Harlow Expansion 1974.*

322

TABLE A37 CUMULATIVE PROJECT AREA POPULATION AND EMPLOYMENT SUMMARY: CEDAR-RIVERSIDE, MINNEAPOLIS, MINNESOTA

Development Stage	Years	New Population	Total New Employment	Retail Employment	Office Employment	All Other Employment (1)
1	1972-1973	3,247	80	30	—	50
2	1974-1975	6,494	400	150	—	250
3	1976-1977	9,714	1,087	270	457	360
4	1978-1979	12,934	1,317	400	457	460
5	1980-1981	16,154	2,187	490	1,007	690
6	1982-1983	19,172	2,421	570	1,007	844
7	1984-1985	22,192	3,331	620	1,737	974
8	1986-1987	25,212	3,621	670	1,737	1,214
9	1988-1989	28,232	4,288	700	2,287	1,301
10	1990-1991	31,250	4,609	730	2,543	1,336

(1) "All Other" employment includes those working in services such as hotel, health, automotive, cultural and entertainment, day care and educational occupations.

Note:

In addition to employment within the Project area, employment for 9,537 persons in 1991 will result from existing and expanded institutions and new institutional related activities in the non-Project Area. At mature development some 14,146 jobs are projected to be available in the entire Cedar-Riverside area. Institutional employment is projected as follows:

(1) Fairview and St. Mary's Hospitals, 3,008 employees

(2) Augsburg College, 261 employees

(3) St. Mary's Junior College, 108 employees

(4) University of Minnesota West Bank Campus, 6,000 employees

(5) New institutional related, 160 employees

During the Development Period construction should generate more than 2.5 jobs in related occupations per man employed on construction. An average of 500 people per day on construction jobs is anticipated over the 20-year period.

Factors utilized to derive some of the above figures are:
Population, 2.5 persons per household
Retail employment, 500 square feet per employee
Office employment, 219 square feet per employee

Source: *Project Agreement Between the United States of America and Cedar-Riverside Land Company.*

TABLE A38   CUMULATIVE SUMMARY: ST. CHARLES, MARYLAND

Project Years	Total Population	Total Employment	Industrial Employment	Commercial & Service Employment	Educational Employment	Medical Employment (Hospital, Nursing Home)	Dwelling Units		
							Total	Low Density	Medium Density
1	1,700	408	400	8	—	—	500	400	100
2	3,400	838	800	8	30	—	1,000	800	200
3	5,100	1,766	1,200	106	460	—	1,500	1,200	300
4	7,975	2,166	1,600	106	460	—	2,375	1,700	675
5	10,850	2,684	2,080	114	490	—	3,250	2,200	1,050
6	14,706	3,164	2,560	114	490	—	4,452	2,700	1,752
7	18,562	3,682	3,040	122	520	—	5,654	3,200	2,454
8	22,418	4,770	3,600	220	950	—	6,856	3,700	3,156
9	26,274	6,230	4,080	600	1,550	—	8,058	4,200	3,858
10	30,130	6,748	4,560	608	1,580	—	9,260	4,700	4,560
11	34,811	7,228	5,040	608	1,580	—	10,737	5,200	5,537
12	39,492	9,286	5,520	706	2,010	1,050	12,214	5,700	6,514
13	44,173	9,804	6,000	714	2,040	1,050	13,691	6,200	7,491
14	48,959	10,322	6,480	722	2,070	1,050	15,198	6,730	8,468
15	53,745	11,330	6,960	820	2,500	1,050	16,705	7,260	9,445
16	58,825	11,848	7,440	828	2,530	1,050	18,310	7,790	10,520
17	63,905	12,486	8,040	836	2,560	1,050	19,915	8,320	11,595
18	68,985	13,614	8,640	934	2,990	1,050	21,520	8,850	12,670
19	74,065	14,252	9,240	942	3,020	1,050	23,125	9,380	13,745
20	79,145	14,890	9,840	950	3,050	1,050	24,730	9,910	14,820

Source: *Project Agreement Between United States of America and Interstate Land Development Company, Inc.*

TABLE A39   OCCUPATIONS—EAST KILBRIDE, SCOTLAND, MALES (803 HOUSEHOLDS)

Age			Full Time Work		Unemployed/ Incapacitated	Student	Retired	School or under School Age	Total	Percentage
75 and over							10		10	0·7
70 and under 75							11		11	0·8
65 ,,	,,	70	9	1·2%			20		29	2·2
60 ,,	,,	65	25	3·3%	2		2		29	2·2
55 ,,	,,	60	51	6·8%	1				52	3·9
50 ,,	,,	55	67	8·9%	2		1		70	5·2
45 ,,	,,	50	90	12·0%	3				93	7·0
40 ,,	,,	45	99	13·2%	1				100	7·5
35 ,,	,,	40	93	12·4%	1				94	7·0
30 ,,	,,	35	101	13·5%	2	1			104	7·8
25 ,,	,,	30	111	14·8%					111	8·3
20 ,,	,,	25	53	7·1%	3	9			65	4·9
15 ,,	,,	20	51	6·8%	4	5		58	118	8·8
10 ,,	,,	15						132	132	9·9
5 ,,	,,	10						186	186	13·9
Under 5								130	130	9·7
Total			750		19	15	44	506	1334	
Percentage			56·2%		1·4%	1·1%	3·3%	37·9%	100%	100%

NOTE : 3 men stated that they worked part time. It was felt however that these (self-employed) occupations should be included in the Full Time Work since no other job was shown.

Source: *East Kilbride 70.*

TABLE A40   OCCUPATIONS—EAST KILBRIDE, SCOTLAND, FEMALES (803 HOUSEHOLDS)

Age	Housewife		Full Time Work		Part Time Work		Student	School or under School Age	Retired	Total	Percentage
75 and over									52	52	3·5
70 and under 75	3	0·7%							48	51	3·5
65 ,, ,, 70	12	2·9%	2	0·7%	1	0·8%			17	32	2·2
60 ,, ,, 65	16	3·8%	2	0·7%	5	4·2%			18	41	2·8
55 ,, ,, 60	27	6·5%	14	4·6%	9	7·6%			2	52	3·5
50 ,, ,, 55	25	6·0%	26	8·6%	15	12·7%				66	4·5
45 ,, ,, 50	25	6·0%	39	12·9%	19	16·1%	1			84	5·7
40 ,, ,, 45	43	10·3%	36	11·9%	19	16·1%	1			99	6·7
35 ,, ,, 40	61	14·6%	32	10·6%	21	17·8%	2			116	7·9
30 ,, ,, 35	70	16·7%	13	4·3%	16	13·6%				99	6·7
25 ,, ,, 30	101	24·2%	34	11·2%	9	7·6%	1			145	9·9
20 ,, ,, 25	30	7·2%	48	15·8%	4	3·4%	4			86	5·9
15 ,, ,, 20	5	1·2%	57	18·8%			10	41		113	7·7
10 ,, ,, 15								138		138	9·4
5 ,, ,, 10								150		150	10·2
Under 5								145		145	9·9
Total	418		303		118		19	474	137	1469	
Percentage		28·5%		20·6%		8·0%	1·3%	32·3%	9·3%	100%	100%

Source: *East Kilbride 70.*

TABLE A41   PRESENT EMPLOYMENT OF HEAD AND UP TO TWO OTHER MEMBERS OF THE HOUSEHOLD—EAST KILBRIDE, SCOTLAND

	Head of Household		Other Person 1		Other Person 2		Total	
	No.	Percentage	No.	Percentage	No.	Percentage	No.	Percentage
1 Unskilled Manual	53	7·1	23	6·7	13	13·4	89	7·5
2 Semi-skilled Manual	86	11·5	44	12·8	4	4·1	134	11·3
3 Skilled Manual	188	25·1	50	14·6	16	16·5	254	21·4
4 Foreman/Supervisor	85	11·4	14	4·1	1	1·0	100	8·4
5 Clerical	80	10·7	116	33·8	27	27·8	223	18·8
6 Shop-Assistant (employee)	12	1·6	41	12·0	12	12·4	65	5·5
7 Shop (Self employed)	12	1·6	2	0·6	1	1·0	15	1·3
8 Managerial	92	12·3	3	0·9	2	2·1	97	8·2
9 Professional	84	11·2	32	9·3	8	8·2	124	10·4
10 Others	56	7·5	18	5·3	13	13·4	87	7·3
Total	748	100·0	343	100·0	97	100·0	1188	100·0

Source: *East Kilbride 70.*

TABLE A42   PLACE OF WORK OF EAST KILBRIDE, SCOTLAND, RESIDENTS

	Full Time		Part Time	
	No.	Percentage	No.	Percentage
East Kilbride	588	53·9	84	80·8
Glasgow	287	26·3	12	11·5
Elsewhere	215	19·7	8	7·7
Total	1090	100·0	104	100·0

Source: *East Kilbride 70.*

TABLE A43   TYPE OF EMPLOYMENT OF HEAD OF HOUSEHOLD AT TIME OF MOVE TO EAST KILBRIDE, SCOTLAND, COMPARED WITH PRESENT EMPLOYMENT

| | | Present Classification | | | | | | | | | | |
| | | 1 | 2 | 3 | 4 | 5 | 6 | 7 | 8 | 9 | 10 | |
Classification at time of move		Unskilled Manual	Semi-Skilled Manual	Skilled Manual	Foreman/ Supervisor	Clerical	Shop Assistant (Employee)	Shop (Self Employed)	Managerial	Professional	Others	Unclassifiable
	Total	53	86	188	85	80	12	12	92	84	56	
1 Unskilled Manual	34	**22**	4	2	—	—	—	—	1	—	3	2
2 Semi-Skilled Manual	84	9	**53**	5	4	1	1	—	2	—	4	5
3 Skilled Manual	226	4	8	**163**	23	2	—	2	8	7	4	5
4 Foreman/Supervisor	69	2	3	5	**46**	—	—	—	7	3	1	2
5 Clerical	87	3	1	1	2	**62**	1	—	11	3	—	3
6 Shop Assistant (Employee)	10	1	—	—	2	2	**2**	—	1	—	—	2
7 Shop (Self-Employed)	12	—	—	1	—	2	—	**7**	—	—	—	2
8 Managerial	64	—	—	1	2	1	—	1	**53**	2	—	4
9 Professional	64	1	—	1	—	—	—	—	1	**59**	1	1
10 Others	65	2	5	2	2	3	1	1	5	6	**33**	5
Unclassifiable		9	12	7	4	7	7	1	3	4	10	

Source: *East Kilbride 70.*

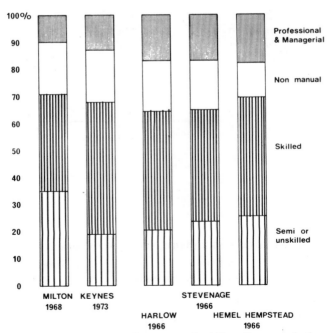

Figure A1. Comparative socioeconomic structures for Milton Keynes and other new towns.
Source: *Four Years On.*

TABLE A44 NORMAL MEANS OF TRAVEL IN EAST KILBRIDE, SCOTLAND

| | Local Shops | | Town Centre Shops | | Out of Town Shops | |
	No.	Percentage	No.	Percentage	No.	Percentage
On Foot	623	81·0	319	40·1	—	—
By Cycle	2	0·3	2	0·3	—	—
By Motor-Cycle	—	—	—	—	—	—
By Car	51	6·6	128	16·1	203	27·7
Car Passenger	20	2·6	53	6·7	101	13·8
By Bus	71	9·2	289	36·4	361	49·2
By Train	1	0·1	3	0·4	68	9·3
Otherwise	1	0·1	1	0·1	—	—
Total	769	100·0	795	100·0	733	100·0

	No.	Percentage
On Foot	107	22·9
By Cycle	1	0·2
By Motor-Cycle	—	—
By Car	207	44·3
As Car Passenger	9	1·9
By Bus	131	28·1
By Train	11	2·4
Otherwise	1	0·2
Total	467	100·0

	No.	Percentage
On Foot	254	72·0
By Cycle	4	1·1
By Motor-Cycle	—	—
By Car	3	0·8
As Car Passenger	8	2·3
By Bus	78	22·0
By Train	4	1·1
Otherwise	2	0·6
Total	353	100·0

	No.	Percentage
On Foot	124	16·6
By Cycle	5	0·7
By Motor-Cycle	—	—
By Car	418	56·0
As Car Passenger	29	3·9
By Bus	156	20·9
By Train	11	1·5
Otherwise	4	0·5
Total	747	100·0

Source: *East Kilbride 70.*

TABLE A45 PROGRESS ON LAND SOLD OR LEASED BY DEVELOPMENT CORPORATIONS/ COMMISSION FOR THE NEW TOWNS, DECEMBER 31, 1974

New Town	Manufacturing		New Shops Completed	Office Space		New Houses and Flats		New Schools	
	No. of Firms	Providing Employment for		Net Sq. Ft. Completed	Net Sq. Ft. under Construction	Completed	Under Construction	No. Completed	No. of Children Provided for
England									
Stevenage	111	19,543	367	464,176	—	20,038	551	41	22,552
Crawley	90	18,319	294	681,885	—	15,652	132	36	20,960
Hemel Hempstead[a]	77	13,675	317	711,120	9,500	14,224	34	44	18,895
Harlow	129	16,280	340	627,899	100,400	22,481	638	37	27,155
Aycliffe	93	9,486	103	25,120	18,250	6,944	353	18	7,190
Peterlee	34	4,079	158	58,369	36,600	7,140	265	23	8,390
Hatfield	20	1,436	118	31,800	10,000	4,517	2	15	5,150
Welwyn Garden City[a]	24	4,002	133	189,184	—	6,648	58	24	9,500
Basildon	187	21,051	378	266,610[b]	299,665[b]	20,875	1,147	29	19,570
Bracknell	38	9,589	197	1,007,927	—	10,897	590	18	7,950
Corby	41	5,319	255	213,348	28,372	8,993	448	33	16,926
Skelmersdale	95	10,107	133	127,068	—	7,724	1,313	20	10,090
Redditch	202+	4,974	95	175,919	15,000	5,558	681	11	6,020
Runcorn	56	3,229	102	292,184	—	6,792	1,229	14	4,740
Washington	152+	5,773	83	215,228	573,387	6,380	1,813	15	6,310

	50+								
Milton Keynes	50+	1,634	40	421,544	239,000	4,041	2,507	16	7,780
Peterborough	91	1,351	19	70,000	527,000	2,410	1,555	3	800
Northampton	84	3,414	6	93,800	—	3,429	1,820	10	3,352
Warrington	10	498	2	—	172,070	810	536	2	600
Telford	133	4,816	58	6,868	—	6,275	1,084	94	3,656
Central Lancashire	.	—	—	—	—	—	—	—	—
Total	1,717	158,575	3,198	5,680,049	2,029,244	182,098	16,756	418	207,586
Wales									
Cwmbran	87	1,970	226	158,009	83,347	8,768	426	20	12,505
Newtown	17	755	1	—	50,000	582	257	—	—
Total	104	2,725	227	158,009	133,347	9,350	683	20	12,505
Scotland									
East Kilbride	155	15,119	227	426,201	231,265	20,628	1,141	26	18,005
Glenrothes	63	6,712	80	151,436	63,400	8,808	824	13	11,530
Cumbernauld	62	4,983	132	190,322	218,000	11,231	873	20	13,375
Livingston	39	3,834	46	71,676	125,000	6,249	1,359	10	6,040
Irvine	37	1,701	29	62,162	105,000	2,114	1,618	5	3,725
Stonehouse	—	—	—	—	—	—	—	—	—
Total	356	32,349	514	901,797	742,665	49,030	5,815	74	52,675

[a] Transferred to Commission for the New Towns.
[b] Amended figure.
Source: Commission for the New Towns, New Town Development.

TABLE A46   SUMMARY OF COMPARATIVE LAND BUDGETS FOR NEW TOWNS—BRITISH AND USA

	British Range in Percentages	U.S.A. Range in Percentages
Residential	30–64%	42–60%
Industry	8–15%	4–21%
Open Space	10–34%	4–23%
Education – Health	5– 6%	3– 9%
Centers	3%	3–40%
Reserve – Recreation	7%	2– 7%
Streets and Services	11–20%	12–16%

Source: *Economic and Financial Feasibility Models for New Community Development.*

TABLE A47   COMPARATIVE LAND BUDGETS AND NEW TOWN SIZES

	BRITISH						U.S.A.					
	Cumbernauld		Hook		Milton Keynes		Reston		Columbia		Pk. Forest So.	
	Acres	%	Acres	%	Acres	%	Acres	%	Acres	%	Acres	%
Residential	832	31	2,025	34	14,100	64	3,900	53	6,520	46	3,795	
Industry	394	15	525	9	2,400	11	1,300	17	3,000	21	679	
Open Space	920	34	1,875	32	2,200	10	1,100	15	3,200	23	1,392[5]	
Education/Health	175	6	150	2	1,100	5	400	5			[5]	
Centers	87	3	144	2	600	3	200	3	780	6	310	
Reserve/Recreation					1,600	7	500[2]	7	500[3]	4	[5]	
Streets & Services	307	11	1,235	21	(4,400)	20[1]	(592)		–		[5]	
TOTAL	2,715	100%	5,954	100%	22,000	100%	7,400	100%	14,000	100%	6,176	
Population	70,000		100,000		250,000		75,000		100,000		94,000[6]	
Gross Density (Persons per Acre)	16		13.3		11.3		10		7.2		15.2	

1/ 20 percent --included in above categories.
2/ Includes lakes and golf course.
3/ Includes lakes.
4/ Reserve sites.
5/ Open space acreage also includes other public lands.
6/ Based on 3.5 persons per housing unit included in developer's program. A total of 110,000 people are projected for all of Park Forest South.

Source: *Economic and Financial Feasibility Models for New Community Development.*

330

TABLE A48 POPULATION AND LAND USE ACRES IN NEW COMMUNITIES (DECEMBER 1972)

New Town	Population	Jobs	Residential	%	Industrial	%	Commercial	%	Schools	%	Open Space and recreation	%	Roads	%	Other	%	Total
Flower Mound	64,141	16,454	2,989	(49)	427	(7)	262	(4)	260	(4)	1,456	(23)	345	(6)	417	(7)	6,156
Woodlands	150,000	40,000	6,339	(37)	2000	(12)	466	(3)	—		4,000	(23)	1,649ᵃ	(8)	2,694ᵇ	(16)	16,939
Riverton	25,632	11,180	1,046	(49)	400	(19)	170	(8)	75	(3)	434ᶜ	(20)	—		—		2,125
Jonathan	49,996	18,152	2,436	(30)	1989	(24)	230	(3)	292	(4)	1,705	(21)	465	(6)	1,073ᵈ	(13)	8,194
Park Forest South	110,000	—	4,871	(60)	1012	(12)	348	(4)	269	(3)	892ᵉ	(1)	—		771ᶠ	(9)	8,163
Cedar-Riverside	31,250	4,609	83	(83)	—		17	(17)	—ᵍ		—ʰ		—		—		100
Lysanderⁱ	18,355	—	910	(34)	795	(30)	168ʲ	(6)	—		597	(22)	—		—		2,670
Maumelleᵏ	45,000	—	2,044	(38)	1071	(20)	86	(2)	238	(4)	1,700	(31)	184	(3)	200	(7)	5,319
St. Charles	79,145	14,890	4,320	(62)	402ˡ	(6)	214	(3)	108	(2)	1,516	(21)	330	(5)	—		6,980
Harbisonⁱ	21,343	6,100	732	(42)	196	(11)	85	(5)	64	(4)	224	(12)	201	(11)	235	(14)	1,739
Soul Cityⁱ	44,000	18,000	1,705	(33)	928	(18)	298ᵐ	(6)	453	(9)	1,495	(28)	200	(4)	101	(2)	5,180
Gananda	55,808	12,890	2,470	(51)	250	(5)	174	(4)	293	(6)	1,010	(21)	480	(10)	54	(1)	4,733
Welfare Islandⁱ	17,000	7,500	40	(27)	—		—ʳ		—ᵍ		49	(34)	33	(20)	21ˢ	(15)	143
San Antonio Ranchⁱ	87,972	17,990	4,249	(46)	1234	(12)	160	(2)		(4)	2,203	(24)	642	(7)	500ᵖ	(5)	9,318
	800,513	197,689q	33,933	(43)							18,336	(24)					78,558

Source: HUD (revised December 1972).

a Includes schools, roads, and other infrastructure.
b Includes an 1,800-acre reserve and 400-acre university.
c "Community space," which includes open space and recreation reserves.
d Church uses, plus agriculture and recreation reserves.
e Residential areas including major open space. Counting 50% of university and schools and residential clusters, total open space is 2,247 or 27%.
f All but 17 acres are for Governor's State University campus.
g Schools included in high-rise buildings and not listed separately.
h Open space is elevated over streets and not computed separately.
i No project agreement signed. Statistics subject to change.
j Acreage includes schools and other community facilities.
k Project agreement covers 12-year development program only. Land-use statistics cover 20-year development period and include 633-acre golf course and 241-acre proposed commercial park, which is owned by an affiliate company and not covered in the project agreement. This land is included in the total plan.

l Excludes 400 acres for industrial land not now acquired, but committed to acquire.
Includes medical and institutional as well as retail uses.
n Excludes "primary reserve" and 1,113 acres, and "land bank" of 4,026 acres.
o Includes industrial preserve.
p Other community facilities and supporting services.
q Total employment computed by taking those projects for which there were no total employment estimates and applying to them the average ratio of jobs to total population for all projects for which statistics are available.
r Commercial included in other structures.
s Hospital.
Source: *The Contemporary New Communities Movement in the United States.*

TABLE A49 LAND DEVELOPMENT SUMMARY (CUMULATIVE AREAS)

Project Year	Total	Residential	Industrial	Comm'l.	Recreational & Open Space	Schools and Community Facilities	Major Roads
1	188	143	20	4	25	1.5	5
2	358	286	40	4	50	1.5	12
3	830	430	60	28	281.5	10.5	20
4	1055	626	84	28	281.5	10.5	29
5	1304	823	108	32	296.0	12.0	37
6	1556	1036	132	32	296.0	12.0	52
7	1828	1248	156	36	310.5	13.5	68
8	2186	1461	180	60	378.5	22.5	84
9	2592	1674	204	114	465.5	35.5	99
10	2900	1887	228	118	515.0	37.0	115
11	3274	2120	252	118	575.0	72.0	137
12	3712	2352	276	142	703.0	81.0	158
13	4061	2584	300	146	777.5	82.5	171
14	4430	2827	324	150	852.0	84.0	193
15	4890	3070	348	174	980.0	93.0	225
16	5284	3319	372	178	1074.5	94.5	246
17	5706	3569	402	182	1189.0	96.0	268
18	6208	3819	432	206	1357.0	105.0	289
19	6600	4069	462	210	1441.5	106.5	311
20	6980	4320	492	214	1516.0	108.0	330
TOTALS	6980	4320	492**	214	1516.0	108*	330

* This includes 73 acres for school buildings and 35 acres for hospital nursing home and public safety center. Libraries, community buildings and churches included in commercial center areas.

** This does not include approximately 400 acres of industrial land to be acquired.

Source: *Project Agreement Between United States of America and Interstate Land Development Company, Inc.*

TABLE A50 LAND USE SUMMARY OF JONATHAN, MINNESOTA (CUMULATIVE)

YEAR	A. TOTAL ACRES DEVELOPED	1) Residential Development	2) Industrial Development	3) Multi-Use Development	4) Educational Development	5) Church Development	6) Open Space Development (Lakes and Greenways)	7) Road Development
1	272.09	65.88	131.0	6.39	—	6.35	148.2	18.5
2	393.79	120.48	227.0	—	14.4	9.45	177.7	27.5
3	529.79	187.78	264.5	—	—	—	230.1	31.5
4	678.29	280.78	304.0	—	—	—	260.3	44.5
5	825.28	377.77	346.9	13.20	18.9	—	290.5	51.6
6	1,099.29	507.17	391.9	—	—	14.45	356.7	56.4
7	1,361.09	636.97	444.7	—	48.9	18.45	448.2	90.9
8	1,718.59	781.37	512.7	19.80	52.9	21.45	559.2	120.4
9	2,102.39	938.47	582.4	66.80	100.9	25.45	668.2	142.9
10	2,526.99	1,121.87	665.2	124.70	105.9	31.45	738.2	180.4
11	3,093.69	1,267.84	765.2	135.23	—	37.79	897.4	208.9
12	3,660.39	1,413.81	865.2	145.76	147.9	—	942.7	237.4
13	4,227.09	1,559.78	965.2	156.29	152.9	44.13	1,038.0	265.9
14	4,793.79	1,705.75	1,065.2	166.82	172.9	—	1,133.3	294.4
15	5,360.49	1,851.72	1,165.2	177.35	177.9	50.47	1,228.6	332.9
16	5,927.19	1,997.69	1,275.2	187.88	182.9	—	1,323.9	351.4
17	6,493.89	2,143.66	1,395.2	198.41	187.9	56.81	1,419.2	379.9
18	7,060.59	2,290.60	1,525.2	208.94	192.9	—	1,514.5	408.4
19	7,627.29	2,436.57	1,665.2	219.47	—	63.14	1,609.8	436.9
20	8,194.00	—	1,815.2	230.00	—	—	1,705.2	465.4
Unde-veloped			173.8		99.2			
Totals	**8,194.00**	**2,436.57**	**1,989.0**	**230.00**	**292.1**	**63.14**	**1,705.2**	**465.4**

Note: Tabular data, columns (1) - (7), does not include land alloted to Recreational Development (556.1 acres), land alloted to Agriculture (440.6 acres), or unassigned land (14.8 acres).

Source: *Jonathan.*

333

Project Year	Single Family Detached D. U.'s	Acres	Single Family Attached D. U.'s	Acres	Moderate Apts. D. U.'s	Acres	Semi-Luxury Apts. D. U.'s	Acres	Luxury Apts. D. U.'s	Acres	Modular Housing D. U.'s	Acres	Annual Acreage Absorption	Cumulative Acreage Absorption
1972	—	—	—	—	—	—	—	—	—	—	—	—	65	65
1973	189	54	30	3	105	7	12	1	—	—	—	—	82	147
1974	242	69	40	4	105	7	24	2	—	—	—	—	87	234
1975	252	72	50	5	120	8	24	2	—	—	—	—	102	336
1976	287	82	50	5	165	11	48	4	—	—	—	—	134	470
1977	371	106	70	7	195	13	36	3	—	—	50	5	154	624
1978	424	121	90	9	240	16	36	3	—	—	50	5	185	809
1979	500	143	110	11	315	21	48	4	—	—	60	6	206	1,015
1980	557	159	110	11	360	24	60	5	—	—	70	7	216	1,231
1981	577	165	110	11	360	24	96	8	—	—	80	8	224	1,455
1982	577	165	120	12	360	24	280	14	—	—	90	9	244	1,699
1983	627	179	130	13	375	25	340	17	—	—	100	10	252	1,951
1984	633	181	140	14	390	26	420	21	—	—	100	10	250	2,201
1985	630	180	170	17	405	27	220	11	100	5	100	10	257	2,458
1986	637	182	190	19	420	28	240	12	120	6	100	10	261	2,719
1987	633	181	210	21	435	29	260	13	140	7	100	10	270	2,989
1988	676	193	230	23	450	30	280	14	160	8	20	2		
TOTAL	7,812	2,232	1,850	185	4,800	320	2,424	134	520	26	920	92	2,989	

Source: *Project Agreement Between The United States of America and Flower Mound New Town, Limited.*

TABLE A52   NEW CITY: PROPOSED LAND USE 1990—TUY MEDIO, VENEZUELA

Land Use		Areas in Hectares
Housing		2300
Industry		1400
Open space:		
City open space, including major parks	700	
Local open space	1225	
		1925
Education:		
Schools	165	
University	80	
		245
Residual:		
Roads	860	
Central area	200	
Cemetery	100	
		1160
Total urban area		7,030
Airport		300
Paraíso del Tuy		1,603
Undeveloped land[1]		6,081
Total land within exporpriation area		15,014

[1]Includes steeply sloping land acquired to prevent large-scale invasion by immigrants.
Source: *Planning Proposals for Tuy Medio, Venezuela.*

TABLE A53   LAND USE IN REDDITCH, ENGLAND

New housing	1409 acres
Education	250 acres
Central area	150 acres
Community facilities and ancillary uses	164 acres
New industry	679 acres
Roads including planting	607 acres
Open space	1040 acres
Golf courses	356 acres
Woodland	390 acres
Cemeteries	31 acres
Hospital	40 acres
Miscellaneous	214 acres
Existing development	1146 acres
Unallocated	744 acres
	7220 acres

Source: *Notes for Students.*

TABLE A54 NEW TOWN OF GRANDE CACHE, CANADA (A COMPANY TOWN)

Breakdown of Land Uses (late 1968)	Acres	Age (%)
Single-family residential	271.5	55.2
Row housing (duplex)	14.3	2.9
Apartments	5.7	1.2
Hospital	13.8	2.8
Commercial and institutional	26.2	5.4
Schools and playgrounds, central park	39.6	8.0
Churches	2.5	0.5
Reserves (buffer and walkways)	32.3	6.6
Industry	49.9	10.1
Highway commercial	9.0	1.8
Trailer courts	13.0	2.7
Main highway	13.5	2.8
Totals	491.3	100.0

Population and residential units	Population	No. of Units	Age (%)
Single family (7 units/acre)	3,916	979	66.7
Row housing (15 units/acre)	856	214	14.6
Apartments (30 units/acre)	684	171	11.6
Trailer courts (18 units/acre)	416	104	7.1
Totals	5,072	1,468	100.0

Total population   5,072
Total area developed   491.3 acres
Gross density   12 persons/acre

Source: "The New Town of Grande Cache."

TABLE A55 LAND USE, 1966 IN WARRINGTON, ENGLAND

	Administrative Zone							
	Warrington County Borough		Warrington Rural District		Runcorn Rural District		Total	
Land Use	Acres	%	Acres	%	Acres	%	Acres	%
Residential [a]	1625	35.1	1,106	10.5	869	25.2	3,600	18.3
Infill [b]	—	—	254	2.3	75	2.2	329	1.8
Industry	832	18.0	378	3.6	27	0.8	1,237	6.6
Commerce	47	1.0	2	—	7	0.2	56	0.3
Education	157	3.4	108	1.0	20	0.6	285	1.5
Motorways	—	—	40	0.3	—	—	40	0.2
Railways	269	5.8	95	0.9	27	0.8	391	2.1
Ship canal	40	0.9	55	0.5	136	3.9	231	1.2
Open space	380	8.2	117	1.1	353	10.2	850	4.6
Utilities	91	2.0	44	0.4	7	0.2	142	0.8
Agriculture	168	3.6	4,593	43.7	1849	53.7	6,610	35.6
Dumping grounds	238	5.1	726	6.9	—	—	964	5.2
Special sites [c]	—	—	2,365	22.4	—	—	2,365	12.7
Other [d]	323	7.0	245	2.3	37	1.1	605	3.2
Vacant	459	9.9	411	3.9	37	1.1	907	4.9
Total	4629	100.0	10,539	100.0	3444	100.0	18,612	100.0

[a] Gross acreage.
[b] Land within the existing built-up area, upon which building has begun, with outstanding planning permission and "white" land.
[c] Includes R.A.F. Burtonwood, and the Risley Ordnance Factory Site.
[d] Includes tidal water, other nontidal water and canals.
Source: *Warrington New Town.*

335

TABLE A56   LAND USE, 1991 IN WARRINGTON, ENGLAND

| | Administrative Zone | | | | | | | |
| | Warrington County Borough | | Warrington Rural District | | Runcorn Rural District | | Total | |
Land Use	Acres	%	Acres	%	Acres	%	Acres	%
Residential [a]	1714	37.0	3,348	31.8	1734	50.3	6,796	36.5
Industry	866	18.7	1,071	10.1	152	4.4	2,089	11.2
Commerce	94	2.0	45	0.4	30	0.9	169	0.9
Education	202	4.4	230	2.2	80	2.3	512	2.8
Motorways	—	—	124	1.2	—	—	124	0.7
Noise buffer zones	—	—	52	0.5	—	—	52	0.4
Railways	241	5.2	108	1.0	27	0.8	376	2.0
Manchester ship canal	40	0.9	55	0.5	136	4.0	231	1.2
Open space	549	11.9	1,802	17.3	669	19.4	3,020	16.2
Utilities	301	6.9	193	1.8	7	0.2	501	2.7
Agriculture	—	—	959	9.1	530	15.4	1,489	8.0
Dumping grounds	272	5.9	940	8.9	—	—	1,212	6.5
Land banks	—	—	1,015	9.6	—	—	1,015	5.5
Other [b]	323	6.9	553	5.2	68	2.0	944	5.1
Total	4629	100.0	10,539	100.0	3444	100.0	18,612	100.0

[a] Gross acreage.

[b] Includes tidal water, other nontidal water and canals.

Note: Holding capacity of designated area, 1966 and 1991—The holding capacity of the designated area is defined as the area available for development at any one time. The estimated capacity for 1966 is 5,400–6,400 acres, including 1,500 acres within existing built-up areas that have been allocated for redevelopment. Taking into account the proposed programe of development, the estimated holding capacity of the designated area in 1991 is 1,000–1,200 acres.

Source: *Warrington New Town*

TABLE A57   LAND USE IN EMMELOORD, THE NETHERLANDS

| | Completed | | | Planned | | Total | | |
	number	area in hectares	as a percentage of the total	number	area in hectares	number	area in hectares	as a percentage of the total
Dwellings (incl. gardens and yards)	1,756	38.2	15.5	113	5.3	1,869	43.5	14.5
Special buildings [1]	51	15.9	6.4		13.8		29.7	9.9
Business premises [2]	166	23.4	9.5		31.0		54.4	18.1
Recreation facilities:								
Sports and Playing fields		32.6	13.2				32.6	11.0
Public parks, incl. roadside planting, etc.		6.9	2.8				6.9	2.3
Woods		71.2	29.0				71.2	23.8
Public roads (incl. roadsides and paths)		39.9	16.2				39.9	13.3
Water		11.2	4.5				11.2	3.7
Miscellaneous [3]		6.7	2.9		3.0		9.7	3.4
Total		246.0	100.0		53.1		299.1	100.0

[1] Schools, churches, hospital, catering establishments, sports buildings, offices, etc.

[2] Shops, garages, workshops and factories

[3] Cemetery, purification plant for sewage

Source: *Planning and Creation of an Environment.*

336

TABLE A58   PROPOSALS FOR THE TUY MEDIO (AREAS PER THOUSAND PERSONS IN HECTARES)

PLACE	Total Urban Area	Housing	Industry	Open-Space	Education	Residual	Comments
New City at Santa Teresa (1190)	16.7	5.5	3.4	4.6	0.4	2.8	Excludes Paraíso del Tuy – Open space includes steep slopes
New City at Ocumare (according to a preliminary study by MOP)	7.24	2.44	1.7	0.7*	0.41*	2.0*	Population 1,000,000
Charallave Development Plan (1990)	16.9	10.7	5.2	0.2	0.3	0.51	
Ocumare (1990)	22.52	14.66*	3.49	2.74	0.37	1.25	* Takes into account low density existing estates
Cúa (1990)	16.0	7.4	3.86	2.38 (*)	0.34	1.9	(*) Includes 21 has. of steeply sloped land at present unused.

Source: *Planning Proposals for Tuy Medio, Venezuela.*

337

TABLE A59 COMMERCIAL PREMISES (OFFICES AND SHOPS) IN 29 BRITISH NEW TOWNS TO DECEMBER 1974

	(a) Offices existing before designation (est.)[1]			(b) Offices completed from designation to 31 Dec. 1974			(c) Offices under construction at 31 Dec. 1974 (est.)		(d) Shops existing before designation (est.)[1]			(e) Shops completed from designation to 31 Dec. 1974		
	No. of offices	No. of employees	Size[2] (sq. ft)	No. of offices	No. of employees	Size[2] (sq. ft)	No. of units	Size[2] (sq. ft)	No. of shops	No. of employees	Size[2] (sq. ft)	No. of shops	No. of employees	Size[2] (sq. ft)
LONDON RING														
Basildon	—	n.k.	n.k.	50	n.k.	366,930	n.k.	301,450	294	n.k.	n.k.	378	n.k.	1,011,276
Bracknell	n.k.	n.k.	n.k.	80	7,000	1,007,927	—	—	85	n.k.	n.k.	197	2,900	578,134
Crawley	—	—	—	63	n.k.	457,645	—	—	177	640	156,873	294	4,060	451,590
Harlow	—	—	—	101	2,700	793,889	—	—	90	240	n.k.	340	3,600	696,581
Hatfield	16	n.k.	n.k.	17	n.k.	32,800	2	138,000	104	n.k.	n.k.	118	n.k.	275,928
Hemel Hempstead	n.k.	n.k.	n.k.	54	3,500	712,620	1 extn	10,000	369[3]	n.k.	n.k.	317	n.k.	576,577
Stevenage	n.k.	n.k.	n.k.	68	3,000	448,000	—	8,000	140	300	n.k.	367	3,300	832,000
Welwyn Gdn City	18	500	18,000	49	750	189,184	—	—	51	700	178,000	133	1,500	219,349
Total: London Ring	—	—	—	482	—	4,008,995	—	475,450	1,310	—	—	2,144	—	4,641,435
OTHERS IN ENGLAND														
Aycliffe	950	33,000	3,000,000	13	110	38,300	n.a.[4]	n.a.[4]	2,067	11,000	3,885,449	90	n.k.	142,100
Central Lancs.	n.k.	n.k.	—	n.a.[4]	n.a.[4]	n.a.[4]	—	—	85	n.k.	n.k.	n.a.[4]	n.a.[4]	n.a.[4]
Corby	n.k.	n.k.	n.k.	39	1,536	213,348	6	26,556	440	n.k.	400,000	255	1,647	405,751
Milton Keynes	n.k.	n.k.	180,000	10	n.a.	278,350	3+2 extns	180,394	1,959	5,697	2,081,345	34	n.k.	69,570
Northampton	491	5,400	965,000	36	6,220	1,026,800	n.k.+1 extn	77,970	800	4,500	1,680,000	112	1,730	552,400
Peterborough	n.k.	5,000[5]	756,250	n.k.	1,700	262,000	—	549,600	—	—	550	n.k.	700	263,000
Peterlee	—	—	—	26	330	67,916	1+1 extn	36,600	420	n.k.	306,790	130	900	199,500
Redditch	180	n.k.	163,727	34	n.k.	233,245	—	30,800	270	1,000	200,000	88	n.k.	246,750
Runcorn[6]	41	n.k.	n.k.	22	2,000	282,805[5]	—	1,300	117	n.k.	67,500	118	1,450	598,760
Skelmersdale	8	21	2,210	29	738	122,718	—	—	650	2,200	650,000	188	n.k.	370,149
Telford	124	1,600[5]	320,000	16	600	75,000	—	70,000	1,350	5,240	1,700,000	98	2,000	560,000
Warrington	n.k.	13,100	533,500	n.a.[4]	n.a.[4]	n.a.[4]	2[4]	165,905[4]	172	500	262,830	9[4]	n.k.[4]	25,660[4]
Washington	n.k.	n.k.	n.k.	47	1,445	215,228	2	573,387				83	939	245,450
Total: Others in England	—	—	—	—	—	2,815,705+	—	1,712,512+	8,331	—	11,234,464+	1,205+	—	3,679,090
WALES														
Cwmbran	n.k.	n.k.	n.k.	23	940	139,510	—	80,000	155	n.k.	n.k.	193	n.k.	497,049
Mid-Wales (Newtown)	28	230	80,000	2	35	10,000	—	50,000	109	384	170,000	3	12	3,000
Total: Wales	—	—	—	25	975	149,510	2	130,000	264	—	—	196	—	500,049
Total: England and Wales	—	—	—	—	—	6,974,210+	—	2,317,962+	9,905	—	—	3,545+	—	8,820,574+
SCOTLAND														
Cumbernauld	1	5	3,200	60	1,175	225,000	multiple	218,000	31	62	25,000	100	1,138	290,000
East Kilbride	9	50	9,470	82	2,800	426,210	n.k.	231,270	33	180	32,040	227	2,200	770,550
Glenrothes	—	—	—	58	905	140,888	1	72,000	3	n.k.	n.k.	81	844	156,178[4]
Irvine[7]	47[5]	1,600	100,000	44	600	60,500	n.k.	135,554	254	1,750	291,622	36	250	49,828
Livingston	—	—	—	24	680	71,676	1	125,000	8	35	6,000	46	340	55,430
Stonehouse	7	30	6,570	—	—	—	—	—	48	200	36,450	—	—	—
Total: Scotland	64	1,685	119,240	268	6,160	924,274	—	781,824	377	2,227	391,112	490	4,772	1,321,986
Total: Great Britain	—	—	—	—	—	7,898,484+	—	3,099,786+	10,282	—	—	4,035+	—	10,142,560+

n.k. – not known. n.a. – not available. [1] Offices and shops existing before designation have frequently been closed or demolished. [2] Gross floor area. [3] 158 since demolished. [4] Figures only available for development carried out by or on behalf of the corporation concerned. [5] Figures revised since 1973. [6] Runcorn estimates under 31.12.74 refer to 1.10.74. [7] Irvine estimates under 31.12.74 refer to 31.3.75.
Source: *Town and Country Planning*, 43, no. 2 (1975). Sources: development corporations and Commission for the New Towns

TABLE A60   COMMERCIAL AND CULTURAL DEVELOPMENT SUMMARY OF CEDAR-RIVERSIDE, MINNEAPOLIS, MINNESOTA: A NEW TOWN IN-TOWN

Development Stage	Years	Land (Acres)	COMMUNITY/COMMERCIAL CENTRUM					NEIGHBORHOOD
			Total Commercial Space (Sq. Ft.)	Retail Space (Sq. Ft.)	Office Space (Sq. Ft.)	Other Commercial(2) Space (Sq. Ft.)	Cultural Space (Sq. Ft.)	Commercial Space (Sq. Ft.)
1	1972-	—	—	—	—	—	—	10,000
	1973	—	—	—	—	—	—	10,000
2	1974-	1.5	214,024	60,024	—	154,000	—	10,000
	1975	1.5(1)	214,024	60,024	—	154,000	—	20,000
3	1976-	3.4	214,024	54,024	120,000	40,000	295,975	10,000
	1977	4.9	428,048	114,048	120,000	194,000	295,975	30,000
4	1978-	1.3	175,120	116,120	—	59,000	—	10,000
	1979	6.2	603,168	230,168	120,000	253,000	—	40,000
5	1980-	1.4	214,024	20,024	162,000	32,000	—	10,000
	1981	7.6	817,192	250,192	282,000	285,000	—	50,000
6	1982-	3.2	107,012	7,012	—	100,000	295,975	10,000
	1983	10.8	924,204	257,204	282,000	385,000	591,950	60,000
7	1984-	1.5	214,024	4,024	180,000	30,000	—	10,000
	1985	12.3	1,138,228	261,228	462,000	415,000	591,950	70,000
8	1986-	1.2	118,899	899	118,000	—	—	10,000
	1987	13.5	1,257,127	262,127	580,000	415,000	591,950	80,000
9	1988-	2.0	—	—	—	—	295,975	10,000
	1989	15.5	1,257,127	262,127	580,000	415,000	887,925	90,000
10	1990-	1.5	242,873	50,873	180,000	12,000	—	10,000
	1991	17.0	1,500,000	313,000	760,000	427,000	887,925	100,000
Totals		17.0	1,500,000	313,000	760,000	427,000	887,925	100,000

(1) Cumulative figures.

(2) "Other Commercial" includes health, hotel, day care and educational.

Source: *Project Agreement Between The United States of America and Cedar-Riverside Land Company.*

TABLE A61   COMMERCIAL DEVELOPMENT IN PARK FOREST SOUTH, ILLINOIS DEVELOPMENT
COMPANY

Construction Year	Retail Space Square Footage		Office Space Square Footage	
	Annual	Cumulative	Annual	Cumulative
1970	10,000	10,000	—	—
71	50,000	60,000	50,000	50,000
72	50,000	110,000	—	50,000
73	50,000	160,000	70,000	120,000
74	50,000	210,000	—	120,000
75	100,000	310,000	40,000	160,000
76	100,000	410,000	40,000	200,000
77	100,000	510,000	40,000	240,000
78	100,000	610,000	40,000	280,000
79	100,000	710,000	40,000	320,000
80	100,000	810,000	40,000	360,000
81	140,000	950,000	60,000	420,000
82	150,000	1,100,000	70,000	490,000
83	150,000	1,250,000	70,000	560,000
84	150,000	1,400,000	70,000	630,000
85	100,000	1,500,000	70,000	700,000
86	100,000	1,600,000	50,000	750,000
87	100,000	1,700,000	50,000	800,000
88	100,000	1,800,000	50,000	850,000
89	50,000	1,850,000	50,000	900,000
90	50,000	1,900,000	50,000	950,000

Source: *Project Agreement Between The United States of America and Park Forest South Development Company.*

TABLE A62   LAND DEVELOPMENT SUMMARY OF CEDAR-RIVERSIDE, MINNEAPOLIS, MINNESOTA

Development Stage	Years	Total Land Acres	NEIGHBORHOOD Residential Land Acres	NEIGHBORHOOD Residential Dwelling Units	NEIGHBORHOOD Commercial Space Sq. Ft.	COMMUNITY/COMMERCIAL CENTRUM Land Acres	COMMUNITY/COMMERCIAL CENTRUM Total Commercial Space Sq. Ft.	Commercial/Cultural Retail Space Sq. Ft.	Commercial/Cultural Office Space Sq. Ft.	Other Commercial(2) Space Sq. Ft.	Cultural Space Sq. Ft.
1	1972-	8.5	8.5	1,299	10,000	—	—	—	—	—	—
	1973	8.5(1)	8.5	1,299	10,000	—	—	—	—	—	—
2	1974-	10.0	8.5	1,299	10,000	1.5	214,024	60,024	—	154,000	—
	1975	18.5	17.0	2,598	20,000	1.5	214,024	60,024	—	154,000	—
3	1976-	11.9	8.5	1,288	10,000	3.4	214,024	54,024	120,000	40,000	295,975
	1977	30.4	25.5	3,886	30,000	4.9	428,048	114,048	120,000	194,000	295,975
4	1978-	9.8	8.5	1,288	10,000	1.3	175,120	116,120	—	59,000	—
	1979	40.2	34.0	5,174	40,000	6.2	603,168	230,168	120,000	253,000	295,975
5	1980-	9.9	8.5	1,288	10,000	1.4	214,024	20,024	162,000	32,000	—
	1981	50.1	42.5	6,462	50,000	7.6	817,192	250,192	282,000	285,000	295,975
6	1982-	11.3	8.1	1,207	10,000	3.2	107,012	7,012	—	100,000	295,975
	1983	61.4	50.6	7,669	60,000	10.8	924,204	257,204	282,000	385,000	591,950
7	1984-	9.6	8.1	1,208	10,000	1.5	214,024	4,024	180,000	30,000	—
	1985	71.0	58.7	8,877	70,000	12.3	1,138,228	261,228	462,000	415,000	591,950
8	1986-	9.3	8.1	1,208	10,000	1.2	118,899	899	118,000	—	—
	1987	80.3	66.8	10,085	80,000	13.5	1,257,127	262,127	580,000	415,000	591,950
9	1988-	10.1	8.1	1,208	10,000	2.0	—	—	—	—	295,975
	1989	90.4	74.9	11,293	90,000	15.5	1,257,127	262,127	580,000	415,000	887,925
10	1990-	9.6	8.1	1,207	10,000	1.5	242,873	50,873	180,000	12,000	295,975
	1991	100.0	83.0	12,500	100,000	17.0	1,500,000	313,000	760,000	427,000	887,925
Totals	………	100.0	83.0	12,500	100,000	17.0	1,500,000	313,000	760,000	427,000	887,925

(1) Cumulative figures.

(2) "Other Commercial" includes health, hotel, day care, and educational.

Source: *Project Agreement Between The United States of America and Cedar-Riverside Land Company*

TABLE A63   HOUSING IN 29 BRITISH NEW TOWNS TO DECEMBER 1974

	(f) Under construction at 31 December 1974 (est.)			(g) To be completed 1975 (est.)			(h) Rented dwellings at 31 December 1974			(i) Owner-occupied dwellings at 31 December 1974	
	DCs & NTC	LA	Others	DCs & NTC	LA	Others	DCs & NTC	LA	Others	DCs & NTC	Others
LONDON RING											
Basildon	1,164	200	180	1,066	243	191	14,271[5]	3,167[4]	1,113[5]	5,480	3,160
Bracknell	507	—	131	399	—	131	7,950	400	n.k.	1,931	n.k.
Crawley	76	596	197	76	300	218	9,864	2,637	n.k.	3,494	n.k.[6]
Harlow	527	57	104	506	100	141	16,824	1,551	150	4,909	1,710
Hatfield	—	176	162	—	176	164	3,296	2,631	32	1,012	1,974
Hemel Hempstead	29	367	200	29	367	200	10,471	3,701	n.k.	2,232	n.k.[7]
Stevenage	400	—	120	300	30	100	13,001	1,377	620	5,977	2,004
Welwyn Gdn City	58	43	40	58	43	40	5,803	3,286	135	2,120	1,876
Total: London Ring	2,761	1,439	1,134	2,434	1,259	1,185	81,480	18,750	—	27,155	—
OTHERS IN ENGLAND											
Aycliffe	266	—	76	236	—	201	5,192	45	n.k.	1,370	n.k.
Central Lancs.	—	205	886	250	220	1,000	100	19,220	11,850	—	56,379
Corby	300	150	215	300	200	130	6,706	3,563	—	1,480	4,108[8]
Milton Keynes	3,009	50	1,240	1,709	100	1,070	2,841[4]	7,685	—	182	10,982
Northampton	1,490	530	480	1,110	380	540	2,452	12,170	6,000	152	32,630
Peterborough	2,533	450	1,600	1,200	440	650	1,905	9,350	—	285	22,343
Peterlee	206	—	14	86	12	18	6,576	229	—	473	435
Redditch	779	109	326	665	248	541	3,580	3,464	n.k.	118	n.k.[11]
Runcorn[12]	1,443	182	187	930	n.k.	n.k.	5,666	763	28	1,164	n.k.
Skelmersdale	1,228	43	125	703	70	175	6,871	1,250	186	159	2,238
Telford	1,289	n.k.	n.k.	684	275	580	5,851	10,846	3,000	—	11,653
Warrington	506	350	330	507	350	200	347	13,294	7,030	—	26,762
Washington	1,781	24	294	1,253	126	407	4,391	4,359	616	370	3,535
Total: Others in England	14,830	2,093	5,773	9,633	2,421+	5,512+	52,478	86,193	—	5,753	—
WALES											
Cwmbran	354	86	100	332	64	80	7,404	2,578	—	1,010	3,737
Mid-Wales (Newtown)	278	—	20	272	—	50	400	714	—	—	1,241
Total: Wales	632	86	120	604	64	130	7,804	3,292	—	1,010	4,978
Total: England & Wales	18,223	3,618	7,027	12,671	3,744+	6,827+	141,762	108,235	—	33,918	—
SCOTLAND											
Cumbernauld	600	—	150	660	28	150	9,626	671	—	1,350	624
East Kilbride	1,050	—	220	1,100	—	275	17,353	459	90	2,590	979
Glenrothes	436	—	155	547	—	221	7,695	365	254	920	253
Irvine[13]	1,840	200	837	1,068	140	533	1,819	10,482	383	—	2,975
Livingston	1,510	—	15	1,049	—	225	5,934	262	21	194	213
Stonehouse	—	41	64	—	41	79	—	1,474	120	—	925
Total: Scotland	5,436	241	1,441	4,424	209	1,483	42,427	13,713	868	5,054	5,969
Total: Great Britain	23,659	3,859	8,468	17,095	3,953+	8,310+	184,189	121,948	—	38,972	—

n.k. not known.

[1] The totals in section (e) will not necessarily equal those in sections (a) and (d) combined or those in sections (h) and (i) combined. This is due to demolitions and acquisitions since designation and to totals in section (e) sometimes being returned as at dates prior to 31.12.74 whereas totals in sections (d), (h) and (i) are estimated at 31.12.74. Dates given if specified.

[2] Details of demolitions given if specified.

[3] Totals in section (e) as at 30.10.74.

[4] Allows for dwellings acquired by the L.A.

[5] Allows for dwellings acquired by the Corporation.

[6] 72 are owner-occupied L.A. built dwellings. Rest not known.

[7] 210 are owner-occupied L.A. built dwellings. Rest not known.

[8] 2,198 of these belonged to Stewarts and Lloyds and were purchased by the Corporation in 1962.

[9] Figures revised since 1973.

[10] 1,978 on Corporation land.

[11] 173 are owner-occupied L.A. built dwellings. Rest not known.

[12] Runcorn estimates under 31.12.74 refer to 1.10.74.

[13] Irvine estimates under 31.12.74 refer to 31.3.75.

[14] 271 have been demolished.

Sources: development corporations and Commission for the New Towns.

	(a) Existing before designation (est.)		(b) Completed at 31 Dec. 1973 (from date of designation)			(c) Completed during 1974 (est.)			(d) Total completed at 31 Dec. 1974 (est.) from date of designation			(e) Total now existing (est.) allowing for demolition since date of designation[1][2]		
	LA	Others	DCs & NTC	LA	Others	DCs & NTC	LA	Others	DCs & NTC	LA	Others	DCs & NTC	LA	Others
LONDON RING														
Basildon	340	7,840	19,255	3,036	1,596	590	95	170	19,845	3,131	1,766	19,684[1][3]	3,120[1][3]	4,008[1][3]
Bracknell	38	1,433	9,537	360	3,031	344	2	155	9,881	362	3,186	9,768[1][3]	400	4,619
Crawley	134	2,028	13,098	2,359	4,530	84	216	134	13,182	2,575	4,664	13,358[5]	2,709	6,516[5]
Harlow	362	678	21,272	1,084	1,094	461	105	88	21,733	1,189	1,182	21,733	1,551	1,860
Hatfield	716	1,648	4,293	1,908	343	—	132	30	4,293	2,040	373	4,308	2,631	2,006
Hemel Hempstead	570	4,325	12,215	3,061	3,374	21	280	210	12,236	3,341	3,584	12,703[5]	3,911	7,909[5]
Stevenage	340	1,600	18,751	997	1,349	227	40	110	18,978	1,037	1,459	18,978	1,377	2,624
Welwyn Gdn City	1,823	3,018	6,348	1,463	558	—	—	10	6,348	1,463	568	7,923	3,286	2,011
Total: London Ring	4,323	22,570	104,769	14,268	15,875	1,727	870	907	106,496	15,138	16,782	108,455	18,985	31,553
OTHERS IN ENGLAND														
Aycliffe	—	—	6,464	45	193	98	—	60	6,562	45	253	6,534[1]	45	234[1]
Central Lancs.	18,800	64,200	—	357	3,549	100	63	480	100	420	4,029	100	19,220	68,229
Corby	1,465	2,705	7,946	2,091	1,259	240	7	144	8,186	2,098	1,403	8,186	3,563	4,108
Milton Keynes	4,844	8,509	1,253	2,492	2,165	1,350	349	728	2,603	2,841	2,893	3,023[5]	7,685	10,982[5]
Northampton	10,255	33,976	1,771	1,650	4,320	833	450	500	2,604	2,100	4,820	2,604	12,350	38,450
Peterborough	7,518[9]	19,893[9]	1,289	1,610[9]	1,755[9]	901	483	434	2,190	2,093	2,189	2,190	9,611	22,082
Peterlee	3,051	30	6,919	74	288	130	155	117	7,049	229	405	7,049	229	435
Redditch	2,650	7,849	3,140	426	1,888	558	160	534	3,698	586	2,422[10]	3,698	3,637	9,290
Runcorn[12]	820	7,150	4,360	680	910	1,306	83	254	5,666	763	1,164	5,666	3,413	8,314
Skelmersdale	9,870	2,380	6,807	410	676	223	20	66	7,030	430	742	7,030	1,250	2,424
Telford	11,060	11,814[9]	4,972	1,250	2,348	653	155	288	5,625	1,405	2,636	5,851[5]	10,846[5]	14,653[5]
Warrington	3,304	32,542	44	1,905	3,381	303	329	292	347	2,234	3,673	347	13,294	33,792
Washington	—	2,670	3,411	927	1,751	1,146	128	292	4,557	1,055	2,043	4,761[5]	4,359	4,151[5]
Total: Others in England	73,637	193,718	48,376	13,917	24,483	7,841	2,382	4,189	56,217	16,299	28,672	57,039	89,502	217,144
WALES														
Cwmbran	530	2,677	8,147	2,036	1,162	114	12	46	8,261	2,048	1,208	8,414[5]	2,578	3,732[5]
Mid-Wales (Newtown)	694	1,103	260	14	168	118	6	26	378	20	194	422[5]	714	1,241[5]
Total: Wales	1,224	3,780	8,407	2,050	1,330	232	18	72	8,639	2,068	1,402	8,836	3,292	4,973
Total: England and Wales	79,184	220,068	161,552	30,235	41,688	9,800	3,270	5,168	171,352	33,505	46,856	174,330	111,779	253,670
SCOTLAND														
Cumbernauld	534[9]	249[9]	10,176	137	284	800	—	91	10,976	137	375	10,976	671	624
East Kilbride	201	343	19,423	258	526	520	—	200	19,943	258	726	19,943	459	1,069
Glenrothes	68	268	8,545	297	177	70	—	62	8,615	297	239	8,615	365	507
Irvine[13]	9,229[9]	2,478[9]	990	1,200	787	796	120	356	1,786	1,320	1,143	1,819	10,482	3,358
Livingston	262	384[14]	5,694	—	109	434	—	12	6,128	—	121	6,128	262	234
Stonehouse	1,470	910	—	—	50	—	4	85	—	4	135	—	1,474	1,045
Total: Scotland	11,764	4,632	44,828	1,892	1,933	2,620	124	806	47,448	2,016	2,739	47,481	13,713	6,837
Total: Great Britain	90,948	224,700	206,380	32,127	43,621	12,420	3,394	5,974	218,800	35,521	49,595	221,811	125,492	260,507

Source: *Town and Country Planning 43*, no. 2 (1975).

TABLE A64 LOW- AND MODERATE-INCOME HOUSING IN NEW COMMUNITIES (DECEMBER 1972)

Project	Low Income		Moderate Income		Combined Low and Moderate		Middle Income		Total Dwelling Units
Maumelle	378	(7%)[a]	842	(16%)[b]	1,220	(23%)[c]	1,214	(23%)	5,293
Park Forest South[d]	—[e]	—	—	—	5,800	(16%)[f]	—	—	37,200
Cedar-Riverside[d]	1,754	(14%)[e]	3,785	(30%)[f]	5,539	(44%)	4,450	(34%)	12,500
Riverton[d]	799[e]	(10%)	2,405	(30%)	3,204	(40%)	—	—	8,010
St. Charles	10%	of rents[a]	—	—	4,946[g]	(20%)	14,838[h]	(60%)	24,730
Flower Mound[d]	—	—	—	—	3,667[i]	(20%)	4,333[i]	(24%)	18,326
Jonathan	—	—	—	—	3,874[k]	(25%)	3,876[l]	(25%)	15,405
Woodlands[d]	6,072	(13%)	6,866	(14%)	12,938	(27%)	—	—	47,375
Gananda	1,245	(7.2%)	2,490	—	3,735	(21%)	—	—	17,200
San Antonio Ranch	2,948	(10%)	7,366	(20%)	10,314	(35%)	—	—	29,476
Harbison[m]	—	—	—	8	2,135	(35%)n	—	—	6,100
Soul City[m]	—	—	—	—	4,980	(37%)	—	—	13,326
Lysander[m]	1,500	(30%)	1,000	(25%)	2,500	(50%)	1,250	(25%)	5,000
Welfare Island[m]	1,500	—	1,250	—	2,750	—	1,000	—	5,000
Total	16,196		26,004		67,502		30,961		245,441

Source: HUD, December 1972.

[a] Less than $5,000.

[b] Figures for Maumelle cover a 12-year period only to 1984. Total d.u.'s are 14,390 per entire development period with percent of low- and moderate-income housing remaining constant. From $5,000 to $7,000 considered moderate income within this project.

[c] $7000 to $10,000.

[d] Subject to renegotiation periodically to ensure their responsiveness to metropolitan income profile.

[e] Rent supplement or public housing level. In Park Forest South, it will constitute 20% of all 236 housing in project.

[f] Includes exception limits not to exceed 15% of subsidized housing in Cedar-Riverside and 40% of subsidized housing in Park Forest South.

[g] Less than $7500.

[h] $7500 to $10,000.

[i] Above 235–236 limits, but below $11,000.

[j] 8% yearly below $7,000.

[k] Below $7800.

[l] $7800 to $10,500.

[m] Project agreement not yet signed.

[n] Estimated time of offer of commitment. Final figure subject to change.

Souce: *The Contemporary New Communities Movement in the United States*.

TABLE A65 DWELLING UNITS FOR LOW- AND MODERATE-INCOME HOUSEHOLDS IN FLOWER MOUND, TEXAS

| Project Year | Annual Dwelling Units | Cumulative Dwelling Units | Low & Moderate Income | |
			Annual D. U.'s	Cumulative D. U.'s
1972	—	—	—	—
1973	336	—	40	40
1974	411	747	84	124
1975	446	1,193	104	228
1976	550	1,743	123	351
1977	722	2,465	143*	494*
1978	840	3,305	168*	662*
1979	1,033	4,338	207*	869*
1980	1,157	5,495	232*	1,101*
1981	1,223	6,718	245*	1,346*
1982	1,427	8,145	285*	1,631*
1983	1,572	9,717	315*	1,946*
1984	1,683	11,400	336*	2,282*
1985	1,625	13,025	325*	2,607*
1986	1,707	14,732	342*	2,949*
1987	1,778	16,510	345*	3,294*
1988	1,816	18,326	373*	3,667*
	18,326			

*The number and proportion of low and moderate income units is subject to change in accordance with Section B-2 of the Development Plan.
**Low income households are those with incomes of $7,000 and below. Moderate income households are those with incomes above $7,000 but within the Income Limits set forth on pages 11 and 12 of this Development Plan.

Source: *Project Agreement Between The United States of America and Flower Mound New Town, Limited.*

TABLE A66   RESIDENTIAL DEVELOPMENT BY NEW COMMUNITY ENTERPRISES IN PARK FOREST SOUTH, ILLINOIS

Year	Totals	Single Family	Low and Moderate Income	Multi-Family	By Others	
					Single Family	Multi-Family
1971	900	150	100	650	—	—
72	1,300	150	200	650	100	200
	2,200					
73	1,500	200	200	600	200	300
	3,700					
74	1,500	200	200	600	200	300
	5,200					
75	1,700	250	250	600	250	350
	6,900					
76	1,700	250	* 250	600	250	350
	8,600					
77	1,900	300	* 300	600	300	400
	10,500					
78	1,900	300	* 300	600	300	400
	12,400					
79	2,000	300	* 300	600	300	500
	14,400					
80	2,000	300	* 300	600	300	500
	16,400					
81	2,000	300	* 300	600	300	500
	18,400					
82	2,000	300	* 300	600	300	500
	20,400					
83	2,050	300	* 350	600	300	500
	22,450					
84	2,050	300	* 350	600	300	500
	24,500					
85	2,050	300	* 350	600	300	500
	26,550					
86	2,150	300	* 350	600	300	600
	28,700					
87	2,150	300	* 350	600	300	600
	30,850					
88	2,150	300	* 350	600	300	600
	33,000					
89	2,250	300	* 350	600	300	700
	35,250					
90	1,950	200	* 350	400	300	700
Totals:	37,200	5,300	*5,800	11,900	5,200	9,000
% to Total	100.00	14.25	* 15.59	31.99	13.98	24.19

* The number and proportion of Low and Moderate Income units is subject to change at the option of the Secretary in accordance with Section B2 of the Development Plan.

Source: *Project Agreement Between The United States of America and Park Forest South Development Company.*

TABLE A67   BUILDUP OF CORPORATION-RENTED DWELLINGS AVAILABLE FOR ALLOCATION IN HARLOW, ENGLAND

Period	New Dwellings	Annual Average of New Dwellings	Cumulative Total of Rented Dwellings	Re-Lets	Annual Average Number of Re-Lets	Dwellings Available for Allocation	Annual Average of Dwellings Available for Allocation
1975-79	2,730	546	19,150	4,505	900	7,235	1,450
1980-84	3,700	740	22,850	5,300	1060	9,000	1,800
1985-89	2,500	500	25,350	6,105	1220	8,605	1,720
Total 1975-89	8,930	595	25,350	15,910	1060	24,840	1,655
1990	nil	-	25,350	1,260	1260	1,260	1,260

Source: *Harlow Expansion 1974.*

TABLE A68   OVERALL RECREATION SYSTEM FOR FLOWER MOUND NEW TOWN, TEXAS

Typology	Activity	Facility	Location	Level of Development	Approximate Acreage	Sponsor
Contemplative	Paths, benches vistas, sculpture gardens, and nature study areas for strolling, talking, sitting, reading, thinking	Environmental corridor and related network of pathways	Throughout all of FMNT	Low	850	Town/MUD
		Residential cluster parks	Adjacent to single family detached dwelling units	Medium	10	Homeowner association or town/MUD
			Adjacent to single family attached and multifamily dwelling units	Medium	30	Developer of dwelling units
	Rooms with tables, chairs, books, sculpture, art, exhibits	Libraries	Town and community centers	High	1	Town or school
		Museum gallery	Town center	High	1	Town, college, or private
Structured play	Trails for hiking, bicycling, horseback riding	Portions of environmental corridor	Throughout all of FMNT	Low	(See above)	Town/MUD
	Areas for camping, trail biking	Lakeshore parks	Grapevine reservoir	Low	(Outside of FMNT)	Army corps of engineers
	Microspaces with piles of dirt, pieces of wood, sand, grass, trees, for random play	Fortuitous open space, odd shaped lots, pathway intersections	Near residences	Low	N.A.	Private, homeowner association, Apartment developen, or Town/MUD
	Small play areas for preschool children	Tot lots	Adjacent to single family attached and multifamily dwelling units	High	10	Developer of dwelling units
	Areas for fishing, boating	Man-made lakes in environmental corridor	In residential areas	Low	(Included above)	Town/MUD
		Lakeshore park	Twin coves area	Medium	50 plus existing corps park	Town
	Rooms with facilities for games, individual crafts, hobbies, indoor sports, excerise, and indoor swimming pools	Bowling alleys	Town and community centers	High	1	Private
		Recreation centers	Town and community centers or schools	High	3	Town or school
			Adjacent to single-family, attached, and multifamily dwelling units	High	5	Developer of dwelling units

Source: *Flower Mound New Town.*

Typology	Activity	Facility	Location	Level of Develop-ment	Approxi-mate Acreage	Sponsor
Structured play	Areas with grass, trees, paved playing surfaces, unlighted playing fields, swimming pools, playground equipment and barbeque and picnic facilities for family outings, informal sports events, random play	Residential cluster playgrounds	Adjacent to elementary schools	High	20	Town or school
			At intersections of pathway network	High	60	Town/MUD
		District playfields	Adjacent to elementary schools	High	45	Town or school
	Lighted playing fields, hard surface courts, and competition swimming pools for organized individual and team sports	District playfields	Adjacent to middle and high schools	High	45	Town or school
		Tennis centers	Town and community centers	High	20	Town/MUD and private
		Golf course	Near community centers	Medium	160	Town/MUD and private
		Olympic pools	Middle and high schools	High	3	Town/MUD or school
	Areas for day camps, competitive sports, arts and crafts	District park	Adjacent to town center	Medium	150	Town
	Indoor facilities for lessons, arts and crafts programs, club meetings, competitive indoor sports	Arts and craft workshops	Town and community centers	High	3	Nonprofit groups
		Recreation centers	Town and community centers or schools	High	(See above)	Town or school
Entertainment	Seating, refreshment, and parking facilities for spectator sports	Stadium	High school or college	High	5	School or college
		Arena	High school or college	High	2	School or college
	Facilities and areas for movies, plays, concerts, legitimate theater, light entertainment, rallies, exhibits, fiestas	Outdoor amphitheater	First community center	High	2	Town/MUD or school.
		Movie theaters	Town and community centers	High	2	Private
		Legitimate theater	Community	High	1	College
		Part of district park	Adjacent to town center	Medium	(See above)	Town
		CATV studio	Town center	High	2	Private
		Concert hall/ convention center	Waterfront	High	4	Town or private
	Facilities for eating, drinking, dancing.	Restaurants and night clubs	Town and first community center, waterfront, second golf course	High	3	Private
		Teen clubs	Community centers	High	1	Church or nonprofit

TABLE A69   OPEN SPACE IN PARK FOREST SOUTH, ILLINOIS

Type of Open Space	Basis of Computation	Acreage	Percentage of Total Site	Acres Per Thousand Population
1. Major open space of town scale. Environmental zones between major components of new town. Woods, ravines, flood plains, lakes, re-forestation areas and cemetery.	100%	892	10.92%	7.51
2. Open space related to neighborhoods, planned unit areas, or districts. Small parks, bicycle paths, playgrounds, recreational areas, pools, and public squares. Major buffer zones and rights-of-way within residential areas.	Single Family Detached at 7.5% of area.	216	2.65	1.82
	Multi-Family Mixed type at 20% of area.	397	4.86	3.34
	100%	225	2.76	1.89
3. Schools and University.	50% of school area as sport field, recreational areas, parks, etc.	134	1.64	1.13
	50% of University land as open space, reforested areas, and sports and recreational areas.	377	4.62	3.17
4. Institutions and Churches.	33% of land as parks, public open spaces.	6	0.07	0.05
		2,247	27.52%	18.91

NOTE: Excluding industrial acreage of 1,011, total % of total site would be 31.42%.

Source: *Project Agreement Between The United States of America and Park Forest South Development Company.*

BIBLIOGRAPHY

Abend, Norman A. "Transportation Inputs in New Town Planning." In *Regional New Towns: Alternatives in Urban Growth for Southeast Michigan.* Detroit: Metropolitan Fund, 1970, pp. 56–63.

Abercrombie, Sir Patrick. *Greater London Plan, 1944.* New York: McGraw-Hill Book Co., 1945; and London: His Majesty's Stationery Office, 1945, 220 pp.

Adamson, J. and J. Fowlie. "New Cities." Mimeo. Ottawa: Central Mortgage and Housing Corporation, 1968.

Aitken, James M. "New and Expanding Towns in Northern Ireland." *Town and Country Planning,* **34,** no. 1 (1966): 11–14.

Akin, Joy. *The Feasibility and Actuality of Modern New Towns for the Poor in the U.S.* Exchange Bibliography No. 167. Monticello, Illinois: Council of Planning Librarians, 1970, 12 pp.

Akzin, Benjamin and Yehizkel Dror. *Israel High Pressure Planning.* National Planning Series. Vol. 5. Syracuse, New York: Syracuse University Press, 1966, 90 pp.

Alanen, Arnold E. "New Towns—2: Tapiola, Finland's Contribution." *Northwest Architect,* **31,** no. 4 (1967): 30–35.

Alayton, William L. "New Cities: Policies and Legislation." In *Planning 1967.* Chicago: American Society of Planning Officials, 1967, pp. 171–73.

Alberta. Department of Municipal Affairs. *Feasibility Study on New Town Status for Hamlet of Smith, Alberta.* Edmonton: Department of Municipal Affairs, 1968.

Alberta. Legislature. "An Act to Provide for the Planning and Development of New Towns." In *Statutes of Alberta, 1969.* Edmonton: Queen's Printer of Alberta, 1969, pp. 1–7.

Alcott, James. "Minnesota Experimental City: A National Proving Ground." *Journal of the American Institute of Architects,* **56,** no. 5 (1971): 37–39.

Aldous, Tony. "Runcorn Report." *Architectural Design,* **42** (1972): 372–78.

Alexander, Donald B. "New Towns: A Proposal for the Appalachia Region." *Planning and Civic Comment,* (1962): 29–30+.

Allen, Irving Lewis. "New Towns and Suburban Ideology: Selling the American Dream." *Sociological Symposium,* no. 12 (1974): 17–40.

————. *The Sociology of New Towns and New Cities: A Classified Bibliography.* Exchange Bibliography No. 518. Monticello, Illinois: Council of Planning Librarians, 1973, 19 pp.

Allen, James B. *The Company Town in the American West.* Norman, Oklahoma: University of Oklahoma Press, 1966, 205 pp.

Allen, Judith A. *The Feasibility of Planning Integration in New Communities.* Chapel Hill, North Carolina: Center for Urban and Regional Studies, University of North Carolina, 1971, 38 pp.

Allen, Muriel I., ed. *New Communities: Challenge for Today.* AIP Background Paper No. 2. Washington, D.C.: American Institute of Planners, 1968, 39 pp.

Alonso, William. "The Economics of Urban Size." *Papers of the Regional Science Association,* **26** (1967): 67–83.

————. "The Mirage of New Towns." *Public Interest,* **19** (1970): 3–17.

————. "The Question of City Size and National Policy." Institute of Urban and Regional Development Working Paper No. 125. Berkeley, California: University of California, Berkeley, January 1970.

————. "What are New Towns For?" *Urban Studies,* **7,** no. 1 (1970): 37–55.

Alonso, William and Chester McGuire. *New Communities in the Bay Area.* San Francisco: Association of Bay Area Governments, 1971, 41 pp.

Alonso, William and Elliott Medrich. "Spontaneous Growth Centers in Twentieth Century American Urbanization." Institute of Urban and Regional Development Working Paper No. 113. Berkeley, California: University of California, Berkeley, January 1970, 28 pp.

Altman, Elizabeth A. and Betsey R. Rosenbaum. "Principles of Planning and Zionist Ideology: The Israeli Development Town." In *Regional Policy: Readings in Theory and Applications,* edited by John Friedmann and William Alonso. Cambridge, Massachusetts: M.I.T. Press, 1975.

American Institute of Architects. "First Report of the National Policy Task Force, Second Edition." Special Issue. *American Institute of Architects Newsletter,* May 1972, pp. 1–18.

American Institute of Planners. "National Planning Policy of the American Institute of Planners." *American Institute of Planners' Newsletter,* **9,** no. 3–4 (1974): 8–28.

————. *Proceedings of the 1964 Annual Conference.* Washington, D.C.: American Institute of Planners, 1965, 302 pp.

American Public Health Association Committee on the Hygiene of Housing. *Planning the Neighborhood.* 2nd ed. Chicago: Public Administration Service, 1960, 94 pp.

Amiran, David H.K. "Eilat: Seaside Town in the Desert of Israel." In *Coastal Deserts: Their Natural and Human Environments,* edited by David H.K. Amiran and Andrew W. Wilson. Tucson: University of Arizona Press, 1973, pp. 171–75.

Amiran, David H.K. and A. Shachar. "Development Towns in Israel." Stencil. Jerusalem: The Hebrew University, 1969, 41 pp.

Andonopoulou-Bogdanou, Myrto and Christopher Ripman. "The City of the Future—Ecumenopolis: Assumptions, Scope, Alternatives." *Ekistics,* **35,** no. 207 (February 1973): 63–77.

Angenbot, L.H.J. and W.J. Bruyon. "The Garden City Idea in the

Netherlands Since 1930." *Stedebouw & Volkshuisvesting* (1963): 108–15.

Anthony, Harry Antoniades. "Ecumenopolis: Solution or Nightmare?" *Journal of the American Institute of Architects,* **52,** no. 4 (1969): 64–68.

———. "Le Corbusier: His Ideas for Cities." *Journal of the American Institute of Planners,* **32,** no. 5 (1966): 279–88.

Antoine, Serge. "A Real Scale Experiment: Le Vaudreuil (France)." *Ekistics,* **30,** no. 179 (October 1970): 286.

Anton, Thomas J. "Politics and Planning in a Swedish Suburb." · *Journal of the American Institute of Planners,* **35,** no. 4 (1969): 253–63.

Antoniou, James. "Planning for Pedestrians." *Traffic Quarterly,* **25,** no. 1 (1971): 55–71.

Apgar, Mahlon IV. "New Business from New Towns." *Harvard Business Review,* **49** (1971): 90–109.

Archer, Hilary M. "A Classification and Definition of Single-enterprise Communities." Master's thesis, University of Manitoba, 1969.

Archer, R.W. "Financing the Development of Canberra as a New City, 1958 to 1971: The Use of the Public Land and Leasehold System." Mimeo. Canberra: Metropolitan Research Trust, 1972, 19 pp.

———. "New Towns for Australia: A Progress Report on the Metrotown Australia Project." Paper presented to the 39th Congress of Australian and New Zealand Association for the Advancement of Science, Melbourne, Australia, January 6, 1967.

———. "From New Towns to Metrotowns and Regional Cities." Parts I and II. *American Journal of Economics and Sociology,* **28** (1969): 257–69 and 385–98.

———. "Private Enterprise New Towns in Britain: Experience, Potential and Policy." *Journal of the Royal Australian Planning Institute,* **11,** no. 4 (1973): 117–21.

Arian, Edward. "Arts Programs for New Towns: A Prescription." *Sociological Symposium,* no. 12 (1974): 99–110.

Aristotle. *Politics and Athenian Constitution.* Translated by John Warrington. London: J.M. Dent and Sons, 1959.

Arizona Department of Economic Planning and Development. *Arizona New Town Development Concepts.* Springfield, Virginia: National Technical Information Services, May 1971, 86 pp.

Armytage, W.H.G. *Heavens Below: Utopian Experiments in Britain 1560–1960.* London: Routledge and Kegan Paul; and Toronto: University of Toronto Press, 1961, 458 pp.

Ascher, Charles S. *Administration of New Towns in the Americas.* New York: United Nations Educational, Scientific, and Cultural Organization, 1960, 38 pp.

Ash, Joan. "New Town in Galilee: Carmel." *Official Architecture and Planning,* **32** (1969): 1193–95.

Ash, Maurice A. "New Towns and the Visual Arts." *Town and Country Planning,* **26,** no. 165 (1958): 8–12.

Ashley, Thomas J. "Planning a New City: Irvine, California." *Town and Country Planning,* **40,** no. 2 (1972): 114–19.

Ashworth, Graham. "Environmental Recovery at Skelmersdale." *Town Planning Review,* **41,** no. 3 (1970): 263–92.

Association for Planning and Regional Reconstruction. *Factors Influencing the Layout of New Towns.* London: Association for Planning and Regional Reconstruction, 1946, 58 pp.

Atkinson, G.A. "Radburn Layouts in Britain: A User Study." *Official Architecture and Planning,* **29,** no. 3 (1966): 380–88.

Audain, Michael. "Citizen Participation in National Urban Policy." Special Issue. *Plan,* **12,** no. 1 (1972): 74–87.

The Austin-Smith/Lord Partnership. *Warrington New Town: Consultants' Proposals for the Draft Master Plan.* London: Warrington New Town Development Corporation, 1969, 471 pp.

Australia. Cities Commission. *Report to the Australian Government: A Recommended New Cities Programme for the Period 1973–1978.* Canberra: Australian Government Publishing Services, 1973, 147 pp.

———. *The Regional City of Albury-Wodonga.* The First Twelve Months January 25, 1973–January 22, 1974. Canberra: Cities Commission, 1974, 20 pp.

———. *Second Annual Report.* July 1, 1973–June 30, 1974. Canberra: Australian Government Publishing Service, 1974, 40 pp.

———. *Summary of Initial Investigations of Urban Centres.* Holsworthy-Campbelltown, New South Wales: an extract from main volume. Canberra: Australian Government Publishing Services, 1973, 18 pp.

———. *Summary of Initial Investigations of Urban Centres.* Monarto, South Australia: an extract from main volume. Canberra: Australian Government Publishing Service, 1973, pp. 138–51.

Australia. Department of Urban and Regional Development. *Urban and Regional Development 1973–1974: Second Annual Report.* Canberra: Australian Government Publishing Service, 1974, 57 pp.

Australia. National Capital Development Commission. *Seventeenth Annual Report.* 1 July 1973 to 30 June 1974. Canberra: Australian Government Publishing Service, 1974, 68 pp.

Australian Institute of Urban Studies. *First Report of the Task Force on New Cities for Australia: Efficient and Humane Alternatives to Overconcentrated Growth.* Canberra: Australian Institute of Urban Studies, 1972, 92 pp.

———. *Seminar on New Cities for Australia: Efficient and Humane Alternatives to Overconcentrated Growth.* Canberra: Australian Institute of Urban Studies, 1972, 49 pp.

Avery, T. Eugene. *Interpretation of Aerial Photographs.* Minneapolis: Burges Publishing Company, 1969.

Ayres, Robert U. et al. "Evaluation of New Urban Transportation Systems." *Highway Research Record,* no. 367 (1971).

Backstrom, Sven and Leif Remius. "Farsta Shopping Centre, Sweden." *Architect and Builder News,* **220** (1961): 855–64.

Bacon, Edmund N. "7 Principles for an Urban Land Policy." *Urban Land,* **30,** no. 4 (1971): 3–8.

Bailey, James, ed. *New Towns in America: The Design and Development Process.* New York: John Wiley and Sons, 1973, 165 pp.

Bain, Henry. *The Reston Express Bus: A Case History of Citizen Action to Improve Urban Transportation.* Washington, D.C.: Washington Center for Metropolitan Studies, 1969, 68 pp.

Ballymena Area Plan. Belfast: Her Majesty's Stationery Office, 1966, 76 pp.

Baltimore Regional Planning Council. *Metrotowns for the Baltimore Region: A Pattern Emerges.* Supporting Data for Planning Report No. 2. Baltimore: Maryland State Planning Department, 1962, 37 pp.

Banovetz, James M., ed. *Managing the Modern City,* Washington, D.C.: International City Management Association, 1971.

Banwell, D.F. "The Economics of Building New Towns." *Town and Country Planning,* **40,** no. 1 (1972): 18–20.

Baranov, N.V. "Building New Towns." In *Planning of Metropolitan Areas and New Towns.* New York: United Nations, 1967, pp. 209–15.

Barber, G. "Growth Determinants in the Central Canada Urban System." In *Urban Systems Development in Central Canada,* L.S. Bourne and R.D. MacKinnan, eds. Toronto: University of Toronto Press, 1972, pp. 147–62.

Barnett, Jonathan. "How are 'Planned Communities' Planned?" *Architectural Record,* **154,** no. 7 (1973): 120–29.

Bateman, Linley H., ed. *History of Harlow.* Harlow, England: Harlow Development Corporation, 1969, 168 pp.

Batty, Michael. "The Impact of a New Town: An Application of the Garinlowry Model." *Journal of the Town Planning Institute,* **55,** no. 10 (1969): 428–35.

Beckman, Norman. "Toward Development of a National Urban Growth Policy: Legislative Review 1971." *Journal of the American Institute of Planners,* **38,** no. 4 (1972): 231–49.

Beckman, Norman and Susan Harding. "Legislative Review: National Urban Growth Policy: 1972 Congressional and Executive Action." *Journal of the American Institute of Planners,* **39,** no. 3 (1973): 229–43.

———. "National Growth Policy 1972." *Urban Land,* **32,** no. 10 (1973): 6–16.

Beckwith, Burnham Putman. *The Next 500 Years: Scientific Predictions of Major Social Trends.* New York: Exposition Press, 1967, xvi + 341 pp.

"Belagievo-Bogorodskogyie." *Ekistics,* **20,** no. 120 (November 1965): 283–87.

Belconnen Town Centre. Braddon, Australia: National Capital Development Commission, 1974, 24 pp.

"Belconnen Town Center, Canberra, Australia." *Architectural Record,* **147,** no. 2 (1970): 132–35.

Bender, Ian. "Land Issues in the Process of New Town Building." Master's thesis, University of Waterloo, School of Urban and Regional Planning, 1970, 183 pp.

Benepe, Barry. "Pedestrian in the City." *Traffic Quarterly,* **19,** no. 1 (1965).

Beresford, Maurice. *New Towns of the Middle Ages: Town Planning in England, Wales, and Gascony.* New York: Praeger, 1967, 670 pp., London: Lutterworth Press, 1967, xx + 670 pp.

———. "The Six New Towns of the Bishops of Winchester, 1200–55." *Medieval Archaeology,* **3** (1959): 187–215.

Berger, P. and Thomas Luckmann. *The Social Construction of Reality.* Garden City, New York: Doubleday and Company, 1967, x + 219 pp.

Berkman, Herman G. "The New Town and Urban Change Form." *Land Economics,* **48,** no. 2 (1972): 93–103.

Berler, Alexander. *New Towns in Israel.* Jerusalem: Israel Universities Press, 1970, 353 pp.

———. *Urban-Rural Relations in Israel: Social and Economic Aspects.* Publications on Problems of Regional Development, Vol. 8. Translated by Hannah Schmorak. Rehovot, Israel: Rehovot Settlement Study Center, 1970, 180 pp.

———. "Urbanization Processes in Israel." *Ekistics,* **17,** no. 78 (January 1964): 26–28.

Berler, Alexander and S. Shaked. *Patterns and Forms of New Urban Settlements.* Amsterdam: United Nations, Economic Commission for Europe, Committee of Housing, 1966.

———. *25 Development Towns in Israel.* Tel Aviv: Ministry of Housing, 1966, 45 pp.

Berry, Brian J. L. and Jack Meltzer, eds. *Goals for Urban America.* Englewood Cliffs, New Jersey: Prentice-Hall, 1967, 152 pp.

Best, Robin H. *Land for New Towns: A Study of Land-Use Densities and Agricultural Displacement.* London: Town and Country Planning Association, 1964, 59 pp.

———. "New Towns in the London Region." In *Greater London,* J.T. Coppock and Hugh C. Prince, eds. London: Faber and Faber, 1964, pp. 313–32.

"The Best Size for Towns: Latest Russian Theory." *Town and Country Planning,* **29,** no. 7 (1961): 282.

Bishop, David. "New Towns and the Church." *Architect and Builder News,* **2** (1969): 63–67.

Black, Gilbert J. " 'New-Town' Style Campus Design Gets Major Test." *College Management,* **6** (1971): 12–14.

Blake, Pat. "Britain's New Towns: Facts and Figures." *Town and Country Planning,* **43,** no. 2 (1975): 81–117.

Blake, Peter. "Paolo Soleri's Visionary City." *Architectural Forum,* **114** (1961): 111–18.

Bland, K.W. "Private Enterprise Housing for New Towns." *Town and Country Planning,* **36,** no. 1–2 (1968): 101–05.

Blenkinshop, Arthur. "The Future of New Towns." *Town and Country Planning,* **38,** no. 1 (1970): 64–65.

Blijstra, Reider. *Town-Planning in The Netherlands Since 1900.* Amsterdam: P.N. Van Kampen and Zoon, N.V., 1965, 74 pp. + plates.

Blowers, Andrew. "Planning Residential Areas." In *Planning and the City.* Milton Keynes, England: The Open University Press, 1973.

Bluestein, Leo I. "Innovative Communication Systems for New Communities." In *Strategy for New Communities Development in the USA,* Gideon Golany, ed. Stroudsburg, Pennsylvania: Dowden, Hutchinson and Ross, 1975.

Blumberg, Donald F. et al. "Computer-Based Socio-Economic Evaluation of New Community Proposals." Jenkintown, Pennsylvania: Decision Sciences Corporation (no date).

Board of the Zuiderzee Works. *A Structure Plan for the Southern Ijsselmeerpolders.* The Hague: Board of the Zuiderzee Works, 1965, 32 pp.

Bodnar, Donald J. *The Enigma of a New Towns Definition: Exercises in Begging the Question.* Chapel Hill, North Carolina: Center for Urban and Regional Studies, University of North Carolina, 1970, 18 pp.

Bodnar, Donald J. and Mark Wassenich. *Implementation: A Critical Limit on the Planner's Role in Planned Community Development.* Chapel Hill, North Carolina: Center for Urban and Regional Studies, University of North Carolina, 1970, 35 pp.

Boley, Robert E. *Industrial Districts: Principles in Practice.* Washington, D.C.: Urban Land Institute, 1970.

———. *Industrial Districts Restudied.* Washington, D.C.: Urban Land Institute, 1969.

Bolwell, L., B. Clarke and D. Stoppard. "Social Class in a New Town: A Comment." *Urban Studies,* **6** (1969): 93–96.

Boothroyd, Peter and Frank Marlyn. "National Urban Policy: A Phrase in Search of a Meaning." *Plan,* **12,** no. 1 (1972): 4–12.

Bor, Walter. "The Changing Concept of New Town Development." *Journal of the Housing Center Trust,* **20** (1971): 72–74.

———. "Designing for New and Expanding Communities in Britain." *Housing Review,* **21,** no. 4 (1972): 125–33.

———. *The Making of Cities.* London: Leonard Hill, 1972.

———. "Milton Keynes: The First Stage of the Planning Process." *Journal of the Town Planning Institute* **54,** no. 5 (1969): 203–08.

———. "Milton Keynes: The Hardware." *RIBA Journal,* **77,** no. 7 (1970): 311–14.

———. "New Towns Within Cities." *Housing Review,* **10,** no. 506 (1961): 81–84.

Bourne, L.S. and R.D. MacKinnon, eds. *Urban Systems Development in Central Canada: Selected Papers.* University of Toronto Department of Geography Research Publications. Toronto: University of Toronto Press, 1972, 243 pp.

Brach, William L. "The Role of Government and the Development of New Communities." In *Land Acquisition and Assembly.* New York: Practicing Law Institute, 1969.

Bramalea Master Plan. Toronto: Canadian Mitchell Associates, 1970, 23 pp.

Branch, M.C. *Selected Bibliography on New Town Planning and Development.* Exchange Bibliography No. 363–364. Monticello, Illinois: Council of Planning Librarians, 1973, 88 pp.

Brandenburg, John G. *The Industrialization of Housing: Implications for New Town Development.* Chapel Hill, North Carolina: Center for Urban and Regional Studies, University of North Carolina, 1970, 48 pp.

———. *New Towns Research Seminar Reports.* Series I: New Town Development Process. Series II: Social Concerns of New Town Development. Series III: Emerging Partnerships in New Community Development. Chapel Hill, North Carolina: Center for Urban and Regional Studies, University of North Carolina, Fall 1969, Spring 1970, Fall 1970, 73 + 132 + 63 pp.

"Brave New Towns That Aged Awkwardly: Radburn, N.J. and Greenbelt, Md." *Business Week,* no. 2157 (January 9, 1971): 22, 24.

Breckenfeld, Gurney. *Columbia and the New Cities.* New York: Ives Washburg, 1971, 332 pp.

Brief History of Reston, Virginia. Reston, Virginia: Gulf Reston, 1971, 30 pp.

"The Briefing Book 1974." Background materials on the Columbia Association and the Village Associations of Columbia. Stencil. Columbia, Maryland: Columbia Association, 1974, 36 pp.

British Information Services. *The New Towns of Britain.* Dorchester, England: Henry Ling, 1974, 30 pp.

"British New Towns." *Town and Country Planning,* **38,** no. 1 (1970): entire issue.

Broady, M. *Planning and People: Essays on the Social Context of Planning.* London: Bedford Square Press, National Council for Social Service, 1968.

Brooks, Richard Oliver. "Interpretation: Social Planning in Columbia." *Journal of the American Institute of Planners,* **37,** no. 6 (1971): 373–79.

———. *New Towns and Communal Values: A Case Study of Columbia, Maryland.* New York: Praeger, 1974, 240 pp.

Brutzkus, Eliezer. "Centralized Versus Decentralized Patterns of Urbanization." *Ekistics,* **36,** no. 214 (September 1973): 189–92.

———. *Physical Planning in Israel: Problems and Achievements.* Jerusalem: E. Brutzkus, 1964, 87 pp.

———. "Planning of Spatial Distribution of Population in Israel." *Ekistics,* **21,** no. 126 (May 1966): 350–55.

———. *Regional Policy in Israel.* Jerusalem: Ministry of Interior, Town and Country Planning Department, 1970, 78 pp.

Bryan, Jack. "New Town/In Town; New Town/Out of Town: Twin Cities of Minneapolis-St. Paul Have Produced a New Set of Twins." *Journal of Housing,* **29,** no. 3 (1972): 119–31.

Buck, Hadley. "Central Areas of New Towns: Planning Successful Commercial Centres." *Town and Country Planning,* **38,** no. 1 (1970): 20–22.

Buckenham, J.R. "A 'New Town' in Virginia: Reston as a Solution to Suburban Sprawl." *County Councils' Gazette,* **58** (1965): 299–310.

Buckthorp, L.W. et al. "Cumbernauld New Town: Some Aspects of Engineering Development." *Journal of the Institute of Municipal Engineers,* **88** (1961): 413–40.

Buder, Stanley. "Ebenezer Howard: The Genesis of a Town Planning Movement." *Journal of the American Institute of Planners,* **35,** no. 6 (1969): 390–98.

"Building the American City: Report from the National Commission on Urban Problems." *Urban Land,* **28,** no. 3 (1969): 1–16.

Building Research Institute. "New Town: Philosophy and Reality." *Building Research,* **3,** no. 1 (1966): 9–34.

Building Systems International and Westinghouse Corporation. *Fort Lincoln New Town, Washington, D.C.: Report of the BSI/Westinghouse Joint Venture.* Washington, D.C.: Marcou, O'Leary and Associates, Subsidiary of Westinghouse Urban Systems Planning and Design Coordinating, 1972, 188 pp.

Bull, D. Ann. "New Town and Town Expansion Schemes." Part 1: An Assessment of Recent Government Planning Reports. Part II: Urban Form and Structure. *Town Planning Review,* **38,** nos. 2–3 (1967): 103–14, 165–86.

———. "New Town and Town Expansion Schemes: Part III, 1, 2, and 3." *Ekistics,* **25,** no. 150 (May 1968): 295–305.

Bunker, Raymond Charles. "Travel in Stevenage." *Town Planning Review,* **38,** no. 4 (1967): 215–32.

Burby, Raymond J., III. "Environmental Amenities and New Community Governance: Results of a Nationwide Study." Paper presented at the 5th Annual Conference, Environmental Design Research Association, Milwaukee, Wisconsin, May 30–June 1, 1974. Chapel Hill, North Carolina: Center for Urban and Regional Studies, University of North Carolina, 1974, 23 pp.

Burby, Raymond J., III, Shirley F. Weiss and Robert Zehner. "Planning for Population Target Groups in New Community Development." Paper prepared for presentation at Confer-In 74, American Institute of Planners Annual Conference, Denver, Colorado, October 27–30, 1974. Chapel Hill, North Carolina: Center for Urban and Regional Studies, University of North Carolina, 1974.

Burchell, Robert W., ed. *Frontiers of Planned Unit Development: A Synthesis of Expert Opinion.* New Brunswick, New Jersey: Center for Urban Policy Research, Rutgers University, 1973, 329 pp.

Burchell, Robert W. with James W. Hughes. *Planned Unit Development: New Communities American Style.* New Brunswick, New Jersey: Center for Urban Policy Research, Rutgers University, 1972, 254 pp.

Burke, Gerald L. "Reclamation of the Zuiderzee." In *Greenhart Metropolis: Planning the Western Netherlands.* London: Macmillan, 1966, pp. 19–46.

Burnett, F.T. "Open Space in New Towns." *Journal of the Town Planning Institute,* **55,** no. 6 (1969): 256–62.

Burns, Leland S. and Leo H. Klaassen. "The Econometrics of Building a New Town." *Review of Economics and Statistics,* **45,** no. 4 (1963): 368–73.

Burns, Wilfred. *New Towns for Old: The Technique of Urban Renewal.* London: Leonard Hill, 1963, 226 pp.

Byron, Carole H. *Basildon: Shopping, Work for Women, Leisure.* Basildon, England: Basildon Development Corporation, 1967, 118 pp.

Cage, E.E.H. "Northern Ireland: Craigavon New Towns." *Town and Country Planning,* **38,** no. 1 (1970): 34–35.

California Institute of Technology. *The Next Ninety Years: Proceedings of a Conference Held at the California Institute of Technology on 7–8 March 1967.* Pasadena, California: California Institute of Technology, 1967, 186 pp.

Camblin, Gilbert. "New Towns and National Parks in Northern Ireland." *Chartered Surveyor,* **98** (1965): 97–101.

Cameron, Kenneth D. "National Urban Growth Strategy in Canada." Master's thesis, University of British Columbia, School of Community and Regional Planning, 1970.

Campbell, Carlos C. "New Towns: Metropolitan Decision-Making and Social Implications." In *Planning 1970.* Chicago: American Society of Planning Officials, 1970, pp. 199–203.

———. "Toward a New Sense of Community: Social Aspects of Industrial Location and New Communities." In *Planning 1971.* Chicago: American Society of Planning Officials, 1971, pp. 440–47.

Campeau, R. *Kanata: A Greenbelt Town.* Ottawa: Queen's Printer of Canada, 1971.

Canadian Provincial Planning Officials. "Planning and Development of New Towns." In *1956 Conference Proceedings: Part 1.* Edmonton: Towns and Rural Planning Branch, Department of Municipal Affairs, 1956, pp. 80–97.

Cannaday, William. *New Schools for New Towns.* New York: Rice University School of Architecture, 1971, 60 pp.

Canty, Donald, ed. *The New City.* New York: Frederick A. Praeger, 1969, 180 pp.

———. "Urbanization: A Proposal for New Cities— and for a New Approach to Land Development." *City,* **3,** no. 3 (1969): 29–36.

———. "What Is This Thing Called Urban Growth Policy?" *City,* **4,** no. 5 (1970): 31–32.

Carpenter, Robert D. "Arizona's New Communities and Large Scale Land Developments." Stencil. Submitted for Presentation at Confer-In '72, American Institute of Planners' Conference, Boston, Massachusetts, 1972, 24 pp.

Carruth, Eleanore. "The Big Move to New Towns." *Fortune,* **84,** no. 3 (1971): 95–96, 147–51.

Carson, John. "A National Urban Growth Policy." *Urban Land,* **31,** no. 2 (1972): 3–10.

Cassidy, Robert. "A New Town with Something New." *Planning,* **40,** no. 9 (1974): 21–25.

Cassie, W. Fisher. "The Satellite Towns: A Study of the Problems Involved in Re-centralised Development." *Journal of Town Planning Institute,* **29,** no. 2 (1943): 53–62.

Caveri, Claudio. "New Cooperative Community: San Miguel, Argentina." *Progressive Architecture,* **47,** no. 5 (1966): 182–83.

Cedar-Riverside Associates. *Cedar-Riverside New Community: Narrative Description.* Minneapolis: Cedar-Riverside Associates, 1972, 25 + pp.

"Central Areas of New Towns: The Design of Present and Future Centres." *Town and Country Planning,* **38,** no. 1 (1970): 15–19.

Central Mortgage and Housing Corporation. *New Towns: Bibliography.* Ottawa: Central Mortage and Housing Corporation, 1969, 36 pp.

Cesio, Godofredo A. *Population Distribution As An Approach to the Future Pattern of Development in the West of the Land and the Borinage-Ruhr Areas.* Comprehensive Planning Course 1965. The Hague: Institute of Social Studies, 1965, 12 pp.

Champion, Anthony. "Recent Trends in New Town Densities." *Town and Country Planning,* **38,** no. 5 (1970): 252–55.

"Chandigarh." *Marg* (December 1961): entire issue.

Chave, S.P.W. "Mental Health in Harlow New Town." *Journal of Psychomatic Research,* **10** (1966): 38–44.

Cheng, Samson. "A New Town of Manitouwadge, Ontario." Master's thesis, University of Manitoba, 1962, 109 pp.

Cheesman, Robert with Walton Lindsay and Martha de Porzecanski. "New Towns: The Data Bank, Its Construction and Organisations." Centre for Land Use and Built Form Studies Working Paper 63. University of Cambridge, 1972.

DeChiara, Joseph and Lee Koppelman. *Planning Design Criteria.* New York: Van Nostrand Reinhold Company, 1969.

Chowdhury, U. Evlie. "Le Corbusier in Chandigarh: Creator and Generator." *Architectural Design,* **35,** no. 4 (1965): 504–13.

Christensen, Boake. "Land Use Control for the New Community." *Harvard Journal of Legislation,* **6** (1969): 496–547.

"Churches for New Towns: Scope for New Structural Techniques." *Building,* **213,** no. 50 (1967): 83–84.

City Building: Experience, Trends and New Directions. Columbia, Maryland: The American City Corporation, 1971, 48 pp.

"The City of the Future." *Ekistics,* **20,** no. 114 (July 1965): 4–52.

Ciudad Guayana Transportation Study Technical Report. Guayana, Venezuela: Corporación Venezolana De Guayana and Alan M. Voorhhes and Associates, 1970, 126 pp.

Clapp, James A. *The New Town Concept: Private Trends and Public Response.* Exchange Bibliography No. 122. Monticello, Illinois: Council of Planning Librarians, 1970, 32 pp.

———. *New Towns and Urban Policy: Planning Metropolitan Growth.* Cambridge, Massachusetts: M.I.T. Press; New York: The Dunellen Company, 1971, 342 pp.

Clark, Colin. "The Economic Functions of City in Relation to its Size." *Econometrica*, **13,** no. 2 (1945): 97–113.

Clark, James A. "The New Towns Concept and Metropolitan Expansion: An Investigation of the Feasibility of an American Program." Ph.D. dissertation, Syracuse University, 1968, 485 pp.

Clarke, E., Director Planning Services. *Forest Hills: Master Plan for a New Community 1974.* Dartmouth, Nova Scotia: Nova Scotia Housing Commission, 1974.

Clawson, Marion and Peter Hall. *Planning and Urban Growth: An Anglo-American Comparison.* Baltimore: Johns Hopkins University Press, 1973, 300 pp.

Clegg, E.T. "A Regional Planning Analysis of a Single Enterprise Community of Settlements." Master's thesis, University of British Columbia, School of Community and Regional Planning, 1958.

Clinchy, Evans. "Dollars and Educational Sense. Some Financial and Educational Options for the Provision of Educational Services in New Towns." Educational Facilities Laboratories and the National Center for Educational Technology Working Paper No. 4. New York, January 1974, 134 pp.

————. "New Towns, New Schools? A Memorandum on The State of the Art of Educational Planning for New Communities in the United States." Educational Facilities Laboratories and the Office of New Communities Development Working Paper No. 1. New York, November 1972, 138 pp.

Coghlan, John F. "Physical Recreation in New Towns." *Royal Society of Health Journal,* **88** (1968): 149–54.

Cohen, E. *The City in Zionist Ideology.* Jerusalem: Institute of Urban and Regional Studies, 1970.

————. "Development Towns: The Social Dynamics of 'Planted' Urban Communities in Israel." In *Integration and Development in Israel,* S.N. Eisenstadt, ed. New York: Praeger, 1970.

Coleman, S.D. *Mental Health and Social Adjustment in a New Town.* An Exploratory Study in East Kilbride. Glasgow: Department of Economic and Social Research, Glasgow University, 1965, 80 pp.

————. "Some Social Problems of New Towns." *Mental Health,* **23** (1965): 61–64.

Colman, William G. "Some Issues and Questions Regarding New Communities." Mimeo. American Society of Planning Officials National Planning Conference, Cincinnati, Ohio, 1969, 6 pp.

The Columbia Association. *Annual Report 1971.* Columbia, Maryland: The Columbia Association, 1971, 25 pp.

Columbia Commission. *Impact of New Town Zoning on Howard County, Maryland.* Report to County Executive and County Council. Ellicott City, Maryland: The Columbia Commission, 1971, 54 pp.

Columbia Conference Committee. *First Annual Columbia Conference on Community Governance, 24–25 March 1972.* Columbia, Maryland: The Columbia Conference Committee on Community Governance, 35 pp.

Columbia Roles Study Committee. *Citizen Participation in Columbia: A Study of Roles, Relationships, and Processes in New Town Governance.* Columbia, Maryland: Columbia Conference Committee, 1972.

Combustion Engineering Association. "Energy for the New Towns." *Journal of Fuel and Heat Technology,* **14** (1967): 9–11, 13–15.

Commonwealth of Pennsylvania. Department of Agriculture. *Final Report with Recommendations to Governor Raymond P. Shafer from the Governor's Committee for the Preservation of Agricultural Land.* Harrisburg: Commonwealth of Pennsylvania, 1969, 31 pp.

Commonwealth of Pennsylvania. State Planning Board. "Pennsylvania New Community Site Survey." Mimeo. Harrisburg: Pennsylvania State Planning Board, 1971, 29 pp.

————. "Phase II: Application for Federal Planning Assistance Funds for a New Town Development Feasibility Study." Stencil. Harrisburg: Commonwealth of Pennsylvania, State Planning Board, 1969, 25 pp.

"Community Facilities in New and Expanded Towns." *Town and Country Planning,* **34,** no. 7 (1966): 348–90.

Connell, Kathleen M. *Regional New Towns and Intergovernmental Relations: Four Case Studies.* Detroit: Metropolitan Fund, 1972, 79 pp.

Cooke, Joan. "Social Balance in New Towns." Master's thesis, University of Illinois, 1967, 104 pp.

Cooley, Charles Horton. *Social Organization: A Study of the Larger Mind.* New York: Charles Scribner's Sons, 1909.

Copcutt, Geoffrey. "Car Parking in Cumbernauld." *Architects' Journal,* **132,** no. 3426 (1960): 862–67.

————. "Cumbernauld New Town Central Area." *Architectural Design,* **33** (1963): 210–25.

Le Corbusier. *The City of Tomorrow.* London: The Architectural Press, 1929.

"Corporations as New Master Builders of Cities." *Progressive Architecture,* **50,** no. 5 (1969): 150–61.

Costain in the New Town of Orleans. Ottawa: Costain Estates Limited, 1971, 29 pp.

Cott, L., B. Hakim and T. Nelson. *The Impact of Technological Growth and Social Change on Physical Design and Planning. Illustrative Application: Lysander New Community.* School of Architecture Report No. 14. Halifax: Nova Scotia Technical College, 1972, 25 pp. + illustrations.

Craigavon Development Corporation. *A New City in Northern Ireland: First Report on the Plan.* London: Her Majesty's Stationery Office, 1964, xviii + 126 pp.

Crane, David A. *Developing New Communities: Application of Technological Innovations.* Washington, D.C.: U.S. Government Printing Office, 1968, 222 pp.

————. *Technologies Study: The Application of Technological Innovation in the Development of a New Community.* Washington, D.C.: National Capital Planning Commission and District of Columbia Government, 1968, 246 pp.

Crane, David A. and Associates. *Lysander New Community: Final Planning Report.* Philadelphia: David A. Crane and Associates, 1971, 97 pp.

Crawley. London: Commission for the New Towns, 1975, 16 pp.

"Creating New Communities: A Symposium on Process and Product." *Journal of the American Institute of Planners,* **33,** no. 5 (1967): 370–409.

"Creation of Communities: Community Facilities in New and Expanded Towns." *Town and Country Planning,* **34,** no. 7 (1966): 384–90.

Creese, Walter L. *Search for Environment: The Garden City, Before and After.* New Haven: Yale University Press, 1966, 360 pp.

de La Crois, Horst. *Military Considerations in City Planning: Fortifications.* New York: George Braziller, 1972.

Cullingworth, J.B. "The Greater London Plan." In *Housing Needs and Planning Policy.* London: Routledge and Kegan Paul, 1960, pp. 72–114.

———. "New Towns: Aims and Achievements: A Review." In *National Urban Development Conference Held on 25–26 March 1971.* London: Centre for Advanced Land Use Studies, College of Estate Management, pp. 1–10.

Cullingworth, J.B. and V.A. Karn. *The Ownership and Management of Housing in the New Towns.* London: Her Majesty's Stationary. Office, 1968, 199 pp.

"Cumbernauld New Town Centre Phase I." *Architects' Journal,* **147,** no. 5 (1968): 293–310.

Curry, David. "Irvine: The Case for a New Kind of Planning." *Cry California,* **6,** no. 1 (1970/71): 18–40.

Dahir, James. *Greendale Comes of Age: The Story of Wisconsin's Best Known Planned Community as it Enters Its Twenty-first Year.* Greendale, Wisconsin: Milwaukee Community Development Corporation, 1958, 32 pp.

Darwent, David. "Externality, Agglomeration Economies and City Size." Institute of Urban and Regional Development Working Paper No. 109. University of California, Berkeley, 1970, 47 pp.

Dascalopolos, Th. "New Aluminum Settlement: Aspra Spitia, Greece." *Ekistics,* **16,** no. 94 (September 1963): 170–83.

Dash, Jacob et al. *National Planning for the Redistribution of Population and the Establishment of New Towns in Israel.* Jerusalem: Ministry of Interior, Planning Department, 1964, 38 pp.

Dash, Jacob and Elisha Efrat. *The Israel Physical Master Plan.* Jerusalem: Ministry of the Interior, Planning Department, 1964, 91 pp.

Davidovitch, V.G. "Satellite Cities and Towns of the U.S.S.R." *Soviet Geography,* **3,** no. 3 (1962): 3–35.

———. *Town Planning in Industrial Districts.* Translated by A. Skotnicki. Jerusalem: Israel Program for Scientific Translations, 1968, 314 pp.

Davis, Jeanne M. "European New Communities." *Building Research,* **6,** no. 3 (1969): 8–15.

———. *Review Draft: Survey of New Towns, Planned Communities, and Other Large Developments in the United States.* Washington, D.C.: Economic Research Service, U.S. Department of Agriculture, 1963.

Deboer, John C. and Alexander Greendale, eds. *Are New Towns for Lower and Middle Income Americans, Too?* New York: Praeger, 1974, 96 pp.

Decision Sciences Corporation. "Basic New Community Simulation System (NUCOMS): Preliminary System Description." Jenkintown, Pennsylvania: Decision Sciences Corporation (no date).

———. "New Community Policy Analysis. Task 1: Impact of HUD Guarantee on New Community Developments." Jenkintown, Pennsylvania: Decision Sciences Corporation, 1974, 33 pp.

———. "New Community Fiscal Impact Evaluation System." Jenkintown, Pennsylvania: Decision Sciences Corporation (no date).

———. "New Communities: Systems for Planning and Evaluation. Executive Summary." Jenkintown, Pennsylvania: Decision Sciences Corporation, 1972, 20 pp.

———. *New Communities: Survey of State of the Art.* PB-206-883. Springfield, Virginia: National Technical Information Service, November 1971, 175 pp.

———. *New Communities: Systems for Planning and Evaluation.* PB-206-882. Springfield, Virginia: National Technical Information Service, November 1971, 375 pp.

Degelman, L.O. *Introductory Manual for Synagraphic Computer Mapping,* version 5, P.S.U. modification 3. University Park, Pennsylvania: Department of Architectural Engineering and the Graduate Interdisciplinary Program in Regional Planning, The Pennsylvania State University, 1969.

Delaware. State Planning Council and State Planning Office. *New Towns: Proceedings of a Symposium Held in Newark, Delaware.* Dover, Delaware: Delaware State Planning Office, 1969, 48 pp.

"Democracy in the New Towns: The Limits of Private Government." *University of Chicago Law Review* (1969): 379–412.

Dempsey, John T. "Prospects for New Towns in Michigan." In *Regional New Towns: Alternatives for Urban Growth.* Detroit: Metropolitan Fund, 1970, pp. 117–21.

Dennis, N. "The Popularity of the Neighbourhood Idea." *Sociological Review,* **6,** no. 2 (1958): 199–206.

Derbyshire, Andrew. "New Town Plans: A Critical Review." *RIBA Journal,* **74,** no. 10 (1967): 430–40.

Derbyshire, Edward. "Notes on the Social Structure of a Canadian Pioneer Town." *Sociological Review,* **8,** no. 1 (1960): 63–75.

Derthick, Martha. *New Towns In-Town: Why a Federal Program Failed.* Washington, D.C.: The Urban Institute, 1972, 103 pp.

Desai, P.B. and Ashish Bose. "Economic Considerations in the Planning and Development of New Towns." In *Planning of Metropolitan Areas and New Towns.* New York: United Nations, 1967, pp. 216–19.

Development of Albury Wodonga. Albury, New South Wales: The Albury Wodonga Development Corporation, 1974, 80 pp.

Dewey, Richard E., ed. *Report of the Howard County Human Services Community Action Seminar.* Howard County, Maryland: Howard County Association of Community Services and Howard Community College, 1972, 67 pp +.

Dickey, John W. and Alan W. Steiss. "Model for Optimizing the Use of Housing in New Towns." *Ekistics,* **28,** no. 164 (July 1969): 45–53.

Dienstfrey, Ted. "A Note on the Economics of Community Building." *Journal of the American Institute of Planners,* **33,** no. 2 (1967): 120–23.

Dietze, S.H. *The Physical Development of Remote Resource Towns.* Ottawa: Central Mortgage and Housing Corporation, 1968.

Dinerstein, Robert A. "Problems in the Development of Park Forest, Illinois." In *Planning 1964.* Chicago: American Society of Planning Officials, 1964, pp. 133–40.

"Domed New City Planned for Minnesota." *Engineering News-Record,* **179,** no. 23 (1967): 21.

Don Mills Developments. "Erin Mills New Town: A Proposal." Toronto: Don Mills Developments, 1969.

Dorney, Roberts. "The Ecologist in Action: How Teamwork Can Produce Ecoplan for 7000 Acre Canadian New Town Site." *Landscape Architecture,* **60,** no. 3 (1970): 196–99.

Downie, Leonard, Jr. *The New Towns of Paris: Reorganizing Suburbs.* Paris: The Alicia Patterson Fund, 1972, 27 pp.

———. *Paris Under Construction.* Paris: The Alicia Patterson Fund, 1972, 18 pp.

Downs, Anthony. "Alternative Forms of Future Urban Growth in the United States." *Journal of the American Institute of Planners,* **36,** no. 1 (1970): 3–11.

———. "Creating the Institutional Framework for Encouraging New Cities." In *Regional New Towns: Alternative in Urban Growth for Southeast Michigan.* Detroit: Metropolitan Fund, 1970, pp. 44–51.

Doxiadis Associates. "Industrial Development in Islamabad." *Ekistics,* **13,** no. 78 (1962): 349–60.

———. "Islamabad: The Scale of the City and Its Central Area." *Ekistics,* **14,** no. 83 (October 1962): 148–60.

———. "The Spirit of Islamabad." *Ekistics,* **12,** no. 72 (November 1961): 315–35.

Doxiadis, Constantinos A. "Cities of the Future." In *Science and Technology in the World of the Future,* Arthur B. Bronwell, ed. New York: John Wiley and Sons, 1970, pp. 61–94.

———. "A City for Human Development: Eighteen Hypotheses." *Ekistics,* **35,** no. 209 (1973): 177–87.

———. "The City (II): Ecumenopolis, World-City of Tomorrow." *The Impact of Science on Society,* **19,** no. 2 (1969): 179–93.

———. "The Coming World-City: Ecumenopolis." In *Cities of Destiny,* Arnold Toynbee, ed. New York: McGraw-Hill Book Company, 1967, pp. 345–63; London: Thames and Hudson, 1967, pp. 336–58.

———. "The Coming Era of Ecumenopolis." *Saturday Review,* **11** (March 18, 1967): 11–14.

———. "Concept of New Cities." *Ekistics,* **36,** no. 212 (July 1973): 4–7.

———. "Ecumenopolis: Tomorrow's City." In *Britannica Book of the Year 1968.* Chicago: Encyclopedia Britannica, 1968, pp. 16–38.

———. "Ecumenopolis: Toward a Universal City." *Ekistics,* **13,** no. 75 (January 1962): 3–18.

———. "How to Build the City of the Future." In *Man in the City of the Future,* Richard Eells and Walton Clarence, eds. New York: MacMillan Company, An Arkville Press Book, 1968, pp. 163–88.

———. "Islamabad: The Creation of New Capital." *Town Planning Review,* **36,** no. 1 (1965): 1–38.

Doxiadis, C.A. and J.G. Papaioannou. "The Concept of Ecumenopolis." *Ekistics,* **33,** no. 199 (June 1972): 428–32.

Dror, Yeheskel. *National Planning in the Netherlands.* Syracuse, New York: Syracuse University Press, 1963, 118 pp.

Dubos, Rene. "The Biological Basis of Urban Design." *Ekistics,* **35,** no. 209 (1973): 199–204.

Duff, Alan Colguhoun. *Britain's New Towns: An Experiment in Living.* London: Pall Mall Press, 1961, 108 pp.

Duncan, Otis Dudley. "Optimum Size of Cities." In *Cities and Society: The Revised Reader in Urban Sociology,* Paul K. Hatt and Albert J. Reiss, Jr., eds. New York: The Free Press, Collier-Macmillan Company, 1957, pp. 759–72.

Dutt, Ashok K. "Regional Planning England and Wales: A Critical Evaluation." *Plan,* **9,** no. 6 (1970): 59–71.

Dutton, Geoffrey. "Foreword: Size and Shape in the Growth of Human Communities." *Ekistics,* **36,** no. 215 (October 1973): 241–43.

Dysart, Etienne R. "Cibuco: A New Regional Growth Center in Puerto Rico." *Ekistics,* **36,** no. 212 (July 1973): 50–63.

East Kilbride: Going to Town. East Kilbride, Scotland: East Kilbride and Stonehouse Development Corporation (no date).

East Kilbride. Recreational Services Group. *Your Guide to Recreation and Leisure.* East Kilbride, Scotland: Burgh of East Kilbride, 1972–1973, 32 pp.

East Kilbride. Town Council. *The Official Guide to East Kilbride.* London: Ed. J. Burrows and Company, 1972, 103 pp.

East Kilbride. Town Council. Health and Social Work Committees. *Community Health and Social Work.* East Kilbride, Scotland: Burgh of East Kilbride, 1973–74, 38 pp.

Economic Associates. *A New Town in Mid-Wales: Consultant's Proposals.* A Report to the Secretary of State for Wales. London: Her Majesty's Stationery Office, 1966, xii + 100 pp.

Economic Commission for Asia and The Far East. *A Case Study of the Damodar Valley Corporation and its Projects.* Flood Control Series no. 16. Bangkok: United Nations, 1960.

Economic Planning Authority. *Targets and Outlines of the Four-Year Plan, 1963/64–1966/67.* Jerusalem: Economic Planning Authority, 1962, 58 pp.

"An Eden for Everyman: California New Towns." *Professional Builder* (1968): 70–80.

Edmonton. Planning Department. *Mill Woods Development Concept.* Edmonton: Planning Department, 1971.

Educational Facilities Laboratories. "Legislation Pertaining to New Communities: A Reference." Educational Facilities Laboratories Working Paper No. 3. New York, June 1973, 68 pp.

———. "Schools for New Towns." Educational Facilities Laboratories Working Paper No. 2. New York, May 1973, 147 pp.

Edwards, Gordon. *Land, People and Policy: The Problems and Techniques of Assembling Land for the Urbanization of 100 Million New Americans.* West Trenton, New Jersey: Chandler-David Publishing Company, 1969, 159 pp.

Eichler, Edward P. "Why New Communities?" In *Shaping an Urban Future,* Bernard T. Frieden and William S. Nash, Jr., eds. Cambridge, Massachusetts: M.I.T. Press, 1969, pp. 95–114.

Eichler, Edward P. and Marshall Kaplan. *The Community Builders.* Berkeley and Los Angeles: University of California Press, 1967, 196 pp.

———. "New Communities." In *Housing Urban America,* Jon Pynoos, Robert Schafer, and Chester W. Hartman, eds. Chicago: Aldine, 1973, pp. 523–31.

Einsweiler, Robert C. and Julius C. Smith. "New Town Locates in a Municipality: Jonathan Saves Money and Chaska Increases Tax Base." *American Institute of Planners Notebook,* **1,** no. 3–4 (1971): entire issue.

Eisenstadt, S.N., ed. *Integration and Development in Israel.* New York: Praeger, 1970, xv + 703 pp.

Eldredge, H. Wentworth. "Lessons Learned from the British New Towns Program." In *How to Manage an Urbanized World,* Vol. II of *Taming Megalopolis,* H. Wentworth Eldredge, ed. New York: Praeger, 1967, pp. 823–37; Garden City, New York: Doubleday and Company, Anchor Books, 1967, pp. 823–28.

Elizabeth, South Australia. Adelaide, South Australia: South Australian Housing Trust, 1971.

"Elliot Lake: A New Town in a Uranium-Ore District in Canada." *International Federation for Housing and Town Planning News Sheet* (1960): 13–16.

Elphick, Peter. "Cramlington: Some Problems Encountered in Building a New Town." *Town Planning Review*, 35, no. 1 (1964): 59–75.

Epstein, David G. *Brasilia: Plan and Reality. A Study of Planned and Spontaneous Settlement.* Berkeley and Los Angeles: University of California Press, 1973, 206 pp.

Erin Mills New Town. Toronto: Don Mills Development, 1969.

Evans, Hazel, ed. *New Towns: The British Experience.* New York: Halstead Press, John Wiley and Sons, 1972, 196 pp.

Evans, Henry K. "Transportation Planning Criteria for New Towns." *Highway Research Record,* no. 97 (1965): 30–51.

Evans, Leonard. "Energy for New Towns." *Town and Country Planning*, 35, no. 1 (1967): 28–31.

Evans, William C. "New Towns: Initial Problems." *Telescope,* 17 (1966): 346–53.

Evenson, Norma. *New Towns—India: Chandigarh.* Berkeley and Los Angeles: University of California Press, 1966, 116 pp. + plates.

———. "The Symbolism of Brasilia." *Landscape,* 18 (1969): 19–28.

———. *Two Brazilian Capitals: Architecture and Urbanism in Rio De Janeiro and Brasilia.* New Haven: Yale University Press, 1973, 225 pp. + illustrations.

Evry New Town Development Corporation. *Presentation Notice of the Evry New Town Competition.* Paris: Ministere de l'Equipement Direction de l'Amenagement Foncier et de l'Urbanisme, 1971, 8 pp.

Ewald, William R., Jr., ed. *Environment and Change: The Next Fifty Years.* Bloomington: Indiana University Press, 1968, xvi + 397 pp.

———. *Environment and Policy: The Next Fifty Years.* Bloomington: Indiana University Press, 1968, xiv + 459.

———. *Environment for Man: The Next Fifty Years.* Bloomington: Indiana University Press, 1967, 308 pp.

"The Expansion of Newtown: Progress Report: 1968–74." Mimeo. Newtown, Wales: Mid-Wales Development Corporation, 1974, 5 pp.

Fahim, Hussein M. "Nubian Resettlement in the Sudan." *Ekistics,* 36, no. 212 (July 1973): 41–49.

Fain, William, Jr. "Learning from Foreign Experience: New Towns in Britain and France." *Architectural Record,* 154, no. 7 (1973): 134–41.

Fairbrother, Nan. *New Towns, New Landscapes: Planning for the 21st Century.* New York: Alfred, 1970, 397 pp.

Faris, Robert E. L. and H. Warren Dunham. *Mental Disorders in Urban Areas.* Chicago: University of Chicago Press, Phoenix Books, 1967.

Faulkner, Sir Percy. *New Towns Act 1946.* London: His Majesty's Stationery Office, 1946, 46 pp.

Fava, Sylvia F. "Blacks in American New Towns: Problems and Prospects." *Sociological Symposium,* no. 12 (1974): 111–29.

———. "The Pop Sociology of Suburbs and New Towns." *American Studies,* 14 (1973): 121–33.

———. "The Sociology of New Towns in the U.S.: 'Balance' of Racial and Income Groups." Mimeo. Paper presented at the American Institute of Planners Confer-In, Minneapolis-St. Paul, Minnesota, October 1970.

Fava, Sylvia F., ed. *Urbanism in World Perspective: A Reader.* New York: Thomas Y. Crowell Company, 1971.

"Federally Assisted New Communities." *Architectural Record,* 154, no. 7 (1973): 88–119.

Feiss, Carl. "New Towns for America." *Journal of the American Institute of Architects,* 33, no. 1 (1960): 85–89.

Fernald, Knowlton, Jr. "Evolution of a New Community: Organization of Management and Decision-Making as Related to the Architect." Mimeo. Paper presented at the American Institute of Architects New Communities Conference, Washington, D.C., November 3–6, 1971, 12 pp.

Field, Donald. "New Town and Town Expansion Schemes—Part III: Five New Towns Planned for Populations of 80,000–100,000." *Town Planning Review,* 39, no. 4 (1968): 196–216.

Finley, William E. "Columbia, Maryland: A New Town for America." *Highway Research Record,* no. 97 (1965): 18–22.

"First Report of the National Policy Task Force." 2nd ed. *Newsletter of the American Institute of Architects,* January 1972.

Fisher, H. Benjamin. *Evaluation of Alternative Plans for New Communities: Toward Application of the Competition-for-Benefits Model.* Chapel Hill, North Carolina: Center for Urban and Regional Studies, University of North Carolina, 1971, 337 pp.

Fitch, Lyle C. "Eight Goals for an Urbanized America." In *The Conscience of the City,* Martin Meyerson, ed. New York: George Braziller, 1970, pp. 51–74.

Fletcher, Robert R. amd Daniel D. Badger. "Economic Impact on a Growth Center Through Development of a New City in a Rural Area." Mimeo. Paper submitted to the Annual Meeting of the American Agricultural Economics Association, Carbondale, Illinois, August 15–18, 1971, 21 pp.

Flower Mound New Town. Dallas: The Raymond D. Nasher Company, 1973, 120 pp.

Flower Mound New Town. General Plan Report. Dallas: Flower Mound New Town, 1972, 120 pp.

Foer, Albert A. "Democracy in the New Towns: The Limits of Private Government." *University of Chicago Law Review,* 36 (1969): 379–412.

Foley, Donald L. *Governing the London Region: Reorganization and Planning in the 1960s.* Berkeley and Los Angeles: University of California Press, 1972, 223 pp.

Fonaroff, Arlene. "The Aesthetic New Town Environment and Its Effect on Community Health." *Sociological Symposium,* no. 12 (1974): 83–98.

Ford, Russell C. *New Towns: Toward an Innovative Leisure Service System.* Chapel Hill, North Carolina: Center for Urban and Regional Studies, University of North Carolina, 1974, 37 pp.

Fox, Karl A. "Population Redistribution Among Functional Economic Areas: A New Strategy for Urban and Rural America." Mimeo. Paper presented at the American Association for the Advancement of Science General Symposium, Washington, D.C., December 30, 1970, 17 pp. + maps.

France, J.C. "Building Societies in the New Towns." *Building Societies' Gazette,* 99 (1966): 284–86.

Frank Schlesinger Associates. *Planning and Architectural Feasibility Study: Lysander New Community.* Washington, D.C.: Frank Schlesinger Associates, 1973, 83 pp.

Fraser, Jack B. "New Towns: What Architects Should Know About Them." *Journal of the American Institute of Architects,* **52,** no. 4 (1969): 1–18.

Freeman, Orville L. "Towards a National Policy on Balanced Communities." *Minnesota Law Review,* **53** (1969): 1163–78.

Fricker, L.J. "A Pedestrian's Experience of the Landscape of Cumbernauld." *Architects' Year Book,* **11** (1965): 259–364.

Friedlander, Gordon. "Birth of a New City: An Exciting Creation." *Institute of Electrical and Electronics Engineers Spectrum,* **4,** no. 4 (1967): 70–82.

Friedmann, John. "The Feasibility of a National Settlement Policy for the USA." *Ekistics,* **32,** no. 192 (November 1971): 320–22.

———. "The Strategy of Deliberate Urbanization." *Journal of the American Institute of Planners,* **34,** no. 5 (1968): 364–73.

"From Three Emerged One: Stockholm, Tapiola, Cumbernauld." *Journal of the American Institute of Architects,* **48,** no. 1 (1967): 36–58.

Fry, E. Maxwell. "Chandigarh: The Capital of the Punjab." *RIBA Journal,* **62,** no. 3 (1955): 87–92.

Fulmer, O. Kline. *Greenbelt.* Washington, D.C.: American Council on Public Affairs, 1941, 46 pp.

Fulmer, O. Kline and Fred N. Severud. "Walled City for the Atomic Age." *Engineering News-Record,* **142,** no. 4 (1949): 18–19.

Gaat, Meshulam and Rice. *Transportation Planning Study of Beersheva: Outline Scheme 1966.* Beersheva, Israel: Beersheva Municipality, 1967.

Gabor, Dennis. *Inventing the Future.* New York: Alfred A. Knopf, 1971, 238 + vii pp.

Galantay, Ervin Y. *New Towns: Antiquity to the Present.* New York: George Braziller, 1975.

Gallagher, Neil. "The Next 100,000,000: Where Will They Live?" *Journal of the American Institute of Architects,* **51,** no. 1 (1969): 30–37.

Gallion, Arthur B. and Simon Eisner. *The Urban Pattern: City Planning and Design.* 2nd ed. Princeton, New Jersey: D. Van Nostrand Company, 1963, 435 pp.

Gandhi, N.K. "New Towns Construction in India: Consideration of Some Vital Aspects." *Quarterly Journal of the Local Self-Government Institute,* **28,** no. 2 (1957): 435–45.

Gans, Herbert J. "The Balanced Community: Homogeneity or Heterogeneity in Residential Areas?" *Journal of the American Institute of Planners,* **27,** no. 3 (1961): 176–84.

———. "How to Succeed in Integrating New Towns." *Design and Environment,* **3,** no. 4 (1972): 28–29, 50, 52.

———. *The Levittowners: Ways of Life and Politics in a New Suburban Community.* New York: Institute of Urban Studies, Columbia University, 1965, 3 vols.; Random House, Vintage Books, 1967, 474 pp.

———. "The Myths of the New Towns." *Equalop* (Winter 1969).

———. *People and Plans: Essays on Urban Problems and Solutions.* New York: Basic Books, 1968, 395 pp.

———. "Planning and Political Participation: A Study of Political Participation in a Planned New Town." *Journal of the American Institute of Planners,* **19,** no. 1 (1953): 3–9.

———. "Planning and Social Life: Friendship and Neighbor Relations in Suburban Communities." *Journal of the American Institute of Planners,* **27,** no. 2 (1961): 134–40.

Garn, Harvey A. *New Cities, New Communities and Growth Centers.* Washington, D.C.: The Urban Institute, 1970, 17 pp.

Garvey, John, Jr. "New Expanding and Renewed Town Concepts." *Assessors Journal,* **4** (1969): 15–56.

———. "What Can Europe Teach Us About Urban Growth?" *Nation's Cities,* **7,** no. 4 (1969): 13–18, 30–31.

Geddes, Sir Patrick. *Cities in Evolution.* New York: Harper and Row, 1968.

General Electric Company-Tempo. *Developing a Methodology for the Evaluation of Proposed New Communities.* PB-207-719. Springfield, Virginia: National Technical Information Service, 1971, 299 pp.

Gertler, L.O., ed. *Planning the Canadian Environment.* Montreal: Harvest House, 1968, 311 pp.

Gertler, L.O. *The Process of New City Planning and Building.* Waterloo, Canada: School of Urban and Regional Planning, University of Waterloo, 1971, x + 90 pp.

———. *Regional Planning in Canada.* Montreal: Harvest House, 1972, 186 pp.

Gibberd, Frederick. "The Architecture of New Towns." *Journal of the Royal Society of Arts,* **106** (1958): 335–50, discussion, 350–53; *Builder,* **194** (1958): 226–27; *Municipal Journal,* **66** (1958): 193–94; *Official Architecture,* **21** (1958): 69–72.

———. "Courthouse at Harlow." *Architect and Builder News,* **219,** no. 19 (1961): 607–12.

———. *Harlow Expansion Survey.* Harlow, England: Harlow Development Corporation, 1963.

———. "Harlow New Town." *Architectural Review,* **117,** no. 701 (1955): 310–29.

———. *Harlow New Town: Master Plan.* Harlow, England: Harlow Development Corporation, 1947, 28 pp.

———. *Harlow New Town: A Plan Prepared for the Harlow Development Corporation.* 2nd ed. Harlow, England: Harlow Development Corporation, 1958, 28 pp.

———. *Town Design.* 5th ed., revised. New York: Praeger, 1967, 372 pp.

Gibbs, A.K. "Cumbernauld New Town, Mark II: A Plan to Master the Motor Vehicle." *Architects' Journal,* **130** (1959): 278–84.

Gibson, John E. "Why Design a New City?" *Institute of Electrical and Electronics Engineers Transactions on Systems, Man & Cybernetics.* SMC-3, no. 1 (1972): 1–10.

Gildea, James J. *Fort Lincoln: A Proposed New Town in the Nation's Capital.* Chapel Hill, North Carolina: Center for Urban and Regional Studies, University of North Carolina, 1970, 21 pp.

———. *GE-UNC New Towns Financial Feasibility Model: A User's Manual for the IBM 360 Short Program.* Chapel Hill, North Carolina: Center for Urban and Regional Studies, University of North Carolina, 1971, 62 pp.

Gimlin, Hoyt. "New Towns." *Editorial Research Report,* **2,** no. 6 (1968): 804–22.

Gipe, Albert B. "Planning a New City: Columbia." *Institute of Electrical and Electronics Engineers Transactions on Industry and General Applications* IGA-2, no. 5 (1966): 423–30.

Gladstone, Robert M. "Does Building a City Make Economic Sense?" *Appraisal Journal*, **34,** no. 3 (1966): 407–12.

————. "Economic and Social Programming: An Overview." Paper presented at the American Institute of Architects New Communities Conference, Washington, D.C., November 3–6, 1971.

————. "New Towns Role in Urban Growth Explored: Public Policy Issues Examined." *Journal of Housing*, **23,** no. 1 (1966): 29–36.

————. "Planned New Communities and Regional Development." In *Proceedings—1965 Government Relations and Planning Policy Conference*. Washington, D.C.: American Institute of Planners, 1965, pp. 44–50.

Gladstone, Robert M. and Harold F. Wise. "New Towns Solve Problems of Urban Growth." In *New Towns: A New Dimension of Urbanism*. Chicago: International City Managers' Association, 1966, pp. 21–31.

Glance, Richard and Eric C. Freund. *The Urban Environment and Residential Satisfaction with an Emphasis on New Towns: An Annotated Bibliography*. Exchange Bibliography No. 429. Monticello, Illinois: Council of Planning Librarians, 1973, 72 pp.

Glavaicki, Milutin. "Novi Beograd: An Example of Planning and Constructing New Settlements in Yugoslavia." Mimeo. Submitted for presentation at the United Nations Interregional Seminar on New Towns, London, June 4–19, 1973, 10 pp.

Glenrothes Development Corporation. Department of Architecture Planning and Quantity Surveying. *Glenrothes New Town: Master Plan/Report*. Glenrothes, Scotland: Glenrothes Development Corporation, 1970, 121 pp.

Glick, Michael B. "Financing of New Towns." In *Regional New Towns: Alternative in Urban Growth for Southeast Michigan*. Detroit: Metropolitan Fund, 1970, pp. 52–55.

Gliege, John G. "New Towns in Arizona: The Impact of the Planned Communities Act." *Arizona State University Public Affairs Bulletin*, **9,** no. 3 (1970): 1–4.

————. "New Towns: Policy Problems in Regulating Development." Tempe, Arizona: Institute of Public Administration, Arizona State University, 1970, 188 pp.

Glikson, Artur. *New Towns in Israel: Guide to the International Town Planning Exhibition, Moscow, July 1958*. Tel Aviv: Association of Engineers and Architects in Israel, Israel Institute of Architects, 1958.

————. *Regional Planning and Development*. Leiden: A.W. Sijthoff's Uitgeversmaatschappij N.V., 1955.

————. "Urban Design in New Towns and Neighborhoods: Israel." *Landscape Architecture*, **52,** no. 3 (1962): 169–72.

Gobar, Alfred. "PUDs as Alternatives to New Towns." *Real Estate Review*, **2** (1971): 72–75.

Godley, David. "Report on the Conference on New Communities in Canada." *Canadian Institute of Planners News*, (June 1975): 3–5.

Godschalk, David. "Comparative New Community Design." *Journal of the American Institute of Planners*, **33,** no. 5 (1967): 371–87.

————. "The Future of Citizen Participation in New Communities." In *Planning for the Social Frontier: New Communities in America*. Gideon Golany, ed., Manuscript under consideration for publication.

————. *Participation, Planning, and Exchange in Old and New Communities: A Collaboration Paradigm*. Chapel Hill, North Carolina: Center for Urban and Regional Studies, University of North Carolina, 1972, 328 pp.

————. "Reforming New Community Planning." *Journal of the American Institute of Planners*, **39,** no. 5 (1973): 306–15.

Godschalk, David R., Donald Balcom, Terrence O'Connor, and Gary Wood. *New Communities and Large Scale Development: Alternative Policies for North Carolina*. Raleigh, North Carolina: North Carolina State Planning Division, 1972, 130 pp.

Goff, Lyman Bullock et al. *Reston: New Town, But for Whom?* Princeton, New Jersey: Princeton University Press, 1968, 161 pp.

Golany, Gideon. *An Analytical Approach to Optimal Future Location and Distribution of Urban Area of "Conurbation Holland" into The Netherlands*. The Hague: Institute of Social Studies, 1965, 30 pp.

————. *City and Regional Planning and Development in Israel*. Exchange Bibliography No. 56. Monticello, Illinois: Council of Planning Librarians, 1968, 30 pp.

————. "New Community for Virginia in the Roanoke Valley: Site Selection and Feasibility Study." State College, Pennsylvania: Gideon Golany Associates, 1972.

————. *New Towns Planning and Development: A World-Wide Bibliography*. Washington, D.C.: Urban Land Institute, 1973, 256 pp.

————. "New Town Site Selection: Method and Criteria." Unpublished study. University Park, Pennsylvania: Department of Architecture, The Pennsylvania State University, 1972.

————. *Planning and Development in Israel and The Netherlands*. Ithaca, New York: Department of City and Regional Planning, Cornell University, 1967, 65 pp.

————. *Planning and Development in The Netherlands: English Bibliographical Guide List*. Haifa: Israel Institute of Technology, Faculty of Architecture and Town Planning, 1965, 80 pp.

————, ed. *Strategy for New Community Development in the United States*. Stroudsburg, Pennsylvania: Dowden, Hutchinson and Ross, 1975, 293 pp.

————. *Urban Survey of Existing Residential Quarters in Jerusalem as a Basis for Rehabilitation*. Part D. Haifa: Israel Institute of Technology, 1965.

Golany, Gideon and Daniel Walden, eds. *The Contemporary New Communities Movement in the United States*. Urbana, Illinois: University of Illinois Press, 1974, 154 pp.

Golany, Gideon et al. *Exton: New Town for Philadelphia*. University Park, Pennsylvania: The Pennsylvania State University, Department of Architecture, Division of Environmental Design and Planning, College of Arts and Architecture, 1974, 50 pp.

Golosov, Il'ia A. *Soviet Cities New and Renewed*. Moscow: Foreign Languages Publishing House, 1939, 30 pp.

Gomez, Benjamin F. "Urbanization in the Philippines: The Need for an Integrated Policy in Urbanization and Development of New Towns." Mimeo. Submitted for presentation at the United Nations Interregional Seminar on New Towns, London, June 4–19, 1973, 15 pp.

Goodey, Brian. "New Towns: Physical Solution or Social Innovation." In *Proceedings of National Urban Development Conference on 25–26 March 1971*. London: Centre for Advanced Land Use Studies, College of Estate Management, 1971, pp. 11–24.

———. *The Public Image of Five British Towns: Perception Studies for Planning.* London: Centre for Urban and Regional Studies, University of Birmingham, 1972.

———. "Social Planning and New Communities: An Historical Introduction." Centre for Urban and Regional Studies Second New Communities Project Working Paper No. 1. University of Birmingham, December 1971.

———. *Social Planning in New Communities: Some Questions for Research and Practice.* Oxford: Oxford Polytechnic, Department of Town Planning, 1970, 27 pp.

———. "Social Research in New Communities." *Build Environment* (1973): 233 +.

Goracz, A., I. Lithwick, and L.O. Stone. *The Urban Future.* Ottawa: Central Mortgage and Housing Corporation, 1971, 139 pp.

Gorynski, Juliuz. "The Problem of Participation in New Town Development: Nowa Huta, Poland." *Ekistics,* **36,** no. 212 (July 1973): 40–41.

Goss, Anthony. "Greater Peterborough: A New City." *Traffic Engineering and Control,* **10** (1969): 606–09.

———. "Neighborhood Units in British New Towns." *Town Planning Review,* **32,** no. 1 (1961): 66–82.

Gottlieb, Manuel. "The Theory of Optimum Population for a Closed Economy." *Journal of Political Economy,* **53,** no. 4 (1945): 289–316.

Gottmann, Jean. *Megalopolis: The Urbanized Northeastern Seaboard of the United States.* Cambridge, Massachusetts: M.I.T. Press, 1965.

Gottschalk, Shimon. *Rural New Towns: Toward a National Policy.* Cambridge, Massachusetts: Center for Community Economic Development, 1971, 27 pp.

Graves, Clifford Wayne. "Public New Town Corporations for California." Master's thesis, University of California at Berkeley, 1961, 113 pp.

Great Britain. *New Towns Act, 1946: 9 & 10 Geo. 6. Ch. 68.* London: His Majesty's Stationery Office, 1946, 46 pp.

———. *New Towns Act, 1959: 7 & 8 Eliz. 2. Ch. 62.* London: Her Majesty's Stationery Office, 1959, 22 pp.

———. *New Towns Act, 1965: Eliz. 2. 1965. Ch. 59.* London: Her Majesty's Stationery Office, 1965, [1] + iv + 88 pp.

———. *New Towns Act, 1967.* London: Her Majesty's Stationery Office, 1967, 80 pp.

Great Britain. Board of Trade. Cmnd. 2206. *The North-East: A Programme for Regional Development and Growth.* London: Her Majesty's Stationery Office, 1963, 48 pp.

Great Britain. British Information Services. *Regional Development in Britain.* New York: British Information Services, 1974, 54 pp.

Great Britain. Central Housing Advisory Committee. *Design of Dwellings.* Report of the Design of Dwellings Subcommittee of the Central Housing Advisory Committee appointed by the Minister of Health and the Minister of Town and Country Planning on site planning and layout in relation to housing. London: His Majesty's Stationery Office, 1944.

Great Britain. Department of Environment. *Long Term Population Distribution in Great Britain: A Study.* London: Her Majesty's Stationery Office, 1971, 205 pp.

———. *New Towns.* London: Her Majesty's Stationery Office, 1973, 154 pp.

Great Britain. Department of the Environment. The Scottish Development Department. The Welsh Office. The Central Office of Information. *The New Towns.* London: Her Majesty's Stationery Office, 1973, 52 pp.

Great Britain. First Secretary of State for Economic Affairs. *The National Plan.* London: Her Majesty's Stationery Office, 1965, xviii + 204 + 239 + 31 pp.

Great Britain. Ministry of Housing and Local Government. *The New Towns.* London: Her Majesty's Stationery Office, 1969, 44 pp.

Great Britain. Ministry of Housing and Local Government Library. "New Towns Bibliography No. 65: 1898–October 1955 and Appendices I–VII." Stencil. London: Ministry of Housing and Local Government Library, 1955–69, 36 + 4 + 19 + 24 + 7 + 15 + 31 + 39 pp.

Great Britain. Ministry of Housing and Local Government. New Towns Division. *Social Provision in New Towns.* London: Ministry of Housing and Local Government, 1959, 53 pp.

Great Britain. Ministry of Housing and Local Government. Sociological Research Unit. *The Impact of Immigrants on the Resident Population of an Expanding Town.* London: Ministry of Housing and Local Government, 1966, 14 pp.

Great Britain. Ministry of Housing and Local Government with the South East Joint Planning Team. *The South East Study: 1961–1981.* London: Her Majesty's Stationery Office, 1964, xv + 146 pp.

Great Britain. Ministry of Housing and Local Government. Welsh Office. Subcommittee of the Central Housing Advisory Committee. *The Needs of New Communities.* London: His Majesty's Stationery Office, 1967, 123 pp.

Great Britain. Ministry of Town and Country Planning. *Greater London Plan: Memorandum on the Report of the Advisory Committee for London Regional Planning.* London: His Majesty's Stationery Office, 1947, 19 pp.

———. *Land Compensation Act, 1961.* London: Her Majesty's Stationery Office, 1970, 43 pp.

Great Britain. Ministry of Town and Country Planning and Department of Health for Scotland. *New Towns Committee Final Report.* London: Her Majesty's Stationery Office, 1946.

Great Britain. Ministry of Town Planning. *New Towns 1898–1948: A Bibliography.* London: His Majesty's Stationery Office, 1948, 13 pp.; Addendum 1950, 4 pp.

Great Britain. Ministry of Transportation. *Traffic in Towns: A Study of the Long Term Problems of Traffic in Urban Areas.* Buchanan Report. London: His Majesty's Stationery Office, 1963.

———. *Traffic in Towns.* Hammondsworth, England: Penguin Books, 1964.

Great Britain. Royal Commission on Distribution of Industrial Population. Cmnd. 6153. *The Barlow Report.* London: His Majesty's Stationery Office, 1940, 320 pp.

Great Britain. Secretary of State for Wales and Minister for Planning and Local Government. "New Towns in England and Wales: A Consultation Document." London: Department of the Environment, The Secretary of State for Wales and the Minister for Planning and Local Government, 1974, 13 pp.

Great Britain. South East Economic Planning Council. *South East*

Study of Subdivisions. London: Her Majesty's Stationery Office, 1970, 149 pp.

————. *A Strategy for the South East: A First Report.* London: Her Majesty's Stationery Office, 1967, 100 pp.

Great Britain. South East Joint Planning Team. *Strategic Plan for the South East.* London: Her Majesty's Stationery Office, 1970, 110 pp.

Greater London Council. *Greater London Development Plan: Report of Studies.* London: Tillotsons (Bolton), 1968, 328 pp.

————. *Greater London Development Plan Statement.* London: Waterlow and Sons, 1968, 78 pp.

————. *Greater London Services 1972 to 1973.* London: Greater London Council, 1973, 96 pp.

————. *The Planning of a New Town: Data and Design Based on a Study for a New Town of 100,000 at Hook, Hampshire.* London: Greater London Council, 1965, 182 pp.

————. *Tomorrow's London: A Background to the Greater London Development Plan.* London: Greater London Council, 1969, 129 pp.

Green, Philip P., Jr. "Land Subdivision." In *Principles and Practice of Urban Planning,* William I. Goodman and Eric C. Freund, eds. Washington, D.C.: International City Managers' Association, 1968.

Greenbie, Barrie B. "Social Territory, Community Health and Urban Planning." *Journal of the American Institute of Planners,* **40,** no. 2 (1974): 74–82.

Griffin, Nathaniel M. *Irvine: The Genesis of a New Community.* A ULI Special Report. Washington, D.C.: Urban Land Institute, 1974, 76 pp.

Grimshaw, Peter N. "Britain's Second-Generation New Towns." *Progress: The Unilever Quarterly,* **53,** no. 4 (1969): 49–54.

Gruen, Victor. "A Critique: The Possible City." Mimeo. Paper presented at the American Institute of Planners' 50th Anniversary Conference, Washington, D.C., October 1–6, 1967.

————. *The Heart of Our Cities: The Urban Crisis—Diagnosis and Cure.* New York: Simon and Schuster, 1964, 368 pp.

Gupta, D.N. "A New Town in the Desert: India." *Annual of Architecture: Structure and Town Planning,* **3** (1962): D35–D42.

Gupta, Sehdev Kumar. "Chandigarh: A Study of Sociological Issues and Urban Development in India." Faculty of Environmental Studies Occasional Paper No. 9. University of Waterloo, 1973, 8 pp.

————. "A Study of Sociological Issues in Chandigarh (Architectural Design)." *Ekistics,* **39,** no. 235 (June 1975): 411–16.

Gutheim, Frederick. "Continental Europe Offers New Town Builders Experience." In *How to Manage an Urbanized World,* Vol. II of *Taming Megalopolis,* H. Wentworth Eldrege, ed. New York: Praeger, 1967, pp. 828–38; Garden City, New York: Doubleday and Company, Anchor Books, 1967, pp. 828–38.

Gutnov, Alexei et al. *The Ideal Communist City.* Translated by Renee Neu Watkins. New York: George Braziller, 1971, 166 pp.

Hagen, Everett E. and F.T. Stephanie White. *Great Britain: Quiet Revolution in Planning.* Syracuse, New York: Syracuse University Press, 1966, 180 pp.

Hall, Oswald. "The New Planned Community." *Canadian Welfare,* **36** (1960): 9–14.

Hall, Peter. *The Theory and Practice of Regional Planning.* London: Pemberton, 1970, vii + 103 pp.

————. *The World Cities.* New York: McGraw-Hill Book Company, World University Library, 1966, 256 pp.

Hallett, Stanley J. *Working Papers in Church Planning: Columbia, Maryland.* New York: National Council of Churches of Christ in the U.S.A. (no date).

Halvarson, Carl M. "Campuses and New Towns." *Journal of the Society for College and University Planning,* **2,** no. 2 (1971): 1–4.

Hancock, Macklin L. "Policies for New Towns." *Ontario Housing,* **11,** no. 3 (1965): 4–11.

Hansen, Niles M. "A Growth Center Strategy for the United States." *Review of Regional Studies,* **1,** no. 1 (1969): 161–73.

Hanson, Royce. "Citizen Participation in New Towns." In *Citizen Participation in the Roles Study,* Joseph Friend et al., eds. Columbia, Maryland: The Columbia Foundation, 1972, p. 59.

————. "The Current Governance of New Towns." *American Country,* **36,** no. 10 (1971): 18–19, 22–25, 29.

————. "Issues in Democratic Development of New Towns." *Ekistics,* **34,** no. 201 (August 1972): 82–85.

————. *Managing Services for New Communities.* Washington, D.C.: Washington Center for Metropolitan Studies, 1972, 21 pp.

————. *New Towns: Laboratories for Democracy.* Report of the Twentieth Century Fund Task Force on Governance of New Towns. New York: The Twentieth Century Fund, 1971, 73 pp.

Hardoy, Jorge E. "The Planning of New Capital Cities and Argentina's Nineteenth-Century New Town." In *Planning of Metropolitan Areas and New Towns.* New York: United Nations, 1967, pp. 176–77, 232–49.

————. "Two New Capital Cities: Brasilia and Islamabad. The Planning of New Capital Cities." *Ekistics,* **18,** no. 108 (November 1964): 320–25.

Hare, E.H. "Mental Health in New Towns: What Next?" *Journal of Psychosomatic Research,* **10,** no. 1 (1966): 53–58.

Harkness, Richard C. *Communication Innovations, Urban Form and Travel Demand: Some Hypotheses and a Bibliography.* Springfield, Virginia: National Technical Information Service, 1972, 55 pp.

Harlap, Amiram, ed. *Israel Builds.* Jerusalem: State of Israel, Ministry of Housing, Planning and Engineering Division, 1973, 271 pp.

Harlow and District Sports Trust. *Harlow Sport Centre.* Harlow, England: Harlow and District Sports Trust, 1968, 16 pp.

Harlow Expansion 1974: Technical Papers. Harlow, England: Harlow Development Corporation, 1974, 60 pp.

Harris, Britton. "New Communities and the Ghetto." *Equalop* (1969).

Harrison, Peter. "Canberra: Case Notes on a New Town." In *Planning 1965.* Chicago: American Society of Planning Officials, 1965, pp. 219–32.

Harvard Graduate School of Design. *New Communities: One Alternative.* Proceedings of 12th Urban Design Conference. Cambridge, Massachusetts: Graduate School of Design, Harvard University, 1968, 125 pp.

Helbock, Richard W. "New Towns in the United States." *Professional Geographer,* **20,** no. 4 (1968): 242–46.

Hellman, Harold. *The City in the World of the Future.* New York: M. Evans and Company, 1970, 186 pp.

Henderson, C. Mc. C. "The Application of the New Town Concept: No. 5, Kitimat, Canada." *International Union of Local Authorities Quarterly,* **10** (1958): 89–92.

Heraud, B.J. "Social Class and the New Towns." *Urban Studies,* **5,** no. 1 (1968): 33–58.

Herbert, Gilbert. "Elizabeth: The Dream and Reality of an Australian New Town." *Hemisphere,* **7,** no. 12 (1963): 11–16.

————. "The Neighborhood Unit Principle and Organic Theory." *Sociological Review,* **11,** no. 2, new series (1963): 171.

Herman, Harold and Michael L. Joroff. "Planning Health Services for New Towns." *American Journal of Public Health,* **57,** no. 4 (1967): 633–40.

Heroux, Richard L. and William A. Wallace. *Financial Analysis and the New Community Development Process.* New York: Praeger, 1973, 172 pp.

Herrero, Michael C. "New Communities and Tele Communications." Research report prepared for the New Towns research seminar. Chapel Hill, North Carolina: Center for Urban and Regional Studies, University of North Carolina, 1973, 71 pp.

Hertel, M.M. *Irvine Community Associations.* Claremont, California: Claremont Urban Research Center, Claremont Graduate School, 1971, 134 pp.

Heywood, Philip. "Regional Planning in the Netherlands." *Ekistics,* **32,** no. 189 (August 1971): 114–19.

Hill, Gerald N. *Alternative Institutions for New Community Development.* Berkeley: Center for Planning and Development Research, University of California, 1965, 37 pp.

Hillman, Ellis, ed. *New Towns, New Cities.* Vol. 2 of *Essays in Local Government Enterprise.* London: Merlin Press, 1965, 192 pp.

Hinojosa, Jesus H. "Urbanization and New Town Planning in Latin America: Hypothetical Insights for the USA." Stencil. Submitted for presentation at Confer-In 72, the American Institute of Planners' Annual Conference, Boston, Massachusetts, 1972, 20 pp. + charts.

Hojayey, D. "Soviet Union to Build New Towns." *Town and Country Planning,* **25,** no. 9 (1957): 373–76.

Holden, Constance. "Le Vaudreuil: French Experiment in Urbanism Without Tears." *Ekistics,* **33,** no. 194 (January 1972): 7–9.

Holden, Matthew et al. *Cities of the Future : Proceedings of the Annual Conference on Urban Policy, 26–28 October 1967.* Iowa City: University of Iowa, 1967, 55 pp.

Hollinshead, Earl D. *Land: Recreation and Leisure.* Washington, D.C.: Urban Land Institute, 1970.

Hopkins, Frank E. "Evaluating the External Effects of Subsidized New Towns." Mimeo. Paper presented at the Northeast Regional Science Conference, Pennsylvania State University, University Park, Pennsylvania, April 14–16, 1972, 26 pp.

Hoppenfeld, Morton. "A Sketch of the Planning-Building Process for Columbia." *Journal of the American Institute of Planners,* **33,** no. 5 (1967): 398–409.

Hornsey College of Art. *Transport for New Towns.* Report of the 3rd Conference on Transportation, held in London, 25 April 1967. London: Hornsey College of Art Advanced Study Group, 1967, 18 pp.

Horrocks, Meryl. "The Organization of Social Development in New Towns." Paper prepared for seminar on social planning at the Centre for Environmental Research, University of Sheffield, 1971.

————. "Social Planning in New Communities." *Building Environment,* **1,** no. 8 (1972): 551–54.

Hosken, Fran P. "France: New Towns Point Way," *The Christian Science Monitor,* September 17, 1971, p. 11.

Hough, Thomas C. and Dilip R. Limaye. "Innovative Concepts for New Communities." Jenkintown, Pennsylvania: Decision Sciences Corporation, 1972.

"HUD: Guaranteed New Communities." *HUD Challenge,* **3,** no. 8 (1972): 17–23.

"HUD Survey and Analysis of Large Developments and New Communities Completed or Under Construction in the United States Since 1947." *Urban Land,* **29,** no. 1 (1970): 11–12.

"How Do You Like Living in a Planned Community?" *Urban Land,* **31,** no. 1 (1972): 3–13.

Howard, Sir Ebenezer. *Garden Cities of Tomorrow,* F.J. Osborne, ed. London: Faber and Faber, 1951, 168 pp.; Cambridge, Massachusetts: M.I.T. Press, 1965, 168 pp.

————. *To-Morrow: A Peaceful Path to Real Reform.* London: Swan Sonnenachein and Company, 1898, 176 pp. Reissued as *Garden Cities of Tomorrow,* 1902, 167 pp.

Howell, Joseph T. *New Towns from the Point of View of the Ghetto Resident: Phase I—Developing a Method of Inquiry.* Chapel Hill, North Carolina: Center for Urban and Regional Studies, University of North Carolina, 1969, 43 pp.

Howes, Robert G. "The New Church in the New Town." *Liturgal Arts,* **37,** no. 4 (1969): 111–14.

Hudson, James W. "We Can Build Space Age Cities Now." *National Wildlife* (September 1970): 5–9.

Hughes, Derek W. "New Town Progress in France." *Town and Country Planning,* **39,** no. 1 (1971): 79–81.

————. "Pontoise: A New Town for Paris." *Town and Country Planning,* **37,** no. 5 (1969): 226–27.

Hunt, Charles B. *Physiography of the United States.* San Francisco and London: W.H. Freeman and Company, 1967.

Hurd, Richard M. "City Problems Require Building of New Towns." *Urban Land,* **25,** no. 3 (1966): 2, 16.

Hyson, John L. "Land Use Controls: Who Watches the Watchers." *Urban Land,* **33,** no. 3 (1974): 5.

"Industrial Location and New Communities." In *Planning 1971.* Chicago: American Society of Planning Officials, pp. 440–56.

Innovation and New Communities? The Princeton University Conference, Meeting No. 102. Princeton, New Jersey: Princeton University School of Architecture and Urban Planning, 1971.

Irvine Development Corporation. *Irvine New Towns Plan.* Irvine, Scotland: Irvine Development Corporation, 1971, 301 pp.

"Islamabad: A Progress Report on Pakistan's New Capital City." *Architectural Review,* **141,** no. 3 (1967): 211–16.

Israel. *Atlas of Settlements in Israel.* Based on the Findings of the Census of Population and Housing, 1961. Publication No. 14. Jerusalem: Prime Minister's Office, Central Bureau of Statistics, 1963, 10 pp. + maps.

————. *Manpower in Development Towns: First Report on Twenty-One Development Towns.* Jerusalem: Ministry of Labour, Man Power Planning Authority, 1964.

————. *Population and Households for Localities and Statistical Areas.* Population and Housing Census 1972, Series 4. Jerusalem: Central Bureau of Statistics, 1974.

Israel. Ministry of Housing. *Carmiel: A New Town in Galilee.* Tel Aviv: Ministry of Housing, Planning Department, 1965, 23 pp.

————. *Israel Builds: Development of Building Methods in Public Housing Projects in Israel.* Tel Aviv: Ministry of Housing, Division of Physical Planning, 1968.

Israel. Ministry of Interior. *National Planning for the Redistribution of Population and the Establishment of New Towns in Israel.* Jerusalem: Ministry of Interior, 1964.

"Israel New Town Honored by American Jury." *Journal of Housing,* **27,** no. 4 (1970): 188–92.

Jackson, Henry M. "Toward a National Land Use Policy." In *Land Use in the United States,* Grant S. McClellan, ed. New York: H.W. Wilson Company, 1971, pp. 10–12.

Jackson, Samuel C. "New Communities." *HUD Challenge,* **3,** no. 8 (1972): 4–7.

————. "A New Generation of New Communities." Mimeo. Paper presented at the American Institute of Architects New Communities Conference, Washington, D.C., November 3–6, 1971, 23 pp.

Jacobsen, George. "Canada's Northern Communities." *North* (November/December 1968): 34–37.

Jamond, Leo. "Islamabad: The Visionary Capital." *Ekistics,* **25,** no. 150 (May 1968): 329–33.

Jay, Maurice. "New Towns in the Negev Desert." *Town and Country Planning,* **33,** nos. 7–8 (1965): 304–09.

Johnson, Byron L. "The Economics of New Innovative Cities in the Arid West." Paper presented at the American Association for Advancement of Science Meeting, Chicago, Illinois, December 27, 1970.

Jonathan Development Corporation. *Jonathan New Town: Design and Development.* Chaska, Minnesota: Jonathan Development Corporation, 1971, 44+ pp.

Jones, Howard. "Flemingdon Park Revisited." *Canadian Architect,* **12,** no. 4 (1967): 41–58.

Kahn, J.H. "A Psychiatrist on New Towns." *Town and Country Planning,* **30,** no. 10 (1961): 410–12.

Kalba, Kas. "Telecommunications for Future Human Settlements: A Planning Framework for Minnesota Experimental City." *Ekistics,* **35,** no. 211 (June 1973): 329–36.

Kanata. Ottowa: Campeau Corporation Limited, no date, 20 pp.

Kaplan, Marshall. *Implementation of the Baltimore Regional Plan Alternatives.* San Francisco: Institute for Planning and Development, 1965, 94 pp.

Karn, Valerie A. *Aycliffe Housing Survey: A Study of a New Town.* Occasional Paper No. 9. Birmingham, England: Centre for Urban and Regional Studies, University of Birmingham, 1970, 69 pp.

————. *Crawley Housing Survey: A Study of a New Town.* Occasional Paper No. 11. Birmingham, England: Centre for Urban and Regional Studies, University of Birmingham, 1970, 74 pp.

————. *East Kilbride Housing Survey: A Study of a New Town.* Occasional Paper No. 8. Birmingham, England: Centre for Urban and Regional Studies, University of Birmingham, 1970, 78 pp.

————. *Stevenage Housing Survey: A Study of a New Town.* Occa-sional Paper No. 10. Birmingham, England: Centre for Urban and Regional Studies, University of Birmingham, 1970, 74 pp.

Keegan, John E. and William Rutzick. "Private Developers and the New Communities Act of 1968." *Georgetown Law Journal,* **57,** no. 6 (1969): 119–57.

Keilhofer, P. and J.W. Parlour. "New Towns: The Canadian Experi-ence." A Discussion Paper. Ottawa: Ministry of State for Urban Affairs, 1972, 53 pp.

Keller, Suzanne. "Neighborhood Concepts in Sociological Perspec-tive." In *Human Identity in the Urban Environment,* edited by Gwen Bell and Jacqueline Tyrwhitt. Hammondsworth, England: Penguin Books, 1972, pp. 276–89.

————. *The Urban Neighborhood: A Sociological Perspective.* New York: Random House, 1968, 201 pp.

Kennedy, Anthony. "Housing Studies for Isolated Communities." *Ekistics,* **25,** no. 150 (May 1968): 361–67.

Kentridge, Leon R. "A Survey of New Towns About Metropolitan Areas with Special Reference to Montreal." Master's thesis, McGill University, 1961, 210 pp.

Kimbrough, John T. "New Towns and Regional Development: Pro-ject Scioto." *Appalachia,* **38** (1970): 5–9.

Klein, Donald. "Problems and Possibilities for Mental Health Prog-rams in New Communities." In *Planning for the Social Frontier: New Communities in the United States,* Gideon Golany, ed. Manus-cript under consideration for publication.

Knittle, Robert E. "New Town Knowledge, Experience, and Theory." *Human Organization,* **32,** no. 1 (1973): 37–48.

Kocken, Manfred. "On Determining the Optimum Size of New Cities." In *Is There an Optimum Level of Population?,* S.F. Singer, ed. New York: McGraw-Hill, 1971, pp. 364–97.

Koenigsberger, Otto H. "New Towns in India." *Town Planning Review,* **23,** no. 2 (1952): 95–132.

Koenigsberger, Otto H. and Michael Safier. "Urban Growth and Planning the Developing Countries of the Commonwealth: A Re-view of Experience from the Past 25 Years." Mimeo. Submitted for presentation at the United Nations Interregional Seminar on New Towns, London, June 4–19, 1973, 55 pp.

Kotler, Milton. *Neighborhood Government: The Local Foundations of Political Life.* New York: The Bobbs-Merrill Company, 1969, 111 pp.

Kozlowski, J. and J.T. Hughes. *Threshold Analysis: A Quantitative Planning Method.* New York: John Wiley and Sons, Halstead Press Division, 1972, 286 pp.

Kudrayavtsav, Aleksy Ozipovich. "Distribution and Planning of New Cities in the U.S.S.R." *Ekistics,* **23** (February 1967): 86.

Lake Havasu City, Arizona: Declaration of Reservations. Scottsdale, Arizona: Holly Development Company, 1966, 43 pp.

Lambert, Barbara. "Milton Keynes." *Habitat,* **15,** no. 1 (1972): 2–8.

Landau, Y.H. *Organizational and Institutional Aspects of Regional Development Planning and Implementation in Greece, Portugal, Spain, Turkey, Yugoslavia and Israel, Comparative Report.* Tel Aviv: Organization for Economic Cooperation and Development, 1964.

Lang, Reg. "Oh Canada, A National Urban Policy?" *Plan,* **12,** no. 1 (1972): 13–32.

Langlois, Claude H. "Urban Lobbying in Canada." *Plan,* **12,** no. 1 (1972): 67–73.

Lansing, John B., Robert W. Marans and Robert B. Zehner. *Planned Residential Environments*. Ann Arbor: Institute for Social Research, the University of Michigan, 1970, 269 pp.

Lapping, Mark B. "Radburn: Planning the American Community." Stencil. Paper presented at the 88th annual meeting of the American Historical Association, New Orleans, Louisiana, December 28, 1972, 23 pp.

Larson, Roy E. and Robert J. Reid. *Transportation–1983: The Minnesota Experimental City*. Minneapolis: North Star Research and Development Institute, 1969, 30 pp.

Layton, Elizabeth. *Administration of New Towns in the United Kingdom, The Netherlands, and Canada*. New York: United Nations, 1960, 50 pp.

League of New Community Developers. "An Imaginary Trip Through Title VII New Communities." *Sociological Symposium*, no. 12 (1974): 41–54.

Lean, W. "Economics of New Town Size and Form." *Ekistics*, **23**, no. 135 (February 1967): 79–82.

Legget, Robert F. *Cities and Geology*. New York: McGraw-Hill Book Company, 1973.

Lenz-Romeiss, Felizitas. *The City: New Town or Home Town?* Translated by James Underwood and Edith Kustner. New York: Praeger, 1973, 153 pp.

LeRoyer, Ann M. "The New Towns Movement in Great Britain and the United States." *Urban and Social Change Review*, **4** (1971): 53–58.

Levin, Earl A. "Lanigan: A New Town for Saskatchewan." *Community Planning Review*, **14**, no. 4 (1964): 13–19.

Lewis, David F. *A Comparative Analysis of Housing and Resident Characteristics in New Communities and Surrounding Areas*. Chapel Hill, North Carolina: Center for Urban and Regional Studies, University of North Carolina, May 1974, 41 pp.

Lichfield, Nathaniel. *Israel's New Towns: A Strategy for Their Growth*. Draft for Discussion, Vol. 1, Stage I: A Report to the Minister of Housing. London: Tavistock House, 1970, 143 pp.

Lichfield, Nathaniel and Paul F. Wendt. "Six English New Towns: A Financial Analysis." *Town Planning Review*, **40**, no. 3 (1969): 283–314.

Lieberman, Myron. "Education in New Cities." *Phi Delta Kappan* (March 1972): 407–11.

Ling, Arthur. *Runcorn New Town: Master Plan*. Runcorn, England: Runcorn Development Corporation, 1967, [18], 137 pp.

Liston, Linda. "The Case for the Airport New Town." *Industrial Development* (July/August 1969): 3–9.

Lithwick, N.H. "Political Innovation: A Case Study." *Plan*, **12**, no. 1 (1972): 45–56.

"Little Aden Cantonment: New Town in the Desert." *Modular Quarterly* (April 1961): 14–23.

Livingstone, Dr. J.M. and Dr. A.J.M. Sykes. *East Kilbride 70: An Economic and Social Survey*. Glasgow, Scotland: University of Strathclyde, no date, 36 pp.

Llewelyn-Davies Associates. *A New Community in Amherst: Interim Report*. New York: Llewelyn-Davies Associates, 1970, 105 pp.

Llewelyn-Davies Weeks Forestier-Walker and Bor. *The Household Survey: Technical Supplement No. 2 to The Plan for Milton Keynes*.

Milton Keynes, England: Milton Keynes Development Corporation, 1970, 163 pp.

————. *Milton Keynes Plan: Interim Report to the Milton Keynes Development Corporation*. London: Llewelyn-Davies Weeks Forestier-Walker and Bor, 1968, viii + 172 pp.

————. *The Plan for Milton Keynes*. 2 vols. Milton Keynes, England: Milton Keynes Development Corporation, 1970, 87 pp. + maps + 356 pp.

————. *Planning Proposals for the Tuy Medio-Venezuela*. London: Llewelyn-Davies Weeks Forestier-Walker and Bor, 1968, 179 pp.

Loewenthal, Norman H. and Raymond J. Burby, III. "Health Care in New Communities." Mimeo. New Communities Policy Application Workshop NSF/RANN/APRT GI-34285, 18 November 1974, 4 pp.

Logue, Edward J. *Goals Guidelines Concerns of the New York State Urban Development Corporation*. New York: New York State Urban Development Corporation, 1971.

————. "The Need for Urban Growth Policies." *Journal of the American Institute of Architects*, **55**, no. 5 (1971): 18–22.

Londonderry Development Commission. *Area Plan 1972 Review Draft*. Londonderry, Northern Ireland: Department of Architecture and Planning, Londonderry Development Commission, October 1972, 78 pp.

Lucas, Rex A. *Minetown, Milltown, Railtown: Life in Canadian Communities*. Toronto: University of Toronto Press, 1971, xiii + 433 pp.

Lynch, Kevin. *Site Planning*. 2nd ed. Cambridge, Massachusetts: M.I.T. Press, 1971.

Lyons, James A., Jr., Howard Moskof and Morton W. Schomer. *New Towns and Planned Communities*. Real Estate Law and Practice Course Handbook No. 42. New York: Practicing Law Institute, 1971, 327 pp.

Lyon, Walter A. "Innovation in Pollution and Environmental Control." In *Innovations for Future Cities*, Gideon Golany, ed. New York: Praeger, in press.

MacCormac, Richard. "Thamesmead." *Architects' Journal*, **154**, no. 41 (1972): 817–32; no. 42 (1972): 879–96.

MacFadyen, Dugland. *Sir Ebenezer Howard and the Town Planning Movement*. Manchester, England: Manchester University Press, and Cambridge, Massachusetts: M.I.T. Press, 1970, 199 pp.

McCoy, Kent. *The Role of the Landscape Architect in Australian New Town Development*. Canberra: National Capital Development Commission, 1974, 241 pp. + Appendices.

McCulloch Properties. *Today's Story of Lake Havasu City, Arizona*. Lake Havasu City, Arizona: McCulloch Properties, 1970, 27 pp.

McDougall, Richard S. "The Administrative Problems of Building a New Town in the United Kingdom." *Journal of Local Administration Overseas*, **8** (1969): 17–25.

McFarland, John R. "The Administration of the Alberta New Towns Program." *Duquesne University Law Review*, no. 3 (1967): 377–91.

McHarg, Ian. *Design with Nature*. Garden City, New York: Doubleday and Company, 1971.

McKeever, J. Ross, ed. *The Community Builders Handbook*. Washington, D.C.: Urban Land Institute, 1968, 526 pp.

McKeever, J. Ross. *Shopping Center Zoning*. Washington, D.C.: Urban Land Institute, 1973.

McLean, Edward. "New Communities and Population Redistribution as Policy Issues." *Urban and Social Change Review* (Spring 1971): 58–61.

Malisz, Boleslaw. "Physical Planning for the Development of New Towns." In *Planning of Metropolitan Areas and New Towns.* New York: United Nations, 1967, pp. 201–208.

———. *Poland Builds New Towns.* Warsaw: Polonia Publishing House, 1962, 173 pp.

Mandelker, Daniel R. "A Legal Strategy for Urban Development." In *Planning for a Nation of Cities,* Sam Bass Warner, Jr., ed. Cambridge, Massachusetts: M.I.T. Press, 1966, 209–26.

Mann, P.H. "The Socially Balanced Neighbourhood Unit." *Town Planning Review,* **29,** no. 2 (1958): 91–98.

Marans, Robert W. "Planning the Experimental Neighborhood at Kiryath Gat, Israel." *Ekistics,* **27,** no. 158 (January 1969): 70–75.

———. "Social and Cultural Influences on New Town Planning: An Israeli Experiment." Mimeo. Paper presented at the Caribbean Research Institute Symposium, St. Thomas, Virgin Islands, November 1967, 28 pp.

———. *Social Integration in Housing: A Case Study of Israel.* Ann Arbor, Michigan: Institute for Social Research, the University of Michigan, 1974.

Marans, Robert W. And Artur Glikson. "The Integral Habitational Unit: An Experiment in Development and Planning." *Ministry of Housing Bulletin,* (Israel, 1967).

Marks, Paul J. *A New Community: Format for Health, Contentment, Security.* Cathedral City, California: Questers Project, 1969, 135 pp.

Marris, Peter. "A Report on Urban Renewal in the United States," In *The Urban Condition: People and Policy in the Metropolis,* Leonard J. Duhl, ed., with the assistance of John Powell. New York: Simon and Schuster, 1963.

Martin, Wendell H. "Remote Land Development or Exploitation?" *Urban Land* (February 1971): 3.

Marz, Roger. "Local Government and New Town Development." In *Regional New Towns: Alternatives for Urban Growth.* Detroit: The Metropolitan Fund, 1970, pp. 40–43.

Mathisson, John S. *Resident Perceptions of Quality of Life in Resource Frontier Communities.* Winnipeg: Centre for Settlement Studies, University of Manitoba, 1970.

Mayer, Albert. *Greenbelt Towns Revisited: In Search of New Directions for New Towns for America.* Washington, D.C.: U.S. Department of Housing and Urban Development, 1968, 34 pp.

———. "Ingredients of an Effective Program for New Towns." In *Proceedings of the 1964 Annual Conference.* Washington, D.C.: American Institute of Planners, 1964, pp. 186–92.

Mayer, Albert with Clarence Stein. "New Towns and Fresh In-City Communities." *Architectural Record,* **136,** no. 2 (1964): 129–38.

Mayer, Harold. "The Pull of Land and Space." In *Metropolis on the Move: Geographers Look at Urban Sprawl,* Jean Gottmann and Robert A. Harper, eds. New York: John Wiley and Sons, 1967, pp. 23–25.

Meadowvale: A New Urban Life Style. Toronto: Markborough Properties, no date, 20 pp.

Mellor, Roy E.H. "The Soviet Town: Characteristics of Soviet Towns Both Old and New." *Town and Country Planning,* **31,** no. 2 (1963): 90–94.

Merlin, Pierre. *New Towns: Regional Planning and Development.* Translated by Margaret Sparks. London: Methuen and Company, 1971, 276 pp.; New York: Barnes and Noble, and Harper and Row, 1971, 276 pp.

Merrill, J.O. "Planning a Town for Atom Workers." *Engineering News-Record,* **143** (1949): 48–49.

Metropolitan Planning Commission Kansas City Region. *Metro/Center: A New Town in Town.* Kansas City, Missouri: Metropolitan Planning Commission, 1971, 20 pp.

Metropolitan Washington Council of Governments. *New Communities in Metropolitan Areas: The Governmental Role.* Washington, D.C.: Metropolitan Washington Council of Governments, 1970, 69 pp.

Mields, Hugh, Jr. *Federally Assisted New Communities: A New Dimension in Urban Development.* A ULI Landmark Report. Washington, D.C.: Urban Land Institute, 1973, 277 pp.

Miles, Simon. "Developing a Canadian Urban Policy: Some Lessons from Abroad." *Plan,* **12,** no. 1 (1972): 88–106.

Miller, Brown, Neil J. Pinney and William S. Saslow. *Innovation in New Communities.* M.I.T. Report No. 23. Cambridge, Massachusetts: M.I.T. Press, 1972, 301 pp. + appendices.

Miller, Myron et al. "The Imperative of Planning Together: Educational Planning in New Communities." Educational Facilities Laboratories and the U.S. Office of Education Working Paper no. 5. January 1974, 119 pp.

Milton Keynes Development Corporation. *Building Conservation in Milton Keynes.* Milton Keynes, England: Milton Keynes Development Corporation, 1971, 123 pp.

———. *A Health Service for Milton Keynes.* Milton Keynes, England: Milton Keynes Development Corporation, 1968, 42 pp.

Minnesota Experimental City. *Minnesota Experimental City (MXC).* Vol. I: A Compendium of Publications Relating to Socio-Culture Aspects. Vol. II: Economic and Physical Aspects. Vol. III: Areas for Study and Experimentation. Vol. IV: Bibliography. Vol. V: Design Strategy Statement. Minneapolis: Experimental City Project, University of Minnesota, 1969.

———. *The Minnesota Experimental City (MXC) Progress Report.* Minneapolis: Experimental City Project, University of Minnesota, 1969.

Mission Viejo Company. *Mission Viejo: The Story of a Plan That Works.* Mission Viejo, California: Mission Viejo Company, 1968.

Mixon, Herman, Jr. and Francis H. Parker. *Soul City: The Initial Stages.* Chapel Hill, North Carolina: Center for Urban and Regional Studies, University of North Carolina, 1971, 46 pp.

More, Sir Thomas. "Utopia." In *Ideal Empires and Republics.* New York: William H. Wise and Company, 1901.

Morrill, Richard L. "The Development of Spatial Distributions of Towns in Sweden: An Historical-Predictive Approach." In *Regional Development and Planning,* John Friedman and William Alonso, eds. Cambridge, Massachusetts: M.I.T. Press, 1964, pp. 173–86.

Morris, M.D. "New Towns in the Desert: Israel Demonstrates How to Create Them." *American City,* **85,** no. 11 (1970): 94–95.

Morris, Robert L. "Transportation Planning for a New Community." *Public Works* (October 1969): 90–100 +.

Morris, William, ed. *The American Heritage Dictionary of the En-*

glish Language. Boston: American Heritage Publishing Company and Houghton Mifflin Company, 1973.

Morrison, Peter A. "A Demographic Assessment of New Cities and Growth Centers as Population Redistribution Strategies." Public Policy, 21, no. 3 (1973): 368–82.

Moynihan, Daniel P., ed. Toward a National Urban Policy. New York: Basic Books, 1970, 348 pp.

Mumford, Lewis. The City in History: Its Origins, Its Transformations, and Its Prospects. New York: Harcourt, Brace and World, 1961, 657 pp.

———. "The Garden City Idea and Modern Planning." In Garden Cities of Tomorrow by Sir Ebenezer Howard. Cambridge, Massachusetts: M.I.T. Press, 1965, pp. 8–29.

———. "The Neighborhood and the Neighborhood Unit." Town Planning Review, 24, no. 4 (1954): 256–70.

———. "Opinions on the New Towns." Town and Country Planning, 24, no. 143 (1956): 161–64.

———. The Story of Utopias. New York: Peter Smith, 1941, 315 pp., The Viking Press, 1971, 315 pp.

———. The Urban Prospect. New York: Harcourt, Brace and World, 1968, 255 pp.

Muncy, Dorothy A. "A Credo for New Communities and Industry." In Planning 1971. Chicago: American Society of Planning Officials, 1971, pp. 447–56.

———. "Planning Guidelines for Industrial Park Development." Urban Land, 29, no. 11 (1970).

Murphy, Judy. The Place of the Arts in New Towns. New York: Educational Facilities Laboratories, 1973, 72 pp.

Murphy, Timothy L. Rural Developments: The Logic of New Communities. Chapel Hill, North Carolina: Center for Urban and Regional Studies, University of North Carolina, 1972, 45 pp.

Nathaniel Litchfield and Associates. Stevenage Public Transport: Cost Benefit Analysis. 2 vols. Stevenage, England: Stevenage Development Corporation, 1970, 141 pp. + illus.

National Association of Homebuilders. New Towns Round Table: A Conference Held at the National Housing Center, Washington, D.C., June 29–30, 1964. Washington, D.C.: National Association of Homebuilders, 1964, 10 pp.

———. Working List of Open Space Communities. Washington, D.C.: National Association of Homebuilders, Land Use and Engineering Department, 1970, 61 pp.

National Capital Development Commission. Tomorrow's Canberra: Planning for Growth and Change. Canberra: Australian National University Press, 1970, xix + 244 pp.

National Commission on Urban Problems. "Building the American City." Urban Land, 28, no. 3 (1969): entire issue.

———. Building the American City. Report of the National Commission on Urban Problems to the Congress and the President of the United States, 91st Congress, 1st Session. Housing Document No. 90-34. Washington, D.C.: U.S. Government Printing Office, 1968, 504 pp.

National Goals Research Staff. Toward Balanced Growth: Quantity with Quality. A Report. Washington, D.C.: National Goals Research Staff, July 4, 1970, 226 pp.

National Housing Act. Ottawa: Information Canada, 1973, 81 pp.

National and University Institute of Agriculture. Regional Cooperation in Israel. Rehovot, Israel: Settlement Study Center (no date).

"National Urban Growth Policies of Other Countries." In Planning 1971. Chicago: American Society of Planning Officials, 1971, pp. 239–86.

Negev, Abraham. Cities in the Desert. Tel Aviv: E. Lewin-Epstein, 1966.

Neilson, Lynsay. "The New Cities Programme." Royal Australian Planning Institute Journal, 12, no. 1 (1974): 14–20.

The Netherlands. Government Physical Planning Service. 1958 Report on the West of the Land. I: The West of the Land. II: Illustrations Belonging to the West of the Land. III: Explanation of the Report. IV: Illustrations Belonging to the Explanation of Report. Comprehensive Planning Course 1965. The Hague: Institute of Social Studies, 1965.

The Netherlands. Ministry of Housing and Physical Planning. The "Randstad:" The Urbanized Zone of The Netherlands. The Hague: Ministry of Housing and Physical Planning, 1970.

———. Second Report on Physical Planning in The Netherlands. Part I: Main Outline of National Physical Planning Policy. Part 2: Future Pattern of Development. Condensed Editions. The Hague: Government Printing Office of The Netherlands, 1966, 50 + 86 pp.

Neufeld, Max. Israel's New Towns: Some Critical Impressions. Pamphlet No. 31. London: Anglo-Israel Association, June 1971, 22 pp.

New City: Milton Keynes 1974. Milton Keynes, England: Milton Keynes Development Corporation, 1974.

"New Communities." HUD Challenge, 3, no. 8 (1972): entire issue.

"New Communities: Business on the Urban Frontier." Special Issue. Saturday Review, 54, no. 20 (1971): entire issue.

"New Community Checklist." Urban Land, 30, no. 4 (1974): 17–19.

New Community Development Project. Community Profiles—Spring 1973: Black Residents in Five New Communities and Two Suburban Control Communities. C.P. Report no. 20. Chapel Hill, North Carolina: Center for Urban and Regional Studies, University of North Carolina, 1974, 18 pp.

———. Community Profile—Spring 1973: Columbia, Maryland. C.P. Report no. 1. Chapel Hill, North Carolina: Center for Urban and Regional Studies, University of North Carolina, 1974, 18 pp.

———. Community Profile—Spring 1973: Comparison of 13 Non-Federally Assisted New Communities and 13 Control Communities. C.P. Report no. 17. Chapel Hill, North Carolina: Center for Urban and Regional Studies, University of North Carolina, 1974, 18 pp. + appendix.

———. Community Profile—Spring 1973: Elk Grove Village, Illinois. C.P. Report no. 2. Chapel Hill, North Carolina: Center for Urban and Regional Studies, University of North Carolina, 1974, 18 pp.

———. Community Profile—Spring 1973: Forest Park, Ohio. C.P. Report no. 3. Chapel Hill, North Carolina: Center for Urban and Regional Studies, University of North Carolina, 1974, 18 pp.

———. Community Profile—Spring 1973: Foster City, California. C.P. Report no. 4. Chapel Hill, North Carolina: Center for Urban and Regional Studies, University of North Carolina, 1974, 18 pp.

———. Community Profile—Spring 1973: Irvine, California. C.P. Report no. 5. Chapel Hill, North Carolina: Center for Urban and Regional Studies, University of North Carolina, 1974, 18 pp.

————. *Community Profile—Spring 1973: Jonathan, Minnesota.* C.P. Report no. 6. Chapel Hill, North Carolina: Center for Urban and Regional Studies, University of North Carolina, 1974, 18 pp.

————. *Community Profile—Spring 1973: Laguna Niguel, California.* C.P. Report no. 7. Chapel Hill, North Carolina: Center for Urban and Regional Studies, University of North Carolina, 1974, 18 pp.

————. *Community Profile: Lake Havasu City, Arizona.* C.P. Report no. 8. Chapel Hill, North Carolina: Center for Urban and Regional Studies, University of North Carolina, 1974, 18 pp.

————. *Community Profile—Spring 1973: North Palm Beach, Florida.* C.P. Report no. 9. Chapel Hill, North Carolina: Center for Urban and Regional Studies, University of North Carolina, 1974, 18 pp.

————. *Community Profile—Spring 1973: Park Forest, Illinois.* C.P. Report no. 10. Chapel Hill, North Carolina: Center for Urban and Regional Studies, University of North Carolina, 1974, 18 pp.

————. *Community Profile—Spring 1973: Park Forest South, Illinois.* C.P. Report no. 11. Chapel Hill, North Carolina: Center for Urban and Regional Studies, University of North Carolina, 1974, 18 pp.

————. *Community Profile—Spring 1973: Reston, Virginia.* C.P. Report no. 12. Chapel Hill, North Carolina: Center for Urban and Regional Studies, University of North Carolina, 1974, 18 pp.

————. *Community Profile—Spring 1973: Retirement Communities. Rossmore Leisure World (Laguna Hills), California; Sun City Center, Florida.* C.P. Report no. 16. Chapel Hill, North Carolina: Center for Urban and Regional Studies, University of North Carolina, 1974, 18 pp.

————. *Community Profile—Spring 1973: Sharpstown, Texas.* C.P. Report no. 13. Chapel Hill, North Carolina: Center for Urban and Regional Studies, University of North Carolina, 1974, 18 pp.

————. *Community Profile—Spring 1973: Subsidized Housing Residents in Five New Communities and Two Suburban Control Communities.* C.P. Report no. 19. Chapel Hill, North Carolina: Center for Urban and Regional Studies, University of North Carolina, 1974, 18 pp.

————. *Community Profile—Spring 1973: Valencia, California.* C.P. Report no. 14. Chapel Hill, North Carolina: Center for Urban and Regional Studies, University of North Carolina, 1974, 18 pp.

————. *Community Profile—1973: Westlake Village, California.* C.P. Report no. 15. Chapel Hill, North Carolina: Center for Urban and Regional Studies, University of North Carolina, 1974, 18 pp.

————. *Community Profile—Spring 1973: Young Adults in 13 Non-Federally Assisted New Communities and 13 Control Communities.* C.P. Report no. 18. Chapel Hill, North Carolina: Center for Urban and Regional Planning, University of North Carolina, 1974, 18 pp.

————. *Elderly Residents in 13 Non-Federally Assisted New Communities, 13 Control Communities, and Two Retirement Communities.* C.P. Report no. 21. Chapel Hill, North Carolina: Center for Urban and Regional Studies, University of North Carolina, 1974, 18 pp.

New Franconia Associates. "New Franconia/New Town In Town: Environmental Inventory." Stencil. Fairfax County, Virginia: New Franconia Associates, 1972, 129 pp. + appendices.

————. "New Franconia/New Town In Town: Urban Residential Planned Community (URPC) Information Document." Stencil. Fairfax County, Virginia: New Franconia Associates, 1972, 74 pp.

New South Wales. State Planning Authority. *The New Cities of Campbelltown, Camden, Appin: Structure Plan.* Sydney: State Planning Authority of New South Wales, 1973, 142 pp.

————. *Sydney Region: Outline Plan 1970–2000 A.D.* Sydney: State Planning Authority of New South Wales, 1968, 111 pp.

"The New Town of Grande Cache." Mimeo. Edmonton: Alberta Provincial Planning Board (no date).

"The New Towns." Special Issue. *Town and Country Planning,* **35,** no. 1 (1967): entire issue.

"New Towns: The Arguments . . . For . . . Against." *American Builder,* **82,** no. 6 (1966): 94–97.

New Towns Association. *New Town Bulletin.* London: New Towns Association, 1973, 4 pp.

"New Towns in Britain." *Town and Country Planning,* **39,** no. 1 (1971): 35–50.

"New Town for Churchill Falls, Labrador." *Community Planning Review,* **18,** no. 1 (1968): 18–21.

"New Towns Come of Age." *Town and Country Planning,* **36,** no. 1–2 (1968): entire issue.

A New Town Comes of Age: Reappraisal of Community Services and Facilities in Hemel Hempstead. Hemel Hempstead, England: Hemel Hempstead Borough Council, 1970, 116 pp.

"New Town, Denmark." *Builder,* **210** (1966): 77–79.

"A New Town Development in Holland." *Architect and Building News,* **215** (1959): 660–63.

"New Towns France." *Town and Country Planning,* **39,** no. 1 (1971): 79–84.

"New Towns: Frontiers or Failures? (Part I)." *Building Research,* **6,** no. 4 (1969): entire issue.

"New Towns: Frontiers or Failures? (Part II)." *Building Research,* **7,** no. 1 (1970): entire issue.

"The New Town of Grenoble-Echirolles." *Architecture, Formes, Functions,* **16** (1971): 277–79.

"New Towns in India." *Town Planning Review,* **23,** no. 1 (1952): 95–131.

"A 'New Town' on an Island." *American City,* **85,** no. 9 (1970): 110–12.

"New Towns: A National Investment." *Town and Country Planning,* **25,** no. 1 (1957): entire issue.

"New Towns in the Picture." *Town and Country Planning,* **33,** no. 1 (1965): entire issue.

"New Towns: Prospects and Problems." In *Planning 1964.* Chicago: American Society of Planning Officials, 1964, pp. 138–60.

"The New Town of Reston, Virginia." *Architectural Record,* **136,** no. 1 (1964): 119–34.

"New Town: Soleri's—Arcosanti, Arizona; Founding July 1970." *Arizona Architect* (March/April 1970): 14–16.

"New Town Statistics." *Town and Country Planning,* **38,** no. 1 (1970): 43–49.

"New Towns: Symposium." *Washington University Law Quarterly* no. 1 (1965): 1–104.

"New Tychy: A New Town in Poland." *Architektura,* **26,** no. 2 (1972): entire issue.

"A New Type of 'New Town' Breaks Ground for Planners." *Business Week*, no. 2081 (1969): 132–36.

New York State Urban Development Corporation. *Lysander New Community: Planning Summary, February 1971*. Syracuse, New York: New York State Urban Development Corporation, Metropolitan Development Association, 1971, 13 pp.

————. *New Communities for New York*. New York: New York State Urban Development Corporation and the New York State Office of Planning Coordination, 1970, 72 pp.

————. *New York State Urban Development Corporation Act, As Amended Through June 1971*. New York: New York State Urban Development Corporation, 1971, 42 pp.

————. *Urban Development Corporation (UDS) in 1973: Annual Report*. New York: New York State Urban Development Corporation, 1974, 95 pp.

————. *Welfare Island: A Planned New Town In Town. An Application for Determination of General Eligibility Under the Housing and Urban Development Act of 1970—Urban Growth and New Community Development, Part B—Development of New Communities*. New York: New York State Urban Development Corporation, 1972.

New York State Urban Development Corporation and Llewelyn-Davies Associates. *A New Community in Amherst*. 2 vols. New York: New York State Urban Development Corporation, 1971, 165 pp.

Nicholas, James C., ed. *New Communities: A Tool to Implement a Policy for the Management of Growth*. Summary Report of the Environmental Land Management Study Committee's Conference on New Communities, Miami, July 15–17, 1973. Tallahassee, Florida: Environmental Land Management Study Committee, 1973.

Nicholson, John H. *New Communities in Britain: Achievements and Problems*. London: National Council of Social Service, 1961, 183 pp.

Nilsson, Sten Ake. *The New Capitals of India, Pakistan and Bangladesh*. Translated by Elizabeth Andreasson. Copenhagen: Scandanavian Institute for Asian Studies, 1973, 230 pp.

Norcross, Carl. "New Towns Under the Microscope: Living Up to Promises?" *Urban Land*, **34**, no. 2 (1975): 3–12.

Norcross, Carl and Sanford Goodkin. *Open Space Communities in the Market Place*. Technical Bulletin 57. Washington, D.C.: Urban Land Institute, 1966.

Norris, Gary Ross. "A Study of the Design Determinants of Five Canadian 'New Towns.' " Master's thesis. University of Manitoba, 1968, 164 pp.

North Pickering Projects: Evaluation of Phase III Modified Concept Plans. Interim Report 2. Toronto: Ministry of Housing, 1975, 97 pp.

North Pickering Project: Summary of Recommended Plan. Toronto: Ministry of Housing, 1975, 36 pp.

Northern Ireland: *New Towns Act (Northern Ireland), 1965. Eliz. 2. 1965. Ch. 13*. London: Her Majesty's Stationery Office, 1965, 50 pp.

North-West Economic Planning Council. *Social Planning in New Communities*. Manchester, England: North-West Economic Planning Council, 1971, 28 pp.

Notes for Students. Redditch, England: Redditch Development Corporation, 1972, 12 pp.

Nott, Christopher. "Does Harlow Work?" *Town and Country Planning*, **39**, no. 1 (1971): 67–72.

Nunn, Douglas, ed. *Newcom: The Psychosocial Environment*. Vol. II. Louisville, Kentucky: The Urban Studies Center, University of Louisville, 1971.

"Nun's Island: A Great Place to Live." *The Gazette* (Montreal), 5 February 1970, pp. 27–38.

Oberlander, H. Peter and Cornelia Oberlander. "A Critique: Canada's New Towns." *Progressive Architecture*, **37,** no. 8 (1956): 113–19.

Ogilvy, A.A. "Employment Expansion and the Development of New Town Hinterlands 1961–66." *Town Planning Review*, **42,** no. 2 (1971): 113–29.

Ogilvy, Audrey A. "The Self-Contained New Town: Employment and Population." *Town Planning Review*, **39,** no. 1 (1968): 38–54.

Omori, K. "Tokyo's Satellite Towns." *Town and Country Planning*, **32,** no. 4 (1964): 190.

Operation Lakhish, Stage 2. Tel Aviv: W. Turnowsky and Son (no date).

Osbron, Frederic J. "The Garden City Movement. A Revolution." *Journal of the Town Planning Institute*, **31,** no. 9 (1945): 193–207.

————. *Genesis of Welwyn Garden City: Some Jubilee Memories*. London: Town and Country Planning Association, 1970, 28 pp.

————. *Green Belt Cities: The British Contribution*. London: Faber and Faber, 1946, 190 pp.; revised edition, London: Evelyn, Adams and Mackay, 1969, 198 pp.; New York: Schocken Books, 1969, 203 pp.

————. "The History of Howard's Social Cities." *Town and Country Planning*, **39,** no. 12 (1971): 539–45.

————. "New Town Density Standards." *Town and Country Planning*, **25,** no. 6 (1957): 241–45.

————. "Population Densities." *Town and Country Planning*, **31,** no. 1 (1963): 52–54.

————. "Sir Ebenezer Howard: The Evolution of His Ideas." *Town Planning Review*, **21,** no. 3 (1950): 221–35.

————. "Transport in New Towns: A Change of Emphasis." *Town and Country Planning*, **35,** no. 8 (1967): 405–07.

Osborn, Frederic J. and Arnold Whittick. *The New Towns: The Answer to Megalopolis*. Introduction by Lewis Mumford. London: Leonard Hill Books, 1963, xvii + 456 pp.; New York: McGraw-Hill Book Company, 1963, 376 pp.

Osborn, Robert J. and Thomas A. Reiner. "Soviet City Planning, Current Issues and Future Perspectives." *Journal of the American Institute of Planners*, **28,** no. 4 (1962): 239–50.

P.G. Pak-Poy and Associates Pty. "Transport Aspects of Structure Plan: Gosford-Wyong." Crows Nest, New South Wales: P.G. Pak-Poy and Associates Pty., 1974, 80 pp.

Paldi, A. *Adaptation of the Physical and Social Environment in a Development Town: Kiriat Malachi*. Tel Aviv: Ministry of Housing, Socio-Economic Research Department, 1967, 77 pp.

Papaioannou, John G. "Future Urbanization Patterns: A Long-Range, World-Wide View." *Ekistics*, **29,** no. 175 (June 1970): 368–81.

Park, Robert E. "The City: Suggestions for the Investigation of Human Behavior in the Urban Environment." In *The City*. Chicago: University of Chicago Press, 1925, pp. 1–46.

Parsons, Kermit et al. *Public Land Acquisition for New Communities* and the Control of Urban Growth: Alternative Strategies. Ithaca, New York: Center for Urban Development Research, Cornell University 1973, 223 pp. + appendices.

Pass, David. Vallingby and Farsta: From Idea to Reality. The New Community Development. Cambridge, Massachusetts: M.I.T. Press, 1973, 190 pp.

Peachey, Paul. New Town, Old Habits: Citizen Participation at Fort Lincoln. Community Governance Paper No. 1. Washington, D.C.: Washington Center for Metropolitan Studies, 1970, 52 pp.

Peat Marwick Kates and Company. The Plan for Milton Keynes Technical Supplement No. 7: Transportation. 2 vols. Milton Keynes, England: Milton Keynes Development Corporation, 1969, 77 + 80 pp.

Penfold, Anthony H. "Ciudad Guyana: Planning a New City in Venezuela." Town Planning Review, 36, no. 4 (1966): 225–48.

Pearson, Norman. "New Towns as Economic Catalysts." In Changes Confronting Small Cities and Towns: A Selection of Papers. Montreal: Canadian Federation of Mayors and Municipalities, 1964, pp. 34–40.

Peng, George T.C. and N.S. Verna. New Town Planning Design and Development: Comprehensive Reference Materials. Lincoln, Nebraska: University of Nebraska, 1971, 108 pp.

Perloff, Harvey S. "New Towns In Town." Journal of the American Institute of Planners, 32, no. 3 (1966): 155–61.

———. "Social Aspects of New Towns." Mimeo. A paper presented at Urban America, Inc., Forum on New Communities, held at UCLA, October 10, 1969, 9 pp.

———. Urban Renewal in a Chicago Neighborhood: An Appraisal of the Hyde Park Kenwood Renewal Program. Chicago: Hyde Park Herald, August 1955.

Perloff, Harvey S. and Royce Hanson. "The Inner City and a New Urban Politics." In Urban America: Goals and Problems. United States Congress, Joint Economic Committee. Materials compiled and prepared for the Subcommittee on Urban Affairs. Washington, D.C.: U.S. Government Printing Office, 1967, pp. 162–69.

Perloff, Harvey S. and Neil C. Sandberg, eds. New Towns: Why?—And for Whom? Praeger Special Studies Program. New York: Praeger, 1973, 250 pp.

Perloff, Harvey S., David Vetter and Thomas Berg. "Lessons from Urban Renewal and Model Cities." In Central City Modernization: The New Town Intown Approach. Vol. 1. Los Angeles: New Town Intown Study, School of Architecture and Urban Planning, UCLA, 1973.

Perloff, Harvey S. et al. "Lessons from New Town Intown Experience." In Central City Modernization: The New Town Intown Approach. Vol. 2. Los Angeles: New Town Intown Study, School of Architecture and Urban Planning, UCLA, 1973.

———. "Lessons from the Experts." In Central City Modernization: The New Town Intown Approach. Vol. 3. Los Angeles: New Town Intown Study, School of Architecture and Urban Planning, UCLA, 1973.

———. "Lessons from an In-Depth Study: The Case of Los Angeles." In Central City Modernization: The New Town Intown Approach. Vol. 4. Los Angeles: New Town Intown Study, School of Architecture and Urban Planning, UCLA, 1973.

———. "Summary and Recommendations." In Central City Modernization: The New Town Intown Approach. Vol. 5. Los Angeles:

New Town Intown Study, School of Architecture and Urban Planning, UCLA, 1973.

Perry, Clarence, "The Neighborhood Unit." In Neighborhood and Community Planning. Vol. 7, Regional Survey of New York and Its Environs. New York: Committee on Regional Plan of New York and Its Environs, 1929, pp. 22–140.

Peterborough Development Corporation. Greater Peterborough Master Plan. Peterborough, England: Peterborough Development Corporation, 1970, 103 pp.

Peterson, David Lee. The Planned Community and the New Investors: Economic and Political Factors in Corporate Real Estate Investment. Special Report No. 4. Berkeley: Center for Real Estate and Urban Economics, Institute of Urban and Regional Development, University of California, 1967, 73 pp.

Peterson, William J. "The Ideological Origins of Britain's New Towns." Journal of the American Institute of Planners, 34, no. 3 (1968): 160–70.

Philadelphia Committee on City Policy. New Towns and Old Cities: Toward a Unified Urban Policy for the State and Nation. Philadelphia: Philadelphia Committee on City Policy, 26 May 1970, 32 pp.

Pickard, Jerome P. "HUD Survey and Analysis of Large Developments and New Communities Completed or Under Construction in the U.S. Since 1947." Urban Land, 29, no. 1 (1970): 11–12.

———. "Is Dispersal the Answer to Urban Overgrowth?" Urban Land, 29, no. 1 (1970): 3–10.

Planners for Equal Opportunity. New Cities for Black and White. New York: Planners for Equal Opportunity, 1970.

Planning Committee of "It's Open for Women." "The Women's Center." Stencil. Columbia, Maryland: Planning Committee of "It's Open for Women," September 1971, 31 pp.

"Planning Health Services for New Towns." American Journal of Public Health (April 1967): 63–40.

"Planning Study: Milton Keynes—New City for the South-East." Architects' Journal, 149, no. 6 (1969): 361–76.

Plato. The Laws. Translated by A.E. Taylor. London: J.M. Dent and Sons, 1934.

Plato. The Republic. Translated by B. Jowett. New York: Vintage Books, A Division of Random House (no date).

Pontchartrain Land Corporation. Application for Pontchartrain NewTown In Town, Presented to the Office of New Community Development, Department of Housing and Urban Development. 2 vols. Dallas: Pontchartrain Land Corporation, 1972.

Porzecanski, Martha de et al. New Towns: The Evolution of Planning Criteria. Prepared within the New Towns Study Supported by the Social Science Research Council. Cambridge: Department of Architecture, 1972, [4] + 42 pp.

Powell, David R. New Towns Bibliography. Exchange Bibliography No. 249. Monticello, Illinois: Council of Planning Librarians, 1972, 34 pp.

Prakash, Ved. New Towns in India. Monograph and Occasional Papers Series, Monograph No. 8. Durham, North Carolina: Duke University, Program in Comparative Studies on Southern Asia, 1969, 149 pp.

Pressman, Norman. A Comprehensive Bibliography on New Towns in Canada. Exchange Bibliography No. 483. Monticello, Illinois: Council of Planning Librarians, 1973, 22 pp.

———. "French Urbanization Policy and the New Towns Program." *Ekistics*, **36,** no. 212 (July 1973): 17–22.

———. "How France Controls Urban Growth." *Landscape Architecture,* **64,** no. 1 (1973): 493–95.

———. *New Towns.* Occasional Paper No. 1. Waterloo, Ontario: Division of Environmental Studies, University of Waterloo, 1972, 19 pp.

———. "Planning New Communities in Canada." Stencil. Waterloo, Ontario: School of Urban and Regional Planning, University of Waterloo, 1974, 128 pp.

———. *A Selected Bibliography on French New Town Planning.* Exchange Bibliography No. 322. Monticello, Illinois: Council of Planning Librarians, 1972, 12 pp.

Pressman, Norman and Paul Brace. "Developing New Towns in France." *Plan,* **13,** no. 1 (1973): 27–44.

Prestridge, J.A. *Case Studies of Six Planned New Towns in the United States.* Lexington, Kentucky: Institute for Environmental Studies, University of Kentucky, 1973, 51 pp.

Princeton University Conference. *Innovation and New Communities?* Princeton, New Jersey: Princeton University School of Architecture and Urban Planning, 1971, 79 pp.

Pritchard, Norman. "Planned Social Provisions in New Towns." *Town Planning Review,* **38,** no. 1 (1967): 25–34.

Purdom, C.B. *The Building of Satellite Towns: A Contribution to the Study of Town Development and Regional Planning.* London: J.M. Dent and Sons, 1925, 368 pp.; 1949, rev. ed., 532 pp.

Qadeer, Mohammed A. "Local Land Market and a New Town: Columbia's Impact on Land Prices in Howard County, Maryland." *Journal of the American Institute of Planners,* **40,** no. 2 (1974): 110–23.

Quoist, M. *La ville et l'homme.* Paris: Les Editions Ouvrieres Economie et Humanisme, 1952.

Ray, William D. "Financing Large Community Developments." *Building Research,* **7,** no. 1 (1970): 94–96.

Real Estate Research Corporation. *The Costs of Sprawl.* Washington, D.C.: U.S. Government Printing Office, 1974.

———. "The Costs of Sprawl." *Real Estate Report,* Special Issue (1974).

———. *Economic and Financial Feasibility Models for New Community Development.* PB-206-925. Springfield, Virginia: National Technical Information Service, August 1971, 86 pp. +.

Regional Economic Development Institute. *Transportation Requirements and Effects of New Communities.* Pittsburgh: Regional Economic Development Institute, 1968, v + 102 pp.

Reilly, William K. and S.J. Schulman. "The State Urban Development Corporation: New York's Innovation." *Urban Lawyer,* **1,** no. 2 (1969): 129–46.

Reiner, Thomas A. *The Place of the Ideal Community in Urban Planning.* Philadelphia: University of Pennsylvania Press, 1963, 194 pp.

Report of the Commission. *Population and the American Future.* New York: The New American Library, 1972.

Report of the Welfare Island Planning and Development Committee. Submitted to John V. Lindsay, Mayor, City of New York, 1969.

Reps, John W. "The Green Belt Concept." *Town and Country Planning,* **28,** no. 7 (1960): 246–50.

———. *The Making of Urban America.* Princeton, New Jersey: Princeton University Press, 1965, 438 pp.

———. *Tidewater Towns: City Planning in Colonial Virginia and Maryland.* Charlottesville, Virginia: University Press of Virginia, 1972, 345 pp.

———. *Town Planning Frontier America.* Princeton, New Jersey: Princeton University Press, 1970, 473 pp.

Research Analysis Corporation. *New Community Development.* 2 vols. McLean, Virginia: Research Analysis Corporation, 1971.

Research and Policy Committee. *Modernizing Local Government.* New York: Committee for Economic Development, 1966.

Reshaping Government in Metropolitan Areas. New York: Research and Policy Committee of the Committee for Economic Development, 1970.

Reston: Density Control Under the Residential Planned Community (RPC) Chapter of the Fairfax County Zoning Ordinance. Reston, Virginia: Gulf Reston, Planning and Engineering Staff, 1970, 32 pp.

Reston, Virginia Foundation for Community Programs. "Social Planning and Programs." Stencil. Reston, Virginia: Reston, Virginia Foundation for Community Programs, 1967, 104 pp.

The Restonian. A newsletter. Reston, Virginia: Gulf Reston, 1974, 8 pp.

Rhode Island University. *Nuclear Energy for a New Town.* Springfield, Virginia: National Technical Information Service, 1971, 64 pp.

Richards, J.M. "New Towns in The Netherlands." *Progress* (1956): 1–11.

Richardson, Harry W. "Optimality in City Size, Systems of Cities and Urban Policy: A Skeptic's View." *Ekistics,* **34,** no. 205 (December 1972): 391–99.

Richardson, H.W. "Regional Development Policy in Spain." *Ekistics,* **32,** no. 192 (November 1971): 374–79.

Richardson, Nigel H. "The Kitimat Region." In *Regional and Resource Planning in Canada,* Ralph K. Krueger et al., eds. Toronto: Holt, Rinehart and Winston of Canada, 1970, pp. 83–89.

Rick, William B. *Planning and Developing Waterfront Property.* Washington, D.C.: Urban Land Institute, 1967.

Ricks, R. Bruce, "Location of New Towns: The Use of Low-Priced Land May Serve to Reduce Development Profits." *Journal of the Federal Home Loan Bank Board,* **3,** no. 6 (1970): 10–15, 24.

———. "New Town Development and the Theory of Location." *Land Economics,* **46,** no. 1 (1970): 5–11.

Ritter, Paul. *Planning for Man and Motor.* London: Pergamon Press, 1964, 384 pp.

Robinson, Albert J. *Economics and New Towns: A Comparative Study of the United States, The United Kingdom, and Australia.* New York: Praeger, 1975, 250 pp.

Robinson, D.C. "Planning in the Commonwealth: Tema, The New Port of Ghana." *Journal of the Town Planning Institute,* **45** (1959): 90–93.

Roderick, W.P. "The London New Towns: Origins of Migrants from Greater London up to December 1968." *Town Planning Review,* **42,** no. 4 (1971): 323–41.

Rodgers, H.B. "Women and Work in New and Expanding Towns." *Town and Country Planning,* **37,** no. 1–2 (1969): 23–27.

Rodwin, Lloyd. *The British New Towns Policy: Problems and Implications.* Harvard City Planning Series, No. 16. Cambridge, Massachusetts: Harvard University Press, 1956, xiii + 252 pp.

————. "Ciudad Guayana: A New City." In *Cities,* edited by *Scientific American.* New York: Alfred A. Knopf, 1967, pp. 88–105.

————. "Economic Problems in Developing New Towns and Expanded Towns." In *Planning of Metropolitan Areas and New Towns.* New York: United Nations, 1967, pp. 149–67.

————. *Nations and Cities: A Comparison of Strategies for Urban Growth.* Boston: Houghton-Mifflin Company, 1970, 395 pp.

————. "Planned Decentralization and Regional Development with Special Reference to British New Towns." *Journal of the American Institute of Planners,* **21,** no. 1 (1955): 43–49.

Rodwin, Lloyd, ed. *Planning Urban Growth and Regional Development: The Experience of the Guayana Program of Venezuela.* Cambridge, Massachusetts: M.I.T. Press, 1969, xix + 524 pp.

Rodwin, Lloyd and Lawrence Susskind. "New Communities and Urban Growth Strategies." Stencil. Cambridge, Massachusetts: Massachusetts Institute of Technology, 1972, 17 pp.

Rogers, David. *The Management of Big Cities Interest Groups and Social Change Strategies.* Beverly Hills, California: Saga Publications, 1971.

Roper, Hugh. "'A New City in Venezuela." *Journal of the Town Planning Institute,* **54** (1968): 437–39.

Rouse Company. *A New City: Columbia, Maryland.* Baltimore: The Rouse Company, 1966, 32 pp.

Rouse, James W. "The City of Columbia, Maryland." In *How to Manage An Urbanized World,* Vol. II of *Taming Megalopolis,* H. Wentworth Eldredge, ed. New York: Praeger, 1967, pp. 838–47; Garden City, New York: Anchor Books, Doubleday and Company, 1967, pp. 838–47.

————. "Columbia: A New Town Built with Private Capital." In *Private Capital for New Towns.* London: Institute of Economic Affairs, 1969, pp. 13–37.

————. "How to Build a Whole New City From Scratch." *Savings Bank Journal,* **47,** no. 8 (1966): 27–32.

Rouse, Willard G. "Practical Aspects of New Town Development." In *Regional New Towns: Alternatives for Urban Growth.* Detroit: The Metropolitan Fund, Inc., 1970, pp. 114–16.

Rowland, Norman and Margaret Drury. *Reston Low-Income Housing Demonstration Program.* Reston, Virginia: The Virginia Reston Foundation for Community Programs, 1969, 196 pp. + appendices.

Roullier, J.E. *Administrative and Financial Problems of Creating New Towns in the Paris Area.* Reprinted from the *Review Techniques et Architecture,* no. 5 (1970): 33 pp.

Roullier, J.Ed., ed. *French New Towns and Innovation.* Reprinted from *Review "2000" Paris,* January 1973, 15 pp.

Royal Institute of Netherlands Architects. *Planning and Creation of an Environment: Experiences in the Ysselmeerpolders.* The Hague: Government of The Netherlands (no date).

Rozhin, I, "Moscow's First New Town." Parts I and II. *Town and Country Planning,* **28,** nos. 3–4 (1960): 98–101, 149–53.

Rubel, John H. "The Aerospace Project Approach Applied to Building New Cities." In *How to Manage An Urbanized World,* Vol. II of *Taming Megalopolis,* H. Wentworth Eldredge, ed. New York: Praeger, 1967, pp. 854–74, Garden City, New York: Anchor Books, Doubleday and Company, 1967, pp. 854–74.

Ruzhnikov, Yevgeni. "A New Town on the Volga." *Architect and Builder News,* **3** (1969): 61–62.

Sagan, Bruce. "The Harper Court Experience." *Journal of the American Institute of Planners,* **32,** no. 3 (1966).

Saini, Balwant Singh. *Building Environment: An Illustrated Analysis of Problems in Hot Dry Lands.* Sydney: Angus and Robertson, Publishers, 1973.

Sainsbury, P. and Joyce Collins. "Some Factors Relating to Mental Illness in a New Town." *Journal of Psychosomatic Research,* **10,** no. 1 (1966): 45–51.

Salley, Marjorie A. "Public Transportation and the Needs of New Communities." *Traffic Quarterly,* **26,** no. 1 (1972): 33–49.

San Antonio New Town. *Final Application for San Antonio New Town.* 3 vols. San Antonio: San Antonio New Town, 1973.

Saskachewan. *A Development Plan for a Proposed Townsite in the Jan Lake Area, Saskatchewan.* Regina: Community Planning Branch, Department of Municipal Affairs, Province of Saskachewan, 1970, 67 pp. + maps.

Scarupa, Harriet. "Youth in Columbia." *Columbia Today,* **3,** no. 4 (1970): 8–19.

Schaffer, Frank. *The New Town Story.* London: MacGibbon and Kee, 1970, 342 pp.

Schaller, Lyle. *Church Planning in New Towns.* Naperville, Illinois: Yokefellow Institute, June 1972, 62 pp.

Schoenauer, Norbert. "New Town Design in the North." Stencil. Montreal: School of Architecture, McGill University, May 1973, 5 pp.

Schon, Donald A. "Techno-Institutional Innovation and New Communities." In *Innovation and New Communities,* a conference sponsored by Princeton University, September 28–29, 1970. Princeton, New Jersey: Princeton University School of Architecture and Urban Planning, 1971, pp. 38–45.

Schulz, Paul O. "The New Town of Wulfen." *Ekistics,* **36,** no. 212 (July 1973): 64–66.

Schwartzman, Daniel, Jules Gregory and George T. Rockrise. "Beersheba: Symbol of a National Policy." *Journal of the American Institute of Architects,* **53,** no. 4 (1970): 27–37.

Science Council of Canada. *Cities for Tomorrow: Some Applications of Science and Technology to Urban Development.* Ottawa: Information Canada, 1971, 67 pp.

Scotland. Scottish Development Department. Cmnd. 2188. *Central Scotland: A Programme for Development and Growth.* Edinburgh: Her Majesty's Stationery Office, 1963, 47 pp.

Scott, F.R. and W.R. Lederman. "A Memorandum Concerning Housing, Urban Development and the Constitution of Canada." *Plan,* **12,** no. 1 (1972): 33–44.

Scott, Randall W. "New Towns as Self-Sufficient Growth Centers: Dream or Feasible Reality." *Urban and Social Change Review,* **5,** no. 1 (1971): 16–19.

Scott, Stanley. "The Large New Communities and Urban Growth: A Broader Perspective and Its Implications." *Public Affairs Report,* **6,** no. 6 (1966): 1–6.

————. "The Large New Communities: Ultimate Self-Government and Other Problems." *Public Affairs Report,* **6,** no. 5 (1965): 1–5.

————. "Local Government and the Large New Communities." *Public Affairs Report,* **6,** no. 3 (1965): 1–5.

————. "New Towns Development and the Role of Government." *Public Affairs Report,* **12** (1964): 1–35.

————. "Urban Growth Challenges New Towns." In *New Towns: A New Dimension of Urbanism.* Chicago: International City Managers' Association, 1966, pp. 44–51.

Sedlar, Sasa. "A Yugoslav New Town." *Town and Country Planning,* **29,** no. 3 (1961): 111–14.

Self, Peter. *Cities in Flood: The Problems of Urban Growth.* London: Faber and Faber, 1957, 189 pp.

————. "New Towns, Greenbelts, and the Urban Region." In *The Metropolitan Future.* Berkeley: University of California, 1963, pp. 32–39.

————. *The New Towns Principle and the Urban Region.* Berkeley and Los Angeles: University of California Press, 1963.

————. *New Towns and Regional Planning from New Towns in the Present and Future.* London: Town and Country Planning Association, 1970.

————. "A New Vision for New Towns." *Town and Country Planning,* **38,** no. 1 (1970): 4–9.

Senior, Derek, ed. *The Regional City: An Anglo-American Discussion of Metropolitan Planning.* London: Longmans, 1966, 192 pp.

"The Senri New Town Central District Center." *Japan Architect,* **45** (1970): 37–64.

"Senri Newtown Neighborhood Centre, Senriyama, Osaka." *Japan Architect,* **39,** no. 12 (1964): 32–35.

"Senri Newtown South Area Centre." *Japan Architect,* **39,** no. 12 (1964): 36–42.

Settlement Study Center. *Regional Cooperation in Israel.* Rehovot, Israel: National and University Institute of Agriculture (no date).

Shacher, A. "Israel's Development Towns, Evaluation of National Urbanization Policy." *Journal of the American Institute of Planners,* **37,** no. 6 (1971): 362–72.

Shaked, S. "New Towns and Housing 1948–67." In *Israel Builds: New Trends in Planning of Housing.* Tel Aviv: Ministry of Housing, Division of Physical Planning, 1968.

Shapiro, Ovadia. *Inhabited Rural Centers in Israel.* Jerusalem: Settlement Study Center, National and University Institute of Agriculture, 1968.

Shindman, B. "An Optimum Size for Cities." In *Readings in Urban Geography,* Harold M. Mayer and Clyde Kohn, eds. Chicago: University of Chicago Press, 1959, pp. 257–60.

Shkvarikov, V., M. Haucke and O. Smirnova. "Recent New Towns: The Building of New Towns in the U.S.S.R." *Ekistics,* **18,** no. 108 (November 1964): 307–19.

Shkvarikov, V., M. Haucke and I. Smoljar. "New Towns." In *The Future: Patterns and Forms of Urban Settlement.* New York: United Nations, 1968, p. 259.

Short, James L. "New Towns or New Communities: Is There a Difference?" *Urban Land,* **31,** no. 11 (1972): 11–17.

Shostak, Arthur B. "Introduction: On Telling a New Town from Any Other—and Listening to it in Turn." *Sociological Symposium,* no. 12 (1974): 1–16.

Shuval, Judith. *Social Problems in Development Towns: A Research Study Towards Planning and Experimental Living Unit at Kiryath Gat.* Jerusalem: Israel Institute of Applied Social Research, Jerusalem, 1959.

Silkin, Lord. "Israel's New Town Programme." *Town and Country Planning,* **35,** no. 3 (1967): 146–47.

————. "Poland's Nova Huta: New Steel Town." *Town and Country Planning,* **24,** no. 142 (1956): 40–42.

Silver, Irving R. "The Role of Social Science Research in Urban Policy." *Plan,* **12,** no. 1 (1972): 107–15.

Silverman, Jane. "Development Towns: Israel's New Frontier." *Urban Land,* **34,** no. 3 (1975): 14–20.

————. "The New Towns of Israel: Unprecedented in Scope and Impact on National Life." *Journal of the American Institute of Architects,* **62** (1974): 46–50.

Simon, Robert E., Jr. "Implementation: New Towns." In *The Regional City,* Derek Senior, ed. Chicago: Aldine Publishing Company, 1966, pp. 113–24.

————. "Site Selection for a Large Scale Community." *Building Research,* **6,** no. 4 (1969): 6–8.

Skaarup, Hans Hartvig. "Heimdal New Town, Norway." *Ekistics,* **36,** no. 212 (July 1973): 67–69.

Skelmersdale Development Corporation. *Population and Social Survey 1972.* Skelmersdale, England: Skelmersdale Development Corporation, 1972, 40 pp.

Sleeswijk, C. Wegener. *The Growth of the City: Urban Extension in Amsterdam.* Amsterdam: Press, Publicity and Information Bureau of the City of Amsterdam, no date, 32 pp.

Slidell, John B. *The Shape of Things to Come? An Evaluation of the Neighborhood Unit as an Organizing Scheme for American New Towns.* Chapel Hill, North Carolina: Center for Urban and Regional Studies, University of North Carolina, 1972, 53 pp.

Slidell, John B. and Shirley F. Weiss. *A Users Guide to the GE-UNC New Towns Financial Feasibility Model: A Long Program.* Chapel Hill, North Carolina: Center for Urban and Regional Studies, University of North Carolina, 1972, 148 pp.

Smith, Brian C. "New Bussa: A New Town on the Niger." *Ekistics,* **25,** no. 147 (February 1968): 101–06; *Urban Studies,* **4,** no. 2 (1967): 149–64.

Smith, L.M., ed. *An Approach to a Total Communications-Electronics System for New Communities.* Revised edition. Waltham, Massachusetts: GTE Laboratories, 1971, 98 pp.

Smith, Leland F. "Is There a Future?" *Urban Land,* **30,** no. 5 (1971).

Smith, P.J. "Changing Objectives in Scottish New Towns Policy." *Ekistics,* **23,** no. 134 (January 1967): 26–33; *Annals of the Association of American Geographers,* **56** (1966): 492–507.

Smith, R. "Planning Schools in New Communities." In *World Year Book of Education 1970,* J.A. Lauwerys and D. Scanlon, eds. London: Evans Brothers, 1970.

Smolski, Chester E. "European New Towns: Focus on London." *Focus,* **22,** no. 6 (1972): 1–8.

Smookler, Helene V. "Economic Integration in New Communities: An Evaluation of Factors Affecting Policies and Implementation."

Mimeo. New Communities Policy Applications Workshop NSF/RANN/APRT GI-34285, November 18, 1974, 4 pp.

Social and Community Planning Research and Milton Keynes Development Corporation. *Four Years On: Milton Keynes Household Survey 1973.* Summary. Milton Keynes, England: Milton Keynes Development Corporation, 1974, 75 pp.

"Social Development in New Communities: Proceedings of a Seminar, March 1972." Research Memorandum No. 12 of the University of Birmingham, Centre for Urban and Regional Studies, April 1972, 66 pp.

Soen, Dan and Baruch Kipnis. "The Functioning of a Cluster of Towns in Israel." *Ekistics,* **34,** no. 205 (December 1972): 400–07.

Soleri, Paolo. *Arcology: The City in the Image of Man.* Cambridge, Massachusetts: M.I.T. Press, 1969, 122 pp.

———. *The Sketchbooks of Paolo Soleri.* Cambridge, Massachusetts: M.I.T. Press, 1971.

South Australia. *Murray New Town (Land Acquisition Act) Act.* Act No. 35 of 1972. Adelaide, South Australia: Government Printer, 1972.

Spencer, P. "Towards a Measure of Social Investment in Communities." *Architectural Research and Teaching,* **1** (1971): 32–38.

Spiegel, Erika. *New Towns in Israel: Urban and Regional Planning and Development.* Translated by Annelie Rookwood. New York: Praeger, 1967, 192 pp., Stuttgart: Karl Kramer Verlog, 1966, 191 pp.

Spilhaus, Athelstan. "The Experimental City." In *America's Changing Environment,* Roger Revelle and Hans H. Landsburg, eds. Boston: Houghton-Mifflin Company, 1970, pp. 219–31.

Stanland, Raymond. *Innovation and New Towns.* Chapel Hill, North Carolina: Center for Urban and Regional Studies, University of North Carolina, 1972, 35 pp.

Stein, Clarence S. *Kitimat Townsite Report.* Kitimat, British Columbia: Corporation of the District of Kitimat, 1960.

———. *Toward New Towns for America.* Introduction by Lewis Mumford. Chicago: Public Administration Service, Liverpool University Press, 1951, 245 pp; New York: Reinhold, 1957, 263 pp; Cambridge, Massachusetts: M.I.T. Press, 1967, 227 pp.

Stein, Clarence et al. "Kitimat Townsite Report." A compilation of reference material and report, 1951–52. Vol 1. Mimeo. New York: British Empire Building, 1952, 270 pp.

Stelter, Gilbert A. "The Origins of a Company Town: Sudbury in the Nineteenth Century." *Laurentian University Review* no. 3 (1971): 3–37.

Stephenson, Glenn V. "Two Newly Created Capitals: Islamabad and Brasilia." *Town Planning Review,* **41,** no. 4 (1970): 317–32.

Stevenage Development Corporation. *Proposals for Expansion.* Volume 2, *Stevenage Expansion 1973.* Stevenage, England: Stevenage Development Corporation, 1973, 91 pp.

Stevenage 72: Updating of the Master Plan 1966. Stevenage, England: Stevenage Development Corporation (no date).

Stevens, Robert D. and George J. Bacalis. "Transportation for a New Town." *Highway Research Record,* no. 367 (1971): 9–16.

Stewart, J.R. "Marine Ecumenopolis." *Ekistics,* **29,** no. 175 (June 1970): 399–418.

Stockholm: Urban Environment. Stockholm: Stockholms Stadsbyggnadskontor, 1972, 169 pp.

Stone, P.A. "Financing the Construction of New Towns." In *Planning of Metropolitan Areas and New Towns.* New York: United Nations, 1967, pp. 220–31.

Strong, Ann Louise. *Planned Urban Environments: Sweden, Finland, Israel, The Netherlands and France.* Baltimore: Johns Hopkins Press, 1971, 406 pp.

Sundquist, James L. "Where Shall They Live?" *Public Interest,* **18** (1970): 88–100.

Suquet-Bonnaud, A. "Introduction" (au numero special sur les villes nouvelles), *Urbanisme* **22,** nos. 25–26 (1953): 3–4. Quoted and translated in Viet, Jean. *New Towns: A Selected Annotated Bibliography,* no. 12, Paris: UNESCO, 1960, p. 16.

Susskind, Lawrence. "Planning for New Towns: The Gap Between Theory and Planning." *Sociological Inquiry,* **43,** no. 3–4 (1973): 291–310.

———. "New Communities and National Urban Growth Strategies—Undergraduate Policy Seminar—42.08." Stencil. Massachusetts Institute of Technology, Department of Urban Studies and Planning, Spring Semester 1971.

Susskind, Lawrence and Gary Hack. "New Communities in a National Urban Growth Strategy." *Technology Review,* **74,** no. 4 (1972): 30–42.

Suttles, Gerald D. *The Social Construction of Communities.* Chicago: University of Chicago Press, 1973.

Swain, Harry and Vern J. Wieler. "Urbanization and Regional Development: The Canadian Experience in Policy Development." Mimeo. Paper Presented at the National Conference of the American Institute of Planners, Boston, Massachusetts, October 7–11, 1972, 13 pp.

"A Synopsis of the Corporation's Planning Proposals for Newtown." Mimeo. Newtown, Wales: Mid-Wales Development Corporation, 1968, 6 pp.

Syracuse, Lee A. "Open Space in New Communities." *Building Research,* **7,** no. 1 (1970): 65–66.

Task Force on Housing and Urban Development. *Report of the Federal Task Force on Housing and Urban Development.* Ottawa: Queen's Printer of Canada, 1969, 85 pp. + illus.

Taubman, William. *Governing Soviet Cities: Bureaucratic Politics and Urban Development in the USSR.* New York: Praeger, 1973.

Taylor, G. Brooke. "Leisure in New Towns." *Town and Country Planning,* **35,** no. 1 (1967): 5–10.

———. "A Policy for Recreation for New Development." *Parks and Sports Grounds,* **32** (1967): 360–62, 364, 366–67.

———. "Recreation in the New Towns." *Town and Country Planning,* **36,** no. 10–11 (1968): 482–84.

———. "Social Planning in New Towns." *Public Health,* **82** (1968): 269–72; discussion, 273–78.

Taylor, Russell D. "New Town in Western Australia." *Journal of the Australian Planning Institute,* **7,** no. 4 (1969): 113–19.

Taylor, Stephen James Lake. *Mental Health in New Communities, 1963.* London: Chadwick Trust, 1963, 8 pp.

Taylor, Lord Stephen James Lake and Sidney Chave. *Mental Health and Environment* (in a New Town.) London: Longmans, 1964, 228 pp.

Tetlow, John and Anthony Goss. *Homes, Towns and Traffic.* London: Faber and Faber, 1965.

Thomas, David. *London's Green Belt.* London: Faber and Faber, 1970, 53 pp.

Thomas, Lucy and Erich Lindemann. "Newcomers' Problems in a Suburban Community."*Journal of the American Institute of Planners,* **27,** no. 3 (1961): 185–93.

Thomas, Ray. *Aycliffe to Cumbernauld: A Study of Seven New Towns in Their Regions.* Broadsheet 516. New York: Committee for Economic Development, 1969, pp. 801–962.

————. *London's New Towns: A Study of Self-Contained Balanced Communities.* London: Political and Economic Planning [PEP], 1969.

————. "Need for Knowledge: The New City Impact." *Town and Country Planning,* **38,** no. 8 (1970): 430–31.

————. "New Towns and New Suburbs: How Spread Out? How Way Out?" *Town and Country Planning,* **39,** no. 1 (1971): 23–26.

Thomas, Ray and Peter Cresswell. *The New Town Idea.* Milton Keynes, England: The Open University Press, 1973, 64 pp.

Thompson, Wayne E. "Prototype City: Design for Tomorrow." In *New Towns: A New Dimension of Urbanism.* Chicago: International City Managers' Association, 1966, pp. 38–43.

Thompson, Wilbur R. "The National System of Cities as an Object of Public Policy." *Urban Studies,* **9,** no. 1 (1972): 99–116.

Thurston, Hazel. "France Finds a New Holiday Coast." *Geographical Magazine,* **41** (1969): 339–45.

Tolley, Rodney S. "Telford New Town: Conception and Reality in West Midlands Industrial Overspill." *Town Planning Review,* **43** (1972): 343–60.

Tomlinson, Richard F., II. *Computer-Aided Space Allocation Technique.* Version 1, modification 0. University Park, Pennsylvania: Department of Architectural Engineering, The Pennsylvania State University, September 1971.

"The Toronto Region's Privately Developed New Communities." *Civic Affairs,* no. 2 (1972): 5–40.

Town and Country Planning Association. *British New Towns.* London: Town and Country Planning Association, 1970.

Towne, Carroll A. "Atomic Energy Commission Community Developments: A Planning Policy Built Upon Enlightening Experience." *Landscape Architecture,* **43** (1953): 119–23.

"Transport in New Towns: A Change of Emphasis." *Town and Country Planning,* **35** (1967): 385–86.

Triton Foundation. *Triton City: A Study of a Prototype Floating Community.* PB 180051. Washington, D.C.: Clearinghouse of the U.S. Department of Commerce, U.S. Government Printing Office, 1968, 120 pp.

Turner, Alan. "A Case for New Towns." *Journal of the American Institute of Architects,* **54,** no. 5 (1970): 28–32.

————. "Tuy Medio." *Architectural Design,* **39,** no. 8 (1969): 439–41.

Turner, Alan and Jonathan Smulian. "New Cities in Venezuela." *Town Planning Review,* **42,** no. 1 (1971): 3–27.

Twentieth Century Fund Task Force for Governance of New Towns. *Newtowns: Laboratories for Democracy.* New York: The Twentieth Century Fund, 1971.

Twenty-Seventh World Congress for Housing and Planning. *National Planning for the Redistribution of Population and the Establishment of New Towns in Israel.* Jerusalem: Ministry of the Interior, 1964.

Tyrwhitte, Jacqueline. "Changes in New Town Policies in Britain 1946–1971." *Ekistics,* **36,** no. 212 (July 1973): 14–16.

Underhill, Jack A. "European New Towns: One Answer to Urban Problems?" *HUD Challenge* (March/April 1970): 19–23.

————. "Federal Role in New Town Development." In *Regional New Towns: Alternatives for Urban Growth.* Detroit: The Metropolitan Fund, 1970, pp. 92–97.

————. "General Observations on British New Town Planning." A report written following participation in the United Nations Seminar on New Towns, held in London, June 4–19, 1973. Mimeo. Washington, D.C.: Department of Housing and Urban Development, Office of International Affairs, 1973, 16 pp. + appendices.

————. "Proposal for Strengthening the Role of New Communities in Implementing National Urban Growth Strategy." Stencil. Washington, D.C.: U.S. Department of Housing and Urban Development, 1971, 32 pp.

United Jewish Appeal. *21 Frontier Towns.* New York: United Jewish Appeal in Cooperation with the Jewish Agency for Israel (no date).

United Nations Center for Housing, Building and Planning. "Selected Conclusions and Recommendations on Regional and Metropolitan Planning: New Towns and Land Policy." *Ekistics,* **23,** no. 135 (February 1967): 87–91.

United Nations. Economic Commission for Asia and the Far East. *A Case Study of The Domodar Valley Corporation and Its Projects.* Flood Control Series No. 16. Bangkok: United Nations Economic Commission for Asia and the Far East, 1960, xii + 110 pp.

United Nations. World Health Organization. *Health and Sanitation Factors in the Planning and Development of New Towns.* United Nations Conference Document No. 12. New York: United Nations, 1964, 15 pp.

United States. "Draft Regulations: Urban Growth and New Community Development Act of 1970." In *Federal Register,* **36** F.R. 14205–14, July 13, 1971.

United States. Advisory Commission on Intergovernmental Relations. *A Look to the North: Canadian Regional Experience.* Commission Report A-46. Substate, Regionalism, and the Federal System Series, Vol. 5. Washington, D.C.: U.S. Government Printing Office, 1974, 134 pp.

————. *Report on New Towns and New Communities: A Bibliography.* Washington, D.C.: U.S. Government Printing Office, 1968.

————. *Urban and Rural America: Policies for Future Growth.* Commission Report A-32. Washington, D.C.: U.S. Government Printing Office, 1968, 186 pp.

United States. Commission on Instructional Technology. *To Improve Learning: A Report to the President and the Congress of the United States.* Washington, D.C.: U.S. Government Printing Office, 1970.

United States. Commission on Population Growth. *Population and the American Future: The Report of the Commission on Population Growth and the American Future.* Washington, D.C.: U.S. Government Printing Office, 1972, xvii + 607 pp.; New York: New American Library, a Signet Special, 1972, 362 pp.

United States. Congress. "Demonstration Cities and Metropolitan

Development Act of 1966." Title IV: Land Development and New Communities. In *United States Statutes at Large,* **80,** Part I (1966): 1271–73.

———. "Housing and Urban Development Act of 1968." Title IV: Guarantees for Financing New Community Land Development. In *United States Statutes at Large,* **82** (1968): 513–18.

———. "Housing and Urban Development Act of 1970." Title VII: Urban Growth and New Community Development. In *United States Statutes at Large,* **84,** Part 2 (1970–71): 1791–1805.

United States. Congress. House. *Drafts of Bills Relating to Housing.* Message from the President. 88th Congress, 2nd Session.

United States. Congress. House. Committee on Banking and Currency. *Population Trends.* Hearings before the Ad Hoc Subcommittee on Urban Growth of the Committee on Banking and Currency, Part 1, 91st Congress, 1st Session. Washington, D.C.: U.S. Government Printing Office, 1969, 803 pp.

———. *The Quality of Urban Life.* Hearings before the Ad Hoc Subcommittee on Urban Growth of the Committee on Banking and Currency, Part 2, 91st Congress, 1st and 2nd sessions. Washington, D.C.: U.S. Government Printing Office, 1970, 765 pp.

United States. Congress. Joint Economic Committee. *Urban America: Goals and Problems.* Materials compiled and prepared for the Subcommittee on Urban Affairs of the Joint Economic Committee, 90th Congress, 1st Session. Washington, D.C.: U.S. Government Printing Office, 1967, 303 pp.

United States. Department of Commerce. Bureau of the Census. *Number of Inhabitants. United States Summary.* Washington, D.C.: U.S. Government Printing Office, 1971, 249 pp.

———. *Statistical Abstracts of the United States 1969.* Washington, D.C.: U.S. Government Printing Office, 1969.

United States. Department of Housing and Urban Development. *Final Environmental Statement on the Proposed Gananda New Community, Wayne County, New York.* Springfield, Virginia: National Technical Information Service, 1972, 123 pp.

———. *Final Environmental Statement on Proposed New Community of Maumelle Pulaski County, Arkansas.* Springfield, Virginia: National Technical Information Service, 1971, 50 pp.

———. *Final Environmental Statement on Proposed New Community of San Antonio Ranch Bexar County, Texas.* Springfield, Virginia: National Technical Information Service, 1972, 206 pp.

———. *Financing New Communities: Government and Private Experience in Europe and the United States.* Washington, D.C.: Office of International Affairs, U.S. Department of Housing and Urban Development, 1973, 59 pp.

———. *Flower Mound New Town, Denton County, Texas Final Environmental Impact Statement.* PB 202338-F. Springfield, Virginia: National Technical Information Service, 1971, 128 pp.

———. "HUD Issues Commitment for First New Community." *HUD News,* February 13, 1970, 5 pp.

———. *Instructions for the Preparation of Porposals and Applications for Guarantee Assistance Under the New Communities Act of 1968.* Washington, D.C.: U.S. Department of Housing and Urban Development, 1970, 15 pp.

———. *New Communities: A Bibliography.* HUD-6-A. Washington, D.C.: U.S. Department of Housing and Urban Development, 1969, 84 pp.

———. *Outline of New Communities Assistance Programs.* Washington, D.C.: U.S. Department of Housing and Urban Development, Office of New Communities Development, 1971, 13 pp.

———. *Project Agreement Between the United States of America and Cedar-Riverside Land Company.* Springfield, Virginia: National Technical Information Service, 1971, 57 pp.

———. *Project Agreement Between the United States of America and Flower Mound New Town, Ltd.* Springfield, Virginia: National Technical Information Service, 1971, 154 pp.

———. *Project Agreement Between the United States of America and Interstate Land Development Company, Inc.* Springfield, Virginia: National Technical Information Service, 1970, 147 pp.

———. *Project Agreement Between the United States of America and Jonathan Development Corporation.* Springfield, Virginia: National Technical Information Service, 1970, 121 pp.

———. *Project Agreement Between the United States of America and Maumelle Land Development, Inc.* Springfield, Virginia: National Technical Information Service, 1971, 182 pp.

———. *Project Agreement Between the United States of America and Park Forest South Development Company.* Springfield, Virginia: National Technical Information Service, 1971, 138 pp.

———. *Proposed New Community of Cedar-Riverside, Minneapolis, Minnesota Final Environmental Impact Statement.* PB 200378-F. Springfield, Virginia: National Technical Information Service, 1971, 70 pp.

———. *The Proposed Riverton New Community, Monroe County, New York Final Environmental Impact Statement.* PB 201391-F. Springfield, Virginia: National Technical Information Service, November 19, 1971, 124 pp.

———. *Proposed New Community of Soul City, Warren County, North Carolina Final Environmental Impact Statement.* PB 203773-F. Springfield, Virginia: National Technical Information Service, February 14, 1972, 122 pp.

———. *Proposed New Community, The Woodlands, North of Houston, Texas Final Environmental Impact Statement.* PB 204498-F. Springfield, Virginia: National Technical Information Service, February 23, 1972, 102 pp.

———. *Special Report on Techniques of Aided Self-Help Housing: Some Examples of U.S. and Overseas Experience.* Washington, D.C.: U.S. Government Printing Office, 1973.

United States. Department of Housing and Urban Development. Office of International Affairs. *Urban Growth Policies in Six European Countries.* Reprint. Washington, D.C.: U.S. Government Printing Office, 1973, 75 pp.

———. *Urban Land Policy: Selected Aspects of European Experiences.* HUD-94-SF. Washington, D.C.: U.S. Department of Housing and Urban Development, Office of International Affairs, 1969, 219 pp.

United States. Executive Office of the President. Domestic Council. Committee on National Growth. *Report on National Growth 1972.* Washington, D.C.: U.S. Government Printing Office, 1972, xii + 74 pp.

United States. President's Committee on Urban Housing. *A Decent Home.* (Kaiser Report). Washington, D.C.: U.S. Government Printing Office, 1969, 252 pp.

United States. Senate. *Housing Legislation of 1964: Hearings Before a Subcommittee*. 88th Congress, 2nd Session, February 19–March 3, 1964.

United States. Urban Growth Policy Study Group. "Urban Growth Policies in Six European Countries." In *National Growth Policy. Part 2: Selected Papers*. Washington, D.C.: U.S. Government Printing Office, 1972, pp. 555–629.

University of Birmingham, Centre for Urban and Regional Studies. *Social Development in New Communities: Proceedings of a Seminar*. Birmingham, England: Centre for Urban and Regional Studies, University of Birmingham, 1972, 66 pp.

University of Kentucky, Department of Architecture. *New Towns for the Appalachian Region: A Case Study Located in Eastern Kentucky*. Lexington, Kentucky: Department of Architecture, University of Kentucky, 1960, 48 pp. +.

University of Louisville, Urban Studies Center. *Turning Problems Into Opportunities: New Community Development as a Means for Realizing Urban and Rural Opportunities*. Louisville, Kentucky: Urban Studies Center, University of Louisville, 1969, 54 pp.

University of Manitoba, Centre for Settlement Studies. *Bibliography: Resource Frontier Communities*. Winnipeg: Centre for Settlement Studies, University of Manitoba, 1969, [v] + no pagination.

————. *Proceedings of the Symposium on Resource Frontier Communities*. Winnipeg: Centre for Settlement Studies, University of Manitoba, 1969, 86 pp.

University of North Carolina. Department of City and Regional Planning. *The Planning Process for New Town Development: Soul City. A Planning Studio Course—Fall 1969*. Chapel Hill, North Carolina: Department of City and Regional Planning, University of North Carolina, 1970, 220 pp.

Urban Land Institute. *The Homes Association Handbook*. Technical Bulletin No. 50. Washington, D.C.: Urban Land Institute, 1964, 422 pp.

————. *Innovations vs. Traditions in Community Development: A Comparative Study in Residential Land Use*. Washington, D.C.: Urban Land Institute, 1963, 111 pp.

————. *Land: Recreation and Leisure*. Washington, D.C.: Urban Land Institute, 1970.

————. *New Approaches to Residential Land Development: A Study of Concepts and Innovations*. Technical Bulletin No. 40. Washington, D.C.: Urban Land Institute, 1961, 151 pp.

————. *Parking Requirements for Shopping Centers: A Survey*. Washington, D.C.: Urban Land Institute, 1965.

————. *The Pros and Cons of Cluster Housing*. Washington, D.C.: Urban Land Institute, 1969.

"Urban Structure and Construction: The Senri Newtown Central District Master Plan." *Japan Architect*, no. 137 (1967): 13–16.

Vagale, L.R. "A Case Study of Chandigarh and Its Growth Potential." *Ekistics*, **23**, no. 135 (February 1967): 98–105.

————. "New Towns in India: Series—Planning and Design Principles." *Journal of the Institute of Town Planners* (India) (December 1966, March 1967): 36–79.

Veale, Alan et al. *Sackville Lakes: Development Plan*. Toronto: Murray V. Jones and Associates, 1970, 112 pp.

Victor Gruen and Associates. *From Farmland to City: Litchfield Park, Arizona*. Litchfield Park, Arizona: Litchfield Park Properties, 1969, 16 pp.

Viet, Jean. *New Towns: A Selected Annotated Bibliography*. Reports and papers in the Social Sciences no. 12. Paris: United Nations Educational, Scientific, and Cultural Organization, 1960, 84 pp.

Vietorisz, Thomas and Peter Bearse. "The Urban Future of New York State: Elements of a New Communities Strategy." Mimeo. Paper presented at the Northeast Regional Science Conference, Pennsylvania State University, University Park, Pennsylvania, April 14–16, 1972, 26 pp.

Villes Nouvelles: Province—Libres Opinions no. 302 (1974–75), 102 pp.

Villes Nouvelles: Region Parisienne no. 301 (1974), 134 pp.

Vincent, Leonard G. "Tema: Ghana's New Town and Harbour." *Town and Country Planning*, **30**, no. 3 (1962): 113–16.

Virginia Division of Environmental and Urban Systems. *Towards an Urban and Rural Development Policy for the State of Virginia*. Blacksburg, Virginia: College of Architecture, Virginia Polytechnic Institute, 1970.

Von Eckardt, Wolf. "The New Community." In *A Place to Live: The Crisis in the Cities*. New York: Delacorte Press, 1967, pp. 347–88.

————. "U.S.A.: The Case for Building 350 New Towns." *Harper's*, **231**, no. 1387 (1965): 85–95; *Town and Country Planning*, **34**, no. 1 (1966): 27–31.

Von Hertzen, Heikki and Paul D. Spreiregen. *Building A New Town: Finland's New Garden City, Tapiola*. Cambridge, Massachusetts: M.I.T. Press, 1971, 234 pp.

Von Moltke, Willo. "Visual Development of Ciudad Guayana." *Connection* (June 1965): 52–60.

Waldorf, Dan. "Recreation Facilities in a New Town." *Official Architecture and Planning*, **29** (1966): 1695–96, 1699–1700.

Walker, David B. "Needed Components of a National Urban General Policy." In *Land Use Policies*, Virginia Curtis, ed. Chicago: American Society of Planning Officials, 1970, 65–74.

Walter, Gerald R. "The Economic Structure of Single Enterprise Communities." Mimeo. Victoria, British Columbia: Department of Economics, University of Victoria, 1971, 15 pp.

Wang, J.Y., ed. *Proceedings of New City Designs Conference*. San Jose, California: Environmental Science Institute, 1969, 102 pp.

Ward, J.H. *The Social Center*. New York: D. Appleton and Company, 1913.

Warrington New Town Outline Plan. Warrington, England: Warrington New Town Development Corporation, 1972, [12], 94 pp.

Washington Center for Metropolitan Studies. *Reston: A Study in Beginning, A History of Reston from the Purchase of the Land in 1961 to the Period of First Occupancy in 1964*. 2 vols. Washington, D.C.: Washington Center for Metropolitan Studies, 1966.

Washnis, George J. *Municipal Decentralization and Neighborhood Resources: Case Studies of Twelve Cities*. Praeger Special Studies in U.S. Economic and Social Development. New York: Praeger, 1972, xxii + 444 pp.

Wassenich, Mark. *New Towns from the Point of View of the Ghetto Resident: Phase II—Evaluating the Game Technique*. Chapel Hill, North Carolina: Center for Urban and Regional Studies, University of North Carolina, 1970, 16 pp. + appendix.

Way, Douglas S. *Terrain Analysis: A Guide to Site Selection Using Aerial Photographic Interpretation*. Stroudsburg, Pennsylvania: Dowden, Hutchinson and Ross, 1973.

Weaver, Robert C. *Dilemmas of Urban America.* Cambridge, Massachusetts: Harvard University Press, 1966, 138 pp.

————. "Planned Communities." *Highway Research Record* no. 97 (1965): 1–6.

Webster, R.H. "New Towns for Old: A Broad Study of Effective Decentralization in Canberra." *Valver,* 22 (1972): 52–67, 114–17.

Weiss, Shirley F. "New Cities." *Panhandle Magazine,* 5, no. 3 (1971): 18–22.

————. *New Town Development in the U.S.: Experiment in Private Entrepreneurship.* Chapel Hill, North Carolina: New Towns Research Seminar, Center for Urban and Regional Studies, University of North Carolina, 1973, 132 pp.

————. "New Town Development in the United States: Public Policy and Private Entrepreneurship." *SAIPA Journal of the Public Administration,* 4, no. 3 (1969): 185–97.

————. "New Towns: Transatlantic Exchange." *Town and Country Planning,* 38, no. 8 (1970): 374–81.

————. *Residential Developer Decisions.* Chapel Hill, North Carolina: Center for Urban and Regional Studies, University of North Carolina, 1967, 94 pp.

Weiss, Shirley F., Raymond J. Burby, III and Robert B.Zehner, eds. *Evaluation of New Communities: Selected Preliminary Findings.* Chapel Hill, North Carolina: Center for Urban and Regional Studies, University of North Carolina, 1974, 38 pp.

Weiss, Shirley F., Edward J. Kaiser, and Raymond J. Burby, III, eds. *New Community Development: Planning Process, Implementation, and Emerging Social Concerns.* 2 vols. Chapel Hill, North Carolina: New Towns Research Seminar, Center for Urban and Regional Studies, University of North Carolina, 1971, 527 + 264 pp.

————. "Toward a Linked Decision Model of the New Town Development Process." *Research Previews,* 16, no. 1 (1969): 12–20.

Weiss, Shirley et al. "New Towns Development: Convergence of Concept and Reality." A research proposal to the National Center for Urban and Industrial Health, Public Health Service, Department of Health, Education, and Welfare, 1968, 16 pp.

————. "New Community Development: A National Study of Environmental Preferences and the Quality of Life." *Research Previews,* 20, no. 1 (1973): 5–15.

Weissbourd, Bernard. "Satellite Communities: For a New Housing Program in the USA." *Ekistics,* 36, no. 212 (July 1973): 33–39.

————. "Satellite Communities: A Proposal for a New Housing Program." *Urban Land,* 31, no. 9 (1972): 3–18.

Weissbourd, Bernard and Herbert Channick. "An Urban Strategy." *Appraisal Journal,* 38, no. 1 (1970): 100–17.

Weitz, Raanan et al. *The Lakhish Region: Background Study for Research in Regional Development Planning.* Rehovot, Israel: Rehovot Settlement Study Center, 1970, 163 pp.

Wejchert, Kazimierz. "Tychy New Town." *Town and Country Planning,* 24 (1956): 214–18.

Wellbank, Michael. "Ideas for Export: British and French Ideas in the Development of a New Town at Pointoise-Cergy." *RIBA Journal,* 75, no. 9 (1968): 414–18.

Welsh, James. "Europe's New Towns: Round Three Coming Up." *Think,* 35, no. 2 (1969): 13–19.

Welwyn Garden City. London: The Commission for the New Towns, 1972, 16 pp.

Wende, Ernest A. "Building a City from Scratch." *Engineering News-Record,* 135 (1945): 149–52.

Wendt, Paul F. and Alan R. Cert. "Investment in Community Development and Urban Development." In *Real Estate Investment: Analysis and Taxation,* Paul F. Wendt and Alan R. Cert, eds. New York: McGraw-Hill, 1969, pp. 230–39.

Werner, Shaun M. et al. "How Do You Like Living in a Planned Community?" *Urban Land,* 31, no. 1 (1972): 3–13.

Werthman, Carl, Jerry S. Mandel and Ted Dienstfrey. *Planning and Purchase Decision: Why People Buy in Planned Communities.* Berkeley: Center for Planning and Development, Institute of Urban and Regional Development Research, University of California, 1965, 229 pp.

West Midlands Planning Authorities Conference. *A Developing Strategy for the West Midlands.* Birmingham, England: West Midlands Planning Authorities Conference, 1972, 26 pp. + maps.

"What Is This Thing Called Urban Growth Policy?" *City,* 4, no. 2 (1970): 31–32.

"What New Towns Ought to Be." In *New Towns: A New Dimension of Urbanism.* Chicago: International City Managers' Association, 1966, pp. 52–54.

Wheaton, William L.C., Albert Mayer and G. Holmes Perkins. "New Towns for American Defense." *Journal of the American Institute of Architects,* 15, no. 1 (1951).

Wheaton, William L.C. and Robert L. Wagner. "The Economic Feasibility of New Towns." Harvard Studies. *Journal of the American Institute of Architects,* 15, no. 1 (1951).

Wheeler, Sir Mortimer. *Civilizations of the Indus Valley and Beyond.* London: Thames and Hudson, 1966.

White, John Robert. "Economic Assessment of Large-Scale Projects." *Appraisal Journal,* 37, no. 3 (1969): 360–71.

White, Lesley E. "The Social Factors Involved in the Planning and Development of New Towns." In *Planning of Metropolitan Areas and New Towns.* New York: United Nations, 1967, pp. 194–200.

Whittick, Arnold. "The Architecture of New Towns." *Town and Country Planning,* 37, no. 1–2 (1969): 28–33.

————. "Central Areas of New Towns: The Design of Present and Future Centers." *Town and Country Planning,* 38, no. 1 (1970): 15–19.

————. "The Plan for Irvine." *Town and Country Planning,* 35, no. 10 (1967): 449–56.

————. "Redditch: The Basic Plan." *Town and Country Planning,* 35, no. 8 (1967): 398–402.

————. "Return to the Garden City: The Interim Proposals for Milton Keynes." *Town and Country Planning,* 37, no. 4 (1969): 151–55.

————. "Transport in New Towns: A Change of Emphasis." *Town and Country Planning,* 35, no. 8 (1967): 385–86.

————. "Washington: The Master Plan." *Town and Country Planning,* 35, no. 5 (1967): 240–44.

"Why Columbia Succeeded Where Others Failed." *Mortgage Banker* (June 1970): 10–20.

Whyte, William H., Jr. *Cluster Development.* New York: American Conservation Association, 1964, 130 pp.

————. *The Last Landscape.* Garden City, New York: Doubleday and Company, 1968, 376 pp., Anchor Books, 1970, 428 pp.

————. *Securing Open Space for Urban America: Conservation Easements.* Washington, D.C.: Urban Land Institute, 1968.

Wiegan, Cameron. *The New Town and Transportation Planning.* Springfield, Virginia: National Technical Information Planning, 1970.

Wiggins, Bruce C.S. "Organized Religion in Columbia: A Discussion of the Social Planning Process." *Sociological Symposium,* no. 12 (1974): 55–64.

Wilburn, M.D. and Robert M. Gladstone. *Optimizing Development Profits in Large Scale Real Estate Projects.* Technical Bulletin No. 67. Washington, D.C.: The Urban Land Institute, 1972, 64 pp.

Wilcoxen, Ralph. *A Short Bibliography on Megastructures.* Exchange Bibliography No. 66. Monticello: Illinois: Council of Planning Librarians, 1969, 18 pp.

Williams, David. "Chandigarh and Islamabad: A Comparative Study of Two New Asian Towns." *Asia Scene* (September 1964): 18–21.

————. "Islamabad." *Architectural Design,* 37 (1967): 49–50.

Williams, George. "Street Furniture in New Towns." *Town and Country Planning,* 21, no. 109 (1953): 236–42.

Willmott, Peter. "Social Research and New Communities." *Journal of the American Institute of Planners,* 33, no. 5 (1967): 387–98.

Wilson, L. Hugh. *Cumbernauld New Town Traffic Analysis Report.* Cumbernauld, Scotland: Cumbernauld Development Corporation, 1958.

————. "New Town Design: Cumbernauld and After." *RIBA Journal,* 71, no. 5 (1964): 191–206.

————. *Skelmersdale New Town Planning Proposals Report on Basic Plan.* Skelmersdale, England: Skelmersdale Development Corporation, 1964.

Wilson, L. Hugh and Lewis Womersley. *Irvine New Town: Final Report on Planning Proposals.* Edinburgh: Scottish Development Department, Her Majesty's Stationery Office, 1967, 240 pp.

Wilson, W.L. and J.C. Knight. "Integrated Heat and Power Services for a New City in Great Britain." *Heating and Ventilating Engineer,* 42 (1968): 299–307.

Wingo, Lowdon, Jr. "Issues in a National Urban Development Strategy for the United States." *Urban Studies,* 9, no. 1 (1972): 3–27.

Winston, Oliver C. "An Urbanization Pattern for the United States: Some Considerations for the Decentralization of Excellence." *Land Economics,* 43, no. 1 (1967): 1–10.

Wolfe, M.R. "Urbanization and a New Town in the Columbia Basin." *Town Planning Review,* 28, no. 6 (1957): 111–30.

Woods, Robert A. "The Neighborhood in Social Reconstruction." *Publications of the American Sociological Society* VII. Meeting held in Boston, Massachusetts, December 28–31, 1912.

Workers Educational Association. Crawley Branch. *The Use of Leisure in a New Town: A Report of a Social Survey.* Crawley, England: Workers Educational Association, 1960, 20 pp.

Working Party of the North West Economic Planning Council. *Social Planning in New Communities.* Manchester: North West Economic Planning Council, 1971.

"Working Session One: Centralization and Decentralization." *Daedalus,* 96, no. 3 (1967): 680–90.

Wright, Doris. "Early Childhood Care and Development and Its Implications for New Communities." In *Planning for the Social Frontier: New Communities in America,* Gideon Golany, ed. Manuscript under consideration for publication.

Wright, Henry Myles. "Radburn Revisited." *Ekistics,* 33, no. 196 (March 1972): 196–201.

Yearwood, Richard M. "Subdivision Law: Timing and Location Control." *Journal of Urban Law,* 44, no. 585 (1967).

Ylvisaker, Paul N. "New Towns: Old Cities." *Jersey Plans,* 17, no. 1 (1970): 19–25.

————. "Socio-Political Innovation and New Communities." In *Innovation and New Communities* Conference Sponsored by Princeton University, September 28–29, 1970. Princeton, New Jersey: Princeton University School of Architecture and Urban Planning, 1971, pp. 5–13.

"Yokkaichi City: Study of Land Use Planning." Government of Japan, Ministry of Construction, Building Research Institute, Occasional Report No. 4, 1961.

Ysselmeer Polders Development Authority. *Almere 1985: First Step Towards a Development Strategy.* Summary of Flevo Report no. 90. Lelystad, The Netherlands: Ysselmeer Polders Development Authority, 1974, 21 pp.

Zehner, Robert B. "Access, Travel, and Transportation in New Communities: Results of a Nationwide Study." Mimeo. New Communities Policy Applications Workshop NSF/RANN/APRT GI-34285. November 18, 1974, 2 pp.

————. "Indicators of the Quality of Life in New Communities." Mimeo. New Communities Policy Applications Workshop NSF/RANN/APRT GI-34285. November 18, 1974, 3 pp.

————. "Neighborhood and Community Satisfaction in New Towns and Less Planned Suburbs." *Journal of the American Institute of Planners,* 37, no. 6 (1971): 379–85.

————. "Participation in Perspective: A Look at New Town Involvement." *Sociological Symposium,* no. 12 (1974): 65–82.

————. "Research Report: Neighborhood and Community Satisfaction in New Towns and Less Planned Suburbs." *Journal of the American Institute of Planners,* 37, no. 6 (1971): 379–85; *Ekistics,* 36, no. 212 (July 1973): 28–30.

————. "Satisfaction with Neighborhoods: The Effects of Social Compatibility, Residential Density and Site Planning." Ph.D. Dissertation, University of Michigan, 1970, 228 pp.

Zehner, Robert B. and Robert W. Marans. *Guidelines for the Provision of Facilities and Services for Timberlake Residents.* Knoxville, Tennessee: The Tennessee Valley Authority, 1972, 47 pp.

————. "Residential Density, Planning Objectives, and Life in Planned Communities." *Journal of the American Institute of Planners,* 39, no. 5 (1973): 337–45.

Zubiena, A., ed. *Urban Centers in French New Towns.* Paris: Ministere De L'equipement Direction De L'amenagement Foncier et De L'urbanisme, 1972, 21 pp.

INDEX